# INTRODUCTIONS TO GERMAN LITERATURE

## GENERAL EDITOR: AUGUST CLOSS

# VOLUME III

# GERMAN LITERATURE OF THE EIGHTEENTH AND NINETEENTH CENTURIES

# GERMAN LITERATURE OF THE EIGHTEENTH AND NINETEENTH CENTURIES

By

### E. L. STAHL

M.A., Ph.D.

*Taylor Professor of the German Language and Literature in the University of Oxford*

and

### W. E. YUILL, M.A.

*Professor of German, Nottingham University*

With chapters on German Painting by Hanna P. Closs and on the Architecture and Sculpture of Germany by M. Q. Smith, M.A., Ph.D., Lecturer in History of European Art, Bristol University

## BARNES & NOBLE, Inc.

### NEW YORK

PUBLISHERS & BOOKSELLERS SINCE 1873

*Published in the United States*
*in 1970*
*by Barnes & Noble Inc.*
*New York, N.Y.*

ISBN 389 03525 4

Printed in Great Britain by
Butler and Tanner Ltd, Frome and London

# CONTENTS

# THE GENERAL EDITOR'S PREFACE

Literature must be seen in relationship to life in general. Any attempt to give a comprehensive account of literature must include at least some discussion and evaluation of such subjects as architecture, painting, sculpture and music as well as economics, history, sociology, science and philosophy. It is imperative to see not only the past but also the present in its proper perspective. These are the considerations that underlie the conception of *Introductions to German Literature*.

The history of the past and its literature can be of essential value if (as is particularly the case in German) it reveals characteristic trends of expression, e.g. in his *History of Modern Germany* (London, 1965) Hajo Holborn points to the 'lasting effects' of the High Middle Ages on Germany: (*a*) the creation of a national consciousness, and (*b*) the establishment of the dependence of the princes on the estates (of prelates and nobility) and the rising power of the cities, finally (*c*) the creation of a secular culture. Medieval roots or references can still be traced in literary images of our age.

In his cycle of finely woven poems, *Die Bücher der Hirten- und Preisgedichte, Der Sagen und Sänge und Der Hängenden Gärten* (1895), Stefan George endeavours to recapture the spirit of Greek serenity and the spirit of the Middle Ages: e.g. themes like the vigil, Parzival mood, the young knight, the dawn-song. Yet in moulding his historical and cultural heritage into timeless utterances Stefan George projected into the Middle Ages some meanings which are not to be found there. His poem *Die Gräber in Speier* (*Der Siebente Ring*, 1907) recalls the contests between Pope and Emperor and conjures up amongst the illustrious names of German rulers the memory of 'the greatest of the Fredericks': Emperor Frederick II, the Stupor Mundi.

Zum Karlen- und Ottonen-plan im blick
Des Morgenlandes ungeheuren traum.
Weisheit der Kabbala und Römerwürde
Feste von Agrigent und Selinunt.

. . . His gaze unites the plans of Ottos, Karls,
With his own boundless dreams of the Levant,
Wisdom of Cabalists and Rome's decorum,
Banquets of Akragas and Selinus.
[tr. by Olga Marx and Ernst Morwitz, 1949,
Univ. of North Carolina Studies]

Another incisive effect on the history, thought and poetry
of modern Europe, and particularly Germany, was created
by the Crusades. In the eleventh century Pope Gregory VII
(Hildebrand) had summoned Christendom to fight the pay-
nim, thereby enabling his successors to weld all the chivalric
ideals and ambitions of the West into *one* formidable weapon
and place it into the hands of the church where it was soon
found useful for purposes other than that of subduing Islam.
Ruthless greed for the earthly 'golden' Jerusalem besmirched
the Crusaders' cause. The capture and desecration of
Constantinople (1204), the Byzantine capital of Christian
civilization for centuries and the guardian of priceless ancient
Greek art treasures, proved an outward victory which brought
dishonour to the spirit of European Christianity. According
to Sir Steven Runciman (*The History of the Crusades*, 3 vols.,
1954/5, Penguin 1965) the Venetians seem to have been the
'most rapacious ones', but the French and the Flemings, too,
destroyed much. 'There was never a greater crime against
humanity than the Fourth Crusade.' Although the Crusades
in the end led to a vast fiasco from which the Moslem power
emerged triumphant, they had brought about the creation
of three military orders: the Templars, the Hospitallers of
St John and the Teutonic Knights. In 1235 these Deutsch-
ordensritter were directed by Emperor Frederick II to
the Baltic regions where they conquered and christianized
the pagan Pruzzen (Prussians), but this domination of the
Northern Slavs began to weaken in the fifteenth century

and has, in our time, been completely reversed by the events of the two World Wars.

The above examples, quite apart from the impact of the age of Reformation and Humanism, will amply demonstrate how past and present are inextricably interlinked in our contemporary scene. An interpretation of the totality of German literature cannot ignore the changing milieu and the interrelationship between philosophy and economics, etc., of a special period, the religious, intellectual and social events at work in Germany and indeed in Western civilization as a whole: e.g. the effect of the Thirty Years War on German literature, thought and society; nor can it ignore mysticism, Leibniz's monadology, the influence of Baroque art and music, the French Revolution and the Wars of Liberation, Hegel's concept of the State as the embodiment of national spirit which is subject to the laws of absolute universal history, Ludwig Feuerbach's and Karl Marx's materialistic philosophy, National Socialism, Communism, and the many other physical and intellectual forces which are reflected in the mirror of present-day Germany, Austria and German-speaking Switzerland. Not least of these is the influence of World-Literature (a term coined by Goethe in *Art and Antiquity*, 6.1.1827), from the Bible, Homer, Dante, Shakespeare, Cervantes and Racine to Sanscrit, Russian, Chinese and other literatures. From earliest times German literature has been heavily influenced by foreign literatures, indeed, some of the earliest Old High German works were glosses. We trust that all these interrelationships will be highlighted by the extensive bibliographies as well as the discussion.

The arrangement of material in these four volumes has been modelled on that in the *Introductions to English Literature*, edited by Professor Bonamy Dobrée. Apart from vol. I, where more space is allowed to the general introductory section covering seven centuries of early German literature, about one-third of each book is taken up by the Introduction dealing with the literature of the period in all its genres and forms, connecting it with the other arts and with religious, social, philosophical and political movements of the time. The remaining two-thirds of each book provide a 'Student's Guide': a general reading list of recommended books dealing with the period as a whole, and also a critically selected bibliography referring to the various categories of works under discussion: poetry, fiction, drama, chronicles, literary periods, etc., and individual authors and their texts. Historical data, references to leading journals, biography and recent scholarly criticism are also included. In view of the vast amount of research published in Europe and America, only the most important relevant studies can be listed in the bibliographies. Naturally, British research is stressed. Wherever possible, modern translations of German literature into English are mentioned, too. The final choice in the selection of the whole material is left to the discretion and considered judgement of each contributor.

The presentation of the *Introductions to German Literature* in four volumes (instead of five) necessitated a drastic restriction of space allotted to the literary works, genres and movements under discussion: vol. I roughly covers the period 800–1500: Old High German, Middle High German Minnesang, Epics and Romances, the Mystics and movements leading up to the Reformation; vol. II the period 1500–1700: Reformation, Renaissance, Baroque, and Aufklärung trends; vol. III is dedicated to the two centuries mainly under Goethe's influence: Enlightenment, Storm and Stress, Classicism, Romanticism, Jungdeutschland, Poetischer Realismus, up to Nietzsche; vol. IV deals with German literature from Nietzsche to our day, i.e. fiction from Thomas Mann, Hermann Hesse, F. Kafka, R. Musil, A. Döblin, etc., up to H. Böll and G. Grass; drama from Gerhart Hauptmann, F. Wedekind, F. Bruckner, G. Kaiser, etc., up to B. Brecht, C. Zuckmayer, M. Frisch, F. Dürrenmatt, R. Hochhuth, P. Weiss and contemporary Hörspiel authors; poetry from Arno Holz, R. Dehmel, Chr. Morgenstern, R. M. Rilke, Stefan George, H. von Hofmannsthal, G. Trakl, to G. Benn,

R. Hagelstange, G. Eich, H. M. Enzensberger and P. Celan, etc. We felt justified in devoting a whole volume to the artistic achievements in German literature of our age.

A work of art, such as *Tristan, Parzival, Faust,* states UNIVERSAL TRUTHS, as does scientific research. But there is a fundamental difference between aesthetic and scientific TRUTHS. If on 4 October 1957 the first Sputnik had not been launched into space, sooner or later it would have been done by the force of technological progress. The same argument would make nonsense in creative art. Without Beethoven we would never have had the *Ninth Symphony* (whatever the human and scientific progress), without Shakespeare no *Hamlet* or *Lear,* without Mozart no *Don Giovanni.* These creations are no Homunculus-productions but aesthetic truths and human self-revelations which vindicate Hölderlin's proud word at the end of his *Empedokles*-tragedy where Empedokles says to Pausanias: 'What are the gods and their spirit if I do not proclaim them?' a phrase which reminds one of the mystic expression by Angelus Silesius (Johann Scheffler): 'God does not live without me: I know that without me God cannot live an instant.'

It is through language that the poet proclaims. Language is the key to literature. Through language we reach the reservoir of man's inmost resources; language preserves the imperishable treasures of the human mind and the human heart; language guarantees the continuity of man's spiritual existence. Ludwig Wittgenstein in his *Tractatus Logico-Philosophicus* remarks: 'The barriers of my language are the barriers of my world.'

In fact, every literary creation is translation, i.e. translation of experience into language. In his *Fragmente* the German Romantic Novalis pointed to the importance of translation. He differentiates between three kinds of translation: grammatical (i.e. literal renderings from one medium into another), interpretative (creative), mythical and symbolical in the highest sense. Novalis saw the whole universe as a symbol: 'Die Welt ist ein Universaltropus des Geistes' (The world is a universal trope of the spirit). To Novalis, Greek mythology is a 'translation' of a national religion into art. In a similiar way the modern cult of the Madonna (mother, virgin, and goddess) is seen as the translation of a myth into a symbol.

Much has in the past years been written about the so-called 'willing suspension of disbelief'. In our view, it is not at all necessary to apply this strictly as a condition to art-appreciation. It is quite possible (cf. Bernard G. Heyl in *New Bearings in Esthetics and Art Criticism. A Study in Semantics and Evaluation*, Yale University Press, 1943, 1957 fourth printing) for an atheist to appreciate Rembrandt's *Christ's Supper* (Christus in Emmaus) intuitively. Moreover, we are not asked, as T. S. Eliot has rightly pointed out, to share Dante's theological creed in order to grasp the poetic greatness of the *Divina Commedia*. One could argue similarly about the revolutionary epic *The Twelve* (1918) by the Russian poet Alexander Blok: the twelve soldiers of the Red Army are not heroes; they are bestial, yet guided by a higher destiny. Christ Himself marches with them, Even Nature is symbolical: 'The wind strolls, the snow dances, / A party of twelve men advances.' Likewise, W. B. Yeats's *Sailing to Byzantium* (1927) reveals a vision of a spiritual empire to the reader without necessarily a 'willing suspension of disbelief': 'That is no country for old men ... caught in that sensual music all neglect / monuments of unageing intellect ... gather me / into the artifice of eternity'.

H. von Hofmannsthal mocks at the seekers of profundity, whom he contrasts with Goethe: 'The important Germans seem to swim continuously under water; only Goethe, like a lonely dolphin, moves along the shining surface' (*Tagebuch-Aufzeichnungen*). Goethe is, of course, not the only exception. Where surface and depth, the outward and inward worlds merge into an artistic unity, perfection is achieved, e.g. in Goethe's *Mailied*, Mörikes' *Mein Fluss*, Rilke's *Die Flamingos*, George's *Teppich des Lebens*, or Heinrich von Morungen's:

Ich hôrt ûf der heide
lûte stimme und süezen sanc.
Dâ von wart ich beide
fröiden rîch und trûrens kranc . . .

I heard in the field
a clear voice, a sweet song,
whence my sorrow grew light,
and my joy waxed strong.
[tr. by Margaret F. Richey in *Medieval
German Lyrics*, 1958]

to mention at random just a few examples, which express poetic truths.

W. B. Yeats is right when he states: 'We can create truths, but we cannot scientifically "know" them'; and Saint-Exupéry says: 'We do not discover truth, we create it.'

The poets, however, who are over-anxious to capture the *Zeitgeist* by using up-to-date scientific nomenclature at any price, are far away from poetic truth. The ineffectiveness of mere actuality is obvious. Neon-lights instead of oil-lamps do not make the poem more original! There is no shortage of topical events: the opening of the first railroad from Nürnberg to Fürth in December 1835 and the first railway journey from Leipzig to Dresden a few years later caused sensation and aroused heated controversies about the 'iron beast'. To Jungdeutschland the locomotive became the symbol of a new era which supplanted Romanticism. Heine's attitude to the 'iron beast' (das eiserne Vieh) is expressed in his *Pferd und Esel*: the horse and the donkey look with melancholy at the new monster. The noble horse is obviously the loser, but the poor ass will survive.

A glance at later versifications of technical achievements (mostly by the time of Impressionism and Expressionism) will prove the outdatedness of such literary effusions. Here are some German examples (apart from many other ones such as W. Whitman's poem on a locomotive in the winter): D. v. Liliencron: *Die neue Eisenbahn*, G. Falke: *Im Schnell-zug*, Gerrit Engelke: *Lokomotive* and *Auf der Strassenbahn*,

H. Lersch: *Die Lokomotive*, Otto zur Linde: *Bau der Untergrund-bahn*, R. Dehmel: *Drohende Aussicht*, H. Carossa: *Der Eisen-wagen*, Günter Eich: *D-Zug München–Frankfurt*, A. Petzold: *Der Werkbahnhof* and *Bergfahrt*, G. Kölwel: *Bahnfahrt durch den Vorfrühling*, A. Wolfenstein: *Fahrt*, Rene Schickele: *Ballade von unserer Lieben Frau im Coupé*, E. Stadler: *Fahrt über die Kölner Rheinbrücke bei Nacht*, G. Benn: *D-Zug*, Th. Fontane: *Die Brücke am Tay*. With a few exceptions, e.g. Fontane's and Benn's poems, almost all the above poems are either forgotten now or live on as specimens of outdatedness. Landscape is still a dominant factor in many of those poems. In our epoch of scientific laboratories and engineering triumphs, the natural order and humanistic scale of Nature have disap-peared from ultra-modern works in favour of an intellectual pattern which claims to be impersonal but also anti-historical and anti-ptolemaic.

It would be misleading to assess twentieth century litera-ture by measuring it solely with the standards of Goethe's concept of organic form and universality of outlook. Instead of totality we now have fragmentation, accompanied by signs of a temporary retreat from language, cf. *The Retreat from the Word* (G. Steiner, *Listener*, 1960). The indisputable fact remains that the 'universal' image is shattered. In his *Second Coming* W. B. Yeats, surely the most inspired European poet of our age, expresses the present dilemma:

> The falcon does not hear the falconer,
> things fall apart; the centre cannot hold . . .

Instead of the 'total' view of poetic vision we are offered pieces of images, like pictures in a kaleidoscope, by rotation of the metal tube. The self-sufficient artist's ego is dethroned or absorbed into the web of bewildering patterns of events, ambitions and manifestations.

Basically, the shattering of the Goethean 'universal' images signifies not only the loss of a once generally accepted world-order, but it also triumphantly declares the supremacy of linguistic artistry over an apparently chaotic fragmentation of the universe. Yet, we should remember that in the creative literature of a nation the resources for renewal are inexhaustible. It is therefore unrealistic to speak of a complete 'tabula rasa', however strongly such a mood must have been felt under the stress of Germany's apocalyptic downfall in and after the last War. But we heartily welcome bold experiments which emerged on the German literary scene since 1945.

To *this* present our thoughts and efforts are directed. In *this* present lie the seeds of our future. Allowing for some variation of the theme, Gottfried's words (which actually refer to the community of the noble hearts, the 'edele herzen') in his 'Prologue' to *Tristan und Isolt* may lend expression to what is our deepest concern:

> . . . dem lebene sî mîn leben ergeben,
> der werlt will ich gewerldet wesen,
> mit ir verderben oder genesen . . .

> . . . To this life my life be dedicated,
> To this world let me belong,
> With it to perish or be saved . . .

A. Closs

# INTRODUCTION

In the eighteenth century a new era begins in German literature: it rises to unprecedented heights and gains European recognition. This does not mean that individual German writers in previous centuries had not won renown abroad. In a sense some of the writers of the seventeenth century were more cosmopolitan than those of the eighteenth: they had far-ranging affiliations with kindred minds in Holland, France and England. These writers belonged to a common European stock and carried forward a recognizable European tradition. In the eighteenth century German writers were no less open to foreign influences, but as the century progressed and ever greater store was laid by originality in literary production, German authors came to establish an autonomous tradition without altogether disavowing the common European heritage.

In this way the writers of the eighteenth century began to realize the aim of founding a 'national' literature, literature with an authentic German stamp. As one result, the sequence of trends and movements which have to be taken into consideration in German literature during this century differ from those in other lands. Conditions peculiar to Germany affected the production of literature, music and philosophy, promoting their growth and leading to a unique series of developments. At the same time these new beginnings are not as radical as they first appear to be: there is more continuity in the development of German literature from the seventeenth to the nineteenth century than has often been avowed and this is even clearer in the kindred fields of music and philosophy where the German contribution is more distinctive in this period than is the case with painting and architecture.

The conditions peculiar to Germany during the eighteenth

century appertain equally to political, social and religious situations. The circumstance that Germany at that time was not a unified state or nation but was composed of a large number of virtually independent kingdoms, duchies, principalities and cities, constituted a handicap in one respect, an advantage in another. There was no single recognized capital for the country as a whole. This meant that literary activity took place in far more numerous centres than was the case in England and France: there is more variety of locale than elsewhere in Europe. As the century progresses and literary schools and movements succeed each other, the focus of attention for the literary historian shifts from Leipzig and Berlin to Hamburg, Halle, Göttingen, Strasbourg; thence to Weimar and Jena and, at the end of the eighteenth century, back to Berlin. Outside Germany proper Copenhagen, Zürich and Berne played important parts in the literary life of the age.

These cities are associated with individual writers and also with schools and movements, since groups of authors often tended to gather together and to collaborate in producing works with a definable trend. At the beginning of the period Leipzig and Berlin were the centres where the twin literary manifestations of Enlightenment and Rococo flourished. The Swiss writers Bodmer and Breitinger expressed their disapproval of these trends from Zürich, while in Berne an author of a different kind again was active at the same time: Albrecht von Haller represents another literary tendency, just as was the case, *mutatis mutandis*, at the other end of the German speaking world in Hamburg, where Brockes lived and Klopstock worked from 1770 until his death in 1803.

When we come to Göttingen and Strasbourg, the progress of German literature is shown in the collaboration by young poets who formed groups and inaugurated new trends. The 'Sturm und Drang', the first phase of which flourished in Strasbourg, leads to Weimar Classicism and this in turn is succeeded by the Romantic Movement with its geographical bases first in Jena and Berlin and later in Heidelberg.

Despite the variety of scene and the widely separated localities where literary activity took place in the eighteenth century, it is remarkable that almost exclusively Protestant parts of Germany are involved. In this century Catholic cities like Munich and Vienna are not in the main stream of literary development: they were not to come into their own or become truly prominent until the nineteenth century. The division between the two forms of the Christian religion determined the course of literary developments more markedly in Germany than elsewhere in Europe.

One manifestation of Protestantism in particular had a profound effect. Pietism is a sectarian movement in which the conscience of the individual in strict adherence to Biblical precept forms the basis of faith and conduct. The practice of self-examination encouraged by this attitude promoted a form of expression which influenced literary production most effectively at a time when the Enlightenment was on the wane. Many great writers of the time, such as Lessing, Klopstock, Goethe, Schiller, Hölderlin and Novalis were affected in one form or another by Pietism and gave expression to its tenets.

In addition to political and religious conditions, the social changes taking place in Germany at that time, at least in some parts of the country, helped to shape the trend of developments. From the middle of the century onwards literature increasingly reflects the rise of the middle classes to power and influence. But equally, the mentality of the German 'Bürger' is a topic of critical interest to German writers like Lessing whose inauguration of 'middle class tragedy' was actuated by motives different from those of encouraging the bourgeois class to achieve that power and influence. Lessing and the Classicists presented the conflict between aristocracy and middle class, between privilege and the demand for equality, with aesthetic objectivity rather than partizan zeal. The contrary trend of revolutionary involvement is only to be found in the 'Sturm und Drang', as again in the 'Junge Deutschland' movement in the nineteenth century.

As German literature unfolds during the eighteenth century it presents a picture of considerable variety and complexity. This is particularly true when we take note of the different trends and movements comprising this expansion, and examine their chronological relationship.

It is customary to distinguish the following trends and movements in the eighteenth century: Enlightenment, Rococo, Sentimentality ('Empfindsamkeit'), 'Sturm und Drang', Classicism, Romanticism. Broadly speaking the first three belong to the earlier part of the century; they go down as far as the sixties, when the impetus leading to the 'Sturm und Drang' makes itself felt, first in the 'Göttinger Hain', then in the work of the Strasbourg group. Two members of this group, Herder and Goethe, albeit in different ways, went on to inaugurate 'Weimar Classicism' during the later seventies, and in the nineties were joined by Schiller who had also had a 'Sturm und Drang' phase. His 'Classicism' differed from that of Goethe, just as his 'Sturm und Drang' had an individual stamp, and yet in both phases their work has features in common which demarcates it from that of the Romantics, the last distinctive group to emerge in the eighteenth century.

The whole range of these movements came into being within a span of seventy years. In all its varied aspects German literature from the Enlightenment to Romanticism is the product of not more than three generations of writers who overlap each other to a considerable extent. The following facts illustrate this feature:

1. The chief representatives of two trends that belong to the earlier part of the century, Klopstock and Wieland, lived to see the inauguration of the Romantic School: they died in 1803 and 1813 respectively. Moreover, during the nineties the young Tieck, a leader in Romanticism, was for a time closely associated with Nicolai, one of the main adherents of the Enlightenment in Berlin. If Romanticism can be said to have begun in reaction to a previous literary trend, that trend was still the Enlightenment rather than Classicism.

2. Weimar Classicism had not fully come into being when Romanticism began. At the time Tieck, Novalis and the Schlegel brothers started to write, in the year 1797, Goethe set out to complete such major 'classical' works as *Faust Part I* (only the 'Fragment' had been published in 1790) and *Wilhelm Meisters Lehrjahre*. Similarly, none of Schiller's 'classical' dramas, the plays from *Wallenstein* onwards, had appeared by 1797.

The complexities inherent in the literary situation during virtually the whole of the eighteenth century makes any straightforwardly chronological account impossible. Instead, one has to find a method of grouping which will do justice both to the large amount of interaction and interpenetration of literary trends that resulted in a high degree of contemporaneity of widely differing trends, and to the marked improvement that can be observed in literary output as the century progressed.

Adopting the traditional, if avowedly ambiguous, categories of literary history, we can say that Classicism and Romanticism are the two dominating trends in the eighteenth century: Realism is only present in its incipient forms in some works belonging mainly to the 'Sturm und Drang'. With some injustice to their autonomous status, it can be said that the literature of the Enlightenment represents an earlier form of Classicism, just as the 'Sturm und Drang' contains recognizably pre-Romantic elements. Thus Enlightenment leads to Classicism, while 'Sturm und Drang' leads to Romanticism.

This statement has enough truth in it to allow us to establish the broad perspective that is needed. Yet it is also inaccurate, since Classicism is just as much a further development of 'Sturm und Drang' (at least in the work of Herder, Goethe and Schiller) as it is the culmination of Enlightenment. On the other hand, Romantic trends are observable in German literature well before the 'Sturm und Drang' began. When Bodmer and Breitinger opposed Gottsched, the chief representative of the literature of Enlightenment in

Germany, they stated a Romantic theory in rudimentary form. Similarly, the work of Klopstock has many pre-Romantic traits.

For all these reasons the division of the century into Classical and Romantic trends fails to do justice to the situation as a whole. It is preferable to attempt a division of the century on a different principle altogether. We can differentiate the literary trends with reference to the human faculties which were called into play at that time in producing and judging literature: the intellect, the senses and the emotions. Each of these facets of human nature had its protagonist in the field of literary theory and practice. Accordingly, three trends stem from the different orientations as indicated by the emphasis placed on each of the three human faculties. They are: Rationalism, Sensualism and 'Irrationalism'. To these trends correspond the three historical manifestations which constitute the literary scene before the 'Sturm und Drang': Enlightenment, Rococo and pre-Romanticism. In each case a leading writer represents the trend at its best and also transcends it. Enlightenment found its culmination in Lessing, Rococo in Wieland, pre-Romanticism in Klopstock.

# I

## RATIONALISM AND ENLIGHTENMENT

The dominant features of German literature in the seventeenth century, inasmuch as they differed from their equivalents in other European countries, may be accounted for by the joint impact of the Counter Reformation and the Thirty Years War. It has already been said that a considerable degree of continuity marks the developments between this century and the next. Yet there is clearly also a reaction against the more extreme forms of Baroque poetry: a new era is heralded with the dawn of the eighteenth century.

The deep-seated discontent and the sense of doom which had found memorable expression in Baroque literature all but vanished at the end of the century. The forms of expression appropriate to these feelings were retained nonetheless by many minor poets and so lost their meaning. It is against such outworn forms of expression that reaction mainly took place. The melancholy mood of seventeenth century poets was supplanted by a new optimism. It was based on that idea of harmony in the universe which had been demonstrated by the astronomers and physicists of the age. The inalterable breach in existence which had obsessed the minds of poets in the seventeenth century was healed when the conviction grew that God had created 'the best of possible worlds' in order that man should find happiness on earth. This creed was not shared by every writer of note: it bore obvious pitfalls of shallowness and triviality. But it was widespread enough to account for the introduction of new themes and the employment of novel forms at the beginning of the century. Harmony and joy are such themes linking together the twin manifestations of this part of the century: Rationalism and Sensualism.

More than ever before intellectual values prevailed in the interpretation of the world, the nature of man, his needs and his works. Reason was assessed to be his highest faculty, while feelings and instincts were subjected to restraint and control. Human conduct and the results of human activity were measured by rationally evolved standards. Common sense was made the chief arbiter of value in literature and became closely linked with good taste. In its more extreme forms this mode of thought led to the rejection of every kind of waywardness or extravagance in favour of what was considered normal and customary. The prohibition was in many cases extended to include the miraculous and the supernatural, particularly in those genres like the drama where the limits of probability could be narrowly drawn.

Acceptance of rational norms encouraged a mode of criticism in which individual works were tested by standards prescribed for the genres to which they belonged rather than by any qualities of originality they might possess. In the production of literature imagination and the intuitive faculties were not merely relegated to a secondary position but were defined, even by their protagonists like Bodmer and Breitinger, in near rationalist terms: prevailingly the imagination was for them a recollective or reproductive, not a creative faculty.

The value placed on the intellect led to a markedly increased emphasis upon theory and criticism. This is the age when the practice of poetry and the drama came to be more dependent upon the findings of the critics than had been the case even in the Renaissance and the seventeenth century. Soon, too, this prescriptive function was to pass from literary reformers such as Gottsched and Lessing, who derived some of their general principles from the study of ancient and contemporary philosophers, to the philosophers themselves. The course of German drama may be mapped by tracing the adherence of writers to the prescriptions of such theorists or to their detachment and declared liberation from them.

The condemnation of extravagance on rational grounds

was in line with the general tendency of the time to reject all forms of transcendentalism in favour of 'natural' and 'purely human' categories of thought. Thus a leading reformer of the time, Christian Thomasius (1655–1728) based his thought on Grotius' tenets of natural law, while Christian Wolff (1679–1754) evolved the first system of Rationalism in Germany from aspects of Leibniz' philosophy and Newton's *Principia*.

In that intellectual climate the principles of causation came to hold a supreme position even in literary production. This meant that the laws of probability were considered of primary importance. Here, too, the progress of German literature during the century may be traced by following the increasingly subtle interpretations of the term 'probability', the shift from external causation to more inward, differentiated, irrational processes of motivation.

Another barrier cramping the free production of poetry in the narrowly rationalist era of the eighteenth century was the prescription of a moral purpose for art. Beauty was linked with truth in such a way that the didactic end was safeguarded, a provision which had particularly limiting effects on many theoretical and some practical demonstrations of what writers of comedies and tragedies should be allowed to do. New assessments were already effecting changes in this outlook when the adherents of 'Sturm und Drang' began to challenge this central rationalist doctrine. It must, however, also be kept in mind that these young writers in some ways merely substituted a new morality based on social justice for the older principles, instead of abandoning didactic purposes altogether.

A genre which underwent similar changes is lyric poetry. Here the temper of Rationalism promoted the writing of instructive and satirical poetry and such genres as the fable and occasional verse which could be easily adapted to the ends of Enlightenment. On the other hand those forms in which unsophisticated feeling or emotional involvement find their finest expression (the song, the ode, the hymn) suffered setbacks. The revival of German poetry in the second half of the century went apace when first the simpler modes and forms of folk poetry (ballad and song), then such complex structures as the hymn, the ode in its Pindaric and Sapphic forms and, later still, the sonnet and other Romance forms were cultivated by poets whose attitude to their art differed radically from that of their predecessors.

One kind of literary activity that was greatly enhanced by the outlook of the Enlightenment was the publication of journals on the model of *The Tatler* and *The Spectator*. In Germany they multiplied as the century advanced and both reflected and influenced the tendencies of the age.

### Drama in the Era of Enlightenment

The principal representative of rationalism in dramatic criticism is Johann Christoph Gottsched. He was born in East Prussia but escaped to Saxony to avoid military service. At Leipzig University he successively became Professor of Poetry (1730) and Professor of Logic and Metaphysics (1734). While his main work lay in literature, he also published *Erste Gründe der gesammten Weltweisheit* in 1734, a corpus of philosophical views based on Wolff's system which is, however, not entirely derivative in character. A severe critic of later Baroque poetry, he set out to reform German literature in accordance with the demands of Good Taste.

Gottsched's 'classicism' was orientated towards the theory and practice of French writers and opposed to that of the English poets and dramatists. It was, however, not a narrowly partizan opposition, since he modelled his literary journals *Die vernünftigen Tadlerinnen* (1725–7) and *Der Biedermann* (1727–9) on those of Addison and Steele and in the Preface to *Deutsche Schaubühne* (1740–5) quotes Shaftesbury. In condemning Milton's 'exaggerations' and Shakespeare's 'excesses' he set a trend that aimed at ridding German literature of what he considered similar faults as shown, above all, by the melodrama of the 'Haupt- und Staatsaktionen' of the time and by the buffoonery of contemporary comedies.

His reforms were salutary in that they provided a starting point of renewal. He promoted the use of a standard literary language (cf. his *Beyträge zur critischen Historie der deutschen Sprache, Poesie und Beredsamkeit*, 1732 ff., and *Grundlegung einer deutschen Sprachkunst*, 1748) and he narrowed the gap between the stage and literary practice by forming an alliance with the acting company of Caroline Neuber, thus assuring the performance of plays acceptable to him, in the place of the tawdry productions generally accessible to theatre-goers at that time. His service to the growing number of members of the middle classes interested in literature was considerable. Yet he was out of tune with the temper of the age in one important respect. In theory as in practice he provided for these classes literary models based on the exploitation of aristocratic rather than bourgeois codes of behaviour.

The unyielding quality of Gottsched's critical thought became evident with the successive publications of his *Versuch einer critischen Dichtkunst vor die Deutschen* (1730). Revised editions appeared in 1737, 1742 and 1751 but he made no substantial concessions to newer trends that had already clearly emerged. He paid mere lip-service to such traditional concepts as inspiration and invention; they are nullified by the rational procedure he recommends in poetic composition. The most frequently quoted example is his prescription for constructing a dramatic plot in the passage beginning: 'Zuerst wähle man sich einen lehrreichen Satz, der dem ganzen Gedicht zugrunde liegen soll . . .' (*Critische Dichtkunst*). The same bent is evident in his interpretation of the three unities which he based on the narrowest concepts of probability. The unity of time, he admits, may be extended to 10 hours. But dramatic actions should not include nightfall when the audience would wish to go home. (Other rationalist critics of the day concede that dramatic actions can be allowed to take place at night if they deal with murders or revolts, on the ground that this is the time when

plots are usually hatched.) A similar line of argument prevails when Gottsched demands the strictest adherence to the
unity of place. The audience, he says, remains seated in the
same place throughout the performance of a play, for which
reason there cannot be any change of scene: 'Wo man ist, da
muss man bleiben.' On the like score of improbability he
eschews the use of monologues and asides, just as he opposed
the opera for being 'unnatural'.

These prescriptions and prohibitions show that Gottsched's
rationalism amounted to a demand for the complete identity
of dramatic and empirical reality. He applied the principle
of Imitation in the interest of reproducing actuality to such
an extent that his rationalism comes to resemble naturalism
as practised in Germany at the end of the nineteenth century,
in several salient respects. One difference between him and
the Naturalists, however, is indicated by his assertion that
dramatic characters should represent types rather than
individuals and that their speech should be 'regular' and
'normal': it should be devoid of all colloquial, dialectal or
idiosyncratic peculiarities. In the post-Rationalist, as in the
post-Naturalist era, the revival of dramatic literature centred
mainly on the renewal of the demand for aesthetic autonomy,
a revival which Lessing began to inaugurate in the eighteenth century.

In all his main contentions Gottsched preserved a rigid
attitude. On one issue he was ready to modify his position
when an inherent illogicality became apparent. In his
*Critische Dichtkunst* he accepted the canon of poetic justice.
But this demand conflicted with the unity of time unless the
law of probability was to be patently violated. In an essay
entitled 'Ob man in theatralischen Gedichten allezeit die
Tugend als belohnt und das Laster als bestraft vorstellen
muss?' (1751) he gave up the claim for poetic justice which
shows that here probability and verisimilitude took precedence over the moral principle.

Gottsched collected plays which he considered exemplary
in his *Deutsche Schaubühne nach den Regeln und Exempeln der alten*

*Griechen und Römern eingerichtet* (1740–5) and *Nötiger Vorrat zur Geschichte der dramatischen Dichtkunst* (1757–65). These were useful compendia. Their usefulness was enhanced by the fact that he arranged the plays in chronological order and so supplied materials for a rudimentary history (a feature acknowledged by Goethe in *Dichtung und Wahrheit*). Historiography did not greatly flourish in Germany during the Enlightenment, but the era is by no means lacking in historical insight. Gottsched himself in a treatise entitled *De temporibus teutonicorum vatum mythicis* (1752) mentioned, among others, Otfrid, Notker, Veldeke, as well as *Williram, Reineke de Vos* and *Der Ackermann aus Böhmen*, but his interest in the historical phenomena of literature remained rudimentary and did not allow him to relax the imposition of standard rules.

Apart from his contributions to criticism, translation and the theatre, Gottsched's importance lies in the fact that he attracted a number of young writers to Leipzig. This School at first tried to put his precepts to the test of dramatic practice, but its more gifted members soon broke away from him and struck out on their own.

Gottsched himself wrote a tragedy to illustrate his rules. *Der sterbende Cato* (1732) is hardly an original work: the first three acts are little more than an adaptation of Addison's play, the last act is taken from Deschamps. At the same time he shows a turn of independence by criticizing Addison for his (Shakespearean) 'weakness' in motivating episodes, and Deschamps for making Cato not a stoic hero (Gottsched's tragic archetype as it was that of dramatists in the Baroque era), but a desperate suicide.

A stronger vein of originality is found in the work of Gottsched's wife Luise Adelgunde (1713–62). Beside translating plays of Destouches and Molière and *The Rape of the Lock*, she wrote comedies such as *Die Pietisterei im Fischbein-Rocke* (1736), *Die ungleiche Heirat* (1745), *Die Hausfranzösin, Der Triumph der Weltweisheit* (1739) and *Das Testament* (1745). They are good examples of that satirical comedy which is the only kind envisaged by Gottsched in his theory: the chief characters embody socially reprehensible qualities, the moral purpose of the comedy consisting in their correction by means of ridicule. Excessive piety is the fault ridiculed in *Die Pietisterei im Fischbein-Rocke*, a play which, like *Das Testament*, also has value in giving a picture of the manners of the day. Altogether, comedy was a genre congenial to the writers of the Enlightenment when they aimed at presenting contemporary society with a measure of realism: they were not bound by classical precedents to the same extent as in tragedy.

This is not the sole reason for the 'death of tragedy' at that time. The optimistic outlook of the age is a more decisive factor. A truly tragic concept did emerge from the tenets of Rationalism once it appeared that human nature cannot be directed towards the avoidance of tragic error and involvement through the mere exercise of rational powers. Oedipus became a symbol of man's struggle against Fate as soon as the efficacy of rational understanding had been denied by Hamann and the members of the 'Sturm und Drang': in different ways the tragedies of later writers such as Schiller, Kleist, Büchner and Grillparzer were based on this awareness.

In the forties and fifties of the eighteenth century it was far from the minds of even the leading dramatists. In addition, they could not bring the tragic potentialities inherent in the outlook of the age to fruition as long as derivative conventions dominated their practice. This is particularly true of the members of the Gottsched School. Their 'Classical' bent is shown in their themes (e.g. J. E. Schlegel's *Die Trojanerinnen*, *Die Geschwister in Taurien* and *Dido*), the formal structures, the invariable use of alexandrines and the elevated language which rarely achieved the highest poetic distinction.

Tragedy suffered more than comedy, for in the latter genre the satirical strain accorded well with the tenor of the age. Satire and mock heroic poetry flourished in the work of writers like C. L. Liscow (1701–60) and G. W. Rabener (1714–71). An outstanding product of this phase of the

Enlightenment is J. F. W. Zachariä's *Der Renomiste* (1744), a mock heroic poem (in the manner of *The Rape of the Lock*) dealing with life at a German university. A good deal of realistic detail found its way into such works as into the comedies written by members of the Gottsched School. Yet, as Goethe pointed out in *Dichtung und Wahrheit*, they lack topical interest and trenchant relevance owing to their tendency to portray types rather than individual characters. This is shown in the titles of representative comedies written by the leading dramatists: J. E. Schlegel's *Die stumme Schönheit* (1748), *Der Geheimnisvolle* and *Die geschäftigen Müssiggänger* (1743), Cronegk's *Der Misstrauische*, Weisse's *Die Misstrauischen gegen sich selbst* and Mylius' *Die Ärzte* and *Der Unerträgliche*.

The first signs of change in the theory and practice of drama appear in the work of Christian Fürchtegott Gellert (1715-69), Gottsched's contemporary at Leipzig, who from 1751 onwards occupied the Chair of Poetry and Rhetoric. He formed an alliance with a group of writers, the 'Bremer Beiträger', chiefly K. C. Gärtner (1712-91), J. A. Cramer (1723-88) and J. A. Ebert (1723-95). They were later joined by the former adherents of Gottsched, J. E. Schlegel, Weisse and Cronegk.

Two factors evident in Gellert's work helped to modify rigid adherence to Rationalist principles. First, there is far greater emphasis on feeling and sentiment. He is a representative of the sentimental trend which became a distinctive feature of European literature during the second half of the century and took on more extreme forms of emotionalism and lachrymosity in Germany than in England and France. Gellert's Inaugural Lecture at Leipzig in 1751, 'Pro Comoedia commovente', a reply to M. D. Chassiron's 'Réflexions sur le comique-larmoyant', contained a plea for the kind of comedy Lessing was to term 'rührendes Lustspiel'. Instead of evoking satirical laughter it aimed to arouse compassion, a purpose Gellert himself had followed in his plays *Die Betschwester* (1745), *Das Loos in der Lotterie* (1746) and *Die zärtlichen Schwestern* (1747). These comedies show that he was no less dependent on his French models (Destouches and Marivaux) than was Gottsched. The difference is that Gellert succeeded in presenting authentic scenes of German life in living speech and thus contributed to the development of German comedy along the lines soon to be followed by Lessing in *Minna von Barnhelm*.

The other solvent of rationalism detectable in Gellert's work is his pietism. Pietism is part of the general trend of the age in that, like the Enlightenment, it opposed orthodoxy, the establishment and institutionalized religion. Its adherents endeavoured to liberate the individual from trammels imposed by the hierarchical system, but instead of intellectual clarification they sought spiritual illumination and the reformation of man through the cultivation of self-examination. Subjectivism was enhanced by this practice of self-analysis, but the reliance on such inward testimony was allied to a firm belief in divine Providence as the supreme external power moulding the life of the individual: it encouraged an attitude of accepting misfortune and of suffering political abuses, until the revolutionary members of the 'Sturm und Drang' brought about a change. More positively, the subjectivity engendered by Pietism advanced the writing of lyric poetry rather than that of drama where action in the modern sense depends upon individual initiative much more than upon fate or Providence. The future course of German drama was influenced to a considerable extent by the interplay of individual responsibility and personal submission: they are attitudes which came to be seen as contradictory or found to be reconcilable, according to whether the works in which they are represented belong to the pre-Romantic or to the Classical trend.

In many ways Gellert's dramas adhered to the principles of Gottsched's *Critische Dichtkunst*, notably in his didacticism. Yet his innovations were far-reaching enough to encourage the 'Bremer Beiträger' when they began to break away from Gottsched. In his theory no less than his practice J. E.

Schlegel became a forerunner of Lessing. In 1741 he wrote the essay 'Vergleichung Shakespeares and Andreas Gryphs' in which admiration for the English poet is not wholehearted but which breaks new ground in critical appreciation: while accusing Shakespeare of bombast in Gottsched's manner, Schlegel praised his creation of individual characters and recognized that the drama of character deserved encouragement in Germany. He insisted that pleasure, not instruction, is 'der wirkliche Endzweck derjenigen Nachahmung, die wir in den Künsten finden' and enunciated novel views on the theory of imitation and the importance of the medium used in artistic production. These are views which show him to have been in advance of contemporary writers on aesthetic subjects: in effect he destroyed the foundation on which Gottsched based his canons of dramatic criticism, by denying the validity of his principle of probability.

No less important are the innovations Schlegel advocated in *Gedanken zur Aufnahme des dänischen Theaters*. He wrote the treatise in 1747 when he was in Copenhagen as secretary of the Saxon ambassador; it was published posthumously in 1764 in time to influence the development of the 'Sturm und Drang,' notably on such issues as the significance of national differences in the use of literary forms and the distinction between 'inner' and 'outer' form. Schlegel did not unequivocally reject the unities: he was sceptical about them, but also recognized their value. In this mediatory role he resembles Lessing: he advanced the development of German drama in two directions: he challenged the prevailing tendency to imitate foreign models but equally endeavoured to maintain the ideal of uniformity of construction. His pioneering position may also be discerned in his later dramatic work. He was a less successful playwright than Lessing, but he was in the van of developments in choosing 'national' themes such as that on 'Hermann der Cherusker' and, in his drama *Canut*, creating at least one rugged individual character, Ulfo.

Among other innovations to be noted in dramas written

during the fifties is the use of blank verse in tragedies by J. W. von Brawe (*Brutus*, 1757), Wieland (*Lady Johanna Gray*, 1756) and C. F. Weisse (*Die Befreiung von Theben* and *Atreus und Thyest*, 1758). These are the first German dramatists who replaced the current alexandrine by a verse form which allowed them greater freedom of expression. More flexibility still was achieved by Lessing when he adopted prose in tragedies as early as 1755 for *Miss Sara Sampson*, a practice he maintained for *Emilia Galotti*. He chose blank verse when he wrote *Nathan der Weise* (1779), eight years before Goethe adopted the same form for *Iphigenie auf Tauris* which had previously been written in prose. Henceforward for many dramatists of the remainder of the century and for the majority during the nineteenth, blank verse became the consecrated classical verse form. It is therefore significant that when it was first adopted in Germany the innovators broke away from Gottsched's constricting example; the later playwrights used it in the interests of the stricter formal requirements which they once more imposed upon tragedy.

The other innovation to be observed in eighteenth-century drama is the writing of 'Singspiele' by C. F. Weisse, e.g. *Die verwandelten Weiber oder Der Teufel ist los* (1752). These are plays which contain lyric interpolations. Such a rudimentary operatic form signalled another challenge to Gottsched who considered opera 'unnatural' because it infringed the laws of probability. The development of 'Singspiele' after the middle of the century was a stride forward: the genre was favoured by many playwrights of the age including Goethe, and helped to mould the 'romantic' form of drama which became more and more pronounced as the century progressed.

### Lessing's theory and practice of drama

In Lessing Germany for the first time in the eighteenth century produced a literary personality whose interests were varied enough to influence a wide range of developments. His contribution was of equal importance in theory and in practice of the drama, in aesthetics and, only to a lesser extent, in theology. On the other hand there are areas of literature like lyric poetry and the novel where he had little or nothing to give.

His critical writings were largely polemical. Invariably he chose to expound his positive ideas by opposing them to opinions with which he disagreed. In this way he imported a dramatic quality into his critical exercises. Another feature was his ability to clarify issues by drawing lucid distinctions of a fundamental kind, such as the difference between terror and fear and between the emotions aroused by, and the passions enacted in, tragedy, the difference between art forms with respective reference to space and to time (cf. *Laokoon*), and the distinction between 'die Religion Christi' and 'die christliche Religion' in his theological writings.

Lessing was not a systematic thinker. His best efforts in criticism were occasional or even haphazard pronouncements, or else they remained fragmentary. Such seminal documents are his contributions to the *Briefe die neueste Literatur betreffend* (1759–65) in which he collaborated with Moses Mendelssohn and Nicolai, notably the Seventeenth Letter where he launched his attack upon Gottsched and championed Shakespeare; *Laokoon oder Über die Grenzen der Malerei und Poesie* (1766) which begins with a critical examination of a statement by Winckelmann on the difference between the Greek statue and Vergil's account of the Trojan episode; the *Hamburgische Dramaturgie* (1767–9) with its critique of French drama, notably works by Corneille and Voltaire, leading to the discussion of salient points of Aristotelian theory; and the controversial writings directed against Samuel Gotthold Lange and against Pastor J. M. Goeze (1768 f. and 1778 respectively).

These critical forays did not stop on the plane of negation or on that of theoretical discussion: they led to positive and practical results, particularly in Lessing's own case. *Laokoon* influenced artistic developments in Germany, the *Hamburgische Dramaturgie* promoted new tragic compositions including the final draft of *Emilia Galotti* (1772) and the theological controversy led to writings as diverse in character as *Nathan der Weise* (1779) and *Die Erziehung des Menschengeschlechts* (1780).

The interrelation of critical clarification and creative composition is most evident in Lessing's dramatic work. In the context of literary activity during the Enlightenment it is significant that he wrote dramas before he wrote about them: the creative impulse had precedence. His first dramatic works are the comedies *Der junge Gelehrte* (1748), *Der Freigeist*, *Die Juden* and *Die alte Jungfer* (all 1749). Then came the critical writings of *Beiträge zur Historie und Aufnahme des Theaters* (1750) and *Theatralische Bibliothek* (1754 onwards), to be followed by the composition of *Miss Sara Sampson* (1755). In 1757 Lessing was engaged with Mendelssohn and Nicolai in writing *Briefe die neueste Literatur betreffend* which continued until 1765. In 1759 he wrote the tragedy *Philotas*. During the later fifties and in the sixties he was occupied with several dramatic experiments such as those on the Faust and Virginia legends. The latter came to fruition in 1772 with the composition of *Emilia Galotti* after Lessing had formulated his mature views on tragedy and kindred subjects in *Hamburgische Dramaturgie* (1767-9) and after writing the comedy *Minna von Barnhelm* (1767). More strikingly than is the case with other writers of the eighteenth century Lessing's creative and critical activities fructified one another and yet remained autonomous expressions of his personality. Undoubtedly he largely followed his own precepts in writing his dramas, so that some of them are best considered in the light of his theories, but the theories were in turn determined in many instances by the experience he had gained from writing his dramas and must be studied in conjunction with them. Of course this does not mean that the dramas cannot be fruitfully examined without primary reference to theory, Lessing's own or that of any other critic.

While remembering that Lessing's theory and practice are mutually dependent, the one upon the other, and fulfil complementary roles in his life and work, it is convenient to treat them separately and to begin with his critical views.

In his theory of tragedy he at first placed the strongest emphasis upon pity which he considered to be the primary tragic emotion, although he later modified his position by greater adherence to Aristotle in stressing fear as well. The earlier position is evident in the correspondence which he carried on with Nicolai and Mendelssohn on the subject of tragedy in 1756 and 1757. Against the former, who maintained that tragedy could arouse any emotion whatever, and against the latter who stated that admiration is an 'emotion' which tragedy should excite in preference to pity and terror, Lessing upheld the view that the purpose of tragedy is specific in that only the two Aristotelian passions, pity and fear, are brought into play with the audience. Of the two emotions, pity is primary, since tragic fear is related to pity as 'das auf uns bezogene Mitleid'. Admiration must be ruled out because it belongs to epic rather than tragic poems. Whatever the justification for Lessing's definition of these emotions, he was original in being the first German critic to attempt an explanation of pity and fear as the sole tragic emotions. He held that they belong together inextricably since an action of a certain kind which arouses fear for ourselves excites pity if it involves another person who is like ourselves.

Such theoretical considerations are grounded in Lessing's wider humanitarian views. He shared the philanthropic sentiments of the age to the extent of maintaining (in the correspondence with Nicolai and Mendelssohn) that 'der beste Mensch ist der mitleidigste Mensch', and asserting the equality of human beings. These principles made him reject heroic tragedy where stoic indifference to suffering is held up to admiration and prevents the release of pity, and led him to postulate a basic similarity between the characters presented on the stage and the average members of the audience. These beliefs formed the mainstay for his opposition to Gottschedian tragedy and for his inauguration of German 'middle class tragedy'.

Lessing brought to bear upon this fundamentally egalitarian outlook other considerations which account for different aspects of his theatrical work. He accepted the differences in national taste, one of his main contentions in the seventeenth 'Literaturbrief'. In effect he came to be regarded as a founder of a 'national' German theatre. Yet his intentions were never narrowly nationalistic and he disavowed all sentiments of patriotism. His attacks on Corneille and Voltaire were vitriolic, but he freely expressed his admiration for Diderot. The more he extended his experience of life and of the theatre, the greater his tendency to uphold aesthetic principles against the prevailing rationalist code. This can best be seen in the *Hamburgische Dramaturgie* when he deals with three topics: genius and the rules; dramatic motivation and probability; catharsis and the purgation of tragic emotions.

Lessing followed English writers of the eighteenth century, such as Edward Young, in claiming exemption from the rules for a work of genius. In this he goes far beyond Gottsched without accepting the tenets advanced by the members of the 'Sturm und Drang'. He maintained that a genius is free without being lawless, in that a true genius follows laws of his own making. There are fundamental requirements which all dramatists must meet if their plays are to be considered real works of art. A genius shuns melodramatic effects. The production of continuous processes rather than disconnected events is what distinguishes the work of a genius from that of a 'wit': 'Das Genie können nur Begebenheiten beschäftigen, die ineinander gegründet sind, nur Ketten von Ursachen und Wirkungen' (*Hamburgische Dramaturgie* no. 30). This means that consistent motivation of action and of character was the primary dramatic requirement for Lessing.

His strictures on Corneille and Voltaire in the *Hamburgische Dramaturgie* concentrate on this problem. To some extent he lacked understanding of the psychological outlook of the French dramatists, so that he was out of touch with their social ideas and misunderstood the meaning of their applied code of honour. This led him to misjudge the motivation of behaviour and the pattern of dramatic construction in the plays he so severely criticized. Lessing's principles of motivation differed to a considerable extent from those of the French tragedians and their German imitators. 'Probability' has come to mean something new in Lessing when we compare his use of the term with Gottsched's. The natural process indicated in his 'Kette von Ursachen und Wirkungen' is far removed from rationalist conceptions of adherence to nature: it brought him noticeably nearer to the position that was to be taken by the 'Stürmer und Dränger'.

Lessing's interpretation of catharsis shows that he took another step in the direction of greater aesthetic freedom. In number 78 of the *Hamburgische Dramaturgie* he does concede that tragedy effects 'die Verwandlung der Leidenschaften in tugendhafte Fertigkeiten'. In a broad sense he thus retained the principle of morality. But his assertion is based on a distinction which he was the first to make. He differentiated between those passions which are presented by the characters of a play and those emotions which the action arouses in the audience. In the narrow moral view the former, which Lessing calls 'die vorgestellten Leidenschaften', are the proper object of purgation—passions like envy and jealousy. This Lessing denies, maintaining that 'die erregten' or 'die erweckten Leidenschaften', that is pity and fear, and these alone, are purified in tragic catharsis, a process which only tragedy among all existing art forms can encompass by virtue of the fact that tragedy, as drama, is a living presentation. 'Bessern sollen uns alle Gattungen der Poesie' he states 'aber alle Gattungen können nicht alles bessern.' What tragedy can do is to stimulate our pity and our fear where they are deficient: it can also reduce them to a proper level when they are exaggerated. This is the double function he now assigned to tragic catharsis. He no longer believed that 'der beste Mensch ist der mitleidigste Mensch' but had come to see that even the greatest virtues are harmful when they are driven to excess.

Not that his fundamental optimism had waned: his humanism represents the best side of the Enlightenment to which he belongs in spite of his advanced thought on many subjects. In numbers 34 and 79 of the *Hamburgische Dramaturgie* he demanded that even tragedy should be a microcosmic representation of the universe which he, like his contemporaries, viewed as a divinely ordained harmonious structure. His Christianity was a 'Christentum der Vernunft' whose historical antecedents and institutional forms he questioned when they lacked rational validity. His attitude to history contrasts with that of later dramatists, notably Schiller and Hebbel. Lessing's historical scepticism did not entail distrust of Providence: on the contrary, his faith increased with the years and reached its culmination when he wrote *Nathan der Weise* and *Die Erziehung des Menschengeschlechts*. He opposed the notion of 'metaphysical' tragedy, the view that in the last resort human suffering was caused by malignant fate or a malevolent deity. Even in its starkest forms tragedy represented for him the results of man's transgressions of the law so enormous that they remain rationally incomprehensible and so escape prevention by legislation, just as comedy is the outcome of infringements which are too petty to fall within the scope of legal jurisdiction.

Lessing expressed this original view in number 7 of the *Hamburgische Dramaturgie*. It would be going too far to claim that all his dramas illustrate the distinctions he draws in that passage. It does, however, prove his desire to relate tragedy and comedy more closely together than is the case with most of his contemporaries and many later dramatists. On the other hand he did not go so far as to accept tragicomedy without reservation. Lope de Vega and Wieland defended it on the ground that it represents the life of daily experience, a claim to be repeated by dramatists of the 'Sturm und Drang'. The contention conflicted with Lessing's idea of imitation: he asked for the representation not of the variety of life's manifestations but of their underlying unity. To this end he accepted a measure of abstraction ('Absonderung') in artistic presentations. Nonetheless he is one of the leading dramatists of the eighteenth century who encouraged the production of a 'mixed' genre. This he did not do in the manner of Shakespeare but by treating serious themes in comic form. He did not consider ridicule to be the true purpose of comedy and wished to take the satirical edge out of comic laughter, to achieve the aim of producing 'Lachen' rather than 'Verlachen'.

From the beginning this was one of Lessing's principal dramatic aims. The best examples in his early work are *Der junge Gelehrte* and *Die Juden*. The former is prevailingly satirical, but in the age of Enlightenment the satirical treatment of intellectual pride has weighty significance. And the presentation of religious and racial intolerance within a comic framework in *Die Juden* is a real innovation, however clearly the theme itself accords with Enlightenment principles. *Minna von Barnhelm* is Lessing's most representative work in the genre. Its novelty at the time it was written consisted in the success with which quite different effects are combined into a coherent artistic whole.

First, the theme is inherently serious in two ways. Tellheim dishonoured is a potentially tragic figure and Minna's playful behaviour towards him aggravates his sense of injury to the extent of bringing their relationship to the verge of rupture. The seriousness is enforced by the topical background of the recently concluded Seven Years War, and it is varied by the broadly sentimental themes Lessing introduces with Werner and the widow Marloff. But it never reaches the degree of intensity demanded from a tragic presentation. The overall effect remains conciliatory. The same result is produced by the comic elements which are no less varied than the serious ones. Farce and satire in the figures of Just, the innkeeper and Riccaut de la Marlinière, wit and gaiety in Minna and Franziska, offset each other and hold the graver action in balance. The satirical humour is of such subordinate quality and is so quickly relieved by the other comic effects that no sense of bitterness remains to any appreciable extent. Moreover, the attention of the spectator is largely absorbed by Minna's intrigue. Above all, the novelty of the work is seen when Tellheim himself is treated humorously, yet with due regard for his human dignity. It was something new in the comedy of that era that the quality so treated is in itself a virtue, not a vice. Tellheim's sense of honour is a butt, not of satirical, yet of humorous portrayal when it becomes excessively scrupulous. It is not an anti-social defect. This substantiates the claim that Lessing successfully associated the two kinds of comedy prevalent in the fifties of the century, and that he combined them with a plot of serious content into a uniform dramatic work.

Viewed in this light Lessing's *Nathan der Weise* may be regarded as a further and yet more profound example of serious comedy. In *Über naive und sentimentalische Dichtung* Schiller suggested that Lessing had failed to write a comedy by overstressing the gravity of its content, but his own attempted adaptation of the play proved unsuccessful. He did not succeed because he restricted the content by thinning out its didactic import: he obscured the fact that Lessing had written the first great German 'Ideendrama' in the comic mode, an achievement from which attention has been diverted by his calling the play 'ein dramatisches Gedicht'. It has a special place in Lessing's dramatic work because of its personal and general topicality: he had given up writing plays when the enforced cessation of the controversy with Pastor Goeze suggested a final and positive reply to his opponent and an appeal to the world at large, in dramatic form.

The 'Parable' of the Rings is the ideological core of the play. It contains inconsistencies on the origin of the first ring and of its copies, when one attempts to translate these facets into religious terms, and it becomes obscure when one considers man's role in bringing the divine plan to fruition. Such logical flaws detract from the poetic value of the work as a whole. Nonetheless it remains Lessing's greatest poetic achievement. He produced a masterpiece by his skilful evocation of the Eastern scene and by his manipulation of the blank verse form. His image of the Orient is not blandly romantic and he intentionally forged a colloquial vehicle of expression by taking many irregularities, variations and realistic turns of speech into his verse. Another poetic device has been much criticized. Lessing based the plot on a traditional pattern of relationships between members of two households and, at the end, in a pantomimic scene, revealed the ties linking both families. Dramatically least convincing, this scene is yet of the essence of the whole dramatic conception because it enforces the doctrine of the Parable: the ideal of human relationship is presented allegorically in terms of family kinships.

The family motif has great significance in drama during the Age of Enlightenment and after. It is a *topos* by which one can assess the changes in German tragedy from Lessing to the 'Sturm und Drang'.

Lessing's first attempt in tragedy has particular interest although it proved abortive. In 1749 he planned to dramatize the story of Samuel Henzi, a Bernese writer who was executed in July of that year for taking part in a plot against the government of the city. The most remarkable feature of Lessing's project is its political topicality; yet it proved a stumbling block for him. He defeated his own ends by endeavouring to portray 'den Aufrührer im Gegensatze mit dem Patrioten und den Unterdrücker im Gegensatze mit dem wahren Oberhaupte'. The generality of his projected presentation shows that he had not yet escaped the prevailing Enlightenment mode of treating dramatic themes. It was left to the later generation of 'Sturm und Drang' writers to solve the technical problems inherent in the dramatization of political material. Lessing only succeeded in completing his first tragedy when he abandoned the notion of choosing a 'Haupt- und Staatsaktion' and wrote a 'bürgerliches Trauerspiel' instead.

In writing *Miss Sara Sampson* he obviously borrowed from

Lillo's *The London Merchant* and Richardson's *Pamela*, but the point must be made that the latter is a more important source than the former. Lessing took over the theme of seduction and many subsidiary motifs from the novel. The main question concerns the nature of the 'middle class' tragedy as he conceived it. He obviously had no intention in this play to present the middle class as subject to social or political victimization. The heroine arouses our sympathy because she is a girl of almost exemplary virtue in spite of having betrayed her father's trust: this moral ambiguity determines the central situation. The middle class quality of Sara's behaviour in that situation comes out in her 'Gelassenheit', her passive acceptance of suffering which is grounded in unquestioning belief in Providence, an attitude engendered in Germany largely by Pietist and similar religious teachings. Lessing located the scene in England: in truth he made little effort to depict an English milieu and to give his characters anything more than borrowed English names. They are prototypes of people behaving in accordance with a pattern which was well understood in the Germany of the time; hence the play's enormous success when it was performed on the stage.

*Miss Sara Sampson* is loosely constructed, verbose and rhetorical. But Lessing keeps dramatic tension in play by using the device of contrast. The contrasts are numerous and varied, the most effective being the different codes of honour upon which Sara, Marwood and Mellefont act, and the different sentiments portrayed in the relationships of the lovers, the rivals, father and daughter, master and servant. The principal dramatic interest lies in these relations and it is in them that the middle class quality of the play must be sought. It is a tragedy without a villain in the usual sense, for Mellefont genuinely loves Sara and we must accept his characteristically middle class reason for not wishing to marry her: he does not want to sacrifice the legacy he has inherited on condition that he remains single.

A manifest weakness of the drama is its melodramatic

dénouement. The same criticism may be made of Lessing's other 'bürgerliches Trauerspiel'. In *Emilia Galotti* as in *Miss Sara Sampson* he found it difficult to devise catastrophes consonant with his conception of tragedies in which family relationships played a ruling part.

A family relationship also enters into Lessing's most uncharacteristic tragedy. *Philotas* is unlike any of his other works of the same genre and, bearing his theoretical statements in mind, an unexpected production, since it is essentially an heroic tragedy. Yet this quality is toned down by the sentimentality he infused into the relation between father and son. Moreover, even in dealing with this domestic theme, *Philotas* differs from Lessing's other plays in which he treats the theme: the relation between father and daughter occupied him far more intensely, particularly when he brought in issues like seduction to portray the middle-class mentality. On the evidence of *Philotas* as of the other tragedies, however, his position may be defined. It was far from Lessing to present the enmity between members of a family which took on such symbolic significance in the work of some leading dramatists of the 'Sturm und Drang'. Middle-class drama as he conceived it dealt with the disruption of family relationships due to outside interference rather than to internecine hatred.

*Emilia Galotti* is his most radical presentation of this domestic theme in that he modified the Virginia legend from which the drama stems, in order to motivate a daughter's death at the hands of her father. The planned abduction and even the seduction of Emilia are by comparison lesser dramatic topics. Again, Lessing's position may be defined by comparing his treatment of these themes with that in such later plays as Goethe's *Clavigo* and *Faust*, and Hebbel's *Maria Magdalene*. The major tragic act in *Emilia Galotti* is Odoardo's final deed, and the greater part of the work contains an action in which the concluding situation is prepared by negative as well as positive motivation. Prevention of escape and personal choice in the end produce the outcome of Emilia's death. In this process of motivation Lessing again gave due emphasis to that sense of honour which provided him with so much material for his dramas, not excluding *Minna von Barnhelm*. As a yardstick of gauging developments, his treatment of this theme may once more be compared with that of Hebbel in *Maria Magdalene*. Lessing's tragedy is remarkable for the lengths he was prepared to go at the risk of improbability: it shows how far he had left Gottschedian principles of motivation behind.

The plot of *Emilia Galotti* is a 'Kette von Ursachen und Wirkungen', a concatenation of events caused by personal desires, impulses and intuitions. It is also a texture of planned happenings and accidental occurrences, design and co-incidence, calmly deliberate and blindly passionate behaviour. Lessing's dramatic procedure is a model of calculation and as such dissatisfied the younger dramatists of the day, but a comparison between the parallel figures of *Miss Sara Sampson* and *Emilia Galotti* shows how much nearer he had got to the position taken up by the 'Stürmer und Dränger'. There is far more vehemence in the conduct and the speech of Odoardo and Orsina than in those of Sir William and Marwood, and Emilia is more resolute than Sara: her attitude is no longer characterized solely by 'Gelassenheit', passive acceptance of suffering. In addition, Lessing achieved greater subtlety by introducing new figures such as Marinelli and Claudia. The former in particular is important as the agent of intrigue accounting for the continuous evocation of fear on Emilia's behalf.

Lessing's greatest tragedy came into its own when Goethe, leaving the 'Sturm und Drang' behind, needed an example of purposeful dramatic construction. The same was the case with Schiller at a later date. The historical significance of *Emilia Galotti* is twofold: in this drama Lessing gave the best that the age of Enlightenment could offer in the tragic genre, but he also went beyond the limits of that age and prepared the way for Weimar Classicism.

## Poetry in the Age of Enlightenment

### 1. Anacreonticism

When Lessing was in Leipzig he wrote a collection of poems to which he gave the title *Lieder von einem anakreontischen Freunde*. This kind of poetry became the predominant form of lyric expression during the first half of the eighteenth century. Its style shows affinities with that of Rococo art. The mode of life reflected in Anacreontic poetry is the bourgeois equivalent of the dignified conviviality at the princely residences portrayed in Rococo paintings. The term Anacreonticism is derived from the *Anacreontea* (1554) of Henricus Stefanus (Henri Estienne), a collection of sixty poems falsely attributed to the Greek poet and widely imitated in European literature. In German literature the style has particular significance.

In the poetry of the Anacreontics as in the thought of the writers of Enlightenment proper, the sombre mood of the Baroque was dispelled through the assertion of new values. Here the resolve prevailed to enjoy the pleasures of life, to engage in sensuous experience as well as in the exercise of rational thought. Anacreonticism is sensualist in origin, its values are based on experience and observation of life and bear traces of the influence of contemporary English philosophy and of Marinism. By contrast, rationalism as it developed in the era of Enlightenment is French in origin. Here the contrast ends. During this era no opposition was felt between the twin manifestations of rationalism and sensualism: opposition came to be voiced much later when, in the 'Sturm und Drang', the senses were 'set free' from intellectual control and sensuality like emotionalism was given unhampered expression. Among the Anacreontics reason retained control of the senses even when the poets made avowals of hedonism. They invariably asserted the need for moderation, whereas the writers of the 'Sturm und Drang' deliberately sought to overleap conventional limits.

Anacreontic poets affirmed the belief in universal harmony for which the philosophers of the Enlightenment had given rational demonstration, and like them discovered its most telling manifestations in nature. To take delight in its beauties was to pay tribute to divine beneficence. This homage also contained a good deal of utilitarian self-interest, particularly in such poets as Barthold Brockes and Albrecht von Haller who clung blandly to a teleological view of nature amounting to the belief that God had created the world not merely for the delectation but also for the profit of mankind.

Hedonism in Anacreontic poetry was not restricted to the enjoyment of nature: it invariably included the pleasures of wine, love and friendship. These themes were often linked together in one and the same poem; their combined effect gives to Anacreontic poetry its individual character, a convivial quality not present to the same extent in previous German poetry. No longer did poets, as in the immediately preceding era, write their songs in melancholic and abstemious isolation. The new social outlook explains why conventionality soon became another feature of Anacreonticism. There is a typical Anacreontic landscape of parks and meadows, groves and grottoes, where the gentle breezes stir and never a tempest rages, where movements are measured and sounds are mellow, nightingales sing and roses never fade. This is the ideal setting for the pursuit of pleasures in which the Greek-named shepherds and shepherdesses endlessly indulge. The scenes and sentiments of such poetry are deliberately stylized in order to express the bourgeois ideals of tranquillity and ease. Clearly, German poetry could not attain its majority until the basis of Anacreontic conventionality, the optimistic regard for happiness and the placid acquiescence, was given up. At the same time it may be said that the Anacreontic poets led the way to new developments after the lyric impetus of the Baroque had waned. They contributed to the vocabulary of German poetry by exploiting the ideals of urbanity and restraint and they cultivated simplicity and grace in their verse forms and their style. With this achievement they set a standard to which later poets often tried to return.

The principal representatives of Anacreonticism are Friedrich von Hagedorn (1708–54) and Johann Wilhelm Ludwig Gleim (1719–1803). Hagedorn's collected verse is contained in *Versuch einiger Gedichte* (1729), *Sammlung neuer Oden und Lieder* (1742–52) and *Moralische Gedichte* (1750), Gleim's in *Versuch in scherzhaften Liedern* (1744–58), *Lieder* (1745), *Lieder nach dem Anacreon* (1766) and *Oden nach dem Horaz* (1769). Beside classical poets, Pope and Prior, Chapelle and Chaulieu were the models of these German authors. But Gleim started another trend with his *Preussische Kriegslieder in den Feldzügen 1756–7 von einem Grenadier* (1758). The poems in these collections depart from Anacreonticism in theme and in style. For his patriotic verse Gleim chose the four-lined *Chevy Chase* ballad stanza of alternately four and three stresses and alternately masculine rhymes. This change did not amount to a break with Anacreonticism or lead to greater achievements. Nonetheless, although Gleim returned to his earlier mode and like Hagedorn was soon overtaken by other poets, his 'Grenadierlieder' have some original qualities.

Anacreontic elements are found in the work of several writers of the period whose principal contribution, however, lies in different directions. This is the case particularly with three poets who rank among the most important in the eighteenth century before Klopstock.

Johann Christian Günther (1695–1723) was long neglected in accounts of German poetry, largely because of Goethe's strictures on him: 'Er wusste sich nicht zu zähmen' he says in *Dichtung und Wahrheit* 'und so zerrann ihm sein Dichten wie sein Leben'. His work is often over-rated and it is, at its best, of unequal merit. But he did produce poetry of an individual kind. He may even be acknowledged as Goethe's predecessor in making poetry out of personal experience, especially in his erotic and his religious poems. His unhappy relations with his father led him into penury which affected his life and his beliefs. Just as he differs from Anacreontic poets (among whose precursors he may be reckoned with some of his work) when he writes love poetry of greater personal truthfulness, so he is one of the first who disavowed the ready optimism of the age and showed himself at times to be a mind in revolt, at others resolved to accept suffering with humility and contrition.

Barthold Heinrich Brockes (1680–1747) wrote a poem in 1720 with the remarkable title 'Der Ursprung des menschlichen Unvergnügens'. It is not his most characteristic work. His main contribution is the compendious *Irdisches Vergnügen in Gott* (1721–48), in nine volumes. Much of it is based on Marini's sensualism which Brockes modified after studying and translating some of the writings of Pope and of Thomson. He has been claimed as an early impressionist, but deism accounts for the considerable difference between his sensualist homage to God and the worldly aims of the nineteenth century poets. Brockes' attitude to nature differs no less from that of the writers of the 'Sturm und Drang': pantheism does not play the same part in his work. If anything he is a follower of Leibniz in regarding God as embracing nature rather than being inherent in it. Repetitive in theme and monotonous in treatment, *Irdisches Vergnügen in Gott* is yet a landmark in the history of German poetry, not least because of the occasional virtuosity Brockes displays in his verse forms and his poetic vocabulary.

As the century progressed the impetus which had been gained from rationalism and from sensualism waned, and other sources were tapped which proved of greater benefit in the composition of lyric poetry. To a limited yet not insignificant extent this is seen in the poetry of Christoph Martin Wieland (1733–1813). A leading representative of all the major trends of the age from Enlightenment to pre-Romanticism and Classicism, with the exception of the 'Sturm und Drang', his best work summed up their essence in an individual way. The changes he underwent from rationalism to, at first, an extreme form of Rococo hedonism until he settled down to a more balanced outlook, were expressions of his complex personality. He also had a stage of 'Schwärmerei' when he came under the spell of Pietism. His most characteristic and lasting poetic productions are those in which he presents, in ironic detachment, the foibles of one-sided enthusiasm and the pitfalls of delusion against backgrounds of legendary make-believe which harbour not a little realistic truth.

Wieland achieved his unique position after embracing the influence of a variety of foreign authors: he was one of the most open-minded writers of the day who knew how to turn diverse styles of European literature to his own account. From Cervantes he took over the theme of experience dispelling self-deception. Shakespeare and Fielding in their different ways attracted him because they portrayed reality with unswerving truth, while Sterne and Voltaire taught him the art of viewing human nature with ironic detachment. In his positive evaluation of social conduct he made Shaftesbury's ideal of the virtuoso and the concept of moral grace his own: they formed the basis of his idea of personal culture ('Bildung') which became one of the principal intellectual concerns of German writers until far into the nineteenth century.

It is Wieland's distinction that he was able to present this idea not only in the novel, which became its customary vehicle, but in his poetry as well. As poet he began in the didactic eighteenth century manner with an imitation of Lucretius' *De rerum natura* (*Die Natur der Dinge*, 1751) and with *Zwölf moralische Briefe in Versen* (1752), both composed in alexandrines. He radically changed this manner in *Komische Erzählungen* (1762–5) four satirical verse tales on mythological subjects. *Musarion* (1766–8) is his first poetic presentation of a conversion from the extremes of 'Pythagorean' otherworldliness and cynical materialism to a balanced acceptance of life's sensual pleasures. The poems that followed, *Idris und Zenide* (1768) and *Der neue Amadis* (1771) testify above all to Wieland's skill in the free use of complex thematic material wholly imaginative in character,

and his adept and individual handling of traditional verse
forms like the Ottava Rima.

This is particularly true of his major poetic work, *Oberon*
(1780), a romantic epic in twelve cantos dealing with three
main actions: the adventures of Huon in obedience to the
command of the Emperor Charles; his love affair with the
Sultan's daughter Rezia; and the quarrel and subsequent
reconciliation of Oberon and Titania. The Oberon-Titania
action is expertly linked to that of Huon and Rezia through
the themes of transgression condoned and fidelity vindicated,
a triumph of the fusion of apparently incompatible literary
sources: *The Arabian Nights*, the medieval French story *Huon
de Bordeaux* and the episode culled from Chaucer's *Merchant's
Tale* and *Midsummer Night's Dream*. Wieland rightly claimed
in his Prefatory Note that this fusion produced 'die eigen-
tümlichste Schönheit des Plans und der Komposition dieses
Gedichts'. It is the best expression of his 'Geist Capriccio'
which was not inconsistent with a desire and a talent for
careful planning. *Oberon* has an evocative appeal which the
poetry of few of his contemporaries could equal. It has a
special place in German poetry at a time when narrative
skill fell below the ability to express ideas. His verse tales are
charged with incident and episodic events of the most varied
kind. In this and in his choice of the Ottava Rima (which he
deliberately made more flexible than Ariosto had done) he
was ahead of his time: from Klopstock's *Der Messias* to Voss's
*Luise* and Goethe's *Hermann und Dorothea* epic poems in the
eighteenth century were written in hexameters, while many
lyric poets also preferred classical Greek and Latin forms
beside native German ones such as the 'Lied'. Wieland
opened up the world of Romance forms, a pioneering effort
that was to bear fruit among those very poets of the Romantic
movement who paid scant tribute to him.

## 2. *Pre-Romantic Poetry and Klopstock*

The advent of Romanticism was heralded in German poetry
in different ways. While Wieland perfected the rationalist

and the sensualist elements prevailing in the Enlightenment and the Rococo phases, another trend was emerging which was developed by writers of a different temper. They did not share the optimistic outlook of Enlightenment and Rococo authors and disdained to search for worldly pleasure: they had a graver and more critical spiritual bias. Their poetry has a fundamentally religious character and it contains a basic disparagement of sophisticated social values. These poets sought peace in nature far removed from haunts of urban pleasure. It has been shown that Joy is a theme running through a great deal of eighteenth century poetry from Brockes to Schiller. The poets now under review replaced it by graver elegiac motifs and expressed themselves in more dynamic modes which quickened the poetic style of the age and infused new passion into it.

Some of these features are first found in the poetry of Albrecht von Haller (1708–77) who came of patrician Bernese stock. An exact contemporary and a friend of Hagedorn, he, too, was influenced by English poets of the day. But whereas Hagedorn chose as his models some of the poems of Cowper, Prior and Herrick, Haller preferred the metaphysical poets. 'Ich hatte indessen', he says, 'die englischen Dichter mir bekannt gemacht und den Vorzug der schweren Dichtung angenommen.' His didactic gravity led him to protest against the current overestimation of man's intellectual powers. A noted scientist (he occupied the chair of medicine at Göttingen from 1736 until 1753), he never became a convinced rationalist. His critique of human reason is stated in a couplet which elicited Goethe's disapproval:

> Ins Innere der Natur dringt kein erschaffener Geist
> Zu glücklich, wann sie noch die äussre Schale weist!

He versified the *Theodicy* of Leibniz in his *Vom Ursprung des Übels* (1732), but his best work is contained in *Versuch schweizerischer Gedichte* of the same year, particularly in the long descriptive and didactic poem *Die Alpen*. In this work he sets forth a view of man and nature which is pre-Romantic in contrast to that of the Anacreonticists. In the place of their urbanized landscapes Haller presents nature in all her sublime grandeur beyond man's control.

This image of sublimity he bequeathed to later poets in the century, an achievement which outweighs that of his fellow countryman Salomon Gessner (1730–88) whose *Dafnis* (1754), *Idyllen* (1756) and *Der Tod Abels* (1758) gained European renown but lacked Haller's profounder insights. Gessner's shepherds and peasants are portrayed in deliberately idealized contours: he turned away from realism, as he admitted in a letter to Gleim: 'Ich kann den Käse und die Nüsse im Gedicht nicht zu oft ausstehen.' Yet he shared the growing distrust in urban civilization and the delight in bucolic simplicity which are among the features of pre-Romanticism.

In the Anacreontic poetry of the time similar moods are occasionally expressed, for example by Hagedorn in 'Wünsche' and by Gleim in 'An Herrn von Kleist', but these protestations lack conviction. By contrast, Ewald von Kleist (1715–59) was able to treat the theme with success because he genuinely experienced the dichotomy of life and had some power to express it. His beginnings were conventionally Anacreontic. Then his life as an officer in the Seven Years War led him to write patriotic and heroic verse, such as his 'Ode an die preussische Armee' (1557) and the epic in three cantos *Cissides und Paches* (1759) in which he also glorified friendship. Other characteristic poems are 'Sehnsucht nach Ruhe' and the melancholy 'Grablied' together with its counterpart 'Geburtslied'. His most influential work is the descriptive poem 'Der Frühling' (1749) which evokes comparison with Schiller's 'Spaziergang'. The landscape is improbably composite for a day's walk—comprising lowland country, snowclad mountains and the ocean—but there are also vignettes of realistically observed detail:

> Ein Teich glänzt mitten im Hofe
> Mit grünem Flosskraut bestreut, wodurch aus scheinbarer Tiefe

Des Himmels Ebenbild blinkt. Er wimmelt von zahmen
  Bewohnern.
Die Henne jammert ums Ufer und ruft die gleitenden
  Entchen,
Die sie gebrütet; sie fliehn der Stiefmutter Stimme,
  durchplätschern
Die Flut und nagen am Schilf . . .

In such passages Ewald von Kleist contributed considerably
to the development of a new poetic style.

A different form of patriotism from that of Kleist is found
in poems by Johann Peter Uz (1720–96), such as 'Das
bedrängte Deutschland', 'Die alten und die heutigen
deutschen Sitten' and 'An die Deutschen'. Uz laments
German disunity and decadence and contrasts past and
present times as Haller contrasts nature and civilization. In
this mode and in his religious poetry he is more like Klopstock than any other poet of the time. He differs from Brockes
in passing from the description of external natural phenomena to the evocation of cosmic events, for example in 'Gott
im Ungewitter', 'Gott im Frühling' and 'Gott der Welt-
schöpfer'. In 'Theodicee', a Leibnizian work like Haller's
poem, Uz subscribes to the current concept of universal
harmony, but he expresses it with urgency and personal
involvement such as only Klopstock at that time summoned:

Mit sonnenvollem Angesichte
Flieg' ich zur Gottheit auf! Ein Strahl von ihrem Lichte
Glänzt auf mein Saitenspiel, das nie erhabner klang,
Durch welche Töne wälzt mein heiliger Gesang
Wie eine Flut von furchtbarn Klippen
Sich strömend fort und braust von meinen Lippen!

But whereas his language shows the new trend of passionate
utterance, his stanzas are more evenly constructed. In this
he differs from Klopstock who achieved a new style with his
free verse.

Two other poets show the way German poetry now began
to develop. Samuel Gotthold Lange (1711–81) was a
follower of Anacreonticism and a supporter of Gottsched

until he met Immanuel Jakob Pyra (1715–44) and in 1733 founded together with him a 'Gesellschaft zur Förderung der deutschen Sprache, Poesie und Beredsamkeit'. Pyra showed greater vigour in composing 'Der Tempel der wahren Dichtkunst' (1737) on the lines of Pope's 'Temple of Fame', and in writing, together with Lange, *Thirsis und Damons freundschaftliche Lieder* (1745). The collection contains a mixture of Anacreontic and religious verse, as some of the titles indicate: 'Des Thirsis Vereinigung mit Damon und Doris den Himmel zu besingen' and 'Damons Zufriedenheit mit dem Himmel, der Dichtkunst, dem Thirsis und der Doris'. The poetry is remarkable only for two features which place it in line with Klopstock's. In the place of the Anacreontics' conception of poetry as a form of recreation, Pyra and Lange gave it consecrated meaning:

> Verbleibe du mir stets, o meine Poesie,
> In deiner hohen Reinigkeit.
> ('Des Thirsis Ruhe in Damons Freundschaft')

They also practised a form of free verse, giving up rhyme and adopting rhythmic variations in order to achieve a more intensely emotional utterance.

It was left to Friedrich Gottlieb Klopstock (1724–1803) to bring about the most far-reaching innovations in epic and lyric poetry, and, to a lesser extent, in the drama. In his poem 'Mein Vaterland' he states that he first saw his poetic task as a patriotic mission but then transferred his allegiance to the 'Vaterland des Menschengeschlechts' and chose the theme of his religious epic. Cantos 1–3 of *Der Messias* came out in *Bremer Beiträge* in 1748, a revised version, together with Cantos 4 and 5 appeared in 1751. Ten cantos in all were published in 1755, five more in 1768. The whole work was completed in twenty cantos in 1773 and revised in 1780 and 1800. Only the first three cantos made (and still make) an immediate impact, but *Der Messias* retains its historic significance in being a representative epic work of the eighteenth century, while embodying an idiosyncratic quality characteristic of the author: lyric evocation in the place of the presentation of events which traditionally belong to the epic genre.

Klopstock achieved his aim of sustaining emotional expressiveness by the cadence of his verse and the quality of his language. After some hesitation he decided on the hexameter as the form most suited to his purpose, but he gave it an individual stamp by introducing an additional syllable before the caesura, varying the stresses in different lines and grouping them into significant entities. His language is characterized by a similar dynamism. Against Gottsched he maintained the poet's right to coin phrases and invent new word-combinations. His poetry abounds in such expressive neologisms as 'Gewittergedanken', 'finsterverwachsene Wälder', 'tiefaufstöhnende Ströme', he used words without their customary prefixes for poetic emphasis ('Folger' for 'Verfolger', 'schatten' for 'beschatten') and omitted conjunctions to heighten emotional utterance. To the same end he changed the normal word order, a practice he defended in his essay 'Über die Wortfolge'. Finally, he confined his language as much as possible to words of Germanic origin and eschewed Latin or Romance forms which he described in another essay *Vom edlen Ausdrucke*, as 'fremde und zugleich widerwärtige Worte'.

Klopstock restricted the scope of his poem to the Passion and the Resurrection and sparingly used the epic poet's traditional device of exploiting episodic material. The work as a whole lacks tension and architectonic interest, although Klopstock attempted to give it more design by using parallelism and antithesis in grouping his characters. *Der Messias* is a landmark in the development of Romantic rather than Classical German poetry.

Thematically, Klopstock's dramas fall into two groups: biblical and national, the former comprising *Der Tod Adams* (1757), *Salomo* (1764) and *David* (1772), the latter containing the trilogy *Hermanns Schlacht* (1769), *Hermann und die Fürsten* (1784) and *Hermanns Tod* (1787). These 'Bardiete' show his

inability to give concrete presentations of political man-
oeuvres and military enterprise. The best part of the trilogy
is the last: the hero's death provided Klopstock with the
occasion for the kind of emotive evocation in which he
excelled. In the same way the biblical dramas stand out
when he comes to present topics such as Solomon's change
of heart and, above all, the leitmotiv of *Der Tod Adams*. This
is a work of considerable originality, a drama of uniquely
lyric character. The action is purely inward, representing
the stages of Adam's realization of the true meaning of the
words spoken by the Angel of Death: 'Einige deiner Nach-
kommen werden entschlummern, einige sterben; aber du
sollst des Todes sterben.' With the recurrent phrase 'du sollst
des Todes sterben' Klopstock uses a *leitmotiv* technique
which makes his short play in three 'Handlungen' a memorable product of the age. It also heralds the coming age with
Adam's last words to his children: 'Der sei der grösste Mann
unter euch, der der menschlichste ist!'

Klopstock's humanitarian idealism has many facets. It was
religious in origin, but it was not unworldly, as the odes 'Der
Eislauf', 'Winterfreuden', 'Der Rheinwein' and 'Der Cap-
wein und der Johannisberger' attest. He later turned it to
account in his poems on the French and the American
Revolution both in eulogizing freedom and in condemning
the reign of terror. This is, however, not his greatest poetry.
The collection of odes and elegies he published in 1771 marks
the height of his literary achievement. The odes written
between 1747 and 1759 on themes such as faith, friendship
and love, composed in his most characteristic free verse with
metre and length of line determined solely by the sweep of
emotional movement, place Klopstock among the leading
poets of the eighteenth century and testify to the grandeur
of his poetic dedication. His odes and elegies have one feature
in common: despite his close attachment to the objects of
nature and the human world, he practised a form of abstraction which gives the poems a quality all their own.

In his most characteristic love poetry he deals not with a

real person but with 'die künftige Geliebte', an attitude
which endeared him to Rilke. Moreover, he spiritualizes
love to the extent of making true union possible only in
death, just as he links death and friendship closely together
(cf. 'An Fanny', 'Wingolt', 'An Ebert', 'Die frühen Gräber').
Klopstock's treatment of these themes marks the difference
between him and the Anacreontics. In his odes he likewise
opened up new perspectives by associating nature with the
manifestation of the deity, most markedly in 'Die Frühlings-
feier' and in poems like 'Dem Allgegenwärtigen', 'Das An-
schauen Gottes' and 'Der Erbarmer'. Here one observes his
emotional pantheism which is so different from the impressionistic sensualism of Brockes:

> Ich hebe mein Aug' auf und seh'!
> Und, siehe, der Herr ist überall!
>
> Mit heiligem Schauer
> Brech' ich die Blum' ab;
> Gott machte sie,
> Gott ist, wo die Blum' ist.
> ('Dem Allgegenwärtigen')

Klopstock's religious fervour enabled him to fashion
another significant link between two lyric themes. He exulted
at the prospect of death, as Novalis was to do later with full
Romantic passion, because death brings about the union
with the beloved and betokens resurrection in the presence
of God:

> Freue dich deines Todes, o Leib!
> Wo du verwesen wirst,
> Wird er sein,
> Der Ewige.
> ('Dem Allgegenwärtigen'. cf. also
> 'Der Tod' and 'Die Glückseligkeit aller')

The best of his 'geistliche Lieder' deal with this particular
theme.

Abstraction is a feature of Klopstock's patriotic poetry as
it is of his poems on nature and on love. Unlike Gleim and

Ewald von Kleist he looked away from the Germany of his day in order to evoke the distant past or a nebulous future. The pseudo-Ossianic 'Bardiete' he wrote from 1766 onwards reveal much of the confusion ruling his mind on this subject. The poems have little value and are only significant because they point in the direction which much German poetry was soon to follow. In the era of growing Hellenism Klopstock confronted the Greek world with the Nordic in poems like 'Der Hügel und der Hain' and 'Der Bach'. In this he revealed the limitations as well as the strength of his intellectual convictions.

His critical writings should not suffer neglect: they are valuable indications of new trends in literary thinking, especially in his advocacy of the principle of 'Darstellung' in the place of the still current theory of imitation. We may define his position in the literary evolution of the time in terms of his dissociation from the main trends of Enlightenment and his leaning towards those of emergent Romanticism.

## Prose Fiction in the Eighteenth Century

It is during the eighteenth century that the novel begins finally to oust the verse epic, to develop more concise and distinctive forms and to approach the predominance that it currently enjoys. Already in the 17th century the sheer volume of novel production makes it necessary to select for discussion only those works of typical significance or of intrinsic merit. With the widening of the reading public in the eighteenth and nineteenth centuries there developed a vast literature of entertainment, largely in the form of novels and short stories. In any account of prose fiction in this period it must be borne in mind that one is dealing with peaks and landmarks—at most with the contours of a vast landscape. It goes without saying that the celebrated works of any era are frequently surrounded in their historical context by a host of imitations, sequels and parodies.

At the beginning of the eighteenth century the German

literary landscape was arid enough: the broad stream of
the heroic courtly novel had either dried up or crept into
stagnant backwaters. Books like *Die asiatische Banise* continued to be reprinted, emulated and read well into the
century, but immediately after 1700 the character of original
works becomes less distinctive. The fairly well-defined categories of the previous age—courtly, popular, 'political' and
pastoral novels—either disappear, are modified to suit a
changing taste, or tend to merge with each other. It has been
remarked, with much truth, that the history of the German
novel between 1700 and 1740 is a literary history without
names. And yet before the century was over, the novel in
Germany had achieved its most characteristic forms and a
climax of excellence. This development involved a fundamental change of emphasis from sensational event to psychological analysis, as well as a transition from a more or less
dogmatic Christian morality to a secular ideal of harmonious
personal development.

The decline of the ornate and fanciful baroque novel and
the evolution of a new tradition during the first half of the
new century were both associated with sociological changes
and with the emergence of fresh intellectual and religious
factors. Prominent among the relevant influences was the increasing status of the middle-class. Literary interest was no
longer centred in the courts, but began to be disseminated
through wider circles. Although the pressure of middle-class
aspirations could scarcely make itself felt in the political
sphere, it becomes apparent in a reaction against the culture
and manners of the courts: the temper and style of the novel
as well as the drama tend to become more rational, more
topical, more realistic and—for a time, at least—ethically
more rigorous. During the first half of the century the prose
narrative in Germany tends to be increasingly assimilated
to contemporary social life, and it is not until the advent of
Wieland and the development of an aesthetic mode of sensibility that the literary imagination begins to come fully into
its own again.

Two very different intellectual forces fostered the development of the novel and first imparted to it that inwardness and philosophical propensity which have remained characteristic of the German tradition: pietism and rationalism, forces which were by no means mutually exclusive, but often strangely interwoven. Both of these movements were virtually confined to the Protestant parts of Germany, and it is in these areas that the novel began to develop anew.

The evangelical movement named after the *Pia Desideria* (1675) and the *Collegia pietatis* of Jakob Spener (1635–1705) embraced a wide range of religious thought and experience and had other equally prominent leaders, such as Gottfried Arnold (1666–1714), August Hermann Francke (1662–1727) and Nikolaus Ludwig von Zinzendorf (1700–60), but common to all was the concern with inner experience and the practice of soul-searching. Pietism not only encouraged the free flow of pious sentiment, it also criticized implicitly the morals of aristocratic society and fostered a sense of social justice. The influence of the pietists on many individual writers from Schnabel to Karl Philipp Moritz and Goethe could easily be demonstrated, and there is little doubt that this influence—exerted through the reading public—affected the style and themes of many novels during the 18th century.

The optimistic rationalist philosophy propagated by Christian Wolff (1679–1754) and J. C. Gottsched (1700–66) looked to literature as an instrument of moral instruction and particularly as a means of satirizing ancient abuses and modish follies and also of furthering social and moral reform. Although Gottsched did not think highly of the novel and looked more to the drama as the instrument for improving public taste and morals, many of his like-minded contemporaries and successors used the novel for similar purposes. The rationalists' interest in empirical psychology, and particularly in human motivation, as well as in the influences of environment and the potentialities of education is reflected in many didactic novels of the age. The demand for reason, moderation, correctness and plausibility as a reaction against the ornate manner of the preceding baroque age fostered a sober and prosaic style.

The development of the novel during the century was guided and much accelerated by the influence of foreign— particularly of English—models. In turn Defoe, Richardson, Fielding, Sterne and Goldsmith all affected the themes and techniques of German novelists.

Before these factors begin to operate, however, it is difficult to detect any very positive trend: of the existing novel forms the pastoral novel seems to be largely defunct by 1700; the satirical 'political' novel of Christian Weise found a few imitators (*Die kluge und närrische Welt* . . . von S. M., 1723), but Friedrich Hunold's *Satyrischer Roman* (1705) was little more than a scurrilous attack on leading figures in Hamburg and of minimal literary significance; the picaresque novel was largely reduced to collections of scandalous erotic anecdotes, although it found a brief new lease of life in the 'Avanturier-romane', imitations of Nicolas Heinsius' *De vermakelijke Avanturier* (1695—translated into German in 1714). It is possible to see in the so-called 'galante Roman', however, a development of at least minor significance. This was in effect a continuation of the monumental baroque courtly novel, adapted to suit the taste of a rising bourgeoisie which was fascinated by courtly culture but remote from its inner values. The baroque models are stripped of their metaphysical implications, emptied of their ethical substance and largely shorn of their rhetoric: the reigning deity is no longer Fortuna but Amor. The prolific August Bohse may be regarded as the initiator of this comparatively short-lived genre; its most successful practitioner was Christian Friedrich Hunold ('Menantes'), whose *Liebens-Würdige Adalie* (1702) enjoyed a success excelled only by his *Satyrischer Roman*. Like the latter, *Die Liebens-Würdige Adalie* owed something of its popularity to topical interest: the plot reflects the actual career of a Frenchwoman of relatively humble origins who rose from the position of mistress to Duke Georg Wilhelm of Lüneburg-Celle to be his consort. Essentially, both the main plot and the almost equally elaborate sub-plot of this novel follow the characteristic pattern of the heroic novel: lovers' meeting, lovers' parting and subsequent quest, culminating in happy marriage. Such plots in the baroque novel, however, had metaphysical and political implications and were calculated above all to demonstrate the absolute constancy of the loving couples and their resistance to every tribulation and temptation. Rosantes, the hero of *Adalie*, and Renard, his counterpart in the sub-plot, show nothing of this traditional superhuman fidelity: although the proprieties are preserved, both Rosantes and Renard flirt with temptation and revel in equivocal situations. Sexual morality is handled with a sophistication and insouciance that contrast with the heroic ethic of the baroque novel on the one hand and the Christian morality of the later eighteenth-century novel on the other. The society depicted here inhabits a rococo world in which taste and good humour are the arbiters, and the chief offender is the spoil-sport. The same tone prevails in the novels of Johann Leonhard Rost ('Meletaon'), 'Selaminte' and 'Melissus'. The prevalence of pseudonyms amongst the authors of 'galant' novels may perhaps be significant of a decline in the status of the genre from the time when it numbered courtiers and at least one sovereign prince amongst its practitioners. Certainly, the new generation of writers appear to be of lower social standing and themselves inclined to look upon the composition of novels as, at best, a youthful folly. The 'galant' novel had in any case largely vanished by about 1740; it seems to have had no deep roots and possibly no very large public. It was succeeded by more edifying works, and its rococo style comes into its own again only with the advent of Wieland some forty years later.

A new impulse in the development of the novel in Germany was provided by the success of Defoe's *Robinson Crusoe* (1719). Although not the first novel in England or Germany to exploit the fate of the castaway, *Crusoe* was the first to explore imaginatively the religious, psychological and social implications of a situation which provided unique opportunities both for speculation on the development of man's rational faculties and for reflection on God's dealings with man through Providence. Defoe's work inspired in Germany a flood of 'Robinsonaden': almost every province and profession claimed its 'Robinson'—male or female—and the genre flourished, with growing emphasis on its didactic potentialities for the young, well into the nineteenth century. It even made its way back to Crusoe's homeland in the very popular *Swiss Family Robinson* of Johann David Wyss.

Almost alone among the early 'Robinsonaden' in its originality was J. G. Schnabel's *Wunderliche Fata einiger See-Fahrer absonderlich Alberti Julii eines geborenen Sachsen*, better known as *Insel Felsenburg*, the first volume of which appeared in 1731 under the pseudonym Gisander, with sequels in 1732, 1736 and 1743. Schnabel, a prolific journalist, perpetrated among other works a typical 'galant' novel under the title of *Der im Garten der Liebe herumtaumelnde Cavalier* (1738), in which the usual erotic exploits are tardily and perfunctorily revoked by the intervention of divine Providence. The *Wunderliche Fata* retains something of the extravagant plot of the baroque novel: it proceeds from a tale of elopement and violence to the description of a Utopia founded by four castaways and their later recruits under the patriarchal rule of Albertus Julius. It is a work which combines rational optimism with pietistic sentiment. The fate of the original castaways and the interpolated biographies of subsequent settlers suggest a revulsion against the depravity and corruption of 'civilized' societies and a longing for a new start based on the Christian principles in which Schnabel, as a pietistically inclined Lutheran, clearly believed.

As a 'Staatsroman' *Felsenburg* implies a protest against the 'political' ideal with its emphasis on guile, intrigue and self-seeking that had developed during the seventeenth century. Literary Utopias were not unknown in the seventeenth century, but their re-emergence in association with the Crusoe situation during the first half of the eighteenth century may be symptomatic of a certain social and political ferment. It is perhaps characteristic of the German novel, however, that where it impinges on the political sphere, it tends towards the Utopian or idyllic rather than towards the pragmatic and the satirical: that is, criticism of existing conditions tends to be implicit rather than direct. The long continuation of absolutism in Germany would alone account for this trend, but the phenomenon of German Classicism with its continuing prestige suggests that what we have here may be an ideological preference. In that most admired example of the German novel, Goethe's *Wilhelm Meister*, the ideal society is envisaged more in terms of an élite than as a political foundation; it involves essentially an 'inner emigration' as well as the actual colonization planned at the end of the *Wanderjahre*.

The ideal community described in another 'Staatsroman' of the time, J. M. von Loen's *Der redliche Mann am Hofe* (1740), is not literally a 'Utopia', for it is located in the Harz mountains. Loen's 'Christianopolis' is a more practical affair than the patriarchal society of Albertus Julius; it is the product of rational reform under the guidance of an enlightened sovereign who may well be an idealized portrait of Frederick II of Prussia. *Der redliche Mann am Hofe* is perhaps more of a 'Fürstenspiegel' than a pure Utopia, and can be regarded in this respect both as a successor to novels of the seventeenth century and a forerunner of works by Albrecht von Haller and Wieland. As in *Felsenburg*, however, there is a counterpoint of Utopian vision and topical criticism: the description of Christianopolis is balanced by the representation of misrule as a consequence of religious bigotry in 'Alpina'. Moreover the idealized hero, as the title implies, is the victim of intriguing courtiers and gains the favour of the sovereign only with difficulty. Although Loen is politically conservative and although he gives his hero an aristocratic title, the ideology of the novel is that of a progressive middle-class. The author is more rationalistic and also more sophisticated than Schnabel, and among the targets of his occasional satire are the equivocal raptures of pietism. Both the style and the compendious structure of *Der redliche Mann am Hofe* perpetuate something of the baroque courtly novel, and the love-story which is linked with the political action turns on the traditional virtue of *constantia*. Nevertheless, the emotional conflicts of some of the characters foreshadow an era in which the novel becomes progressively concerned with psychological factors. From about 1740 its themes grow increasingly domestic, its idiom more realistic; it becomes simpler in structure, less rhetorical in expression; character tends to become more important than events, virtue—and its preservation—becomes a central theme. In particular, the tension between the morality of the court and that of the middle-class family constitutes an increasingly prominent topic in the novel as well as in the drama. It is possible to distinguish two stages in these developments, corresponding to the generation of writers who flourished in the forties and fifties of the century, and those who succeeded them in the sixties and seventies. The older generation is eminently sober, rationalistic, orthodox in its Christian morality, concerned with establishing patterns of behaviour appropriate to the middle-class family. For them the ideal community has quietistic features, it is a family of well-tempered souls, bound to each other by equable affection. The ideal individual is conceived as pious and passively submissive to the workings of Providence. The ultimate virtue is 'Gelassenheit'—'equanimity'.

The younger writers who were active during the sixties and seventies were no longer content with this passive ideal, nor content to identify themselves with the ethos of a particular class. The claims of individual feeling are asserted against the laws of objective morality: each man tends to become a law unto himself and seek fulfilment not as a member of a philadelphian association but in terms of his own personality. New tragic potentialities are born of the refusal to accept persecution or mischance as the workings of divine Providence. It is this striving for the emancipation of the individual that culminates in the 'Sturm und Drang' period and, reinforced by the philosophy of idealism, generates the modern, essentially subjectivistic mode of feeling.

The initial stages of this development, in so far as it involves the German novel, would hardly be conceivable without the influence of English models, and the stages are in fact epitomized in the response of different generations to these models. The earliest English novelists to enjoy a vogue in Germany after Defoe were Richardson and Fielding, and the titles and settings of a multitude of German novels in the eighteenth century bear witness to their influence. German critics did not at first detect the significant differences between the two English authors: Bodmer, Gottsched and Haller saw only edifying elements in both; it was not until after 1760 that Richardson and Fielding became pawns in a literary quarrel between German 'idealists' and 'satirists'. For the older generation, however, Richardson was from the beginning pre-eminent. Brockes praised Pamela as a model of virtuous conduct, Gottsched declared *Grandison* indubitably the best novel ever written, Gellert set Richardson above Homer. It was largely in emulation of Richardson that Gellert wrote his *Leben der schwedischen Gräfin von G.* (1747–8). The heroine of this work embodies the ideal of 'Gelassenheit': passions and personal choices she calmly subordinates to the dictates of Providence. Forced to flee from court by the advances of a prince who contrives the disgrace and, seemingly, the death of her husband, the countess finds refuge in Holland and marries a commoner, Herr R., the life-long friend of her husband. After an interval of years the count returns from Siberian captivity and the original marriage is re-established; the home is shared, however, not only with Herr R. but also with Karoline, a former mistress of the count. On the death of the count, the widow rejects an offer of marriage from the remorseful prince, and a resumption of her partnership with Herr R. is prevented only by the death of the latter. The situation of the ménage à trois—or even à quatre—which may strike the modern reader as tasteless or absurd is designed to demonstrate the impersonal nature of well-tempered love which adjusts itself rationally to providential changes in circumstance. The destructive power of unbridled passion is illustrated, on the other hand, in the contrapuntal sub-plot involving Karlson, Karoline's son by the count: this unfortunate youth marries a girl who subsequently turns out, as fate—or Providence—will have it, to be his sister. Unable to revert to a proper fraternal affection, Karlson enlists in the army, hoping to find death. He dies indeed, not in battle, but from a lingering sickness. The sister/widow marries his friend Dormund, only to discover that the latter has poisoned Karlson in order to gain her hand: in despair, she kills herself. The novel, the latter part of which consists of the count's letters written during his Siberian exile, is in a stoically unemphatic style which contrasts with the melodramatic plot; it is not without a certain elegance worthy of an author considered the leading stylist of his generation.

The response of a younger generation to Richardson is epitomized in Sophie von La Roche's *Geschichte des Fräuleins von Sternheim* (1770) edited and published, with considerable misgivings, by Wieland. The plot has initial affinities with that of Gellert's novel as well as with Richardson's *Sir Charles Grandison*: Sophie von Sternheim, nurtured in idyllic middle-class surroundings, is introduced to life at court by a scheming aunt who hopes to profit by the prince's passion for her niece. More sinister still are the machinations of Lord Derby, who tricks Sophie into a bogus marriage and later, fearing she will prevent his marrying a wealthy heiress, has her abducted to the inhospitable mountains of Scotland. Rescued by Lord Seymour and Lord Rich, Sophie finds herself, like the Swedish countess, placed between two men equally worthy of her gratitude. Rich magnanimously yields to the prior claim of Seymour, and Sophie becomes an ideal wife, mother and lady of the manor. Sophie's virtue proves, like that of the Swedish countess, impregnable, but her attitude is less passive: she is tormented by religious doubts and moral scruples.

The Swedish countess was stoically committed to virtue; Sophie is passionately, almost hysterically, devoted to it. The letter form in which the novel is cast allowed opportunities for the unbridled expression of emotion and gave to the book the immediacy of a confession. Its readers were enraptured by Sophie's combination of temperament, spirited virtue and piety: they might well agree with Lord Derby who wrote in wonder and frustration about his fair quarry: 'Das Mädchen war eine ganz neue Gattung von Charakter.' The young writers of the 'Sturm und Drang' greeted the work with enthusiasm: for Herder it was 'einzig und weit mehr als die Clarisse', and Goethe rebuked its rationalistic critics in his review: 'Die Herren irren sich, wenn sie glauben sie beurteilen ein Buch—es ist eine Menschenseele.' In *Das Fräulein von Sternheim* there is no more than an inkling of the emotional intensity of *Werther* and the dawning appreciation of the beauties of Nature is as yet stiff, utilitarian and rationalistic. In fact, the modern reader will be struck by the dry rational morality of the novel, which must have been so much a part of the contemporary intellectual climate that it was taken for granted. The moral and religious near-hysteria of the heroine is superficial, the froth on a profound self-righteousness which is as placid as that of the Swedish countess. In spite of all the sound and fury the novel is an unproblematic work.

In Germany, as in England, a reaction against Richardsonian sentimentality soon developed which not unnaturally looked to Fielding as a model. J. K. A. Musäus parodied the prudish perfection of Richardson's characters in his *Grandison der Zweite* (1760), and there was an increasing demand for greater realism and more local colour. The critic Resewitz called for a German Fielding, 'der die Sitten der Deutschen ebenso genau zeichnete, als jener die Sitten der Engelländer gezeichnet hat'. Among the most ambitious attempts to meet this demand was *Sophiens Reise von Memel nach Sachsen* (1770–2) by J. T. Hermes, whose first novel, *Miss Fanny Wilkes* (1766) had been little more than an imitation of

*Grandison. Sophiens Reise*, one of the most widely read books of the later eighteenth century, does indeed give a picture of life in Germany during the Seven Years War, but it is diffuse, complicated and sensational in its plot. There is, too, something incongruous in the contrast between Hermes' manifest moral purpose and an attempted raciness in the description of situation; Hermes belongs essentially to the old school of objective moralists and finds himself compelled, for reasons which will hardly appeal to a modern reader, to condemn his high-spirited heroine for her 'Sprödigkeit', that is, her reluctance to follow custom and reason rather than inclination and taste in choosing a husband. The incidental realism of the work—which even attempts to reproduce dialect speech—and the depiction of certain eccentric figures are not without appeal, but *Sophiens Reise* is too prolix and pedestrian to rank as a work of art.

Among other aspirants to the title of German Fielding may be mentioned Johann Gottwerth Müller, who wrote in his *Siegfried von Lindenberg* (1779), 'Studiere den *Tom Jones* und schreibe nicht eher, bis du den beurteilen und nahe an ihn dich emporschwingen kannst.' Lindenberg gives an entertaining account of the pretensions and eccentricities of a Pomeranian squire and is not lacking in acute observation and psychological insight.

Both Hermes and Müller are admirers of Sterne as well as of Fielding, and many popular novels of the eighties and nineties show the influence of both these writers—sometimes dubiously combined in more or less satirical 'comic novels'. *The Sentimental Journey* had scarcely been translated into German before it was emulated by J. G. Schummel in a popular didactic novel, *Empfindsame Reise durch Deutschland* (1770-2). Even the rationalist Friedrich Nicolai was not immune from the influence of Sterne: it is not only the title of his satirical *Leben und Meinungen des Herrn Magister Sebaldus Nothanker* (1773-6) which recalls Shandy. Nothanker—abducted, incidentally, from Thümmel's popular prose idyll *Wilhelmine* (1764)—a good-natured and liberal-minded pastor persecuted by his orthodox superiors, clings through thick and thin to his 'hobby'—a revolutionary interpretation of the Apocalyptic books. The targets of Nicolai's attack include not only religious bigotry but also the affected sentimentality of the Jacobi circle, represented here by the poet Säugling. Something of the whimsical Sterneian concern with the fortuitous influence of environment is also shown by Johann Karl Wezel in his *Lebensgeschichte Tobias Knauths des Weisen sonst Stammler genannt* (1776). Although he attacks callow idealism and the cult of sentiment in *Belphegor* (1776) and *Wilhelmine Arend* (1782) respectively, Wezel is a much less thorough-going rationalist than Nicolai: he was himself an unstable character, and his best novel, *Herrmann und Ulrike* (1780), reflects in its problematic hero the situation of a man poised between the confident rationalism of the Enlightenment and the subjectivism of 'Sturm und Drang'. *Herrmann und Ulrike* is more genuinely symptomatic of the intellectual ferment of the time than *Das Fräulein von Sternheim*; the situation and development of Herrmann have much in common with *Wilhelm Meisters Theatralische Sendung*.

From a host of other 'Lebensgeschichten' and 'Reisen' of a sentimental or satirical complexion only one or two stand out. Theodor Gottlieb von Hippel's *Lebensläufe nach aufsteigender Linie* (1778–81) not only employs many of Sterne's narrative tricks, but also has something of the typical mixture of sentiment and wit. A brooding concern with death and the increasingly edifying tone of the 'Beilagen' are evidence of pietistic influence. Hippel's style and sensibility foreshadow the novels of Jean Paul. Moritz August von Thümmel followed the path of Sterne both literally and metaphorically in his *Reise in die mittäglichen Provinzen von Frankreich* (1791–1805); the enlightened traveller is horrified by evidences of corruption and superstition and urges a reform of education and a return to a more natural way of life. The elegance and urbanity of Thümmel's style place him on a footing with Wieland.

# II

## STURM UND DRANG

After Klopstock and the intervening group of poets called the 'Göttinger Hain', the writers of the 'Sturm und Drang' represent the culmination of the pre-Romantic trends which began with Bodmer and Breitinger's opposition to Gottsched well within the era of Enlightenment. But although these writers decisively reacted against the Enlightenment, the complexity of the historical processes leading to the 'Sturm und Drang' is so great and the impetus behind the Enlightenment so considerable, that in several important respects the 'Sturm und Drang' appears as a further development of the 'Aufklärung' as much as its revocation.

In both movements writers demanded social equality and individual autonomy, but equality and freedom meant different things in the two cases. Adherents of the 'Sturm und Drang' no longer believed that progress was assured by the 'enlightenment' of the human mind and they rejected the rationalists' view of the relationship between individual and society. Social criticism became much sharper and was principally directed against abuses of privilege by the upper classes. The lower orders are therefore shown in a new light and a host of figures appear in literature who had not been previously written about in the same way—simple folk from the countryside as well as from the cities. Rousseau was a powerful influence: his ideas on nature and society determined much of the thought of 'Sturm und Drang' writers. New distinctions were made or were newly emphasized, such as those between society and community, state and people, civilization and 'culture', the positive valuation in each case resting on the second entity.

Rousseau's primitivism came to be allied to another view

of nature. A characteristic feature of 'Sturm und Drang' thinking here is the interest in organic and dynamic processes as against the static image of nature prevalent in the previous era. Genesis, origin, development are the categories which now claim primary attention. They influenced the production and the evaluation of literature to a considerable extent. Stress was laid on energy of character and strength of feeling. Passionate involvement was ranked above intellectual detachment in life as in artistic presentation. This led to a form of expressionism in language and style. At the same time the interest in hitherto neglected representatives of society—the life led by simple people and the downtrodden classes—brought a greater measure of realism, even a kind of naturalism, into the dramatic literature of the movement. Here the pre-Romantic character of the 'Sturm und Drang' gives way to different trends which will reach full expansion only in the nineteenth century.

The cult of energy enabled the writers of the movement to evolve a new heroic ideal: the strong individual as leader, the creative mind rivalling the deity in fashioning human beings in its own image, genius proclaiming and demonstrating its autonomy in life and art. These predilections reveal a dichotomy of values which the members of the 'Sturm und Drang' could not resolve until they reached classical maturity. The common man and the heroic 'titan' ('Kraftkerl') are brought together in many works, novels as well as dramas, and frequently clash in the motivation of the actions presented in them. A similar discrepancy appears in the evaluation of literature and art. The supreme artist, a 'genius' like Shakespeare, was regarded as autonomous and in his works appeared to be a law unto himself. On the other hand such a genius was seen to be the spokesman of his times, and no less a product of the age in which he lived, the country in which he had his being, than its ordinary citizens. As Herder put it in his review on Thomas Abbt: 'Der führende Geist . . . steht in seinem Jahrhundert wie ein Baum in dem Erdreich wurzelt, aus welchem er Säfte zieht.' In his essay on Shakespeare it is difficult to reconcile the image of Promethean creativity with the idea of conditioned art whereby he accounts for the difference between the types of tragedy written in ancient Greece and the Elizabethan age.

Many conditioning factors were now recognized as contributing to the processes of history. Compared with the views put forward in the 'Aufklärung', 'Sturm und Drang' concepts of history placed far greater emphasis on the process itself than on its ultimate goal. More than one writer disavowed teleological thought, even in its Aristotelian form, and eschewed rationalist beliefs in progress, affirming instead the differences between individual historical manifestations. 'Sturm und Drang' individualism contrasts with the abstract idealism of the Enlightenment. Moreover, its primitivism led writers to pay increased attention to the origins as well as the processes of historical development. The essence of a phenomenon was seen to lie in its original form, as Herder stated in *Fragmente*: 'In dem Ursprung eines Phänomens liegt aller Schatz der Erklärung, durch welche die Erklärung desselben genetisch wird.' This point of view explains why the beginnings of individual and collective man, childhood and primitive society, came to occupy an increasingly important place in the literary interests of the 'Sturm und Drang' period.

Primitivism also accounts for the revival of folk poetry which had been given an inferior position by Gottsched and most of his followers. 'Sturm und Drang' individualism likewise enhanced the expression of personal experiences in poetry. By contrast, the assessment of poetry as a craft tended to be neglected and remained in abeyance until the advent of Classicism.

In spite of the prominence given to originality in 'Sturm und Drang' thought, foreign influences decisively affected the trends of the movement. In dramatic theory and practice Sebastien Mercier's essay on dramatic art was translated by Heinrich Leopold Wagner and this helped to sharpen the break with the drama of the preceding period. His eulogy of Shakespeare's genius was linked with opposition to the canons of Aristotelian criticism and so went far beyond Lessing who still attempted to justify Shakespeare in Aristotelian terms. Shakespeare was the major foreign influence: different aspects of his dramatic art engaged most German dramatists in the later eighteenth century as well as throughout the nineteenth. In the 'Sturm und Drang' Shakespeare criticism was largely moulded by English writers like Edward Young in whose *Conjectures on Original Composition* of 1759 (translated by Teubner in 1760) many of Herder's thoughts on genius, the rules, imagination and creativity are prefigured.

In poetry major English influences were James Macpherson's *Fragments of Ancient Poetry* (1760–3), and Percy's *Reliques of Ancient English Poetry* (1765). They helped 'Sturm und Drang' writers to formulate their views on the nature of poetic language and composition and on the difference between 'natural' and 'artificial' modes of expression. These trends were enforced by the revaluations of Vergil and Homer contained in Wood's *Essay on the Original Genius and Writings of Homer* of 1769.

Within Germany Johann Georg Hamann (1730–88) made the strongest impact on writers of the 'Sturm und Drang'. A radical critic of the Enlightenment, he arrived at his 'irrationalist' view of human nature after his religious conversion during a visit to London. His opposition to rationalism allowed him to exalt feeling, intuition and the imagination above man's intellectual faculties and to propound the principle of 'docta ignorantia' (*Sokratische Denkwürdigkeiten*, 1759). His own unsystematic fragmentary writings are full of improvisations and contradictions and his style, like that of his pupil, the young Herder, is a compact of oracular, allusive and associative utterances. One of the most influential ideas he stated in his *Aesthetica in nuce*, a chapter of *Kreuzzüge des Philologen, eine kabbalistische Rhapsodie* (1762), is contained in the parallel he drew between divine and human creativity: God is 'der Poet am Anfang der Tage'. His creation is 'Weltdichtung', a work of art. Aesthetically this view is of doubtful value since it tends to obscure the essential quality of any work of art. The young Schiller similarly equated the divine creation with a human work of art: he did not advance towards a truer estimate of aesthetic phenomena until he adopted Kantian principles under the guidance of J. G. Körner. Hamann's aesthetic ideas had greater validity when he applied them to literary topics. He described poetry as an imitation of the 'Tatendichtung Gottes', human language as the medium of revelation, poetry as the 'mother tongue' of mankind. The Old Testament, 'älteste Urkunde des Menschengeschlechts', is essentially a poetic work. Hamann viewed the poetry of primitive people in the same way and prepared the ground for Herder to enunciate his ideas on language and poetry in *Fragmente über die neuere deutsche Literatur* (1767–8) and *Kritische Wälder* (1769) which represents the authentic 'Sturm und Drang' doctrine on these topics.

Johann Gottfried Herder (1744–1803) was the intellectual leader of those 'Sturm und Drang' writers who gathered in Strasbourg during the formative years of the movement. His conversation made an even greater impact on his disciples than his writings, many of which remained fragmentary. He inaugurated a new era in criticism by rejecting judgements based on the application of set standards and instead relating individual works and authors to embracing historical trends. His importance lies in the fact that he contributed in equal measure to the formulation of 'Sturm und Drang', Classical and Romantic ideas.

During his first phase his most influential work was on drama and poetry. It is contained in his essay on Shakespeare and in *Briefwechsel über Ossian und die Lieder alter Völker*, from *Von deutscher Art und Kunst*, a collection of essays by different hands which he edited in 1773. No contemporary writer stated the new ideas on lyric style more suggestively and forcibly than Herder did in his appreciation of Ossian's

songs. Such 'popular' poetry represents the direct communi-
cation of feeling through irregular rhythmic patterns, concrete and sensuous imagery, impromptu and 'dance-like'
articulation (Würfe und Sprünge), obscure and even ineffable sentiments, dynamic word combinations and the use
of inversions and repetitions without regard for logical consistency. He followed up the essay with the collection of
*Volkslieder* (1778, later called *Stimmen der Völker in Liedern*),
which contains poems by Pindar, Sappho and Shakespeare
as well as folksongs from a large number of countries including Iceland and Peru. He helped to mould the 'Sturm
und Drang' style of German poetry until, with the advent
of Classicism, the practice of craftsmanship again prevailed
over spontaneity. Herder himself promoted the change as
early as 1775 when, in *Ursachen des gesunkenen Geschmacks bei
den verschiedenen Völkern da er geblühet*, he commented adversely
on the excesses which his own enthusiastic pronouncements
had in good part fostered, and demanded the renewed
exercise of Good Taste in the interests of order and harmony.

Herder had an intuitive grasp of lyric values. By contrast,
his contribution to dramatic theory has less significance.
The essay on Shakespeare in *Von deutscher Art und Kunst*
(1773) makes an interesting comparison with Goethe's *Rede
zum Shakespeare Tag*. Goethe praised Shakespeare's Promethean creativity; Herder's interest was largely historical. In
his 'Sturm und Drang' phase one of his main concerns was
to establish the relativism of history against the view held
by Enlightenment thinkers, to demonstrate the individuality
of each era and to show how it differed from other eras: he
put greater emphasis on the variety of historical phenomena
than upon their fundamental uniformity. This is the principal theme of the treatise *Auch eine Philosophie der Geschichte zur
Bildung der Menschheit* (1774) where he states: 'Jede Nation
(und freilich auch jede Zeit) hat ihren Mittelpunkt der
Glückseligkeit in sich, wie jede Kugel ihren Schwerpunkt.'
Thus all ages must be judged by their own standards, none
is essentially more perfect than any other, each represents a

characteristic totality of constituent forces. Later, in his Classical phase, Herder sought to find the force that links the ages of history together and eventually discovered it in the idea of 'Humanität'.

His 'Sturm und Drang' attitude is also evident in *Kritische Wälder*, especially in the influential dissertations on the origins of language and on the 'Laokoon' problem. In the latter essay he went further than Lessing had done by distinguishing more clearly between poetry and music on the one hand, and between painting and sculpture on the other. In characteristic 'Sturm und Drang' fashion he described poetry as a manifestation of energy ('Kraft') and explained sculpture in terms of tactile sensation ('Gefühl') which exhibits its three-dimensionality. This point of view enabled him to add the category 'In- und Hintereinander' to Lessing's 'Nacheinander' and 'Nebeneinander'; it again demonstrates a focal quality of 'Sturm und Drang' thought.

## Drama

The conflicts presented in the dramatic works of 'Sturm und Drang' writers reflect the current ideas on the rights of man, particularly the claims of vigorous personalities against an effete society. A strongly propagandist strain enters the depiction of those conflicts where in the previous era even Lessing had sought to moderate the political bias. Similarly, whereas Lessing had avoided metaphysical issues, the dramatists now showed their heroes as representatives of mankind battling against tyrannous supernatural forces. For this reason they used ancient myths and legends more often than had been the case hitherto: Prometheus was the prototype of the hero in revolt. The favourite historical background, however, was the Renaissance, from which dramatists of the 'Sturm und Drang' took some of their leading figures. Their attitude of revolt went beyond the choice of theme in their disregard for the traditional rules of dramatic composition.

In a revised version of his essay Herder asserted that Shakespeare portrayed events ('Begebenheiten'), while the Greek dramatists presented actions ('Handlungen'). This distinction is symptomatic of the practice followed in the 'Sturm und Drang'. Rejecting the unities dramatists now tended to present a series of episodes in preference to constructing actions in the strict sense: their works have an epic quality. Moreover, disregarding one of the main contentions Lessing had made in *Laokoon* on the difference between the pictorial arts and poetry, they used the words 'Gemälde' and 'Schilderung' for their dramatic presentations. The blurring of distinctions between tragedies and comedies led in the same direction. With their lyric interpolations, dramatic structures resembling the Romantic 'Gesamtkunstwerk' in rudimentary form resulted from these efforts to combine effects from different areas of art and literature.

The first plays to show 'Sturm und Drang' features are *Julie* (1767) by Helfrich Peter Sturz (1736–79) and *Ugolino* by Heinrich Wilhelm Gerstenberg (1737–1823). In the former play the heroine's refusal to submit to parental authority and the attention paid to environmental conditions show the new trends. But Sturz observes the unities, as does Gerstenberg in *Ugolino* (1768), although here the theme enforced observance of the unity of place. The play is a dramatization of an episode from Dante's *Divine Comedy*, the action representing the last phase when father and sons are faced with death by starvation. The principal interest aroused in this remarkable work are the different reactions of the characters to their situation, the contrasts of mood and expression ranging from the heroic to the macabre. In theme and tone German drama took a new turn with *Ugolino* which was written five years before Lessing completed *Emilia Galotti*.

The first 'Sturm und Drang' drama in the technical sense is Goethe's *Götz von Berlichingen* (1773), a model for many contemporary playwrights. But while these dramatists conformed to one and the same trend, they also showed individual predilections in their choice of themes and their treatment of common topics. Criticism of contemporary society is not the salient feature of Goethe's dramatic work as it is that of much of the dramatic work of Lenz, Wagner and the young Schiller. Klinger shared with Goethe a preference for dramatizing the fortunes of 'titanic' individuals in conflict with their times rather than with their society. In his 'Sturm und Drang' period Goethe treated this theme by choosing historical figures who had become legendary, such as Götz von Berlichingen and Faust, while Klinger also used contemporary material.

In his earliest plays, *Die Laune des Verliebten* (1768) and *Die Mitschuldigen* (1769), Goethe to a large extent followed the Rococo fashion, although in the former work he modified the idyllic theme by introducing touches of psychological realism while the latter play bears the stamp of Goethe's style in the handling of the rhyming alexandrine couplets: he frequently splits up individual lines by distributing parts among two or more speakers, thus loosening the traditional form. This indicates a certain break with convention and foreshadows the greater changes represented in the composition of *Götz von Berlichingen* which began in 1771.

Goethe's idea of tragedy in his 'Sturm und Drang' is best seen in his *Rede* on Shakespeare. He follows the trend of the time in pointing to Shakespeare's plays as examples of Promethean creativity: 'Er wetteiferte mit dem Prometheus, bildete ihm Zug vor Zug seine Menschen nach, nur in Kolossalischer Grösse.' In a later passage he reads into these works a problem that is in fact more his own than Shakespeare's, the clash between the claims of individual freedom and external necessity: 'Seine Stücke drehen sich alle um den geheimen Punkt . . . in dem das Eigentümliche unseres Ichs, die prätendierte Freiheit unseres Wollens mit dem notwendigen Gang des Ganzen zusammenstösst.' This is the problem of 'Sturm und Drang' titanism which Goethe, unlike other dramatists of the movement, from the beginning saw as a tragic issue. He did not exaggerate the claims of the

individual against society to the same extent as Klinger, and
he took more trouble to portray the conditions which
fashioned the attitude of his titanic heroes, especially of
Götz and Faust. In dramatizing the autobiography of the
German knight he does present a 'grosser Kerl' who fights
for his own right and that of others. But Götz is also the last
of the barons who opposes social change, the 'notwendige
Gang des Ganzen' that led to the rise of the middle class.
Götz is politically a reactionary far more than a revolutionary, the defender of an outworn system, not a protagonist of
social progress. Here Goethe's play differs from those 'Sturm
und Drang' works which advocate social change outspokenly
or implicitly.

In other respects, however, Goethe gave a lead which his
contemporaries followed. He presented a series of events in
Herder's sense and included two sub-plots. The first concerns
the relations between Adelheid (a 'Machtweib' modelled
on Lady Macbeth) and Weislingen, and brings in the theme
of infidelity, a motif which Goethe also treated in his other
'Sturm und Drang' plays, Faust, Clavigo and Stella. The
second sub-plot of Götz von Berlichingen sketches the historical
background of the Peasants War and the Reformation
(represented in Bruder Martin). This diversity of scene and
action endangers the unity of the work: only Goethe's skilful
control avoided the pitfall of formlessness to which other
dramatists of the time succumbed. But he chose a technique
of multiple scene changes which atomized the action and
made Herder deplore the excess to which his own commenda-
tion of Shakespeare had led. Goethe accepted the censure
and acted upon it when revising the play for publication.
This second version lost in liveliness what it gained in co-
hesiveness. In making these changes Goethe studied Emilia
Galotti and so laid the foundation for his later 'classical'
technique.

At this time he planned to write dramas on several legendary or historically attested 'titanic' figures: Faust, Prometheus, Socrates, Caesar and Mohammed. None materialized

except the first. *Faust* became Goethe's life work because the material allowed him the greatest scope for diversification. In its first stage (the 'Urfaust') the unity of conception was endangered by the disparity of the Faust–Mephistopheles and the Faust–Gretchen actions. The latter is a 'bürgerliches Trauerspiel' in strong contrast with the supernatural aspects of the Faust–Mephisto action. Lessing had met the same difficulty when he began to dramatize the Faust legend. His two plans show that the supernatural elements presented him with a problem which he proposed to solve either by making Mephistopheles into a human being ('Erzbösewicht') or by presenting the hero's temptation in a dream sequence to enable him to escape damnation. It is not known whether Goethe from the beginning likewise planned to save Faust: his 'Sturm und Drang' idea of tragedy makes this unlikely. The first extant version lacks the scenes when Mephisto makes his appearance and when he concludes the pact with Faust. This 'grosse Lücke' may be due to the fact that Goethe hesitated at that stage of writing the work about the question of Faust's damnation: upon this issue the terms of the pact clearly depend. The solution he finally arrived at takes us into his classical era.

The principal tragic theme in the 'Urfaust' is centred on Faust's seduction of Gretchen and her act of infanticide. These are favourite topics with those 'Sturm und Drang' writers who wished to voice their social criticism. Goethe is not among them, nor is his dramatization of Faust's urge to achieve universal knowledge characteristic of the period. He gave titanism a tragic bias by allowing it to reveal the limitations of the hero's nature and to provide the motivation for Faust's practice of magic as well as his search for experience to which Gretchen falls victim.

Although the work remained a fragment for many years, even the 'Urfaust' is Goethe's most representative 'Sturm und Drang' creation in real no less than potential achievement. This is shown in his formal and structural virtuosity. He fashioned a flexible medium comprising 'Knittelvers', prose and song with which he expressed a great variety of moods and feelings in monologue, dialogue and repartee, in reflective and emotional utterance.

Faust's dualism has its origin in religious doubt. By comparison, *Clavigo* (1774), based on the memoirs of Beaumarchais, presents the problem less searchingly. Carlos is a representative of 'Sturm und Drang' morality, but Clavigo himself falls short of it. He is a 'genius', yet a vacillating character. By divorcing strength from genius, Goethe cast doubt on a salient aspect of 'Sturm und Drang' ideology. He also moderated his own earlier practices of dramatic construction and expression. The inconclusive end of *Stella* (1776) where, with infidelity forgiven, general accord prevails, indicates a similar transition from 'Sturm und Drang' radicalism towards acceptance of the 'classical' principles of harmony and reconciliation.

*Egmont*, begun in 1775 but not completed until 1788, testifies to the transition in a different way. As Goethe reports in Book XX of *Dichtung und Wahrheit*, a new awareness gained ground with him at the time he began to write the drama. The 'daimonic' impulse he describes here is different from the titanic urge of his 'Sturm und Drang' heroes. Goethe saw it operating within the individual as well as externally in nature, and manifesting itself in contradictory attributes, rational and irrational, beneficent and malevolent. Accepting the reality of this 'incalculable' power, he transmuted his experience of it into poetic images: 'Ich suchte mich vor diesem furchtbaren Wesen zu retten, indem ich mich nach meiner Gewohnheit hinter ein Bild flüchtete.' He also says: 'Am furchtbarsten aber erscheint dieses Dämonische, wenn es in irgend einem Menschen überwiegend hervortritt.' When 'der grosse Kerl' of 'Sturm und Drang' provenance is ruled by this daimonic power it inspires fear. In other circumstances it evokes admiration and love. Such is the case with Egmont: in him it appears merely as carefree bravery, but nonetheless leads him to doom.

The play is an historical drama different from *Götz von*

*Berlichingen* although both deal with the theme of liberty. Exercising the right of poetic licence in dealing with his material, Goethe invented the figure of Klärchen and made Egmont her lover for obvious dramatic reasons which Schiller failed to recognize in his review of the play. Some of the broadly epic features of Goethe's earlier drama recur in *Egmont*, particularly in the crowd scenes. But Goethe succeeded in exploiting the dramatic potentialities of the historical material in a new way. He amplified the technique of contrast which he had practised in *Götz* and *Faust* and produced even greater diversity of interest within a more balanced total action. The final scenes show his new approach. They have, without justice, been called 'operatic', if this is a term of censure. They are intentionally untragic. Egmont's resignation and his vision of Klärchen as an emblem of freedom achieved, prefigure the kind of conclusion Goethe was to find for *Faust* nearly sixty years later. More immediately, *Egmont* points to Goethe's mature style of dramatic language. He did not finish the work until he had written *Iphigenie auf Tauris*. Embedded in the prose of the final act are numerous blank verse lines, the metre he chose for his classical plays.

None of the other 'Sturm und Drang' dramatists except Schiller had the talent or good fortune to progress far beyond the confines of that movement. Jakob Michael Reinhold Lenz (1751–92) had the gift to do so but succumbed to madness. There is much tragic violence in the plays he called 'comedies'. He used the term in a more than ordinarily embracing sense: he combined tragic and comic effects for purposes of realistic presentation: 'Daher müssen unsere deutschen Komödienschreiber komisch und tragisch zugleich schreiben, weil das Volk . . . ein solcher Mischmasch von Kultur und Rohigkeit, Sittigkeit und Wildheit ist.' He shared with his 'Sturm und Drang' contemporaries a strong antipathy against the abuse of privilege but avoided one-sided motivation of its consequences. In *Der Hofmeister* (1774) the tutor Läuffer and Gustchen's parents are equally to blame.

In true 'Sturm und Drang' manner, however, Lenz treats his main theme against a composite background. He includes a satirical portrayal of student life and introduces much realistic detail in characterizing such figures as the schoolmaster Wenzeslaus and the musician Rehaar. The epic interest is sustained to an excessive degree: for the thirty-five scenes there is an inordinate number of changes of locality.

Lenz practised a similarly impressionistic and epic technique in *Die Soldaten* (1776) with the aim of impartially presenting the privileged position of the officer class and the moral instability of the lower middle class section of society. As a play devoid of heroic intent it entitles Lenz to be called a 'Maler der menschlichen Gesellschaft'. His objectivity eschews the idealistic quality this attitude begins to assume in German Classicism, but it won the approval of Bertolt Brecht and gives his dramas their modern appeal.

The dramas of Friedrich Maximilian Klinger (1752–1831) have a more subjective bias. The deprivations he suffered in youth made him an outspoken critic of society. Following Rousseau, his chosen theme is the thwarting effect of institutions and conventions upon the self-esteem and freedom of action of exceptional human beings. He modelled his first tragedy, *Otto* (1775), on *Götz von Berlichingen* but added the favourite 'Sturm und Drang' theme of family feuds and treated it in characteristically explosive language. Fratricide resulting from the hero's revolt against the law of primogeniture is the content of *Die Zwillinge* (1776), emancipation and the battle against oppression the subjects Klinger treated with equal vigour in *Das leidende Weib* (1775) and *Die neue Arria* (1776). His next two plays, *Simsone Grisaldo* and *Sturm und Drang* (originally called *Wirrwarr*) are again written in this uninhibited manner, but they indicate the beginning of a change in his outlook: the feuds and conflicts end in reconciliation. In the oddly chosen setting of *Sturm und Drang*, in America, there are typical characters like the 'Kraftkerl'. Wild, violent passions and intentionally chaotic scenes: so much so that the work appears to be an ironic presentation of those features of the movement to which it gave its name.

Klinger was in Weimar on a visit to Goethe when he wrote the play. It shows him in process of outgrowing his youthful exuberance. Among his later dramatic works are the comedies *Der Derwisch* (1780), *Stilpo und seine Kinder* (1780) and *Die falschen Spieler* (1782). They treat some of his 'Sturm und Drang' themes with greater restraint. Despite his association with the Seyler group of actors, he did not succeed in the theatre but turned instead to writing 'philosophical' novels after entering the Russian military and civil services where he achieved considerable eminence. His farewell to the 'Sturm und Drang' is the satirical novel *Plimplamplasko oder Der hohe Geist (heut Genie)*.

Heinrich Leopold Wagner (1747–79) was an even more outspoken critic of society than Klinger. After imitating Wieland's *Komische Erzählungen* in his *Confiskable Erzählungen* (1774) and the satire *Prometheus, Deukalion und seine Rezensenten* (1775), he wrote two dramas which are characterized by stark realism bordering on naturalism. In theme and style *Die Reue nach der Tat* (1775) anticipates the late-nineteenth-century treatments of love frustrated by class prejudice. Wagner's frankly propagandist intentions are evident from his characterization of the coachman Walz who, like Wenzeslaus in *Der Hofmeister* and Wesener in *Die Soldaten*, represents human nature unspoilt by civilized society. The butcher Humbrecht in *Die Kindermörderin* (1776) is another sympathetically drawn man of the people but here Wagner's presentation is less partial than in his earlier play. His condemnation of the privileged class is not so sweeping as in *Die Reue nach der Tat*. His main concern in writing *Die Kindermörderin* appears to have been a plea for legal reform in the punishment of infanticide. Evchen Humbrecht's seduction and its aftermath have striking similarities with Gretchen's tragedy in *Faust*, justifying Goethe's accusation of plagiarism. But Wagner's realism and his propagandist line resulted in a play that is quite different from Goethe's, even in the treatment of the 'Kindermörderin' motif.

Johann Anton Leisewitz (1752–1806) treated the other favourite 'Sturm und Drang' theme, fratricide, in *Julius von Tarent* (1776). However, he was not a member of the Strasbourg group (he did not meet Herder and Goethe until he went to Weimar in 1780) but rather of the 'Göttinger Hain'. Unlike Klinger he focussed attention on the weaker brother and divorced the tragic issue from social criticism. On the other hand he followed the trend in condemning tyranny when he wrote the 'Dramoletten' *Der Besuch um Mitternacht* and *Die Pfändung*.

Aspects of the 'Sturm und Drang' are also apparent in the work of Friedrich ('Maler') Müller (1749–1825). Like Goethe he dramatized legends in *Niobe* (1778) and the fragmentary *Fausts Leben dramatisiert* (1778). In a Preface to the latter work he stated his reasons for treating his material in the 'Sturm und Drang' manner: 'Faust war in meiner Kindheit immer einer meiner Lieblingshelden, weil ich ihn gleich vor einen grossen Kerl nahm; ein Kerl, der alle seine Kraft gefühlt, gefühlt den Zügel, den Glück und Schicksal ihm anhielt, den er zerbrechen wollt' und Mittel und Wege sucht—Mut genug hat, alles niederzuwerfen, was im Weg trat und ihn verhindern will—Wärme genug in seinem Busen trägt, sich in Liebe an einen Teufel zu hängen, der ihm offen und vertraulich entgegentritt.' This is a good statement of 'Sturm und Drang' ideology, but in the parts of the play which Müller executed, the titanic side of Faust's character is not much in evidence. Instead, Müller dwells largely on the domestic side of his hero's life and the reasons (among them lack of money) which led him to make the pact with the devil. Maler Müller did not have Goethe's gift of portraying a forceful personality: his strength lay in depicting the student and merchant milieu at Ingolstadt where the action takes place.

His 'painterly' approach to his subjects comes out in the idylls he wrote in 1775 and 1776: *Der Satyr Mopsus, Bacchidon und Milon, Die Schaf-Schur, Das Nusskernen.* Here he succeeds remarkably in evoking the actuality of life in the Palatinate countryside. He was not equipped to write a drama in the 'Sturm und Drang' style. This is confirmed by *Golo und Genoveva* written between the years 1775 and 1781, in which he again aimed at portraying titanic figures in the unscrupulous Golo and in Mathilde, a virago with obvious likeness to Adelheid in *Götz von Berlichingen*. Instead, he succeeded well in creating 'Stimmung', the forest atmosphere of medieval Germany. The play contains scenes of great poetic beauty and for this reason, not because of its realization of 'Sturm und Drang' qualities, it may be ranked as one of the best dramatic productions of the time.

The last representative 'Sturm und Drang' writer was Friedrich Schiller. When he began writing, the movement had lost its impetus, nor was he associated with any member of the Strasbourg group until he went to Weimar at a time when the movement was a thing of the past and he had himself changed. His literary antecedents were different from those of the other 'Sturm und Drang' dramatists. Swabian pietism and relics of Enlightenment philosophy determined his outlook even when he revolted against the political and social inequalities of the time. His protests have a strongly religious flavour and when he wrote his defence of the stage, justifying it as a 'moralische Anstalt', he paid more than lip-service to the philosophy of the 'Aufklärung', retaining, in particular, the belief in universal harmony until his friend Körner disproved it in Kantian terms. His youthful poem 'Die Kindesmörderin' has far more moral fervour directed against the seducer than is found in Goethe's and Wagner's plays.

The starting point of Schiller's 'Sturm und Drang' was different from Goethe's: he did not go through a Rococo phase. From the beginning he showed keener awareness of social problems. In a sense Goethe amalgamated his two earlier phases (Rococo and 'Sturm und Drang') when he evolved his Classicism. Schiller moved away from his 'Sturm

und Drang' in a straighter line. The more Goethe developed
as a dramatist, the less he concerned himself with historical
themes: for Schiller history yielded increasingly rewarding
topics the more he outgrew his 'Sturm und Drang'. He
became the first consistent writer of historical dramas in
modern German literature.

The 'Sturm und Drang' ethos of his first three plays is
very pronounced. It is unmistakable in their themes and
their language. Yet there are characteristic differences which
place them apart and account for the direction of Schiller's
later development. In *Die Räuber* (1777–80) he does deal
with fraternal enmity, the theme stated in the sub-title. It
may have been the subject of Schiller's original conception
and only later gave way to the robber motif. At any rate,
both aspects of the plot show his 'Sturm und Drang' interest
in crime as a social phenomenon. Franz Moor is the younger
'disinherited' son of 'Sturm und Drang' tragedies on fratricide without being a 'grosser Kerl': in *Die Räuber* Karl Moor
fulfils this function and he is the avenger of social injustice.
By distributing the roles in this way and making such a
combination of themes, Schiller produced a new kind of
'Sturm und Drang' drama.

Furthermore, he added another facet: Franz represents
frustrated materialism, Karl embodies idealism gone astray.
The antithetic structure of the whole work is characteristic of
Schiller's art. It accounts for the superiority of his dramas
as theatre over the 'epic' forms chosen by his predecessors.
By turning his 'grosser Kerl' into a misguided idealist he was
able to include in his dramatic scheme a credible presentation
of change of heart, thus safeguarding his moral priorities.
Karl Moor comes to recognize his own guilt and atones for
it with an act of generous magnanimity. This is a motif
which Schiller found capable of further development in his
classical phase. In this sense Karl prefigures the later 'sublime' heroes.

Schiller's second tragedy, *Die Verschwörung des Fiesco zu
Genua* (1782), is noteworthy for being his first attempt at

dramatizing historical material. It remained an immature endeavour because he had not made a careful study of historical sources as he was to do for his later plays, but relied on a secondary account of dubiously 'romantic' character. The interest accordingly lies less in the dramatization of a phase of Genoese history than in Schiller's handling of a psychological motif: the corruption of Fiesco the republican idealist through the lure of power, the making of a potential tyrant out of a genuine lover of freedom. This project involved Schiller in dealing largely with deceit and intrigue. He made skilful use of imagery denoting acts of cloaking, veiling and masquerading, a motif which runs through the work and culminates in Fiesco's killing his wife when she is in male disguise. He had not yet mastered the technique of weaving love intrigues and political cabals together, a problem he faced more successfully in his next play. But he was able to put the love episodes to good account in constructing his tragedy on antithetical lines. *Fiesco* has many shifts of mood and attitude in language of appropriate diversity; its main feature is the contrasts Schiller establishes between the representatives of the two political camps as well as within the Republican fold.

Antithesis and variety of mood and language characterize Schiller's next play, the 'bürgerliches Trauerspiel' *Kabale und Liebe* (1783). An improvement of his technique is evinced by his ability to exploit contrasts of personality and to express them by differentiating the speech of the lovers Ferdinand and Luise from that of the courtiers and of the heroine's middle-class parents. In Hofmarschall von Kalb he also satirized the Gallic mannerisms affected in aristocratic speech of the day. In this way he developed the realism of 'Sturm und Drang' drama without going to the lengths practised by Wagner.

A further indication of Schiller's originality within the current tradition is his treatment of the middle-class theme. Social distinctions and their destructive effect for the individual are still the principal content of *Kabale und Liebe*, but

Schiller went beyond the traditional scope by adding an internal process of disintegration to the externally motivated destruction. The relationship between Ferdinand and Luise is undermined and their love destroyed no less by Ferdinand's jealousy than by Wurm's machinations. If Shakespeare is an influence here it has changed its quality since the days of Strasbourg. By amalgamating themes from *Othello* and *Romeo and Juliet* Schiller gave a more mature presentation of dramatic conflict than he had hitherto achieved. This meant that the way lay open to him to evolve a new style at about the same time as Goethe did when he published his first classical play. An important figure in *Kabale und Liebe* is Lady Milford. She had the makings of an Orsina or of a 'Sturm und Drang' virago. Instead, she acts on principles which Schiller increasingly used in his later dramas to demonstrate sublimity in his heroes and heroines.

*Don Carlos* (begun in 1782, completed in 1787) is the great work of Schiller's transition from 'Sturm und Drang' to Classicism. His original theme, enmity between father and son, became less important for him in the course of writing the play. This is partly accounted for by the fact that while his original intention was to write a 'domestic tragedy', it could not have been a 'bürgerliches Trauerspiel'. The plot was fairly easily shorn of its 'Sturm und Drang' bias when Schiller's growing historical interests influenced his writing. At the beginning he had based himself largely on Real's romantic fabrication, but as he realized the potentialities of his material he went more carefully into the historical background with the result that the rivalry between King Philip and Don Carlos in their love for the queen faded into relative insignificance. Marquis Posa, a character of subordinate interest in Schiller's first draft, now gained in importance as he came to represent the ideal of freedom in the struggle of the Netherlands against Spain.

Again, however, what might have remained a 'Sturm und Drang' conflict between a tyrant king and one of his liberal-minded subjects changed when Schiller made Posa into an egotistical schemer, an idealist who resorts to intrigue and deceit in carrying out his plans. Now a revision of the king's character became possible: in the completed work he is no longer the traditional tyrant but an intensely vulnerable man who is capable of generous acts yet demeans himself by outrageous behaviour towards his queen. Elisabeth, by contrast, gains in majesty in persuading Don Carlos to give up his love for her. Posa shares in the process of rehabilitation when he sacrifices himself for Carlos. But the defeat of idealism is made finally manifest when the Grand Inquisitor rebukes King Philip at the final juncture of the play and when he is seen to exercise real power over him.

This drama of inordinate length is best remembered for isolated scenes such as the confrontation between the king and Posa in Act III. It compares in dramatic interest with that between Nathan and Saladin in Lessing's play. *Don Carlos* is likewise written in blank verse, a medium which Schiller made his own in a remarkably short time after writing his previous tragedy. Its cadence of eloquence compares with Lessing's conversational and Goethe's poetic use of the form. These three writers fashioned the medium of classical German drama in less than a decade and in different ways impressed upon it the stamp of their personalities.

*Poetry*

Elements of the 'Sturm und Drang' are first to be found in the work of some members of the 'Göttinger Hain', a group of poets at the Hanoverian university in the sixties and early seventies. Klopstock's influence was paramount (the name of the association derives from his poem 'Der Hügel und der Hain'), while Wieland was rejected as representing alien trends. A 'Bund' was formed by contributors to the *Göttinger Musenalmanach* which Heinrich Christian Boie (1744–1806) and Friedrich Wilhelm Gotter (1746–97) began to edit in 1770. When Gotter, who later became an opponent of the 'Sturm und Drang', left Göttingen, Boie enlisted the aid of

Bürger for a short while; the *Almanach* was edited by Johann Heinrich Voss during the years 1776–80. In the later issues Voss, Hölty and Miller became contributors, as did Klopstock, Wieland, Herder, Leisewitz, Goethe, the brothers Stolberg and Claudius at different times. None of the last named except Klopstock and the Stolbergs joined the 'Bund'. It ceased to exist in 1776 while the *Almanach* continued to be published from Hamburg until the end of the century.

The poets of the 'Göttinger Hain' formed an organized group. They held regular meetings at which they discussed each others' poetry and they kept a record of these transactions which has been lost. They were agreed on some general matters such as the need to promote national feeling in poetry and shared a love of nature and of country life, but there are considerable differences in the content and the quality of the poetry they produced. In terms of literary history, the work of some members points towards Classicism, that of others towards Romanticism. The most important representatives are Voss, Friedrich Leopold Stolberg and Hölty: it is in their work that these divergent trends are most clearly seen.

Johann Heinrich Voss (1751–1826) had the greatest influence with his hexameter translations (1781–93) of Greek and Latin poets, especially Homer and Virgil; they became standard works and continued the dissemination of classical literature begun by Lessing and Winckelmann. In his original verse he showed a preference for pastoral and idyllic poetry, his most successful work being the idyll *Luise*. It first appeared in the form of three cantos in the *Göttinger Musenalmanach* of 1783 but was re-issued in 1795 and in 1800 with many prosaic additions in the form of an epic under the title *Luise, ein ländliches Gedicht*. In other examples of idyllic poetry Voss introduced a polemical note on contemporary social topics. He attacked aristocratic privileges in the 'Sturm und Drang' manner. On the other hand he also wrote idylls with the aim of spreading

'Volksaufklärung' by attacking superstition and ignorance. Here the continuance of Enlightenment tradition is evident. As time went on he increasingly showed this side of his interests: he became an outspoken critic of some aspects of romanticism, notably opposing the Catholic trends of the Heidelberg School, especially in *Anti-Symbolik*.

Friedrich Leopold Graf zu Stolberg (1750–1819) had little sympathy with the Enlightenment. When he belonged to the 'Göttinger Hain' he wrote defiant and forceful odes and hymns on freedom and kindred subjects, e.g. 'Die Freiheit', 'Freiheitsgesang'. The 'Sturm und Drang' quality of his verse is also evident in the language, metre and themes of his mature poetry. At the same time he showed a liking for idyllic scenes and tranquil moods of nature. The coexistence of both attitudes in Stolberg's work shows itself in his treatment of similar themes with contrasting effect as in 'Die Meere' and 'An das Meer', 'Der Felsenstrom' and 'An die Wende bei Göttingen'. This conjunction of the revolutionary and the pacific is a feature of the poetry of the whole period. Stolberg's idyllic trend is best seen in poems like 'Die Ruhe' and 'Der Abend'. It increased in significance after the death of his first wife in 1789. When he was converted to Catholicism in 1800 he belonged to the circle of Gräfin Gallitzin which played an important part in the development of Romanticism in Germany. In Stolberg's later poetry Romantic features are frequently found, for example in 'Lied auf dem Wasser zu singen' (1782), 'Die Bitte' (1789) and 'Sehnsucht' (1790). These melodious and suggestive poems are among his best work.

Stolberg's treatment of the quest for tranquillity when he was a member of the 'Göttinger Hain' is paralleled in the poetry of another adherent, Ludwig Christoph Heinrich Hölty (1748–76). His early death prevented him from fulfilling the promise he amply showed. He began as a follower of Anacreonticism and in this phase wrote some of his best known poems, such as 'Lebenspflichten'. When Bürger introduced him to Boie and he became a founding member of the 'Bund' he developed a different style and treated new themes. This is shown in his nature poetry, particularly in the groups of poems he called 'Mai- und Mondlieder' and 'Erntelieder'. The 'Mondlieder' are clearly pre-Romantic in theme if not in treatment. In none of his mature work are 'Sturm und Drang' features noticeable, although he wrote many poems in the 'Volkslied' style and in his ballads was influenced by Percy's *Reliques*. Another English writer whose work he followed was Thomas Gray. Hölty wrote a number of elegies between 1770 ('Elegie auf eine Rose') and 1775 ('Elegie bei dem Grabe meines Vaters'). His imitation of Gray's elegy as well as his relative independence can best be seen in the two poems he wrote in 1771, 'Elegie auf einen Dorfkirchhof' and 'Elegie auf einen Stadtkirchhof'. By making the contrast between village and city, Hölty introduced a rudimentary form of social criticism into the subject matter of Gray's poem and so showed some affinity with 'Sturm und Drang' tendencies.

Matthias Claudius (1740–1815) shared little of the growing interest in these tendencies. He cultivated the simple style of folk poetry without accepting Herder's theories, and distrusted the fervent expressiveness of *Der Messias*. It is one of the works he admitted finding incomprehensible. He spent most of his adult life in rural parts of Westphalia writing poetry which differs from that of his contemporaries in that it is genuinely 'naiv' in Schiller's sense of the term. His cradle songs ('Ein Wiegenlied beim Mondschein zu singen' and 'Noch ein Wiegenlied') and the poems on death, including the justly famed 'Der Tod und das Mädchen', are among his best work. His fundamentally affirmative attitude enabled him to indulge a quizzical sense of humour devoid of satirical thrust. An example is 'Wandsbeck—eine Art von Romanze'.

Some of the diverse influences brought to bear on German poetry between Anacreonticism and the Classical era show themselves in the work of Gottfried August Bürger (1747–94). His outstanding achievement was the creation of a new kind of ballad at a time when Gottsched's condemnation of the genre was still influential. 'Lenore' justly gained for its author a European reputation. It is his best known work but not the only one of its kind: he wrote other ballads in a comparable style.

Before writing 'Lenore', Bürger had an Anacreontic phase, traces of which remained in his later work. However, he deepened the Rococo mood in his treatment of love as a cosmic force, e.g. in 'Die Nachtfeier der Venus' (1769), 'Die Elemente' (1776) and similar poems. He published 'Lenore' in the Göttinger Musenalmanach for 1774. It is one of the first works partly written under the impact of Herder's Ossian essay. But it is essentially not 'folk poetry' in Herder's sense: far from being a spontaneous effusion of feeling proceeding in a series of 'Würfe und Sprünge', it is carefully composed and it achieves its telling effect with an intricately assembled stanza form and a judicious mixture of repetition and variation, narration and dialogue, description and onomatopoeic jingle. These devices enabled Bürger to convey speedy movement and the mounting tension of the ghostly atmosphere. He wrote other poems, e.g. 'Die Entführung', in the same style but with less success. In some ballads ('Das Lied vom braven Mann', 'Der Ritter und sein Liebchen', 'Der wilde Jäger') a moral tone which he kept under control in 'Lenore' became obtrusive. In a further group ('Der Kaiser und der Abbt', 'Die Weiber von Weinsberg', 'Frau Schnipps', 'Jupiter und Europa') Bürger employed satire, in yet another he used 'Sturm und Drang' motifs that deal with oppression ('Der Raubgraf', 'Der Bauer') and infanticide ('Des Pfarrers Tochter von Taubenheim').

He is in line with 'Sturm und Drang' writers in another respect. His 'Mollylieder' are examples of 'confessional' poetry. In these he did not achieve Goethe's distinction of creatively transmuting personal experience. In 1791 Schiller severely criticized this side of Bürger's work, unjustly, since he was not given to write his poetry to Schiller's precept:

'Nur die heitere, die ruhige Seele gebiert das Vollkommene.' But without reaching such classical perfection, Bürger did attempt formal control by composing sonnets. He did this at a time when few German poets wrote in the genre. His enterprise in this field has no little merit, but his place in the history of German literature is mainly assured by his writing 'Lenore' and by translating and expanding Raspe's *Münchhausen* (1786).

Goethe's poetic pre-eminence during the 'Sturm und Drang' remained unchallenged. The range and depth of his experiences and, more tellingly, his creative apprehension of them in the process of composing his poetry, qualified him as 'Erlebnisdichter' in a unique and unrivalled way. He achieved this distinction not only because of his ability to express his experiences in memorable form but because these very experiences were of a poetic order: experience and creation were complementary manifestations of Goethe's personality.

As in his dramatic work, so in his poetry he began by adopting established conventions. His first collections *Annette* (1767) and *Neue Lieder* (1770) owe much to Anacreontic models. Even here, however, some of his abiding themes make their appearance, as in his use of images like water and moonlight which he employed more significantly than other poets at that time. But a fuller realization of his true potentialities came with the composition of the three odes to his friend Behrisch which are notably original in theme and style.

During the years 1770–5 Goethe brought 'Sturm und Drang' poetry to full efflorescence. He has no equal in any of the different forms practised by the members of the group. The ballads, songs, odes and hymns he wrote in Strasbourg and Frankfurt are supreme examples of pre-Romantic poetry excelling even Klopstock's contribution in depth and range. The quality of his achievement may be gauged from the richly varied poetic dispositions he had at his command: directly communicative expression of emotion

('Mailied', 'Willkommen und Abschied'), suggestive narration and the evocation of mysterious presences in nature ('Der Fischer', 'Erlkönig'), idyllic description ('Anacreons Grab'), defiant challenge ('Prometheus', 'An Schwager Chronos'), rapture in acceptance of personal destiny ('Mahomets Gesang', 'Ganymed', 'Wanderers Sturmlied'), humorous self-assertion ('Lilis Park').

Goethe's lyric dynamism was greater than at any other time. This is shown by his preference for expressions denoting movement and by the actions he incorporated in poems like 'Wanderers Sturmlied', 'Auf dem See', 'Mahomets Gesang' and 'Ganymed'. These poems illustrate two other features in which he differed from some of his fellow 'Stürmer und Dränger'. The will to shape was strong in Goethe long before it found supreme fruition in his Classical era. Even when his 'Sturm und Drang' dynamism was in full spate he made this pronouncement: 'Ich finde, dass jeder Künstler, so lange seine Hände nicht plastisch arbeiten, nichts ist.'

The second characteristic feature is his choice of images which were capable of embodying his personal experience in correlative form. Such an image is the 'Wanderer' in 'Wanderers Sturmlied', 'Der Wanderer' and the two 'Wanderers Nachtlied' poems. Another instance is the imagery derived from natural phenomena like water and moonlight ('Mahomets Gesang', 'An den Mond'). From his use of these images we can trace the continuity and the changes of his poetry in transition from 'Sturm und Drang' to Classicism.

The last representative writer of the 'Sturm und Drang' in poetry as in drama is Friedrich Schiller. He is one of the major poets of the age (Hölderlin is another) whose lyric style was not moulded by the revival of the 'Volkslied'. It also lacks the quality of song which Goethe so eminently possesses. Some of his poems were occasioned by actual events, such as the death of a friend, but Schiller invariably left the occasion behind in order to dwell in cosmic realms of the imagination. His early poetry is characterized by the kind of abstraction he later censured in Klopstock, a typical example being 'Die Grösse der Welt'. His love poetry in particular is strangely unreal. If it is appropriate to call such poems as 'Die Entzückung an Laura', 'Melancholie an Laura', 'Phantasie an Laura' and 'Laura am Klavier' products of the 'Sturm und Drang', the difference between them and Goethe's 'Friederikelieder' is unmistakable. Similarly, Schiller's evocation of spring in 'An den Frühling' is less direct than Goethe's in 'Mailied': his feelings towards the world around him were far from sanguine. There is a strain of pessimism, a sense of bitterness and rancour in all his early work which derives from personal deprivations but can also be analysed as frustrated idealism. These notes are heard in poems like 'An Minna' and 'Eine Leichen-phantasie'. Compared with Hölty's gentle laments, Schiller's 'Elegie auf den Tod eines Jünglings' is intentionally macabre and acrimonious.

Yet even at its most exaggerated Schiller's lyric utterance had potentialities of development towards more balanced forms. The intellectual bent of his imagination remained inviolate, and when he subjected it to new influences he found the strength to produce an individual kind of Classical poetry.

## Novel

Although Goethe's *Die Leiden des jungen Werthers* (1774) may belong superficially to the category of the 'sentimental' novel inspired by Richardson and Rousseau's *Nouvelle Heloise*, it goes far beyond the other members of this category, both in its radically subjective morality and its aesthetic quality. What Goethe had said of *Sternheim* applies with even greater force to his own novel: it is indeed a human soul that is laid bare. Gone are all the sensational elements that had marked the novel up till now: *Werther* appealed to its contemporaries, and appeals to us still, by its artistic economy, and by its authentic emotional intensity. The 'plot' may be summed up in a few words: Werther, still smarting from an unhappy love affair, makes the acquaintance of Lotte, idealizes her and falls in love with her, only to find that she is engaged to Albert, whom he cannot but respect; he tears himself away and seeks distraction in a career which brings him only frustration and rebuffs. He is drawn back to Lotte, now married to Albert, ultimately confesses his love, and then shoots himself with one of Albert's pistols. The story rings true, not simply because it is known that these events reflect, on the one hand, Goethe's situation in Wetzlar vis-à-vis his friend Kestner and Charlotte Buff, and, on the other, the suicide of a colleague at the 'Reichskammergericht', but because the character of the hero is so utterly consistent. Werther, typical of his generation, is incapable of mastering a situation resolved with relative ease by Gellert's Swedish countess. His suicide is, however, not merely the consequence of a forbidden passion, much less the heroic solution which he conceives it to be. It is the inevitable end of an unstable character, whose idealistic visions and ineffable experiences could not be accommodated to the prosaic circumstances of his time. Unhappiness in love is compounded by disgust with pedantry and social prejudice; Lotte merely focusses a wider experience of rejection. Werther plunges helplessly from rapture to despair, for he has nothing of the rationalist's 'Gelassenheit'. His perception of the world is constantly coloured by his emotions. Nature captivates him with mystic intimations of divine unity, or horrifies him as a destructive monster, he turns from the sunny world of Homer to Ossian's Celtic twilight. The integration of every detail and circumstance to form a picture of a mind in torment gives *Werther* its inner form and carries it from the sphere of fiction into the realm of poetry. It is unique in its age and one of the first characteristically modern works of literature. It articulates the sense of alienation that goes with the purely subjective mode of feeling and demonstrates that suffering may spring not from guilt and malice but from sheer discord of mind and milieu. Goethe draws the tragic conclusion from which Rousseau, with his basically optimistic morality and didactic purpose, still shrank.

*Werther* was the first German novel to achieve almost world-wide fame. It fired the imagination of youth and incensed the older generation; it stimulated imitation and provoked parody in almost every country of Europe. Its German successors include J. M. Miller's *Beiträge zur Geschichte der Zärtlichkeit* (1776) and his more famous *Siegwart, eine Klostergeschichte* (1776), J. M. R. Lenz's thinly disguised account of life in the Weimar circle, *Der Waldbruder* (written 1776), and F. H. Jacobi's *Aus Eduard Allwills Papieren* and *Woldemar*. Such works represent the more elegiac and sentimental aspect of the 'Sturm und Drang' as it was satirized by Nicolai in his *Freuden des jungen Werthers* (1775). The aggressive titanism of the movement which so revolutionized the drama is less evident in the novel and manifested only in relatively late works by Wilhelm Heinse and F. M. Klinger. Heinse's *Ardinghello oder die glücklichen Inseln* (1787) is a Utopia glorifying vitalism and the aesthetic life. Heinse's enthusiasm for a return to nature is more vigorous than Rousseau's, his advocacy of Greek sensuality more robust than Wieland's, his vision of a Greece restored to pristine glory cruder than Hölderlin's, but he has affinities with all three. The dionysiac amorism of Heinse's work disturbed Goethe and Schiller, but he exercised a strong influence on the Romantics and has even been seen as a forerunner of Nietzsche.

In a cycle of ten novels, of which nine were more or less completed, Klinger sought to 'embrace the entire moral existence of man'. The archetypal figure of Faust recurs again and again as the author grapples with a welter of philosophical and political problems: the nature of evil, free will and necessity; the conflict of nature and culture; the dialogue of poet and pragmatist; the abrogation of aristocratic privilege and the improvement of the peasant's lot. The ultimate view of man's destiny is embodied in the Faustian philosophy of constant striving—even although God remains inscrutable and mute: 'nichts beantwortet dieses schreckliche Schweigen als unsere innere moralische Kraft, und auch sie selbst nur durch ihr Wirken.' In his concern with the corrupting effects of civilization Klinger is linked to Rousseau and Wieland; his vision of man's triadic development from innocence through depravity to higher harmony anticipates a typical Romantic pattern of thought. Klinger employs a variety of forms and idioms—myth, Märchen and satire, and it is hardly surprising that the vast enterprise barely achieves the unity he sought and that its extravagance reminds us of the baroque novels of an earlier age.

# III

# WEIMAR CLASSICISM

The roots of German Classicism in the eighteenth century go back to the Renaissance, but they also lie, more immediately, in the 'Aufklärung'. The ruling concepts of these antecedents were immeasurably deepened and broadened by the leading Weimar writers Herder, Goethe and Schiller. To them must be added a group of authors who made their own individual contributions—Wilhelm von Humboldt (1767–1835) and Karl Philipp Moritz (1756–93) above all—while others again, like Jean Paul, Heinrich von Kleist and Hölderlin stood aside from the main stream of Classical developments without dissociating themselves entirely from them.

The unique character of Weimar Classicism resulted from the fact that nowhere else in Europe did the equivalent trends emerge from the successive movements that make up its pattern: even in Austria the precursory 'Sturm und Drang' element is lacking, and this is true of other parts of the German speaking world as well. Weimar Classicism is largely a product of the Protestant parts of Germany, while in Romanticism the Catholic component becomes more prominent, if not at the inception of this movement, yet increasingly as it developed.

Weimar Classicism is also unique in being the work of writers who underwent similar, though not identical, intellectual and personal experiences. What Herder, Goethe and Schiller have in common in their transition from 'Sturm und Drang', is the search for new standards, universally acceptable norms, in the place of their earlier affirmation of personal freedom and individual predilection, partisan precepts and liberty of expression. The common link in the new outlook of these three writers may be seen in their concept of law in its most embracing sense: it is the foundation of the intellectual edifice which they built between the eras of 'Sturm und Drang' and Romanticism. At the same time this concept is different in their three cases and thus reveals the complexity as well as the uniformity of the Classical outlook.

To begin with Herder and Goethe based their idea of law on the exploration of natural processes, while Schiller's was more prescriptive and thus tended towards the assertion of morally valid principles. The difference is accounted for by the three writers' philosophical interests: Spinoza's thought for Herder and Goethe, Kant's for Schiller. In addition, science became Goethe's primary non-literary interest, history and aesthetics that of Schiller. Herder bridges the gap: his Classical thought is based equally on the idea of nature and of history.

Herder's Classicism began when he sought to discover the links binding together the different phases of human culture which he had so clearly set apart in his 'Sturm und Drang' period. From *Auch eine Philosophie der Geschichte zur Bildung der Menschheit* (1774) to *Älteste Urkunde des Menschengeschlechts* (1774-6), *Ideen zur Philosophie der Geschichte der Menschheit* (1784-91) and finally *Briefe zur Beförderung der Humanität* (1793-7), we can trace the emergence of his idea of 'Humanität' and his growing emphasis upon predestination and immortality—Christian elements which are essential to his Classical thought. It is grounded in pantheism—most clearly expressed in the treatise *Gott* (1787)—yet also transcendentally orientated, as shown in his belief in Providence as well as Nemesis (cf. especially *Briefe zur Beförderung der Humanität* and *Adrastea*).

Providence and Fate are forces moulding human existence which Goethe and Schiller likewise came to accept in their Classical periods: they must be included in any assessment of the basic concepts of Weimar Classicism. But again the individual differences are no less important than the affinities. This may be shown in an examination of the idea of Necessity which runs through much of Goethe's and Schiller's thought and influenced their dramatic output. Without disavowing human responsibility Goethe placed less emphasis upon freedom of choice than Schiller; he accepted the determination of individual and generic life through chance and necessity, as the poem 'Urworte Orphisch' explicitly states and the Classical dramas implicitly demonstrate. For Schiller the human will was paramount: 'Der Mensch ist das Wesen welches will,' he says in 'Uber das Erhabene', and likewise, 'Der Wille ist der Geschlechts-charakter des Menschen.' In his view necessity is a power which human beings can overcome by force of moral independence even when it destroys them physically. He refused to recognize its supremacy while Goethe came to terms with it.

Schiller arrived at his position after studying first history and then Kant's moral and aesthetic treatises. These disciplines gave him a new set of values. In any form classicism implies the acceptance of norms. Schiller's acceptance came from his assessment of man's role in the evolution of civilized forms of life, Goethe's from that of man's relation to universal natural laws. The relevance of Goethe's scientific work for his literary output may be studied by comparing two of his central concepts, 'Bildung' and 'Metamorphose'. Both concern the achievement of shape ('Bild') after a process of evolution. Like other representative writers in the era of Classicism, for example Herder and Wilhelm von Humboldt, Goethe's idea of 'Bildung' combined what was originally a religious concept involving notions of the divine image in man realized in a process of correction, with eighteenth-century biological theories on epigenesis and preformation. The synthesis of these ideas resulted in the notion that individual human development should represent both the greatest possible actualization of talent and the renunciation of what lies beyond its proper scope. Goethe's retention of Christian notions within the Classical frame is evident in his doctrine of 'Entsagung' and in the image of 'Menschlichkeit' he presented in *Iphigenie auf Tauris*.

'Bildung' and kindred concepts represent Goethe's Classical solution of the problems inherent in 'Sturm und Drang' individualism. Social integration is placed above self-assertion. In Weimar this ideal was promoted by the paternalistic form of political life, though the ideal remained unfulfilled. To this extent Weimar Classicism is the product of contingent circumstances, just as the form it took in Goethe's work was fortuitously governed by chance factors such as the presence of Frau von Stein at the court. Another factor was less fortuitous: Goethe's Italian journey (1786–8) was as much an outcome of his Classical leanings as a leading influence in their furtherance: the art and the landscape of Italy moulded his growing aesthetic awareness and account for the change in his sense of artistic form. In the place of what he had called 'characteristic' art entailing expressiveness and the cult of variety (cf. his essay on the Strasbourg cathedral), the principles he propounded in the journals *Propyläen* (1798–1800) and *Über Kunst und Altertum* (1816–32) after his return from Italy embraced the control of form through the practice of symmetry and proportion.

If uniformity was a guiding principle in aesthetic thought at the height of the 'Aufklärung', and during the 'Sturm und Drang' variety took its place, the classical precept to which both Goethe and Schiller subscribed was uniformity within variety ('Einheit in der Mannigfaltigkeit'). The impact of this change in artistic outlook is most clearly seen when one compares the formal values of the dramas and the poetry of both authors belonging to their 'Sturm und Drang' with those from the years 1786–1800.

In this respect, as in many others, Weimar Classicism represents a more sophisticated and elevated form of rationalism than that prevalent in the Gottsched era. Viewed from this angle 'Aufklärung' is pre-classical just as 'Sturm und Drang' is pre-romantic. Weimar Classicism also represents the zenith of developments in bringing about a synthesis of both movements.

With Winckelmann and Lessing, Hellenism became an

abiding feature of modern German literature. Goethe and Schiller imbued the Greek ideal with new forms of deepened comprehension, to be succeeded in even greater measure of insight by Hölderlin. In Weimar Classicism Greek legends appeared capable of embodying contemporary German as well as wider human problems. If violence was done to the real meaning of these legends and if this method of presenting contemporary problems seemed evasive, at least it curbed some forms of growing nationalism in literature and promoted the renewed acceptance of more universal values. This trend was supported by a return to French standards of artistic production, for example in Goethe's and Schiller's re-assessment of the formal values of classical French tragedy. Shakespeare retained his importance as a model, but no longer as predominantly as in the days of 'Sturm und Drang'.

The doctrines of universality and humanity current in the Classical era may be said to betoken an over-idealistic belief in man's goodness and a propensity to ignore the actuality of evil in the world. Goethe shunned exposure of the starker facts of Orest's matricide in *Iphigenie auf Tauris* and of the deaths of Philemon and Baucis in *Faust*. The reality of evil appears to be relativized in Weimar Classicism by the postulation of absolution through the exercise of 'Humanität'. However, this doctrine did not imply a total rejection of traditional religious beliefs. 'Sturm und Drang' defiance gave way to the acceptance of supramundane authority. This is evident in many of Goethe's poems written after 1775, in the completed *Faust Part I* and in *Iphigenie auf Tauris*. Schiller's idea of sublimity is based on the belief that man's spiritual strength transcends nature's power. But even these solutions were found wanting by the next generation of writers. The limitations in the position taken up by Herder, Goethe and Schiller led to the presentation of different ideas by Heinrich von Kleist, Jean Paul and the Romantics and, later still, by the adherents of Realism in the nineteenth century. Goethe's most

## Goethe's and Schiller's Classical Dramas

important Classical dramas were written between 1779 and 1810. They are: *Iphigenie auf Tauris* (1779–1787), *Torquato Tasso* (1790), *Die natürliche Tochter* (1803) and those parts of *Faust* which were composed during the same years. After 1810 it is no longer so meaningful to talk of Goethe's work as being 'classical': in *Faust* and in the poetry he wrote after the first decade of the new century trends appear which can be aligned with Romanticism but which more significantly achieve a quality entirely Goethe's own.

The Classical features of *Iphigenie auf Tauris* and *Torquato Tasso* are conceptual as well as formal. The former play is the more representative since the three versions Goethe wrote between 1779 and 1787 mark the progress of his dramatic output in transition from 'Sturm und Drang'. Compared with the dramas belonging to this movement, *Iphigenie* displays objectivity and the new ethical outlook. At the core is the religious conflict brought about by the oracle which appears to enforce an act of bloodshed upon the heroine in opposition to her innate moral sense. All other characters are drawn into this conflict. In treating their individual differences, Goethe shows his newly developed dramatic impartiality. The formal equivalents of this objectivity are the symmetrical arrangement of the scenes, the regular alternation of monologue and dialogue (particularly significant in the fourth act) and the predominant, though not uniform, use of blank verse which, in the final version, took the place of the prose and the free verse of the earlier drafts.

Similar features are found in the structure of *Torquato Tasso* which began, like *Iphigenie auf Tauris*, in the wake of Goethe's 'Sturm und Drang'. He transformed the original theme of misunderstood and exploited genius by putting his hero in the wrong when he aspires to a position which his true gifts do not entitle him to occupy. 'Entsagung' is the implicit demand voiced in this drama as in *Faust*, for while the claims of creative genius remain upheld against the prejudices of the world as represented by Antonio, the rights of this world are affirmed in almost equal measure. Tasso regains his poetic integrity at the end of the finely balanced action, although it is not clear whether Goethe intended his recovery to be a permanent one: the final scene is charged with tragic potentialities.

Considering all the aspects of the dénouements of these two plays, it is not justifiable to speak of Goethe's 'avoidance' of tragedy, however important the principle of reconciliation became for him in his Classical period. In *Faust* he solved the tragic issue inherent in the first draft by raising the whole action to a plane of symbolic import. Faust now became a representative of mankind, a Job-like figure for whose soul Heaven and Hell contend. The final solution is clearly adumbrated in the *Prologue in Heaven*, yet the dramatic interest is kept alive, if often strenuously, in a variety of incidents, moods and scenes. In what may appear to be a welter of events engaging a multitude of characters, the main themes of Faust's striving and temptation, sin and crime, and his eventual salvation and ultimate purification on the path to Heaven, are never entirely lost to sight. Despite all 'digressions and abandonments', Goethe was able to safeguard the unity of his theme and to enforce its dramatic continuity. In order to achieve this he applied some of the devices he had learned during his Classical apprenticeship: symmetry, parallelism and repetition in setting and character, as in the two 'Walpurgisnacht' and 'Studierzimmer' scenes, and in the analogies to be drawn between Faust and Homunkulus, Gretchen and Helena. He also preserved the integrity of dramatic impression by ensuring the almost continuous presence of one or other of the principal characters upon the stage. Nonetheless, this most representative of Goethe's works cannot be assessed in dramatic terms alone: in form and theme *Faust*, as Goethe contrived its monumental structure over sixty years of his creative life, came to outgrow the limits of any literary category or literary trend evolved in the eighteenth and nineteenth centuries.

By comparison, Goethe's other dramas are more traditional in design. He wrote two plays dealing with aspects of the French Revolution, the comedy *Der Bürgergeneral* (1793), and the tragedy *Die natürliche Tochter*. Of unusual interest are the 'Festspiele' *Pandora* (1808) and *Des Epimenides Erwachen* (1815). The stylized language of *Die natürliche Tochter* and the matchless poetry of *Pandora* and *Des Epimenides Erwachen* ensure for these plays a unique position in the literature of the time.

Schiller's path to Classicism is first seen in his historical writings. *Geschichte des Abfalls der vereinigten Niederlande* (1788) and *Geschichte des dreissigjährigen Kriegs* (1791 f.) testify to his increasing insight into the clash of interests and the moral principles involved in political action, an awareness which deepened into a profound understanding of the cultural issues involved when he wrote his major work on aesthetics, *Über die ästhetische Erziehung des Menschen* (1793 f.) and his most important critical study, *Über naive und sentimentalische Dichtung* (1795 f.).

From these studies his mature dramas gained considerable import. Compared with his earlier plays, the plots and the characters are authentic in a new sense: his Classicism has a core of realism which derives from his careful preparatory work on historical sources. But Schiller's realism differs from that of later dramatists; his attention to historical detail is only one side of his Classical art. More important is his acceptance of the leading principles from Kant's *Kritik der praktischen Vernunft* and *Kritik der Urteilskraft*. Kant's categorical imperative and his concept of sublimity were fundamental to Schiller's mature theory of tragedy as he stated it in the essays he wrote between 1790 and 1800: 'Über den Grund des Vergnügens an tragischen Gegenständen', 'Über die tragische Kunst', 'Über das Pathetische' and 'Über das Erhabene'. They determined his portrayal of historical characters in which he departed from the stricter tenets of realistic presentation.

*Wallenstein* (1798 f.), the first of the post-Kantian tragedies, is widely held to be Schiller's finest dramatic work: more firmly rooted in historical reality than the succeeding plays, the tragedy enacted yet has wider scope and harsher inevitability. But even in *Wallenstein* he safeguarded his idealism by inventing Max Piccolomini and in other ways too, modifying received tradition in order to lift historical reality into higher sublimity: the clash of interests results in the physical defeat of the representatives of idealism and realism alike.

This theme Schiller abandoned in his next plays. In *Maria Stuart* (1800) and *Die Jungfrau von Orleans* (1801) he carried his theoretical precepts into practice in a way he had not done in *Wallenstein* by presenting the heroines' spiritual triumph in their hour of physical annihilation. With these two dramas he went farther than before in violating historical veracity in the interest of artistic truth. They also show that he was not given to writing the same kind of tragedy twice in succession: the structure of *Die Jungfrau von Orleans* materially differs from that of *Maria Stuart*. The latter has a tautly antithetical pattern with a clearly marked climax in the third act, while *Die Jungfrau von Orleans*, like *Wilhelm Tell* (1804), has a more open, 'romantic' form. The same contrast prevails in *Die Braut von Messina* (1803), a tragedy of classical theme and proportions (including the use of a chorus), and the fragmentary *Demetrius* (1804 f.) with its colourful variegation of scene.

In all these differing dramatic designs, however, the continuity of Schiller's Classical practice is attested by his treatment of moral issues inherent in historically authenticated situations and events. It gives his tragedies their individual stamp distinguishing them from those of his contemporaries no less than the dramas of succeeding writers.

This becomes clear when we compare his tragedies with Heinrich von Kleist's. Both writers were influenced by

Kant's philosophy, but they registered its impact differently. Schiller took the lead from the philosopher's ethical and aesthetic principles, Kleist from his epistemological theory as well. For Schiller the power of the human will is supreme: man can break the bondage of physical necessity either by voluntarily submitting to it or by actively triumphing over it: Don Cesar in *Die Braut von Messina*, like the other 'sublime' heroes, freely seeks his own death. Misinterpreting Kant's statements on 'das Ding an sich', Kleist believed them to signify that human beings are incapable of distinguishing between falsehood and truth and that they are given over to an inscrutable higher power.

This conviction was confirmed by the occurrence of chance events in his own life, and they led him to present an idiosyncratic pattern of behaviour in his dramas. A striking feature in the conduct of his characters is the ease with which they fall victim to error and the violence, often amounting to brutality and sadism, which they display in reacting to situations they cannot understand and make no effort to comprehend. In part this is due to their innate weakness, in part to the intervention of malignant external powers, which Kleist keeps hidden in the tragedies *Robert Guiskard* (published 1808) and *Die Familie Schroffenstein* (1803), makes ambiguously manifest in *Penthesilea* (1808) and explicitly reveals in the 'comedy' *Amphitryon* (1807). In this play a characteristically Kleistian development takes place when Jupiter's seduction of Alkmene gives her a sense of higher existence but eventually leads her to lose her self-assurance, just as Amphitryon is robbed of his sense of personal identity. Loss of self-awareness in the ambiguous situations of life and deprivation of personal integrity in the storms of passion evoked by these situations, are recurrent psychological features of Kleist's tragedies, the mark of originality which was without parallel at the time he wrote them.

Chronologically these plays fall into the era of Weimar Classicism, but their intellectual and emotional substance is the antithesis of that in Goethe's and Schiller's Classical dramas. Kleist's comedies are no less unique. They have tragic undertones, more marked in *Amphitryon* than in *Der zerbrochene Krug* (completed 1808, publ. 1811) which is still unlike any previous work of the same genre. Some of his later plays have affinities with those of the Romantics, notably the fairy-tale drama *Das Käthchen von Heilbronn* (publ. 1810) and the propagandist patriotic play *Die Hermannsschlacht* (publ. 1821). They are not without interest, but they do not show Kleist at his best. His last work, *Prinz Friedrich von Homburg* (publ. 1821), is his dramatic masterpiece in that it represents a more universally valid attempt to resolve the tragic dilemmas inherent in his earlier plays. While it does not have the dramatic power of *Penthesilea*, its balanced construction and subtle motivation rival the achievements of his greatest contemporaries. Kleist's forthright psychological veracity untinged by idealism entitles him to be considered the foremost of the dramatists who adumbrate the transition from Classicism and Romanticism to the literature of the new age of Realism.

## Poetry in the Era of Classicism

While 'Erlebnis' remained a formative element in Goethe's poetry during his Classical phase, he transformed the expression of his personal experiences by exercising greater restraint and aiming at more impersonally valid presentations. He took up again many of the themes he had treated before; his new poetry is characterized by the changed meaning these themes gained for him. This accounts for the idealized contours he now gave to nature and to love, the relief he sought for his former doubts and griefs, and the forms he chose to state these mature experiences and beliefs. His earlier modes of passionate expression in song, hymn and ode gave way to more measured compositions in which descriptive, narrative and reflective elements are stronger components than before.

Reflection is inherent in all Goethe's poetry: even his

most intuitive lyric work in the 'Sturm und Drang' era is not devoid of it. But his growing sense of responsibility, acceptance of human limitations and affirmation of universal laws gave wider scope to the reflective element and enabled him to fashion a new kind of poetry.

These changes may be seen in the poems he wrote just before going to Weimar and in his first years there, for example in 'Grenzen der Menschheit' (1781) and 'Das Göttliche' (1783) with their calculated didactic content, 'Ilmenau' (1783) and 'Harzreise im Winter' with their new sense of mission and accountability. A similar awareness of professional responsibility prevails in such occasional verse as 'Auf Miedings Tod', while the extension of personal desires into timeless transcendence is the mark of love poems like those addressed to Charlotte von Stein. The same trends are seen in the ballads Goethe then wrote. They were brought to fruition during, and immediately after, the journey to Italy (1786–8) when he concentrated upon narrative and reflective poetry. In the latter genre *Römische Elegien* (1795) and *Venezianische Epigramme* (1796) are the principal yield, while the culmination of his work in the former category are *Reineke Fuchs* (1794), *Alexis und Dora* (1796) and *Hermann und Dorothea* (1797). This last work, a love story enacted against the aftermath of the French Revolution, is a masterpiece of balanced construction and idealized presentation of actuality. Like the other epic writings it is composed in hexameters, a form which Goethe practised with much success, even to express the prevailingly bourgeois sentiments of *Hermann und Dorothea*.

This phase of Goethe's Classicism came to an end when he wrote to Schiller in August 1797 that he proposed to explore symbolism in poetry. In this endeavour his later poetry ran parallel with that of Hölderlin and some of the Romantics, although the differences between them all remain considerable. Goethe's poetic symbolism is based on the insights he gained from his scientific studies, and on his intimations of the correspondence between cosmic and terrestrial life. Thus in the poems 'Metamorphose der Pflanzen' and 'Metamorphose der Tiere' phases of plant and animal structure symbolize aspects of human relationship. Another case is 'Gingo Biloba' with its relevance for the poet's love, while 'An vollen Büschelzweigen' adds a further facet by including his creative process. Exceeding in scope even this poetic mode are Goethe's mature reflective poems which he grouped together under the heading 'Gott und Welt'. They are unrivalled [for their evocative power and intellectual penetration, particularly in such supreme examples as 'Eins und Alles', 'Dauer im Wechsel', 'Weltseele', 'Selige Sehnuscht', 'Proömion' and 'Urworte Orphisch' (1820).

While writing poetry of this unique kind, Goethe continued to exploit his more personal experiences: the characteristic works in the later stages of his life are *West-östlicher Divan* (1814–19) and 'Trilogie der Leidenschaft (1827). The former collection is a creative experiment in love poetry representing the voices of both partners and masking the actuality of their relationship as well as that of contemporary events in an Eastern setting and in an adaptation of Hafis' lyric forms. 'Trilogie der Leidenschaft', most poignant and renunciatory of Goethe's 'Erlebnisdichtung', points the parallel with the experience of Werther and achieves a new resolution through the power of music.

Schiller's closest collaboration with Goethe occurred during the years 1796 and 1797 when they jointly composed the collection of satirical epigrammatic verse *Xenien* and, severally, a series of ballads. Schiller's poetry, no less than his drama, had undergone considerable change since his 'Sturm und Drang'. The Classical direction first showed itself in attempts to curb the excessive pessimism to which he had been prone. The friendship with C. G. Körner proved most formative in bringing about the change. An early indication is found in 'An die Freude' (1786), an ode in which Schiller took up a favourite Anacreontic theme and into which he imported his own cosmic vision. A new readiness to experience pleasure also asserted itself against the earlier rigour in poems like 'Der Kampf' and 'Resignation' which belong to the same time (1786).

Schiller's attitude to the contemporary world in another group of poems headed by 'Die Götter Griechenlands' (1788) and 'Die vier Weltalter' was still largely negative, although he had now found a positive ideal with which to contrast his own age. The former poem is a dirge lamenting the loss of the beauty and richness of the Greek heritage, but it harbours recognition of potential recuperation. The aesthetic basis of Schiller's classicism begins to show itself and finds its first complete expression in the long philosophical poem 'Die Künstler' (1789). Here for the first time he treats the cardinal tenet of his Classicism: the conviction that art and beauty are true agents of culture through which man passes from savagery to civilization, from sensuality to rational behaviour. The argument of 'Die Künstler' is often confused and Schiller had yet to find a more adequate form than the verse sections of varied length and the allegorical imagery which often obscures the progress of his thought. The advance he made in composing philosophical poetry may be gauged when we compare his handling of the theme of 'Die Künstler' with that of 'Der Spaziergang' (1795) where he traces phases in the history of man's social and political organization correlatively with different scenes he encountered during a country walk. He adopted a similar technique in 'Die Erwartung' and 'Der Tanz' where his performance, as in 'Der Spaziergang', is perhaps more impressive than in 'Das Lied von der Glocke' (1800) with its rigid alternation between passages describing bell-making and observations on the crucial situations of private and civic life. Schiller's Kantian legacy is also seen in 'Das Ideal und das Leben' (1795), where he postulates the need for order and harmony, and in 'Die Klage der Ceres' and 'Das Eleusische Fest' (1798) which celebrate productive human activity within a framework of elegiac lament.

Philosophical poetry in elegiac verse is Schiller's principal form of expression in the Classical manner before he collaborated with Goethe. The ballads he wrote in 1797 demonstrate the difference between his contribution to Weimar Classicism and Goethe's. They show his greater dramatic vigour but equally his more readily apprehensible didactic purpose. Goethe's subtle motivations in 'Die Braut von Korinth' and 'Der Gott und die Bajadere' encompass deliberately ambiguous meanings in contrast to Schiller's overt presentation of moral stamina in his most characteristic ballads, such as 'Der Taucher', 'Die Kraniche des Ibykus', 'Die Bürgschaft', 'Der Gang zum Eisenhammer'. The composition of these ballads had a special significance for Schiller in that it prepared him for writing his later tragedies both formally, in that the structure of the ballad resembles that of the drama, and conceptually, since his most successful poems in this genre contain a first poetic intimation of sublimity which he had explored in theory and was about to put into dramatic practice.

Friedrich Hölderlin (1770–1843) is the poet living in the era of Classicism who had, at the beginning of his poetic career, the closest affinities with Schiller. The poems he wrote before 1797 are a tribute to this allegiance but they are his least characteristic work: they embody an abstract form of idealism allegorically conveyed in a style of no great distinction. The year 1797 marks a crucial juncture. Estrangement from Schiller, love for Suzette Gontard, new intellectual interests in association with Hegel and Schelling who had been his contemporaries at the 'Tübinger Stift' from 1788 to 1793, the impact of the French Revolution and the campaigns of Napoleon whom he fervently admired, travels in Germany, Switzerland and France, preoccupation with the masterpieces of Greek literature and Greek thought —these formative experiences combined to produce in Hölderlin an aptitude to write some of the greatest poetry in the German language.

He limited his production by disregarding popular forms

like the ballad and the 'Lied' and even eschewing Romance
genres like the sonnet which had become a part of the
German lyric tradition. Instead, he concentrated upon the
stateliest genres—ode, hymn, idyll and elegy—and here
achieved lasting success. He became a master in handling
Pindaric, Sapphic and Alcaic stanza forms and, more
important, evolved a 'triadic' structural principle and a
theory of 'Wechsel der Töne' entirely his own which he
put into effect in his most considerable compositions such as
'Der Rhein', 'Brot und Wein' and 'Patmos'.

His characteristic themes are small in number but
profoundly searching; they are contained in his idiosyncratic ideas on history and religion linking together Hellas
and 'Hesperien', the gods of the ancient world and Christianity, remotely historical and narrowly contemporary
events. Among his unrivalled evocations are the Greek
scenes of 'Der Archipelagus' and the German ones of
'Heidelberg' and 'Stuttgart'. Hölderlin's poetry is an almost
self-contained world with its own correlations of landscapes
and seasons, myths and symbols, visions and perceptions.
The same is true of his quite unusual tragedy *Empedokles*, the
three versions of which (1797–1800) remained fragmentary.
Neither Goethe nor Schiller had the measure of his greatness
which, however, had not come to poetic fruition when they
got to know him personally. Nor was it fully recognized
before the twentieth century, although some of the Romantics
and, later in the nineteenth century, Mörike and Nietzsche
had more than an inkling. A Hellenist unlike any other of
the eighteenth century, a religious poet more individual and
profound than even Novalis, Hölderlin is of the age of
German Classicism and Romanticism without in essence
belonging to either literary trend.

## The Classical Novel

A noteworthy attempt to establish a theory of the novel and
to formulate principles on which it might develop was made

by Friedrich von Blanckenburg in a *Versuch über den Roman* (1774) which manifests both the perspicacity and the limitations of the rationalist critic. Blanckenburg believed that the novel occupied in modern society the place taken in antiquity by the epic; it differs essentially from the epic, however, in that it is concerned not with the 'Bürger', which is the term Blanckenburg uses for the member of a community, but with the individual personality—'der Mensch'. For Blanckenburg, all literature must have a plain moral purpose, and the chief concern of the poet should be to serve this purpose even as he entertains his readers: 'Der Dichter soll in seinen Lesern auf die Art, wie er es durch seine Mittel vorzüglich kann, Vorstellungen und Empfindungen erzeugen, die die Vervollkommnung des Menschen und seine Bestimmung befördern können.' To achieve this the poet creates a microcosm in which the order of the universe, too vast otherwise for our comprehension, is intelligibly mirrored. Since the dynamic order of the universe—'alles ist werdend in der Natur'—is determined by the sequence of cause and effect, the novelist as poet must show us the development of his hero in graphic terms of cause and effect. The novel should achieve its moral aim not by preaching or by the depiction of improbably perfect characters but by the plausible development of the hero through influences of education and experience to a degree of perfection which is convincing in human terms. In this sense Richardson and his German imitators fall short and are criticized by Blanckenburg, who sets against them the examples of *Tom Jones* and Wieland's *Agathon*. In the latter Blanckenburg sees a new category of psychological novel which will supersede the merely 'narrative' novel of the past. In Agathon 'sehen wir, *wie* er zu all den Eigenschaften gelangt ist, die ihn uns so schätzbar machen'.

This praise, warm as it is, does Wieland's novel only partial justice. From his standpoint as rational moralist Blanckenburg cannot command an entire aspect of the work which makes it the first of the great German 'Bildungsromane': this is the element of personal involvement of 'confession'. In the attempts of the hero to establish the nice balance between indulgence and the demands of morality, between reason and sensuality, Wieland is rehearsing, not for the first or last time, his own inner conflict. In his youth he had subscribed to a Christian equivalent of Agathon's high-flown Platonic idealism. He had formed part of a sentimentally religious coterie in Zürich, imitated the morbid transports of Edward Young and Elizabeth Rowe, fashioned the Clementina di Porretta episode of *Grandison* into a drama, allowed himself to be adopted by Bodmer as the protagonist of a 'seraphic' school of poetry. In later years he commented ironically that such 'spiritual debaucheries' had done his health more harm than physical indulgence had. The reaction against the 'seraphic' period is amusingly recorded in the satirical novel modelled on Cervantes, *Don Sylvio von Rosalva* (1764), sub-titled *Der Sieg der Natur über die Schwärmerey*, in which the young hero is converted from his belief in fairies and achieves a congenial sensuality.

*Agathon*, as a positive statement of its author's views, is a much more ambitious work. Begun at the same time as *Don Sylvio*, it occupied Wieland, in various redactions, for many years. In a characteristic way it exploits parallels between the philosophical creeds of Ancient Greece and varieties of contemporary religious experience. Like much of Wieland's work it has—both in its ideology and its form— a somewhat eclectic character. The hero of the story is exposed to disillusioning experiences in love, resists the blandishments of Hippias, a rational hedonist, is caught up in intrigue and suffers imprisonment. He finds harmony and contentment under the guidance of the sage Archytas, his passion for the hetaera Danae tempered to affectionate friendship, his ethereal love for Psyche readily moderated by the discovery that she is his long-lost sister. Ultimate wisdom consists in the realization that man can progress only by coming to terms with his dual nature, 'dass der

Mensch—auf der einen Seite den Tieren des Feldes, auf der anderen den höheren Wesen und der Gottheit selbst verwandt—zwar ebenso unfähig sei, ein blosses Tier als ein blosser Geist zu sein, aber dass er nur alsdann seiner Natur gemäss lebe, wenn er immer emporsteige; dass jede höhere Stufe der Weisheit und Tugend, die er erstiegen hat, seine Glückseligkeit erhöhe.' Not even the final version of 1794, however, in which the exemplary career of Archytas gives Agathon new confidence, has an entirely convincing conclusion.

In his belief in the perfectibility of man and his confidence in the power of reason to govern passion, Wieland is a representative of Enlightenment humanism with its watchwords of Nature and Reason; in his ideal of harmonious development of the personality, in his irony and in the liberality of his aesthetic imagination, in his informed devotion to Greek antiquity as a model in life and art, in the elegance and sophistication of his style, he is the first founder of Weimar Classicism. His other novels are inspired by the same ideals, marked by the same qualities. *Die Geschichte der Abderiten* is based on the legendary follies of the Greek city-state of Abdera: Wieland contrives both to satirize the philistinism of German provincial life and to dampen the uncritical enthusiasm for Classical ideals which had been fired by J. J. Winckelmann's *Gedanken über die Nachahmung der griechischen Werke in der Malerei und Bildkunst* (1755) and *Geschichte der Kunst des Altertums* (1764). *Agathodämon* reverts to the Utopian model in describing an ideal community established on the principles of nature and reason. *Peregrinus Proteus* concerns itself with a problem that occupied Wieland for much of his life, the authenticity and validity of mystical experiences. *Aristipp und einige seiner Zeitgenossen* takes as its hero a pupil of Socrates, the hedonist philosopher Aristippos; the letters of which the work consists conjure up a nostalgic picture of a golden age very different from the turbulent and uncongenial era in which Wieland lived out the last years of his life. At heart he remained a cosmopolitan of the eighteenth century, a rococo figure, undoubtedly—and perhaps happily—lacking the sense of incommensurable and demonic forces in human destiny, unable to relinquish optimistic notions of Providence and progress. The conflict between man's higher and lower selves repeatedly epitomized in Wieland's heroes is, in a sense, the conflict of Faust's two souls, but Wieland never seems to have been fully aware of the tragic potentialities of this conflict: one feels that he was never more than 'un homme moyen sensuel'.

With *Agathon* Wieland established the most characteristic species of the German novel—the 'Bildungsroman'. Fundamental to the 'Bildungsroman' is the idea of the hero's organic development—under formative influences of chance and environment, it is true—but essentially from his inner resources. This idea may owe something to the Leibnizian theory of preformation, but it is also an aspect of the general process of secularization termed the Enlightenment that visualized the emergence of man from his self-imposed minority into a condition of autonomy. It gained strength from analogy with discoveries in the natural sciences as well as from progress in educational theories and constituted an essential part of Classicism.

The 'Bildungsroman' tends to be at least an inner biography of its author, an amalgam of truth and fiction; it could perhaps be visualized as occupying the centre of the broad spectrum of the 'Entwicklungsroman', ranging from the didactic paedagogical novel (Erziehungsroman) on the one hand to the thinly disguised autobiography on the other. At one extreme we might place Pestalozzi's *Lienhard und Gertrud* (1781–7), which describes the rescue of a Swiss village from ignorance, superstition and corruption and its rehabilitation by practical economic measures. As moralist and educator Pestalozzi embodies a distinct national tradition which is continued in Jeremias Gotthelf and Gottfried Keller. The 'Fürstenspiegel', through which eighteenth-century philosophers still hoped to breed enlightened despots, is a special category of 'Erziehungsroman'.

Wieland provides an example in his *Goldner Spiegel oder Die König von Scheschian* (1772), a characteristically urbane treatise which seeks to balance divine right and social contract, absolutism and democracy, clericalism and free thought. As a diplomatic statement of the liberal policies expected of the Emperor Joseph II it was intended to secure for its author a situation at the court of Vienna. It brought him to Weimar instead.

At the other end of the scale represented by the 'Entwicklungsroman' in general one finds such autobiographical works as Heinrich Jung-Stilling's *Lebensgeschichte* (1777–8) and Karl Philipp Moritz's *Anton Reiser. Ein psychologischer Roman* (1785–90). Both these novels are strongly influenced by the pietistic background of their authors. Jung-Stilling's retrospect of an arduous youth and distinguished career as physician and scholar seeks to demonstrate the benign workings of Providence; Goethe wrote of him in *Dichtung und Wahrheit*: 'Das Element seiner Energie war ein unverwüstlicher Glaube an Gott und an eine unmittelbar von daher fliessende Hülfe, die sich in einer ununterbrochenen Vorsorge und in einer unfehlbaren Rettung aus aller Not von jedem Übel augenscheinlich bestätigte.' Moritz, describing a childhood and adolescence crippled by poverty and humiliation, takes a more sombre view of the fervid pietism of his home. He writes of the narrowness of artisan life, of religious raptures and wretchedness, of the pathological ambition and despair experienced by a talented boy forced into uncongenial work and dependence on charity. Moritz's novel is remarkable for its keen analysis of environmental influences and of the traumatic effect of apparently trivial incidents. In seeking refuge from the frustrations of middle-class life in the art of the theatre Anton Reiser opens up a path of escape followed by an increasing number of heroes of the 'Bildungsroman': with the advent of Romanticism and its confrontation of artist and philistine the novel tends to become more and more estranged from common life and values, to become defiantly a 'Künstlerroman'.

The most celebrated 'Bildungsroman' springs from the conflict of aesthetic and practical values and involves an attempt to balance the claims of each. Goethe's *Wilhelm Meisters Lehrjahre* and its sequel, *Wilhelm Meisters Wanderjahre*, constitute together a complex work that is as urbane, ironic and sage as *Werther* was impassioned, lyrical and tormented. The genesis of *Wilhelm Meister* was exceptionally long and complex: the first five books of the *Lehrjahre* were written during the early years of Goethe's residence in Weimar, but the work was then neglected until about 1793, when it was re-written and completed for publication in 1795–6. The *Wanderjahre* is a work of Goethe's old age, first published in 1821 and in a revised version in 1829.

A manuscript copy of the earliest version, known as *Wilhelm Meisters theatralische Sendung*, came to light only in 1910 and revealed that the work had undergone fundamental changes before its publication in 1795–6. The 'Theatrical Mission' is concerned with one of the great intellectual ambitions of eighteenth-century Germany—the project to establish a national theatre as a focus of cultural and patriotic awareness in a country lacking political unity. Wilhelm, the son of a merchant, has his imagination fired as a child by a puppet-theatre and subsequently falls victim to the glamour of the stage, particularly as it is embodied in the actress Mariane. Even her apparent infidelity does not cure him finally of his infatuation. Seeking the self-fulfilment which he cannot find in the commercial pursuits praised by his prosaic brother-in-law Werner, Wilhelm throws responsibility to the winds and joins a troupe of itinerant actors. He shares their trials and modest triumphs, and in their company makes his first acquaintance with the life of the nobility. The story breaks off at the point where Wilhelm is about to sign a contract with the actor-manager Serlo.

In this version Wilhelm appears as an impulsive young man, committed to his mission and loyal to the feckless actors who constitute the imperfect instrument for its achievement. Character, milieu and event are described with irony and graphic force, but there are also intimations of mystery and poetic longing in the figure of Mignon, as well as sombre hints of sin and madness in the character of the old minstrel. These two figures suggest ramifications of plot and a depth of meaning that are realized only in the changed perspectives of the *Lehrjahre*. Wilhelm's passion for the stage is now seen as an aberration; it gives way to his apprenticeship to life under the guidance of a mysterious 'Society of the Tower'. True cultivation of the hero's personality begins when he renounces the aim of total self-fulfilment and thus becomes one of a company of 'Renunciants' who are described in the final part of the work, the *Wanderjahre*. In an 'era of specialisms' each member of this society has developed a particular craft or skill, so as to make of himself an 'organ' of the communal body. Nevertheless, each retains his individuality, for it is precisely individual character and experience which dictate the choice of calling. For the adept, his craft has a symbolic as well as a practical value: 'wenn er Eins tut, tut er alles, oder, um weniger paradox zu sein, in dem Einen, was er recht tut, sieht er das Gleichnis von allem, was recht getan wird.' Wilhelm no longer wishes to be an actor—that is, all things to all men—but to be a surgeon. In dedication to this practical aim true 'Bildung' may be found: 'Eines recht wissen und ausüben gibt höhere Bildung als Halbheiten im Hundertfältigen.'

Wilhelm plays a much less prominent part in the *Wanderjahre*, for here it is the cultivation of the community rather than the individual which is the principal theme. The title has its own deeper significance: it refers not only to the 'journeyman years' of Wilhelm, but to the age itself. The migrant groups of artisans with which the narrative is largely concerned convey Goethe's awareness of impending changes in European society. But the plans of the Society of the Tower and others to establish new communities in America and an inhospitable part of Europe should not be regarded too literally, as Goethe's economic solution to the evils of industrialization: they stand, rather, for an 'inner emigration', a discipline of the spirit, the dedication of the individual in service to an organic community as a defence against the mass society.

*Wilhelm Meister* cannot be judged by the normal criteria of the novel, any more than the second part of *Faust* can be judged by the criteria of the 'well-made play'. In particular, the unity of the *Wanderjahre* is not a narrative unity, nor is it any longer even the unity of the hero's experience. The work is a compendium of Goethe's mature wisdom, conveyed in an inter-related set of paradigmatic tales, situations and figures. The tone is assured: there is no sharp conflict, no negative principle as there is in *Faust*. There are polarities, however: thought and action, the individual and the community, private and public life, passion and renunciation, kinesis and stasis, rationalism and mysticism. This is the bible of Goethean 'Weltfrömmigkeit', a secular faith that embraces both the practical projects of the migrants and the nature mysticism of the cosmic 'saint', Makarie. The style is by turns circumstantial and laconic, gnomic and sententious. The *Wanderjahre* could never be a popular work: it demands much of the reader, for Goethe conveys his thought by hints and subtle accentuation: as often as not the 'Novellen' which are intertwined with the main action break off abruptly and leave the reader to draw the intended conclusion. It was too individual a work to serve as a model. The *Lehrjahre*, on the other hand, graphic, self-assured and seductively ironic in style, made a mark on the subsequent development of the novel that was deep and lasting.

## The Short Story in the Eighteenth Century

Amongst the first short prose works to achieve both popularity and literary distinction were the *Idyllen* (1756) of Salomon Gessner, written in the peace and security of Zürich but widely read in a Germany ravaged by the Seven Years War. These rococo fantasies proved that

German prose could be delicate, urbane and musical. At
the same time, the progressive thinkers of the Enlightenment
demanded something less escapist, more topical and utilitarian. The 'moral weeklies' inspired by English periodicals
like *The Tatler*, *The Spectator* and *The Guardian* were interested
in contemporary men and manners; they provided a public
and a market for writers of short stories, who took as their
models English and French 'character sketches' by Labru-
yère, John Earle and Samuel Butler. From the 'characters'
there developed 'family portraits' and modest narratives of
an improving sort—for example, Wieland's *Bonifaz Schleicher*,
Lenz's *Zerbin*, Merck's *Geschichte des Herrn Oheim*, Sturz's
*Reise nach dem Deister*, Wezel's *Satirische Erzählungen*. French
fairy-tales of both the naive and the satirical kind as well as
dubious 'contes licencieux' also found translators and
imitators in collections like *Die Abendstunden* and *Die Neuen
Abendstunden* and Wieland's *Dschinnistan, oder auserlesene Feen-
und Geistermärchen* (1786–9). Johann Karl August Musäus
went beyond his French sources and adapted German folk-
tales to express the scepticism and the rationalistic morality
of the Enlightenment, a technique continued in Friedrich
Nicolai's *Straussfedern* until this collection was sabotaged in
the Romantic interest by Ludwig Tieck.

The moral and philosophical tales of Marmontel,
Hamilton and Voltaire were also widely emulated—by
Sophie von La Roche, August Gottlieb Meissner and August
Lafontaine amongst others. Many of Meissner's *Kriminal-
geschichten* (1778–96) represent an appeal for more humane
administration of the law and better understanding of
criminal motives. C. H. Spiess shares Meissner's aims in
his *Selbstmörderbiographien* (1785) and *Biographien der Wahnsinnigen* (1795), and Schiller's story, *Der Verbrecher aus Infamie*
(1786) is also an attempt to understand the mind of a
criminal.

More imaginative are the elegant tales of Christian
Leberecht Heyne (Anton-Wall), who often adopts the
Oriental costume then popular with French writers. His

*Omar* (1783) praises in a delightful way the joys of the simple life. *Baruch, oder der Schüler der Weisheit* (1783) relates with wry humour the fate of an ingénu who comes to the city, is admired and prospers because he murders a rival in love and comes to grief because of his virtue. The theme resembles that of *Candide*, but Anton-Wall's satire is milder than that of Voltaire. Amongst other popular authors of 'moralische Erzählungen' were Johann Christoph Ludwig Haken and Friedrich Rochlitz. Haken's *Der Liederliche* (1790) is a Hogarthian 'Rake's Progress' based on twelve engravings by Daniel Chodowiecki. The work consists of a series of letters and dialogues in a remarkable variety of styles—illiterate and semi-literate epistles from servants and riding-masters, the Yiddish of a money-lender, stilted professorial prose, thieves' slang, the jargon of physicians and the sentimental effusions of deceived women. The author reveals a fascinating familiarity with the techniques of eighteenth-century confidence tricksters. Rochlitz deals with stereotyped situations—the perils of seduction, the virtues of contented domesticity—but he is capable, as in *Die Landmädchen* (1799), of sound psychological observation and characterization.

A traditional form of short story aimed at an unsophisticated audience was the moralizing anecdote incorporated into rural calendars, which were often the only secular reading-matter of the farming community. These tales were later raised to a high literary standard in J. P. Hebel's *Schatzkästlein des Rheinischen Hausfreundes* (1816–19), which goes back for much of its material to Jörg Wickram's *Rollwagenbüchlein* of 1555. Many cruder stories from such collections, both German and foreign, continued to be reproduced in the eighteenth century—for example, in Karl Grosse's *Des Grafen von Vargas Novellen* (1792). The moral crudity of these works is seldom redeemed by artistic qualities: they tend to be prolix and ill-fashioned.

## The Novel between Classicism and Romanticism

The last decade of the eighteenth century was a time of
intellectual as well as political turmoil: philosophical
thinking was revolutionized by Kant's 'Critiques' just as
European society was shaken by the unprecedented up-
heaval in France. In literature, superannuated leaders of
the Enlightenment fought a losing battle against the sophisticated aesthetic theories of the Classical writers and the
irrational heritage of the 'Sturm und Drang', which soon
acquired a fresh impulse from the new generation of Romantic writers. The intellectual cross-currents of this period are
nowhere more mingled than in the novels of Jean Paul, who
stands Janus-like on the threshold of the old and new
centuries, looking back to the sentimentality of the sixties
and seventies and forward to the unruly fantasies of Romanticism. Jean Paul groped for the Classical ideal of harmony,
but he found its criteria too clinical and could confine
neither the amplitude of his sentiment nor his teeming
imagination within the formal limits that Goethe and
Schiller prescribed: for Goethe he was 'a Chinaman in
Rome'. Although Jean Paul was repelled by the solipsism of
the Romantics, whom he termed 'poetic nihilists', and by
their apparent immorality, his work is Romantic in its
transcendentalism, in its ecstatic feeling for Nature and its
belief in the unity of man with the created universe.

Jean Paul began his literary career with attempts at
social satire which were largely ineffectual because he knew
the world of fashionable culture only from books. It was not
until he 'closed the vinegar factory' and began to work the
veins of whimsical humour and sentimental idealism that
ran through his nature that he achieved a popular success
with *Die unsichtbare Loge* (1793). This is a biographical novel
of a strongly paedagogical complexion in which a secret
society plays an even more dominant part in the hero's
education than was the case in *Wilhelm Meister*. *Hesperus*
(1795), *Siebenkäs* (1796–7) and many of the succeeding

novels—*Titan* (1800-3), *Flegeljahre* (1804-5), *Dr Katzenbergers Badereise* (1809), *Der Komet* (1820)—also have plots
which may seem pointlessly bizarre; in fact the mistaken or
masked identities, cryptic events and sensational revelations
often have an ulterior significance—they are emblems of
psychological states and crises, spiritual deaths, rejuvena-
tions and resurrections. Alongside—and sometimes even
embedded within—the tangled intrigues of these stories
with their sublime or demonic characters are studies of
idyllic contentment in cheerful 'poverty or portraits of
amiable eccentricity: *Das Leben des Quintus Fixlein* (1796),
*Das Leben des vergnügten Schulmeisterlein Wuz in Auenthal*
(annexed to *Die unsichtbare Loge*), *Des Feldpredigers Schmelzle
Reise nach Flätz* (1809). Jean Paul attempts to map out a
middle path between the ethereal yearnings of his 'hohe
Menschen' and the doggedly myopic happiness of the
village dominie. It is this attempt which gives his work its
ambivalence and its typically iridescent emotional colouring
makes it, in the words of his admirer, Thomas Carlyle,
'fantastic, many-coloured, far-grasping, everywhere perplexed and extraordinary.' The poetic realism of the idylls
and the comic episodes forms the counterpoint to vast and
gloomy visions like the 'Rede des toten Christus vom
Weltgebäude herab, dass kein Gott sei' in *Siebenkäs*; scurrilous
wit succeeds enthusiastic adoration of nature, ecstasy is shot
through with irony. The twin aspects of Jean Paul's sensibility are embodied in the twin brothers of *Flegeljahre*—
Walt, the 'still, soft-hearted, tearful enthusiast', as Carlyle
describes him, and Vult, 'a madcap humorist . . . bursting
out on all hands with the strangest explosions, speculative
and practical.'

Jean Paul's style is mercilessly metaphorical, embroidered
with arabesque patterns of allusion, ballasted with paren-
theses and footnotes to the point where it might seem that
he is incapable of making a plain statement but is being
dragged helplessly through thickets of association. In fact
his critical manifesto, *Vorschule der Ästhetik* (1804 and 1813),

which is remarkable for point and clarity, makes it obvious that 'his singularity was professed and deliberate'. Jean Paul is a master of the mannered style which has flourished intermittently in periods such as the Elizabethan age and the German baroque.

Whereas Jean Paul may be said to have bridged the gulf between the eighteenth and the nineteenth century and between 'Classicism' and 'Romanticism', Friedrich Hölderlin long inhabited a kind of limbo between these recognized schools. Hölderlin's inspiration is not assimilated, like Jean Paul's, from the emotional atmosphere of the time, it is essentially inward; his genius is not nourished by a network of intellectual channels, but springs essentially from a single fountain-head —an intuitive sympathy with the cultural and religious ideals of Classical Greece as epitomizing beauty and harmony with Nature. His mature poetry invokes a vision of the mystic unity of man, God and Nature; the tone of his odes is solemn, impassioned, mantic, their rhythms—modelled on Classical metres—are incantatory. In Hölderlin's one novel, *Hyperion oder der Eremit in Griechenland* (1797–9), the vision of Greece is not bathed in a nostalgic afterglow as it was in the historical–philosophical novels of Wieland; it is radiant with the dawning hope of contemporary events—the aftermath of the French Revolution and the efforts of the Greeks to overthrow their Turkish rulers. It is in this patriotic struggle of the Greeks that the hero of the novel, a young Greek, is involved, and the work consists mainly of his letters to Bellarmin, a friend in Germany. The battles and the naval engagement in which Hyperion is gravely wounded are only dimly seen, however; the novel is not an adventure story but a lyrical portrait of an idealistic spirit in conflict with a prosaic age and the realities of a political struggle. Hyperion's association with the ruthless patriot, Alabanda, and with cut-throat partisans can bring him nothing but disillusionment. The death of his hopes is linked to the death of his beloved Diotima, who embodied ideals of beauty and harmony. Hyperion returns to Germany, to find there a cold, denatured race—'tief unfähig jeden göttlichen Gefühls ... dumpf und harmonielos.' His only comfort is in the elemental forces of Nature manifested in the northern spring. Contemplation of the oneness, timelessness and beauty of Nature initiates a final modulation of the novel into a religious key: in surging rhythms Hyperion visualizes his reunion with Diotima in the cosmic harmony.

Hölderlin enjoyed nothing of the popular success of Jean Paul, and even his spiritual peers looked at him askance: Goethe seems to have been disturbed by the visionary tone of his poetry, and Schiller, who could not deny a temperamental affinity with his fellow-Swabian, was no doubt uncomfortably reminded of youthful enthusiasms long moderated. Of the Romantics, perhaps only Josef Görres appreciated the tragic idealism and indignation of this 'broken-winged eagle'. In spite of its insight into the condition of man in modern society *Hyperion* found little resonance and no successors even among Romantics—whose gaze was focussed on another model: Goethe's *Wilhelm Meisters Lehrjahre.*

# IV

# ROMANTICISM

Because of its discreditable association with medieval tales the word 'romantic' had in the seventeenth and early eighteenth century the meaning of 'fantastic', 'extravagant' or simply 'false'. During the latter part of the eighteenth century, however, as a consequence of a general change in taste, it acquired more positive connotations as a term used to describe the awe and nostalgia inspired by wild landscape or venerable ruins. With the development of the historical sense and increasing interest in the middle ages the word also came to be used (by Herder, for instance) to denote the culture and the vernacular literatures of medieval Europe as opposed to the traditions of Greece and Rome. All these associations, as well as the link with the contemporary 'Roman', were no doubt welcomed by Friedrich Schlegel when he chose 'romantisch' to characterize trends in philosophy, literature and political life during the last decade of the eighteenth century and to serve as the slogan for a 'poetry of the future'. At this time features of Romanticism appear to develop spontaneously in England, France and Italy as well as in Germany, but it is in German thought and art that the Romantic spirit achieves its most characteristic, coherent and comprehensive expression. With Romanticism German literature first gained a dominant position in Europe and exerted massive influence in many countries. It may be considered the most typically German of intellectual attitudes and its effects on German history were profound and enduring.

Like most intellectual movements, Romanticism is easier to illustrate than to define, but definition is perhaps less hazardous in the case of German Romanticism than with

Romantic movements in other countries. In its origins the early German Romantic school is intimately linked with the Classicism of Goethe and Schiller, but its emergence is marked with some precision by the formation of a relatively closely knit group of individuals with critical views held in common and expressed in particular works and journals. It has proved possible also, without doing too much violence to the nature of things, to distinguish phases or schools in the development of Romanticism in Germany—although it tends, as it evolves, to change its nature from a literary movement to something more diffuse and pervasive, a kind of intellectual climate.

The antecedents of the Romantic schools during the eighteenth century are those scattered symptoms which asserted themselves in opposition to rationalism. In the Romantic schools they took more effective shape when the leading writers conformed to the principles of post-Kantian idealism, particularly in its Fichtean form. The crucial historical fact is that this happened at the time when Schiller began to put into practice the ideas he had formed under Kant's influence. The initiators of the first Romantic school in the persons of the Schlegel brothers and Novalis started to formulate their views around 1795. Schiller's aesthetic writings and Fichte's *Wissenschaftslehre* (1794) were their starting points. This accounts for both the similarity in the arguments of Schiller's *Über naive und sentimentalische Dichtung* and Friedrich Schlegel's *Über das Studium der griechischen Poesie* and for their no less striking divergence.

The difference between Schiller's (and Goethe's) Classical precepts and the doctrines of the Romantics may be defined in terms of the principle from which the poetics of both Classicism and Romanticism ultimately stem. In both trends imitation is rejected in favour of creative autonomy through the exercise of man's imaginative rather than his rational powers. According to the Classical canon the artist's imagination transmutes the lineaments of reality, Schiller's 'wirkliche Natur', into the ennobled form he called 'wahre

Natur' (*Über naive und sentimentalische Dichtung*). Empirically observed reality is to be purged of its inessential or deforming elements in order to produce an idealized image or a quintessential analogue of that reality.

In the Romantic view the imagination transcends reality: the severance is complete. Poetic creativity transgresses even the limits set by perception, which is itself seen as a creative act in the philosophy of subjective idealism which Fichte had developed in the wake of that 'Copernican Revolution' by which Kant established the ineluctable function of the mind in shaping our impressions of the world around us. The imagination is accorded entire autonomy and is allowed to become productive in the sense of achieving the presentation of what lies beyond the sensible world. 'Der Sinn der Poesie', says Novalis, 'ist der Sinn für das Unbekannte, Geheimnisvolle, zu Offenbarende . . . Er stellt das Undarstellbare dar. Er sieht das Unsichtbare, fühlt das Unfühlbare.' In this he sanctions the kind of abstraction Schiller had censured in *Über naive und sentimentalische Dichtung*.

Friedrich Schlegel carried the emancipation of the freely operating creative imagination a step further with his conception of 'Ironie'. He called it 'die Stimmung, welche alles übersieht, und sich über alles Bedingte unendlich überhebt, auch über die eigne Kunst, Tugend oder Genialität'. In this view the total freedom of the creative mind manifests itself in the artist's desire and ability to destroy as well as to produce a form of reality. This Fichtean 'Selbstvernichtung' succeeding 'Selbstschöpfung' is the Romantic counterpart of the process of aesthetic distancing which Schiller demanded in his review of Bürger's poetry.

Friedrich Schlegel stated another cardinal Romantic principle in his *Gespräch über Poesie*: 'Die höchste Schönheit, ja die höchste Ordnung ist denn doch nur die des Chaos.' He held the poet's task to be 'den Gang und die Gesetze der vernünftig denkenden Vernunft aufzuheben und uns wieder in die schöne Verwirrung der Phantasie, in das ursprüngliche Chaos zu versetzen.' Such statements indicate what the

Romantics envisaged to be the essence of poetic form. Like Kant they considered arabesques as the prototype of 'free' composition and 'pure' non-representational art.

Perhaps the most characteristic Romantic concept regarding poetic form is contained in Friedrich Schlegel's statement: 'Die romantische Poesie ist eine progressive Universalpoesie . . . Ihre Bestimmung ist nicht bloss, alle getrennten Gattungen der Poesie wieder zu vereinigen, und die Poesie mit der Philosophie und Rhetorik in Berührung zu setzen. Sie will und soll auch Poesie und Prosa, Genialität und Kritik, Kunstpoesie und Naturpoesie bald mischen, bald verschmelzen . . .' As with many other sweeping pronouncements of this kind, practice fell considerably behind theory, but Schlegel's concept is sufficiently authoritative to account for some typical features of Romantic literature.

This universalistic view of the Romantics was not confined to literature: attempts were made to break down traditional intellectual barriers wherever they existed—between individual arts, between philosophy and art, religion and art, art and life. In the light of Fichtean idealism even the long-established division of the universe into mind and matter seemed no longer absolute. Schelling declared mind and nature to be polar aspects or reality, with art as the sphere in which they were assimilated. Dreams, visions and subconscious life not only acquired increased psychological significance but were seen as evidence of the mind's cosmic dimensions. In the speculations of Novalis and in G. H. Schubert's *Ansichten von der Nachtseite der Naturwissenschaften* (1808) discoveries in magnetism were linked with hypnotic phenomena as evidence of a homogeneous force pervading man and inorganic nature. Religion, too, became, in the early stages of the movement at least, simply a cosmic sense, 'Gefühl der schlechthinnigen Abhängigkeit vom Unendlichen', in Schleiermacher's phrase; the mystical theories of Jakob Böhme were revived by Franz von Baader and Schelling.

Romantic thinking is fundamentally anti-rationalistic—

although not always irrational. It is difficult to summarise, for it is often speculative in an undisciplined way and full of contrasts and paradoxes implicit in a universalistic world-view. Romantic writers can be by turns—and often well-nigh simultaneously—rational and emotional, naive and sophisticated, ironical and impassioned. There are, however, typical patterns of Romantic thought, amongst which perhaps the most prominent is the triad of thesis—antithesis—synthesis, applied, for instance, to the stages of man's spiritual or cultural development from primal innocence to some as yet unrealised state of perfection. Romantic 'Sehnsucht' often takes the form of a yearning for an ultimate synthesis in which the dichotomies of life as we now know it would be resolved by some intellectual or mystical *tour de force*, or for a return on a higher plane to the lost state of innocence—a 'circumnavigation of the globe', as Kleist calls it in his essay on the marionettes. The entry into a new mode of existence in which there are no longer dualities like mind and nature, reason and emotion, intellect and sensuality, duty and desire is visualized as being achieved through ecstasy in religious experience or in love or through identification of the individual with a historical tradition or an ethnic community. What is sought ultimately is an escape from an imperfectly ordered society and from inner conflict.

The principal but by no means the only begetter of Romantic theory was Friedrich Schlegel, a brilliant intuitive critic who was most at home in short essays and aphorisms. It was his brother, August Wilhelm, who undertook the task of interpreting the panorama of Europeon literature in terms of the Romantic view of history. This he accomplished in lectures on *Schöne Literatur und Kunst* (Berlin, 1801-4) and on *Dramatische Kunst und Literatur* (Vienna, 1808).

Neither of the Schlegels was distinguished as an original poet. The creative impulse of early Romanticism issued from other writers—Tieck, Wackenroder and Novalis. Tieck and Wackenroder, unencumbered by philosophical premise or critical conjecture, experienced the beauty of Renaissance and baroque art and music as a revelation after the dry rational climate of their native Berlin. In the poems and sketches of *Herzensergiessungen eines kunstliebenden Klosterbruders* (1797) Wackenroder celebrated the divine inspiration of great art and wrote of the raptures and misery of genius from his own heart and experience. Tieck, a facile and impressionable talent and already a professional writer from a tender age, not only imitated the rhapsodic style of his friend but also excelled in the writing of atmospheric tales in which nature reflects the moods of man and folk-tale motifs are invested, through some intuitive subtlety, with acute psychological meaning. Novalis combined the philosophical acumen of Fichte and the Schlegels with a poetic talent unsurpassed in all of Romanticism. His philosophy of 'magic idealism' sought to reconcile mysticism and natural science, and the poems inspired by the death of his fiancée fuse religious and erotic emotion in a way that is typical of Romanticism. More than any other writer Novalis gave the movement its hallmark of infinite yearning and other-worldliness. It was Novalis also who, with his essay, *Die Christenheit oder Europa* (1799, publ. 1826), helped to establish the nostalgia for the faith and ideals of the Middle Ages that marks the later phases of Romanticism.

By 1801 both Wackenroder and Novalis were dead and the early Romantic group associated with Berlin and Jena had dissolved. A rather looser association of Romantic writers settled in Heidelberg between 1805 and 1808. Its most prominent members were Arnim, Brentano, Eichendorff and Josef Görres, but the journal they edited, *Die Zeitung für Einsiedler* (1808) also included contributions from the Schlegels, Tieck, Fouqué, the brothers Jakob and Wilhelm Grimm, Uhland, Kerner and the painter, Philipp Otto Runge. The interests of the Heidelberg Romantics are more purely literary and poetic, less philosophical than had been the case with some of their fore-runners; Romanticism began to lose its speculative and revolutionary character, it became politically conservative and manifestly Christian, often specifically Roman Catholic. Enthusiasm for national traditions and popular poetry is reflected in the collection and editing of ballads and stories: Arnim and Brentano's *Des Knaben Wunderhorn* (1805–8), Görres's *Teutsche Volksbücher* (1807) and the famous *Kinder- und Hausmärchen* (1812–15) of the brothers Grimm. Nostalgia for the past and admiration for the ethnic soul are expressed in historical novels by Arnim and in Brentano's fictitious chronicle, *Aus der Chronika eines fahrenden Schülers* (1803, publ. 1818). Conversely, the moral laxity and philistinism of contemporary society are satirically attacked.

In the period from about 1810 onwards until the victorrious outcome of the War of Liberation (1813–14) Romanticism became more and more identified with the national cause. Berlin was again the centre of a Romantic group, formed this time round a political society, the Christlich–Deutsche Tischgesellschaft, which numbered Arnim, Brentano, Eichendorff, Kleist, Fouqué and Chamisso amongst its members. It was Kleist who edited the journals of this later Romantic school: *Phöbus* (1808), which contained almost exclusively contributions by himself and the conservative political theorist Adam Müller, and the *Berliner Abendblätter* (1810–11), to which most of the members of the Christlich–Deutsche Tischgesellschaft contributed; his patriotic dramas, along with Fichte's *Reden an die deutsche Nation* (1808) and the martial poetry of Arndt, Körner, Schenkendorf and Rückert helped to inspire the national rising against Napoleon in 1813.

After the political restoration of 1815 this patriotic fervour was quickly repressed as subversive of the old dynastic loyalties. Romanticism lost much of its impetus and although individuals like the Grimms, Arndt and Uhland retained liberal opinions right down to the revolutions of 1848 it tended to be associated more and more with religious orthodoxy and political reaction and to be assimilated to the canny culture of Biedermeier. Individual writers like Hoffmann, Eichendorff and, of course, Heine continued to

produce works that were characteristically Romantic, but
the movement had lost its coherence after 1815. It was left
to Heine, 'the last abdicated king of Romanticism', in whose
work and personality lyricism and irony are so closely
blended, to describe the movement as a historical phenomenon in *Zur Geschichte der neueren schönen Literatur in Deutschland* (1833; 1836 as *Die romantische Schule*), a work which, for
all its satire, still constitutes the most brilliant account of
Romanticism ever written.

The character of Romantic writing is very varied—
mystical, for instance, with Novalis, satirical with Friedrich
Schlegel, both with Brentano. It is often remarkable for
fantasy, ingenuity and the mannered virtuosity which revels
in devices like synaesthesia and onomatopeia. On the other
hand, it can be moving or forceful through sheer simplicity.
The most memorable Romantic literary achievements are
almost certainly in the field of the lyric and the short story,
where simplicity of theme and the salutary influence of folk
models curbed a tendency to formlessness that stemmed
sometimes from principle, sometimes from ineptitude. Very
few Romantic novels ever reached a satisfactory conclusion
and Romantic dramas, apart from some satirical comedies by
Tieck and one or two works by Zacharias Werner, rarely
proved effective on the stage. Perhaps the greatest gift of the
Romantic movement to the German theatre was the translation of Shakespeare by A. W. Schlegel and Tieck. The
achievements of the Romantics generally as translators and
interpreters of foreign literatures in Germany should not be
forgotten: Schlegel translated Calderon as well as Shakespeare, Tieck translated *Don Quixote*, Schleiermacher rendered Plato into German and J. D. Gries translated the
Italian poets Boiardo, Ariosto and Tasso as well as Calderon,
while W. Grimm translated and commented on old Norse
epics.

## The Romantic novel

Friedrich Schlegel who, in 1798, praised the subtlety, the irony and the intricate 'musical' form of *Wilhelm Meister* could proclaim with considerable justification in a review of Goethe's collected works just ten years later: 'Der *Meister* . . . hat auf das Ganze der deutschen Literatur sichtbar wie wenige andere Erscheinungen gewirkt, und recht eigentlich Epoche gemacht, indem er . . . die Sprache nach einer ganz neuen Seite hin mehr bereicherte, als es vielleicht in irgend einer Gattung durch ein einzelnes Werk auf einmal geschehen ist.' Certainly the pattern of Goethe's novel—the hero's journey and the dual theme of apprenticeship to art and to life—recurs in many novels throughout the Romantic era while the fey descendants of Mignon haunt the pages of novels down to Immermann's *Epigonen* and even Spielhagen's *Problematische Naturen* (1861–2). Numerous authors seek, too, to emulate both Goethe's philosophical purpose and the sovereign artistry of his style. Needless to say, however, the model is modified by other literary influences, by ideological change and by idiosyncrasies of temperament. This was only to be expected of the Romantics, in whose name Friedrich Schlegel had proclaimed the absolute autonomy of every novel—'jeder Roman (ist) eigentlich ein abgesondertes Individuum für sich.' His own *Lucinde* has little enough in common with Goethe's work apart from a rudimentary notion of cultivation of the personality through experience and a caricatured version of the poetic autonomy which Schlegel so admired in Goethe and which he here expresses in the declaration, 'dass ich gleich anfangs das, was wir Ordnung nennen, vernichte . . . und mir das Recht einer reizenden Verwirrung deutlich zueigne und durch die Tat behaupte.' The work is a loose collection of reflections, 'rhapsodies', letters and conversations superficially linked to Goethe's novel by a chapter entitled 'Lehrjahre der Männlichkeit'. *Lucinde* is essentially an account of Schlegel's love affair with Dorothea Veit; as an early symptom of Romantic rebellion against philistine convention it caused much offence, in spite of Schleiermacher's attempt to justify it in *Vertraute Briefe über Friedrich Schlegels Lucinde*. *Florentin*, an unfinished novel by 'Lucinde' herself, also seeks to promote a more liberal ideal of wedlock in which both partners, as equal 'soul-mates', would share the same quality of affection. A serious concern with sexual morality and the ethics of marriage is apparent in a number of novels of the period down to Goethe's *Wahlverwandtschaften* and its Romantic counterparts, Arnim's *Gräfin Dolores* and Eichendorff's *Ahnung und Gegenwart*. In its technique *Florentin* is much more conventional than *Lucinde*: its description of the life of the landed gentry and their philanthropic projects is reminiscent of *Wilhelm Meister*, Eleonore has a strong resemblance to Goethe's Natalie, Clementine is a 'beautiful soul'. The hero, however, is no naive and impressionable middle-class youth but an Italian nobleman of mysterious antecedents: he has the manly melancholy attractiveness that later became known as 'Byronic'. Florentin's Italian adventures—sere-nades, seductions, the attempt to abduct a novice from the threshold of the convent—as well as the crude anti-clericalism of these episodes—no doubt owe much to the popular novel of the eighteenth century: picaresque and buccaneering exploits are part of a common pattern that recurs in *Sternbald*, *Godwi*, *Die Gräfin Dolores*, *Ahnung und Gegenwart*, Immermann's *Epigonen*, Keller's *Grüner Heinrich* and countless lesser products of the Romantic and Biedermeier period.

An awareness of the gulf between inner experience and social realities that is less defiant and more tragic than Schlegel's is expressed in the Josef Berglinger items from W. H. Wackenroder's *Herzensergiessungen eines kunstliebenden Klosterbruders* and *Phantasien über die Kunst*. To the musician Berglinger his art comes to seem a 'seductive forbidden fruit', a poison that kills the charitable impulse and turns the artist into an actor, for whom suffering is a study and sym-pathy a pose. Berglinger is an ancestor of Hoffmann's Johannes Kreisler and foreshadows the dilemma of heroes in works by Thomas and Heinrich Mann. In his account of the *malheur d'être poète*, his exaltation of the aesthetic response and his sensitivity to the moods of Nature Wackenroder strikes typical Romantic chords.

It is certain episodes of the *Herzensergiessungen* which provide the seeds of Ludwig Tieck's *Franz Sternbalds Wanderungen*; the soil, however, had already been prepared by the example of *Wilhelm Meister*, to which Tieck's instantaneous and characteristic response had been the sketch of a novel called *Der junge Tischlermeister*. To Goethe's worldly wisdom and Wackenroder's artistic religiosity was added—as Coleridge observed—a dash of Heinse's Bohemian vitalism. Sternbald, a youthful pupil of Dürer, pursues his education in art and life through Germany, Holland and Italy: he is faced with a choice between art and commerce, consorts with noble patrons, falls in love with a beautiful stranger, is tantalized by hints of secret affinities with those he encounters on his journeys. Like all the early Romantic novels, Sternbald is unfinished, but it is not ill-fashioned and possesses something of the charm of Eichendorff's *Taugenichts*. It is remarkable for its stereotyped but effective evocations of 'romantic' landscapes and lyrical moods of Nature. As Goethe drily remarked, 'Es sind viele hübsche Sonnenaufgänge darin.'

None of the early Romantic writers reacted more strongly to *Wilhelm Meisters Lehrjahre* than Friedrich von Hardenberg, who passed swiftly from adulation to execration. But even when Goethe's novel seemed to him a 'Candide gegen die Poesie ... ein fatales und albernes Buch', Hardenberg continued to admire its artistry and tried to emulate its style in *Heinrich von Ofterdingen*, the Romantic counterpart and challenge to *Meister*. Where Goethe's novel—for all its enigmatic characters and secret societies—is firmly fixed in a social context of the eighteenth century, *Ofterdingen* floats in a misty medieval setting. It is a metaphysical novel, in which the poet as hero plays a chiliastic role; its hall-mark is otherworldliness. Ofterdingen moves on a predestined path towards an apotheosis which is conceived as an act of universal redemption; his experiences do not mould him, they strike responsive chords within and confirm his presentiments. The novel is the poetic expression of Hardenberg's idealistic philosophy and of the Romantic belief in the symbolic nature of reality: our world is a veil cast over a vaster life to which we have access fleetingly in dreams or visions and ultimately in death. Hardenberg penetrates even more deeply into the 'Weltinnenraum' than Jean Paul; world and mind are one, mystic introspection yields the key to the universe: 'Nach innen geht der geheimnisvolle Weg.' The first part of the novel culminates in *Klingsohrs Märchen*, an allegorical fantasy in which the dichotomies of life—love and the moral imperative, reason and sentiment, sensuality and intellect, chance and design, freedom and necessity—are resolved. In psychological terms the author might seem to be groping towards an understanding of the subconscious mind, but Hardenberg himself insists on sublimating into a metaphysical and religious parable the release of inner tensions which he seeks: he is certainly unlikely to have been aware of the latent eroticism of much of his imagery.

Only the first part of the novel, *Die Erwartung*, was completed; *Die Erfüllung* consists, apart from fragmentary notes of a single chapter, but the structure of the work, as far as it goes, is meticulously regular. Reality and dream alternate, and the growing profundity of Ofterdingen's experience points to the ultimate transition from mundane experience to a higher world adumbrated in dreams. 'Die Welt wird Traum, der Traum wird Welt.' Apart from the dazzling Goethean imagery of *Klingsohrs Märchen* which anticipates this conclusion the world of *Ofterdingen* is pale and limpid, transparent to the gaze of the seer-poet.

The remaining novel of the early Romantic group, Clemens Brentano's *Godwi*, is intertwined in plot and motif with familiar models—*Meister*, *Lucinde*, *Sternbald*, even *William Lovell*, *Florentin*, works by Jean Paul and Heinse, the popular thriller—but in its defiant individualism it is perhaps the most original of them all. It calls itself 'ein verwilderter

Roman', but it is not so much tangled as intricate: two main plots closely interwoven, a variety of narrative techniques and styles, contrasts of sensual and sentimental abandon among its characters, an ironic breaking of illusion that involves the death of the alleged author and the finishing of the story by the hero himself. *Godwi* is the most subjective of Romantic novels: it is essentially an expression of Brentano's restless moods and longings, his desire to shake off the trammels of society; it is a proclamation of the individual's spiritual autonomy—each man should learn to understand himself and act in conformity with the law of his own being. To Godwi life seems like a dream, but his vision has none of the serenity of Ofterdingen's: he longs for emotional fulfilment—'Leben heisst fühlen und fühlen machen'—and conceives 'Glück und Genuss' as the aims of living. He pours scorn alike on barbaric squireens and the bourgeois philistines with their gospel of useful labour. But as with many Romantic novels, the most memorable features of *Godwi* are, after all, the interpolated lyrics and ballads—of which one, 'Zu Bacharach am Rheine', literally founded the popular 'legend' of the Lorelei.

Goethe's third novel, *Die Wahlverwandtschaften* (1809), had less contemporary impact than his *Lehrjahre* but it too found a response among Romantic writers. This is a work of great symbolic intricacy in which Goethe reflects on the problematic analogy between natural laws, such as that which prescribes an 'elective affinity' amongst chemical elements, and the laws of social morality which operate by free choice: he demonstrates the triumph, through self-sacrifice, of freedom over necessity, of moral law and the social interest over biological attraction. The precarious harmony of Eduard's marriage to Charlotte is upset by the arrival of a 'Hauptmann' and of Charlotte's niece Ottilie. The chiastic situation is epitomized in a 'spiritual adultery', of which the offspring, a child of Eduard and Charlotte, is seen to bear the features of Ottilie and the Hauptmann. Ottilie is involved in the death of the child and construes this as an omen: rather than accept the rational solution of divorce and re-marriage which offers itself, Ottilie exalts the sanctity of wedlock by willing her own death. As in the final act of *Faust II* Goethe has recourse to Christian legend to represent the saintliness of Ottilie in her transfigured state; the dogmatic morality of the Church is, on the other hand, grimly satirized in the blundering cleric, Mittler. The story, which betrays in its economy and the striking theme of 'spiritual adultery' its first conception as a 'Novelle', is amplified by the introduction of parallel or contrasting characters and situations, by the symbolic involvement of nature and the landscape and by reflective passages represented as being from Ottilie's diary. The whole is formed into a complex structure of superb cogency.

In spite of its manifest spirituality and rigorous morality, *Die Wahlverwandtschaften* was regarded by many as scandalous or obscene: Friedrich Jacobi, with unbelievable obtuseness, considered it an 'apotheosis of wicked sensuality' and even Jean Paul disapproved of its 'immoral elements'. There was much in the novel, however, that appealed to the discerning mind of the Romantics: its concern with the spiritual meaning of marriage, certain mortuary undertones and the suggestion of a morbid mysticism, the traffic with fashionable notions of 'galvanism'. Achim von Arnim's *Reichtum, Armut, Schuld und Busse der Gräfin Dolores* (1810) traces the spiritual and psychological progress of its heroine from youthful frivolity through sin to repentance and atonement. Arnim is committed to Christian morality, and the story is characteristically loose-knit and lurid at times, but the common theme suggests than *Gräfin Dolores* is both affirmation of and reply to *Die Wahlverwandtschaften*. The views and activities of the hero, Karl, and incidental satire of upper-class life indicate that the reforming impulse is no longer revolutionary as it was in Schlegel's *Lucinde* but reactionary: Arnim seeks a return to established values rather than an advance to a new morality. The same tendency is even clearer in Eichendorff's *Ahnung und Gegenwart* (1815), a work that has unmistakable incidental resemblances to *Meister*, *Florentin* and *Godwi*, as well as to *Gräfin Dolores*. Eichendorff visualizes a spiritual rather than a political cure for the moral ills of the turbulent years that succeeded the Napoleonic wars: in the conviction that a shattered society can be restored only by spiritual rebirth and a return to the religious life, Friedrich, the hero, ultimately enters a monastery:

'Wenn die Gemüter auf solche Weise von den göttlichen Wahrheiten der Religion ... gereinigt und wahrhaft durchdrungen würden, dass der Geist Gottes und das Grosse im öffentlichen Leben wieder Raum in ihnen gewännen, dann erst wird es Zeit sein, unmittelbar zu handeln und das alte Recht, die alte Freiheit, Ehre und Ruhm in das wiedereroberte Reich zurückzuführen. Und in dieser Gesinnung', concludes Friedrich, 'bleibe ich in Deutschland und wähle mir das Kreuz zum Schwert.'

The interplay of elemental and psychological forces that is suggested in *Die Wahlverwandtschaften* fascinated many Romantic writers. Tieck's early stories were full of intimations of demonic forces at work in man's environment; with an intuition that was truer than he knew, he linked the supernatural elements of fairy-tales with hysteria and pathological states of mind. Discoveries in electrical magnetism were linked with the phenomenon of hypnotism and a growing awareness of a subconscious mind to form theories of dreams and 'animal magnetism' that were propounded in books like G. H. Schubert's *Ansichten von der Nachtseite der Naturwissenschaft* (1808). It is this interest in the uncanny and in the psycho-pathological that informs the macabre and grotesque variety of the Romantic novel. *Die Nachtwachen des Bonaventura*, a work attributed at first to Schelling or E. T. A. Hoffmann but now believed to be by Friedrich Gottlob Wetzel, accompanies a half-demented night-watchman on his rounds through a small German town. Diabolical and apocalyptic visions are invoked to attack the absolute corruption of Church and state. But the attack goes beyond mere radicalism to a hysterical nihilism. 'Bonaventura' sees men as puppets or automata, their personalities as masks or successive layers, which, when peeled away, leave precisely nothing. The concept of a mechanical universe, which inspired the 'Aufklärer' has become a nightmare which haunts not only E. T. A. Hoffmann but also the dramatist Büchner. The ordered limits of the eighteenth-century world seem suddenly to have receded to infinity, and behind the flimsy façade of reality yawns the void. The transcendentalism that comforted Hardenberg, his vision of 'doppelte Welten', can be a terror as well as a solace: 'der Weg nach innen' may no longer lead to an apotheosis but to madness or oblivion. Even in this existence man may lose the attributes of his substantiality—be symbolically deprived of his shadow or his reflection, become a phantom.

It is on the uncanny juxtaposition of the prosaic world and the daemonic world—which we are at liberty to construe as the world of insanity—that the effectiveness of E. T. A. Hoffmann's stories is balanced. Reality and fantasy are inextricably mingled: familiar features dissolve and change, a door-knocker momentarily becomes a witch, a character steps across a threshold and finds himself in another world. Hoffmann's tales may be read simply as ghost stories, but they are also descriptions of enraptured or inflamed minds, in which spirits and demons represent ineffable longings or psychological injuries. Music, above all, is the element of the daemonic in which the mind hovers between ecstasy and delirium.

*Die Elixiere des Teufels* (1815–16), a tale of seduction and murder that is reminiscent of Matthew Gregory Lewis's novel *Ambrosio or the Monk* (1796), employs the fate motif of the contemporary 'Schicksalstragödie'. The nightmare career of Brother Medardus, and especially his encounters with his 'Doppelgänger', conjure up the spectre of insanity which seems to have haunted Hoffmann: 'Warum denke ich schlafend oder wachend so oft an den Wahnsinn?' he wrote. *Lebensansichten des Katers Murr nebst fragmentarischer Biographie des Kapellmeisters Johannes Kreisler in zufälligen Makulaturblättern* (1820–1) intersperses, through a whimsical fiction, the burlesque or banal autobiography of a philistine tom-cat with the sensational intrigues and mystifications that surround the career of the musician Johannes Kreisler: social satire alternates with Gothic fantasy, plot and passion. The confessions of Murr are cut short by his untimely death; the story of Kreisler remains unresolved as the work was never completed.

The evolution of the short story in Germany during the nineteenth century is dominated by the Novelle, to which a vast amount of critical attention has been devoted. The term was adopted into German from the collections of brief tales common in Romance literatures of the Renaissance— Boccaccio's *Decamerone* (1353), the anonymous *Cent Nouvelles Nouvelles* (ca. 1440), the *Heptameron* (1558) of Marguerite de Navarre. Karl Grosse and Meissner (*Novellen des Rittmeister Schuster*, 1786) used the term, but it was not until the advent of the Romantics that it acquired special significance, became disengaged from the Romance prototype and developed many varieties. German critics have expended much effort in defining the Novelle. A good deal of what they have written is specious and speculative nonsense and many of the criteria so painfully deduced—succinctness, ulterior significance, striking incident, turning-points and symbols—are simply features of any good short story. More recent criticism has tended to abandon the canonical approach and use terms like 'novellistic narrative' rather than 'Novelle'. It remains true, however, that many leading authors of the nineteenth century show a theoretical and practical interest in strictly fashioned short narratives with mainly realistic social settings and with philosophical or psychological implications.

It was Goethe who initiated the development of the Novelle. His *Unterhaltungen deutscher Ausgewanderten* (1795) is linked to the original Romance form less by the stories themselves than by the 'framework' situation: aristocratic families have fled from the French invasion of the Rheinland as Boccaccio's story-tellers had fled from the perils of the plague in Florence. The purpose of the story-telling in Goethe's case, however, is not merely entertainment but the restoration of polite and urbane intercourse after the group has been disrupted by heated discussion of the French Revolution. The tales range from ghost stories to 'moralische Erzählungen'; some are original, some borrowed from known sources, some mere anecdotes, others highly elaborate. Apart from Goethe's *Märchen*, which crowns the collection, the two most substantial stories are the tale of the honest procurator from the *Cent Nouvelles Nouvelles*, and the story of Friedrich. The former describes a ruse by which a young wife is induced to remain faithful to her absent husband: she is tricked into a fast which puts her physically beyond temptation. Goethe turns a sly anecdote into a study of renunciation that anticipates the fate of Ottilie in *Die Wahlverwandtschaften*, itself a work originally designed as a Novelle for inclusion in *Wilhelm Meisters Wanderjahre*. The story of Friedrich belongs to the category of the 'family portrait'. It describes how the hero, having accidentally discovered a way of rifling his father's desk, redeems himself, escapes from the emotional situation that prompted the crime and settles down with a worthy wife to train his children in the virtue of renunciation.

Goethe's *Märchen* is an imaginative myth which suggests some chiliastic change in the history of man and nature. Its symbolism operates with traditional objects and patterns— the river, the snake, the giant, gold, light and darkness, mystic numbers—but it is too individual and intricate to yield to rational analysis. Religious, aesthetic and even political analogies glint here and there in the finely worked texture of the tale but the laws of this poetic universe and its truths spring from a level of the mind deeper than the reason and can be assimilated best at that level: it can only be said that *Das Märchen* revolves round self-sacrifice, redemption and apotheosis. The story's iridescent symbolism attracted the Romantics, and it was on Goethe's work, for instance, that Novalis based *Klingsohrs Märchen*, which forms the climax of the first part of *Heinrich von Ofterdingen*.

The pattern of the *Decamerone* revived by Goethe was adopted by Wieland in his *Hexameron von Rosenhain* (1805), a collection of three Novellen and three Märchen, by Achim von Arnim in his *Wintergarten* (1809) and by Tieck in his *Phantasus* (1811). Goethe wove Novellen into the fabric of *Wilhelm Meister* and *Die Wahlverwandtschaften*, but it was not until much later that he turned to the autonomous Novelle that had by then become the rule. His *Novelle* (1827) has acquired canonical status because of its title and because of the remark which Goethe made about it to Eckermann: 'Was ist eine Novelle anders als eine unerhörte, sich ereignete Begebenheit.' The theme of his *Novelle* is defined by Goethe: 'Zu zeigen, wie das Unbändige, Unüberwindliche oft besser durch Liebe und Frömmigkeit als durch Gewalt bezwungen werde . . .' A lion and a tiger escape from a menagerie and cross the path of an aristocratic riding-party. The tiger is shot by a young nobleman who believes that it threatens the Princess; the lion, which has taken refuge in the courtyard of a ruined castle, is led back to captivity by the music of a child:

> So beschwören, fest zu bannen
> Liebem Sohn ans zarte Knie
> Ihn, des Waldes Hochtyrannen,
> Frommer Sinn und Melodie.

The moral of these events is delicately reflected in the relationship of the page Honorio to the Princess and in almost every detail of the landscape. There can be few works of literature in which the central idea so ingeniously and so completely informs plot and circumstance.

In the Romance tradition adopted and developed by Goethe and Wieland the Novelle is concerned with manifold aspects of social behaviour and presumes the ethos of a cultured community. Its tone is fundamentally rational, controlled, urbane; irrational forces are discounted or kept consciously at bay. The Romantics, on the other hand, express in the Novelle a sense of wonder or of horror, a belief in daemonic forces linking man and nature, an awareness of man's vulnerability to fate or chance, an interest in folk tales and superstitions. Their stories are atmospheric; events and characters are surrounded by a penumbra of mystery. A striking example is Tieck's *Der blonde Eckbert* (1797), a story of shifting perspectives flickering between past and present. Eckbert and his wife Bertha wander in a world of witchcraft and taboo, perplexed by premonitions and changing identities, haunted by the memory of lost innocence that rings in the strange cry of 'Waldeinsamkeit'. In *Der Runenberg* (1802) a beautiful woman personifies the spell of wild nature. The focus of this story changes dramatically from visions of gold and gems in the mind of the hero to the horrified view of his wife, who sees nothing but a madman gloating over worthless flints. The effect here is more contrived than in *Der blonde Eckbert*, and *Die Elfen* (1811) is more remote still from the authentic folk motifs of the earlier stories. The thrill of horror that renders *Eckbert* memorable is lacking here, and the tone of the story is arch and falsely naive. Tieck's later Novellen revert to social themes and often embody prosaic attacks on literary and political foibles of the day.

With Tieck it is dark forces of nature that seduce or imperil the mind. In E. T. A. Hoffmann's stories supernatural powers enthrall men through art and music. The *Fantasiestücke in Callots Manier* (1814–15) and *Die Serapionsbrüder* (1819–21) are thronged with half-crazed geniuses who have fallen victim to their art. Hoffmann cultivates ambiguities by which grotesque and gruesome events are presented at one point as objective truth, only to appear elsewhere as hallucinations bred in the fevered brains of his characters: the reader is tantalized with rational explanations as an escape from nightmare. Uncanny figures glide through humdrum urban scenes; without warning a philistine Dresden drawing-room in *Der goldene Topf* dissolves fleetingly into fairyland. This story is both a comment on Hoffmann's dual existence as lawyer and poet and an allegory on the magic of the creative imagination. Even in those stories which dispense with supernatural elements Hoffmann tends to deal with lurid events and monstrous characters—like the criminal goldsmith

Cardillac in that rudimentary detective-story, *Das Fräulein von Scudéry*.

Hoffmann had numerous associates and imitators, amongst them the French émigrés Friedrich de la Motte Fouqué and Adalbert von Chamisso. It was on the basis of Fouqué's *Undine* (1811) that Hoffmann composed an opera. This is a moving story of a waternymph betrayed by the mortal to whom she is wed and whom she is compelled by the laws of her elemental nature to destroy. Chamisso's *Peter Schlemihls wundersame Geschichte* (1814) combines the motifs of the inexhaustible purse and the seven-league boots with the tale of the man who sold his shadow to the Devil. There are no doubt psychological implications in this transaction: the distrust and hostility which Schlemihl's singular condition attracts may well reflect Chamisso's experience as an exile. Schlemihl's travels in the latter part of the story involve the botanical interests of the author, who later accompanied a Russian scientific expedition on a voyage round the world and ultimately became curator of the Berlin Botanical Gardens.

The short stories of Heinrich von Kleist are akin to his dramas in their determination to explore the foundations of the ethical world. The moral problems with which his characters are faced acquire metaphysical significance in that their faith in the intelligible order of the universe depends on the resolution of these problems. The fantasy by which the Romantics widened and deepened the limits of the Novelle gives way in Kleist to a dogged quest for truth. Not that the stories are openly speculative or reflective: on the contrary, Kleist's probing into the workings of Fate and 'the unsound nature of the world' is implied in convulsive events and impulsive acts—earthquake, revolution, murder and rape. Plots hinge on paradox and on the astonishing disparity between cause and effect: Michael Kohlhaas, 'one of the most just and most terrible men of his time', ravages his homeland for the sake of two horses unjustly seized from him; an earthquake snatches ill-starred lovers from despair and impending death in *Das Erdbeben in Chili* and allows them a fleeting paradise before they fall victim again to the inhumanity of man; a twist of fate leads the hero of *Die Verlobung in St. Domingo* to misconstrue the actions of the girl who loves him and has saved his life; in *Die Marquise von O.* and *Der Zweikampf* it seems that the laws of nature and even the judgement of God deny the innocence of the heroine, so that the characters are plunged into a potentially tragic confusion of feeling before a near-miraculous turn of events restores their faith. Kleist's Novellen—he himself called them simply 'Erzählungen'—are, as it were, erratic blocks in the geology of the genre. They are inimitable, and only the use of exotic and historical themes and of stupendous events may be said to have influenced succeeding writers.

Arnim, Brentano and Eichendorff, no less than Tieck, Hoffmann and Kleist, express in their works belief in a transcendental world, but in their case the organ by which this higher world is intuited is not so much the imagination or the philosophical intellect as the religious sense, particularly as it is manifested in folk tales, superstitions and legends. Mandrake and golem play a part in Arnim's *Isabella von Ägypten* (1812), and the hero in his *Majoratsherren* (1820) is gifted with second sight. A number of Arnim's stories have settings in the remote past, but what is perhaps his best-known Novelle, *Der tolle Invalide auf dem Fort Ratonneau* (1818), is based on an anecdote from the Seven Years War. Sergeant Francoeur is driven insane by an old head-wound and holds the city of Marseilles to ransom with the guns of his fort until he is induced to surrender by the self-sacrificing love of his wife. By discreet use of ambivalent symbols and incidents Arnim gives the story a theological perspective: beyond the rationally explicable psychological and physiological factors in the action he suggests a struggle between divine and diabolical powers which ends triumphantly in the words:

> Gnade löst den Fluch der Sünde,
> Liebe treibt den Teufel aus.

Brentano's characteristic mixture of religious faith and satirical wit manifests itself in many of his *Märchen* (1805–11, and in many revised versions). These are frequently based on French or Italian originals, the best-known of them, for instance, *Gockel, Hinkel and Gackeleia*, being taken from Giambattista Basile's collection of Neapolitan fairy-tales, *Il Pentamerone*. Possibly the best of Brentano's *Novellen* is the balladesque *Geschichte vom braven Kasperl und dem schönen Annerl* (1817). During a fine summer night the writer hears from an old peasant woman the doubly tragic tale of Kasperl, her soldier grandson, who has shot himself from shame on learning that his father and brother are scoundrels, and of Kasperl's fiancée, who is to be beheaded in the morning for the murder of her child, fruit of her seduction by an aristocratic officer. The writer's vain attempt to save Annerl seems officious and foolish in the face of the old woman's acceptance of an exemplary atonement that not only saves her god-child's immortal part but moves sinners to repentance. The tale is worked through with folk superstitions and epitomizes Brentano's ideal of a deeply rooted religious morality.

Eichendorff's *Das Marmorbild* (1819), which he described as 'Novelle oder Märchen', is reminiscent of the Tannhäuser legend. Although the power of Venus has been broken by the Virgin and Child, her phantom returns each spring to the magically restored temple and lures men to destruction. The young nobleman Florio is rescued from the temptations of the pagan goddess when he hears the words of an old hymn; the seductive vision vanishes leaving behind shattered statues and overgrown gardens, Florio is liberated from lust and feels a holier love growing in his heart.

There are no supernatural elements in Eichendorff's famous *Aus dem Leben eines Taugenichts* (1826), but it has all the shining optimism of a fairy-tale. The career of Eichendorff's happy wanderer expresses the gay wanderlust of Romanticism tinged with an irony that saves the story from outright sentimentality. Like a vagabond Orpheus the good-for-nothing fiddles his way from Vienna to Rome and back again, through sunlit landscapes and moonlit forests, to the accompaniment of nightingales and posthorns. It is a rococo world seen with the comfortable nostalgia of Biedermeier, a world which is never cold or cruel, in which the pangs of love are bitter-sweet and privation is never for long, a world in which every menace turns out to be a comic illusion, a world of flowered dressing-gowns and churchwarden pipes and cottage gardens. Nothing can go amiss in the end: the good-for-nothing is united with his beloved and the story finishes with a *feu-de-joie* and a cry of joyous affirmation:

> Sie lächelte still und sah mich recht vergnügt und freundlich an, und von fern schallte immerfort die Musik herüber, und Leuchtkugeln flogen vom Schloss durch die stille Nacht über die Gärten und die Donau rauschte dazwischen herauf—und es war alles, alles gut.

It would perhaps be ungracious to recall that this charming idyll was written in an age of brutal political repression; certainly, the lyrical beauty of the songs strewn throughout the story—'Wem Gott will rechte Gunst erweisen' and 'Das Lied der Prager Studenten', for instance—transcends such considerations and constitutes a monument to all that is finest in Romanticism.

One of the most important literary and scholarly initiatives of the Romantic movement was the collection and investigation of folk-tales by the brothers Jacob and Wilhelm Grimm. In their *Kinder- und Hausmärchen* (vol. I, 1812, vol. II, 1815), originally planned as a counterpart to *Des Knaben Wunderhorn*, they rescued some 200 tales from a dying oral tradition and made them part of the national literary heritage. The main geographical basis of the collection was Hesse, but tales from many other areas were included, most from oral tradition but many from manuscripts and earlier prints. In spite of individual differences between them—Jacob's versions are laconic, Wilhelm's more elaborate, detailed and colourful— the brothers evolved a more or less uniform style which is quite distinctive, has been imitated ever since and recognized by generations of Germans as the 'traditional' idiom of the folk-tale. The assimilation of many dialects and styles to a standard so widely understood and accepted was in itself a remarkable feat of imagination and literary skill. The Grimms did not hesitate to reconstruct and adapt in the light of their philological studies the stories that they gathered, for they considered that popular tales embodied splinters of prehistoric beliefs and myths. 'In diesen Volksmärchen liegt lauter urdeutscher Mythus, den man für verloren gehalten', wrote Wilhelm Grimm in the preface to the second volume. Jacob insisted, 'Das Märchenbuch ist mir gar nicht für Kinder geschrieben', nevertheless the compilers were delighted that it appealed to children, and the *Kleine Ausgabe*, published in 1825 and reprinted innumerable times, was aimed specially at the young. The example of the Grimms stimulated investigation into the folk-tales of many lands and led to the compilation of collections all over the world. In Germany the most popular successor to them was Ludwig Bechstein, whose *Deutsches Märchenbuch* (1845), with fine illustrations by Ludwig Richter, sold 63,000 copies within seven years. Bechstein's style is somewhat more sophisticated than that of the Grimms, he aims rather more clearly at moral improvement and is fond of a faintly ironic tone.

### The Romantic Drama

Drama is not the genre most successfully practised in the Romantic era. Criticism outweighed creative performance, and where originality was achieved, the contribution was greater in comedy than in tragedy. The reason may be found in the emphasis which the Romantics excessively placed on the supernatural aspects of tragedy, whereas in the field of comedy they succeeded in accomplishing a new satirical form.

The accent upon the supernatural is seen first in the motivation of tragic issues as a concatenation of fated events. The 'Schicksalstragödie' came to be a distinctive type, beginning with Tieck's *Karl von Berneck* (1793–5). It reached its zenith with Zacharias Werner's *Der vierundzwanzigste Februar* (1809) and its nadir with Adolf Müllner's *Die Schuld* (1816). This kind of tragedy has little intrinsic merit; it is historically significant only in being based on a then widely held notion that the salient feature differentiating Greek tragedy from its Shakespearean and other 'modern' forms was the motivating power of fate rather than individual human initiative.

A more advanced form of Romantic drama is the kind advocated by Friedrich Schlegel and Adam Müller. When Schlegel wrote *Über das Studium der griechischen Poesie* he ranked *Hamlet* as a pinnacle of 'philosophical' tragedy, the expression of disharmony ruling the modern mind in contrast to the balanced presentations to be found in the work of Greek tragedians, Sophocles in particular. After his conversion to Catholicism he assessed Calderon's Christian dramas to be an even higher fulfilment of the ideal of tragedy in projecting the reconciliation of human disharmonies not in this life but in the next. Adam Müller postulated the need for a 'Himmelfahrtsmoment' in tragedy after the 'Todesmoment' of the catastrophe. Traditionally, death represents the ultimate 'tragic moment'; in Romantic drama this is followed by a representation of the hero's salvation in the beyond. *Faust Part II* may be said to conform with Romantic tragic theory, although Goethe adapted Christian mythology in a manner contrary to Friedrich Schlegel's and Adam Müller's orthodox ideas.

Romantic Christian tragedy heralds a return to the 'martyr-dramas' exemplified in the work of certain writers of the Baroque era. In his lectures *Über dramatische Kunst und Literatur* (1809–11), August Wilhelm Schlegel adopted a principle contravening Lessing's rejection of this type of tragedy: 'Die Freudigkeit, somit die Märtyrer in Qual und Tod gingen, war nicht Unempfindlichkeit, sondern der Heldenmut der höchsten Liebe.' The most successful treatment of this theme in the Romantic manner is Tieck's *Leben und Tod der heiligen Genoveva* (1800). This play has some of the characteristic qualities of Romantic drama which are similarly revealed in his *Kaiser Oktavianus* (1804). The subject matter is taken from medieval Christian or popular legend and treated with spacious breadth in multiple lyric forms, including sonnet and *terza rima*. The vast scope of Romantic dramas and their composite formal structures jeopardized overall dramatic consistency, but through their episodic structure and their frequent lyric interpolations they often made room for scenes of great poetic beauty.

Another example is Brentano's *Die Gründung Prags* (1815), while Fouqué's trilogy *Der Held des Nordens* (1808–10), a first attempt to dramatize the Siegfried story, is constructed on stricter lines, although the lyric element frequently also preponderates. A different kind is represented by Zacharias Werner's tragedies with their overt didactic religious intent: *Die Söhne des Tals* (1803), *Das Kreuz an der Ostsee* and *Martin Luther oder Die Weihe der Kraft* (1806). A. W. Schlegel's *Jon* (1802) and Friedrich Schlegel's *Alarcos* (1802), influenced respectively by Goethe's *Iphigenie* and Calderon's work, are tragedies on more traditional lines yet also possess distinctly Romantic formal and thematic features.

The Romantics made a considerably greater contribution in comedy. Opposition to prevalent social conditions and intellectual trends, particularly in their 'philistine' rationalist form, was part of the Romantic attitude at the outset and expressed itself in the outspokenly parodistic and satirical utterances of some of the leading writers. This led to a new kind of comedy represented in its best form by Tieck in *Der gestiefelte Kater* (1797), *Prinz Zerbino oder Die Reise nach dem guten Geschmack* (1799) and *Die verkehrte Welt* (1798). Basing his plots on well-known fairy tales and using the 'play within the play' technique, he was able to dispense with any pretext of realistic portrayal and yet, by including unmistakably topical allusions, to satirize the literary and social conditions of the day. He held up the philistine opinions of the common theatre-goer to ridicule and parodied the writings of Kotzebue and Böttiger, disreputable figures in the eyes of some Romantics.

The novelty of this kind of comedy is its inversion of the satirical principle ruling in the earlier eighteenth century. In the era of Enlightenment, satirists spoke in the name of society and directed their wit at those individuals or professional groups who acted eccentrically or egotistically against the common interest. In Tieck's comedies the position is reversed; accepted social and other norms become the focus of satirical attention. Apart from their attendant didactic purpose these comedies display greater sense of fun than those of many earlier or later writers. This accords with Friedrich Schlegel's views who, in his essay 'Über den ästhetischen Wert der griechischen Komödie' lauded 'Freude' and 'Rausch der Fröhlichkeit' as the outstanding virtues of the genre. A feeling of irresponsibility, a playfulness and aesthetic unconcern prevailed with Brentano when he wrote his farce *Gustav Wasa* (1800) containing parodies of Kotzebue, Schiller, Schelling and Herder. By comparison, his other work in the comic genre, *Ponce de Leon* (1804), while not devoid of what Brentano himself called his 'Mutwille', has a fundament of seriousness, largely reflecting the author's personal experiences.

## Romantic Poetry

The emphasis upon deliberate creative processes so evident in the doctrine of Irony, is only one side of the concept of literary production in the Romantic movement. This is shown by the equal importance given to the 'irrational' apprehension of the substratum of reality, to occult phenomena, intuitions, dreams and presentiments. In his Vienna lectures of 1808 A. W. Schlegel stated the Romantic equivalent of Schiller's distinction between ancient and modern poetry: 'Die Poesie der Alten war die des Besitzes, die unsrige ist die der Sehnsucht; jene steht fest auf dem Boden der Gegenwart, diese wiegt sich zwischen Erinnerung und Ahnung.'

Escapism is too negative a term for such an attitude towards reality. Like the Weimar poets, the Romantics eschewed reality in its actual forms, but instead of giving it heightened, idealized contours, they presented an imaginatively apprehended form in which dreams, fairy tales, visions, legends and myths constituted notable ingredients. In 'Gespräch über Poesie' Friedrich Schlegel demanded the creation of new myths based on modern philosophy. This project remained unfulfilled at the time, for like other members of the movement Friedrich Schlegel came to accept the Christian tradition when he joined the Catholic Church. That decision put an end to his Romanticism in its speculative form.

The speculative critical and aesthetic contribution of the movement comes from the members of the First School at Jena and in Berlin as represented by the Schlegel brothers and Novalis. The Second (Heidelberg) School with Achim von Arnim, Clemens Brentano and Joseph Freiherr von Eichendorff as its principal figures, and the Swabian School, notably Justus Kerner and Ludwig Uhland, covered a narrower field in their literary work. But however great the disparity in the poetic works of these different branches, they have shared features which distinguish them from the poetry of earlier and later movements.

The common Romantic attitude is most clearly seen in the prevailing predilection for secret and faraway places, for darkness and the indefinable vagueness given to landscapes by distance ('blaue Ferne'), for the deep stillness of forest and sky and, in another dimension, of death. The symbolic human figures embodying the longing for these experiences are the wanderer and the hermit, solitaries who have abandoned the confines of artificial urban life and seek communion with nature, with the undifferentiated life of the 'Volk' and with God. Their yearning for a unitary mode of existence on whatever level, physical or spiritual, differs essentially from the ideal propounded in the era of Classicism. Here the demand for integration predominates, in Romanticism the longing for complete fusion. In Classical ideology the individual preserves his function of remaining an identifiable part of a totality, in Romanticism he is spurred by 'Sehnsucht' to merge utterly with the embracing whole.

These are valid distinctions, although there were many variations of attitude and technique on both sides which brought their adherents together. Moreover, the original difference, increased by personal animosities between Goethe and Schiller on the one hand and the Schlegels on the other, became blurred when changes took place within the Romantic movement itself. As it progressed, a certain contraction of outlook occurred. From Novalis to Brentano and Eichendorff the scope of poetry narrowed, although it did not necessarily lose in poetic substantiality. The sum and substance of German Romantic poetry in its different forms is represented by Novalis' *Hymnen an die Nacht* (1797–1800) and *Geistliche Lieder* (1802), Arnim's and Brentano's *Des Knaben Wunderhorn* (1806–8), Brentano's poetry including *Romanzen vom Rosenkranz* (1803–11) and Eichendorff's lyric work. The major contribution of Tieck and the brothers Schlegel, who are not negligible poets, is in other fields. This is also true of Chamisso. Within the Swabian School Uhland's ballads are of greater historical significance than his lyric pieces, not, however, forgetting 'Der gute Kamerad' and perhaps 'Die Kapelle'.

*Hymnen an die Nacht* is the profoundest single poetic work of the Romantic movement. Novalis here brought the hymn to new heights of significance after the earlier achievements of Klopstock, Goethe and Hölderlin. He endowed it with a new content and gave it individual form. In stating his themes on day and night, life and death, nature and mind, love and belief, he presents a progressive poetic argument using varied forms of rhythmic prose and verse, complex imagery, oblique statement and direct address, and succeeded in fusing them all into an integrated pattern. In his own work and in that of other Romantic writers *Hymnen an die Nacht* remains a work unequalled for its speculative poetic fervour. The *Geistliche Lieder* are on a more traditional scale, a less sophisticated profession of faith. They would seem to indicate that when Novalis died at the age of twenty-nine, he was already approaching the end of his idiosyncratic form of Romanticism.

Clemens Brentano (1778–1842) and Achim von Arnim (1781–1831) made their mark with *Des Knaben Wunderhorn*, a collection of 'Volkslieder' and 'Kinderlieder' from the Middle Ages onwards. Although the versions they recorded often lack authenticity and despite the enfeebling changes they made in later editions, the collection is one of the most influential of its kind and helped to fashion the writing of this genre of poetry throughout the nineteenth century.

Brentano's own most ambitious individual work is his fragmentary *Romanzen vom Rosenkranz*, twenty intricately assembled poems forming an epic cycle. The action is located in medieval Bologna and deals with a complex series of religious themes. The work reveals Brentano's powers of composing poetry of the utmost richness of texture and musicality, but likewise his inability to sustain a lengthy poetic argument. Among his other lyric work his achievement is best seen in the subtly varied and melodious compositions of 'Sprich aus der Ferne' and 'Frühlingsschrei eines Knechtes aus der Tiefe'.

Eichendorff's lyric production is more restricted in theme and uniform in tone. Yet in volume it is the most representative collection of verse by an individual Romantic author. His favourite form is the 'Lied' with its regularly constructed stanzas containing alternately rhymed lines and its invariably reiterated Romantic themes of 'Wanderlust' and love of nature. The musicality of Eichendorff's verse is less intricate than Brentano's, but no less haunting. Nor does his repetitiveness obscure the individual quality of his 'geistliche Lieder' or of such memorable and far from optimistic poems as 'Der verspätete Wanderer' and 'Die zwei Gesellen'.

A different aspect of German Romanticism is found in the work of the 'Freiheitsdichter' Ernst Moritz Arndt (1769–

1860), Max von Schenkendorff (1783–1817) and Karl Theodor Körner (1791–1813). It is of minor importance but it represents the phase when Romanticism in its most distinctive form comes to an end. The patriotic verse of these soldier-poets expresses the satisfaction of an urge to share in communal life. In the same way conversion to Catholicism fulfils religious Romantic longings. Patriotic activity and traditional religiosity cause the primary Romantic impulses to abate and new attitudes to prevail. The wanderer returns home and settles down to perform his acknowledged civic and domestic tasks. The age of 'bürgerlicher Realismus' begins with this change in outlook which was imposed on German writers by the social developments and the political events of the post-Napoleonic era.

# V

## BIEDERMEIER AND YOUNG GERMANY

German literature in the years between 1820 and 1850, basically realistic in its idiom, has many transitional features: Romanticism was in decay, Realism not yet fully established; the deaths of Goethe, Hegel, F. Schlegel, Arnim and Schleiermacher between 1829 and 1834 seemed to mark the end of an era to which there was no obvious sequel; the idealism of Classicism and Romanticism was manifestly beginning to clash with the materialism of the nineteenth century. It has always been difficult to put a name to the distinctive but amorphous culture of the period. It is true that the vigorous and relatively coherent Young German movement falls within these years, but its clamour for moral and political emancipation by no means represented the canny, reactionary spirit of the age, and it included, apart from Heine, few notable poets. It was not until the 1920s that the term 'Biedermeier' began to be applied to certain major aspects of the literature of this time, and although its validity has been disputed it is now widely accepted. The word requires some explanation. The pseudonym 'Biedermeier' was attached to a collection of parodies (*Auserlesene Gedichte von weiland Gottlieb Biedermaier, Schulmeister in Schwaben* ...) that first appeared in the periodical *Fliegende Blätter* between 1855 and 1857. The authors, Adolf Kussmaul and Ludwig Eichrodt, had based their work on the quaint verses of Samuel Friedrich Sauter (*Sämmtliche Gedichte*, 1845) which epitomized the cosy, complacent respectability of the 'antediluvian' years before 1848, 'wo Teutschland noch im Schatten kühler Sauerkrautköpfe ass ...'. In the hectic 'Gründerzeit' between 1870 and 1910, however, the unassuming Biedermeier taste in art and furnishings seemed no longer comic but a nostalgic reminder of 'the good old days'. The Berlin centennial exhibition of 1906 and books like Max von Boehn's *Biedermeier: Deutschland von 1815 bis 1847* (1910) helped to free the word from its ironic implications and established it in art criticism, from where it soon spread to the literary field.

'Biedermeier', as the name implies, is a middle-class culture. It is predominantly provincial and parochial in character and reflects the political stagnation of an era in which the established order in church and state was largely accepted. Most educated individuals were resigned to political abstinence and tended to withdraw into the family circle or into a sphere of private interests—professional or dilettante —which were sometimes pursued to the point of eccentricity. Drawing-room and poet's garret, as the settings of cultured domesticity and cheerful poverty respectively, feature in the contemporary genre paintings of Spitzweg and Hasenclever. Spitzweg's pictures of sleepy provincial towns show us a world of slippered ease, of window-boxes, night caps and mighty church-warden pipes. It is an eclectic culture, conservative in every sense, imitative rather than creative: it contains something of the Enlightenment's belief in reason and progress and a good deal of Jean Paulesque whimsy and sentimentality, as well as the Romantic feeling for atmosphere and idyllic nature—although it totally lacks the dynamism, the conscious ambivalence and the extravagant fantasy of Romanticism. The heritage of Classicism dictates a concern for decorum and an anxious cultivation of good taste: this was the time when Berlin and Munich were transformed by the neo-Classical buildings of K. F. Schinkel and Leo von Klenze. It was Klenze who declared categorically: 'Es gab und gibt nur eine Baukunst und wird nur eine Baukunst geben, nämlich diejenige, welche in der griechischen Geschichts- und Bildungsepoche ihre Vollendung erhielt.' The attempt to compromise between idealism and realism marks the idyllic but meticulously accurate landscapes by

F. G. Waldmüller and the careful portraits of Franz Krüger: it is no less characteristic of much Biedermeier poetry.

Popular literature tended to be escapist or 'romantic' in a trivial sense. It was the heyday of the historical novels of Scott, Hugo, Dumas père and Hauff and of the maudlin or lubricous tales of Carl Heun (pseudonym: H. Clauren)— the latter counterfeited rather than parodied by Hauff in *Der Mann im Monde* (1826). Drawing-room poetry flourished —almanacs and album verses, lyrical vignettes, ballads and refined folk-songs like those of W. Müller's *Schöne Müllerin* (1824) and *Winterreise* (1827), which would be deservedly forgotten but for Schubert's musical settings. Short stories and Märchen were much in vogue. In the case of the fairy-tale, Biedermeier writers—in keeping with the underlying trend to realism and in contrast with the Romantics—are careful to mark clearly the boundary between reality and fantasy. There is often a didactic strain in such stories, for example in Heinrich Hoffmann's sadistically edifying *Struwwelpeter* (1848).

Apart from the work of the Viennese dramatists—Raimund, Nestroy and Grillparzer (some of whose major plays were not published until after his death),—the drama of Biedermeier was undistinguished. The stilted Schillerian tragedies of Uechtritz found little response, and the repertoire was dominated by the fustian historical and legendary dramas of Halm and Raupach or by Charlotte Birch-Pfeiffer's adaptations of Hugo, Dumas and Charlotte Brontë. The provincialism of Biedermeier accounts for the popularity of local comedies, amongst which Niebergall's Darmstadt dialect tragi-comedy *Datterich* (1841) stands out as a rare classic. It was not until the 1840s that Hebbel began to infuse new blood into the German theatre, while the dramas of Büchner and Grabbe, revolutionary in theme and style alike, did not find their way on to the stage until many years later still.

Certain Romantics, for example Eichendorff and Tieck, adjust to the Biedermeier taste: a story like Tieck's *Des Lebens*

*Überfluss* is thoroughly Biedermeier in feeling. Traces of Biedermeier have even been detected in the elderly Goethe —the marked didacticism, a belief in prudent renunciation, a fondness for collecting objects d'art and an undue concern with tasteful furnishings. There are, however, distinguished writers specifically identified with Biedermeier, who, in giving poetic expression to its values as well as its problematic features, transcend its inherent limitations. Unlike the Romantics they do not form a symbiotic group, they tend to be solitary by disposition as well as by situation. Only Immermann and Gotthelf, among these writers, are capable of being vigorously affirmative in their outlook; Droste-Hülshoff, Grillparzer, Lenau, Mörike, Raimund and Stifter are fundamentally pessimistic. All of them suffer under the stifling atmosphere of the age and experience the discordance of the ideal and the real, or art and life, as a fate to be mastered by resignation, dedication and studied control of the passions. Overshadowed by the Classicism on which their style is largely modelled, they were disconsolately aware that poetry was losing its pre-eminence in intellectual life and that the poet—as opposed to the journalist—could no longer claim the status of prophet and leader. Droste-Hüls-hoff and Stifter absorb themselves in registering the sights and sounds of nature as intelligible manifestations of the cosmic order or in compiling simple annals of the poor in spirit who yet should inherit the earth. 'Andacht zum Kleinen' is Stifter's motto. Mörike gazes back nostalgically to the beauty of rococo art, broods on the mortality of genius and shrinks from the dubious bounty of experience: 'Lass, o Welt, o lass mich sein! Locket nicht mit Liebesgaben . . .' The burden of Grillparzer's work is resignation—tragic in the case of Rudolf II in *Ein Bruderzwist,* precariously affirmative in the case of Rustan in *Der Traum ein Leben.* A morbid strain latent in Biedermeier emerges in these poets, who are aware of daemonic forces in man blandly ignored by most of their contemporaries. The lives of nearly all of them were shadowed by disappointment and hypochondria. Grillparzer ended his life practically as a recluse. Mörike suffered much unhappiness from a protracted love-affair, Lenau died mad, both Raimund and Stifter, whose *Nachsommer* is the very vade-mecum of spiritual hygiene, committed suicide. The inner tensions and frustrations of an era that seems on the surface so snug, smug and innocently contented are sadly apparent in the life and work of these perceptive individuals.

On 10 December 1835 the Bundestag passed a resolution enjoining member states to proceed with the full rigour of the law against the 'literary school' of 'das junge Deutschland' or 'die junge Literatur ... deren Bemühungen unverhohlen dahin gehen, in belletristischen, für alle Klassen von Lesern zugänglichen Schriften die christliche Religion auf die frechste Weise anzugreifen, die bestehenden sozialen Verhältnisse herabzuwürdigen und alle Zucht und Sittlichkeit zu zerstören'. As is often the way with governments, the Bundestag credited its opponents with a greater degree of co-ordinated purpose than actually existed: 'Young Germany' was certainly not a 'school' and although, in relation to the general stagnation of the time, it may be considered a 'movement', it was largely spontaneous and unco-ordinated. It united more or less fortuitously a number of writers—the resolution named Heine, Gutzkow, Wienbarg, Mundt and Laube—who supported progressive ideas like German unification, constitutional rule and the emancipation of women. The term was used on occasion by these writers on the analogy of contemporary political movements such as Mazzini's 'Young Italy' and 'Young Europe'; it did not imply the close personal relationships that characterized the Romantic movement, and 'Young German' authors were more often rivals than friends. The liberal ideas that constitute what might be considered a Young German programme are in fact widely disseminated and outlast anything that could be called a Young German movement. Apart from the authors named, L. Börne, Ernst Willkomm, Adolf Glassbrenner, Gustav Kühne, August Lewald and H. J. König have at least a 'Young German' phase, while Prince

Pückler-Muskau, Immermann, Alexis, Ungern-Sternberg and H. Marggraf all show traces of 'Young German' influence.

Attacks on the reactionary régimes of the Metternich era had been mounted by Börne and Heine before 1830, but it was the July Revolution of that year that unleashed the sudden clamour of liberal opinion sometimes known as 'Jungdeutscher Sturm und Drang'. 'Die Revolution tritt in die Literatur', wrote Heine jubilantly, but, in Germany at least, the revolution remained largely confined to literature, for the political fragmentation of the country and its backward economy had prevented the growth of a commercial middle-class powerful enough to challenge the monarchical order. Seeking reform if not revolution, a liberal minority turned to literature as their forum. The insulation of poetry from contemporary life and the 'indifferentism' of Romanticism in its Biedermeier mutation were condemned, a concern with social and political issues was encouraged. The sovereignty of aesthetic judgements, so laboriously established during the eighteenth century, was revoked—they were no longer to be considered as absolute but as relative to the national culture of the day. 'Schön ist', wrote Theodor Mundt, 'was den nationalen Formen der jedesmal herausgetretenen Weltanschauung einer Zeit und eines Volkes gemäss und harmonisch ist.' The established order in Church and State was attacked: outmoded conventions were to be swept away, Christian transcendentalism and asceticism driven out by a healthily hedonistic 'modern' outlook under the slogan of 'emancipation of the flesh'. 'Das Leben ist des Lebens höchster Zweck', proclaimed Ludolf Wienbarg. Laube put the demand for moral and physical hygiene even more drastically—'Deutschland, geh ins Bad!'

The main intellectual roots as well as some of the literary models of 'Young Germany' are to be found in France—in the half-rationalistic, half-religious sociology and ethics of Saint-Simon, Prosper Enfantin and Armand Bazard—but the dialectical method of Hegel, if not his philosophy as such, also had much influence, through the so-called 'Junghegelianer'. The materialism of Ludwig Feuerbach, important for Marx and Engels as well as for Gottfried Keller, F. T. Vischer, Anzengruber and many other writers, had a Hegelian basis. Feuerbach's *Wesen des Christentums* (1841) was an even more fundamental challenge to Christian tradition than D. F. Strauss's *Leben Jesu* (1835), which scandalized the orthodox by suggesting that much Christian dogma was myth or legend. With the advance of the physical and biological sciences, epitomized for example in Darwin's theory of the origin of species, the influence of Hegel declined and the basis of the critical movement became increasingly pragmatic. The second half of the nineteenth century was dominated by a positivism derived from the kind of faith in modern science expressed by Ludwig Büchner in his popular *Kraft und Stoff* (1855). These later developments, however, outstripped the thought of the 'Young Germans', who saw themselves as the heirs of a humanistic tradition established by progressive writers of the eighteenth century—Lessing, the 'Sturm und Drang' authors of the 1770s, Schiller, Jean Paul and Wilhelm Heinse.

Most of the 'Young Germans' were professional writers and their works were journalistic by necessity as much as by choice. The plan for a major 'Young German' organ, *Die Deutsche Revue*, to be edited by Gutzkow and Wienbarg, was nipped in the bud by the censor, but Gutzkow, Mundt, Laube and August Lewald all edited various other periodicals. The literary forms preferred were naturally such as could be accommodated in magazines for general circulation and in the feuilletons of newspapers—character sketches, vignettes of social life, diaries, letters, Novellen, travel journals and serial novels—all of them in what the aggrieved Prussian censor called 'halb witzige, halb poetische Einkleidung'. Attention was focussed on man rather than nature, on varieties of social organization and characteristic features of economic life, with prominence given to 'human interest'. The 'Reisebilder' and 'Reisenovellen' attempted to give a rapid impression of a national or regional culture under the fashionable heading of 'Zustände' and in a style that departed deliberately from sedate tradition. The nature of their topics as well as the manner of publication prompted the 'Young Germans' to write in prose rather than in verse. There is no lyric in the traditional sense of the term that could be labelled 'Young German'—the categories are pretty well mutually exclusive—although the 'Vormärz', the period preceding the 1848 revolution, can show some fine political verse in satirical or rhetorical vein by Herwegh, Freiligrath, Fallersleben, Prutz and Anastasius Grün. In his *Kunst der deutschen Prosa* (1837) Mundt argued for the primacy of prose in the modern world and urged the 'emancipation' of German from its customary cumbersome patterns. The ideal of a flexible, graphic, witty and ironically allusive style was best realized by Heine and Wienbarg; the writings of Mundt himself, Willkomm, Glassbrenner and some other minor authors are often hectic and negligent. Most 'Young German' prose is devoid of atmosphere and is functional rather than poetic: its sheer topicality disqualifies it from aesthetic judgement. Even the better 'Young German' works have never been popular in Germany for they lack the warmth and soulful intensity associated with the concept of 'Gemüt'. Their main literary merits consist in a flair for significant descriptive detail and the acute analysis of motivation as the product of personality and environment. The 'Young Germans' are nevertheless nowhere near as objectively realistic as they pretend. Their accounts of institutions and social life are shaped by political ideals, prejudices and assumptions, or else coloured by the jaundiced eye of that modish, quasi-Byronic figure, 'der Zerrissene'.

The 'Sturm und Drang' phase of 'Young Germany' culminated in 1835 with major works by Wienbarg, Mundt, Kühne and Gutzkow and was succeeded by a more temperate phase in which the racy idiom and journalistic format yielded to a rather more careful style and increasingly ambitious literary forms. The Bundestag resolution may have had its effect on some individuals. Certainly ideological as well as stylistic moderation may be observed in the later parts of Laube's *Das junge Europa* (*Die Krieger*; *Die Bürger*, 1837) and in Mundt's historical novels. The successful plays of Gutzkow and Laube are conventional enough in technique and express views that are no more than moderately liberal, while the social realism of Gutzkow's long novels, *Die Ritter vom Geiste* (1850/1) and *Der Zauberer von Rom* (1858/61) is superimposed on a foundation of liberal idealism that seemed by that time innocuously outdated.

Even in the earliest phase of 'Jungdeutschland' there had been differences of political outlook between constitutional liberals, such as Gutzkow, Laube, Wienbarg and Mundt essentially were, and radical democrats like Georg Büchner and Ludwig Weidig, who sought to appeal, in *Der hessische Landbote* (1834) for example, more directly to the working population. After 1840 the radical wing was philosophically strengthened by the 'Junghegelianer', who used their journal, variously titled *Hallesche Jahrbücher für deutsche Kunst und Wissenschaft* and *Deutsche Jahrbücher für Kunst und Wissenschaft*, to attack the liberals as self-indulgent idealists. Prominent among the radicals were Karl Marx and Friedrich Engels. As increasing industrialization made more obvious the plight of the working class, social evils and the demand for social justice replaced constitutional and conscientious liberty as the themes of progressive writers. The later novels of Ernst Willkomm, the works of Robert Prutz and Luise Otto, and even some of the novels of F. W. Hackländer, show the transition from liberalism to socialism, and although they are not free from fantastic and melodramatic elements, they are more firmly rooted in material realities and show more understanding of economic processes than the novels of Laube and Gutzkow.

The 1848 revolution revealed even more clearly the ideological confusion of its protagonists and the gulf that had developed between the middle-class liberals whose aim was reform, and the radicals who put their faith in proletarian revolution. Communism, with its materialistic basis and its appeal to the working classes, superseded the old liberalism as the most persuasive philosophy of social change. As an allegedly scientific system with a deterministic view of history and society communism seems to have had less recourse than 'Young German' liberalism to imaginative literature as a means of expression. After the collapse of liberal hopes in 1848 middle-class authors tended to turn away from political engagement to a more 'poetic' form of realism—which was an undoubted aesthetic gain— and although 'Young German' ideas persisted here and there beyond 1848 the failure of the Frankfurt Parliament may be seen as the effective end of a movement that began explosively with the revolution of 1830. Generally speaking, German literature did not again assume a radical political aspect until the end of the nineteenth century.

# VI

# REALISM

The terms 'poetischer Realismus', 'bürgerlicher Realismus' and 'psychologischer Realismus' are often used in connection with literary works of the period 1850–80. They do not denote distinct literary schools so much as different aspects of the same idiom. 'Realism' might be applied, in fact, not only to the literary style but to the whole mood and intellectual atmosphere of the era. The philosophical edifice of rational idealism that had dominated German thought from Leibniz to Hegel was one of the casualties in the collapse of the 1848 revolution and the Frankfurt parliament. This collapse was a traumatic experience for the intellectual middle-class, which was made to realize both its impotence and its vulnerability and compelled to revise its thinking in the direction of empiricism. There was a distinct fall in the political temperature, the liberal movement lost its élan and the enthusiasms that had inspired or buffeted the nation ever since the Napoleonic wars were succeeded by a spirit of caution and compromise: 'Die Zeit der Ideale ist vorüber', declared the liberal politician Miquel. The second half of the century is significantly the period of Bismarck's 'Realpolitik', of the calculated challenge to Austrian hegemony and of bold but specious solutions to social and cultural problems. At the same time the increasing tempo of economic life affected the relationship of the social classes and created great differences between urban and rural life. Political theorists like Proudhon, Max Stirner, Marx and Engels questioned the concept of private property and the basis of capitalist society while, on the other hand, an increasingly self-confident bourgeoisie identified property and material success with culture. This bourgeoisie, although the political hopes of its liberal element had been disappointed, supported the authoritarian state for the guarantee of social order which it furnished and, by abdicating its full political responsibilities, helped to create the gulf between thought and action, intellect and authority, cultural and political aspiration that has since so balefully affected German history. German unity, the liberal dream, was realized in 1871 under the auspices of military alliance rather than through democratic initiative, and the cultural sterility of the new Reich was justly exposed by Nietzsche in his *Unzeitgemässe Betrachtungen* (1873–6). In these circumstances many intellectuals relinquished 'impractical' ideals and contented themselves with the cultivation of private 'domestic' virtues—conscientiousness, diligence, thrift, loyalty. 'Work' was assigned a high ethical value and the happy end of human endeavour conceived as a well-regulated and economically secure family life: 'Wir treiben jetzt Familienglück', wrote Heine sarcastically in 1849.

The advent of realism in politics coincided with advances in the physical and biological sciences and in technology that led to the formulation of scientific hypotheses about the nature of the universe and man's place in it. In his *Kraft und Stoff* (1855) Ludwig Büchner popularized the theory of materialism, and both he and the distinguished zoologist Ernst Haeckel (*Natürliche Schöpfungsgeschichte*, 1868) did much to spread the influence of Darwin's theory of natural selection and to propagate a philosophy of 'monism', described by Haeckel as 'the link between religion and the sciences'. The abstract system of Hegel with its claim to universal validity was superseded either by pure empiricism or by philosophies that were anthropologically or historically interpretative and aimed to appeal to the individual in an existential situation. Feuerbach's fundamentally optimistic view of man as the procreator of his own idea of perfection, destined to fulfil himself individually and socially, physically, emotionally and intellectually within the limits of the natural universe, found many adherents in an age of reaction against transcendentalism. On the other hand, Schopenhauer's pessimistic philosophy of resignation, which represented the world as a battlefield of conflicting wills and the very exertion of will as the source of suffering, enjoyed a belated vogue among those who were disillusioned or dismayed by the turmoil of the times. For what might seem in historical perspective to be a period of relative stability and prosperity seemed to many who lived then to be a time of ferment and crisis. J. G. Droysen wrote in 1854: 'So ist die Gegenwart: Alles im Wanken, in unermesslicher Zerrüttung, Gärung, Verwilderung. Alles Alte verbraucht, gefälscht, wurmstichig, rettungslos. Und das Neue noch formlos, ziellos, chaotisch, nur zerstörend. ... Wir stehen in einer jener grossen Krisen, welche von einer Weltepoche zu einer anderen hinüber leiten.'

Many poets and writers were indeed aware of living in a time of convulsive change and of transition from traditional values and ways of life to a much more dynamic economy and a materialistic society. Much intellectual effort was expended in the attempt to conserve humanistic values while assimilating the new scientific doctrines of determinism. The poets of realism treated with reserve the theory that man was subject to forces of heredity and environment, they saw him in conflict with these forces rather than ineluctably determined by them. The tone of much realist writing is laconic and detached, the humour that characterizes the work of all the realists with the possible exception of Storm often has a wry note and seems to serve as a means of evading commitment, as an emollient for the asperities of a changing world.

The poetic realist concedes the autonomy of the physical universe and tries to form through the power of imagination a coherent picture of our experience of this universe without recourse to ulterior concepts like God or Fate. The world is conceived as a mechanical organism which may evoke wonder or aesthetic pleasure but is in itself ethically indifferent, the irrational and fantastic are granted only subjective validity, language is not, as it was for the Romantics, a quasi-magic incantatory power, or, as it was for

'Jungdeutschland', a vehicle for polemics, but a reproductive and evocative instrument for articulating experience. 'Speak as you find' might be a motto for the poetic realists: the world is to be judged in the light of experience, with good and evil, the beautiful and the ugly equally worthy of representation. Overt comment, false poetic effects and crude ethical dualism are to be avoided, to this end the author often effaces himself behind a 'framework', a narrator or the fiction of a chronicle. Characters are depicted generally in everyday middle-class settings, attention is paid to details of milieu and calling and to plausibility of motivation. Raabe's *Hungerpastor* and Keller's *Der grüne Heinrich* represent the development of their heroes as determined by economic circumstance to a degree which is foreign to the Classical 'Bildungsroman'. The moral code of realism is a less ambitious and more utilitarian version of Classical humanism, in which self-discipline and altruistic service to the community play a leading part. Ultimate wisdom often takes the form of stoic resignation, and writers like Raabe, Storm and Fontane seem disinclined to probe too deeply into the tragic implications of the situations they describe.

The novel and the Novelle were the most favoured forms amongst realist writers. Foreign models had some influence: Balzac remained popular, the psychological subtlety of Stendhal found belated recognition and Flaubert's clinical detachment, the precision of his style and his descriptions of provincial life made a deep impression in Germany. The example of Dickens focussed attention on the social problems of urban life and also inspired many attempts to emulate the whimsical humour of *Pickwick Papers*. On the whole, however, realism in Germany retained a kind of demure Biedermeier blandness that is characteristic—there is an element of the idyllic in it which robs it of the harshness that marks the contemporary novels of other nations. This idyllic quality is linked to the provincial and regional character of German realism, and no doubt owes something to Romantic notions of ethnic virtues and a nostalgic belief in the soundness of life in small organic communities. Realist novels and Novellen are generally artistically constructed with an eye to the symbolism of character and circumstance. Keller, Storm, C. F. Meyer and Otto Ludwig restored the Novelle to a strict aesthetic form but allowed themselves psychological analysis and description of milieu and atmosphere on a scale unknown in the Italian or even the German Classical Novelle. The historical novel and short story reached their peak in the period of realism, when the study of history flourished as never before and methods of historical research were used—amongst others by the historians Scheffel, Riehl, Dahn and Ebers—not only to represent the great figures of history but to reconstruct the conditions of everyday life in the past. Such 'Professoren-Romane' served in a more responsible fashion the didactic purposes of the heroic and gallant novels of the seventeenth century, they are written in a similar colourful vein and subscribe to the same kind of ethical dualism.

Realism, as opposed to Naturalism, made no very distinctive contribution to the drama; its temper was perhaps too laconic to be dramatically effective. Ludwig never achieved much success as a dramatist and Hebbel, after his rehabilitation of the 'bürgerliches Trauerspiel' with *Maria Magdalene* (1844) abandoned the realistic idiom for historical and mythical themes which seemed better adapted to fulfil the essential function of the drama as a representation of the historical process itself; realistic details of milieu would here have been unnecessary, irrelevant and a distraction from the philosophical import of the plays. The popular dramatists of the time, now largely forgotten, were indebted for themes and technique to French playwrights—Dumas fils, Sardou, Feuillet. They included Adolf Wilbrandt, Oskar Blumenthal, Gustav Kadelburg, Adolph L'Arronge and Hugo Lubliner.

Among the realist writers of the second half of the century only Storm, Meyer and, to a lesser extent, Keller had outstanding gifts as lyric poets. The literary 'Gesellschaft der Krokodile' founded by Maximilan II of Bavaria in 1842 included lyric poets like Geibel, Bodenstedt, Graf Schack, Leuthold and Lingg among its members but they were not in any sense realists. On the contrary, they revived the classical cult of pure form on the model of Leconte de Lisle's 'Parnassiens' with their doctrine of 'L'art pour l'art' and were certainly opposed to the tendentiousness of the Naturalists. The Berlin literary club founded by M. G. Saphir, 'Der Tunnel über der Spree', with its annual publication *Argo* and the periodical *Die Grenzboten*—at least during the years when it was edited by Julian Schmidt and Gustav Freytag (1848–57)—attracted a number of realist poets and provided vehicles for the discussion of realism, but it would hardly be possible to speak of a realist programme.

### Narrative prose from Biedermeier to Realism

The years between 1815 and 1848 were politically stagnant in Germany: the exuberant liberalism of the Liberation Wars, in which literary Romanticism became identified with the patriotic cause, soon gave way to political repression, producing resignation, disillusion, scepticism. At the same time the economic and social changes associated with industrialization, although imperfectly recognized, generated unrest and uncertainty. Laube summed the situation up in the words: 'Wir leben . . . auf der Brücke zweier Zeiten'. Materialism became a more powerful intellectual force, literature became, in one way or another, increasingly 'realistic'. The novel, with its direct social relevance, reflected these changes more clearly than most other genres.

In two major works, *Die Epigonen* (1836) and *Münchhausen* (1838/9), Karl Immermann sees his generation as demoralized 'latecomers' and dilettanti: 'Wir sind, um mit einem Wort das ganze Elend auszusprechen, Epigonen und tragen an der Last, die jeder Erb- und Nachgeborenschaft anzukleben pflegt.' It is an age of play-acting and disingenuousness. It is also an age of conflict between the landed aristocracy and a middle-class growing ever more powerful through the spread of industry: Immermann, in fact, delineates the problem adumbrated in *Wilhelm Meisters Wanderjahre*. Hermann, the hero of *Die Epigonen*, finds himself torn between the gracious world of the old aristocracy, now effete and bereft of its political function, and the dynamic world of the industrial financier. By an archaic literary device Immermann does not hesitate to make him literally the heir to both these worlds. Hermann refuses, however, to regard himself as anything but a trustee of his inherited wealth. He resolves to save at least an island from the tide of industrialization by closing his late uncle's factories and restoring the duke's estates to the plough: 'Die Erde gehört dem Pfluge, dem Sonnenschein und Regen, welcher das Samenkorn entfaltet, der fleissigen einfach arbeitenden Hand.'

In *Münchhausen* the aristocracy is caricatured in the bizarre household of Schloss Schnick-Schnack-Schnurr—the eccentric Baron von Schnuck, and his elderly daughter Emerentia with her romantic memories of an ancient love-affair. Their guest, the legendary Freiherr von Münchhausen, with his interminable tales and his project for using solidified air as a building-material, embodies the mendacious and fraudulent spirit of the age. But from the decay of Schnick-Schnack-Schnurr springs—like an orchid from a rotting log, to use Immermann's image—the beautiful and virtuous Lisbeth, whom we must suppose to be the issue of the erstwhile affair between Emerentia and Münchhausen, alias Rucciopuccio. Lisbeth belongs more properly to the quasi-idyllic setting of the Westphalian 'Oberhof' than to Schnick-Schnack-Schnurr, and it is here that she is discovered by the Swabian Graf Oswald. The more or less autonomous 'Oberhof' episodes form the counterpart to the decaying world of Baron von Schnuck, the patriarchal 'Hofschulze' personifies Germanic tribal foundations underlying the edifice of the modern state. Although he and his like are to Immermann's mind 'the granite of society', the 'Hofschulze' is not unduly idealized: he is callous and ruthless and ready to accept fraudulent evidence in support of his authority. In the union of Oswald and Lisbeth Immermann seeks to symbolize the birth of a new race from the best elements of the old.

In both novels Immerman takes occasion to satirize a multitude of intellectual frauds and fads—the unstable enthusiasms and the puerile plots of student demagogues, the preciosity of Berlin salons, the reactionary politics of Joseph Görres, the pretensions of A. W. Schlegel, the mystical obscurantism of Justinus Kerner, the dandyism of the globe-trotting Prince Pückler-Muskau, the educational excursions of Basedow and of *Wilhelm Meisters Wanderjahre*. The diversity of these targets is symptomatic of the complexity of a transitional age, and Immermann is himself in many senses a transitional figure. For his literary techniques he is indebted to Classicism and Romanticism in general, to Goethe's *Wilhelm Meister* and to Jean Paul in particular. At the same time, the topicality and local colour of his novels link him to the realistic idiom that increasingly dominates the nineteenth century. Plot and character are fashioned with a disregard for plausibility in order to illustrate principles and ideas, but the concern with detail and local colour—particularly in *Oberhof*—makes Immermann a forerunner of the realistic 'Dorfgeschichte'. The satirical tone of Münchhausen is reminiscent of much Romantic writing: Immermann cannot resist the devices of 'Romantic irony'—the binding of chapters out of their proper order, as in Hoffmann's *Kater Murr*, and the introduction of the author himself into the action of the story, as in Brentano's *Godwi* or Tieck's satirical comedies. Again, in his intellectual position, Immermann stands somewhere between Biedermeier and Jungdeutschland: he shares the longing for stability and the preservation of ideals that is characteristic of the former; on the other hand, although as a devoted monarchist Immermann cannot approve the revolutionary sentiments of the Young German writers, his bitter social satire and his protest against the lunacies of re-instated princelings have a 'Young German' ring.

Switzerland, no less than Germany, was affected by radical changes between 1798 and 1831, but development was here more uniformly progressive. The challenge was to nurture and guide those classes of the population who were emancipated as a result of the French Revolution, Napoleonic intervention and the civic reforms of 1830/1. Immermann's contemporary, Albert Bitzius, who took his pseudonym, Jeremias Gotthelf, from his own first novel (*Der Bauernspiegel*, 1837) was able by character, calling and national destiny to adopt a more unequivocal stand on social and political issues. Gotthelf had recourse to literature as an extension of parochial work and a substitute for the political activity from which his cloth debarred him. He did not hesitate to construct stories round causes as prosaic as inoculation against smallpox (*Anne Bäbi Jowäger*, 1843/4) or the establishment of co-operative dairies (*Die Molkerei in der Vehfreude*, 1850), or to attack the vice of alcoholism (*Wie fünf Mädchen im Branntwein jämmerlich umkommen*, 1838; *Dursli der Weinbrandsäufer*, 1839). These didactic purposes in the tradition of Gotthelf's master and model, Heinrich Pestalozzi, are not, however, the measure of his excellence. Gotthelf has a vigorous natural talent, largely untrammelled by literary traditions. But he is not simply a provincial novelist, his imagination is not limited to his parish boundaries. In works like *Die Armennot* (1840) he deploys a reasoned political philosophy in which practical Christianity is seen as the antidote to materialism and assigned an active part in overcoming the social evils of industrialization. Gotthelf's acquaintance with rural life was necessarily more intimate than Immermann's and *Uli der Knecht* (1841), for instance, is a vigorous picture of farming life in Canton Berne. The Swiss ethos in general and Gotthelf's immediate didactic purpose in this novel account for the simple correlation between integrity on the one hand and prosperity on the other as well as for an obtrusive element of caricature (the figure of Elisi, for example). In its sequel, *Uli der Pächter* (1848), and in other works like *Geld und Geist* (1843) and

*Käthi die Grossmutter* (1847), Gotthelf takes a more problematic view of providence and prosperity, and like latter-day Swiss dramatists he warns his countrymen against the dangers of materialism. The unrest and violence of 1848 and the preceding years confirmed his pessimistic view and in *Jakobs des Handwerkers Wanderungen durch die Schweiz* (1846/7) and *Zeitgeist und Berner Geist* (1849) he attacks the irreligious and demagogic spirit of the age. The latter work pursues a Romeo and Juliet theme with a wealth of topical reference but stops short of a tragic issue.

Both Immermann and Gotthelf are caught up in a contemporary dialectic of political forces and their polemical conservatism represents the interaction of individual minds and circumstances. The conservatism of Adalbert Stifter is of a fundamental philosophical nature; the novels and short stories in which it is expressed dispense largely with topicality and tension. Stifter adapts classical ideals of harmony, objectivity and restraint so that they match the sensibility of the Austrian Biedermeier: schooling and sublimation of the passions, quietistic absorption in the nature of things, integration of the individual in family and state. For Stifter, spiritual values and processes must be measured by their own scale which is unrelated to measures of physical grandeur or historical significance: 'Ein ganzes Leben voll Gerechtigkeit, Einfachheit, Bezwingung seiner selbst, Verstandesgemässheit, Wirksamkeit in seinem Kreise, Bewunderung des Schönen, verbunden mit einem heiteren gelassenen Streben, halte ich für gross ... Wir wollen das sanfte Gesetz zu erblicken suchen, wodurch das menschliche Geschlecht geleitet wird.'

*Nachsommer* (1857) is a quasi-utopian 'Bildungsroman' in which the hero is spared growing-pains. Stifter deliberately eschews the false starts, inner conflicts and daemonic undercurrents of Goethe's *Wilhelm Meister* and concerns himself with the cultivation of 'beautiful souls'. The education of Heinrich Drendorf revolves round the rose-bowered villa of the Freiherr von Risach where, with infinite solicitude, he is initiated into mysteries of art and nature and listens dutifully to his mentor's sedate account of happiness forfeited, or at least deferred, by juvenile wilfulness. The bond which forms between Heinrich and Nathalie, the daughter of von Risach's former love, leads, with due circumspection, to marriage. Modern readers may find this account of lives so decorously ordered unrealistic or even smug, but the work may not be judged by realistic standards—in spite of its incidental realism. It attempts by style as well as by episode and characterization to suggest an ideal of emotional maturity. That Stifter was aware of tragic potentialities is evident from stories like *Abdias*—and from his own life and melancholy death.

*Witiko* (1865/7) is Stifter's political testament, a declaration of faith in the Habsburg Empire, transposed into the age immediately preceding its founding. The novel describes the evolution of the ideal state much as *Nachsommer* described the education of an ideal individual. Affinities with the historical dramas of Grillparzer are not hard to detect. The Bohemian leader Witiko, a paragon of valour and loyalty, stands by the duke whose authority he has recognized, helps him to suppress repeated rebellions and finally lives to see established a state founded on trust and Christian forgiveness, linked in harmony with the other nations of the Empire. *Witiko* is Stifter's characteristic response both to the insurrections of 1848 and to the Prussian bid for hegemony manifested in the war of 1866 against Austria. He masks the topicality of his theme by setting it in the twelfth century and also seeks to give it universality and objectivity by employing a monumental epic style modelled on Homer, the Bible and the Nibelungenlied. The result is anachronistically mannered.

## The Novel of 'Young Germany'

The writers of 'Jungdeutschland' are even more uncompromising than Stifter and Gotthelf in their view of literature as propaganda. The lack of representative institutions drove these liberal thinkers to literature as their forum. Their aims, which may be summed up as the political unification of Germany, democratic advance, social equality and liberalization of moral standards, are practical rather than aesthetic, their methods as much journalistic as literary. The form of their works is determined by these aims and methods—by the practice of serial publication in newspapers, for instance, or by the need to hoodwink the censor. They are little concerned with questions of literary genre or aesthetic autonomy: they do not distinguish, for instance, between 'Roman' and 'Novelle' and they prize topical appeal above universal validity. Their most significant contribution to the development of the novel in Germany consists probably in the introduction of what Gutzkow in the introduction to his *Ritter vom Geiste* called 'der Roman des Nebeneinander':

> 'Der frühere Roman hat das Nacheinander kunstvoller verschlungener Begebenheiten dargestellt, der neue Roman ist dagegen der Roman des Nebeneinander. Da liegt die ganze Welt; da begegnen sich Könige und Bettler—Thron und Hütte sind zusammengerückt!'

In their major political novels Gutzkow and Laube try to present 'a panorama of the age': the single hero gives way to a group of typical figures, individual psychology is less important than social relationships—'die wechselseitige Befruchtung eines Menschenzustandes durch einen andern'. The synchronic narrative pattern had been developed by Balzac and Eugène Sue; Gutzkow saw it as particularly apt to represent the diversity of political and social circumstances in the German states.

In Laube's novels political themes are frequently intertwined with erotic adventures, the argument concerns sexual as well as political emancipation, free love as well as free elections. According to Valerius in *Die Poeten* these issues are inseparable: the supreme aim is 'die fröhlichste, ungebundenste Allherrschaft, wo jede Individualität gilt, weil jede sich gesetzmässig ist und in ihrer Veredelung das neben ihr wandelnde Gesetz nicht stört.' Such idealism is characteristic of this first part of Laube's trilogy, *Das junge Europa*. The two succeeding volumes, *Die Krieger* and *Die Bürger*, show an increasing realism both in technique and outlook, for Laube learned a bitter lesson from nine months of brutal imprisonment. At the end of *Die Krieger* Valerius voices the resigned mood of some 'Young Germans':

> Wer sich töricht unterfängt, in Schnelligkeit die Weltge-schichte meistern zu wollen, wie wir in den letzten Jahren als eine Kleinigkeit versuchten, der beklage sich nicht, wenn er zu Grunde geht. Handle, wer sich berufen fühlt, aber keiner wage ins Einzelne vorauszubestimmen, was werden soll; wir kennen die Welt nur einen Schritt weit. Ich will in meine Heimat gehen, mir eine Hütte bauen, das Weite auch ferner betrachten, aber nur für's Nächste wirken.

The scale of *Das junge Europa*, grandiose as it was, was exceeded by Gutzkow's *Ritter vom Geiste* (1850–1) and *Der Zauberer von Rom* (1858–61), which attempt such an elaborate picture of society that the author compares them to section-alized drawings of a battleship or a coal-mine. The first of these nine-volume novels revolves round a democratic secret society of the kind which led a more or less phantom existence in the era of Metternich. It has a host of characters and—in spite of realism of detail—depends heavily on coincidence and mystification; not surprisingly, it lacks proportion and shows signs of flagging energy in the later volumes. *Der Zauberer von Rom* is directed against the re-actionary and disruptive influence of the Roman Church in Germany: 'Die Dichtung will beitragen helfen, die vater-ländische Einheit zu fördern', claimed Gutzkow. The plot is even more involved and implausible than that of *Die Ritter vom Geiste*. It culminates in the elevation to the papal throne of the main character, Bonaventura, who proceeds to inaugurate a reformed 'German' Catholicism. In both of these works Gutzkow shows himself as an idealistic liberal of an older school which was being increasingly eclipsed by more materialistic socialist creeds. He appears, too, as the heir of a tradition in the novel which attached much importance to intrigue and symbolic configuration of plot and character. At the same time, the sociological complexity, the local colour and the topicality of these novels foreshadow the work of realists—poetic or otherwise—such as Spielhagen, Keller, Raabe, Freytag and Fontane.

Other varieties of Young German novel are perhaps less obviously in the main stream of development. In his earliest works Gutzkow had veiled his criticisms in satire, adopting, for instance, the fiction of insanity in his *Briefe eines Narren an eine Närrin* (1832). The beloved to whom these love-letters are directed is a sadly deranged Germany, the hero's protestations are effusions of political idealism ironically branded as 'crazy'. This work, as well as a hackneyed political metaphor derived from the disastrous cholera epidemic in which Hegel died, probably suggested to Gustav Kühne the satirical guise of his 'pathology of modern life', *Eine Quarantäne im Irrenhause* (1835). The madness with which the young hero wrestles represents the contemporary obsession with the Hegelian philosophy, his paroxysms in the padded cell epitomize the plight of German liberalism.

Theodor Mundt's Salzschreiber Seeliger in *Moderne Lebenswirren* (1834) is not confined but he, too, suffers grave mental distress. Even in the stagnant Biedermeier seclusion of 'Kleinweltwinkel' he cannot escape the political distemper of the age: 'Der Zeitgeist tut weh in mir, Esperance', he writes to his symbolically named fiancée. In his 'craving for a rejuvenation of Germany' Seeliger is both inspired and baffled by his conversations with a political Mephistopheles, Herr Zodiakus, who casts a bewildering series of political horoscopes for his benefit. Both Kühne's work and Mundt's end on a note which may be construed as optimistic— although in the *Quarantäne* there are ironic implications: the reactionary 'Präsident' who had his nephew committed to the lunatic asylum suffers a condign fate and is himself infected by the liberal 'madness'. 'Ich glaube an eine schöne

Zukunft des Erdenlebens', he babbles. 'Die Menschheit geht einer grossen Frühlingszeit entgegen.' Esperance summons Seeliger to employment as a teacher of history and exhorts him: 'Fortschritt, Freiheit, Zukunft! sind und bleiben die schönsten Worte der Menschheit. Sie sind unser aller Gebet.'

In setting his *Maha Guru* (1833) in a remote land Gutzkow was following time-honoured satirical precedent but also exploiting a contemporary vogue for *chinoiserie*. There is an assortment of targets—transcendentalism in general, hypocritical and scheming clerics, superstition, the mandarin pretensions of the Prussian ruling class and the man-worship of a political system still unregenerately absolutist. Maha Guru, chosen as Dalai Lama, finds that his divine authority is illusory, he is the tool of the priests. To his relief he is deposed by an insurrection and henceforth lives an idyllic life with his bride, Gyllupsa, whom—allegedly in Tibetan fashion—he shares with his brother. The moral: 'Es ist ein Glück ein Mensch zu sein.'

Gutzkow's *Blasedow und seine Söhne* (1838-9) is a more direct satire. Beginning as a lampoon on the system of vocational education devised by J. B. Basedow—which had already been ridiculed, incidentally, by Schummel in his *Spitzbart* (1779) and by Immermann in *Die Epigonen* (Part I, Book 3)—it soon becomes a rambling tale in which the aristocracy, fraudulent industrial projects of the Münchhausen type, the military caste, and various literary foibles are attacked. The style is indigestibly Jean Paulesque, and many of the topical allusions must have been obscure even to contemporaries.

The early satires of 'Young Germany' were either too furtive or too esoteric to provoke public or official reaction. The storm of indignation broke only when Gutzkow ventured openly on the hallowed ground of Christian faith and morality with a serious polemical work. *Wally, die Zweiflerin* (1835) is a hybrid product. The heroine's religious doubts serve as the pretext for a defence of D. F. Strauss's rationalistic

*Leben Jesu* (1835) in the form of the tract 'Geständnisse über Religion und Christentum', attributed to the story's hero, Cäsar, but based in fact on the fragments of Reimarus, the publication of which had involved Lessing in his famous dispute with Pastor Goeze. The work is also a vehicle for Gutzkow's views on sexual morality in the spirit of Heinse, Schlegel's *Lucinde* and the French disciples of Saint-Simon. Its conclusion was motivated by the notorious suicide of Charlotte Stieglitz. A work fashioned to match such diverse and topical interests could hardly be other than 'aphoristisch, skizzenartig, lakonisch hingeworfen'. The psychological portrait of Wally is nevertheless highly plausible. She is naive, vain, sensuous, 'ein humoristisches Kapriccio animalischer Natur', a spoilt child suffering from a nameless malaise, railing against the triviality of women's education and the futility of lives that she compares to those of handsome caged animals. At the same time, Wally clings to the frivolity of her social existence for fear of the metaphysical void which she senses near at hand. Sickened by a hateful marriage and deserted by the sceptical Cäsar, in whose rational arguments she can find no comfort, she ultimately stabs herself.

Gutzkow shows an acute understanding, not only of the female psyche, but also of the spiritual sickness of the society in which he moved. *Wally* is symptomatic, a *Werther* of its time. Cäsar is a representative of the disillusioned, hedonistic, quasi-Byronic raisonneurs who find their time is out of joint and have lost the will to put it right. The modish expression for the adherents of this 'new religion', sardonically so called in W. Alexis' *Haus Düsterweg*, is 'die Zerrissenen'; they appear as such in Ungern-Sternberg's novel (1832), but also as Ernst Willkomm's *Die Europamüden* (1838), and even some thirty years later as Spielhagen's *Problematische Naturen* (1861–2). Wally herself epitomizes the troubled mind of women on the verge of emancipation but ill-prepared for it.

Wally's tragic prototype, Charlotte Stieglitz, also pro-

G L—G

vided the model for less tragic heroines—Esperance in *Moderne Lebenswirren* and Maria in Theodor Mundt's *Madonna* (1835). Maria is a 'Weltheilige' who has achieved, through tribulation, the harmony of spirit and senses that constitutes in Mundt's expression 'die Wiedereinsetzung des Bildes', hence the reconciliation of elements which he, like Heine, believes have been put asunder in the Nazarene tradition of Christianity: 'Die Trennung von Fleisch und Geist ist der unsühnbare Selbstmord des menschlichen Geistes.' The narrator in *Madonna* stands enraptured before Titian's Venus and feels himself restored to full humanity by that miraculous fusion of the spiritual and the sensual response that is worked by artistic beauty:

> Denn der Geist ist nicht ohne den Körper, und der Körper ist nicht ohne den Geist, sondern beide ineinander sind das Bild, also das ich erscheine. Darum bin ich gesund, ich bin heiter, weil ich ein Bild bin, und ich würde krank sein, wie ganze Jahrhunderte krank waren, wenn ich auseinanderfiele in Geist und Leib, in Diesseits und Jenseits!

Wally and Mundt's Maria have numerous contemporaries in fact and fiction—it is often hard to tell fact from fiction. Bettina von Brentano, with that talent for documentary fabrication manifested in *Goethes Briefwechsel mit einem Kinde* (1835) and *Dies Buch gehört dem König* (1843), fashioned a novel from the tragic love of Caroline von Günderode, a friend of her youth (*Die Günderode*, 1840). Varnhagen von Ense commemorated his talented wife in *Rahel, ein Buch des Andenkens für ihre Freunde* (1833), Theodor Mundt did the same for Charlotte Stieglitz in *Charlotte Stieglitz, ein Denkmal*, while the novels of the colourful Ida, Gräfin Hahn-Hahn, particularly *Ilda Schönholm* (1838) and *Gräfin Faustine* (1841) have manifest autobiographical features, as do those of her rival, Fanny Lewald. Both of these novelists concern themselves with the 'freedom of feeling' that is associated with the Young German movement, but from very different points of view. Faustine is arrogant and tempestuous, an insatiable femme fatale: 'sie will Befriedigung, dauernde,

ewige, unerschöpfliche ... Die Essenz ihres Wesens ist
schöngeistiger Egoismus, der alles ausschliesst, was Opfer
und Entsagung ist, und der sich im Streben nach der
missverstandenen Entwicklung und Befriedigung ausbildet.'
For her the cloister provides a somewhat jejune conclusion
to a career of flamboyant self-indulgence. Fanny Lewald
invokes a morality more soberly consistent in the almost
excessively virtuous heroine of *Clementine* (1842) who dutifully preserves her marriage against the renewed advances
of a faithless former lover. *Jenny* (1854), a tragic tale of the
conscientious scruples entailed in marriage between Gentile
and converted Jew, reflects something of Fanny Lewald's
own experience and illuminates the imperfect realization of
Jewish emancipation.

## Novelle and Short Story: Biedermeier

There are elements of 'Biedermeier' in late Romantic works
like *Taugenichts*, and the stories of Tieck, once in the vanguard
of Romanticism, became more and more 'Biedermeier'
during the later part of his long life. In his case the transition
is, in a metaphorical as well as a literal sense, that from
youth to age—marked by a slackening of intellectual sinews,
growing prosiness and conformism and a tendency to
shapelessness. Tieck's later Novellen represent a return to
topicality and social themes after the fantasy and exoticism
of his Romantic phase. Although he insisted in theory on
formal criteria like the 'turning-point' these later Novellen
are stylistically undistinguished for the most part and
distended by discursive elements; in many of them Tieck
attacks intellectual or political foibles of the day—*Die
Vogelscheuche* (1835), for instance, derides effete pseudo-
Romantics, *Eigensinn und Laune* (1835) deplores Young
German ideas on the emancipation of women. The historical
tales are, on the whole, among the best: in *Ein Dichterleben*
(1825-9) Tieck deploys his knowledge of Shakespeare and
the Elizabethan age. The story of the religious war against
the Huguenot Camisards, *Der Aufruhr in den Cevennen* (1826),

and the Renaissance novel *Vittoria Accorombona* (1840), testify to his skill as a writer of historical fiction and anticipate the work of C. F. Meyer. One of the more entertaining Novellen is *Des Lebens Überfluss* (1838), a typical piece of Biedermeier whimsy in which an impoverished young man makes a virtue of necessity by proving philosophically to his wife that almost all material amenities are superfluous. These include the staircase, which is demolished step by step to provide fuel, so that the couple in their attic are finally cut off from the outside world altogether.

The literature of 'Biedermeier' is capable of greater intellectual force and formal excellence than are to be found in Tieck. Stifter's stories best express the precarious quietism and sense of propriety that characterize Biedermeier: if ever Novellen earned the description 'exemplary' it is these. At times Stifter's men and women seem little more than figures in a landscape, diminished by distance to the scale of the flowers and flints that occupy the foreground. Works like *Bergkristall* (1845) and *Kalkstein* (1848) are based on the simplest of episodes. Events are purged of violence by being relegated to memory, viewed metaphorically—and sometimes literally—through a telescope. Hardly a tremor of contemporary political upheavals penetrates to the still centre of Stifter's world. His heroes pass through tribulation to end as ideal husbands or sage recluses who, like Freiherr von Risach in *Nachsommer*, dispense to docile youth the wisdom of self-discipline and renunciation. There is rarely anything malignant in these characters: jealous impulses are expiated in years of soul-searching, shattered selfish hopes compensated for by dedication to altruistic purposes, disillusion accepted with dignity. Man and nature alike bow to the 'gentle law' of the universe. The stories have a sedative charm, but the unremitting highmindedness of most of the characters can seem unreal and insipid.

No other writer articulates so clearly and comprehensively the ideals of 'Biedermeier' culture, but the 'Biedermeier' spirit informs individual works of great artistry by Grillparzer and Mörike. The hero of Grillparzer's *Der arme Spielmann* (1848), who has features of the author, combines with his timid ineffectuality and apparent artistic ineptitude the saint-like innocence of Stifter's recluses. The propriety of the old bachelor's life is symbolized in the meticulous tidiness of his corner in the attic which he shares with two artisans, his nobility is shown in unspectacular heroism that leads to his death in the waters of a flood. This kind of attic existence, so beloved by the painter Spitzweg, might almost be termed a 'Biedermeier' syndrome. It represents a shrinking from public life into a shell of modest felicity.

Mörike's exquisite *Mozart auf der Reise nach Prag* (1856) imagines that the composer, on his way to conduct a performance of *Don Giovanni* in 1787, wanders into the garden of a country-house, absent-mindedly plucks a cherished orange and thus makes the acquaintance of a family celebrating their daughter's betrothal. After a day of festivity and music, Mozart and his wife travel on in a carriage presented to them by their host. The gay rococo world figured here is shadowed by omens of mortality—a phial of perfume spilled, a rare fruit plucked before its time, the chilling finale to *Don Giovanni*—'Wie von entlegenen Sternenkreisen fallen die Töne aus silbernen Posaunen, eiskalt, Mark und Seele durchschneidend . . .'—a sombre song left on the piano as a memento mori: 'Ein Tännlein grünet wo, wer weiss, im Walde.' This is not simply a character sketch of Mozart but a complex evocation of a problematic creative spirit, of the doomed charm of the ancien régime and of Mörike's own melancholy cast of mind.

## Short Story: Young Germany

The writers of Young Germany, being primarily concerned with propaganda, paid scant attention to literary canons. They aimed to voice political opinions and describe in detail actual social conditions—as in Gustav Kühne's *Wartburgfeier* (1831) or Theodor Mundt's *Madelon, oder die Romantiker in Paris* (1832), for example. The austere economy of the artistic Novelle did not interest them. Mundt, in the preface to *Moderne Lebenswirren* (1834), although postulating an aesthetic form for the Novelle as 'eine Cirkellinie', describes it otherwise simply as a useful vehicle for the dissemination of radical ideas. These writers went even further than Tieck in stretching the limits of the 'short' story and made, on principle, no distinction between 'Novelle' and 'Roman'. Ernst Willkomm applied the term Novelle to *Julius Kühn* (1833), which was virtually a 'Bildungsroman' in two volumes, and Gutzkow's *Die Nihilisten* (1853), a somewhat critical retrospective portrait of Young German intellectuals, is also more of a novel than a Novelle. Laube's *Reisenovellen* (1834–7) could more properly be called 'Reisebilder' on the model of Heine. The great majority of Young German short stories published in journals and almanacs has not even the literary interest of the major novels of the school. Laube's *Die Bandomire* (1843) has some merit as a picture of life in Kurland in the eighteenth century, and Gutzkow's *Emporblick* (1852) ('eine Novelle aus dem Volksleben') is interesting as an attempt to divert attention from the popular 'Dorfgeschichte' to the plight of the urban proletariat. One of the few memorable short stories by a writer associated with Jungdeutschland, Georg Büchner's *Lenz* (1839), has no distinctively Young German features: it is an uncannily convincing study of the madness of the 'Sturm und Drang' poet and friend of Goethe, J. M. R. Lenz.

## Travel Literature

During the nineteenth century German society, in common with other Western European societies, became increasingly mobile. This tendency was not simply a consequence of improved communications; it reflects generally the restlessness and intellectual curiosity of the age, a widening of mental as well as physical horizons. It is not only the liberal writers, the members of 'the movement', who are infected with Wanderlust: the moods and motives of the travellers are diverse—some are still in search of the Romantic 'blue flower', others are on the run from the police, the journeys are satirical as well as sentimental. Biedermeier has its feckless vagabonds as well as its village dominies: Eichendorff's *Taugenichts* set out on his whimsical way in the same year in which Heine began his *Reisebilder* with *Die Harzreise* (1826). Daniel Lessmann's *Wanderbuch eines Schwermütigen* (1831) reads like a belated echo of Thümmel's sentimental and splenetic travels. Karl von Holtei's hero, Anton Hahn, pursues an unrepentant theatrical mission through the half-world of theatre and circus in *Die Vagabunden* (1852), in which historical figures like the actor Ludwig Devrient, Paganini and E. T. A. Hoffman rub shoulders with gipsies and jugglers. Freiherr von Gaudy follows in the footsteps of countless literary journeymen with *Aus dem Tagebuch eines wandernden Schneidergesellen* (1836) and *Mein Römerzug* (1836). To this world of moonlight, posthorns and rococo gardens Theodor Mundt bids farewell in *Madonna* (1835), in which the city and not the countryside is envisaged as the characteristic setting for coming generations. The Biedermeier figures of the wandering scholar and craftsman give way to the journalist, the tourist, the political refugee.

It is only in the 1830s that the German novel begins belatedly to embrace themes and settings beyond the confines of Europe in authentic rather than purely fanciful terms. The experiences of aristocratic tourists, scholars and humble emigrants begin to fertilize German literature in the way in which English literature had long been fertilized by colonial connections. Prince Pückler-Muskau roamed from Newmarket to the Nile in search of physical gratification and mental stimulus. He returned to look sardonically on the religious and moral sanctions of his homeland and assert man's right to pleasure in the spirit of Saint-Simon: 'Unser Leben ist kurz—doch Vergnügen verlängert die Tage. Der Mensch ist für den Genuss gemacht.'

An even more remarkable career is that of Charles Sealsfield, alias Karl Postl who rebelled against the stagnant atmosphere of Metternich's Europe and his own calling as a monk. Postl made his way to the United States and his first novel was published in English—*Tokeah, or the White Rose* (1828; in German: *Der Legitime und die Republikaner*, 1833). It describes with a wealth of local colour the confused struggles of 1812, with the Indians fighting a losing battle against white settlers and the English waging war on the Americans in the Mississippi valley. *Der Virey und die Aristokraten* (1835) is set in Mexico at the same period and deals with an equally complex conflict for power and independence involving the multifarious races and classes of the Spanish colony. *Nathan, der Squatter-regulator* (1837) and *Das Kajütenbuch* (1841) give thrilling accounts of the settlement of Texas and Louisiana by the hard-bitten American pioneers. Among the tales of *Das Kajütenbuch* is *Die Prärie am Jacinto*, one of the finest adventure stories in the whole of German literature.

Sealsfield's novels are more than merely tales of adventure. They show understanding of ethnic character, of political and economic changes and the conflict of cultures entailed in the break-up of colonial empires and the expansion of the United States. Sealsfield is in sympathy with the vigorous new forces that seemed to him to be disrupting an effete hierarchical society—not only through the confrontation in America but throughout the economic cosmos. His novel *Morton, oder die grosse Tour* (1835), like Immermann's *Epigonen*, visualizes the triumph of bankers and industrialists over the old aristocracy. Sealsfield has a talent for graphic description, but otherwise the form and style of his works do not match the originality of his perception: he is trammelled by a tradition that favoured intrigue, mystification and the monumental style. The stories of Friedrich Gerstäcker who emulated Sealsfield in a veritable Cook's tour of America and the Pacific suffer from the same defects, but lack the intellectual content of Sealsfield's work. They are little more than sensational crime stories in exotic settings.

## The Historical Novel

By 'historical novels' we commonly understand works in which the main interest derives from the circumstantial account of important incidents and characters, or from the evocation of the general culture of an earlier period in the national life. Not all tales with their settings in the past are necessarily 'historical' in this sense. In spite of elaborate local colour Wieland's 'Greek' novels are more properly philosophical than historical. The Enlightenment, with its cosmopolitan ideal, its belief in progress, its general lack of historical sense and its contempt for the 'dark ages' was unsympathetic towards historical fiction; it was the germinating irrationalism and patriotic sentiment of men like Bodmer, Klopstock, Herder and Justus Möser that fostered its development. The transition from the novel of classical antiquity to that of the national past may be observed, incidentally, in Wieland's imitators August Gottlieb Meissner and Ignatz Aurelius Fessler.

Apart from Goethe's *Götz* and Schiller's *Räuber*, the literary products of this interest in the national past are relatively low-grade. Leonhard Wächter, who wrote under the pseudonym of Veit Weber, published, for instance, seven volumes of *Sagen der Vorzeit* between the years 1787 and 1798. These tales are unsophisticated vulgarizations: Wächter, although he had a rudimentary historical training, had little understanding of the spirit of the Middle Ages. He simply exploits the glamour of swashbuckling knights, noble ladies and languishing troubadours. His products are at least less crude than those of his rivals, C. G. Cramer and C. H. Spiess, in which the historical novel is linked, through the Gothic setting and such figures as the chivalrous bandit, with the ghost story and the crime thriller. Amongst the most popular practitioners of the latter was Goethe's brother-in-law, C. A. Vulpius, who achieved sustained success with *Rinaldo Rinaldini, der Räuberhauptmann* (1798) and its sequels. Even Schiller, with his *Geisterseher* (1789) succumbed to the vogue for novels of mystery and criminal intrigue.

A marginally more authentic and certainly less sensational account of the past is presented in the voluminous works of Benedikte Naubert, whose themes embrace practically every century from the ninth to the sixteenth. She is perhaps the best informed and the most ambitious historical novelist of her generation but her insight into past cultures is limited by her rationalistic education and essentially middle-class common-sense: affairs of state tend to be seen in terms of minor commercial transactions, momentous movements like the Crusades regarded as irresponsible follies.

The early Romantic novelists showed themselves to be more in tune with the ideals of the Middle Ages and the Renaissance, and although works like Novalis' *Heinrich von Ofterdingen*, E. T. A. Hoffmann's *Kampf der Sänger* (1819) and Tieck's *Franz Sternbald* were not primarily designed as historical novels they do recapture something of the spirit of the past. It was in the Romantic period, too, that the historical novel began to be used as oblique comment on the contemporary age. Achim von Arnim manifestly has such a tendentious purpose with his *Kronenwächter* (1817; fragmentary second part, 1854), which describes the efforts of a secret society in the sixteenth century to guide and restore to power the surviving members of the Hohenstaufen dynasty. The concept of such masonic associations seems indispensable to many novelists of the period, from Goethe to Vulpius. Arnim's hero, Berthold, whose mission, love-life and vacillation between commerce and art suggest an affinity with Wilhelm Meister, embodies the author's views on the contemporary situation when he conceives the regeneration of the Empire in spiritual rather than purely political terms.

Historical fiction in Germany as in other countries was revolutionized by the example of Sir Walter Scott, who had himself been inspired—at second hand—by Goethe's *Götz* and works of Benedikte Naubert. Scott imparted to his imitators the local patriotism, the subtler psychology and the sounder antiquarian foundation which marks the historical novel in the nineteenth century. Something of this development was no doubt spontaneous in Germany: Carl van der Velde, for instance, apparently did not know Scott's works when he began to produce novels hailed as worthy of a German Scott. One of the first self-confessed imitators was Wilhelm Hauff, whose *Lichtenstein* (1826) is set in Swabia at the beginning of the sixteenth century. The impetuous young hero, Georg Sturmfeder, is caught up in the feud between the Swabian League and Duke Ulrich of Württemberg and is torn by conflicting loyalties when he falls in love with the daughter of one of the duke's supporters. There are appropriate alarms, excursions, midnight encounters and sojourns in dark caverns. It is a colourful and exciting tale, but the characterization—especially of the women—is far below that of Hauff's models.

Among the countless imitators of Scott, K. A. von Witzleben, who wrote under the pseudonym of August von Tromlitz, Philipp Joseph von Rehfues and Karl Spindler were the most prolific and popular in their day. Of Spindler's 102 volumes, however, only *Der Jesuit* (1828–9) and *Der Jude* (1827)—which is reminiscent of *Ivanhoe*—have any literary distinction and continuing interest. Heinrich Zschokke, whose works embrace crude thrillers like *Abällino* (1794) and edifying tales of rehabilitation in the spirit of Pestalozzi and Gotthelf (*Das Goldmacherdorf*, 1817; *Die Weinbrandpest*, 1837), also recognized the vogue for historical novels in his tales of the Swiss past, e.g. *Der Freihof von Aarau* (1823) and *Addrich im Moos* (1824).

Wilhelm Häring (pseudonym: Willibald Alexis) achieved his first literary success with stories purporting to be trans-lations from Scott—*Walladmor* (1823) and *Schloss Avalon* (1827)—but proceeded to develop a not inconsiderable original talent in a series of novels dealing with the history of Brandenburg and Prussia from the fourteenth century to the Napoleonic era. The more mature works of Alexis are marked less by Scott's nostalgic romanticism than by the middle-class liberalism of 'Young Germany', while to the novelists of that movement he owes his relatively realistic style. Unlike Scott, Alexis concentrates less on over-simplified dramatic historical confrontation than on the complexity of national life and the continuity of national aspirations. His ultimate hero is the Prussian people. At the same time, the characterization in the novels, particularly that of the women, is surprisingly subtle. In this respect Alexis is a not unworthy fore-runner of Theodor Fontane.

Alexis' *Ruhe ist die erste Bürgerpflicht* (1852) and *Isegrimm* (1854) carried his historical survey to the threshold of his own age, and there are a number of other writers whose historical tales have well-nigh contemporary settings. The implications of such works are often tendentious in a Young German sense. As early as 1814 Ulrich Hegner gave in *Salys Revolutionstage* a vivid account of the repercussions in Switzerland of the French Revolution. Ludwig Rellstab described Napoleon's Russian campaign in *1812* (1834) and the extreme radical, Heinrich Josef König deals with the short-lived Republic in Mainz in *Die Klubbisten in Mainz* (1847). Heinrich Laube, who had written a typically monumental novel about the Thirty Years War (*Der deutsche Krieg*, 1863–6) also turned to the recent past in his final novel, *Die Böhminger* (1880), which deals with the aftermath of the July Revolution.

## The Novel and the Industrial Revolution

In the years immediately preceding and following the revolutions of 1848 many novelists were concerned with the social evils created by the industrial revolution: George Sand, Eugène Sue and Balzac in France, Dickens, Mrs Gaskell and Charles Kingsley in England, had all cast a more or less lurid light on the plight of the urban poor. Industrialization came rather later in Germany and the social situation was possibly less acute, but here, too, novelists as well as political thinkers turned to social themes. J. K. Rodbertus in his *Zur Kenntnis unserer staatswissenschaftlichen Zustände* (1842) and Marx and Engels in *Das kommunistische Manifest* (1848) offered, respectively, conservative and revolutionary remedies for the economic problems of the age. There was widespread disillusion with the constitutional liberalism that had inspired the revolution of 1830: the socialist writer Robert Prutz condemned the 'liberals'

> Die nur reden, die nur prahlen,
> Nur mit Worten stets bezahlen,
> Aber arm an Taten sind.

In *Moderne Titanen* (1850) Heinrich Gisecke attacked the middle-class leaders of the 1848 revolution as confused, unstable idealists, 'small men in a time of greatness'. Gutzkow, on the other hand, like many of his generation, viewed with alarm the rise of the 'proletariat' and what Marx himself called 'the spectre of Communism'. The demagogue Fritz Hackert in Gutzkow's *Ritter vom Geiste* (1850/1) personifies this fear of the working class as a slumbering 'Caliban'.

Even before the riots among Silesian weavers in 1844, Bettina von Arnim had drawn attention in *Dies Buch gehört dem König* (1843) to the misery of urban workers. Ernst Willkomm's *Weisse Sklaven oder die Leiden des Volks* (1845) seems to have been inspired by the Silesian troubles. Eduard Ehrenreich (Johann Eduard Ehrenreich Eichenholz) also describes the weavers' wretched existence in *Schicksale eines Proletariers* (1846), but at least allows his hero to rise to the dignity of Bürgermeister and to devote his life to improving the workers' lot. Luise Otto's socialistic *Schloss und Fabrik* (1846) caused as great a scandal in Germany as Mrs Gaskell's *Mary Barton* in England, and was temporarily suppressed. Few socialist writers, however, had as close an acquaintance with industry as Georg Weerth, a friend and associate of Karl Marx. Apart from his satire on the aristocracy, *Leben und Taten des berühmten Ritters Schnapphahnski* (1849)—which cost him three months in prison—Weerth left a fragmentary novel based on experience in the textile industry in Bradford and the Rhineland. In Weerth's novel the decline of the land-owning aristocracy, already adumbrated by Immermann, is epitomized in the ruin of the Baron d'Eyncourt at the hands of the rapacious industrialist, Preiss. The heroic figure of Eduard Martin, who returns from England fired with revolutionary zeal, symbolizes the rise of a class-conscious proletariat. Preiss's son August embodies the largely ineffectual conscientious scruples of the liberal middle-class. Harrowing, but less tendentious accounts of the sufferings of the poor are to be found in *Bilder aus dem Leben* (1850) and *Europäisches Sklavenleben* (1854) by the successful novelist, F. W. Hackländer. A peripheral product of the interest in the urban masses was the crime story, represented, for instance, by Ernst Dronke's *Polizeige-schichten* (1846) and *Berlin* (1846).

Few of these works achieve literary distinction. This is not simply because their authors are inept, but also because they are handicapped by an inherited 'literary' style ill-adapted to their topics and to the social status of many of their characters. Very few of them had a sustained and intimate knowledge of the conditions they are describing, so that they tend to exaggerate. Characterization is often stereotyped: effete aristocrats, villainous or benevolent employers, rascally subordinates, suffering or defiant workers. Plots are melodramatic, and the authors seem incapable of registering changing class relationships other than by novelistic devices like illegitimate birth and mésalliance. Machines they tend to look upon with awe, as infernal and malevolent. Robert Prutz's novel, *Das Engelchen* (1851), has a typical climax in which a machine is made to go berserk by its crazed inventor so that it destroys both him and the factory in which it is installed. Even the Marxist, Georg Weerth, the most knowledgeable of these writers, cannot resist apostrophizing his characters ('Sieh, alter Preiss, das ist deine Welt! Was hast du getan?') and describing their emotional reactions in hyperbolic terms:

> Scham und Wut röteten Augusts Stirne, wild schoss das Blut durch seine Brust, seine Augen blitzten, die Stimme versagte ihm den Dienst . . .

The stridency of 'social' novels and the incongruity of their style and content are signs of literary bankruptcy: a return to solvency, as it were, could be achieved only by the revival of aesthetic standards, a more objective view of reality, a renewed concern with the moral and psychological development of the individual in a well-defined social context, and modernization of the novelist's language. All this was achieved in the years between 1850 and 1880, in which the middle class consolidated its economic position. The result was a variety of realistic idioms ('bürgerlicher Realismus'; 'psychologischer Realismus'; 'poetischer Realismus') which provided a firmer basis for the renewed concern with social themes that issued in the 'Naturalism' of the last two decades of the century.

## Novel and Short Story: Realism

Realist writers found the novel and short story well adapted to their aims and raised these forms to a pitch of excellence generally beyond the drama of the same period. Concentration on milieu, historical or contemporary, and on characteristic dialogue tended to give the movement a diversified regional character, and although the Berlin literary club 'Der Tunnel über der Spree' and the periodicals *Argo* and *Die Grenzboten* provided rallying-points, Realist poets throughout the German-speaking countries developed a rich variety of landscapes, characters and idioms. North Germany was represented, for instance, by Storm and Fritz Reuter, the Mark Brandenburg by Willibald Alexis and Theodor Fontane, Switzerland by Gottfried Keller and Conrad Ferdinand Meyer, Austria by Maria von Ebner-Eschenbach and Peter Rosegger, central Germany by Otto Ludwig and Louise von François, Swabia by Berthold Auerbach and Viktor von Scheffel, Silesia by Gustav Freytag.

The ethos of most of these writers is sturdily, sometimes aggressively, middle-class. In a less uncritical way they continue the tradition of 'Biedermeier', stressing domestic virtues and trying to adapt the heritage of Classical humanism to the circumstances of middle-class life. They believe in moderation and in prudent adaptation to social circumstances, they praise devotion to practical affairs and cast on farm or counting-house a poetic and often humorous light.

This is a golden age of the Novelle, which is adopted by nearly all the leading writers of the time—Storm, Keller, Ludwig, Raabe and Meyer, Although the Novelle of Realism is generally a pretty substantial narrative and it is sometimes difficult, in point of length and complexity, to distinguish in individual cases between Novelle and novel, it has recovered the shapeliness it tended to lose in Biedermeier and Young German examples. Storm, in making the highest claims for the genre, points to a distinctive inner form:

> Sie ist nicht mehr, wie einst, 'die kurzgehaltene Darstellung einer durch ihre Ungewöhnlichkeit fesselnde und einen überraschenden Wendepunkt darbietenden Begebenheit'; die heutige Novelle ist die Schwester des Dramas und die strengste Form der Prosadichtung. Gleich dem Drama behandelt sie die tiefsten Probleme des Menschenlebens; gleich diesem verlangt sie zu ihrer Vollendung einen im Mittelpunkt stehenden Konflikt, von welchem aus das Ganze sich organisiert, und demzufolge die geschlossenste Form und die Ausschliessung alles Unwesentlichen; sie duldet nicht nur, sie stellt auch die höchsten Forderungen der Kunst.

Gottfried Keller was more sceptical about the craze for Novellen—'Mich beschleicht das Gefühl', he wrote, 'dass die Novelliererei eine allgemeine Nivelliererei geworden sei . . .' Nevertheless, there is no doubt that the Novellen of the second half of the nineteenth century include some fine writing—a good deal of it by Keller himself.

A prelude to the full flourishing of the realistic short story may be seen in rural tales by Annette von Droste-Hülshoff and Jeremias Gotthelf. Droste-Hülshoff's *Die Judenbuche* (1842) is a murder story set in Westphalia in which the identity of the murderer is veiled until the end when he is found hanged on the beech-tree under which he had killed the Jew Aaron, drawn back to the scene of the crime after

many years of exile by the Hebrew inscription on the tree
'Wenn du dich diesem Orte nahest, so wird es dir ergehen,
wie du mir getan hast.' Gotthelf's *Schwarze Spinne* (1842) is
an even more uncanny story with the force of a parable.
The people of a Swiss village enlist the aid of the Devil
against their tyrannical overlord and then cheat him of his
promised due—the soul of a newly born child. The Evil
One inflicts on them a plague of spiders and turns Christine,
the moving spirit among them, into one of these venomous
creatures. The curse is intermittently renewed throughout
the ages whenever true Christian faith flags. The *Schwarzwälder Dorfgeschichten* (1843–53) of Berthold Auerbach
mainly lack the elemental force and moral passion of
Gotthelf's work; they represent to some extent facile literary
exploitation of the more picturesque aspects of rural life, but
they do have political undertones as well as a concern for
authentic detail and ethnic character.

Later Realists are equally at home in urban settings, but
they tend to concern themselves with scenes from provincial
rather than metropolitan life and with the private fate of
individuals and families rather than with the political
issues clamorously argued by Young German and Socialist
novelists. Auerbach's stories, in fact, with their echoes of
Young German liberalism and anti-clericalism, mark the
transition from the tendentiousness of Gutzkow and Laube
to a more subtle and poetic representation of individual
lives in familiar and undramatic settings. Auerbach inclines
to sentimental moralizing and conventional happy endings;
he idealizes rural life and compares it with the artificiality
and impersonality of life in the city—for example, in *Die
Frau Professorin* (1846). The problematic outcome of this
story of cultural mésalliance, however, is a tribute to the
author's psychological as well as his circumstantial realism.
Here, as in *Lucifer* (1847), the story of an agnostic peasant's
feud with the village parson, Auerbach showed himself
capable of resisting the happy ending. In *Die Geschichte
Diethelms von Buchenberg* (1853) and *Der Lehnhold* (1853) he

achieved tragic heights and a dramatic power at least approaching that of Gotthelf. These tales of savage peasant rivalries and murderous ambition anticipate the rustic novels of the Austrians, Anzengruber and Rosegger.

It was Otto Ludwig who coined the term 'poetic realism', which he defined as 'ein erhöhtes Spiegelbild des Gegenstandes, aber nach dem Gesetz der Malerei zu klarer Ordnung gediehen'. His own tales of farmers and artisans are essentially picturesque and combine well-defined moral themes with delicately drawn impressions of Thuringian village life and character. The combination is well illustrated in *Zwischen Himmel und Erde* (1856), in which the struggle between good and evil brothers, Apollonius and Fritz Nettenmaier, has deep moral implications, but is fought out against the humdrum background of a small provincial town. The brothers are steeplejacks, and the circumstances of their perilous calling 'between Heaven and earth' are given symbolic significance. Fritz plunges to his death in the course of an attempt to murder his brother. Apollonius cares for his brother's widow, whom he has long secretly loved, but because of the circumstances of Fritz's death he cannot bring himself to marry her. The realism of the setting and the psychological analysis of Apollonius as a moral hypochondriac are almost unique in their time and make the story a forerunner of the Naturalist school.

The short stories of Theodor Storm are almost obsessively centred on Schleswig-Holstein, his characters are rooted there or drawn back inevitably to their native heath. Storm's imagination carries him into shadowy labyrinths of the past, rarely into distant places. The remark he makes about a character in the story *Abseits* (1863) characterises his work in general: 'Immer hingebender blickte sie in die Perspective der Vergangenheit, wo eine Aussicht immer tiefer als die andere sich eröffnete.' The idyllic moments of his stories lie mostly in the past and are dimmed by awareness of inevitable decay, lust for life derives its keenest thrill from the sense of mortality: 'Jener Schauer, der aus dem Verlangen nach

Erdenlust und dem schmerzlichen Gefühl ihrer Vergäng-
lichkeit so wunderbar gemischt ist.' Storm's heroes are often
mild, morose, limp or low-spirited, mourning what might
have been—the hero of *Ein stiller Musikant* (1874/5), who so
closely resembles Grillparzer's *Armer Spielmann*, the old
doctor of *Drüben am Markt* (1860), Harre in *In St Jürgen*
(1867), Ehrhard in *Angelika* (1855). Even in the earliest of
Storm's stories, *Immensee* (1849), written when he was
thirty-two, he chooses the perspective of an old man remembering a lost love. It is perhaps Storm's craving for the
sheltered life that prompts him to recollect his emotions in
tranquillity, to embalm them in nostalgia, 'wohlverwahrt
in dem sicheren Lande der Vergangenheit', as he puts it in
*Eine Halligfahrt* (1870). Many of the earlier stories are little
more than lyrical sketches, in which atmospheric pictures
of moonlit gardens or sundrenched moors reflect the moods of
characters whose physical presence is sketchily realized. It is
in his few Märchen (e.g. *Die Regentrude*, 1864, and *Bulemanns
Haus*, 1864) and, paradoxically, in the works of his old age,
culminating in *Der Schimmelreiter* (1888), that he achieves
his most vivid feats of imagination and develops his greatest
narrative verve. The Deichgraf Hauke Haien in the grim
and uncanny *Schimmelreiter*, with his defiant struggle against
the sea, is for once a figure of real heroic stature, the whole
story is effectively pervaded by a sense of impending doom.

Here, as in so many of his stories, Storm sets his tale
within a narrative 'framework'; elsewhere he loves to
construct the narrative from fictional documents—although
the simulated chronicle style is often inept and unconvincing.
His descriptive talents are lyrical and evocative rather than
graphic, and he has the lyric poet's facility in the use of
symbols. His landscapes are more colourless than even the
heath and the flat coast of his native region warrant and
they can verge at times on stereotype.

It was not only the sentiment and the Biedermeier
domesticity of Storm that appealed to his middle-class
readers. He embodies many of the social and cultural

values of the professional class to which he belonged—the patriotism inflamed by Danish annexation of his native province, the hostility towards the aristocracy and the commercial class that lies behind stories like *Auf dem Staatshof* (1858), *Im Schloss* (1861) and *Aquis Submersus* (1875/6), the secularism, and in particular the antagonism to Roman Catholicism, that marks *Veronika* (1861). Storm's poetic power is somehow impaired by the narrowness of his social horizon as well as by his sombre temperament.

An earthier variety of regional realism is that of Fritz Reuter, whose most successful works are in the Low German dialect of Mecklenburg. Reuter's main prose works, collected under the title of *Olle Kamellen* (1859–68), are largely autobiographical and have a sometimes forced humour which illuminates even the account of his seven years of harsh imprisonment (*Ut mine Festungstid*, 1862). *Ut mine Stromtid* (1865) records the author's experiences as a farmer and features the comic figure of Inspektor Zacharias Bräsig, who personifies the homely wit and wisdom of the Mecklenburger. From Reuter's work there emerges a picture of sturdy country-folk, democratically united and modestly proud of their ethnic individuality.

Rural realism is represented in Austria by Marie von Ebner-Eschenbach, Ludwig Anzengruber and Peter Rosegger, all of them indebted in some degree to the example of Stifter. Ebner-Eschenbach is the most perceptive and accomplished of the three: her works are essentially exemplary tales of dedication or rehabilitation. *Das Gemeindekind* (1887), for example, describes how the maligned child of a murderer, reluctantly adopted by the parish, overcomes the bitterness in his heart and gains the respect of the community. The priest in *Glaubenlos?* (1893) and the doctor in *Der Kreisphysikus* (1883) overcome doubt and cynicism and dedicate themselves to the service of humanity. The authoress has a shrewd eye for human foibles and the seamier side of village life as well as a concern for social justice, but her stories by no means lack humour—as is evident, for instance, from *Die Freiherren von Gemperlein* (1881), a wry story of two brothers whose eccentricity and ineptitude frustrate their marriage plans and entail the extinction of their line of descent.

Both Anzengruber and Rosegger have a fondness for stark situation and picturesque character which can lapse at times into melodrama and stereotype. Their best novels, however—Anzengruber's *Schandfleck* (1877) and *Sternsteinhof* (1884), for example—are convincingly authentic in setting and characterization. In a number of novels (e.g. *Jakob der Letzte*, 1888, and *Das ewige Licht*, 1897) Rosegger expresses anxiety about the corruption of peasant life by industry and tourism. In *Erdsegen* (1900), the story of a journalist who, for a bet, becomes a farm labourer and is ultimately moved to settle on the land, Rosegger pleads for a return to nature.

Such rural stories had intrinsic limitations of motif and intellectual interest and no doubt owed much of their popularity in the second half of the nineteenth century to the nostalgia of an increasingly artificial urban society for a venerable way of life that was threatened with extinction. Talented writers turned eventually to more sophisticated themes and more complex and articulate characters, but in the hands of less illustrious authors rustic tales remained very popular. The banal novels of Ludwig Ganghofer, for instance, are still much read and have reached the widest possible public in their adaptations as notorious 'Heimatfilme'.

## The Middle-class Novel (1850–80)

The political ambitions of the middle class may have been checked by the failure of the 1848 revolution but there was no halting its rise to economic pre-eminence, fostered as it was by the growing unity and power of Germany. F. W. Hackländer heralded the emergence of the commercial class in *Handel und Wandel* (1850); the typical ethos of this class is celebrated in Gustav Freytag's *Soll und Haben* (1855), which takes as its motto Julian Schmidt's statement: 'Der Roman soll das deutsche Volk da suchen, wo es in seiner

Tüchtigkeit zu finden ist, nämlich bei seiner Arbeit.' Freytag idealizes the efficiency and integrity of the German merchant and compares him with the inept nobleman and the rascally Jew (one of the repulsive features of the work is its anti-Semitism). The young hero, Anton Wohlfahrt, is temporarily dazzled by the glamour of the aristocracy and, in particular, by the beauty of Leonore von Rothsattel; ungratefully spurned because of his lowly birth, he finds a worthier bride in the sister of his principal as well as fulfilment of his vocation in a partnership in the firm. *Die verlorene Handschrift* (1864) is an academic counterpart to *Soll und Haben*: a young professor married to the daughter of a prosperous farmer is flattered by royal patronage, but finds himself involved in the professional jealousies and social rivalries of a provincial capital. His wife's reputation is threatened by the attentions of the crown prince, and the couple are happy to escape from the pitfalls of court life to the obscurity of a university town. Freytag's apotheosis of the middle class culminates in a series of novels (*Die Ahnen*, 1872–80) which traces successive generations of a German family from the fourth to the nineteenth century. The rivalry between aristocracy and middle class is raised to a pitch of hostility in F. Spielhagen's novels, *Problematische Naturen* (1861), *In Reih und Glied* (1867) and *Sturmflut* (1877): the plebeian heroes of these works, lovers of aristocratic women or illegitimate sons of noblemen, suffer from their ambivalent situation. Spielhagen himself adopts an ambiguous attitude towards the bourgeoisie, particularly in *Sturmflut*, which describes the speculative boom of the 'Gründerzeit', the years following the foundation of the Reich.

In spite of their gifts as vigorous storytellers, neither of these writers is capable of giving balanced artistic expression to the inner values of bourgeois culture, of which Freytag's philistinism is a pinchbeck counterfeit. It is in the works of Gottfried Keller and Wilhelm Raabe that these values achieve persuasive aesthetic form.

Although Keller discarded Christianity for Feuerbach's

materialistic humanism, he stands in the didactic tradition of his clerical fellow-countryman, Jeremias Gotthelf, and the ethical values he proclaims are of the prosaic and slightly puritanical Swiss kind: strict honesty and conscientiousness, prudence, probity, self-denial and compassion. His thought and expression are less provincial than Gotthelf's, however, for Keller laid claim to the entire heritage of German culture.

Keller's Novellen are mostly set in Switzerland and range in time from the Middle Ages to his own day. They are cautionary tales of fecklessness rather than vice, of self-discovery and self-improvement. The most celebrated of them are associated with the fictitious town of Seldwyla and the follies of its good-natured, indolent inhabitants. Occasionally a tragic shadow falls across this 'fair and sunny spot', as in the poignant story of the village Romeo and Juliet, but generally the tone is indulgently ironic. However, in the introduction to the second volume of *Die Leute von Seldwyla* (1874) the author sounds a wryly elegiac note: the Seldwyler have in a sense come into their own, for the entire country has become indolent and irresponsible, but they have changed, too, to conform to the new age; they have become mean and meretricious, shady business men rather than engaging ne'er-do-weels, so that the later stories are 'gleanings from happier times'. These comments reflect Keller's dismay at the unhealthy inflation of the country's economy and the political opportunism that marked the 'Gründerjahre' in Switzerland as well as Germany. This is the theme of the novel, *Martin Salander* (1886), in which Keller tries, not altogether successfully, to adopt something of the Naturalist style.

Keller's major contribution to the tradition of the German novel is *Der grüne Heinrich*, a largely autobiographical 'Bildungsroman', the two versions of which (1854/5 and 1879/80) mark the author's progress from a romantically subjective to a more realistic and critical attitude, as well as from relative ineptitude to near mastery of the novel form. Heinrich Lee is the victim of tensions and conflicts repeatedly embodied in the 'Bildungsroman': he is torn between love for the delicate Anna and passion for the voluptuous young widow, Judith, and he struggles through years of vain artistic endeavour as a landscape painter before settling down in humdrum but useful employment as a village clerk. Heinrich's life is dominated by feelings of guilt towards his self-sacrificing widowed mother, and it is largely this sense of guilt which undermines his relations with women and draws him back to his native soil. In the account of Heinrich's youth, which constitutes the finest part of the work, Keller conveys with unique sensitivity his hero's and his own wrestling with religion, the unfolding of his creative imagination on the frontier between poetic fiction and criminal fabrication, the frustrating attempt to nourish a puny talent, and the painful raptures of adolescent sex. The latter parts of the novel have longueurs, but the vitality and psychological acumen of the 'Jugendgeschichte' have seldom been surpassed. Keller transposes the problems of Agathon and Meister from a philosophical to a more personal plane; he translates the idiom of Classicism into the less resonant but more incisive terms of the modern world and provides a bridge by which the 'Bildungsroman' may enter the twentieth century.

Wilhelm Raabe is a writer easy to underrate. He is not what he seems at first sight, simply a tardy representative of Biedermeier sentiment, but a novelist whose realism is truly poetic and not merely picturesque and whose admitted philistinism has a gleam of true wisdom. The laconic or whimsical tone of much that he wrote is deceptive: unemphatic remarks by simple old people like Sophie Grünhagen and Marten in *Das Horn von Wanza* (1881), the capricious asides of eccentrics like Peter Uhusen in *Im alten Eisen* (1887) and Heinrich Schaumann in *Stopfkuchen* (1891) turn out, once the tale is complete, to be quintessential truths. Raabe is often called a pessimist, but his novels include the idyllic *Horacker* (1876) as well as the morbid beauty of *Unruhige Gäste* (1886). His 'pessimism' is simply an acknowledgement of the inscrutable fitness of things, whether the outcome be cheerful or tragic.

Some of Raabe's works have a topical bent: *Pfisters Mühle*, for instance, gives a glimpse of the destruction of the old Germany by the new—but the main concern of his work is existential rather than topical. He attempts to capture the flavour of life and, in particular, to see the here and now as a nodal point in the fabric of time and space. Raabe is fascinated by the mysteries of simultaneity and sequence. This is reflected in the narrative method of his best novels, in which he concentrates the action into the smallest possible compass of time but sinks shafts of reminiscence into the past and spins a web of historical and mythical association round places and things. Raabe escapes the tyranny of the monolinear narrative and supersedes the multiple narrative of the Young Germans with what one might call the narrative of vertical integration—'Roman des Durcheinander'—the deity of which, 'die Göttin des Durcheinander', is invoked by Rudolf Haeseler in *Der Dräumling* (1872). What seems to be an instinctive mastery of complex narration is evident in Raabe's first novel, *Aus der Chronik der Sperlingsgasse* (1856); it is less obvious in his most popular works, *Der Hungerpastor* (1864), *Abu Telfan* (1867) and *Der Schüdderump* (1870), but it re-appears in his later novels. The incidental pleasures of Raabe's stories are many and varied: his characterization—often reciprocally conveyed through the characters themselves—is precise and colourful; within the body of his work he creates on the soil of the Harz a kind of poetic province that has been justly compared with Hardy's Wessex. His faults are few— an excessive whimsicality at times, some jejune symbolism, a strain of anti-Semitism in *Der Hungerpastor*. As far as the atmosphere and ethos of his novels is concerned, Raabe represents a climax of middle-class realism, but although his narrative techniques in some ways anticipate Thomas Mann he has no obvious successors and is a curiously isolated figure.

## Realism and Historical Fiction

The effect on fiction of more exact historical study was paradoxically demonstrated in W. Meinhold's adroit counterfeit of a seventeenth-century witch trial, *Die Bernsteinhexe* (1843), originally published as a hoax to prove the unreliability of contemporary textual criticism. This effect became even more marked in the period of realism. Not all writers of historical tales were capable of welding topical relevance, personal experience and antiquarian interest: Viktor von Scheffel's *Ekkehard* (1855), a romance about the author of the medieval Latin epic, *Waltharius*, is an outstandingly successful example which is not matched by many of the numerous 'Professorenromane' of the second half of the century. W. H. Riehl's *Kulturgeschichtliche Novellen* (1856) had the special aim of re-creating with fictional characters the social conditions and the mentality of past ages as background to the great men and movements which properly concern the historian. Felix Dahn undertook a more ambitious task in *Ein Kampf um Rom* (1876), a reconstruction of the decline and fall of the Ostrogothic empire in Italy. The work is of more than trivial or academic interest, for it echoes the political events of the nineteenth century, while one of its fictional characters, the ruthless, intriguing Roman Cethegus, anticipates the Nietzschean 'Machtmensch'.

Not all historical novelists of the time chose patriotic themes: as in the novel of German life a certain regionalism developed. Georg Ebers wrote a number of stories about ancient Egypt, of which the most successful was *Eine ägyptische Königstochter* (1874). Ernst Eckstein took ancient Rome as his province, with *Der Claudier* (1881), *Prusias* (1883) and *Nero* (1889). Robert Hamerling wrote about classical Greece in *Aspasia* (1876).

Few historical novelists of the time enter into the minds of their protagonists in quite as problematic a way as C. F. Meyer. In the unadventurous life of this rather prim patrician the men of the Italian Renaissance and the religious wars of the seventeenth century seem to have offered a substitute for real experience. He once wrote to a friend:

> Je me sers de la forme de la nouvelle historique purement et simplement pour y loger mes expériences et mes sentiments personnels, la préférant au 'Zeitroman' parcequ'elle me masque mieux . . .

Meyer is a tireless craftsman, obsessed with symmetry and picturesque contrast: his principal characters are set off dramatically against each other—gay Catholic and sombre Calvinist in *Das Amulett* (1873), ruthless renegade and saintly soldier in *Jürg Jenatsch* (1874-6), gross Norman king and the ascetic Saxon archbishop Thomas Becket in *Der Heilige* (1880), the vicious Lukrezia and the virtuous Angela in *Angela Borgia* (1891). The hero of *Die Hochzeit des Mönchs* (1884) is dragged from the cloister to the plot and passion of a Renaissance court; death commonly comes to these people like a bolt of lightning at the climactic moment of life. The violent plots of Meyer's stories themselves contrast with the tense discipline of the imagery and style: brilliant tableaux and statuesque groupings abound and there is something oppressively sumptuous about the settings. In the later stories there is a distinct morbidity, a whiff of decadence and traces of the repressed hectic temper that Heinrich Mann called 'hysterische Renaissance'.

The last two decades of the nineteenth century were a time of experiment and theorizing of which the first phase was dominated by the slogan 'Naturalism'. Ultimately Naturalism came to stand for the rejection of idealism and the utterly consistent application of the principles of realism, but as used initially by the brothers Heinrich and Julius Hart in the *Deutsche Monatsblätter* (1878) and *Kritische Waffengänge* (1882-4) it implied a revolt against the residual aesthetic formalism of the realist writers, a demand for new vigour, a return to nature, in fact, and to the deepest creative forces of the national soul. The Harts link 'Naturalismus' with 'das Elementare, das Genie' and talk of poetic creation 'aus der germanischen Volksseele heraus'; both they and

Karl Bleibtreu in his *Revolution der Literatur* (1886) revert to the Sturm und Drang writers as their spiritual ancestors. At the same time the younger generation of writers in the 1880s were very conscious of living in a 'modern' world: 'Unsere Welt ist nicht mehr klassisch, / Unsere Welt ist nicht mehr romantisch, / Unsere Welt ist modern', wrote Arno Holz, and 'die Moderne' was used by Eugen Wolff to denote contemporary urbanized industrial society in contrast to the anachronistic 'Antike' which had dominated Classicism and its prolonged aftermath. The use of this term and of the expression 'Das Jüngste Deutschland' for certain writers of early Naturalism points to an affinity with the radical movement of the 1830s and 1840s. In the context of 'die Moderne' a return to nature could no longer be a matter of intuition and pantheistic feeling; it had to take account of scientific determinism, of psychological advance and of the ever more acute 'social problem'; it had to penetrate beneath the bland surface of middle-class realism and observe human behaviour with scientific precision as a function of heredity and environment, shirking none of its more repulsive aspects. The ideal of scientific objectivity conflicted, it is true, with the commitment to social reform felt by many Naturalists: Otto Brahm tried to solve this dilemma by stating that Naturalism sought 'nicht Wahrheit im objektiven (das ist keinem Kämpfer möglich), sondern im subjektiven Sinn'. The connection between literature and socialism in the Naturalist movement was to some extent fortuitous, however, and did not last very long—the attempt to create solidarity between writers and workers by the foundation of a 'Freie Volksbühne', for instance, was short-lived. At the height of the movement, however, the obsession of Naturalist dramatists and novelists with the socially sordid, morbid and lurid associated them in the public mind at least with the propaganda of social democracy.

The most radical and consistent theorist of Naturalism in Germany was Arno Holz, the advocate of 'konsequenter Naturalismus'. Holz exposed the speciousness of Zola's theory of the experimental novel and, in his essay *Die Kunst, ihr Wesen und ihre Gesetze* (1891), deduced from the principles of representational art the maxim 'Die Kunst hat die Tendenz wieder Natur zu sein, sie wird sie nach Massgabe ihrer Mittel und deren Handhabung'—or, in brief formula, 'Kunst = Natur − $x$', where $x$ represents the discrepancy between the object and its representation. The excellence of a work of art may thus be measured by its approximation to total identification with reality; logically, the artist's aim must be total assimilation of form to content. To do Holz justice it must be mentioned that he construes 'Natur' in a wide sense to include the world of intellect and imagination as well as the physical world. The application of the principle of perfect illusion turned the Naturalists towards the drama, where in fact they achieved their most convincing successes. It was Holz himself, in collaboration with Johannes Schlaf, who provided the best examples of the style appropriate to consistent naturalism, a 'Sekundenstil' of microscopic precision which registered every detail of setting, every inflection of speech and nuance of atmosphere.

The young critics of the 1880s—Heinrich and Julius Hart, M. G. Conrad, Konrad Alberti, Karl Bleibtreu, Bruno Wille and the rest—were confused and divided about definitions of Realism and Naturalism and about the exact nature of proposed reforms but they were united in their criticism of most contemporary fiction—on the grounds, largely, that it *was* no more than 'fiction'. As prophets of a new age of science, technology and psychological analysis they looked to France, Russia and Scandinavia for their models, to Zola, Tolstoy and Dostojevski, J. P. Jacobsen, Arne Garborg and Alexander Kielland, to Ibsen, Björnson and Strindberg. The novel, they felt, must be rescued from mere 'writers' like Spielhagen and Paul Lindau and become once again the concern of poets. But even in their choice of targets these 'Jüngstdeutsche' were not entirely unanimous or consistent: Freytag and Keller are praised by some, damned by others, Alexis was lauded, Ebers reviled. They nearly all agree, however, in their execration of Paul Heyse, who seemed to them the personification of everything false and effete in the age. 'Heyse lesen heisst, ein Mensch ohne Geschmack sein— Heyse bewundern, heisst ein Lump sein', declared Konrad Alberti. It is true that Heyse's countless Novellen are more remarkable for elegant construction, colourful settings and polished style than for deep feeling or profound thought. His enormously popular novel *Kinder der Welt* (1873) is a jejune attack on religious dogmatism and a facile defence of secularism. *Im Paradies* (1875) describes the genteel Bohemianism of the better sort of Munich artist and mounts a guarded attack on the conventional ethics of marriage.

The critics of Heyse had themselves remarkably little success as novelists. The versatile Conrad set out to emulate Zola's *Rougon-Macquart* in a cycle of novels based on Munich life and no doubt designed as a foil to Heyse's unproblematic work. Conrad did not possess the stamina, much less the genius of his model, and he produced only a trilogy: *Was die Isar rauscht* (1887), *Die klugen Jungfrauen* (1889) and *Die Beichte des Narren* (1889–90). The first of these is the most readable as an account of the unhealthy prosperity of the 'Gründerjahre'. In the figure and fate of Max von Drillinger there is already something of the *fin de siècle* neurosis that marks the disillusioned and degenerate heroes of Hermann Conradi's *Adam Mensch* (1889) and Otto Julius Bierbaum's *Stilpe* (1897). Graf Krastinik, the hero of Bleibtreu's *Grössenwahn* (1888), although betrayed in love and disappointed in literature, discovers a darkly prophetic purpose when he re-enters the Austrian army in expectation of an Armageddon that will shatter and cleanse the culture of Europe. The most interesting part of the work is the lightly disguised account of contemporary literary feuds in Berlin.

Conrad and Bleibtreu believed they had found their 'German Zola' in Max Kretzer, whose novels of proletatian life were based on personal experience in factories. *Meister Timpe* (1888) describes the ruin of an honest craftsman by the power of capital and the defection of his own son to an unscrupulously efficient rival. Kretzer acknowledged the influence of Dickens and the despised Freytag as well as of Zola, but his work stands comparison with none of these models: it is melodramatic in plot and motivation, crude in characterization and unredeemably prosaic in style. In his analysis of social and economic problems he hardly goes beyond the socialist novelists of the 1840s and 1850s.

Naturalism is largely a phenomenon of urban life—in its final phase Conrad himself spoke of the 'konsequenter Naturalismus' of Holz and Schlaf as 'Asphaltpflanze der Grossstadtgasse, ohne Duft, ohne Samen, ein erstaunliches Wunder der Technik'. Nevertheless, some novels of rural life have naturalistic features. Ludwig Anzengruber's stories and the early novels of Clara Viebig are realistic to the point of naturalism. Hermann Sudermann, whose effective but facile naturalist dramas caused a great furore in Berlin, described the struggle of a young East Prussian farmer against debt, misfortune and a degenerate father in *Frau Sorge* (1887). Wilhelm von Polenz reverted in his fine novel *Der Büttner-bauer* (1895) to problems treated by Auerbach in *Der Lehnhold* and Rosegger in *Jakob der Letzte:* the splitting up of farms by inheritance and the encroachment of capitalist speculators into rural life, with the consequent destruction of the peasant family and culture. The development of regional 'Heimat-dichtung' during the first decades of the twentieth century is a consequence of the spread of naturalism to the countryside.

As far as technique is concerned, most 'naturalist' novels differ little from the novels of the Young Germans. The only significant advance in this ultimate phase of realism is to be found in shorter narrative forms, in the few cases, in fact, where a new style is developed. The most notable example is *Papa Hamlet* (1889) by Arno Holz and Johannes Schlaf, three sketches of squalid life and wretched death in which the impressionistic 'Sekundenstil' registers every nuance of setting and atmosphere, every idiosyncrasy of dialogue. The prominence of dialogue and the manifest impossibility of employing this microscopic technique on the scale of a novel are significant for the trend of Naturalism towards the drama. Apart from *Papa Hamlet* Gerhart Hauptmann's *Bahnwärter Thiel* (1887) is perhaps the only narrative product of the Naturalist group that could be unhesitatingly described as a masterpiece—on grounds of its symbolism and Hauptmann's insight into the pathological mysticism of the protagonist rather than for specifically naturalistic qualities.

Naturalism as such made little impression on the development of the German novel. Its social impulse soon flagged; what remained was the refinement of perception and sensibility and a fascination by neurosis. Zola gave way to Paul Bourget and Huysmans, the cult of Nietzsche replaced the compassionate socialism of the Naturalists, the morbid aestheticism of the *fin de siècle* made its appearance in the first stories of Heinrich and Thomas Mann.

What is possibly the finest achievement of the German novel in the last phase of the nineteenth century cannot be credited to the younger generation. It belongs to a writer born in 1819—Theodor Fontane. Fontane's approach to the novel was leisurely—from journalism through lyric, ballads and volumes of travel literature. When he first ventured on the novel form he clung to recognized models—Alexis in the case of *Vor dem Sturm* (1878), a story of the Wars of Liberation, Storm in the case of *Grete Minde* (1880), set in the seventeenth century, and *Ellernklipp*, a tale of the eighteenth century. It was not until he turned to the Berlin of his own time that he discovered the setting most congenial to him. The first of his 'Berlin' novels, *L'Adultera* (1882), is reminiscent of Paul Heyse, but with *Cécile* (1887) and the works which followed Fontane achieved distinctive mastery as a shrewd, urbane but compassionate commentator on the social life of the time.

Fontane is perhaps most at home in dealing with the upper classes of society. His sympathies, discreetly revealed, tend to be with the often impoverished old aristocracy, his sharpest irony is reserved for the parvenus and nouveaux riches—'das Schlechteste, was einer sein kann'. The life of the working-class, where it enters into his stories, tends to be unobtrusively idealized; his workers live in homes that are humble rather than squalid, their speech may be brusque and down-to-earth but it is always seemly. He is essentially a humane conservative, aware of the pathos or tragedy which may issue from the double standards involved in rigid class distinctions, but prepared to tolerate such distinctions as part of an organic social order sufficiently right to justify the occasional curbing or marring of individual happiness.

It is in dialogue and in the spare precision of his descriptions that Fontane excels. Through conversation, with the minimum of discursive comment, he outlines the mental constitution of his characters and reflects their hidden impulses and reactions. Fontane's exact topographical descriptions, often enchanting in themselves, are more than background: individual details have meaning both for the characters and for the reader. Their accumulation, combination and recurrence constitute a network of symbols and leitmotifs relevant to the theme of the story. Few novelists between Goethe and Thomas Mann have wrought to such a pitch the fine art of selective allusion.

Fontane's work was fittingly crowned in the last year of his life by the publication of *Der Stechlin* (1898), the story of the declining years of a country squire, a man of no great accomplishments but the representative, in his integrity, humour and charm, of a vanishing aristocratic culture. In the conversation of Dubslav von Stechlin, wry, witty and wise, Fontane embodies his own scepticism about political opportunists and about the brash new Prussian state, while through the liberal Pastor Lorenzen he voices a modest hope for a better future. The novel as a whole is a testimonial to its author's tolerance and wisdom. It is not difficult to see in Stechlin features of Fontane himself, and the words of Pastor Lorenzen at Dubslav's funeral form a proper epilogue to the work of a great novelist: 'Nichts Menschliches war ihm fremd, weil er sich selbst als Mensch empfand und sich eigner menschlicher Schwäche jederzeit bewusst war.'

### The Drama from Biedermeier to Realism

The new trend which followed upon Romanticism shows many different sides. Political, social, historical and psychological factors all play their part in determining the new contents of literary production after 1820. There are also divergent kinds of expression according to the genres chosen by individual writers: different forms prevail in the drama and in lyric poetry. Moreover, some phases of the trend in German literature conform to those in Europe at large, while others like 'Biedermeier', 'Das junge Deutschland' and 'Poetic Realism' are peculiar to Germany and Austria. The complexity of the situation in the nineteenth century is also shown by the persistence or revival of the Classical and Romantic heritage and, in the case of 'Das junge Deutschland', even of Enlightenment and 'Storm and Stress' traditions. Thus the Age of Realism is a term which conveniently applies to kindred but not identical literary manifestations between the Napoleonic Wars and the foundation of the Empire in 1870.

In drama the tradition of satirical comedy continues in the work of the Austrians Ferdinand Raimund (1790–1836) and Johann Nepomuk Nestroy (1801–62), but, with characteristically Viennese admixtures from the repertoire of the earlier 'Zauberpossen' and 'Verwandlungsstücke', as well as from such diverse sources as the Commedia dell' Arte and the dramas of Goldoni and Lope de Vega. These different elements cohered to form a living stage tradition of popular entertainment. Although amusement was Raimund's main concern, he also treated serious themes in works like *Der Alpenkönig und der Menschenfeind* (1828) which has been compared with Grillparzer's *Der Traum ein Leben*. Whereas Raimund greatly admired Grillparzer, Nestroy parodied his *Ein treuer Diener seines Herrn* in *Der Einsilbige oder Ein dummer Diener seines Herrn* (1829), just as he burlesqued Raimund's *Der Verschwender* (1834) and Hebbel's *Judith*. In his best known plays *Der böse Geist Lumpacivagabundus oder das liederliche*

*Kleeblatt* (1833), *Zu ebener Erde und im ersten Stock* (1835), *Einen Jux will er sich machen* (1842) and *Der Zerrissene* (1845) he showed greater awareness of realist trends. None of these comedies could vie in literary merit with Grillparzer's *Weh dem der lügt*, although they had far greater popular success.

German Romantic comedy lived on in brilliantly fanciful and ironic works like Christian Dietrich Grabbe's *Scherz, Satire, Ironie und tiefere Bedeutung* (written 1822, publ. 1827) and Georg Büchner's *Leonce und Lena* (written 1836, publ. 1842). In *Die Journalisten* (1852) Gustav Freytag wrote a more strictly realistic piece in which he kept to the tradition of ridiculing with good humour the professional life of a section of society. 'Das junge Deutschland' produced no great writer of comedies in the realist manner with the possible exception of Karl Gutzkow who had some success but established no new trend with his plays *Zopf und Schwert* (1844), a satire on life at the court of Frederich William the First, *Das Urbild des Tartüffe* (1844), a comedy of literary intrigue, and *Der Königsleutnant* (1852), a dramatization of episodes from the young Goethe's life.

Coming to tragedy, with the exception of Büchner's *Woyzeck*, the only notable works written between 1820 and 1870 with the aim of portraying actuality are the 'bürgerliche Trauerspiele' of Otto Ludwig and Hebbel. The overwhelming number of dramas belonging to this period deal with historical and legendary subjects and it is in the handling of such material that realism, in the widest sense, achieves its best results in German dramatic literature. The representative writers, Grillparzer, Hebbel, Otto Ludwig, Grabbe and Büchner are not a concerted group: they differ from one another in important respects and therefore cannot be said to belong to a School like that of the Romantics or to a movement like the Classicists'. They did not even influence each other in a pronounced way. Nonetheless they all shared in establishing what has been appropriately termed the literature of 'bürgerlicher Realismus'.

Franz Grillparzer's antecedents are different from those of his German contemporaries. He was heir to a tradition in which neither the German 'Aufklärung' nor the 'Sturm und Drang' played important parts, but his links with the Baroque remained close. On the other hand he acknowledged his indebtedness to the Weimar Classicists. Essentially, he represents the spirit of Austrian 'Biedermeier'. The ruling principle of this attitude as it appears in his work is stated in the lines from *Der Traum ein Leben*:

> Eines nur ist Glück hienieden
> Eins: des Innern stiller Frieden
> Und die schuldbefreite Brust.

The last line is as important as the second in defining Grillparzer's outlook, but it is true that he prized withdrawal into contemplative tranquillity above participation in life's turmoil. Napoleon's defeat impressed him and those who thought like him to the extent of causing them to disavow all ambition or liking for adventure. Beyond this Grillparzer was keenly aware of the conflicts engendered by the incongruity of personality and desire, art and life. The tragedy of incompatibles became a ruling motif of his work whether he chose his material from Greek legend or from Austrian history. Exploitation of this theme with psychological veracity and artistic skill is his outstanding contribution to literature in the Age of Realism.

His first drama, *Die Ahnfrau* (1817), follows the pattern of earlier fate-tragedies without adhering to it completely: Grillparzer gave more weight to the characters' individuality than his predecessors allowed. Yet he had not found his own métier in writing this work. He began *Der Traum ein Leben* only a year later with the projected title *Traum und Wahrheit*, but did not complete it until 1831 when he had fully developed his personal style. This fairy tale in dramatic form in the 'Zauberstück' tradition nonetheless differs from his other mature work in that here he avoids the tragic issue of his specific themes: the problem of Rustan's ambition is solved when he realizes its consequences in a dream. Other exceptional features are Calderon's predominant influence and Grillparzer's choice of a trochaic verse form.

He came fully into his own when he composed his dramas based on well-known Greek legends: *Sappho* (written as early as 1817), the trilogy *Das goldene Vliess* (1818–21) and *Des Meeres und der Liebe Wellen* (begun in 1819 but not completed until 1829). *Sappho* parallels Goethe's *Torquato Tasso* in dramatizing the contrast between art and life, but Grillparzer sharpened the resultant conflicts by introducing a second love theme in Phaon's relations with the poetess's handmaiden Melitta and developing the deterioration of the heroine's character to the point where suicide is the only way out for her. Another instance of the clash between love and vocation is *Des Meeres und der Liebe Wellen*, a dramatization of the Hero and Leander legend. The distinctive quality of Grillparzer's rendering is Hero's aspiration to be a priestess, a vocation to which she is not called by her nature. She exemplifies the disparity between native character and ambition which is one of Grillparzer's key themes. When she has fallen in love with Leander after taking the vow, the priest, whose warnings she had not heeded, exacts vengeance, so that Leander is drowned in swimming the Hellespont. But the real issue concerns Hero: she is as tragically engulfed by love as Leander is by the waves of the ocean.

The trilogy *Das goldene Vliess* is Grillparzer's most elaborate dramatic composition. The action progresses steadily in the first two parts, *Der Gastfreund* (1818) and *Die Argonauten* (1818–20), and reaches its culmination in the third (*Medea*), yet each part contains its own tragic problem. *Das goldene Vliess* can be called a fate tragedy if weight is given to the curse which rests upon Jason, and indeed his crimes are fearfully avenged. But it is a 'Schicksalstragödie' on a far higher level of conception and execution than *Die Ahnfrau*: it embodies Grillparzer's central dramatic idea in showing forth the vanity of ambitious enterprise. At the root of the tragic entanglements also lies Jason's and Medea's mutual incompatibility as representatives of the different societies to which they belong. An intensified motif from *Sappho* is present in the last part of the trilogy when Medea's love turns into hideous revulsion and unnatural cruelty. An arresting feature of the tragic dénouement, it is a measure of the distance that began to separate Grillparzer from the Weimar Classicists when he wrote this work. It marks his relative approximation to realism. (This also comes out in his deliberate variations of speech and alternation of blank verse and free verse to express the contrasting moods of individual characters.) The impact Medea's crime makes is more immediate than the perpetration of a similar deed as reported by the heroine in Goethe's *Iphigenie auf Tauris*. Without going to radical lengths Grillparzer is here more in line with dramatists like Kleist and Grabbe who do not shrink from presenting the brutal side of human nature.

For his other plays Grillparzer chose episodes from Austrian, Hungarian, Bohemian and Spanish history. All his ruling themes appear in them, although frequently with altered emphasis. In *König Ottokars Glück und Ende* (1823) the Bohemian ruler's unscrupulous bid for the Imperial crown is sharply contrasted with Rudolf of Habsburg's integrity. (Ottokar's actions also have topical interest in recalling events from Napoleon's later career.) The hero of *Ein treuer Diener seines Herrn* (1826–7) is an even more intensely tragic figure. Bancbanus loyally tries to administer the stewardship entrusted to him by his king but lacks the strength to carry it through. In *Ein Bruderzwist in Habsburg* (completed in 1848) Rudolf's passivity prevents effective political action and shows the tragically guilty aspect of a life dedicated to contemplation. The reverse holds good for Libussa, the eponymous heroine of the drama Grillparzer completed in the same year. She is embroiled in uncongenial political activity when she gives up her divinely ordained rulership and marries Primislaus. This leads to the foundation of the city of Prague and the establishment of a new order in the place of Libussa's outdated matriarchy. A similarly positive result following upon the violent severance of an incompatible relationship is given in *Die Jüdin von Toledo* (completed after 1850). After the grandees of Spain have instigated Rahel's murder, King Alfonso overcomes his infatuation and repents the neglect of his regal duties with the words: 'Besiegter Fehl ist all der Menschen Tugend.'

None of the plays Grillparzer wrote after *Weh dem, der lügt* was performed during his lifetime: the unfavourable reception of this work led him to withhold them even from publication. Yet he wrote them all for the stage. He was an austere critic of his own dramas and always had their actability in mind. His stagecraft is unrivalled. In his theoretical writings, which have considerable importance (acknowledged, for example, by George Sainsbury), he stressed the fact that a drama is above all 'eine Gegenwart', a scenic presentation. Not the least of his achievements is the pictorial effect he produces in all his major plays, with his skill in exploiting contrasts and his sense of modulation and tone.

In many ways Friedrich Hebbel's idea of tragedy is the antithesis of Grillparzer's. We can see this when we compare *Die Jüdin von Toledo* with *Agnes Bernauer* (1852). In both plays murder is condoned in the interests of the state. Where Hebbel differs from Grillparzer is in treating the theme as a conflict between a father and his son and representing it as a clash of individual desire against collective responsibility. In this respect, too *Agnes Bernauer* is strikingly unlike any 'Sturm und Drang' drama where the enmity of father and son signified the conflict between an older conservative generation and a progressive younger one. In Hebbel's play the father (Herzog Ernst) upholds a more advanced view than his son (Albrecht) when the occasion for their quarrel is considered in relation to the ultimate welfare of the state. The crux of the issue as Hebbel presents it is not the right of any individual to freedom of choice within the law, but his responsibility if the welfare of the community is at stake.

Hebbel's tragic conceptions emerge in several other

features of this play. Agnes is existentially guilty in provoking the conflict through her inordinate beauty. In Hebbelian terms excess of any quality, however good in itself and however involuntarily come by, of any immoderate assertion of selfhood, upsets the balance of forces in the universe which must be restored by violent means. Another aspect of Hebbel's idea of tragedy comes out when we consider the historical setting. The action of *Agnes Bernauer* takes place in an age of transition during which ideas of rulership were changing and princes were slowly assuming the task of serving their subjects instead of imposing their will upon them. The rise of the middle class which provoked that change is also incorporated in this inverted 'bürgerliches Trauerspiel'. Thirdly, after the murder of Agnes, on the verge of the battle between father and son, Albrecht comes to acknowledge the justice of Herzog Ernst's case. An essential part of Hebbel's mature tragedies is an act or manifestation of reconciliation which brings the drama to a close.

One of his principal contributions to German tragedy is his presentation of clashes between strong-willed individuals (often, but not invariably, of opposite sex) and his employment of Hegelian concepts of history in dramatizing such conflicts. His originality lies in creating a kind of historical tragedy where the essence of historicity consists not so much in the events or the characters as in the process of change which these events demonstrate in leading to the emergence of new moral values. One of the protagonists in a given play by Hebbel invariably represents the old order, his (or occasionally, her) opponent, the coming age. Two of Hebbel's most important dramas, *Herodes und Mariamne* (1849) and *Die Nibelungen* (1861) deal with conflicts in localities where Christianity established the new order—in the first against prevailing Hebrew and Roman, in the other against Germanic codes of behaviour. In *Gyges und sein Ring* (1856) the Greek impact upon conservative Eastern mentality adumbrated a comparable change, though with less dramatic plausibility.

In all these plays the test of morality is love. Herodes' egotism represents the old order. Mariamne's love adumbrates the Christian idea. In *Die Nibelungen* Hagen embodies the Germanic principle of blood kinship against Kriemhild's more Christian notion of the primacy of marital ties. A noteworthy feature of both works is that the heroines also show that they still belong to the passing order by their vengeful actions devoid of Christian charity.

Hebbel did not start his career with this distinctive idea of tragedy in mind. His first dramas, *Judith* (1840), *Genoveva* (1843) and *Maria Magdalene* (1844), represent its antecedent forms. Tragic excess is already present in *Judith*, where Hebbel also gives a first rendering of the conflict between the sexes. But the tragedy mainly resides in the heroine's defection of her mission in killing Holofernes primarily in order to avenge her outraged womanhood rather than to rescue Bethulia. Nor does a clear image of Hebbel's historical outlook emerge from *Genoveva*, a tragedy differing from those of Maler Müller and Tieck on the same subject. Hebbel focussed attention on the character of Golo; the drama amounts to a study of knavery without penetrating to the level of psychological realism.

In the 'bürgerliches Trauerspiel' *Maria Magdalene* Hebbel goes beyond the traditional scheme followed by Lessing and Schiller in *Emilia Galotti* and *Kabale und Liebe* by placing the conflict within the middle class rather than locating it in the clash between representatives of the lower and higher social orders. *Maria Magdalene* is the most directly realist of Hebbel's tragedies. His evocation of the lower middle class milieu makes an immediate impact: it is his only play in which he treats the manifestations of changing morality in a palpably contemporary setting, so that his brand of historical tragedy is implied rather than explicit, except in Meister Anton's final words: 'Ich verstehe die Welt nicht mehr'. In the Preface to the work Hebbel claims too much for it in terms of the progressive interiorization of tragic conflicts from the time of ancient Greece onwards. But it is one of his characteristic products, illustrating as it does the principle he noted in his diary: 'Der Einzelne kann sich der Welt gar nicht gegenüber stellen, ohne sein kleines Recht in ein grosses Unrecht zu verwandeln.'

Hebbel's conception of tragedy is ultimately metaphysical, based on his own pronouncement: 'Alles Leben ist Kampf des Individuellen mit dem Universum'. It is also centred on the idea of divine ordinance, the tragic situation of human beings chosen by God to fulfil a mission and abandoned by Him in the course of its execution. In his diary he explicitly stated this to be the theme of the apocryphal story of Judith which, he felt, is also the story of Joan of Arc unrealized in Schiller's drama. Religious themes occupied him over many years: he planned tragedies on Christ and on Moloch, but they did not come to fruition. He also failed to complete dramas on Saul, Moses, Julian the Apostate and Martin Luther. Another fragment is his *Demetrius*, four acts of which he had completed when he died in 1863. Here he again vied with Schiller and, as in *Judith*, re-interpreted the story by basing his conception on a Hegelian conflict between two kinds of duty.

Hebbel tried his hand at two other dramatic forms: tragicomedy in *Ein Trauerspiel in Sizilien* (1851), comedy in *Der Diamant* (1847) and *Der Rubin* (1851). They are not among his best work, largely because of his inability to raise the comic elements above the levels of caricature and grotesque satire.

Otto Ludwig is the principal theorist of Poetic Realism. When we compare his dramas with his theory, however, we see him placed in an ambiguous position. In his major critical work, *Shakespeare-Studien* (1871), he opposed the 'idealistic' mode of tragedy which he one-sidedly attributed to Schiller, and upheld a more realistic manner of motivating character and action. His 'bürgerliches Trauerspiel' *Der Erbförster* (1850) succeeds well enough in evoking the stubborn character of the gamekeeper and capturing the atmosphere of life among a section of the middle classes in

Thuringia. But he failed to carry out his own critical precepts by giving too much scope to chance and coincidence in the economy of the tragic action. His earlier dramatization of E. T. A. Hoffmann's *Das Fräulein von Scudéri* (1848) and the tragedies in blank verse, *Die Makkabäer* (1854) and *Der Engel von Augsburg* (1846) (a version of the Agnes Bernauer story), contain some forceful scenes. But Otto Ludwig's performance remains uneven and inconsistent. His eclecticism comes out in his attempts to work over material which had in his day become time-honoured, such as Arminius, Mary Queen of Scots, Genoveva and Wallenstein, beside plans for tragedies on Christ, Jud Süss and Charlotte Corday.

The dramatic yield of the Young German movement is scarcely more noteworthy than that of Poetic Realism, particularly in tragedy. Gutzkow's *Uriel Acosta* (1846) is one of the few exceptions. In its 'Tendenz' as a plea for religious liberalism it recalls the Enlightenment. Heinrich Laube's plays, the most important of which are *Die Karlsschüler* (1846), on Schiller's conflict with Duke Karl Eugen, *Struensee* (1847) and *Graf Essex* (1856) are more tendentiously political in purpose though historical or biographical in scope.

Within the German context the term 'realistic' is applied with greater relevance to aspects of the work of two dramatists who wrote during the earlier part of the century. Christian Dietrich Grabbe, a dissolute genius, has been called a precursor of Nietzsche in uncovering the brutal side of human nature with outspoken frankness. Scenes of crude violence abound in his tragedies. They make a direct impact, not least because of the dramatic technique Grabbe employed. He anticipated later developments by avoiding the construction of continuous actions. His dramas move in impetuous bursts, just as his characters express themselves in explosive images and staccato rhythms. He produced his most powerful effects when he presented conflicts between sharply contrasting figures, as in *Marius und Sulla* (1827), *Don Juan und Faust* (1829), *Die Hohenstaufen* (1829) and *Die Her-*

*mannsschalcht* (1838). His strength also lay in handling crowd scenes, particularly in *Napoleon oder Die Hundert Tage* (1831). This is his most effective play in which, as in *Hannibal* (1835), he gave a picture of political action doomed to failure. Disillusionment over the futility of heroic enterprise links Grabbe with the representatives of 'Biedermeier', but in the place of their reliance upon solid possessions and traditions, he had no solution to offer: with him melancholy sharpened into a sense of futility.

The same disillusionment characterizes the work of Georg Büchner. His literary output was small, but it has far greater intellectual and artistic significance than Grabbe's. Although he took as his model the dramas of Lenz (which Tieck published in 1828), originality is an outstanding feature of his work. In outlook and style it marks a decisive break with the previous age and, while representing German realism in one of its most sharply contoured forms, foreshadows developments to come that led to Expressionism and the Surrealist trend.

Büchner's competence as dramatist grew as his interest in politics waned. His two tragedies are unique products of an artistic impulse released after his revolutionary activities were terminated by threatened police prosecution. In *Dantons Tod* (1835) he pushed political disillusionment beyond pessimism into a new kind of humanitarian feeling. He evokes sympathy devoid of heroic admiration for Danton, the victim of Robespierre's fanaticism, the victim, too, of the revolutionary fervour he had himself fanned but which has now faded in his case into bored indifference. The ugly truth of history had never been revealed with so much candour: in this portrayal Büchner was far ahead of his day.

With the same humanitarian sympathy and psychological insight he laid bare the sufferings of Woyzeck, a helpless victim *par excellence*, partly the dupe of unscrupulous superiors and fellow-men, partly the prey of his own incomprehensions. The technique Büchner used in these plays anticipates the collage effects of the modern 'Stationendrama' in giving a series of dramatic impressions rather than an action which, in Lessing's sense, links events in a chain of cause and effect. *Woyzeck* has a loosely organized scheme that allows considerable freedom of interpretation, particularly at the end of the tragedy, without detriment to the spectator's understanding of the total dramatic intent. Büchner's modernity is shown in this handling of dramatic form no less than in his choice of tragic themes.

There is considerable similarity in theme if not in performance between *Dantons Tod* and Robert Griepenkerl's political plays *Maximilian Robespierre* (1851) and *Die Girondisten* (1852). The failure of revolutionary action is also treated, in another métier, in Ferdinand Lassalle's *Franz von Sickingen* (1857-8). It challenges comparison with *Götz von Berlichingen*. But whereas Goethe presented his hero as attempting to arrest the march of social change and involving himself in political guilt by his association with the peasants, Lassalle's Sickingen is a revolutionary who fails because he does not unambiguously support the peasants in their uprising. For Karl Marx and Friedrich Engels this did not go far enough: in their correspondence with Lassalle they criticized him for placing a 'Schillerian' hero rather than the revolutionary movement into the centre of the action.

Within the Age of Realism the only remaining dramatists of note are Ludwig Anzengruber and Ernst von Wildenbruch. The latter was most successful with his patriotic dramas on historical lines, particularly with *Die Karolinger* (1881), *Heinrich und Heinrichs Geschlecht* (1896) and *Die Rabensteinerin* (1907). He was also influenced by the Naturalists in writing *Die Haubenlerche* (1891).

Anzengruber is one of the few Austrian dramatists during this period whose realism consisted in social criticism. He differs from the Naturalists in espousing the cause not of the city proletariat but of the peasantry, and, moreover, in the interests of 'Volksaufklärung', not for political ends. He used a stylized form of dialect rather than actual peasant speech. Even with these limitations he revolutionized the Vienna theatre. His tragedies *Der Pfarrer von Kirchfeld* (1870), *Der Meineidbauer* (1871), *Die Kreuzlschreiber* (1872) and *Der G'wissenswurm* (1874) made a strong impression and are still effective stage pieces. He also transformed the traditional 'Posse' with his comedy *Doppelselbstmord* (1876), a parody of *Romeo and Juliet*. He treated the same theme as a middle-class tragedy in *Das Vierte Gebot* (1877).

## Poetry from Biedermeier to Realism

Romanticism did not come to a halt with the end of the movement from which it takes its name: it persists as an enduring trend whenever attempts are made in literature to probe beyond the here and now into the past or the future, beyond the phenomenal world conveyed by the senses into the realms apprehended through intuition and presentiment, beyond life into death, across the barriers of known reality into outer cosmic or inward spiritual dimensions.

In the third decade of the nineteenth century preoccupation with such themes was curtailed by the practical tasks which poets felt the new age enjoined upon them. Romanticism continued to flourish, often in combination with a leavening of Classical ingredients, in the work of some leading poets like Platen and Mörike. This conjunction produced unique results. But the novel feature of German poetry written during the decades following the Napoleonic Wars was the quality given to it by the prevailing realist trend. The term realism can only be used to describe lyric poetry in a limited sense: it is more readily applied to the novel and the drama. The clearest poetic manifestations are in the 'Tendenzdichtung' of 'Das junge Deutschland'; in the political poetry of Anastasius Grün, Herwegh, Hoffmann von Fallersleben, and Freiligrath; in the narrative forms that gained increasing prestige as the century progressed, and in those lyric genres where poets could state their emotional stresses with absolute psychological veracity.

Tradition and innovation held equal sway from the middle of the century onwards. Adherence to what went before is seen in the cultivation of the multiple verse forms from German, Romance, Classical and Oriental sources. In general the 'Lied' and the ballad are more widely represented than some of the intricate Romance and Oriental structures favoured by the Romantics. The innovations appear as three kinds of poetry that emerged in a new way during the nineteenth century: 'Zeitgedichte', 'Dinggedichte' and Symbolist poetry. For the greater part poetry was written in accordance with the established view, as represented among others in the aesthetic writings of Hegel, Schopenhauer and Hebbel, that lyric utterance is essentially subjective in contrast to the 'objective' presentations of the drama and the novel. The expression of an individual poet's feelings was everywhere held to be the hallmark of good lyric writing: the lyric ego manifests itself in the articulation of personal experiences, in 'Erlebnisdichtung'. Such over-simplified valuations began to be modified with the appearance of the above-mentioned innovations. Just as Büchner and Grabbe anticipated the 'Stationendrama' of the twentieth century, so Mörike paved the way for 'Dinggedichte', C. F. Meyer for Symbolism, Heine for the political poetry of the present century.

The work of these three initiators represents a growing tendency to fashion more objective poetry. In addition to the form and the substance of individual poems, this propensity is seen in the care taken by Heine and C. F. Meyer in composing cycles of poems and in planning their volumes of collected verse on architectonic lines. In doing so they reduced the importance of an isolated lyric utterance and made it part of an integrated design.

Different combinations of Classical and Romantic elements can be discerned in the poetry of Friedrich Rückert and August Graf von Platen-Hallermünde. In his patriotic verse, the best of which is *Geharnischte Sonette* (1814), Rückert failed to make the same impact as Körner and the other 'Freiheitsdichter'. He had more success with *Liebesfrühling* (1844) and, posthumously, with *Kindertotenlieder* (written in 1834 but not published until 1872). Both collections are examples of

'Erlebnisdichtung', largely of indifferent quality. His out-standing contributions are his translations from Oriental literatures, notably from the Arabic and the Persian, as in *Die Makamen des Hariri* (1826–37), *Die Weisheit des Brahmanen* (1836–9), *Rostem und Suhrab* (1838). In this field he continued the work begun by Goethe and Friedrich Schlegel, and with greater authority: he studied Oriental languages under Joseph von Hammer-Purgstall in Vienna. Rückert also wrote dramas, for example *Napoleon* (1815–18), a trilogy, *Saul und David* (1843), *Herodes der Grosse* (1844), *Christofero Colombo* (1845); they have little intrinsic value.

Platen's dramas have greater significance, if only in historical perspective. They belong to the genre of 'Märchen-spiele', for example *Der gläserne Pantoffel* (1823), or are satirical comedies such as *Die verhängnisvolle Gabel* (1826) and *Der romantische Ödipus* (1829) directed, respectively, against the modish 'Schicksalstragödie' and against Heine and Immer-mann. These caricatures indicate Platen's hostile attitude towards some of the literary trends of the day.

His poetry shows the influence of Goethe and Rückert in his collections *Ghaselen* (1821) and *Neue Ghaselen* (1823). He also wrote a number of ballads, the best known being 'Das Grab im Busento' and, following another literary convention of the time, a series of poems on the condition of Poland. But his most distinguished work lies in his handling of such diverse forms as the sonnet (especially in *Sonette aus Venedig*, 1825), eclogue, ode, idyll and hymn. In the poems belonging to these latter genres he based himself on Theocritus and Pindar and so kept alive the tradition of the Weimar Classi-cists and of Hölderlin. He is a classicist in that he gave controlled expression to his personal afflictions and inward uncertainties. His dissatisfaction with conditions in con-temporary Germany and his devotion to southern art led him into voluntary exile in Italy where he gained the same kind of inspiration for his poetry as Goethe had done forty years earlier, without, however, achieving an enduring sense of liberation.

Nikolaus Lenau (Nikolaus Franz, Edler von Strehlenau) experienced a similar feeling of dissatisfaction but expressed it differently. His 'Weltschmerz' belongs to a trend that came down from the 'Sturm und Drang' and turned into deepest pessimism. This is the characteristic shown throughout the collections of poetry he published in 1832, 1838, 1844 and in the volume published posthumously by Anastasius Grün in 1851. In poems like 'Herbstklage' and the sonnets 'Einsamkeit', autumn becomes a season not of bounty but of impending decay, and Romantic longing is turned into despair. The steppes of Hungary, the plains and forests of Germany, American and Canadian prairies are all imbued with foreboding. The whispered sounds described in the 'Schilflieder', a distinctive series of poems, evoke a like feeling. Lenau wrote few poems celebrating human companionship and his love poetry conveys little sense of satisfaction. He took up Klopstock's theme of 'die künftige Geliebte' but treated it with far less assurance and exhilaration.

As with the image of nature, so with that of humanity. He differs from both Classicists and Romantics in his preference for the outcasts of society. His wanderers suffer sharper unease than even Eichendorff's 'verspäteter Wanderer'. The subjects of his 'Polenlieder' are refugees rather than fighters for the freedom of their country, his Red Indians dispossessed beings in despair, the gypsies of 'Die drei Zigeuner' carefree only because they have contempt for life. The same predilection accounts for his choosing Faust and Don Juan as subjects for semi-dramatic, semi-lyrical works: they are prototypes of nihilistic despair. Towards the end of his creative life he wrote *Die Albigenser* (1842), an epic work like the earlier *Savonarola* of 1837. A study of Hegel's philosophy of history gave Lenau new insights and offered possibilities of escape from his ingrained despondency through revolutionary action. But this approach to realism remained unachieved.

His influence confirmed strains of melancholy in two poets of similar temperament but inferior talent, Heinrich Leuthold (1827–79) and Ferdinand von Saar whose best poetic works are, respectively *Lieder der Riviera* (1837) and *Wiener Elegien* (1893).

Without going to the extremes of Lenau's pessimism, the most notable writings of almost every major poet of the post-Romantic era are fraught with expressions of uncertainty and doubt. Annette, Freiin von Droste-Hülshoff is no exception. Taken as a whole her work is epic rather than lyric. Even discounting her prose fiction and such considerable narrative poems as 'Das Hospiz auf dem grossen Sankt Bernhard' (1827–34), 'Des Arztes Vermächtnis' (1828–30), 'Die Schlacht im Loener Bruch' (1836–8) and 'Der Spiritus familiaris des Rosstauschers' (1842), her collections of verse published in 1838 and 1844 reveal her aptness for objective presentation. They contain beside her ballads, a number of 'Zeitbilder' and descriptive poems in the sections 'Heidebilder' and 'Fels, Wald und See'. In cultivating these genres she moved in the direction of Realism, but it is Realism of an individual kind. She possessed considerable powers of observation and exercised her skill in registering the details of vegetative and insect life and in evoking the atmosphere of her native Westfalian landscape, especially the aura of dread which emanates from its heaths and moorlands (e.g. in 'Geierpfiff', 'Der Knabe im Moor').

But her poetry is deceptively impersonal. She wrote no love poems and tried to conceal the inner world of her being, yet in many passages of her posthumous works *Letzte Gaben* and in *Das geistliche Jahr* (publ. 1851) a different mood prevails. In this latter cycle of 72 poems written between 1818 and 1839 she had planned to offer straightforward explanations of the most significant days in the Christian calendar, but they grew into disclosures of her own profoundly disturbed religious life. Subjective utterance here took unintentional precedence. A similar bias comes out in much of her best poetry, for example 'Spiegelbild' and 'Durchwachte Nacht'. Her work has been one-sidedly classified as belonging to the 'Biedermeier' trend. Far from testifying to her successful withdrawal into an inner sanctuary of calm or to her unhesitating acceptance of traditional values, her work exhibits a characteristic combination of extroversion and pre-occupation with a turbulent world of inward doubts and fears.

Eduard Mörike can be cited as a representative of 'Bieder-meier' with greater justification. The claim may be sub-stantiated from his life by his avoidance of involvement with the enigmatic adventuress Maria Meyer who yet held the greatest fascination for him, and, from his work, by poems like 'Verborgenheit', the epic 'Idylle vom Bodensee' (1846) and the genre piece 'Der alte Turmhahn' (1852). His readi-ness to flee from threatened turmoil, however, is matched by an enduring interest in the occult and in the natural manifes-tations of dynamic vitality. In poems such as 'An einem Wintermorgen, vor Sonnenaufgang', 'Nachts' and 'Um Mitternacht' he achieved his most memorable effects when depicting the interplay of light and dark, movement and repose in imagery of inimitable suggestiveness and rhythms of great subtlety.

In his other work he cultivated a larger range of lyric forms than most of his contemporaries. He went back to the German Anacreontics of the eighteenth century and further back still to the Greek and Roman originals. In 1840 and 1855 he published selections from the poetry of Theocritus and Catullus and in 1864 edited Degen's *Anakreon und die soge-nannten anakreontischen Lieder*. This side of his work is unique in nineteenth-century German poetry: the revival of Anacreon-ticism redressed the balance which the laments of solitaries like Lenau had upset. Humour is rare in German poetry at this time except in the form of satire as practised by Heine and, differently, by Wilhelm Busch. Mörike's 'Der alte Turmhahn' has genuine humour born of detachment and disengagement. His poems 'Der Kehlkopf' and 'Die Streich-kröte' even look forward to the work of Christian Morgen-stern and of twentieth-century writers of nonsense verse.

His technical skill is exceptional in the handling of such diverse forms as hexameters, the Sapphic ode, sonnets, alexandrines, 'Knittelvers' and free verse. He wrote with equal dexterity in the idiom of German folk poetry and balladry ('Das verlassene Mägdlein', 'Schön-Rohtraut', 'Die Geister am Mummelsee', 'Die traurige Krönung') and in his own style created subtly differentiating and balancing effects. His contribution to German poetry went further: with his short yet pregnant poem 'Auf eine Lampe' he offered a 'Dinggedicht' of the kind later poets were to cultivate more extensively.

The interplay of tradition and innovation takes a different turn in the poetry of Heinrich Heine. He is the first great politically committed writer of the nineteenth century who changed from metaphysical 'Weltschmerz' to social criticism. He played a dual role, even an ambivalent part. Most successful in assuring the continuance of Romanticism, he also cut it short by exercising an extreme form of its own irony. In his hands Romantic Irony became a Realist's antidote to sentimental self-indulgence. The range of lyric forms at his command was relatively small; on the whole he confined himself to writing 'Lieder', ballads, free verse and sonnets; even in his longer poetic works he employed the basic folksong modes. But he used them in a way they had never been used before.

Heine's political interests developed fully only after he had settled in Paris in 1831. In *Das Buch der Lieder* (1827), his first comprehensive collection containing most of his previously published poetic work, tradition still outweighs innovation as far as choice of themes is concerned. What is already new is the impact of his personality in the evocation of feeling and the exercise of wit. No less significant is what has come to be recognized as the impersonal nature of much of this poetry. It has been shown that the love poems of *Junge Leiden* and *Die Heimkehr* are not autobiographical in the usual sense; at least they do not truly reflect his love relations with his cousins Therese and Amalie. Even at this early stage Heine's poetry represents his desire to transcend subjectivity by constructing poetic fictions rather than rendering autobiographical facts. Increasing awareness of this truth has led to keener recognition of his methods of objectification. Barker Fairley has traced the recurrent images in his work drawn from music and dance, theatre and ceremony, carnival and costume as well as from the animal world. These images occur in his later poetry as much as his earlier, and give his work a greater measure of consistency than is allowed by those who only stress his palpable self-contradictions.

The continuity as well as the originality of Heine's work can be demonstrated by reference to one of his leading themes. Exile is a state which goes beyond his personal experience: he saw it as a fundamental condition of existence in the modern world. Accepting Schiller's and Schlegel's distinctions between ancient Greek and modern European poetry and affirming Hegel's philosophy of history, he lamented the exile of the Greek gods. For Heine they have not, as for Hölderlin, departed in order to reappear when the era of night has passed: they have been banished irretrievably and live in degrading exile. Nor did he envisage, as Nietzsche did, a process of eternal recurrence. His solution was social reform or, if unavailing, revolution, in the belief that man can create a heaven on earth. This is the source of his accepting Saint Simonian and Marxist views. He expressed them in much of his later writing while also venting his revulsion from what their realization would entail.

An important aspect of Heine's craftsmanship may be seen in the way he fashioned his collections, namely *Neue Gedichte* (1844) containing the greater number of political 'Zeitgedichte'; *Der Romanzero* (1851) comprising *Historien, Lamentationen* and *Hebräische Melodien*; and the posthumous *Letzte Gedichte* (1869). He changed individual poems that had already appeared elsewhere to conform with the remainder of the volume in which they now found a place, and he arranged them in such a way that they formed structures of carefully graduated moods and melodies. The greatness of Heine's poetry lies in its combination of haunting appeal to the emotions and pungent intellectual stimulation. Its unity can best be seen not in the consistency with which he expressed feelings and convictions but in his ability to create antithetic yet integrated aesthetic compositions.

The unique quality of his achievement may be assessed by comparing his political verse with that of his immediate contemporaries. The authors of 'Das junge Deutschland' were singularly lacking in lyric talent: their best energy went into writing novels, dramas and critical or polemical tracts. Among other poets whose work shows political bias, Anastasius Grün played a part with his criticism of Metternich in *Spaziergänge eines Wiener Poeten* (1831), likewise Franz von Dingelstedt with *Lieder eines kosmopolitischen Nachtwächters* (1840). Among the Germans, August Heinrich Hoffmann von Fallersleben in *Unpolitische Lieder* (1840), and Ferdinand Freiligrath in *Ein Glaubensbekenntnis* (1844) and *Ça ira!* (1846) achieved notable examples of political verse without rivalling Heine's incisiveness. After 1848 Fallersleben and Freiligrath gave up revolutionary politics and wrote patriotic verse instead. Georg Herwegh is the only poet in this group who, in his best known collection *Gedichte eines Lebendigen* (1841), as well as in his later poetry, equalled some of Heine's achievements.

Political verse is of minor importance in the poetry of Theodor Storm and of Gottfried Keller. The Romantic heritage subsists in Storm's 'Erinnerungslyrik' with its recollective nostalgia, while his leaning towards Poetic Realism is manifested in his evocations of scenes from the landscape of Schleswig-Holstein and from his own domestic life. He began with publishing, in the company of the Mommsen brothers, *Liederbuch dreier Freunde* in 1843, followed by *Sommergeschichten und Lieder* in 1851. His collected verse appeared in 1852. Although enlargements of this collection came out in different editions as late as 1885, Storm's lyric productivity, unlike his output of fiction, reached its culmination during the first decades of his literary career. He excelled in writing songs of appealing simplicity and alluring musicality, but he showed little liking for larger or more intricate forms.

Gottfried Keller's poetry has greater range. He is the most

representative lyricist whose work can be assigned to Poetic Realism. His political verse, which he included in his first collection of poems (1846) under the title *Lebendig begraben*, belongs only to his earliest phase when he associated with Freiligrath and Herwegh. In his later work he maintained his interest in the cause of civic liberty, but increasingly followed a conservative course, as may be seen in the epic *Der Apotheker von Chamounix* (1860), a parody of Heine's *Romanzero*. In the *Neuere Gedichte* of 1851 Keller's brand of realism is evident in his treatment of familiar themes as in 'Winternacht', 'Stille der Nacht', 'Abendlied' and the cycle 'Waldlieder'. Balladry and narrative poetry come to the fore in his *Gesammelte Gedichte* of 1883. These volumes show where his most individual contribution lies. After surmounting the difficulties of his early life, he came under the influence of agnostic philosophers like D. F. Strauss and L. Feuerbach. He gained a cheerful hold on life which he expressed with unremitting zeal tempered only by a form of mysticism he took over from Angelus Silesius.

At a further remove from Romanticism than many of his contemporaries is Friedrich Hebbel. As a poet he went through his apprenticeship by undergoing the influence first of Schiller then of Uhland. This is evident in the ballads contained in the 1842 collection of his verse. The *Gesamtausgabe* of 1857 shows his more original achievement which consists mainly in his ability to fuse the reflective and emotional modes in an unusual way. His poems are invariably graver in tone than Keller's similar attempts, particularly in his experimental use of sonnets and epigrams.

Like Hebbel, Theodor Fontane began with writing ballads, a collection of which appeared in 1861. He modelled himself rather more on Percy's *Reliques* and Sir Walter Scott's *Minstrelsy*, than on German examples of the genre. He took his subject matter from Nordic, English, Scottish and Prussian history and legend and, at a later stage, included quite modern material, for example in 'Die Brück' am Tay'. The 'Romanzen' cycle 'Von der schönen Rosamunde' appeared in 1850, a collection of ballads in 1861. A feature of his other poetry is his treatment of themes showing his sense of social justice. Here again he found a stimulus in English poets. Compared with this side of his work his patriotic poems occasioned by the wars of 1866 and 1870 have less intrinsic value. Editions of his collections appeared in 1851, 1875, 1889 and 1892. The last of these shows an increase in epigrammatic and didactic verse where Fontane displays the same ironic sympathy with human foibles which so eminently characterizes his best narrative work.

Conrad Ferdinand Meyer resembles Fontane in dividing his attention between prose fiction and poetry. In the latter category he published three volumes: *Zwanzig Balladen von einem Schweizer* (1864), *Romanzen und Bilder* (1869) and *Gedichte* (first published in 1882). His originality is most easily recognized when one compares the changes he made in the five editions of his *Gedichte* he published between 1882 and 1892, with Fontane's method of enlarging his collections. The artistry of Meyer's procedure has been shown to consist in an architectonic arrangement by which he pursued an increasingly objective design. Thus the final volume represents an integrated structure although the poems of which it is composed were written over a large number of years. Meyer did not include them in the form in which he first composed or published them: the new place he assigned to them exacted textual alterations of more than passing significance. Arrangement of poetry in coordinated cycles became a feature of German poetry in the nineteenth century. None achieved a greater degree of craftsmanship in this area than C. F. Meyer, although his individual poems do not always measure up in intrinsic value to those of many of his predecessors or contemporaries.

His poetry represents a culmination of nineteenth century developments in another respect. Biographical facts are on the whole irrelevant for the interpretation of his best work. There are, for example, no poems about friends or about cities like Zürich and Lausanne where he spent so much of his time. He almost completely ignored modern conditions of life in his poetry. This shows how different his realism is from that of his contemporaries. He is a realist in constantly striving to externalize his inward experiences. He is not an 'Erlebnisdichter' in the accepted sense, but a poet who transmuted outward objects into analogues of his own states of mind and into paradigms of transcendent reality. Thus he became in essence a Symbolist even as a creator of 'Ding-gedichte'.

Meyer also wrote cycles of poems in a genre differing from those of his volume of *Gedichte*. The seventy-one parts of *Huttens letzte Tage* (1871) form a series of vignettes on the exile of the great Humanist whom Zwingli befriended and harboured at the end of his life. The work is written in iambic couplets which give it an epigrammatic rather than a consistently epic quality. It established Meyer's reputation although, like the comparable *Engelberg* (1872), it is a contribution to German literature of lesser distinction than some of his 'Novellen' or his other poetry.

A feature of German literature during the second half of the nineteenth century is the revival of verse narratives in line with such earlier examples as Wieland's *Oberon*, Voss's *Luise* and Goethe's *Hermann und Dorothea*. The genre gained in popularity as the century progressed, but not to the same extent as the prose 'Novelle'. While Joseph Victor von Scheffel achieved great success with a mixture of romance and humour in *Der Trompeter von Säckingen* (1854), Hebbel failed when he treated a combination of social and domestic themes in *Mutter und Kind* (1859). Fritz Reuter depicted the feudal conditions of his native Mecklenburg with much greater force and candour in *Kein Hüsung* (1857) but lessened its impact through using Low German dialect. An epic work of different scope and less intrinsic quality is Wilhelm Jordan's *Nibelunge* (1867–74) which, however, enjoyed great esteem during the last decades of the century.

Before the advent of Naturalism a group of poets who formed the 'Münchner Dichterschule' made a similarly widespread appeal. The principal members are Emanuel Geibel whose *Gedichte*, first published in 1840, reached their hundredth edition in 1884; Friedrich Bodenstedt author of the widely read *Die Lieder des Mirza Schaffy* (1851), Hermann Lingg and Paul Heyse (1830–1914) whose voluminous production includes 'Novellen' written in verse. The work of all these writers may now be considered to have at most historical interest, particularly in one respect. None of the great poets of the nineteenth century after the Romantics belonged to an organized group or a literary school, except Fontane who for a time was associated with a literary club 'Tunnel über der Spree' and whose journal *Argo* he helped to edit in 1854. The members of the 'Münchner Dichterkreis' belonged to the 'Gesellschaft der Krokodile', a literary society which flourished from 1856 until 1883. They contemptuously dismissed the work of Gottfried Kinkel, Victor von Scheffel and Rudolf Baumbach as 'Butzenscheibenlyrik', but in historical perspective there is little difference between them. Both parties opposed 'Tendenz' in poetry and almost exclusively cultivated its traditional themes and forms, often with considerable technical skill. The Naturalist attack was largely directed against the literary conservatism represented by these two groups of writers.

# Select Bibliography

# SELECT BIBLIOGRAPHY

# 1. GENERAL WORKS OF REFERENCE

P. Merker, W. Stammler (eds.), *Reallexikon der dt. Lit.gesch.*, 4 vols. 1925–31; 2nd ed. W. Kohlschmidt, W. Mohr in progress (A–O, 2 vols., 1955–65). Definitions and histories of literary forms and topics.

W. Stammler (ed.) *Dt. Philologie im Aufriss*, 3 vols., 1952–7; 2nd ed. 1957–62. Substantial monographs on major topics of German language and literature, e.g. novel, Novelle, drama.

R. v. Liliencron, F. X. v. Wegele (eds.), *Allgemeine dt. Biographie*, 56 vols., 1875–1912; repr. in progress, 1967 ff.

*Neue dt. Biographie*, 1953 ff., ed. Hist. Kommission bei der Bayerischen Akademie der Wissenschaften.

Separate reference to these primary sources is not generally made below.

# 2. BIBLIOGRAPHICAL AIDS

K. Goedeke, *Grundriss zur Gesch. der dt. Dichtung*, 13 vols., 2nd ed. 1884–1953; vol. 14, 1959; vol. 15, first fascicule, 1964; 3rd ed. so far only vol. 4 (Gottsched-Goethe), 1960. The most comprehensive catalogue of work on German authors and the history of German literature from the Middle Ages to 1830. Vol. 1 of the new series of Goedeke (1955–62) covers the period 1830–80.

J. Körner, *Bibl. Handbuch des dt. Schrifttums*, 1949. Lists in highly condensed form standard eds and secondary literature up till 1948; more useful than Goedeke for rapid reference.

W. Kosch, *Dt. Lit.-Lexikon*, 4 vols., 1927–30; 2nd ed. 1949–58.

F. A. Schmitt, *Stoff- u. Motivgesch. der dt. Lit., Eine Bibl.*, 1959; 2nd ed. 1965. Lists secondary lit. on the history and occurrence of lit. themes and motifs.

H. W. Eppelsheimer, C. Köttelwesch, *Bibl. der dt. Lit.wissenschaft*, 1957 ff. Current bibl. of secondary lit. since 1945; annually since vol. 3.

*Germanistik*, 1960 ff. Quarterly bibl. of current work with annual index and reviews of major items.

*Publications of the Modern Language Association of America. Annual Bibl.*, 1922 ff. Comprehensive annual list of work published all over the world.

*The Year's Work in Modern Language Studies*, 1931 ff. Selective critical annual bibl.

P. Raabe, *Einführung in die Bücherkunde zur dt. Lit.wissenschaft*, 5th ed. 1966.

J. Hansel, *Bücherkunde f. Germanisten. Studienausgabe*, 1961; 4th ed. 1967. Concise guide to bibl. aids.

J. Hansel, *Personalbibl. zur dt. Lit. gesch. Studienausgabe*, 1967. Lists bibl. information under individual authors.

D. K. Johnson, 'German lang. and lit. serials', *International Library Rev.*, 1969.

# 3. COLLECTIONS OF TEXTS

DL  **Dt.** *Literatur in Entwicklungsreihen*, ed. H. Kindermann, 109 of 250 vols. planned, 1928–43. Some series are much less complete than others; a certain number of volumes have been reprinted. The relevant series are: *Aufklärung, Irrationalismus, Klassik, Romantik, Politische Dichtung, Naturalismus, Vom Naturalismus zur neueren Volksdichtung, Dt. Selbstzeugnisse.*

DLD  *Dt. Literaturdenkmale des 18. und 19. Jahrhunderts*, 1881–1914; new series (vol. 1 only) 1924.

DN  *Dt. Neudrucke. Reihe Texte des 18. Jahrhunderts*, 1965 ff.

DNL  *Dt. Nationallitteratur*, 1882–99. 164 vols. down to Immermann and Lenau.

ND  *Neudrucke dt. Literaturwerke: Neue Folge*, 1961 ff.

# 4. ABBREVIATIONS

| PBB | *Beitragen zur Geschichte der deutschen Sprache und Literatur*, 1874 ff. |
| PEGS | *Publications of the English Goethe Society*, 1886–1912; new series 1924 ff. |
| PMLA | *Publications of the Modern Language Association of America*, 1886 ff. |
| RLC | *Revue de littérature comparée*, 1921 ff. |
| SuF | *Sinn und Form*, 1949 ff. |
| WB | *Weimarer Beiträge*, 1955 ff. |
| WW | *Wirkendes Wort*, 1950 ff. |
| ZfdA | *Zeitschrift für deutsches Altertum und deutsche Literatur*, 1841 ff. |
| ZdU | *Zeitschrift für deutschen Unterricht* (from 1920: *Z. für Deutschkunde*), 1887–1963. |
| ZfdPh | *Zeitschrift für deutsche Philologie*, 1869 ff. |

## TEXTUAL ABBREVIATIONS

| bibl. | bibliography, Bibliographie; bibliographical, -isch |
| bio. | biography, Biographie; biographical, -isch |
| dt. | deutsch (and all inflexions) |
| diss. | dissertation, Dissertation |
| ed. | edition; edited (by) |
| f. | für |
| Fs. | Festschrift (followed by name of scholar to whom it was presented) |
| Ger. | German |
| Germ. | Germanic, germanisch |
| Gesch. | Geschichte, geschichtlich |
| hist. | history, historical |
| Jb. | Jahrbuch |
| Jh. | Jahrhundert |
| lit. | literature, Literatur; literary, -isch |
| repr. | reprinted |
| rev. | revised (by) |
| u. | und |
| Zs. | Zeitschrift |

# 5. GENERAL POLITICAL AND ECONOMIC HISTORIES

(See also below, *The Eighteenth Century* and *The Nineteenth Century*)
*New Cambridge modern history* (relevant sections in vols. 7–11).

J. Roach, *A bibl. of modern history*, 1968 (companion vol. to *New Cambridge Modern History*).

B. Gebhart, *Handbuch der dt. Gesch.*, 4 vols., 8th ed., 1954–9 ed. H. Grundmann.

G. Barraclough, *The origins of modern Germany*, 1946; 2nd, rev. ed. 1947; repr. 1966.

K. S. Pinson, *Modern Germany: its history and civilization*, 2nd ed. 1966.

H. S. Steinberg, *A short history of Germany*, 1946.

P. Kampfmeyer, *Gesch. der modernen Gesellschaftsklassen in Deutschland* 1910.

W. Sombart, *Der Bourgeois*, 1913.

G. P. Gooch, *Germany and the French Revolution*, 1920.

K. Epstein, *The genesis of German Conservatism*, 1966.

# 6. HISTORY OF IDEAS AND CULTURE

J. Bithell, *Germany: a companion to German Studies*, 1932; 5th ed. 1955.

A. Farquharson (ed.), *The German mind and outlook*, 1945.

H. Gollwitzer, *Europabild u. Europagedanke. Beiträge zur dt. Geistes-Gesch. des 18. u. 19. Jhs*, 1951.

A. Kleinberg, *Die dt. Dichtung in ihrem sozialen, zeit- und geistesgesch. Bedingungen*, 1927.

H. Kohn, *The mind of Germany: the education of a nation*, 1961.

W. Mönch, *Dt. Kultur von der Aufklärung bis zur Gegenwart*, 1962.

G. Steinhausen, *Kulturgesch. der Deutschen in der Neuzeit*, 2nd ed. 1918.

G. Steinhausen, *Gesch. der dt. Kultur*, 3rd ed. 1929.

K. Viëtor, *Dt. Dichten u. Denken von der Aufklärung bis zum Realismus*, 3rd ed. 1958.

O. F. Walzel, *Vom Geistesleben des 18. und 19. Jhs.*, 1911.

H. Boeschenstein, *Dt. Gefühlskultur*, 2 vols., 1954, 1966.

E. M. Butler, *The tyranny of Greece over Germany*, 1935.

I. M. Barth, *Das lit. Weimar*, 1969.

A. Müller, *Landschaftserlebnis u. Landschaftsbild. Studien zur dt. Dichtung des 18. Jhs. u. der Romantik*, 1955.

G. C. Schoolfield, *The figure of the musician in German lit.*, 1956.

A. Schöne, *Säkularisation als sprachbildende Kraft. Studien zur Dichtung dt. Pfarrersöhne*, Pal 226 (1958).

G. Könnecke, *Bilderatlas zur Gesch. der dt. Lit.*, 2nd ed. 1912.

G. v. Wilpert, *Dt. Lit. in Bildern*, 2nd ed. 1965.

K. H. Halbach, *Vergleichende Zeittafel zur dt. Lit.-Gesch.*, 1952.

F. Schmitt, G. Fricke, *Dt. Lit. gesch. in Tabellen*, 3 vols., 2nd ed. 1960 ff.

J. M. Ritchie, *Periods in German lit.*, vol. 1, 1966, vol. 2, 1969.

F. Paulsen, *Das dt. Bildungswesen in seiner gesch. Entwicklung*, 1920.

O. Fambach, *Ein Jh. Literaturkritik 1750–1850*, 4 vols. (of 6), 1959–63 (reviews and correspondence thematically arranged).

D. W. Schumann, 'The Latecomer', *GQ*, 1966.

H. Mayer (ed.) *Meisterwerke dt. Literaturkritik*, 2 parts in 3 vols.,

237

1954–6 (selection of major critical texts from early eighteenth down to twentieth century).

H. Hatzfeld, *Wechselbeziehungen zwischen der dt. Lit. u. den anderen europäischen Literaturen*, 1927.

L. M. Price, *English-German literary influences: bibl. and survey*, 1919/20.

L. M. Price, *The reception of English lit. in Germany*, 1932.

L. M. Price, *English lit. in Germany*, 1953.

L. M. Price, 'The English domestic novel in Germany 1740–1799', *Libris et litteris*, Fs. H. Tiemann (1959).

# 7. AESTHETICS AND CRITICISM

## GENERAL

B. Bosanquet, *A history of aesthetics*, 1892.

E. Utitz, *Gesch. der Ästhetik*, 1932.

K. Gilbert, H. Kuhn, *A history of aesthetics*, 1953.

R. Bayer, *Histoire de l'esthetique*, 1961.

H. v. Stein, *Die Entstehung der neueren Ästhetik*, 1886.

E. Auerbach, *Mimesis*, 1946; English transl. 1953.

E. R. Curtius, *Europäische Lit. u. lateinisches Mittelalter*, 1948.

R. Wellek, A. Warren, *Theory of literature*, 1954.

R. Wellek, *A history of modern criticism*, 4 vols, 1955–66.

H. Lotze, *Gesch. der Ästhetik in Deutschland*, 1868.

B. Markwardt, *Gesch. der dt. Poetik*, 5 vols., 1937–65.

E. Staiger, *Grundbegriffe der Poetik*, 1956.

H. Seidler, *Die Dichtung. Wesen, Form u. Dasein*, 1959.

W. Kayser, *Die Wahrheit der Dichter*, 1959.

J. Volkelt, *Ästhetik des Tragischen*, 1917.

H. Kreuzer (ed.), *Mathematik u. Dichtung. Versuch zur Frage einer exakten Literaturwissenschaft*, 1965; 2nd ed. 1967.

W. Iser (ed.), *Immanente Ästhetik. Ästhetische Reflexion. Lyrik als Paradigma der Moderne*, 1966.

## EIGHTEENTH CENTURY

F. Schlümer, *Das Problem der Ästhetik in der Philosophie des 18. Jhs*, 1941.

K. R. Scherpe, *Gattungspoetik im 18. Jh. Entwicklung von Gottsched bis Herder*, 1968.

A. Pellegrini, *Gottsched, Bodmer, Breitinger e la poetica dell' Aufklärung*, 1952.

F. Braitmaier, *Gesch. der poetischen Theorie u. Kritik von den Diskursen der Maler bis Lessing*, 1889; repr. 1947.

R. Sommer, *Grundzüge einer Gesch. der dt. Psychologie u. Ästhetik von Wolff-Baumgarten bis Kant-Schiller*, 1892.

E. Utitz, *J.J.W. Heinse u. die Ästhetik zur Zeit der dt. Aufklärung*, 1907.

H. Wolf, *Versuch einer Gesch. des Geniebegriffs in der Ästhetik*, 1923.

B. Rosenthal, *Der Geniebegriff des Aufklärungszeitalters*, 1933.

P. Grappin, *La théorie du génie dans le préclassicisme allemand*, 1952.

A. Nivelle, *Les théories esthétiques en Allemagne de Baumgarten à Kant*, 1955.

A. Bäumler, *Kants Kritik der Urteilskraft. Das Irrationalitätsproblem in der Ästhetik u. Logik des 18. Jhs*, 1923.

G. Jacobs, *Herders und Kants Ästhetik*, 1907.

F. Kühnemann, *Kants und Schillers Begründung der Ästhetik*, 1895.

J. Vorländer, *Kant–Goethe–Schiller*, 1907.

O. Harnack, *Die klassische Ästhetik der Deutschen*, 1892.

H. Stocker, *Zur Kunstanschauung des 18. Jhs von Winckelmann bis zu Wackenroder*, 1904.

## ROMANTICISM AND NINETEENTH CENTURY

B. A. Sørensen, *Symbol u. Symbolismus in den ästhetischen Theorien des 18. Jhs u. der dt. Romantik*, 1963.

F. Brie, *Ästhetische Weltanschauung in der Lit. des 19. Jhs*, 1921.

E. v. Hartmann, *Die dt. Ästhetik seit Kant*, 1886.

L. Knox, *The aesthetic theories of Kant, Hegel and Schopenhauer*, 1936.

P. Demetz, *Marx, Engels u. die Dichter*, 1959.

H. Kuhn, *Die Vollendung der klassischen dt. Ästhetik durch Hegel*, 1931.

C. D. Pflaum, *Die Poetik der dt. Romantiker*, 1909.

O. Walzel, *Romantisches*, 1934.

H. v. Kleinmayr, *Welt- u. Kunstanschauung des Jungen Deutschland*, 1930.

H. Reinhardt, *Die Dichtungstheorie der sogenannten poetischen Realisten*, 1939.

# 8. GENERAL THEORY AND HISTORY OF LITERARY FORMS

## PROSE NARRATIVE

F. Martini, 'Gesch. u. Poetik des Romans. Ein Literaturbericht', *DU* 3 (1951).

C. H. Handschin, 'Bibl. zur Technik des neueren dt. Romans', *MLN* 24, 25 (1909, 1910).

J. R. Frey, 'Bibl. zur Theorie und Technik des dt. Romans 1910–1953', *MLN* 54, 69 (1939, 1954).

N. Pabst, 'Literatur zur Theorie des Romans' *DVLG* 34 (1960).

R. Grimm (ed.), *Dt. Romantheorien*, 1968.

M. L. Wolff, *Gesch. der Romantheorie. Von den Anfängen bis zur Mitte des 18. Jhs*, diss. Munich, 1915

H. Keiter, *Versuch einer Theorie des Romans u. der Erzählkunst*, 1876; 4th ed. by T. Kellen, *Der Roman*, 1912.

F. Spielhagen, *Beiträge zur Theorie u. Technik des Romans*, 1883.

R. Koskimies, *Theorie des Romans*, 1935, repr. 1966.

G. Lukács, *Die Theorie des Romans*, 1920, repr. 1963.

E. G. Kolbenheyer, 'The art of the German novel', *GLL* 1 (1936).

V. Klotz (ed.), *Zur Poetik des Romans*, 1965.

N. Miller (ed.), *Romananfänge. Versuch zu einer Poetik des Romans*, 1965.

H. Meyer, *Das Zitat in der Erzählkunst. Zur Gesch. u. Poetik des europäischen Romans*, 1961.

P. P. Sagave, *Recherches sur le roman social en Allemagne*, 1960 (on Goethe, Freytag, Fontane, Th. Mann and E. v. Salomon).

F. Bobertag, *Gesch. des Romans u. der ihm verwandten Dichtungsgattungen in Deutschland*, 2 vols., 1876–84.

H. H. Borcherdt, *Gesch. des Romans u. der Novelle in Deutschland* 1926 (from early Middle Ages to Wieland).

H. H. Borcherdt, *Der Roman der Goethezeit*, 1949.

H. Mielke, *Gesch. des dt. Romans*, 1904; 3rd ed. 1913.

H. Spiero, *Gesch. des dt. Romans*, 1950.

H. C. Hatfield, 'Realism in the German novel', *CL* 3 (1951) (from Jörg Wickram to Mann and Hesse).

R. Pascal, *The German novel*, 1956.

H. M. Waidson, *The changing pattern of the German novel*, 1961.

B. v. Wiese, *Der dt. Roman. Vom Barock bis zur Gegenwart. Struktur u. Gesch.*, 2 vols., 1963; 2nd ed. 1965.

H. Granzow, *Künstler u. Gesellschaft im Roman der Goethezeit*, diss. Bonn, 1960.

J. Schillemeit (ed.), *Interpretationen*, vol. 3, 1966.

W. Olbrich, J. Beer, *Der Romanführer*, vols. 1 and 2, 1950/1; 2nd ed. 1960.

J. Beer, W. Schuster, *Reclams Romanführer*, 1962 (with useful introductions).

V. Klotz (ed.), *Zur Poetik des Romans*, 1965.

F. C. Maatje, *Der Doppelroman: eine literatursystematische Studie über duplikative Erzählstrukturen*, 1964.

## VARIETIES OF THE NOVEL

### 'Robinsonaden' and other Voyages

H. Ullrich, *Defoes Robinson Crusoe, die Gesch. eines Weltbuches*, 1924.

F. Brüggemann, *Utopie u. Robinsonade*, 1914.

H. Ullrich, *Robinson u. Robinsonade*, 1898; *Nachtrag, Zs. f. Bücherfreunde* 11 (1907–8).

O. Deneke, *Robinson Crusoe in Deutschland. Die Frühdrucke* 1720–80, 1934.

L. Brandl, 'Vordefoesche Robinsonaden in der Weltlit.', *GRM* 5 (1913).

T. C. van Stockum, 'Robinson Crusoe, Vorrobinsonaden u. Robinsonaden', *Von F. Nicolai bis Th. Mann*, 1962.

A. Kippenberg, *Robinson in Deutschland bis zur Insel Felsenburg*, 1892.

H. F. Wagner, *Robinson u. Robinsonaden in unserer Jugendliteratur*, 1903.

B. Doerk, *Reiseroman u. Reisenovelle in Deutschland von Hermes bis Heine*, diss. Münster, 1925.

M. Link, *Der Reisebericht als lit. Kunstform von Goethe bis Heine*, diss. Köln, 1963.

P. B. Gove, *The imaginary voyage in prose fiction*, 1941.

R. Riemann, *Die Entwicklung des exotischen Romans in Deutschland*, 1910.

F. L. Lamport: 'Utopia' and 'Robinsonade', *OGS*, 1, 1966.

### Historical novel

A. v. Grolman, 'Über das Wesen des hist. Romans', *DVLG* 7 (1929).

G. Lukacs, *Der hist. Roman*, 1955; repr. 1965.

H. Stresau, 'Der hist. Roman', *Neue Rundschau* 47 (1936).

M. Wehrli, 'Der hist. Roman. Versuch einer Übersicht', *Helicon* 3 (1941).

R. du Moulin-Eckart, *Der hist. Roman in Deutschland*, 1905.

V. Klemperer, 'Die Arten der hist. Dichtung', *DVLG* 1 (1923).

H. Bock, K. Weitzel, *Der hist. Roman als Begleiter der Weltgesch.*, 3 vols, 1922–31.

G. Schmidt, 'Anmerkungen zum hist. Roman', *Die neue Literatur* 6 (1941).

R. Bauer, *Der hist. Trivialroman in Deutschland im ausgehenden 18. Jh.*, diss. Munich, 1930.

J. W. Appel, *Die Ritter-, Räuber- u. Schauerromantik*, 1889.

A. G. Murphy, *Banditry, chivalry and terror in German fiction 1790–1830*, diss. Chicago, 1936.

C. Müller-Fraureuth, *Die Ritter- und Räuberromane*, 1894; repr. 1965.

H. Garte, *Kunstform Schauerroman*, diss. Leipzig, 1935.

K. Fuss, *Der frühgotische Roman*, diss. Königsberg, 1941.

### 'Bildungsroman'

F. Martini, 'Der Bildungsroman: zur Gesch. des Wortes u. der Theorie', *DVLG* 35 (1961).

H. H. Borcherdt, 'Der dt. Bildungsroman', *Von dt. Art in Sprache und Dichtung* 5 (1941).

E. L. Stahl, *Die religiöse u. die humanitätsphilosophische Bildungsidee u. die Entstehung des dt. Bildungsromans im 18. Jh.*, 1934.

A. Bach, 'Das epische Bild im Bildungsroman von Goethe bis Thomas Mann', *GRM* 43 (1962).

M. Gerhard, *Der dt. Entwicklungsroman bis zu Goethes 'Wilhelm Meister'*, 1926.

K. Scheuten, *Seelengeschichte u. Entwicklungsroman*, diss. Bonn, 1934.

H. Germer, *The German novel of education from 1792 to 1805*, 1968.

L. Köhn, 'Entwicklungs- u. Bildungsroman. Ein Forschungsbericht', *DVLG* 42 (1968).

H. Reiss, *Goethe's novels*, 1969.

*Other types of novel*

E. Birch, *Der biographische Roman*, diss. Heidelberg, 1936.

K. Forstreuter, 'Die dt. Icherzählung. Eine Studie zu ihrer Gesch. u. Technik', *Germ. Stud.* 33 (1924).

K. R. Mendelkow, 'Der dt. Briefroman. Zum Problem der Polyperspektive im Epischen', *N.* 44 (1960).

G. Weymar, *Der dt. Briefroman*, diss. Hamburg, 1942.

E. T. Voss, *Erzählprobleme des Briefromans*, diss. Bonn, 1960.

E. Neumann, *Probleme des dt.-protestantischen Pfarrerstandes im Spiegel des Pfarrer-Romans*, diss. Freiburg i. Br., 1938.

A. Krüger, *Der humoristische Roman mit gegensätzlich verschränkter Bauform*, 1952.

R. Riemann, *Die Entwicklung des politischen Romans in Deutschland*, 1911.

R. v. Mohl, *Die Staats-Romane, ein Beitrag zur Lit. der Staats-Wissenschaften*, vol. 1 of *Gesch. u. Lit. der Staatswissenschaften*, 1855.

F. Kleinwächter, *Die Staatsromane*, 1891.

A. Voigt, *Die sozialen Utopien*, 1912.

G. Schmidt-Henkel (ed.), *Trivialliteratur*, 1964.

W. Nutz, *Der Trivialroman. Seine Formen u. seine Hersteller.* 1962.

M. Thalmann, *Der Trivialroman des 18. Jhs. u. der romantische Roman*, 1923.

M. Greiner, *Die Entstehung der modernen Unterhaltungsliteratur*, 1964.

K. I. Flessau, *Der moralische Roman. Studien zur gesellschaftskritischen Trivialliteratur der Goethezeit*, 1968.

H. F. Foltin, 'Die minderwertige Prosaliteratur. Einteilung und Bezeichnungen', *DVLG* 39 (1965).

R. Hackmann, *Die Anfänge des Romans in der Zeitung*, diss. Berlin 1938.

## NOVELLE AND OTHER PROSE FORMS

A. Hirsch, 'Der Gattungsbegriff 'Novelle' ', *Germ. Stud.* 64 (1928).

B. v. Arx, *Novellistisches Dasein. Spielraum einer Gattung in der Goethezeit*, diss. Zürich, 1954.

N. Pabst, 'Die Theorie der Novelle in Deutschland', *Romanistisches Jb.* 2 (1949).

K. K. Polheim, *Novellentheorie u. Novellenforschung 1945-64*, 1965.

E. K. Bennett, *A history of the German Novelle*, 1934; rev. and continued by H. M. Waidson, 1961.

H. Himmel, *Gesch. der dt. Novelle*, 1963.

J. Klein, *Gesch. der dt. Novelle von Goethe bis zur Gegenwart*, 4th ed. 1960.

B. v. Wiese, *Novelle*, 1963.

B. v. Wiese, *Die dt. Novelle von Goethe bis Kafka*, 2 vols. 1956, 1962.

F. Lockemann, *Gestalt u. Wandlungen der dt. Novelle*, 1957.

F. Lockemann, 'Die Bedeutung des Rahmens in der dt. Novellendichtung', *WW* 6 (1955/6).

H. O. Burger, 'Theorie und Wissenschaft von der dt. Novelle'. *DU* 3 (1951).

H. H. Malmede, *Wege zur Novelle. Theorie u. Interpretation der Gattung in der dt. Literaturwissenschaft*, 1966.

J. Schillemeit (ed.), *Interpretationen*, vol. 4, 1966.

J. Müller, 'Novelle und Erzählung', *EG* 16 (1961).

M. Lüthi, *Märchen*, 1962, 2nd ed. 1964.

K. J. Obenauer, *Das Märchen. Dichtung u. Deutung*, 1959.

A. Wesselski, *Versuch einer Theorie des Märchens*, Prager dt. Studien 45 (1931).

F. v. d. Leyen, K. Schier, *Das Märchen. Ein Versuch*, 4th ed. 1958.

L. Mackensen (ed.), *Handwörterbuch des dt. Märchens*, 2 vols. (A–G), 1930–40.

M. Lüthi, *Volksmärchen und Volkssage. Zwei Grundformen erzählender Dichtung*, 1961; 2nd ed. 1966.

A. Jolles, *Einfache Formen. Legende—Sage—Mythe—Rätsel—Kasus—Memorabile—Märchen—Witz*, 1930; 3rd ed. 1965.

G. Pfohl (ed.) *Das Epigramm*, 1969.

B. Berger, *Der Essay*, 1964.

L. Rohner, *Der dt. Essay. Materialien zur Gesch. u. Ästhetik einer Gattung*, 1966.

G. Hass, *Studien zur Form des Essays u. zu seinen Vorformen im Roman*, 1966.

K. Lazarowicz, *Verkehrte Welt. Vorstudien zu einer Gesch. der dt. Satire*, 1963.

H. Küntzel, *Essay u. Aufklärung*, 1969.

POETRY

*Theory*

E. Geiger, *Beiträge zu einer Ästhetik der Lyrik*, 1905.

H. Henel, 'Erlebnisdichtung u. Symbolismus', *DVLG* 32 (1958).

M. Kommerell, *Gedanken über Gedichte*, 1943.

R. N. Maier, *Das Gedicht. Über die Natur des Dichterischen u. der dichterischen Formen*, 1961.

G. Müller, *Grundformen der dt. Lyrik*, 1941.

K. Opfert, 'Das Dinggedicht', *DVLG* 4 (1926).

R. Petsch, *Die lyrische Dichtkunst*, 1939.

J. Pfeiffer, *Das lyrische Gedicht als ästhetisches Gebilde*, 1931.

E. Reitmeier, *Studien zum Problem der Dichtsammlung*, 1935.

H. Rosenfeld, *Das dt. Bildgedicht. Seine antiken Vorbilder und seine Entwicklung bis zur Gegenwart*, *Pal.* 90 (1935).

E. Witkop, *Das Wesen der Lyrik*, 1907.

H. O. Burger, *Wesen u. Ursprung der dt. Lyrik*, 1936.

### History

A. Closs, *The genius of the German lyric*, 1938; revised and enlarged 1965.

J. Klein, *Gesch. der dt. Lyrik von Luther bis zum Ausgang des 2. Weltkriegs*, 1957; repr. 1960.

R. Findeis, *Gesch. der dt. Lyrik*, 1914.

P. Witkop, *Die dt. Lyriker von Luther bis Nietzsche*, 1921.

R. Haller, *Gesch. der dt. Lyrik vom Ausgang des Mittelalters bis zu Goethes Tod*, 1967.

E. Ermatinger, *Die dt. Lyrik seit Herder*, 3 vols., 1925.

N. Macleod, *German lyric poetry*, 1930.

### Metre

A. Heusler, *Dt. Versgeschichte*, 3 vols., 1925–9; 2nd ed. 1956.

W. Kayser, *Gesch. des dt. Verses*, 1960.

W. Kayser, *Kleine dt. Versschule*, 1946; repr. 1965.

S. Chatman, *A theory of meter*, 1965.

O. Paul, *Dt. Metrik*, 1930; 5th ed. 1964.

F. Lockemann, *Der Rhythmus des dt. Verses*, 1960.

W. Bennett, *German verse in classical metres*, 1963.

### Interpretations

H. O. Burger (ed.), *Gedicht u. Gedanke*, 1942.

A. Closs (ed.), *Reality and creative vision in German lyrical poetry*, 1963, and *Medusa's Mirror*, 1957.

R. Hirschenauer, A. Weber (ed.), *Wege zum Gedicht*, 2 vols., 1956–63.

J. Schillemeit (ed.), *Interpretationen, Bd 1. Dt. Lyrik von Weckherlin bis Benn*, 1965.

B. von Weise (ed.), *Die dt. Lyrik. Form u. Gesch.*, 1956; repr. 1959.

W. Killy, *Wandlungen des lyrischen Bildes*, 1961.

K. May, *Form u. Bedeutung*, 1957.

S. S. Prawer, *German lyric poetry: a critical analysis of selected poems from Klopstock to Rilke*, 1952.

E. Staiger, *Die Zeit als Einbildungskraft des Dichters*, 1963. (Goethe, Brentano, Keller).

B. Blume, A. E. Schröder, 'Interpretations of German poetry (1936–56). A bibl', *Monatshefte* 49 (1957).

## Genres

H. Maiworm, *Neue dt. Epik*, 1968.

L. L. Albertsen, *Das Lehrgedicht*, 1967.

P. Schaaf, 'Das philosophische Gedicht', *DVLG* 6 (1928).

F. Beissner, *Gesch. der dt. Elegie*, 1936; 3rd ed. 1965.

K. Viëtor, *Gesch. der dt. Ode*, 1923; repr. 1961.

R. Böschenstein, *Idylle*, 1967.

A. Götze, *Das dt. Volkslied*, 1929; repr. 1948.

G. Müller, *Gesch. des dt. Liedes vom Zeitalter des Barock bis zur Gegenwart*, 1925; repr. 1961.

W. Kayser, *Gesch. der dt. Ballade*, 1936.

J. Müller, 'Romanze u. Ballade', *GRM* 40 (1959).

A. Closs, *Die freien Rhythmen in der dt. Lyrik*, 1947.

H. M. Mustard, *The lyric cycle in German lit.*, 1946.

H. Welti, *Gesch. des Sonettes in der dt. Dichtung*, 1884.

W. Mönch, *Das Sonett. Gestalt u. Geschichte*, 1955.

J. U. Fechner (ed.), *Das dt. Sonett*, 1968.

G. Wilker-Guersch, *Gehalt u. Form im dt. Sonett von Goethe bis Rilke*, 1952.

W. v. Ruttkowski, *Das lit. Chanson in Deutschland*, 1966.

## DRAMA

### Theory

R. Peacock, *The art of drama*, 1957.

H. Petsch, *Wesen u. Form des Dramas*, 1945.

V. Klotz, *Geschlossene u. offene Form im Drama*, 1960.

W. Wittkowski, 'Zur Ästhetik u. Interpretation des Dramas. Ein Lit.–Bericht', *DU* 15 (1963).

R. F. Arnold, *Das dt. Drama*, 1925.

B. v. Wiese (ed.), *Das dt. Drama*, 1958.

J. Schillemeit, *Interpretationen, Bd. 2. Dt. Dramen von Gryphius bis Brecht*, 1965.

A. Perger, *Grundlagen der Dramaturgie*, 1952.

H. A. Bulthaupt, *Dramaturgie des Schauspiels*, 1893–1905.

M. Dietrich, P. Stefanek, *Dt. Dramaturgie von Gryphius bis Brecht*, 1965.

W. Flemming, *Epik u. Dramatik*, 1925; repr. 1955.

## History

W. Creizenach, *Gesch. des neueren Dramas*, 5 vols., 1911–23.

O. Mann, *Gesch. des dt. Dramas*, 1960.

F. Sengle, 'Lit. zur Gesch. des neueren dt. Dramas u. Theaters', *DVLG* 27 (1953).

F. Sengle, 'Klassik im dt. Drama', *Arbeiten zur dt. Lit.*, 1965.

W. Kayser, 'Formtypen des dt. Dramas um 1800', *Die Vortragsreise*, 1958.

## Tragedy

O. Mann, *Poetik der Tragödie*, 1958.

J. Volkelt, *Ästhetik des Tragischen*, 3rd ed., 1917.

P. Szondi, *Versuch über das Tragische*, 1961.

C. Steinweg, *Studien zur Entwicklungsgesch. der Tragödie*, 1905–1924.

B. v. Wiese, *Die dt. Tragödie von Lessing bis Hebbel*, 1952; repr. 1961.

E. Busch, *Die Idee des Tragischen in der dt. Klassik*, 1942.

M. C. Ives, 'The problem of identity in German tragedy between 1770 and 1808', *PEGS* 36 (1966).

G. Steiner, *The death of tragedy*, 1961.

J. Minor, *Die Schicksalstragödie in ihren Hauptvertretern*, 1883.

A. Görland, *Die Idee des Schicksals in der Gesch. der Tragödie*, 1913.

## Comedy

K. Holl, *Zur Gesch. der Lustspieltheorie*, 1910.

H. Steffen (ed.), *Das dt. Lustspiel*, 1968.

K. Holl, *Gesch. des dt. Lustspiels*, 1923; repr. 1964.

H. Prang, *Gesch. des Lustspiels*, 1968.

H. Arntzen, *Die ernste Komödie. Das dt. Lustspiel von Lessing bis Kleist*, 1968.

M. Beare, *Die Theorie der Komödie von Gottsched bis Jean Paul*, 1928.

O. Rommel, *Die Alt-Wiener Volkskomödie*, 1952.

C. P. Magill, 'Austrian comedy', *GLL*, new series, 4 (1950–1).

A. Vogel, *Die Weimarer Klassik u. das Lustspiel*, diss. Zürich, 1952.

### Other Varieties and Aspects of the Drama

K. S. Guthke, *Gesch. u. Poetik der dt. Tragikomödie*, 1961.

A. Eloesser, *Das bürgerliche Drama. Seine Gesch. im 18. u. 19. Jh.*, 1898.

H. Ulmann, *Das dt. Bürgertum in dt. Tragödien des 18. u. 19. Jhs*, 1923.

E. Dosenheimer, *Das dt. soziale Drama von Lessing bis Sternheim*, 1949.

F. Sengle, *Das dt. Geschichtsdrama*, 1952.

O. Brahm, *Das dt. Ritterdrama*, 1880.

C. Steinweg, *Das Seelendrama*, 1924.

W. Liepe, *Das Religionsproblem im neueren Drama von Lessing bis zur Romantik*, 1914.

M. J. Rudwin, *A hist. and bibl. survey of the German religious drama*, 1924.

E. W. Helmrich, *A history of the chorus in the German drama*, 1912; repr. 1966.

I. Hürsch, *Der Monolog im dt. Drama von Lessing bis Hebbel*, diss. Zürich, 1947.

F. Gundolf, *Shakespeare u. der dt. Geist*, 1911.

R. Pascal, *Shakespeare in Germany, 1740–1815*, 1937.

E. L. Stahl, *Shakespeare u. das dt. Theater*, 1947.

W. H. Bruford, *Theatre, drama and audience in Goethe's Germany*, 1950.

J. Gregor, *Der Schauspielführer*, vol. 1: *Das dt. Schauspiel vom Mittelalter bis zum Expressionismus*, 1953.

V. Arpe, *Knaurs Schauspielführer. Eine Gesch. des Dramas*, 3rd ed., 1959.

O. A. zur Nedden, K. H. Ruppel (eds), *Reclams Schauspielführer*, 1960.

W. Kosch, *Dt. Theaterlexikon*, 1951– .

H. Kindermann, *Theatergesch. der Goethezeit*, 1949.

H. Knudsen, *Dt. Theatergeschichte*, 1959.

H. Calm, *Kulturbilder aus der dt. Theatergesch.*, 1925.

E. Devrient, *Gesch. der dt. Schauspielkunst*, ed. W. Stuhlfeld, 1929.

R. Petsch, 'Drama u. Theater. Ein Forschungsbericht', *DVLG*, 14–16 (1936–8).

# 9. THE EIGHTEENTH CENTURY

## POLITICAL AND ECONOMIC HISTORY

W. Goetz, *Propyläen-Weltgeschichte*, vol. 6, 'Das Zeitalter des Absolutismus', 1931.

H. Holborn, *A history of modern Germany 1648–1840*, 1965.

C. T. Atkinson, *A history of Germany 1715–1815*, 1908.

F. C. Schlosser, *Gesch. des 18. Jhs*, 5th ed. 1879.

F. Wagner, *Europa im Zeitalter des Absolutismus 1648–1789*, 1948.

R. Lorenz, *Die Grundlegung des Absolutismus*, 1939–40.

L. Just, *Der aufgeklärte Absolutismus*, 1952.

W. Fränzel, *Deutschland im Jahrhundert Friedrichs des Grossen*, 1921.

F. Meinecke, *Die Idee der Staatsräson*, 1924; 3rd ed. 1929.

B. Erdmannsdörffer, *Dt. Gesch. vom Westfälischen Frieden bis zum Regierungsantritt Friedrichs des Grossen*, 2 vols., 1892–3.

F. Valjavec, *Die Entstehung der politischen Strömungen in Deutschland 1770–1815*, 1951.

## HISTORY OF IDEAS AND CULTURE

P. Hazard, *La Pensée européenne au 18 ième siècle: de Montesquieu à Lessing*, 1946.

B. Willey, *The 18th century background: studies in the idea of Nature in the thought of the period*, 1941.

C. L. Becker, *The heavenly city of the 18th century philosophers*, 1932; repr. 1959.

R. U. Rockwood, *Carl Becker's heavenly City revisited*, 1958.

H. N. Fairchild, *The Noble Savage*, 1928.

K. Biedermann, *Deutschland im 18. Jh.*, 5 vols., 1854–80; 2nd ed. 1880, repr. 1969.

M. v. Boehn, *Deutschland im 18. Jh.*, 2 vols., 1921–2.

W. H. Dawson, *The Germany of the 18th century*, 1929.

W. H. Bruford, *Germany in the 18th century: the social background to the literary revival*, 1935.

F. Koch, *Dt. Kultur des Idealismus*, 1935/6.

G. L. Kriegk, *Dt. Kulturbilder aus dem 18. Jh.*, 1874.

A. Schultz, *Alltagsleben einer dt. Frau zu Anfang des 18. Jhs*, 1880.

M. v. Boehn, *Die Mode, Menschen und Moden im 18. Jh.*, 1909; 2nd ed. 1919.

H. Schöffler, *Dt. Geist im 18. Jh. Essays zur Geistes- und Religionsgesch.*, ed. G. v. Selle, 1956.

J. W. Appel, *Werther u. seine Zeit*, 4th ed. 1896.

L. Balet, E. Gerhard, *Die Verbürgerlichung der Kunst im 18. Jh.*, 1936.

F. Brüggemann, 'Der Kampf um die bürgerliche Welt- und Lebensanschauung in der Lit. des 18. Jhs', *DVLG* 3 (1925).

H. W. zur Nieden, *Die religiösen Bewegungen im 18. Jh.*, 1910.

G. Schnürer, *Katholische Kirche u. Kultur im 18. Jh.*, 1937.

A. Ritschl, *Gesch. des Pietismus*, 3 vols., 1880–6.

W. Mahrholz, *Der dt. Pietismus*, 1921.

M. Schmidt, W. Jannasch (eds.), *Das Zeitalter des Pietismus*, 1965.

F. W. Kantzenbach, *Die Erweckungsbewegung. Studien zur Gesch. ihrer Entstehung u. ersten Ausbreitung in Deutschland*, 1957.

G. Meyer, '*Gnadenfrei*', *eine Herrnhuter Siedlung des schlesischen Pietismus im 18. Jh.*, 1950.

F. Stemme, 'Die Säkularisation des Pietismus zur Erfahrungsseelenkunde', *Zs. f. dt. Philosophie* 72 (1953).

G. Kaiser, *Pietismus u. Patriotismus im lit. Deutschland*, 1961; 2nd ed. 1964.

K. S. Pinson, *Pietism as a factor in the rise of German nationalism*, 1934.

W. Hubrig, *Die patriotischen Gesellschaften des 18. Jhs*, 1957.

K. Schwarze, *Der 7-jährige Krieg in der zeitgenössischen dt. Lit.*, 1936.

M. Kawczynski, *Studien zur Lit.gesch. des 18. Jhs. Moralische Zeitschriften*, diss. Leipzig, 1880.

E. Milburg, *Die moralischen Wochenschriften des 18. Jhs*, 1880.

K. Jacoby, *Die ersten moralischen Wochenschriften am Anfang des 18. Jhs*, 1888.

W. Oberkampf, *Die zeitungskundliche Bedeutung der moralischen Wochenschriften*, 1934.

M. Stecher, *Die Erziehungsbestrebungen der dt. moralischen Wochenschriften*, 1914.

M. Gaus, *Das Idealbild der Familie in den moralischen Wochenschriften u. seine Auswirkung in der dt. Lit. des 18. Jhs*, 1937.

U. Menck, *Die Auffassung der Frau in den frühen moralischen Wochenschriften*, diss. Hamburg, 1940.

P. Currie, 'Moral weeklies and the reading public in Germany, 1711–1750', *OGS* 3 (1968).

W. Martens, *Die Botschaft der Tugend. Die Aufklärung im Spiegel der dt. moralischen Wochenschriften*, 1968.

P. Kluckhohn, *Die Auffassung der Liebe in der Lit. des 18. Jhs u. in der dt. Romantik*, 1931; 3rd ed. 1966.

L. Mittner, 'Freundschaft u. Liebe in der dt. Dichtung des 18. Jhs', *Stoffe, Formen, Strukturen*, Fs. Borcherdt, ed. A. Fuchs, H. Motekat.

W. Rasch, *Freundschaftskult u. Freundschaftsdichtung im dt. Schrifttum des 18. Jhs*, 1936.

P. Grappin, *La théorie du génie dans le préclassicisme allemand*, 1952.

W. F. Mainland, *Freedom: some German thoughts from the 18th century*, 1954.

A. Nivelle, *Kunst- u. Dichtungstheorien zwischen Aufklärung u. Klassik*, 1960.

H. Stöcker, *Zur Kunstanschauung des 18. Jhs. Von Winckelmann bis zu Wackenroder*, 1904.

B. A. Sørensen, *Symbol u. Symbolismus in den ästhetischen Theorien des 18. Jhs. u. der dt. Romantik*, 1963.

H. Hettner, *Gesch. der dt. Lit. im 18. Jh.*, 6 vols., 1856–70; repr., 2 vols., 1961.

D. W. Schumann, 'Neuorientierung im 18. Jh.', *MLQ* 9 (1948).

E. Purdie, *Studies in German lit. of the 18th century*, 1965.

A. Langen, *Anschauungsformen in der dt. Dichtung des 18. Jhs*, 1934; repr. 1965.

E. A. Blackall, *The emergence of German as a literary language 1700–1775*, 1959.

W. Hafen, *Studien zur Gesch. der dt. Prosa im 18. Jh.*, diss. Zürich, 1952.

U. Wendland, *Die Theoretiker u. Theorie der sogenannten galanten Stilepoche u. die dt. Sprache*, 1930.

C. Wiedemann (ed.), *Der galante Stil, 1690–1720*, 1969.

H. Sperber, 'Der Einfluss des Pietismus auf die Sprache des 18. Jhs', *DVLG* 8 (1930).

A. Langen, *Der Wortschatz des dt. Pietismus*, 1954; 2nd ed. 1968.

A. Langen, 'Zum Problem der sprachlichen Säkularisation in der dt. Dichtung des 18. u. 19. Jhs', *ZfdPh* 83, (1964).

A. Schöne, *Säkularisation als sprachbildende Kraft*, *Pal* 226 (1958); 2nd ed. 1968.

A. Langen, 'Der Wortschatz des 18. Jhs', *Dt. Wortgesch.*, ed. F. Maurer, F. Stroh, vol. 2, 1959.

W. Feldmann, 'Modewörter des 18. Jhs', *Zs. für dt. Wortforschung* 6 (1906).

M. B. Price, *The publication of English lit. in Germany in the 18th century*, 1934.

G. N. Davis, *German thought and culture in England, 1700–70*, 1969.

*Aufklärung*

M. v. Geismar, *Bibliothek der dt. Aufklärer des 18. Jhs*, 1846; repr., 2 vols., 1963/4.

G. Funke (ed.), *Die Aufklärung.* In ausgewählten Texten dargestellt u. eingeleitet von G. Funke, 1963.

E. Cassirer, *Die Philosophie der Aufklärung*, 1932; English trans. 1951.

H. Friedrich, F. Schalk (eds), *Europäische Aufklärung*, Fs. Dieckmann, 1967.

P. Gay, *The Enlightenment: an interpretation*, 1967.

H. M. Wolff, *Die Weltanschauung der Aufklärung in gesch. Entwicklung*, 2nd ed. 1963.

N. Hampson, *The Enlightenment*, 1968.

F. Valjavec, *Gesch. der abendländischen Aufklärung*, 1961.

F. Valjavec, 'Die politischen Wirkungen der Aufklärung', *Ostdt. Wissenschaft* 2 (1955).

E. Ermatinger, *Dt. Kultur im Zeitalter der Aufklärung*, 1935.

P. Hazard, *La crise de la conscience européenne 1680–1715*, 1935.

W. Philipp, *Das Werden der Aufklärung in theologischer Sicht*, 1957.

L. Leiste, *Der Humanitätsgedanke in der Popularphilosophie der dt. Aufklärung*, 1932.

M. Horkheimer, T. W. Adorno, *Dialektik der Aufklärung*, 1947.

G. Müller, 'Die Wende vom Barock zur Aufklärung', *Lit. wissenschaftliches Jahrbuch der Görresgesellschaft* 8 (1933).

H. K. Kettler, *Baroque tradition in the lit. of the German Enlightenment, 1700–1750*, 1943.

W. Promies, *Die Bürger u. der Narr oder das Risiko der Phantasie. Eine Untersuchung über das Irrationale in der Lit. des Rationalismus*, diss. Munich, 1962. (1966).

H. O. Burger, *Die Geschichte der unvergnügten Seele*, 1961.

A. L. Veit, *Das Aufklärungsschrifttum des 18. Jhs u. die katholische Kirche*, 1937.

C. Meyer, *Österreich u. die Aufklärung im 18. Jh.*, 1896.

W. Krauss, *Die französische Aufklärung im Spiegel der dt. Literatur des 18. Jhs*, 1963.

T. W. Danzel, *Gottsched u. seine Zeit*, 2nd ed. 1855.

J. Crüger, *J. C. Gottsched u. die Schweizer J. J. Bodmer und J. J. Breitinger*, 1884; repr. 1965.

B. Rosenthal, *Der Geniebegriff des Aufklärungszeitalters: Lessing und die Popularphilosophen*, 1933.

J. Jungius-Gesellschaft (ed.), *Lessing u. die Zeit der Aufklärung*, 1968.

G. Kaiser, *Von der Aufklärung bis zum Sturm und Drang. 1730 bis 1789*, 1966.

R. Wilhelm, *F. J. Riedel u. die Ästhetik der Aufklärung*, 1933.

W. Scheibe, *Die Krisis der Aufklärung. Studie zum Kampf der Sturm- und Drangbewegung gegen den Rationalismus der Aufklärung des 18. Jhs*, diss. Göttingen, 1936.

W. Rasch, 'Die Lit. der Aufklärungszeit: ein Forschungsbericht', *DVLG* 30 (1956).

H. Prang, 'Literaturbericht zur dt. Vorklassik', *WW* 2 (1951/2).

A. Köster, *Die dt. Literatur der Aufklärungszeit*, 1925.

H. Sperber, 'Die Sprache der Aufklärung', *ZdU* 43 (1929).

*Rococo and Empfindsamkeit*

V. Klemperer, 'Der Begriff Rokoko' *Jb. f. Philologie 1* (1925).

V. Tornius *Dt. Rokoko*, 1935.

I. S. Stamm, 'German lit. rococo', *GR* 36 (1961).

H. Heckel, *Zu Begriff Wesen des lit. Rokoko in Deutschland*, Fs. Th. Siebs, 1933.

A. Anger, *Literarisches Rokoko*, 1962.

A. Anger (ed.), *Dichtung des Rokoko nach Motiven geordnet*, 1958.

A. Anger, *Dt. Rokokodichtung*, 1963.

E. Ermatinger, *Barock und Rokoko in der dt. Dichtung*, 1926.

B. A. Sørensen, 'Das dt. Rokoko u. die Verserzählung im 18. Jh.', *Euph* 48 (1954).

M. Wieser, *Der sentimentale Mensch*, 1924.

R. Unger, 'Hamann u. die Empfindsamkeit', *Euph* 30 (1936).

W. Schmitz, *Die Empfindsamkeit Jean Pauls*, 1930.

N. Miller, *Der empfindsame Erzähler*, 1968.

H. Friedrich, *Abbé Prévost in Deutschland. Ein Beitrag zur Gesch. der Empfindsamkeit*, 1929.

E. Erämetsä, *Englische Lehnprägungen in der dt. Empfindsamkeit des 18. Jhs*, 1955.

### Göttinger Hain and Sturm und Drang

A. Lübbering (ed.), '*Klopstock.' Ein Gedichtband des Göttinger Hains*, 1957.

K. A. Schleiden, 'Die Dichter des Göttinger Hains', *DU* 10 (1958).

E. Metelmann, *Zur Gesch. des Göttinger Dichterbundes 1772–74*, 1965.

R. Bäsken, *Die Dichter des Göttinger Hains u. die Bürgerlichkeit*, diss. Königsberg, 1937.

A. Wicke, *Die Dichter des Göttinger Hains in ihrem Verhältnis zur englischen Lit. und Ästhetik*, diss. Göttingen, 1929.

C. Redlich, (ed.), *Göttinger Musenalmanach auf 1770–72*, DLD 49/50, 52/53, 64/65.

R. Strasser (ed.), *Sturm und Drang*, 3 vols., 1966.

N. H. Verbeek (ed.), *Sturm und Drang, eine Auswahl dichtungstheoretischer Schriften*, 1948.

E. Loewenthal (ed.), *Sturm und Drang. Kritische Schriften*, 1949.

A. Wald, *The aesthetic theories of the German Storm and Stress movement*, diss. Chicago, 1924.

E. Zilsel, *Die Entstehung des Geniebegriffs*, 1926.

H. Wolf, *Versuch einer Gesch. des Geniebegriffs 1: von Gottsched bis Lessing*, 1923.

H. B. Garland, *Storm and Stress*, 1952.

R. Pascal, *The German Sturm und Drang*, 1953.

H. Kindermann, *Die Entwicklung der Sturm- und Drangbewegung*, 1925.

F. J. Schneider, *Die dt. Dichtung der Geniezeit*, 1952.

E. A. Runge, *Primitivism and related ideas in Sturm und Drang lit.*, 1946.

K. S. Guthke, *Englische Vorromantik u. dt. Sturm und Drang. M. G. Lewis' Stellung in der Gesch. der dt.–englischen Literaturbeziehungen*, 1958.

H. Hecht, *T. Percy, R. Wood, and J. D. Michaelis: ein Beitrag zur Lit.gesch. der Genieperiode*, 1933.

A. Beck, *Griechisch-dt. Begegnung: das dt. Griechenerlebnis im Sturm und Drang*, 1947.

E. Braemer, *Goethes Prometheus u. die Grundpositionen des Sturm und Drang*, 2nd ed., 1963.

E. A. Blackall, 'The language of Sturm und Drang', *Stil- und Formprobleme in der Literatur*, ed. P. Böckmann, 1959.

### Classicism and Romanticism ('*Goethezeit*')

H. A. Korff, *Geist der Geothezeit*, 4 parts, 1923–53; 2nd ed. 1964.

H. Grimm, *Das Jahrhundert Goethes*, 1948.

F. Schultz, *Klassik u. Romantik der Deutschen*, 2 vols., 1935–40; 3rd ed. 1959.

F. Strich, *Dt. Klassik u. Romantik*, 1922; 5th ed. 1962.

F. Martini, *Die Goethezeit*, 1949.

W. v. d. Steinen, *Das Zeitalter Goethes*, 1949.

G. Lukács, *Goethe u. seine Zeit*, 1947.

J. Körner, *Romantiker u. Klassiker*, 1924.

B. v. Wiese, *Von Lessing bis Grabbe. Studien zur dt. Klassik u. Romantik*, 1968.

W. Folkierski, *Entre le classicisme et le romanticisme, étude sur l'esthétique et les esthéticiens du 18e siècle*, 1925.

P. Kluckhohn, *Die Idee des Menschen in der Goethezeit*, 1947.

W. Kohlschmidt, *Form u. Innerlichkeit. Beiträge zur Gesch. und Wirkung der dt. Klassik u. Romantik*, 1955.

N. Hartmann, *Die Philosophie des dt. Idealismus*, 2 vols, 1923–9.

M. Kronenberg, *Gesch. des dt. Idealismus*, 2 vols, 1909–12.

W. Lütgert, *Die Religion des dt. Idealismus u. ihr Ende*, 4 parts, 1923–30.

L. W. Kahn, *Social ideas in German lit. 1770–1830*, 1938.

W. Rehm, *Griechentum u. Goethezeit*, 1936; 2nd ed. 1938.

W. Dilthey, *Das Erlebnis u. die Dichtung*, 1905; 14th ed. 1965.

P. Raabe, 'Zur Bibl. der Goethezeit', *Euph* 48 (1954).

### Classicism

G. Highet, *The classical tradition. Greek and Roman influences on Western lit.*, 1949.

A. Heussler, *Klassik u. Klassizismus in der dt. Lit. Studie über zwei literarhistorische Begriffe*, 1952.

H. A. Korff (ed.), *Edel sei der Mensch*, 2 vols., 1947 (texts).

R. H. Thomas, *The classical ideal in German lit. 1755–1805: introduction and anthology*, 1939.

F. Bobertag (ed.) DNL 136–7 (texts).

L. A. Willoughby, *The Classical age of German lit.*, 1926.

O. Harnack, *Der dt. Klassizismus im Zeitalter Goethes*, 1906.

R. Benz, *Die Zeit der dt. Klassik. Kultur des 18. Jhs. 1750–1800*, 1953.

G. Albrecht, J. Mittenzwei, *Klassik (Erläuterungen zur dt. Lit. 3)*, 2nd ed. 1960.

M. Enzinger, *Der Humanismus der dt. Klassik*, 1947.

E. Franz, *Dt. Klassik u. Reformation*, 1937.

E. v. Sydow, *Die Kultur des dt. Klassizismus*, 1926.

M. Kommerell, *Der Dichter als Führer in der dt. Klassik*, 2nd ed. 1942.

J. Müller, *Wirlichkeit u. Klassik. Beiträge zur dt. Lit.gesch. von Lessing bis Heine*, 1955.

H. Hatfield, *Aesthetic paganism in German lit. from Winckelmann to the death of Goethe*, 1964.

E. M. Wilkinson, 'Form and content in the aesthetics of German classicism', *Stil und Formprobleme in der Lit.*, ed. P. Böckmann, 1959.

W. H. Bruford, *Culture and society in Classical Weimar, 1775–1806*, 1962.

V. Tornius, *Das klassische Weimar*, 1949.

F. Kühnlenz, *Weimarer Porträts, Neue Folge*, 1965.

K. Toggenburger, *Die Werkstatt der Klassik. Goethes u. Schillers Diskussion des künstlerischen Schaffens*, diss. Zürich, 1948.

A. Bettex, *Der Kampf um das klassische Weimar, 1788–98*, 1935.

K. Hammer, H. Henning, S. Seifert, 'Internationale Bibl. zur dt. Klassik 1750–1850', *WB* 1960 ff.

## Romanticism

R. Mowat, *The Romantic age: Europe in the early 19th century*, 1937.

L. R. Fürst, *Romanticism in perspective*, 1969.

P. van Tieghem, *Le romantisme dans la littérature européenne*, 1948.

A. O. Lovejoy, 'On the discrimination of romanticisms', *PMLA* 29 (1924).

R. Wellek, 'The concept of romanticism in lit. history', *CL* 1 (1949).

R. Ullmann, H. Gotthard, *Gesch. des Begriffs 'romantisch' in Deutschland*, 1927.

A. O. Lovejoy, 'The meaning of "Romantic" in early German romanticism', *Essays in the history of ideas*, 2nd ed. 1952.

E. C. Mason, *Dt. u. englische Romantik. Eine Gegenüberstellung*, 1959; 2nd ed. 1966.

H. Marquardt, *Henry Crabb Robinson u. seine dt. Freunde*, 2 vols., 1964–7.

J. G. Robertson, *Studies in the genesis of romantic theory in the 18th century*, 1923.

H. Schanze, *Romantik u. Aufklärung*, 1966.

P. van Tieghem, *Préromantisme*, 3 vols., 1924–48.

R. Ayrault, *La genèse du romantisme allemand. Situation spirituelle de l'Allemagne dans la deuxième moitié du 18e siècle*, 2 vols., 1961.

J. Petersen, *Die Wesensbestimmung der dt. Romantik*, 1926.

R. Haym, *Die romantische Schule*, 1870; 5th ed. by O. Walzel 1928; 1870 ed. repr. 1961.

R. Huch, *Die Romantik. Ausbreitung, Blütezeit u. Zerfall*, 2 vo 1899–1902; repr. 1964.

O. Walzel, *Dt. Romantik*, 2 vols., 1908, 1926.

K. Breul, *The Romantic movement in German lit.*, 1927.

L. A. Willoughby, *The Romantic movement in Germany*, 1930; repr. 1966.

R. Benz, *Die dt. Romantik*, 1937.

H. Steffen (ed.), *Die dt. Romantik. Poetik, Formen u. Motive*, 1967.

F. Gundolf, *Romantiker*, 2 vols., 1930–1.

P. Kluckhohn, *Das Ideengut der dt. Romantik*, 1941, 5th ed. 1966.

F. Lion, *Romantik als dt. Schicksal*, 1947.

Th. Steinbüchel (ed.), *Romantik. Ein Zyklus Tübinger Vorlesungen*, 1948.

R. Benz, *Lebenswelt der Romantik. Dokumente romantischen Denkens u. Seins*, 1948.

R. Tymms, *German Romantic lit.*, 1955.

R. Benz, *Romantik. Aus Schriften, Briefen, Tagebüchern*, 1955.

G. Bianquis, *La vie quotidienne en Allemagne à l'époque romantique*, 1958.

H. H. Borcherdt, *Schiller u. die Romantiker*, 1950.

R. Haller, *Die Romantik in der Zeit der Umkehr: die Anfänge der jüngeren Romantik 1800–1808*, 1941.

W. D. Robson-Scott, *The lit. background of the Gothic revival in Germany*, 1965.

A. Stockmann, *Die jüngere Romantik*, 1923.

H. Apfelstedt, *Selbsterziehung u. Sebstbildung in der dt. Frühromantik. F. Schlegel, Novalis, Wackenroder, Tieck*, diss. Munich, 1958.

M. Brion, *L'Allemagne romantique. Kleist, Brentano, Wackenroder, Tieck, C. von Günderode*, 1962.

P. Reiff, *Die Ästhetik der dt. Frühromantik*, 1946.

H. Lippuner, *Wackenroder/Tieck u. die bildende Kunst. Grundlegung der romantischen Ästhetik*, 1965.

J. Körner, *Krisenjahre der Frühromantik*, 3 vols., 1936–58.

H. Levin, *Die Heidelberger Romantik*, 1922.

J. Nadler, *Die Berliner Romantik*, 1921.

H. O. Burger, *Schwäbische Romantik. Studien zur Charakteristik des Uhland-Kreises*, 1928.

O. Ackermann, *Schwabentum u. Romantik: geistesgesch. Untersuchungen über J. Kerner u. L. Uhland*, 1939.

O. E. Schmidt, *Die Romantik in Sachsen*, 1938.

K. E. Winter, 'Die österreichische Romantik', *Allgemeine Rundschau* 26 (1929).

G. Peterli, *Zerfall u. Nachklang. Studien zur dt. Spatromantik*, 1958.

K. S. Thornton, *Religion in early romantic novels*, diss. Columbia Univ., 1955.

S. Schultze, *Das Naturgefühl der Romantik*, 1911.

C. Bernouilli, H. Kern (eds.), *Romantische Naturwissenschaft*, 1926.

H. Petrich, *Drei Kapitel vom romantischen Stil*, 1878.

M. Thalmann, *Romantik u. Manierismus*, 1963.

E. Fiesel, *Die Sprachphilosophie der dt. Romantik*, 1927.

F. Brüggemann, *Die Ironie als entwicklungsgesch. Element*, 1909.

F. Ernst, *Die romantische Ironie*, diss. Zürich, 1917.

K. Friedemann, 'Die romantische Ironie', *Zs. f. Ästhetik* 13 (1919).

O. Walzel, 'Romantische Ironie', *Romantisches*, 1934.

J. Strohschneider-Kohrs, *Die romantische Ironie in Theorie und Gestaltung*, 1960.

B. Heimreich, *Fiktion u. Fiktionsironie in Theorie u. Dichtung der dt. Romantik*, 1968.

W. Bausch, *Theorien des epischen Erzählens in der dt. Frühromantik*, 1964.

K. Wenger, *Historische Romane dt. Romantiker*, 1905.

J. Ramming, *Die Bedeutung der Magie in der Dichtung der dt. Romantik*, diss. Zürich, 1948.

M. Thalmann, *Märchen u. Moderne. Zum Begriff der Surrealität im Märchen der Romantik*, 1961; 2nd ed. 1966.

R. Benz, *Märchendichtung der Romantiker*, 1908; 2nd ed. 1926.

R. Aris, *History of political thought in Germany, 1789–1815*, 1937.

H. S. Reiss, 'The political ideas of the German Romantic movement; *GLL* 8 (1954/55).

H. S. Reiss, *Politisches Denken in der dt. Romantik*, 1966.

F. Arnold, *Die Dichter der Befreiungskriege*, 2 vols., 1908.

P. Eberhard, *Die politischen Anschauungen der christlich-dt. Tischgesellschaft*, 1937.

J. Droz, *Le romantisme allemand et l'Etat*, 1966.

### THEORY AND HISTORY OF LITERARY FORMS
### IN THE EIGHTEENTH CENTURY
(not including Romanticism)

*Prose Narrative*

J. v. Eichendorff, *Der dt. Roman des 18. Jhs*, 1851.

H. Rausse, *Gesch. des dt. Romans bis 1800*, 1914.

I. Arndt, *Die seelische Welt im Roman des 18. Jhs*, diss. Giessen, 1940.

W. Kayser, 'Die Anfänge des modernen Romans im 18. Jh. u. seine heutige Krise', *DVLG* 27 (1954).

K. Minners, *Die Theorie des Romans in der dt. Aufklärung*, diss. Hamburg, 1922.

M. Sommerfeld, 'Romantheorie u. Romantypus der dt. Aufklärung', *DVLG* 4 (1926).

D. Kimpel, *Der Roman der Aufklärung*, 1967.

A. Hirsch, 'Barockroman u. Aufklärungsroman', *EG* 9 (1954).

A. Hirsch, *Bürgertum u. Barock im dt. Roman*, ed. H. Singer; 2nd ed. 1957.

H. Singer, *Der dt. Roman zwischen Barock u. Rokoko*, 1963.

H. Singer, *Der galante Roman*, 1961.

I. Eder, *Untersuchungen zur Gesch. des empfindsamen Romans in Deutschland*, diss. Vienna, 1953.

M. Götz, *Der frühe bürgerliche Roman in Deutschland*, diss. Munich, 1958 (typescript).

N. Miller, *Der empfindsame Erzähler. Untersuchungen an Romananfängen des 18. Jhs*, 1968.

K. I. Flessau, *Der moralische Roman*, 1968.

C. Heine, *Der Roman in Deutschland 1774–78*, 1892.

E. Becker, *Der dt. Roman um 1780*, 1964.

H. Rötteken, 'Weltflucht u. Idylle in Deutschland von 1720

bis zur Insel Felsenburg', *Zs. für vergleichende Lit. gesch.*, new series, 9 (1896).

B. Mildebrath, *Die dt. Avanturiers des 18. Jhs*, diss. Würzburg, 1907.

E. Roth, *Die Bildgestaltung der Persönlichkeit, ein Beitrag zur Formgesch. des Romans vom Sturm und Drang bis zur Romantik*, diss. Munich, 1942.

H. J. Skorna, *Das Wanderermotiv im Roman der Goethezeit*, diss. Cologne, 1961.

W. Nowack, *Liebe u. Ehe im dt. Roman zu Rousseaus Zeiten*, 1906.

W. Gebhardt, *Religionssoziologische Probleme im Roman der dt. Aufklärung*, diss. Giessen, 1931.

P. A. Graber, *Religious types in some representative German novels of the enlightenment*, diss. Univ. of Iowa, 1953.

C. L. Hornaday, *Nature in the German novel of the late 18th century*, 1940.

V. Lange, 'Erzählformen im Roman des 18. Jhs', *Stil- und Formprobleme in der Literatur*, ed. P. Böckmann, 1959.

M. Wesley, *Das junge Mädchen im dt. Roman des 18. Jhs, bis zum Beginn des Sturm und Dranges*, diss. Leipzig, 1933.

C. Touaillon, *Der dt. Frauenroman des 18. Jhs*, 1919.

N. Halparin, *Die dt. Schriftstellerinnen in der zweiten Hälfte des 19. Jhs*, 1935.

L. E. Kurth, 'Historiographie u. historischer Roman. Kritik und Theorie im 18. Jh.', *MLN* 79 (1963).

M. Beaujean, *Der Trivialroman in der zweiten Hälfte des 18. Jhs. Die Ursprünge des modernen Unterhaltungsromans*, 1964.

R. Bauer, *Der historische Trivialroman in Deutschland im ausgehenden 18. Jh.*, diss. Munich, 1930.

M. Spiegel, *Der Roman u. sein Publikum im früheren 18. Jh. 1700–1767*, 1967.

H. Riefstahl, *Dichter u. Publikum in der ersten Hälfte des 18. Jhs, dargestellt an der Gesch. der Vorrede*, diss. Frankfurt a. M., 1934.

R. Engelsing, 'Der Bürger als Leser. Die Bildung der protestantischen Bevölkerung Deutschlands im 17. und 18. Jh.', *Börsenblatt f. den dt. Buchhandel* 16 (1960).

W. Rumpf, *Das lit. Publikum u. sein Geschmack in den Jahren 1760–1770*, diss. Frankfurt a. M., 1924.

W. Wittmann, *Beruf u. Buch im 18. Jh.*, diss. Frankfurt a. M., 1934.

L. M. Price, 'On the reception of Richardson in Germany', *JEGP* 25 (1926).

E. Schmidt, *Richardson, Rousseau u. Goethe. Ein Beitrag zur Gesch. des Romans im 18. Jh.*, 1924.

K. Harris, *Beiträge zur Wirkung Fieldings in Deutschland*, diss. Göttingen, 1961.

G. Stern, *Fielding, Wieland and Goethe. A study in the development of the novel*, diss. Columbia Univ., 1954.

J. Czerny, *Sterne, Hippel u. Jean Paul. Ein Beitrag zur Gesch. des humoristischen Romans in Deutschland*, 1904.

P. Michelsen, *Laurence Sterne u. der dt. Roman des 18. Jhs*, 1962.

W. Beyer, *Die moralische Erzählung in Deutschland bis zu Heinrich von Kleist*, 1941.

R. Fürst (ed.), *Dt. Erzähler des 18. Jhs*, DLD. 66–69, 1897.

R. Fürst, *Die Vorläufer der modernen Novelle im 18. Jh.*, 1897.

U. Borchmeyer, *Die dt. Prosaerzählungen des 18. Jhs*, diss. Münster, 1955 (typescript).

## Poetry (*18th century*)

M. Colleville, *La renaissance du lyrisme dans la poésie allemande au 18ième siècle*, 1936.

M. Paustian, *Die Lyrik der Aufklärung 1710–70*, 1933.

P. Böckmann, '18th century hymnic verse', *Reality and creative vision in German lyrical poetry*, ed. A. Closs, 1963.

W. Lüthi, *Ein Beitrag zur Gesch. der Stimmungen im 18. Jh. Die Entfaltung des Lyrischen*, diss. Zürich, 1951.

S. Behm-Cierpka, *Die optimistische Weltanschauung in der dt. Gedanken-Lyrik der Aufklärungszeit*, diss. Heidelberg, 1933.

G. Weissert, *Das Mildheimische Liederbuch. Studien zur volkspädagogischen Lit. der Aufklärung*, 1966.

K. Berger, *Barock u. Aufklärung im geistlichen Lied*, 1951.

T. Erb, *Die Pointe in der Dichtung von Barock u. Aufklärung*, 1929.

C. Kahn, *Die Melancholie in der dt. Lyrik des 18, Jhs*, 1932.

H. Joswig, *Leidenschaft u. Gelassenheit in der dt. Lyrik des 18. Jhs*, 1938.

G. Schütze, *Das Naturgefühl um die Mitte des 18. Jhs in der Lyrik von Pyra bis Claudius*, diss. Leipzig, 1933.

W. Rasch, *Freundschaft u. Freundschaftsdichtung im dt. Schrifttum des 18. Jhs*, 1936.

E. Ehrmann, *Die bardische Lyrik im 18. Jh.* 1925.

A. Pülzl, *Studien zur Entwicklung der dt. Bardendichtung*, diss. Vienna, 1950.

E. A. G. Albrecht, *Primitivism and related ideas in 18th century German lyric poetry, 1680–1740*, diss. Johns Hopkins Univ., 1950.

P. Fledelius, *Volkslieder u. Poesie des Hainbundes*, 1960.

O. Uebel, *Grays Einfluss auf die dt. Lyrik im 18. Jh.*, diss. Heidelberg, 1914.

P. Stöcklein, 'Vom barocken zum Goetheschen Liebesgedicht', *Wege zum späten Goethe*, 1960.

E. Trunz, 'Die Formen der dt. Lyrik in der Goethezeit', *DU* 16 (1964).

A. Krättli, *Die Farben in der Lyrik der Goethezeit*, diss. Zürich 1949.

A. G. de Capua, 'Early poetical anthologies for schools. A contribution to the history of the lyrical anthology in Germany before 1770', *Monatshefte* 49 (1957).

B. A. Sørensen, 'Das dt. Rokoko u. die Verserzählung im 18. Jh.', *Euph* 48 (1954).

F. Ernst, 'Die Entdeckung der Volkspoesie im 18. Jh.', *Späte Essais*, 1963.

H. J. Schrimpf, 'Vers ist tanzhafte Rede. Ein Beitrag zur dt. Prosodie aus dem 18. Jh.', Fs. Trier, 1964 (1965).

## Drama (*18th century*)

C. Heine, *Das Schauspiel der dt. Wanderbühne vor Gottsched*, 1889.

G. Schubart-Fikentscher, *Zur Stellung der Komödianten im 17. u. 18. Jh.*, 1963.

W. Schaer, *Die Gesellschaft im dt. bürgerlichen Drama des 18. Jhs*, 1963.

M. R. Scherrer, *Technik u. Auffassung des Kampfes im dt. Drama des 18. Jhs.*, 1917.

E. Staiger, 'Rasende Weiber in der dt. Tragödie des 18. Jhs', *ZfdPh* 80 (1961); also *Stilwandel*, 1963.

S. E. Schreiber, *The German woman in the age of the enlightenment: a study in the drama from Gottsched to Lessing*, 1948.

R. R. Heitner, 'The Iphigenia in Tauris theme in the drama of the 18th century', *CL* 16 (1964).

E. Birnbaum, *The drama of sensibility, 1696–1780*, 1915.

F. Rühle, *Das dt. Schäferspiel des 18. Jhs*, 1885.

J. Schmidt, *Studien zum Bibeldrama der Empfindsamkeit*, diss. Breslau, 1933.

R. Götte, *Die Tochter im Familiendrama des 18. Jhs*, 1964.

K. H. v. Stockmayer, *Das dt. Soldatenstück des 18. Jhs seit Lessings Minna von Barnhelm*, 1898.

E. Loewenthal, L. Schneider (eds.), *Sturm u. Drang. Dramatische Schriften*, 2 vols, 1959.

S. Melchinger, *Dramaturgie des Sturms u. Drangs*, 1929.

H. Ruppert, *Die Darstellung der Affekte u. Liedenschaften im Drama des Sturmes und Dranges*, 1941.

G. Mattenklott, *Melancholie in der Dramatik des Sturm und Drang*, 1968.

H. Hüchting, *Die Literatursatire der Sturm- u. Drangbewegung*, 1942.

C. Stockmeyer, *Soziale Probleme im Drama des Sturmes u. Dranges*, 1922.

G. Keckeis, *Dramaturgische Probleme im Sturm u. Drang*, 1907.

J. Zorn, *Die Motive der Sturm- u. Drang-Dramatiker*, diss. Bonn, 1909.

M. Poensgen, *Gesch. der Theorie der Tragödie von Gottsched bis Lessing*, 1899.

M. Kommerell, *Lessing u. Aristotles. Untersuchung über die Theorie der Tragödie*, 2nd ed. 1957.

K. A. Dickson, 'Lessing's creative misinterpretation of Aristotle', *Greece and Rome*, 2nd series, 14 (1967).

R. R. Heitner, *German tragedy in the age of enlightenment*, 1963.

R. Daunicht, *Die Entstehung des bürgerlichen Trauerspiels in Deutschland*, 1963.

J. Pinatel, *Le drame bourgeois en Allemagne au 18ième siècle*, 1938.

H. Selver, *Die Auffassung des Bürgers im dt. bürgerlichen Drama des 18. Jhs*, 1931.

L. Pikulik, *Bürgerliches Trauerspiel u. Empfindsamkeit*, 1966.

W. Hinck, *Das dt. Lustspiel des 17. u. 18. Jhs u. die italienische Commedia dell' arte u. Théatre italien*, 1965.

G. Wicke, *Die Struktur des dt. Lustspiels der Aufklärung*, 1965.

H. Steinmetz, *Die Komödie der Aufklärung*, 1966.

H. Steinmetz, 'Der Harlekin. Seine Rolle in der dt. Komödientheorie u. -dichtung des 18. Jhs', *N* 50 (1966).

B. Aiken-Sneath, *Comedy in Germany in the first half of the 18th century*, 1936.

H. Friederici, *Das dt. bürgerliche Lustspiel der Frühaufklärung (1736–50)*, 1957.

# 10. THE NINETEENTH CENTURY

## POLITICAL AND ECONOMIC HISTORY

D. Thomson, *Europe since Napoleon*, 1957; rev. ed. 1966.

D. Sternberger, *Panorama oder Ansichten vom 19. Jh.*, 1938; 3rd ed. 1955.

H. M. Chadwick, *The nationalities of Europe and the growth of national ideologies*, 1945.

F. Schnabel, *Dt. Gesch. im 19. Jh.*, 4 vols., 2nd ed. 1948–51.

P. Sethe, *Dt. Gesch. im letzten Jh.*, 1960.

G. Mann, *Dt. Gesch. des 19. und 20. Jhs*, 1961.

A. Ramm, *Germany 1789–1919. A political history*, 1967.

W. Sombart, *Die dt. Volkswirtschaft im 19. Jh.*, 5th ed. 1921.

A. W. Ward, *Germany 1815–1890*, 3 vols., 1916–18.

C. J. Passant, *A short history of Germany 1815–1945*, 1959.

W. Wohlrabe, *Die Freiheitskriege*, 2 vols., 1933 (vol. 2: *Im Spiegel der Roman- und Dramenlit.*).

F. Meinecke, *Das Zeitalter der dt. Erhebung*, 1905; 2nd ed. 1941.

T. S. Hamerow, *Restoration, Revolution, Reaction. Economics and politics in Germany, 1815–71*, 1958.

E. Troeltsch, *Die Restaurationsepoche am Anfang des 19. Jhs*, 1913.

A. E. Zucker, *The Forty-Eighters*, 1950.

W. Goetz (ed.), *Propyläen-Weltgeschichte*, vol. 8, 'Liberalismus und Nationalismus 1848–90', 1930.

F. Hartung, *Dt. Geschichte 1871–1919*, 1920; 4th ed. 1939.

W. Oncken, *Das Zeitalter Wilhelms I*, 2 vols., 1890–2.

W. F. Bruck, *Social and economic history of Germany from William II to Hitler, 1888–1938*, 1938.

## HISTORY OF IDEAS AND CULTURE

E. Bergmann, *Der Geist des 19. Jhs*, 2nd ed. 1927.

J. T. Merz, *A History of European Thought in the 19th century*, 1904–12; repr. 1965.

O. Walzel, *Die Geistesströmungen des 19. Jhs*, 2nd ed. 1929.

T. Ziegler, *Die geistigen und sozialen Strömungen des 19. Jhs*, 1900.

W. Bauer, *Dt. Kultur 1830–70*, 1939–42.

M. v. Boehn, *Die Mode, Menschen und Moden im 19. Jh.*, 4 vols, 1908–19.

W. Mack, *Metternich's Europe*, 1968.

H. Tietze, *Das vormärzliche Wien in Wort und Bild*, 1925.

H. R. Doering-Manteuffel, *Dresden und sein Geistesleben im Vormärz*, 1935.

S. Lublinski, *Lit. u. Gesellschaft im 19. Jh.*, 4 vols, 1899–1900.

F. Sengle, 'Voraussetzungen u. Erscheinungsformen der dt. Restaurationslit.', *Arbeiten zur dt. Lit. 1750–1850*, 1965.

J. Dresch, 'La révolution de 1848 et la littérature allemande', *RLC* 22 (1948).

C. P. Magill, 'The German author and his public in the mid-nineteenth century', *MLR* 43 (1948).

R. H. Thomas, *Liberalism, nationalism, and the German intellectuals*, 1951.

G. Steinhausen, *Dt. Geistes- und Kulturgesch. 1870 bis zur Gegenwart*, 1931.

D. M. v. Abbé, *Image of a people. The Germans and their creative writing under and since Bismarck*, 1964.

R. Weitbrecht, 'Der Protestantismus in der dt. Dichtung des 19. Jhs', C. Werckshagen: *Der Prot. am Ende des 19. Jhs.*, vol. 2, 1902.

A. Hübotter, *Das Schicksal der Humanität im 19. Jh.*, 1929.

P. Ernst, *Der Zusammenbruch des dt. Idealismus*, 3rd ed. 1931.

W. Lütgert, *Das Ende des Idealismus im Zeitalter Bismarcks*, 1930.

F. A. Lange, *Gesch. des Materialismus*, 1866; 10th ed. 1926.

H. Cysarz, *Von Schiller zu Nietzsche. Hauptfragen der dt. Dichtungs- und Bildungsgesch. des jüngsten Jhs*, 1928.

H. Marcuse, *Reason and revolution: Hegel and the rise of social theory*, 1941.

K. Löwith, *Von Hegel zu Nietzsche*, 1941.

P. Vogel, *Hegels Gesellschaftsbegriff u. seine gesch. Fortbildung durch L. v. Stein, Marx, Engels u. Lassalle*, 1926.

H. Pross, *Lit. u. Politik. Gesch. u. Programm der politischlit. Zeitschriften im dt. Sprachgebiet seit 1870*, 1963.

E. K. Bramstedt, *Aristocracy and the middle classes in Germany. Social types in German lit. 1830–70*, 2nd ed. 1964.

R. Wellek, *Confrontations. Studies in the intellectual and lit. relations between Germany, England and the United States during the 19th century*, 1965.

F. W. Schirmer, *Der Einfluss der dt. Lit. auf die englische im 19. Jh.*, 1947.

H. Jantz, 'Sequence and continuity in 19th century German lit.', *GR* 38 (1963).

F. Brie, *Ästhetische Weltanschauung in der Lit. des 19. Jhs*, 1921.

F. Koch, *Idee u. Wirklichkeit. Dt. Dichtung zwischen Romantik u. Naturalismus*, 2 vols., 1956.

W. Höllerer, *Zwischen Klassik u. Moderne*, 1958.

H. Bieber, *Der Kampf um die Tradition. Die dt. Dichtung im europäischen Geistesleben 1830–80*, 1928.

G. Sainsbury, *The later nineteenth century*, 1923 (pp. 195–252).

E. Alker, *Gesch. der dt. Lit. von Goethes Tod bis zur Gegenwart*, 2 vols., 1949–50 (also as *Die dt. Lit. im 19. Jh.*, 1962).

H. Boeschenstein, *German lit. of the 19th century*, 1969.

R. Gray, *The German tradition in lit. 1871–1945*, 1965.

G. Lukács, *Dt. Lit. im Zeitalter des Imperialismus*, 1945; 6th ed. 1950.

C. David, *Zwischen Romantik u. Symbolismus, 1820–85*, 1966.

V. Lange, *Modern German lit. 1870–1940*, 1945.

J. Bithell, *Modern German lit. 1880–1950*, 3rd ed. 1959.

P. E. H. Lüthi, *Literatur als Geschichte: dt. Dichtung 1885–1947*, 1947.

W. Stammler, *Dt. Lit. vom Naturalismus bis zur Gegenwart*, 1924; 2nd ed. 1927.

H. Steinhauser, *Die dt. Dichtung 1880–1933*, 2 vols., 1941.

A. Soergel, C. Hohoff, *Dichter u. Dichtung der Zeit*, 2 vols., 1961–1963.

W. Mahrholz, *Dt. Dichtung der Gegenwart*, 1926; 2nd ed. 1930.

F. Schlawe, *Lit. Zeitschriften 1885–1910*, 1961; 2nd ed. 1965.

W. Rose, *Men, myths and movements in German lit.*, 1931.

G. Minde-Pouet, E. Rothe (eds.), *Goedekes Grundriss zur Gesch. der dt. Dichtung*, new series 1, 1962.

J. P. Stern, *Re-interpretations. 7 studies in 19th century German lit.*, 1964.

E. Staiger, *Meisterwerke dt. Sprache aus dem 19. Jh.*, 1948; 3rd ed. 1957.

B. v. Wiese (ed.), *Dt. Dichter des 19. Jhs: ihr Leben u. Werk*, 1969.
Mod. Lang. Ass. of America. 'German lit. of the 19th century, 1830–80. A current bibl.', *Modern Language Forum* 34–7 (1949–52), *GR* 28–35 (1953–60).

*Biedermeier*

C. A. Williams, 'Notes on the origin and history of the earlier "Biedermaier" ', *JEGP* 57 (1958).

M. v. Boehn, *Biedermeier. Deutschland von 1815 bis 1847*, n.d. (1911); 3rd ed. 1922.

G. Hermann, *Das Biedermeier im Spiegel seiner Zeit*, 1913; repr. 1965.

H. H. Houben, *Der gefesselte Biedermeier*, 1924.

H. H. Houben, *Kleine Blumen, Kleine Blätter aus Biedermeier und Vormärz*, 1925.

O. Zausmer, *Lebendes, schaffendes Biedermeier*, 1936.

E. E. Pauls, *Der Beginn der bürgerlichen Zeit: Biedermeier-Schicksale*, 1924.

P. F. Schmidt, *Biedermeiermalerei*, 1922; 2nd ed. 1923.

H. Funck, 'Musikalisches Biedermeier', *DVLG* 14 (1936).

K. Simon, 'Biedermeier in der bildenden Kunst', *DVLG* 13 (1935).

E. Kalkschmidt, *Biedermeiers Glück und Ende*, 1957.

M. Wundt, 'Die Philosophie in der Zeit des Biedermeier', *DVLG* 13 (1935).

H. Hoffmann, *Die Zersetzung des dt. Idealismus in der Biedermeierzeit*, 1939.

E. E. Pauls, *Der politische Biedermeier*, 1925.

P. Kluckhohn, 'Biedermeier als literarische Epochenbezeichnung', *DVLG* 13 (1935) and 'Zur Biedermeier-Diskussion', *DVLG* 14 (1936).

G. Weydt, 'Literarisches Biedermeier', *DVLG* 9 (1931) and 13 (1935).

R. Majut, 'Das literarische Biedermeier', *GRM* 20 (1932).

J. Hermand, *Die literarische Formenwelt des Biedermeiers*, 1958.

M. Greiner, *Zwischen Biedermeier u. Bourgeoisie. Ein Kapitel dt. Lit. gesch. im Zeichen H. Heines*, 1953.

F. Sengle, 'Stilistische Sorglosigkeit u. gesellschaftliche Bewährung. Zur Literatur der Biedermeierzeit', *Arbeiten zur dt. Literatur*, 1965.

F. H. Körber (ed.) *Heinrich Laube. Reise durch das Biedermeier*, 1965.

M. Zuber, 'Die dt. Musenalmanche u. schöngeistigen Taschenbücher des Biedermeier 1815–48', *Archiv für die Gesch. des Buchwesens* 1 (1958).

H. Liebing, *Die Erzählungen H. Claurens als Ausdruck der bürger-lichen Welt- u. Lebensanschauung in der beginnenden Biedermeier-zeit*, diss. Halle, 1931.

W. Bietak, *Das Lebensgefühl des Biedermeier in der österreichischen Dichtung*, 1931.

K. Wietfeld, *Biedermeierisches beim alten Goethe*, diss. Munster, 1938.

R. Haller, 'Goethe u. die Welt des Biedermeiers', *DVLG* 14 (1936).

E. H. Zeydel, 'L. Tieck u. das Biedermeier', *GRM* 26 (1938).

G. Weydt, *Naturschilderung bei Annette v. Droste-Hülshoff und A. Stifter: Beiträge zum Biedermeierstil*, 1930.

V. Sandomirsky, *E. Mörikes Verhältnis zum Biedermeier*, 1935.

G. Weydt, 'Biedermeier u. Junges Deutschland', *DVLG* 25 (1951).

A. B. Berkhout, *Biedermeier u. poetischer Realismus*, diss. Amsterdam, 1942.

id., *Der dt. Vormärz. Texte und Dokumente*, 1967.


*Young Germany*

J. Hermand (ed.), *Das Junge Deutschland. Texte und Dokumente*, 1966.

H. G. Keller, *Das 'Junge Europa' 1834–36*, 1938.

J. Proelss, *Das junge Deutschland. Ein Buch dt. Geistesgesch.*, 1892.

H. H. Houben, *Jungdeutscher Sturm und Drang*, 1911.

H. v. Kleinmeyer, *Welt- u. Kunstanschauung des Jungen Deutsch-land*, 1930.

C. P. Magill, 'Young Germany: a revaluation', *Germ. Studies pre-sented to L. A. Willoughby*, 1952.

K. Hecker, *Mensch u. Masse*, 1933.

H. Bloesch, *Das Junge Deutschland in seinen Beziehungen zu Frank-reich*, 1903.

L. Geiger, 'Das Junge Deutschland und Österreich'. *DRs* 127 (1906).

J. Whyte, *Young Germany in its relations to Britain*, 1917.

E. v. Pustau, *Die Stellung der Frau im Leben u. im Roman des Jungen Deutschland*, diss. Frankfurt a. M., 1928.

G. Bäumer, *Der Frauentypus des Jungen Deutschland*, 1911.

H. Gulde, *Studien zum jungdt. Frauenroman*, diss. Tübingen, 1931.

E. Royen, *Die Auffassung der Liebe im Jungen Deutschland*, diss. Münster, 1928.

G. Thrum, *Der Typ des Zerrissenen*, 1931.

E. Gamper, *Dichter u. Dichtertum zur Zeit des Jungen Deutschland*, diss. Zürich, 1932.

A. Wildhaber, *Das Bild der Reformation in der jungdeutschen Epoche*, diss. Berne, 1936.

E. M. Butler, *The Saint-Simonian religion in Germany*, 1926.

W. Suhge, *Saint-Simonismus u. Junges Deutschland*, 1935.

H. J. Whyte, 'The attitude of Das junge Deutschland towards the historical novel', *GR* 3 (1928).

V. Eichstädt, *Die dt. Publizistik von 1830*, 1933.

W. Dietze, *Junges Deutschland und dt. Klassik*, 2nd ed. 1958; 3rd ed. 1962.

A. C. de Noé, *Das Junge Deutschland u. Goethe*, diss. Chicago, 1910.

J. Dresch, *Goethe et la Jeune Allemagne*, *Publ. de la Faculté des lettres de Strasbourg* 57 (1932).

M. Holzmann (ed.), *Stimmen aus dem Lager der Goethe-Gegner*, DLD 129 (1904).

F. Petitpierre, *Heinse in den Jugendschriften des Jungen Deutschland*, diss. Berne, 1916.

T. K. Brown, *Young Germany's view of Romanticism*, 1941.

E. Jenal, 'Der Kampf gegen die jungdeutsche Lit.', *ZfdPh* 58 (1933).

E. M. Butler, 'The Persecution of the Young Germans', *MLR* 19 (1924).

H. Friedrich: *Die religionsphilosophischen, soziologischen und politischen Elemente in den Prosadichtungen des Jungen Deutschlands*, diss. Leipzig, 1907.

J. Weil, *Das Junge Deutschland u. die Juden*, 1836.

### Realism and Naturalism

J. M. Ritchie, 'The ambivalence of "Realism" in German literature 1830–80', *Orbis litterarum*, 15 (1960).

E. L. Stahl, 'Bürgerlicher Realismus', *MLR* 59 (1964).

R. Brinkmann, *Wirklichkeit und Illusion. Studien über Gehalt u. Grenzen des Begriffs Realismus f. die erzählende Dichtung des 19. Jhs*, 1957; 2nd ed. 1966.

R. Brinkmann, *Begriffsbestimmung des lit. Realismus*, 1969.

F. Martini, *Dt. Lit. im bürgerlichen Realismus 1848–98*, 1962; 2nd ed. 1964.

W. Linden, 'Das Zeitalter des Realismus 1830–85', *Zs. f. dt. Unterricht* 44 (1930).

S. v. Lempicki, 'Wurzeln u. Typen des dt. Realismus im 19. Jh., Fs. J. Petersen, 1938.

H. Reinhardt, *Die Dichtungstheorien der sogenannten poetischen Realisten*, diss. Tübingen, 1939.

G. Lukács, *Essays über Realismus*, 1948.

G. Lukács, *Dt. Realisten des 19. Jhs*, 1951; 2nd ed. 1952.

H. Ohl, *Bild u. Wirklichkeit. Studien zur Romankunst Raabes u. Fontanes*, 1968.

N. Fuerst, *The Victorian age of German lit. 8 essays*, 1966.

W. Preisendanz, *Humor als dichterische Einbildungskraft. Studien zur Erzählkunst des poetischen Realismus*, 1963.

M. L. Gansberg, *Der Prosa-Wortschatz des dt. Realismus*, 1964.

K. Fehr, *Der Realismus in der schweizerischen Lit.*, 1965.

F. Stuckert, 'Zur Dichtung des Realismus und des Jh.-endes. Ein Literaturbericht', *DVLG* 19 (1941).

F. Martini, *Forschungsbericht zur dt. Lit. des Realismus*, 1962.

H. Röhl, *Der Naturalismus*, 1927.

R. Hamann, J. Hermand, *Naturalismus. Dt. Kunst u. Kultur von der Gründerzeit bis zum Expressionismus*, vol. 2, 1959.

U. Münchow, *Dt. Naturalismus*, 1968.

L. Fischer, *Der Kampf um den Naturalismus*, diss. Rostock, 1930.

H. Claus, *Deutung des Frühnaturalismus*, 1933.

O. E. Lessing, *Die neue Form*, 1910.

E. Utitz, 'Naturalistische Kunsttheorie', *Zs. f. Ästhetik* 5 (1911).

H. Vetter, *Formerneuerungsversuche in der dt. Dichtung im 9. Jahrzehnt des 19. Jhs*, diss. Leipzig, 1931.

E. Ruprecht (ed.), *Literarische Manifeste des Naturalismus 1880–92*, 1962.

L. H. Wolf, *Die ästhetische Grundlage der Literaturrevolution: die 'Kritschen Waffengänge' der Gebrüder Hart*, diss. Berne, 1921.

G. P. Gooch, 'Berlin in the 'nineties', *GLL* 9 (1955–6).

W. Spohr, *O ihr Tage von Friedrichshagen! Erinnerungen aus der Werdezeit des dt. lit. Realismus*, 1949.

W. H. Root, 'Optimism in the naturalistic Weltanschauung', *GR* 12 (1937).

W. R. Gaede, 'Zur geistesgesch. Deutung des Früh-Naturalismus', *GR* 11 (1936).

H. Hlauschek, *Der Entwicklungsbegriff in den theoretischen Programm-schriften des Frühnaturalismus*, diss. Munich, 1941.

H. Kasten, *Die Idee der Dichtung und des Dichters in den lit. Theorien des sogenannten 'Dt. Naturalismus'*, diss. Königsberg, 1936.

L. Rausch, *Die Gestalt des Künstlers in der Dichtung des Naturalismus*, diss. Giessen, 1932.

K. Remmers, *Die Frau im Früh-Naturalismus*. diss. Bonn, 1931.

H. Guntrum, *Die Emanzipierte in der Dichtung des Naturalismus*, diss. Giessen, 1928.

J. Saueracker, *Paul Bourget u. der Naturalismus*, 1936.

I. Günther, *Die Einwirkung des skandinavischen Romans auf den dt. Naturalismus 1870–1900*, diss. Giessen, 1934.

W. H. Eller, *Ibsen in Germany 1870–1900*, 1918.

M. Thalmann, *Ibsen. ein Erlebnis der Deutschen*, 1928.

J. W. McFarlane, 'Hauptmann, Ibsen and the concept of Natur-alismus', *Hauptmann Centenary Lectures*, ed. F. Norman, 1964.

G. Kersten, *G. Hauptmann u. Lev Nikolajević Tolstoy. Studien zur Wirkungsgesch. von L. N. Tolstoy in Deutschland 1885–1910*, 1966.

W. Halm, 'Wechselbeziehungen zwischen Tolstoi u. der dt. Lit.', *Archiv f. slavische Philologie* 35 (1911).

T. Kampmann, *Dostojevsky in Deutschland*, 1931.

V. Eckert, *Vom Naturalismus zum Neuidealismus*, 1914.

D. W. Schumann, 'Motifs of cultural eschatology in German poetry from naturalism to expressionism', *PMLA* 58 (1943).

W. Duwe, *Ausdrucksformen dt. Dichtung vom Naturalismus bis zur Gegenwart*, 1965.

D. Sternberger, *Über den Jugendstil u. andere Essays*, 1956.

J. Hermand, *Jugendstil*, 1965.

## THEORY AND HISTORY OF LITERARY FORMS

### Prose Narrative

H. Mielke, H. J. Homann, *Der dt. Roman*, 5th ed. 1921 (nineteenth and twentieth century).

L. Pineau, *L'évolution du roman en Allemagne au 19e siècle*, 1908.

F. Sengle, 'Der Romanbegriff in der ersten Hälfte des 19. Jhs', *Arbeiten zur dt. Lit.*, 1965.

H. Mayer, 'Der dt. Roman im 19. Jh.', *Dt. Lit. u. Weltlit.*, 1957.

W. Killy, *Wirklichkeit u. Kunstcharakter: neun Romane des 19. Jhs*, 1963.

L. B. Jennings, *The ludicrous demon. Aspects of the grotesque in German post-romantic prose*, 1963.

P. Scheidweiler, *Der Roman der dt. Romantik*, 1916.

F. Lübbe, *Die Wendung vom Individualismus zur sozialen Gemeinschaft im romantischen Roman*, 1931.

E. Voerster, *Märchen u. Novellen im klassisch-romantischen Roman*, 1964; 2nd ed. 1966.

M. Schian, *Der dt. Roman seit Goethe*, 1904.

F. Martini, 'Zur Theorie des Romans im dt. "Realismus" ', Fs. Ed. Berend, 1959.

F. Martini, ' "Bürgerlicher" Realismus u. der dt. Roman im 19. Jh.' *WW* 1 (1950).

R. Horovitz, *Vom Roman des Jungen Deutschland zum Roman der Gartenlaube*, diss. Basel, 1937.

E. A. Greatwood, *Die dichterische Selbstdarstellung im Roman des Jungen Deutschland*, 1935.

H. Grünauer, *Typen des historischen Romans der Jungdeutschen*, diss. Vienna, 1946.

O. Krauss, *Der Professorenroman*, 1884.

O. Sieper, *Der historische Roman u. die historische Novelle bei Raabe u. Fontane*, 1930.

W. Manggold, *Der dt. Adels-Roman im 19. Jh.*, diss. Freiburg, 1934.

H. Reider, *Liberalismus als Lebensform in der dt. Prosaepik des 19. Jhs*, 1939.

H. Gulde, *Studien zum jungdt. Frauenroman*, diss. Tübingen, 1932.

H. Sallenbach, *Georges Sand u. der dt. Emanzipationsroman*, diss. Zürich, 1942.

R. Zellweger, *Les débuts du roman rustique: Suisse, Allemagne, France 1836–56*, 1941.

R. Hallgarten, *Die Anfänge der schweizer Dorfgeschichte*, 1906.

F. Altvater, *Wesen u. Form der dt. Dorfgeschichte im 19. Jh.*, 1930.

H. Lemaire, *Das Stadt-Land-Problem u. seine Gestaltung im dt. Roman des 19. und 20. Jhr.*, diss. Bonn, 1933.

H. Kirchner-Klemperer, 'Der dt. soziale Roman der vierziger Jahre des 19. Jhs', *Wissenschaftliche Zs. der Humboldt-Univ. Berlin* 11 (1962).

K. Helmer, *Die Frauenbewegung im Spiegel des dt. Frauenromans von 1830–50*, diss. Vienna, 1922.

G. Strecker, *Frauenträume, Frauentränen. Über den dt. Frauenroman*, 1969.

J. Dresch, *Le roman social en Allemagne 1850–1900*, 1913.

K. Mehle, *Die soziale Frage im dt. Roman während der zweiten Hälfte des 19. Jhs*, diss. Halle, 1924.

A. Behrens, *Der entwurzelte Mensch im Familienroman 1880 bis zur Gegenwart*, diss. Bonn, 1932.

G. Gräfe, *Die Gestalt des Literaten im Zeitroman des 19. Jhs*, 1937.

E. Diem, *Wesen u. Entwicklung des dt. naturalistischen Romans*, diss. Munich, 1923.

L. Niemann, *Soziologie des naturalistischen Romans*, Germ. Stud. 148 (1934).

D. Huber, *Romanstoffe in den bürgerlichen Zeitungen des 19. Jhs*, diss. Berlin, 1943.

B. v. Wiese, *Die dt. Novelle von Goethe bis Kafka*, 2 vols., 1956, 1962.

K. Ewald, *Die dt. Novelle im ersten Drittel des 19. Jhs*, 1907.

J. Kunz, *Die dt. Novelle zwischen Klassik u. Romantik*, 1966.

P. Bastier, *La nouvelle individualiste en Allemagne de Goethe à Gottfried Keller*, 1910.

G. Schüler, *Die Novelle des Jungen Deutschland*, diss. Berlin, 1941.

F. Martini, 'Die dt. Novelle im bürgerlichen Realismus. Überlegungen zur gesch. Bestimmung des Formtypus', *WW* 10 (1960).

W. Wilz, *Realism and reality, studies in the German novelle of poetic realism*, 1965.

J. M. Ritchie, 'Drama and melodrama in the 19th century Novelle', *AUMLA*, 1963.

*Poetry*

P. Böckmann, 'Dt. Lyrik im 19. Jh.', *Formkräfte der dt. Dichtung*, 1963.

H. J. Schueler, *The German verse epic in the 19th and 20th century*, diss. Toronto, 1965.

H. Schlaffer, 'Das Dichtergedicht im 19. Jh. Topos u. Ideologie', *JDSG* 10 (1966).

R. Bernheim, *Die Terzine in der dt. Dichtung von Goethe bis Hofmannsthal*, diss. Berne, 1954.

R. Ibel, *Weltschau dt. Dichter*, 1948 (Novalis, Eichendorff, Mörike, Droste-Hülshoff).

P. Böckmann, *Klang u. Bild in der Stimmungslyrik der Romantik*, Fs. R. Benz, 1954.

R. Kienzerle, *Aufbauformen romantischer Lyrik aufgezeigt an Tieck, Brentano u. Eichendorff*, diss. Tübingen, 1947.

G. Scholz, *Die Balladendichtung der Frühromantik*, 1935.

J. Hermand, *Die lit. Formenwelt des Biedermeier*, 1958.

J. Bithell, *An anthology of German poetry*, vol. 1 (1830–80), vol. 2 (1880–1940), 1956.

C. Petzet, *Die Blütezeit der dt. politischen Lyrik 1840–50*, 1903.

O. Rommel, *Die politische Lyrik des Vormärz u. des Sturmjahres*, 1912.

H. E. Tièche, *Die politische Lyrik in der dt. Schweiz 1830–50*, 1917.

W. Roer, *Die soziale Bewegung vor der dt. Revolution 1848 im Spiegel der zeitgenössischen politischen Lyrik*, 1933.

H. Schlaffer, *Lyrik im Realismus. Studien über Raum u. Zeit in den Gedichten Mörikes, der Droste u. Liliencrons*, 1966.

L. Bianchi, *Von der Droste bis Liliencron*, 1922.

S. Liptzin, *Lyric pioneers of modern Germany: studies in German social poetry*, 1928.

J. Hundt, *Das Proletariat u. die soziale Frage im Spiegel der naturalistischen Dichtung 1884–90*, diss. Rostock, 1933.

W. Sieber, *Der Münchener Dichterkreis u. die Romantik*, diss. Berne, 1937.

F. Burwick, *Die Kunsttheorie des Münchener Dichterkreises*, diss. Greifswald, 1932.

R. F. Egan, *The genesis of the theory of 'Art for Art's sake' in Germany and England*, 2 parts, 1922–24.

*Drama*

G. Witkowski, *Das dt. Drama im 19. Jh.*, 1904.

W. Kosch, *Das dt. Theater u. Drama im 19. u. 20. Jh.*, 3rd ed., 1939.

F. W. Kaufmann, *German dramatists of the 19th century*, 1940.

M. Dietrich, *Europäische Dramaturgie im 19 Jh.*, 1961.

M. Martersteig, *Das dt. Theater im 19. Jh., eine kulturgesch. Darstellung*, 2nd ed., 1924.

B. E. Schatzky, 'The German stage in the 19th century', *GLL* 13 (1959–60).

B. E. Schatzky, 'Genre painting and the German tragedy of common life', *MLR* 54 (1959).

K. Ziegler, 'Stiltypen des dt. Dramas im 19. Jh.', *Formkräfte der dt. Dichtung*, 1963.

R. Ullshöfer, *Die Theorie des Dramas in der dt. Romantik*, 1935.

E. Gross, *Die ältere Romantik u. das Theater*, 1960.

K. G. Wendriner, *Das romantische Drama*, 1909.

W. Kayser, 'Formtypen des dt. Dramas um 1800', *Stil- u. Formprobleme*, ed. P. Böckmann, 1959; also in *Die Vortragsreise*, 1958.

E. Morschel, *Der Sprechstil der idealistischen Schauspielkunst in der ersten Hälfte des 19. Jhs*, 1956.

A. Fuchs, 'Der Verfall der dt. dramatischen Form im 19. Jh.' *Bull. de la Fac. des Lettres, Strasbourg*, 1955–56.

W. Schlunk, *Hegels Theorie des Dramas*, diss. Tübingen, 1936.

H. Hettner, 'Die Komödie der Gegenwart' (1852), *Meisterwerke dt. Lit.kritik*, ed. H. Mayer, II.

O-R. Dithmar, *Dt. Dramaturgie zwischen Hegel u. Hettner um die Wende von 1840*, diss. Heidelberg, 1965.

U. Münchow, 'Die ersten Anfänge der sozialistischen Dramatik in Deutschland', *WB* 9 (1963).

H. Förster, *Studien zum jungdeutschen Begriff des Dramas*, diss. Breslau, 1930.

P. Malthan, *Das Junge Deutschland u. das Lustspiel*, 1930.

H. Bessler, *Studien zum historischen Drama des Jungen Deutschland*, diss. Leipzig, 1935.

G. Engelmann, *Das historische Drama im ausgehenden 19. Jh.*, diss. Munich, 1957.

B. v. Wiese, 'Probleme der dt. Tragödie im 19. Jh.', *WW* 1 (1950–51).

B. v. Wiese, 'Schiller u. die dt. Tragödie des 19. Jhs', *DVLG* 25 (1951).

W. Weier, 'Entwicklungsphasen des Todesproblems in der dt. Tragödie zwischen Idealismus u. Realismus', *Lit.wiss. Jb.* 5 (1964).

G. Kluge, 'Das Lustspiel der dt. Romantik', *Das dt. Lustspiel*, ed. H. Steffen, 1968.

G. Kluge, *Spiel u. Witz im romantischen Lustspiel*, diss. Köln, 1963.

F. Güttinger, *Die romantische Komödie u. das dt. Lustspiel*, 1939.

M. Pulver, *Romantische Ironie u. romantische Komödie*, diss. Freiburg i. Br., 1912.

# 11. BIOGRAPHIES AND BIBLIOGRAPHIES OF INDIVIDUAL AUTHORS

## WILLIBALD ALEXIS (WILHELM HÄRING)

Häring, who took as his pseudonym the Latin equivalent of his surname, was born 29 June 1798 in Breslau. He fought in the War of Liberation in 1815 then studied law in Berlin and Breslau. He quickly abandoned his legal career, however, and became journalist, bookseller and estate agent. In 1849 he joined the editorial staff of the *Vossische Zeitung*, but his success as a novelist enabled him to retire to Arnstadt in 1851. In 1856 he suffered a cerebral stroke and never fully recovered. He died 16 Dec. 1871. Alexis began his career with Novellen in the manner of Tieck but made his reputation as the author of historical tales in emulation of Scott. His travel journals and his *Pitaval*, a chronicle of contemporary crimes and criminals, are of cultural and sociological interest. The novels and short stories combine romantic antiquarianism and the patriotic liberalism of Young Germany. The sharp observation of social detail which Alexis had no doubt learned in his journalistic career anticipated the work of Fontane and other realistic novelists.

## Works

*Der Schatz der Tempelherren*, 1823
*Walladmor*, 1823
*Heer- u. Querstrassen*, 1824 ff. (travel journal)
*Schloss Avalon*, 1827
*Herbstreise durch Skandinavien*, 1828
*Gesammelte Novellen*, 4 vols., 1830 ff.
*Cabanis*, 1832
*Das Haus Düsterweg*, 1835
*Neue Novellen*, 2 vols., 1836
*Zwölf Nächte*, 1838
*Der Roland von Berlin*, 1840
*Der falsche Woldemar*, 1842
*Der neue Pitaval*, ed. with J. E. Hitzig, 30 vols., 1842 ff.

*Die Hosen des Herrn von Bredow*, 1846
*Der Wärwolf*, 1848
*Ruhe ist die erste Bürgerpflicht*, 1852; repr. ed. H. Poschmann, 1969
*Isegrimm*, 1854
*Dorothee*, 1856
*Gesammelte Werke*, 18 vols., 1861–6; 20 vols., 1874

Literature

L. H. C. Thomas, *Willibald Alexis. A German writer of the 19th century*, 1964
T. Fontane, 'Willibald Alexis', 1883; repr. *Aufsätze zur Lit.*, ed. K. Schreiner, 1963
H. Haasen, *Der junge Willibald Alexis*, diss. Bonn, 1920
H. A. Korff, *Scott u. Alexis*, diss. Heidelberg, 1907
W. Beutin, *Königtum u. Adel in den historischen Romanen von Willibald Alexis*, 1966
P. K. Richter, *Willibald Alexis als Lit.- u. Theaterkritiker*, Germ. Stud. 107 (1931)
M. Ewert, F. Hasselberg (eds.), *Jahresbericht* (later: *Jb.*) des *Willibald Alexis-Bundes*, 1927–37

## LUDWIG ANZENGRUBER (pseud. L. GRUBER)

Born 29 Nov. 1839 in Vienna, Anzengruber started life as an apprentice in the book-trade but joined an itinerant troupe of actors in 1858. From 1868 he earned his living as a journalist with various Viennese periodicals and it was at this time that he wrote his most popular drama, the anti-clerical *Pfarrer von Kirchfeld*; from then on he was immensely prolific and popular. He tended to model his naturalistic plays and tales on Zola. From 1882–5 Anzengruber was editor-in-chief of the magazine, *Die Heimat*, and from 1885–9 editor of the humorous journal *Figaro*. He died in Vienna on 10 Dec. 1889.

Works

*Der Pfarrer von Kirchfeld*, 1871
*Der Meineidbauer*, 1872 (tragedy)
*Die Kreuzelschreiber*, 1872 (comedy)
*Elfriede*, 1873 (drama)
*Die Tochter des Wucherers*, 1873 (drama)
*Der G'wissenswurm*, 1874 (comedy)

*Ein Geschworener*, 1876 (drama)
*Der Schandfleck*, 1877 (novel)
*Der ledige Hof*, 1877 (drama)
*Das vierte Gebot*, 1878 (drama)
*Ein Faustschlag*, 1878 (drama)
*'s Jungferngift*, 1878 (comedy)
*Die Trutzige*, 1879 (drama)
*Alte Wiener*, 1879 (drama)
*Die umkehrte Freit*, 1879 (drama)
*Dorfgänge*, 2 vols., 1879 (short stories)
*Aus 'm g'wöhnlichen G'leis*, 1880 (drama)
*Brave Leut' vom Grund*, 1880 (drama)
*Der Sternsteinhof*, 1885 (novel)
*Heimg'funden*, 1885 (comedy)
*Stahl und Stein*, 1887 (drama)
*Wolken und Sunn'schein*, 1888 (collected tales)
*Der Fleck auf der Ehr'*, 1889 (drama)
*Letzte Dorfgänge*, 1894
*Gesammelte Werke*, ed. A. Bettelheim *et al.*, 10 vols., 1890; *Briefe*, 2 vols., 1902
*Sämtliche Werke*, ed. R. Latzke, O. Rommel, 17 vols., 1920–2

Literature

A. Bettelheim, *Anzengruber. Der Mann, sein Werk u. seine Weltanschauung*, 1891; 2nd ed. 1898
A. Kleinberg, *Ludwig Anzengruber*, 1921
L. Koessler, *Le théâtre d'Anzengruber*, 1943
F. Weber, *Anzengrubers Naturalismus*, diss. Tübingen, 1928
J. C. Blankenagel, 'Naturalistic tendencies in Anzengruber's *Das vierte Gebot*', *GR* 10 (1935)
W. Martin, *Der kämpferische Atheismus Anzengrubers*, diss. East Berlin, 1960
W. Martin, 'Anzengruber und das Volksstück', *Neue Dt. Lit.* 9 (1961)
W. E. Yates, 'Nestroysche Stilelemente bei Anzengruber', *Maske u. Kothurn* 24 (1968)

ERNST MORITZ ARNDT

Born 26 Dec. 1769 at Gross-Schoritz on the island of Rügen, died 29 Jan. 1860 in Bonn. He studied theology and history at

Greifswald and Jena; at the latter university he attended Fichte's lectures, which made a strong impression on him. From 1796–8 he earned his living as a tutor and during the next two years journeyed on foot in Austria, Hungary, France and Belgium; in 1805 he became Professor of History at Greifswald. He took an active part in opposing Napoleon and fled to Stockholm in 1806, returning to Greifswald in 1810. In the following year he resigned his professorship and until 1818 acted as Freiherr von Stein's secretary in St. Petersburg, Königsberg, Leipzig and Frankfurt. In 1818 he accepted a professorship of history at the newly founded University of Bonn. He was dismissed in 1821 because of his association with the 'Burschenschaften' but was reinstated in 1840. He became a member of the Frankfurt Parliament in 1848. His political writings are no less characteristic than his patriotic verse, the best known tract being 'Der Rhein, Teutschlands Strom, aber nicht Teutschlands Grenze' (1813).

## Works

*Gedichte, 1803*
*Lieder für Deutsche*, 1813; ed. O. Anwand, 1935
*Gedichte*, 1818
*Werke*, ed. H. Meisner and H. Rösch, 1892–1903

## Literature

R. Thiele, *Ernst Moritz Arndt*, 1894
G. Lange, *Der Dichter Arndt*, 1910
H. Frömbgen, *Arndt u. die dt. Romantik*, 1927

## Ludwig Achim von Arnim

Born in Berlin, 26 Jan. 1781, died at Wiepersdorf, Mark Brandenburg, 21 Jan. 1831. He studied physics at Halle and Göttingen from 1798 to 1801. His friendship with Clemens Brentano began in this year. He travelled in France and England (1802–4). In 1805 he joined Brentano in Heidelberg where they collaborated in collecting material for *Des Knaben Wunderhorn*. With Brentano, Tieck, Görres, the brothers Grimm and Runge he edited the *Zeitung für Einsiedler* (1808–12), one of the most representative and influential journals of the Second Romantic

School, particularly notable for its polemics against the Classicists and against Voss. In 1811 Arnim collaborated with Brentano, H. v. Kleist, Adam Müller, Chamisso and Fouqué in founding the 'Christlich-deutsche Tischgesellschaft'. He served in the 1813 campaign, edited the *Preussische Korrespondent* from Oct. 1813 until Jan. 1814, then retired to his estate at Wiepersdorf. He married Bettina, Clemens Brentano's sister in 1811.

Works

*Des Knaben Wunderhorn*, ed. with C. Brentano, 1806–8
*Kriegslieder*, 1806
*Armut, Reichtum, Schuld, und Busse der Gräfin Dolores*, 1810 (novel)
*Halle und Jerusalem*, 1811 (drama)
*Isabella von Ägypten*, 1812 (short story)
*Die Kronenwächter*, 1817 (novel)
*Der tolle Invalide auf dem Fort Ratonneau*, 1818 (short story)
*Die Gleichen*, 1819 (drama)
*Sämtliche Werke*, ed. W. Grimm, 1839–56
*Ausgewählte Werke*, ed. R. Steig, 1911; M. Morris, 1916
Correspondence with Bettina, ed. W. Vortriede, 1961
*Sämtliche Romane u. Erzählungen*, ed. W. Migge, 1961 ff.

Literature

R. Steig, *Achim von Arnim*, 3 vols., 1894–1913
R. Guignard, *Achim von Arnim*, 1936; repr. 1953
I. Seidel, *Achim von Arnim*, 1944
G. Rudolph, *Studien zur dichterischen Welt Achim v. Arnims*, 1958
G. Falkner, *Die Dramen Achim v. Arnims*, 1962
Bibliography by O. Mallon, 1925; repr. 1965

BERTHOLD AUERBACH (MOSES BARUCH AUERBACHER; pseud. THEOBALD CHAUBER)

Born 28 Feb. 1812 at Nordstetten in the Black Forest, died 8 Feb. 1882 in Cannes; his parents intended him to become a rabbi but in 1830 he took up the study of law in Tübingen. He was arrested several times and once imprisoned because of connections with the liberal Burschenschaft, failed to qualify and took up journalism in Frankfurt, becoming editor of a newspaper in Karlsruhe in 1841. After the success of his *Dorfgeschichten* Auerbach settled for a time in Dresden but in the following years moved to a number of different places, including Berlin and Bingen. Auerbach helped in the founding of Julius Rodenberg's *Deutsche Rundschau*. He fought throughout his life for the improvement of popular education and the emancipation of the Jews and at one time enjoyed a European reputation.

## Works

*Das Judentum u. die neueste Literatur*, 1836
*Spinoza*, 1837 (historical novel)
*Andree Hofer*, 1850 (tragedy)
*Neues Leben*, 3 vols., 1852
*Der Wahlbruder*, 1855 (tragedy)
*Barfüssele*, 1856
*Joseph im Schnee*, 1860
*Auf der Höhe*, 3 vols., 1865
*Das Landhaus am Rhein*, 5 vols., 1869
*Waldfried*, 3 vols., 1874
*Lorle, die Frau Professorin*, 1874
*Landolin von Reutershöfen*, 1878
*Der Forstmeister*, 2 vols., 1879
*Brigitta*, 1880
*Schwarzwälder Dorfgeschichten*, 10 vols., 1843–54; ed. A. Bettelheim, 1913
*Gesammelte Schriften*, 3rd ed., 18 vols., 1892–5
*Werke*, 12 vols., 1911; sel. and ed. C. Christiansen, 2 vols., 1926
*Erzählungen*, sel. and ed. W. Hagen, 1962

## Literature

A. Bettelheim, *B. Auerbach, der Mann, sein Werk, sein Nachlass*, 1907
W. Hagen, 'B. Auerbach, Dichter und Schriftsteller', *Lebensbilder aus Schwaben und Franken* 7 (1960)
A. Weber, *Berthold Auerbachs Weltanschauung*, diss. Zürich, 1922
W. Dietz, *Weltanschauung u. Reflexion bei B. Auerbach*, diss. Würzburg, 1925
M. G. Zwick, *B. Auerbachs sozialpolitischer u. ethischer Liberalismus*, 1933
J. Kill, *B. Auerbach als Schriftsteller*, diss. Bonn, 1924
R. Danek, *Neue Untersuchungen über B. Auerbach an Hand seines Romans 'Neues Leben'*, diss. Vienna, 1950

E. H. Spitz, *Studien zu den Schwarzwälder Dorfgeschichten B. Auerbachs*, 1957

W. Hagen, 'B. Auerbach über E. Mörike', *JDSG* 6 (1962)

S. B. Puknat, 'Auerbach and Channing', *PMLA* 72 (1957)

see also: Goedeke's *Grundriss*, new series, vol. 1 (1962)

## FRANZ XAVER VON BAADER

Baader was born in Munich on 27 March 1765. Trained originally as a physician, he became director of mines, a member of the Bavarian Academy of Sciences and honorary professor at the University of Munich. He died in Munich on 23 May 1841. Baader's philosophy was influenced by the mystic, Jakob Böhme (1575–1624) and influenced in turn the thinking of many Romantics, particularly Schelling. Although Baader was a Roman Catholic his theosophical idea of God's presence in individual consciousness ('Cogitor ergo cogito et sum') and also his social views brought him into conflict with the Church. As a forerunner of Christian Socialism, Baader came into renewed prominence in the twenties of the present century.

Works

*Fermenta cognitionis*, 1822

*Über das dermalige Verhältnis der Vermögenslosen oder Proletairs zu den Vermögen besitzenden Klassen der Societät*, 1835

*Grundzüge der Sozietätsphilosophie*, 1837

*Revision der Philosopheme der Hegelschen Schule*, 1839

*Sämtliche Werke*, ed. F. Hoffmann, 16 vols., 1851–60

Literature

J. Claassen, *Franz von Baaders Leben und theosophische Werke*, 2 vols., 1886–7

F. Lieb, *Franz von Baaders Jugendgeschichte*, 1926

D. Baumgardt, *Franz von Baader und die philosophische Romantik*, 1927

J. Sauter, *Die Sozialphilosophie Franz von Baaders*, diss. Munich, 1926

J. Sauter, *Baader und Kant*, 1928

E. Susini, *Franz von Baader et le romantisme mystique*, 2 vols., 1942

J. Siegel, *Franz von Baader*, 1957

K. Hemmerle, *Franz von Baaders Gedanke der Schöpfung*, 1963

J. Jost, *Bibliographie der Schriften Baaders*, 1926

## ALEXANDER GOTTLIEB BAUMGARTEN

Born 17 July 1714 in Berlin, a pupil of Christian Wolff, became professor at Frankfurt an der Oder, where he died, 27 May 1762. He is the founder of aesthetics as a separate philosophical discipline and influenced every succeeding writer on the subject in the eighteenth century.

Works
*Meditations philosophicae de nonnullis ad poema pertinentibus*, 1735
    (transl. with the original text by K. Aschenbrunner and
    W. B. Holther, 1954)
*Aesthetica*, 1750

Literature
H. Sommer, *Die poetische Lehre Baumgartens*, 1911
A. Riemann, *Die Ästhetik A. Baumgartens*, 1928
A. Nivelle, *Les théories esthétiques en Allemagne de Baumgarten à Kant*,
    1955

## CHARLOTTE BIRCH-PFEIFFER

Born Stuttgart, 23 June 1800, died Berlin 25 Aug. 1868. Celebrated actress, producer and author of popular dramas, often adapted from successful novels, e.g. by A. Dumas and Charlotte Bronte.

Works
*Das Pfefferrösel*, 1828
*Hinko*, 1829
*Der Glöckner von Notre Dame*, 1847
*Dorf und Stadt*, 1847
*Die Waise von Lowood*, 1855
*Die Grille*, 1856
*Gesammelte Novellen u. Erzählungen*, 3 vols., 1863–5
*Gesammelte dramatische Werke*, 23 vols., 1863–80

Literature
E. Hess, *Charlotte Birch-Pfeiffer als Dramatikerin*, 1914
A. v. Weilen, *K. Gutzkow u. Charlotte Birch-Pfeiffer*, 1918

CHRISTIAN FRIEDRICH VON BLANCKENBURG

Born in Kolberg on 24 Jan. 1744, Blanckenburg followed the example of his uncle, Ewald von Kleist, in combining literary interests with a military career. After serving with a Prussian dragoon regiment he obtained his discharge in 1777 and settled in Leipzig, where he devoted himself to literary and aesthetic studies and became a close friend of the dramatist C. F. Weisse. Apart from his essay on the novel, the first major study of the genre in German, he wrote part of a novel himself, translated Samuel Johnson's *Lives of the most eminent English poets* and produced a new ed. of J. G. Sulzer's authoritative *Theorie der schönen Künste*. Among his many reviews the most notable was that of Goethe's Werther in the *Neue Bibliothek der schönen Wissenschaften* (1775), reprinted in J. W. Braun, *Goethe im Urteil seiner Zeitgenossen* (1883–5). He died in Leipzig on 4 May 1796.

Works

*Versuch über den Roman*, 1774; repr. with critical study by E. Lämmert, 1965
*Beiträge zur Geschichte deutschen Reichs und deutscher Sitten, I Teil*, 1775

Literature

K. Wölfel, 'Friedrich von Blanckenburgs *Versuch über den Roman*', *Dt. Romantheorien*, 1968
M. C. Schioler, 'Blankenburg's advocacy of Shakespeare', *Monatshefte* 42 (1950)

FRIEDRICH (VON) BODENSTEDT

Born 22 April 1819 at Peine near Hanover, studied philology at Göttingen, Munich and Berlin from 1840 to 1844. He became a teacher, first in Moscow (1844–5), then in Tiflis. Here his friend Mirza Schaffy taught him Oriental languages. In 1854 King Maximilian of Bavaria invited him to Munich where he was appointed to a professorship in Slavic languages. He travelled to England in 1859 and to America in 1880. From 1867 until 1869 he directed the theatre at Meiningen. He died 18 April 1892 in Wiesbaden.

Works
*Die Lieder des Mirza Schaffy*, 1851
*Erzählungen und Romane*, 1871–2
*Gesammelte Schriften*, 1865–9

Literature
G. Schenk, *Friedrich Bodenstedt*, 1893
K. Sundermayer, *Bodenstedt u. die Lieder des Mirza Schaffy*, 1932

JOHANN JAKOB BODMER

Born in Greifensee, near Zürich, on 19 July 1698, Bodmer
studied theology and began a career as a bookseller before
becoming professor of Swiss history at the Gymnasium in Zürich
in 1725. He enjoyed great local esteem and was made a member
of the Grand Council in 1737. His enthusiasm for Milton, whose
*Paradise Lost* he translated, and the relatively important part he
was prepared to assign to creative imagination and the irrational
in poetry led him into the celebrated feud with Gottsched and
the Leipzig school of critics. Bodmer published his views first in
conjunction with Breitinger and other Swiss men of letters in
*Die Discourse der Mahlern* and subsequently in numerous critical
and stylistic treatises. He adopted first Klopstock and then
Wieland as his protégés and prospective champions and also
tried to implement his theories in his own epics and dramas on
Biblical, classical and patriotic topics. He attacked his opponents
in parodies and satires, but neither these nor his more ambitious
works have any substantial literary worth. On the other hand,
his endeavours to restore a vigorous literary diction powerful in
metaphor were meritorious and historically significant. His
investigations into Middle High German poetry and his publication of medieval epics and lyrics from the Manesse manuscript
also showed him to be perceptively in advance of his time.
He died in Schönenberg, near Zürich, 2 Jan. 1783.

Works
*Die Discourse der Mahlern*, 1721–3 (ed. T. Vetter, 1891)
*Von dem Einfluss und Gebrauch der Einbildungskraft*, 1727 (with
   Breitinger)
*Johann Miltons Verlust des Paradieses. Ein Heldengedicht*, 1732; repr.
   1965 (ed. W. Bender)

*Briefwechsel von der Natur des poetischen Geschmackes,* 1736; repr.
    1966 (ed. W. Bender)
*Critische Abhandlung von dem Wunderbaren in der Poesie und dessen
    Verbindung mit dem Wahrscheinlichen,* 1740
*Critische Betrachtungen über die poetischen Gemälde der Dichter,* 1741
*Proben der alten schwäbischen Poesie des 13. Jahrhunderts,* 1748
*Noah, ein Heldengedicht,* 1750–2
*Crito. Eine Monat-Schrift,* 1751
*Jacob und Joseph: ein Gedicht in 3 Gesängen,* 1751–4
*Jacob und Rahel, ein Gedicht in zween Gesängen,* 1752
*Der Parcival, ein Gedicht in Wolframs von Eschilbach Denkart,* 1753
*Der erkannte Joseph und der keusche Joseph. Zwei tragische Stücke,*
    1754
*Edward Grandisons Geschichte in Görlitz,* 1755
*Fabeln aus den Zeiten der Minnesänger,* 1757
*Chriemhilden Rache und die Klage,* 1757
*Sammlung von Minnesingern aus dem schwäbischen Zeitpunkte,* 1758
*Electra oder die gerechte Übeltat. Ein Trauerspiel,* 1760
*Ulysses, Telemachs Sohn. Ein Trauerspiel,* 1760
*Julius Cäsar, Ein Trauerspiel,* 1763
*Die Grundsätze der deutschen Sprache,* 1768
*Karl von Burgund, ein Trauerspiel,* 1771 (repr. DLD 9, 1883)
*Schweizerische Schauspiele (Wilhelm Tell; Gesslers Tod; Der alte
    Heinrich von Melchthal),* 1775
*Patroclus, ein Trauerspiel,* 1778
*Odoardo Galotti, Vater der Emilia. Ein Pendant zu Emilia,* 1778
*Homers Werke,* 1778 (translation)
*Altenglische und altschwäbische Balladen,* 1781
Selections from Bodmer's work are contained in DNL 42, ed.
    J. Crueger

Literature

J. Crueger (ed.), *J. C. Gottsched u. die Schweizer J. J. Bodmer und
    J. J. Breitinger,* 1884 (DNL 42); repr. 1965
S. Hildebrand, *Die Discourse der Mahlern.* diss. Uppsala, 1923
C. L. Long, *Die Zeitschriften der dt. Schweiz 1694–1798,* 1939
E. Meissner, *Bodmer als Parodist,* diss. Leipzig, 1904
F. Budde, *Wieland u. Bodmer,* 1910
A. Scenna, *The treatment of ancient legend and history in Bodmer,* 1910
M. Wehrli, *Bodmer u. die Gesch. der Lit.,* 1936

J. Schmitter, *Bodmers Ubersetzungen von Miltons Verlorenem Paradies sprachlich verglichen*, diss. Zürich, 1913

F. Servaes, *Johann Jakob Bodmer zum 200. Geburtstag*, 1900 (with bibl. by T. Vetter)

A. Brown, 'John Locke's essay and Bodmer and Breitinger', *MLQ* 10 (1949)

D. Knight, 'Thomas Blackwell and J. J. Bodmer: the establishment of a lit. link between Homeric Greece and medieval Germany', *GLL* 6 (1952/3)

E. K. Grotegut, 'Bodmer contra Gellert', *MLQ* 23 (1962)

W. Bender, 'J. J. Bodmer u. Johann Miltons *Verlorenes Paradies*', *JDSG* 11 (1967)

F. Servaes, *Die Poetik Gottscheds und der Schweizer*, 1887

F. Ernst, 'J. J. Bodmer', *Essays I* (1946)

E. A. Blackall, *The Emergence of German as a lit. language 1700–75*, 1959, Chap. 9

## Ludwig Börne

Born 6 May 1786 in Frankfurt am Main, died 13 Feb. 1837 in Paris. He studied medicine in Berlin and there frequented the salons of Rahel Varnhagen and Henriette Herz. Later he studied law and politics in Heidelberg and Giessen. He was dismissed from a post in 1811 because of his Jewish origin and in 1818 converted to the Christian faith. During the rest of his life he was engaged in journalism, founding *Die Wage* in 1818 and editing *Zeitschwingen* in 1819. Between 1820 and 1822 and from 1830 until his death he lived in Paris. A leading member of 'Das junge Deutschland' he expressed radical views in numerous articles, essays and reviews. His best known works are his *Denkrede auf Jean Paul* (1826) and *Briefe aus Paris* (1832–4). The distribution of the latter was prohibited by the Bundestag.

Works
*Gesammelte Schriften*, 8 vols., 1829–31
*Werke*, ed. L. Geiger, 1911–19; I. and P. Rippmann, 1964–6

Literature
A. Kuh, *Ludwig Börne, der Zeitgenosse*, 1922
L. Marcuse, *Revolutionär und Patriot. Das Leben Ludwig Börnes*, 1929
H. Bock, *Ludwig Börne*, 1962

## August Bohse ('Talander')

Born 1661 in Halle, died 1730 as professor in Liegnitz, author of many comic and modish tales, of which only a typical selection is mentioned here.

### Works
*Liebeskabinett der Damen*, 1685
*Der getreuen Bellamira wohlbelohnte Liebesprobe*, 1692
*Der Liebe Irregarten*, 1696
*Die Amazoninnen aus dem Kloster*, 1696
*Ariadnens, Königlicher Prinzessin von Toledo, Staats- u. Liebes-Geschichte*, 1699
*Die verliebten Verwirrungen der Sicilianischen Höfe*, 1725

### Literature
E. Schubert, *Augustus Bohse, genannt Talander*, 1911
H. Tiemann, *Die heroisch-galanten Romane August Bohses*, diss. Kiel, 1932
O. Heinlein, *August Bohse-Talander*, diss. Greifswald, 1939
H. Singer, *Der galante Roman*, 1961

## Heinrich Christian Boie

Born 19 July 1744 at Meldorf, Holstein, studied in Jena and Göttingen where he was a member of the 'Hainbund' and founded, with Gotter, the *Göttinger Musenalmanach*. Distinguished career as administrator, editor of *Deutsches Museum* (1776–88) and *Neues Deutsches Museum* (1789–91). Died in Meldorf, 3 March 1806. His work consists mainly of lyric poetry.

### Literature
K. Weinhold, *Heinrich Christian Boie*, 1868; repr. 1969
W. Hofstätter, *Das Deutsche u. Das Neue Deutsche Museum*, 1908

## Joachim Wilhelm Freiherr von Brawe

Born 4 Feb. 1738 in Weissenfels, died 7 April 1758 in Dresden; studied law in Leipzig. With Lessing's encouragement he wrote one of the first blank verse dramas in German (*Brutus*, 1757) and a tragedy in prose, *Der Freigeist*.

Works
*Der Freigeist*, 1758
*Brutus*, 1768
*Trauerspiele*, 1768

Literature
A. Sauer, *J. W. von Brawe, der Schüler Lessings*, 1878

# Johann Jakob Breitinger

Born in Zürich on 1 March 1701. After theological and classical studies he became professor at the Carolinum in Zürich, first of Hebrew (1731), then of Greek (1745). He was a close friend and ally of Bodmer in the latter's feud with Gottsched. He was the more scholarly of the two, less flamboyant and aggressive than Bodmer, whose literary ambition he lacked: Bodmer tended to provide the original ideas and Breitinger the systematic exposition of them. The two men collaborated in producing *Discourse der Mahlern* and the editions of medieval texts which they published owed a great deal to Breitinger's exact philological methods. His *Critische Dichtkunst*, a reply to Gottsched's work of the same name, advocated a more imaginative approach to literature and proposed English rather than French models. Breitinger died in Zürich on 15 December 1776.

Works
*Critische Abhandlung von der Natur, den Absichten und dem Gebrauch der Gleichnisse*, 1740; repr. 1967
*Critische Dichtkunst*, 1740; repr. 1966

Literature
J. C. Mörikofer, *Breitinger und Zürich*, 1874
H. Bodmer, *J. J. Breitinger*, diss. Zürich, 1897
H. Schöffler, *Das lit. Zürich 1700 bis 1750*, 1925
J. Bing, *Die Nachahmungstheorie bei Gottsched u. den Schweizern*, 1935
J. W. Eaton, *Bodmer and Breitinger and European lit. theory*, 1941
J. Bräker, *Der erzieherische Gehalt in J. J. Breitingers 'Critische Dichtkunst'*, 195

Cf. also: J. G. Robertson, *Studies in the genesis of Romantic theory in the eighteenth century*, 1923; E. A. Blackall, *The emergence of German as a lit. language 1700–1775*, 1959

## CLEMENS BRENTANO

Born 8 Sep. 1778 at Ehrenbreitstein, the son of an Italian merchant. He studied at Bonn University and, after working in his father's business, at the Universities of Halle and Jena. Much of the time he spent in the company of literary men like Herder, Wieland, Goethe, the Schlegels and Tieck. In 1803 he married Sophie Mereau who had been the wife of a professor at Jena, and after her death in 1807, Auguste Busmann. This marriage soon failed. A prominent member of the Second Romantic School, he collaborated with Achim von Arnim in composing *Des Knaben Wunderhorn* and forming the 'Christlich-deutsche Tischgesellschaft', in which he was associated with Kleist, Eichendorff and other eminent writers. He went to Vienna in 1813 where Adam Müller, F. Schlegel and Eichendorff also were. In 1816 he met Luise Hensel who was instrumental in his returning to the Catholic faith. From 1819 until 1824 he was at Dülmen in Westphalia recording the visions of a nun Katharina Emmerich. After her death he led an unsettled life, staying, among other places, in Frankfurt and Munich. He died 28 July 1842 in Aschaffenburg at the home of his brother Christian.

Works
*Gustav Wasa*, 1800 (drama)
*Godwi*, 1801
*Ponce de Leon*, 1804 (drama)
*Des Knaben Wunderhorn*, ed. with A. v. Arnim, 1806–8
*Die Gründung Prags*, 1815 (drama)
*Victoria und ihre Geschwister*, 1817 (drama)
*Geschichte vom braven Kasperl und dem schönen Annerl*, 1838
*Gockel, Hinckel und Gackeleia*, 1838
*Gedichte*, 1854
*Romanzen vom Rosenkranz*, 1912
*Gesammelte Schriften*, ed. C. Brentano, 1852–5
*Sämtliche Werke*, ed. C. Schüddekopf and H. Amelung, 1909–1
*Selected Works*, ed. F. Kemp, 1965–6

Literature
R. Steig, *Arnim und Brentano*, 1894
H. Jaeger, *Brentanos Frühlyrik*, 1926
K. Schubert, *Brentanos weltliche Lyrik*, 1910
W. Kosch, *Clemens Brentano. Sein Leben und Schaffen*, 1943
I. Seidel, *Clemens Brentano*, 1944
H. M. Enzensberger, *Brentanos Poetik*, 1961
W. Hoffmann, *Clemens Brentano, Leben und Werk*, 1966
O. Mallon, *Brentano-Bibl.*, 1926; repr. 1965

BARTHOLD HEINRICH BROCKES

Born 22 Sep. 1680 in Hamburg, where he lived all his life except
for his travels in different countries, including England; died
Ritzebüttel, 16 Jan. 1747. He became a Senator of his native
city in 1720 and later undertook diplomatic missions to Vienna,
Copenhagen and Berlin. In 1714 he founded, together with
König and Richey, a Society which was first called 'Teutsch-
übende Gesellschaft' and later 'Patriotische Gesellschaft'. From
1724–6 he edited the weekly 'Der Patriot'.

Works
The 9 books of *Irdisches Vergnügen in Gott* appeared between 1721
and 1748, the collected works, in 5 vols., in 1800. See the selection
in DNL, vol. 39, and the facsimile of the 1738 ed. of *Irdisches
Vergnügen in Gott*, ed. D. Bode, 1965

Literature
A. Brandl, *B. H. Brockes*, 1878
K. Lohmeyer, *Brockes in seinen Gedichten*, 1935
H. W. Pfund, *Studien zu Wort und Bild bei Brockes*, 1935
W. F. Mainland, 'Brockes and the limitations of imitation',
    *Reality and creative vision in German lyrical poetry*, ed. A. Closs,
    1963

GEORG BÜCHNER

Born 17 Oct. 1813 at Goddelau near Darmstadt. From 1831 until
1834 he studied medicine at Strasbourg and philosophy at
Giessen. Here he founded a secret society ('Gesellschaft für
Menschenrechte') and edited the socialist *Hessischer Landbote*.

He was threatened with police action and fled first to Darmstadt and, in 1835, to Strasbourg. He gave up politics and went to Zürich where he took his doctorate with a thesis on the nervous system and in 1836 qualified as a lecturer in comparative anatomy with a thesis 'Über Schädelnerven'. He died after a brief illness, 19 Feb. 1837.

Works
*Dantons Tod*, 1835
*Lenz*, 1839
*Leonce und Lena*, 1842
*Woyzeck*, 1879
*Sämtl. Werke*, ed. K. Franzos, 1879
*Werke und Briefe*, ed. F. Bergemann, 1922; repr. 1965

Literature
A. Renker, *Büchner und das Lustspiel der Romantik*, 1924
H. Mayer, *G. Büchner und seine Zeit*, 1946; repr. 1960
ibid. 'Büchners ästhetische Anschauungen', *ZfdPh*, 1954
E. Diem, *G. Büchner*, 1946
K. Viëtor, *G. Büchner. Politik, Dichtung, Wissenschaft*, 1949
A. H. J. Knight, *G. Büchner*, 1951
H. Oppel, *Die tragische Dichtung Büchners*, 1951
G. Lukács in *Dt. Realisten des 19. Jh.*, 1952
M. Hamburger in *Reason and Energy*, 1957
W. Höllerer in *Zwischen Klassik und Moderne*, 1958

LUDWIG BÜCHNER (pseud. KARL LUDWIG)

Born Darmstadt, 28 March 1824. Like his elder brother Georg, the dramatist, Ludwig studied medicine; he became a prolific popularizer of Darwinism and the materialist philosophy in Germany. President of the German League of Free-Thinkers, delegate to the Landtag of Hesse. Died Darmstadt, 1 May 1899.

Works
*Kraft und Stoff*, 1855
*Natur und Geist*, 1857
*Die Darwinsche Theorie von der Entstehung u. Umwandlung der Lebewelt*, 1868
*Der Gottesbegriff u. dessen Bedeutung in der Gegenwart*, 1874

*Am Sterbelager des Jahrhunderts*, 1894
*Im Dienste der Wahrheit*, 1899

Literature

F. A. Lange, *Gesch. des Materialismus*, 2 vols., 10th ed., 1921
W. Hof, 'Pessimismus u. Fortschrittsglaube. Zu L. Büchners Jugendgedichten', *Rationalität, Phänomenalität, Individualität* (Fs. H. u. M. Glockner), ed. W. Ritzel, 1966

## GOTTFRIED AUGUST BÜRGER

Born 31 Dec. 1747 at Molmerswende near Halberstadt, died Molmerswende (Harz), 8 June 1794. He studied theology and law at Göttingen where he met the leading members of the 'Hain'. From 1772 until 1784 he acted as a magistrate in different places near Göttingen and in 1784 began teaching at the university. He was appointed Professor of Aesthetics in 1789. He married Dorette Leonhart in 1774, an unhappy relationship owing to his love for his wife's sister Auguste, the Molly of his poetry. He married her in 1785 after Dorette's death. Auguste died in 1786. Bürger's third marriage (to Elise Hahn) ended in divorce. These experiences form the basis for much of his 'Erlebnisdichtung'. In addition to poetry he wrote treatises on aesthetics and poetics. He also translated from English, notably *Macbeth* (1783) and Raspe's Münchhausen tales (1785–8). The notable features of his writings on aesthetics are his development of Klopstock's principle of 'Darstellung', his observations on some neglected aspects of poetic style and his views on popular poetry.

Works

*Gedichte*, 1789; ed. E. Consensius, 1914
*Werke* ed. L. Kaim and S. Streller, 1956
*Baron Münchhausens Erzählungen*, 1786 ed. C. W. Schmidt, 1943
'Herzensausguss über Volkspoesie', 1776
'Von der Popularität der Poesie', 1778
*Lehrbuch der Ästhetik*, 1825
*Lehrbuch des deutschen Stiles*, 1826

Literature

W. v. Wurzbach, *G. A. Bürfer*, 1900
F. Kiesel, *Bürger als Balladendichter*, 1907

E. Krienitz, *G. A. Bürgers Jugendlyrik*, diss. Greifswald, 1929
F. Gundolf, 'Bürgers Lenore als Volkslied', *Sitzungsberichte der Heidelberger Akademie der Wissenschaften*, 1929–30
H. Schöffler, 'Bürgers Lenore' in *Die Sammlung*, 1947
C. Janentzky, *G. A. Bürgers Ästhetik*, 1909

## ADALBERT (or ADELBERT) VON CHAMISSO

The youngest son of an aristocratic French family, born at the Château de Boncourt in Champagne on 30 Jan. 1781, Chamisso accompanied his family when they fled to Germany during the Revolution and remained there when his parents returned to France. From 1801–6 he served as a lieutenant in the Prussian army, but his interests were essentially literary and academic. During a stay in Switzerland he belatedly discovered his métier as botanist and, at the age of thirty-one, began studies at the University of Berlin. From 1815–18 he accompanied a Russian scientific expedition on a voyage round the world and on his return was appointed a custodian of the Berlin Botanical Gardens. He died in Berlin on 21 Aug. 1838. None of Chamisso's other works had anything like the success of *Peter Schlemihl*, but the lyrics and ballads which he contributed to the *Musenalmanache* he helped to edit were popular in their day and he is remembered for his *Frauenliebe und- leben* in the setting by Robert Schumann.

### Works
*Faust*, 1803
*Musenalmanach auf das Jahr 1804, 1805, 1806*
*Adelberts Fabel*, 1806
*Fortunati Glückseckel und Wunschhütlein*, 1806
*Peter Schlemihls wundersame Geschichte*, 1814; ed. K. J. Northcott, 1955
*Gedichte*, 1831
*Musenalmanache*, 1830–8

### Literature
K. Fulda, *Chamisso und seine Zeit*, 1881
G. Hofmeister, *Adalbert von Chamisso*, 1883
B. Croce, 'Chamisso', *Poesie und Nichtpoesie*, 1925
T. Mann, 'Chamisso', *Adel des Geistes*, 1948

U. Baumgartner, *Chamissos Peter Schlemihl*, 1944

B. v. Wiese, 'Peter Schlemihls wundersame Geschichte', *Die dt. Novelle von Goethe bis Kafka*, 1956

E. Loeb, 'Symbol und Wirklichkeit des Schattens in Chamissos *Peter Schlemihl*', *GRM*, new series, 15 (1965)

H. J. Weigand, 'Peter Schlemihl', *Surveys and Soundings in European lit.*, 1966

S. Atkins, 'Peter Schlemihl in relation to the popular novel of the Romantic period', *GR* 21 (1946)

## MATTHIAS CLAUDIUS

Born at Reinfeld in Holstein 15 Aug. 1740. He studied theology and law at Jena. After acting as secretary to Graf Holstein in Copenhagen and as an editor of the *Hamburger Neue Zeitung*, he went to Wandsbeck. Here he edited the *Wandsbecker Bote* from 1771 until 1775. In 1776 he obtained a post in Darmstadt with Herder's support and in 1777 returned to Wandsbeck. He lived here as a free-lance writer until 1814 when he went to Hamburg. Died Hamburg, 21 Jan. 1815.

Works

His collected works appeared as *Asmus omnia sua portans oder Sämtliche Werke des Wandsbecker Boten*, 1775–1812. New ed. by U. Roedl, 1960; repr. 1965.

See also *Werke* ed. C. Redlich, 1902

Literature

U. Roedl, *M. Claudius*, 1934, repr. 1950

J. Pfeiffer, *M. Claudius*, 1949

I. Rüttenauer, *M. Claudius*, 1952

## CARL GOTTLOB CRAMER

Born 3 March 1758 in Pädelitz, died 7 June 1817 at Dreissigacker, Meiningen. Prolific author of thrillers and popular tales of chivalry, genres epitomized in his *Hasper a Spada*. His dramas on similar themes are now forgotten.

Works

*Adelheim*, 1786

*Leben und Meinungen Erasmus Schleichers*, 1789

*Der deutsche Alcibiades*, 1790
*Hasper a Spada*, 2 vols., 1792 f.
etc., etc.

Literature
J. W. Appell, *Die Ritter-, Räuber- u. Schauerromantik*, 1859
K. Müller-Fraureuth, *Die Ritter- u. Räuberromane*, 1894


JOHANN ANDREAS CRAMER

Born 29 Jan. 1723 at Jöhstadt, Saxony, died Kiel, 12 June 1788.
One of the original 'Bremer Beiträger' and editor of the 'moral
weekly' *Der nordische Aufseher*, court preacher and professor of
theology in Copenhagen, later professor of theology in Kiel and
chancellor of the university there.


Works
*Vermischte Schriften*, 1757
*Neue geistliche Oden und Lieder*, 1766–75
*Gellerts Leben*, 1774
*Sämtliche Gedichte*, ed. C. F. Cramer, 1791

Literature
M. Luers, *Der nordische Aufseher*, diss. Copenhagen, 1922
C. Reichmann, 'J. A. Cramer u. die dt. Geschichtsprosa der
    Aufklärung', *Monatshefte* 54 (1962)


JOHANN FRIEDRICH REICHSHERR VON CRONEGK

Born at Ansbach, the son of a general, on 2 Sep. 1730. He studied
law at Halle and Leipzig. After travelling in Italy and France
be became 'Hofrat' at the Ansbach court. From 1754 until 1756
he edited, together with Uz, the journal *Der Freund*. Died 31 Dec.
1757 in Nürnberg.


Works
*Codrus*, 1760
*Der Misstrauische*, ed. S. Roth, 1969
*Olinth und Sophronia*, 1760
*Schriften* ed. J. P. Uz, 1760 f.

Literature
W. Gensel, *J. F. Cronegk. Sein Leben und seine Schriften*, 1894
S. Roth, *Die Dramen J. F. Cronegks*, 1964
K. Briegleb, 'Zu J. F. v. Cronegks Lyrik', *Unterscheidung u. Bewährung* (Fs. Kunisch), ed. K. Lazarowicz, W. Kron, 1961

## FELIX DAHN (pseud. LUDWIG SOPHUS)

Born 9 Feb. 1834 in Hamburg, died 3 Jan. 1912 in Breslau. Prolific writer of erudite historical novels of patriotic complexion ('Professorenromane'). Member of 'Tunnel über der Spree' and Munich 'Krokodil'.

Works
*Gedichte*, 1857
*Ein Kampf um Rom*, 1876
*Kleine Romane aus der Völkerwanderung*, 13 vols., 1882 ff.
*Sämtliche Werke poetischen Inhalts*, 21 vols., 1898

Literature
H. Meyer, *Felix Dahn*, 1913
J. Weisser, *Studien zu den germanischen Romanen Dahns*, diss. Cologne, 1922
A. Ludwig, 'Dahn, Fouqué, Stevenson', *Euph* 17 (1910)
T. Siebs, *Felix Dahn u. J. Scheffel*, 1914
H. Eckenroth, *F. Dahn als Dramatiker*, diss. Würzburg, 1921

## FRANZ (VON) DINGELSTEDT

Born 30 June 1814 at Halsdorf, Ober-Hessen, son of a non-commissioned officer, studied theology and philology in Marburg and became a teacher at the English college in Ricklingen near Hannover. Dingelstedt co-operated with Gustav Schwab and Chamisso in editing their *Musenalmanach* and later became editor of the literary supplement to the *Kurhessische Allgemeine Landeszeitung*. Because of his links with Young Germany and liberal ideas in his satirical *Bilder aus Hessen-Kassel* he was removed from the teaching post he had obtained in Kassel and sent to Fulda, where he formed a friendship with the liberal writer Heinrich

König. Deprived of his doctorate and his salary by the reactionary government of Kurhessen Dingelstedt moved in 1841 to Stuttgart. During a period as foreign correspondent for Cotta in Paris and London his views became steadily more conservative. In 1842 he married the celebrated singer Jenny Lutzer in Vienna and began to cut a figure in Viennese society. In the following year he was appointed librarian and reader to the King of Württemberg. There followed appointments as Intendant at the court theatres of Stuttgart and Munich, where he was raised to the nobility by King Maximilian II. After a period as director of the theatre and orchestra in Weimar Dingelstedt moved back to Vienna as director of the Burgtheater (1876). He died in Vienna on 15 May 1881. Dingelstedt's best original work is probably the political lyric of his youth, but he distinguished himself also by translations and productions of Shakespeare's historical dramas. He was a founder of the Shakespeare-Gesellschaft.

## Works

*Gedichte*, 1838

*Licht und Schatten in der Liebe*, 1838

*Frauenspiegel*, 1838

*Wanderbuch*, 2 vols., 1839–43

*Die neuen Argonauten*, 1839 (novel); repr. ed. P. Heidelbach, 1931

*Das Gespenst der Ehre*, 1840 (drama)

*Unter der Erde*, 2 vols., 1840; 2nd ed. 1877

*Lieder eines kosmopolitischen Nachtwächters*, 1841; repr. ed. H. Houben, 1923

*Heptameron*, 2 vols., 1844

*Sieben friedliche Erzählungen*, 3 vols., 1844

*Gedichte*, 1845; 2nd ed. 1858

*Das Haus der Barneveldt*, 1850 (drama)

*Nacht und Morgen*, 1851

*Novellenbuch*, 1856

*Der Erntekranz*, 1858

*Studien und Kopien nach Shakespeare*, 1858

*Shakespeares Historien*, 2 vols., 1868 (translations)

*Die Amazone*, 2 vols., 1868; 2nd ed. 1877

*Eine Faust-Trilogie*, 1876 (dramatic study)

*Bade-Novellen*, 1877

*Künstlergeschichten,* 1877
*Lyrische Dichtungen,* 2 vols., 1877
*Bunte Reihe,* 1877 (stories)
*Theater,* 4 vols., 1877 (mostly translations of Shakespeare)
*Literarisches Bilderbuch,* 1878
*Sämtliche Werke,* 12 vols., 1877
*Blätter aus Dingelstedts Nachlass,* 2 vols., ed. J. Rodenberg, 1891
*Briefwechsel mit J. Hartmann,* ed. W. Deetjen, 1923

Literature
H. Knudsen, 'Franz von Dingelstedt', *Lebensbilder aus Kurhessen* 2
    (1939)
H. Knudsen, *Aus Dingelstedts hessischer Jugendzeit,* 1964
B. Klostermann, *Dingelstedts Jugendleben und politische Dichtung,*
    diss. Münster, 1912
O. Liebscher, *F. Dingelstedt, seine dramaturgische Entwicklung und
    Tätigkeit bis 1857,* diss. Munich, 1910


ANNETTE FREIIN VON DROSTE-HÜLSHOFF

Born at Schloss Hülshoff, near Münster, 14 Jan. 1797. In this
neighbourhood she spent much of her uneventful youth. She
travelled to Cologne and Bonn in 1825, when she met A. W.
Schlegel and Adele Schopenhauer. She made a second journey
to the Rhine in 1828. After her father's death in 1826 she went
to live on her mother's estate at Rüschhaus. From 1835-7 she lived
in Switzerland at the home of her sister who had married
Freiherr von Lassberg and from 1841-4 in their other home at
Schloss Meersburg on Lake Constance. Her love for the writer
Levin Schücking (1814-83) proved a painful experience,
particularly after the publication of his novel, *Die Ritterbürtigen*
(1846). She bought a property at Meersburg in 1844 and died
there, 24 May 1848. In addition to writing poetry and prose
fiction she helped the brothers Grimm with their collection of
fairy tales, Uhland with his 'Volkslieder' and Levin Schücking
with *Das malerische und romantische Westfalen* (1841; repr. 1961).

Works
*Gedichte,* 1838 and 1844
*Die Judenbuche,* 1842

*Das geistliche Jahr*, 1851
*Letzte Gaben*, 1860
*Sämtliche Werke*, ed. K. Schulte-Kemminghausen, 1925–30; ed.
    C. Heselhaus, 1963
*Correspondence*, ed. K. Schulte-Kemminghausen, 1945

Literature
H. Hüffer, *Annette v. Droste-Hülshoff u. ihre Werke*, 1910
E. Staiger, *Annette v. Droste-Hülshoff*, 1933
C. Heselhaus, *A. v. Droste-Hülshoff. Die Entdeckung des Seins in der
    Dichtung des 19. Jhs*, (1943)
W. Höllerer, 'A. v. Droste-Hülshoff', *Zwischen Klassik u. Moderne*,
    1958
B. E. Schatzky, 'A. v. Droste-Hülshoff', *German men of letters I*,
    ed. A. Natan, 1961
M. Mare, *Annette von Droste-Hülshoff*, 1965
G. Frühbrodt, *Der Impressionismus in der Lyrik der A. v. Droste-
    Hülshoff*, 1930
J. W. Miller, *Poetic strategy and metaphorical structure. A study of A. v.
    Droste-Hülshoff's 'Das geistliche Jahr'*, 1965
H. Henel, 'A. v. Droste-Hülshoff: Erzählstil u. Wirklichkert's
    Fs. i. B. Blume, 1967

GEORG EBERS

Born 1 March 1837 in Berlin, professor of Egyptology in Leipzig,
made revolutionary contributions to the subject. Premature
retirement because of ill-health gave him the opportunity to
write popular stories of medieval and ancient Egyptian life.
Died in Tübingen, 7 Aug. 1898.

Works
*Eine ägyptische Königstochter*, 1874
*Uarda*, 1877
*Homo sum*, 1878
*Der Kaiser*, 1881
*Serapis*, 1885
*Die Nilbraut*, 1887
*Die Gred*, 1889
*Per aspera*, 1892
*Kleopatra*, 1894

*Barbara Blomberg,* 1897
*Arachne,* 1898
*Geschichte meines Lebens,* 1893
*Gesammelte Werke,* 32 vols., 1893–7

Literature
O. Kraus, *Der Professorenroman,* 1884
E. Meyer, 'Georg Ebers', *Biographisches Jahrbuch* 3 (1900)

## MARIE VON EBNER-ESCHENBACH

Born Gräfin Dubsky, 13 Sept. 1830, at Schloss Zdislawitz in Moravia, married Moritz, Freiherr v. Ebner-Eschanbach in 1848, died 12 March 1916 in Vienna, where she had lived, apart from occasional residence abroad (e.g. in Rome), since 1863. Her lyric and her early dramas in the Classical vein earned the approbation of Grillparzer but she did not achieve popular success until 1889, when her Novelle, *Lotti, die Uhrmacherin,* appeared in the *Deutsche Rundschau.* The realism of Ebner-Eschenbach's stories extends to the psychological motivation of the characters. Although she was a devout Roman Catholic the religious feeling in her work is complex and not always orthodox; at times she seems to approach the materialistic outlook of Gottfried Keller and Ludwig Anzengruber. In spite of her aristocratic birth and background she showed a progressive attitude to social problems of her day.

Works
*Maria von Schottland,* 1860 (tragedy)
*Marie Roland,* 1867 (tragedy)
*Männertreue,* 1874 (comedy)
*Erzählungen,* 1875
*Božena,* 1876
*Dorf- und Schlossgeschichten,* 1884
*Die Unverstandene auf dem Dorfe,* 1886
*Das Gemeindekind,* 1887
*Miterlebtes,* 1889
*Neue Erzählungen,* 1889
*Lotti, die Uhrmacherin,* 1889
*Ein kleiner Roman,* 1889
*Unsühnbar,* 1890

*Margarete,* 1891
*Drei Novellen,* 1892
*Parabeln, Märchen und Gedichte,* 1892; repr. ed. E. Gross, 1960
*Glaubenslos,* 1893
*Rittmeister Brandt,* 1896
*Bertram Vogelweid,* 1896
*Alte Schule,* 1897
*Wiener Kinder,* 1897
*Aus Spätherbsttagen,* 2 vols., 1901
*Agave,* 1903
*Die arme Kleine,* 1903
*Die unbesiegbare Macht,* 1905
*Meine Kinderjahre,* 1906; repr. ed. E. Gross, 1960; ed. F. Minckwitz, 1967
*Altweibersommer,* 1909
*Genrebilder,* 1910
*Ausgewählte Erzählungen,* 3 vols., 1910
*Gesammelte Schriften,* 10 vols., 1911 ff.
*Sämtliche Werke,* 12 vols., 1928
*Gesammelte Werke,* ed. E. Gross, 1961

Literature

A. Bettelheim, *M. v. Ebner-Eschenbachs Wirken u. Vermächtnis,* 1920
E. M. O'Connor, *Marie Ebner,* 1928
K. Benesch, *Die Frau mit den hundert Schicksalen. Das Leben der M. v. Ebner-Eschenbach,* 1966
M. Alkemade, *Die Lebens- u. Weltanschauung der M. v. Ebner-Eschenbach,* 1935
M. R. Doyle, *Catholic atmosphere in M. v. Ebner-Eschenbach,* diss. Washington, 1936
K. Offergeld, *M. v. Ebner-Eschenbach. Untersuchungen über ihre Erzählungstechnik,* diss. Münster, 1917
E. Fischer, *Die Soziologie Mährens in der zweiten Hälfte des 19. Jhs als Hintergrund der Werke M. v. Ebner-Eschenbachs,* 1939
I. Geserick, 'M. v. Ebner-Eschenbach u. Ivan Turgenev', *Zs. f. Slavistik* 3 (1958)

JOSEPH VON EICHENDORFF

Eichendorff was born on 10 March 1788 at Schloss Lubowitz in Upper Silesia. During his studies in Halle, Heidelberg, Berlin and Vienna he made the acquaintance of practically all the eminent Romantic writers. After serving as a volunteer in the Wars of Liberation against Napoleon he entered the civil service in Breslau, moving subsequently to Danzig, Berlin and Königsberg and then finally to the Ministry of Education in Berlin, where he was responsible for the supervision of Catholic schools in Prussia. He retired in 1844 with the rank of Geheimer Regierungsrat and lived in Vienna, Berlin, Köthen and Dresden before moving to Neisse, where he died on 26 Nov. 1857. Eichendorff is a remarkably prolific and versatile poet who represents the climax of literary Romanticism. His fame rests principally on stories like *Taugenichts* and lyrics of superbly musical simpllicity like 'O Täler weit, o Höhen' and 'In einem kühlen Grunde' which epitomize the nostalgic charm of a rural Germany since overwhelmed by industrialization and political turmoil, but he could also write in ironical and satirical vein against the smug vulgarity of a philistine society. His Roman Catholic faith furnished him throughout his life with the solid moral foundation to his poetry. Eichendorff's interest in Spanish literature of the Golden Age was reflected in numerous translations from Calderon and Cervantes.

Works

*Sagen und Märchen aus Oberschlesien*, 1808
*Ahnung und Gegenwart*, 1815
*Das Marmorbild*, 1819
*Krieg den Philistern*, 1824 (dramatic satire)
*Aus dem Leben eines Taugenichts*, 1826
*Meierbeths Glück und Ende*, 1827 (dramatic satire on fate tragedy)
*Ezzelin von Romano*, 1828 (tragedy)
*Der letzte Held von Marienburg*, 1830
*Über Pressfreiheit*, 1832
*Viel Lärm um nichts*, 1832
*Die Freier*, 1833 (comedy)
*Dichter und ihre Gesellen*, 1834
*Eine Meerfahrt*, 1835
*Das Schloss Durande*, 1837
*Gedichte*, 1837
*Die Entführung*, 1839
*Die Glücksritter*, 1841

*Incognito*, 1841 (puppet play)

*Über die ethische und religiöse Bedeutung der neueren romantischen Poesie
    in Deutschland*, 1847

*Libertas und ihre Freier*, 1849

*Der deutsche Roman des 18. Jahrhunderts in seinem Verhältnis zum
    Christentum*, 1851

*Julian*, 1853

*Zur Geschichte des Dramas*, 1854

*Robert und Guiscard*, 1855

*Lucius*, 1857

*Erlebtes*, 1857; repr. 1967

*Geschichte der poetischen Literatur Deutschlands*, 1857


Literature

H. v. Eichendorff, *J. v. Eichendorff, sein Leben und seine Schriften*,
    1864; 3rd ed. by K. v. Eichendorff und W. Kosch, 1923

H. Brandenburg, *J. v. Eichendorff. Sein Leben und sein Werk*, 1922

F. Strich, *J. v. Eichendorff*, 1928

W. Köhler, *Eichendorff*, 1937

J. Kunz, *Eichendorff, Höhepunkt und Krise der Spatromantik*, 1951

O. Seidlin, *Versuche über Eichendorff*, 1965

W. Köhler, *J. v. Eichendorff, Ein Dichterleben*, 1957

G. Möbus, *Der andere Eichendorff*, 1960

G. Rodger, 'J. v. Eichendorff'; *German Men of Letters I*, ed. A. Natan,
    1961

P. Stöcklein, *J. v. Eichendorff in Zelbstzeugnissen und Bilddokumenten*,
    1963

W. Rehm, 'Prinz Rokoko im Alten Garten. Eine Eichendorff-
    Studie', *Späte Studien*, 1964

O. Seidlin, *Versuche über Eichendorff*, 1965

H. J. Lüthi, *Dichtung und Dichter bei J. v. Eichendorff*, 1966

J. Nadler, *Eichendorffs Lyrik*, 1908

G. Jahn, *Studien zu Eichendorffs Prosastil*, Pal. 206 (1937)

W. Kohlschmidt, 'Die symbolische Formelhaftigkeit von Eichen-
    dorffs Prosastil', *Orbis Litterarum* 8 (1950).

D. W. Schumann, 'Eichendorff's Taugenichts and Romanticism',
    *GQ* 9 (1936)

B. v. Wiese, 'Aus dem Leben eines Taugenichts', *Der dt. Roman
    von Goethe bis Kafka*, 1956

G. T. Hughes, *Eichendorff: Aus dem Leben eines Taugenichts*, 1961

E. Stopp, 'The metaphor of death in Eichendorff', *OGS* 4 (1969)

P. Stöcklein (ed.), *Eichendorff heute*, 1960; 2nd ed. 1966

J. Müller, 'Der Stand der Eichendorff-Forschung', *Forschungen und Fortschritte* 37 (1963)

Cf. also *Aurora, Eichendorff-Almanach*, 1931–43 and 1953 ff. (cumulative bibl. of work on Eichendorff)

## IGNAZ AURELIUS FESSLER

Born 18 May 1756 at Zürndorf, Hungary, died 15 Dec. 1839 in St. Petersburg. Fessler was for a time a Jesuit priest and professor of Oriental studies at Lemberg but converted to Protestantism in 1791 and became a leading light in the Masonic order. He was professor in St. Petersburg and rose to a high administrative position there. He was the author of historical novels of an erudite kind dealing with themes of Antiquity and the Middle Ages as well as of Masonic tracts.

Works
*Sidney*, 1784 (tragedy)
*Mark Aurel*, 1790–2
*Aristides und Themistokles*, 1792
*Matthias Corvinus, König der Ungarn*, 1793 f.
*Attila, König der Hunnen*, 1794
*Alexander der Eroberer*, 1797
*Sämtliche Schriften über die Freimaurerei*, 1805
*Abälard und Héloise*, 1807
etc., etc.
*Rückblick auf meine siebzigjährige Pilgerschaft*, 1826; 2nd ed. by F. Bülau, 1851

Literature
L. Fensch, *Fessler, sein Leben u. seine maurerische Wirksamkeit* (*Bücherei f. Freimaurer 21–22*), 1909

O. Kahle, *Ignaz Aurelius Fessler* (*Concordia Bibl. freimaurerischer Vorträge*, 9–11), 1920

## LUDWIG FEUERBACH

Born 28 July 1804 in Landshut, died Nürnberg, 13 Sept. 1872. Philosopher of sensualism and pure materialism: 'Der Mensch ist, was er isst'. Intepreted religion as a system of sublimated human desires and needs; important influence on Marx, Gottfried Keller, Nietzsche and Freud.

Works

*Gedanken über Tod und Unsterblichkeit,* 1830
*Darstellung der Geschichte der neueren Philosophie,* 1833–8
*Das Wesen des Christentums,* 1841; repr. ed. W. Schuffenhauer, 2 vols., 1956
*Grundsätze der Philosophie der Zukunft,* 1843
*Das Wesen der Religion,* 1845
*Theogonie,* 1857
*Sämtliche Werke,* 10 vols., 1846 ff.; repr. ed. W. Bolin, F. Jodl, 1903
*Kleine philosophische Schriften,* 1842–5; repr. ed. M. G. Lange, 1950

Literature

F. Engels, *L. Feuerbach u. der Ausgang der dt. klassischen Philosophie,* 1888
F. Jodl, *Ludwig Feuerbach,* 1904; 2nd ed. 1921
S. Rawidowicz, *Ludwig Feuerbachs Philosophie,* 1931; 2nd ed. 1964
W. Schuffenhauer, *Ludwig Feuerbach und der junge Marx,* 1965

## Theodor Fontane

Born 30 Sep. 1819 in Neuruppin, descendant of a Huguenot refugee family, educated at the Gewerbeschule in Berlin in his father's calling of dispenser. After military service he travelled to England, then settled in Berlin where he was a member of the literary club 'Tunnel über der Spree' and soon became a full-time journalist and theatrical critic. A second journey to England followed in 1852 and a third in 1855, Fontane remaining in England on this occasion for some four years as journalist and correspondent. He acted as a war correspondent in the Prussian campaigns of 1866 and 1870, being captured by the French in 1871 and briefly imprisoned. In 1874–5 he travelled in Italy and was then for a short time secretary of the Akademie der Künste in Berlin. He died in Berlin, 20 Sep. 1898. Fontane began his literary career with ballads and travel journals and progressed via historical tales to novels of contemporary life in Berlin and Brandenburg. His stories are remarkable for sharpness of observation and unforced symbolism as well as for the author's urbane wisdom and humour. In many respects he may be seen as a forerunner to Thomas Mann. He is also a notable poet.

Works

*Gedichte*, 1851

*Ein Sommer in London*, 1854

*Wanderungen durch die Mark Brandenburg*, 4 vols., 1862–82

*Vor dem Sturm*, 1878

*Grete Minde*, 1880

*Ellernklipp*, 1881

*L'Adultera*, 1882

*Schach von Wuthenow*, 1883

*Graf Petöfy*, 1884

*Unterm Birnbaum*, 1885

*Cécile*, 1887

*Irrungen, Wirrungen*, 1888

*Stine*, 1890

*Unwiederbringlich*, 1891

*Quitt*, 1891

*Frau Jenny Treibel*, 1893

*Meine Kinderjahre*, 1894

*Effi Briest*, 1895

*Die Poggenpuhls*, 1896

*Der Stechlin*, 1898

*Von Zwanzig bis Dreissig*, 1898 (autobiography)

*Aus England und Schottland*, 1900

*Mathilde Möhring*, 1914

*Gesammelte Werke*, ser. I, vol. 1–10; ser. 2, vol. 1–11, 1905–10

*Sämtliche Werke*, ed. E. Gross, K. Schreinert, 1959 ff.; ed. W. Keitel, 1962 ff.

Literature

C. Wandrey, *Theodor Fontane*, 1919

K. Hayens, *Theodor Fontane, A critical study*, 1920

M. Krammer, *Theodor Fontane*, 1922

H. Spiero, *Fontane*, 1928

R. Pascal, 'Theodor Fontane 1819–98', *The German novel*, 1956

H. Fricke, *Theodor Fontane. Chronik seines Lebens*, 1960

H. B. Garland, 'Theodor Fontane', *German Men of Letters I*, ed. A. Natan, 1961

F. Martini, 'Theodor Fontane', *Dt. Lit. im bürgerlichen Realismus*, 1962

R. Brinkmann, *T. Fontane. Über die Verbindlichkeit des Unverbindlichen*, 1967

H. Nürnberger, *Fontane*, 1968

P. Demetz, *Formen des Realismus. Theodor Fontane*, 1964

V. Günther, *Das Symbol im erzählerischen Werk Fontanes*, 1967

H. Ohl, *Bild u. Wirklichkeit. Studien zur Romankunst Raabes u. Fontanes*, 1968

H. Nürnberger, *Der frühe Fontane: Politik. Poesie. Geschichte 1840–60*, 1967

C. Sieper, *Der hist. Roman u. die hist. Novelle bei Raabe u. Fontane*, 1930

H. Wolter, *Probleme des Bürgertums in T. Fontanes Zeitromanen*, 1935

J. Thanner, *Die Stilistik T. Fontanes*, 1967

J. Petersen, 'Fontanes Altersroman', *Euph* 29 (1928)

G. Lukács, 'Der alte Fontane', *Dt. Realisten des 19. Jhs*, 1952

J. Remak, *The gentle critic. T. Fontane and German politics, 1848–98*, 1964

H. Ritscher, *Fontane. Seine politische Gedankenwelt*, 1953

F. Schönemann, 'T. Fontane und England', *PMLA* 30 (1916)

J. Schobess, *Lit. von u. über Theodor Fontane*, 1965

C. Jolles, 'Zu Fontanes lit. Entwicklung. Bibl. Übersicht über seine Beiträge in Zeitschriften, Almanachen, Kalendern u. Zeitungen 1839–1858/9', *JDSG* 4 (1960)

B. E. Trebein, *T. Fontane as a critic of the drama*, 1916; repr. 1966

## Friedrich Baron de la Motte Fouqué

Born 12 Feb. 1777 in Brandenburg. He spent his childhood near Potsdam and from 1788 lived on an estate at Fehrbellin. He entered the Prussian army in 1794 and took part in several campaigns before he resigned his commission in 1813 for reasons of health. From 1813 to 1840 he lived in Halle and lectured on history and literature. King Frederick William IV recalled him to Berlin in 1840 and he died there on 23 Jan. 1843. A prolific writer using Germanic legendary material, he is best known as the author of *Undine*.

## Works
*Sigurd der Schlangentöter*, 1808 (drama)
*Der Held des Nordens*, 1810 (dramatic trilogy)
*Undine*, 1811
*Der Zauberring*, 1813
*Die Fahrten Thiodolfs des Isländers*, 1815
*Gedichte*, 1816–27
*Heldenspiele*, 1818
*Ausgewählte Werke*, 1841; ed. W. Ziesemer, 1908

## Literature
E. Hagemeister, *Fouqué als Dramatiker*, 1905
F. Braun, *Fouqués Lyrik*, 1907
L. Jenthe, *Fouqué als Erzähler*, 1910
A. Schmidt, *Fouqué u. einige seiner Zeitgenossen. Biographischer Versuch*, 1958
A. R. Neumann, 'La Motte Fouqué, the unmusical musician', *MLQ* 15 (1954)

## MARIE LUISE VON FRANÇOIS

Born 27 June 1817 at Herzberg, Saxony, daughter of an army officer, largely self-educated. After losing most of her fortune and, in consequence, her fiancé, she lived a retired life in Halberstadt, Potsdam and Weissenfels, where she died on 25 Sep. 1893. She corresponded with Marie v. Ebner-Eschenbach and C. F. Meyer, and was herself the author of vigorously realistic novels and tales. G. Freytag made her known to a wider public.

## Works
*Ausgewählte Novellen*, 1867
*Die letzte Reckenburgerin*, 1871
*Erzählungen*, 1871
*Frau Erdmuthens Zwillingssöhne*, 1872

*Hellstädt und andere Erzählungen*, 1874
*Natur und Gnade nebst anderen Erzählungen*, 1876
*Stufenjahre eines Glücklichen*, 1877
*Der Katzenjunker*, 1879
*Phosphorus Hollunder*, 1881
*Zu Füssen des Monarchen*, 1881
*Das Jubiläum und andere Erzählungen*, 1886
*Briefwechsel mit C. F. Meyer*, ed. A. Bettelheim, 1905
*Gesammelte Werke*, 5 vols., 1918

Literature
H. Binder, *Luise v. François*, 1894
E. Krause, *Luise v. François*, 1916
G. Lehmann, *Luise v. François. Ihr Roman Die letzte Reckenburgerin als Ausdruck ihrer Persönlichkeit*, diss. Greifswald, 1919
H. Hossfeld, *Zur Kunst der Erzählung bei L. v. François*, diss. Jena, 1922
T. Urech, *L. v. François. Versuch einer kunstlerischen Würdigung*, diss. Zürich, 1955
F. Oeding, *Bibliographie der L. v. François*, 1937


FERDINAND FREILIGRATH

Born in Detmold, 17 June 1810, taught himself modern languages while serving as a merchant's apprentice in Soest, began writing poetry when he was in a post in Amsterdam and from 1839 devoted himself entirely to writing. In 1842 he received a grant from Frederick William IV but gave it up in 1844 when he joined the Liberals. Fearing persecution he fled to Belgium where he met Karl Marx and then went to Switzerland and England (1845–6). He returned to Germany in 1848 and joined the Communists in Düsseldorf. With Karl Marx he edited the *Neue Rheinische Zeitung* in Cologne and, when it was suppressed, fled to Holland. In 1851 he returned to London and worked in a bank. From 1856–65 he was director of a Swiss bank. He returned to Germany in 1868 and died in Canstatt on 18 March 1876. In addition to his political activities and his poetic work Freiligrath made a considerable contribution in translating French and English authors into German, including Byron, Bret Harte and Walt Whitman.

Works
*Gedichte*, 1838
*Ein Glaubensbekenntnis*, 1844
*Ça ira!*, 1846
*Gesammelte Dichtungen*, 1870 f.
*Sämtliche Werke*, ed. L. Schröder, 1907

Literature
L. Schröder, *Freiligraths Leben und Schaffen*, 1907
E. G. Gudde, *Freiligraths Entwicklung als politischer Dichter*, 1960
H. Eulenberg, *Ferdinand Freiligrath*, 1948
E. Kittel (ed.), *F. Freiligrath als Achtundvierziger u. westfälischer Dichter*, 1960

## GUSTAV FREYTAG

Born 13 July 1816 in Kreuzburg (Silesia), studied in Breslau and Berlin, became Privatdozent for German language and literature in Breslau but resigned in 1844 in order to devote himself to writing. In 1847 Freytag moved to Dresden and from 1848 to 1870 edited the influential Liberal journal *Die Grenzboten*. He represented the National Liberals in the North German Reichstag, was attached to the Prussian headquarters during the war of 1870, achieved the rank of Geheimer Hofrat in 1886 and the title of Exzellenz in 1893. Freytag died on 30 April 1895. His novels and historical writings reflect an ideology that is more national than liberal: they praise the commercial and professional middle-class and exalt the sound German race over Jews and Slavs. The realism of his settings and the topicality of his themes made his stories very popular; apart from *Die Journalisten*, his dramas did not enjoy the same success.

Works
*Bilder aus dem Volke*, 1838–41 (poems)
*Der Gelehrte*, 1844 (drama)
*In Breslau*, 1845 (poems)
*Die Valentine*, 1847 (drama)
*Die Journalisten*, 1854 (comedy); repr. ed. H. Kreissig, 1966
*Soll und Haben*, 1855
*Graf Waldemar*, 1858 (drama)

*Die Fabier*, 1859 (drama)
*Die Technik des Dramas*, 1863; repr. 1965 (with review by W. Dilthey)
*Die verlorene Handschrift*, 1864
*Bilder aus der deutschen Vergangenheit*, 1859–67; repr. ed. E. Brandenburg, 1923
*Die Ahnen*, 1872–81
*Erinnerungen aus meinem Leben*, 1887
*Gesammelte Werke*, 22 vols., 1886–8; 12 vols., ed. H. M. Elster, 1926

Literature
H. Lindau, *Gustav Freytag*, 1907
H. Zuchold, *Gustav Freytag*, 1926
R. Ostwald, *Freytag als Politiker*, 1927
E. Laaths, *Der Nationalliberalismus im Werk Gustav Freytags*, diss. Köln, 1934
J. S. Andrews, 'The impact on 19th cent. Britain of Freytag's Soll und Haben', *Proceedings of Leeds Philos. Soc. Lit. and Hist. Sect.* 8 (1959)
T. E. Carter, 'Freytag's Soll und Haben; a liberal national manifesto as a best seller', *GLL* 21 (1967/8).
Cf. passim: *Veröffentlichungen der Gustav Freytag-Gesellschaft zu Kreuzburg*, vols. 1–6 (1908–16).
   *Gustav-Freytag Blätter*, 1954 ff. (ed. 1954–62 G. W. Freytag; 1962 ff. K. Fleischer)

FRANZ FREIHERR VON GAUDY

Born 19 April 1800 in Frankfurt on Oder, son of a major of Scottish descent, entered the army in 1818 but resigned his commission in 1833 and embarked on a literary career in which he was supported by the Crown Prince later Frederick William IV. The character of Gaudy's lyric and short stories may be described as late Romantic; he edited the *Deutsches Musenalmanach* along with Chamisso. He died in Berlin, 5 Feb. 1840.

Works
*Geschichtliche Gesänge der Polen*, 1833
*Mein Römerzug*, 1836
*Aus dem Tagebuch eines wandernden Schneidergesellen*, 1836
*Bérangers Lieder*, 1838 (transl. with Chamisso)

*Venetianische Novellen,* 1838
*Novellen und Skizzen,* 1839
*Sämtliche Werke,* 24 vols., ed. T. Echtermeyer, A. Ruge, 1844;
    8 vols., ed. A. Müller, 1853 f.
*Ausgewählte Werke,* 3 vols., ed. K. Siegen, 1896

Literature
J. Reiske, *F. Freiherr von Gaudy als Dichter, Pal* 60 (1911)

EMANUEL GEIBEL

Born in Lübeck 17 Oct. 1815. He studied theology and philology at Bonn and Berlin universities. In Berlin he met Bettina
von Arnim who obtained a tutorship for him in the home of the
Russian ambassador in Athens which he held from 1838 to 1840.
In 1852 he was appointed Professor of German literature in
Munich. Here he formed the literary club *Krokodil* and became
a leading member of the Munich School. After the death of
King Maximilian, his patron, he was deprived of a pension
because of his overt Prussian sympathies and retired to Lübeck on
another pension given to him by the King of Prussia. He died
there on 6 April 1894.

Works
*Gedichte,* 1840
*Juniuslieder,* 1848
*Neue Gedichte,* 1856
*Heroldsrufe,* 1871
*Gesammelte Werke,* 1883–4

Literature
K. Goedeke, *E. Geibel,* 1869
C. Leimbach, *Geibels Leben, Werke und Bedeutung,* 1877
W. Scherer, *E. Geibel,* 1884

CHRISTIAN FÜRCHTEGOTT GELLERT

Gellert was born on 4 July 1715 at Hainichen in the Erzgebirge.
He was educated locally and at the Fürstenschule in Meissen. In
1734 he matriculated at the University of Leipzig, where he
studied theology and philosophy; after an interlude as private

tutor he graduated in 1743, began to lecture on poetry and
rhetoric soon after and became 'ausserordentlicher Professor' of
philosophy in 1751. His reputation as teacher and poet spread
throughout Germany, and his death on 13 Dec. 1769 was widely
mourned. Gellert was physically and morally a hypochondriac
given to anxious soul-searching and self-reproach; his modesty
and blameless life became almost a legend and reinforced the
influence of his lectures, poetry and correspondence. A simple
moral code, sentimental piety and unassuming style endeared
him to all classes, from peasants and soldiers to Frederick the
Great himself, who called him 'le plus raisonnable de tous les
savants allemands'. Although Gellert's example encouraged the
return to a clear and natural style, his literary taste was conventional and moralistic: his natural timidity caused him to retreat
from his own mildly anacreontic early *Lieder* and to give only
hesitant support to the 'Bremer Beiträger', who opposed Gottschedian dogmatism. He appreciated none but tamely decorous
talents, largely ignored powerful and problematic writers like
Klopstock, Lessing and Wieland, and was horrified by the
doctrines of Rousseau. Gellert is perhaps at his best in the light
conversational and often humorous idiom of his fables. The
lessons which he is at pains to point so clearly in them form a
slightly incongruous mixture of Christian faith and worldly wisdom. His sentimental comedies broadened the range of the genre
beyond the narrow Gottschedian satirical model; the characterization is occasionally acute, but on the whole the plays are
contrived and prolix and the morality which they embody now
seems either unnatural or materialistic. Gellert was a prey to
facile pathos—he wept floods of tears over Richardson's *Grandison*
—but he shrank from more powerful and potentially destructive
passions: his sacred songs and the novel, *Das Leben der schwedischen
Gräfin von G . . .*, preach control of the passions and praise stoic
equanimity in the face of an inscrutable Providence. Gellert's
literary reputation rapidly perished in the stormy period following
his death but his popular influence, particularly through his
*Geistliche Lieder*, persisted for much longer.

Works
*Lieder*, 1743
*Das Band. Ein Schäferspiel*, 1745

*Sylvia. Ein Schäferspiel*, 1745

*Die Betschwester. Ein Lustspiel in 3 Aufzügen*, 1746

*Das Los in der Lotterie. Lustspiel in 5 Aufzügen*, 1746

*Fabeln und Erzählungen*, 1746–8; repr. 1966

*Leben der schwedischen Gräfin von G . . .*, 1747–8

*Lustspiele*, 1747 (includes, apart from those above, *Die zärtlichen Schwestern, Das Orakel, Die kranke Frau*); repr. 1966, ed. H. Steinmetz

*Pro comoedia commovente*, 1751 (transl. by Lessing, 1754; by Gellert, 1756)

*Lehrgedichte und Erzählungen*, 1754

*Geistliche Oden und Lieder*, 1757; repr. 1965

*Sämtliche Schriften*, 10 vols., 1769–74

*Vermischte Gedichte*, 1770

*Moralische Vorlesungen*, 2 vols., 1770

*Letzte Vorlesungen*, 1770

*Briefe*, 3 vols., 1774

Selections from *Fabeln und Erzählungen* and *Geistliche Oden und Lieder*, DNL 43


Literature

M. Durach, *Christian Fürchtegott Gellert*, 1938

C. Schlingmann, *Gellert. Eine literarhistorische Revision*, 1967

K. O. Frenzel, *Über Gellerts religiöses Wirken*, 1894

I. S. Stamm, 'Gellert: religion and rationalism', *GR* 28 (1953)

H. Handwerk, *Studien über Gellerts Fabelstil*, 1891

G. Ellinger, *Über Gellerts Fabeln und Erzählungen*, 1895

H. Handwerk, *Gellerts älteste Fabeln* (1907)

F. Helber, *Der Stil Gellerts in den Fabeln und Gedichten*, diss. Tübingen, 1938

J. Coym, *Gellerts Lustspiele*, 1898; repr. 1967

T. Dobbmann, *Die Technik von Gellerts Lustspielen*, 1901

L. Capt, *Gellerts Lustspiele*, diss. Zürich, 1949

E. Höhler, *Gellerts moralische Vorlesungen*, diss. Heidelberg, 1917

E. Werth, *Untersuchungen zu Gellerts geistlichen Oden und Liedern*, diss. Breslau, 1936

E. Kretzschmar, *Gellert als Romanschriftsteller*, 1902

F. Brüggemann, *Gellerts schwedische Gräfin*, 1925

K. Russell, 'Das Leben der schwedischen Gräfin von G . . .', *Monatshefte* 6 (1948)

L. Striegel, *Der Leipziger Goethe und Gellert*, diss. Tübingen, 1934

A. Leitzmann, 'Goethe und Gellert', *Goethe* 8 (1943)

E. K. Grotegut, 'Bodmer contra Gellert', *MLQ* 23 (1962)

D. V. Hegemann, 'Boswell's interviews with Gottsched and Gellert', *JEGP* 46 (1947)

E. K. Grotegut, 'Gellert. Wit or sentimentalist?', *Monatshefte* 54 (1962)

G. F. Merkel, 'Gellerts Stellung in der dt. Sprachgesch.', *PBB* (Halle) 82 (1961)

W. Martens, 'Lektüre bei Gellert', Fs. Alewyn, 1967

## Friedrich Gerstäcker

Born 10 May 1816 in Hamburg, trained as a clerk and worked on a farm before emigrating to America in 1837. After an adventurous and varied career there Gerstäcker returned to Germany in 1843. The response to his stories of American life prompted him to undertake a number of other journeys in South and Central America, Australia and the Dutch East Indies. He also accompanied Duke Ernst of Coburg-Gotha to Egypt and Abyssinia. His adventure tales still find many young readers while the 'Sittenbilder' of exotic lands retain a documentary interest.

Works
*Die Regulatoren in Arkansas*, 1845
*Die Flusspiraten des Missisippi*, 1848
*Gold*, 1858
*Unter dem Äquator*, 1860
etc. etc.
*Gesammelte Schriften*, 44 vols., 1872–9
*Ausgewählte Werke*, 24 vols., ed. D. Theden, 1889–91; 3rd ed. by D. Theden, C. Döring, 1906 ff.
*Ausgewählte Erzählungen*, 8 vols., ed. K. Holm, 1903

Literature
F. Jacobstroer, *Die Romantechnik bei F. Gerstäcker*, diss Greifswald, 1914

E. Seyfarth, *F. Gerstäcker. Ein Beitrag zur Gesch. des exotischen Romans in Deutschland*, 1930

A. J. Prahl, 'Seitenlichter auf den Charakter Gerstäckers', *MLN* 49 (1934)

E. Hofacker, 'Über die Entstehung von Gerstäckers Germels-hausen', *GR* 2 (1927)

G. H. R. O'Donnell, 'Gerstäcker in America, 1837–43', *PMLA* 42 (1927)

A. J. Prahl, *Gerstäcker u. die Probleme seiner Zeit*, 1938

H. Plischke, *Von Cooper bis Karl May. Gesch. des völkerkundlichen Reiseromans*, 1951

## HEINRICH WILHELM VON GERSTENBERG

Born at Tondern in Schleswig 23 Jan. 1737. He studied law at Jena and in 1760 entered the Danish service, becoming Consul in Lübeck in 1775. In 1786 he retired to Altona where he spent the rest of his life; he died 1 Nov. 1823. Apart from his dramas and his critical writings his *Prosaische Gedichte*, 1759, repr. 1925, and *Gedicht eines Skalden* are of considerable historical interest.

### Works

*Tändeleyen*, 1759; repr. ed. A. Anger, DN, 1966

*Briefe über Merkwürdigkeiten der Literatur*, 1760–70

*Ariadne auf Naxos*, 1767

*Ugolino*, 1768

*Minona*, 1785

*Vermischte Schriften*, 1815 f.

### Literature

A. M. Wagner, *H. W. von Gerstenberg und der Sturm und Drang*, 1920–4

J. W. Eaton, *Gerstenberg und Lessing*, 1938

K. Gerth, *Studien zu Gerstenbergs Poetik*, *Pal 231*, 1960

## SALOMON GESSNER

Gessner was born in Zürich on 1 April 1730. He showed little academic promise and was sent to Berlin in 1749 to serve an apprenticeship in the printing and book-selling trade so that he might take his place in the family business. The attractions of art and literature proved too strong and he soon abandoned his employment for the company of scholars and poets like J. G.

Sulzer, Hagedorn and Ramler. It was the latter who persuaded Gessner to abandon verse for the rhythmic prose with which he eventually made his reputation. Gessner returned to Zürich in 1750 and devoted himself largely to painting and writing. In 1761 he married Juditha Heidegger, a member of a local patrician family, who played a large part in running the business when Gessner's father died in 1775. In 1765 Gessner was elected to the Grand Council and subsequently occupied various civic offices, enjoying the serene and secure existence of which Keller gives a glimpse in his *Landvogt von Greifensee*. In his later years Gessner devoted himself more to painting and engraving than to writing. He died in Zürich on 2 March 1788. His taste, both in poetry and painting, was classicistic and he distinguished himself in the rococo form of the pastoral idyll. His models were Theocritus and Virgil, whose works he must have known mainly through translations. His sole attempt at the grandiose epic advocated by Bodmer, *Der Tod Abels*, although widely read and praised in its time, was unconvincing, while his plays *Evander und Alcimna* and *Erast* are totally lacking in dramatic merit. His talent was formal and decorative, his themes were trivial, their treatment unproblematic, the sentiment in his work cloying; as Goethe rightly said, his characters are 'Schattenwesen'. On the other hand, his renunciation of verse prompted him to lavish on his prose an unprecedented care which made it a model of polished elegance for many other writers. The delicate charm and insouciance of his idylls made him even more popular in France than in Germany, his works were translated into almost every European language and he became one of the first writers in German to acquire a truly international reputation.

Works
*Die Nacht*, 1753
*Daphnis*, 1754
*Idyllen*, 1756
*Der Tod Abels*, 1758
*Evander und Alcimna*, 1762
*Erast*, 1762
*Der erste Schiffer*, 1762
*Idyllen*, 1772
*Moralische Erzählungen u. Idyllen von Diderot u. Gessner*, 1772
Selections from Gessner's work, ed. A. Frey, DNL 41, I

Literature
P. Leeman van Elck, *Salomon Gessner*, 1930
H. Wölfflin, *Salomon Gessner*, 1889
F. Baldensperger, 'L'épisode de Gessner dans la littérature
   européenne', *Gessner-Gedenkbuch*, 1930
R. Strasser, *Stilprobleme in Gessners Kunst u. Dichtung*, diss. Heidel-
   berg, 1936
W. E. Delp, 'Goethe u. Gessner', *MLR* 20 (1925)
P. van Tieghem, 'Les idylles de Gessner et le rêve pastoral dans le
   préromanticisme européen', *RLC* 4 (1924)
F. Baldensperger, 'Gessner en France', *Revue d'histoire littéraire de
   la France*, 10 (1903)
N. Müller, *Die dt. Theorien der Idylle von Gottsched bis Gessner*, diss.
   Strasbourg, 1911
H. E. Mantz, 'Non-dramatic pastoral in Europe in the 18th
   century', *PMLA* 31 (1916)

ADOLF GLASSBRENNER (pseud. ADOLF BRENNGLAS)

Journalist of liberal views, connoisseur of Berlin humour. Born
27 March 1810 in Berlin, died there 25 Sept. 1876.

Works
*Berlin, wie es ist und—trinkt*, 1832–50
*Die politisierenden Eckensteher*, 1833; rev. ed. 1839
*Buntes Leben*, 1837–53
*Berliner Erzählungen und Lebensbilder*, 1838
*Schilderungen aus dem Berliner Volksleben*, 1842
*Humor im Berliner Volksleben*, 3 vols., 1906

JOHANN WILHELM LUDWIG GLEIM

Born at Ermsleben near Halberstadt, 2 April 1719. He studied law
and philosophy at Halle and there met Uz. He served in the
Second Silesian War and from 1747 to 1791 was secretary to the
Chapter of Halberstadt, where he died on 18 Feb. 1803.

Works
*Preussische Kriegslieder*, ed. A. Sauer, DNL 4 (1882)
*Sämtl. Werke*, ed. W. Korte, 1811–41

Literature

K. Becker, *Gleim der Grenadier und seine Freunde*, 1919
K. Schwarze, 'Gleims Preussische Kriegslieder von einem Grenadier', *GRM* 25 (1937)

## JOSEF GÖRRES

Görres, born in Koblenz on 25 Jan. 1776, was the son of a Rhenish timber-merchant and an Italian mother. His student years coincided with the French occupation of his homeland during the revolutionary wars. As editor of *Das rote Blatt* and *Rübezahl* (1797–8) Görres hailed the revolutionary triumph over the old clerical regimes but attacked the French when it became clear that they did not mean to create the autonomous Rhenish Republic he desired, so that his papers were suppressed by the authorities. As a revolutionary delegate to Paris in 1799 Görres witnessed the rise of Napoleon and returned disillusioned to a post as schoolmaster in Koblenz. In 1806 he moved to the University of Heidelberg where, a brilliant dilettante, he lectured on many topics and joined Arnim and Brentano in their study of German medieval and popular literature. When the Romantic group split up in 1808 Görres returned to Koblenz, but the wars of liberation again called him into the political arena. His *Rheinischer Merkur* was the most influential liberal organ during the false dawn of freedom that followed Napoleon's defeat; his agitation for a united and constitutional German state caused the Prussian government to ban the *Merkur* in 1816 and he escaped arrest in 1819 only by flight abroad. During his exile Görres reverted to the faith of his youth and founded the periodical *Der Katholik* in Strasbourg. In spite of Prussian protests King Ludwig I of Bavaria appointed him Professor of History in the University of Munich in 1826 and for the remainder of his life Görres propagated the Catholic cause with idiosyncratic zeal and an emphasis on mysticism that was not entirely approved by the Church. He died in Munich on 29 Jan. 1848. Görres was a man of vehement temperament and great intellectual vitality who championed very diverse causes during his life. As a scholar he was given to extravagant speculation and his treatises on mythology are no longer regarded as sound, but as a polemical publicist he had few equals: 'Seit Milton', wrote Friedrich Gentz, 'hat keiner erhabener und teuflischer geschrieben als dieser Görres.' Had

Germany possessed parliamentary institutions in his time his influence might have been greater still.

Works

*Der allgemeine Frieden, ein Ideal*, 1798
*Resultate meiner Sendung nach Paris*, 1800
*Glauben und Wissen*, 1805
*Die teutschen Volksbücher*, 1807
*Die wunderbare Geschichte von BOGS dem Uhrmacher*, 1807
*Rheinischer Merkur*, 23 Jan. 1814–10 Jan. 1816
*Teutschlands künftige Verfassung*, 1816
*Altteutsche Volks- und Meisterlieder*, 1817
*Teutschland und die Revolution*, 1819
*Europa und die Revolution*, 1821
*Napoleons Proklamation an die Völker Europas vor seinem Abzug auf die
    Insel Elba*, 1824 (repr. from *Teutscher Merkur*)
*Christliche Mystik*, 1836–42
*Athanasius*, 1837

Literature

J. N. Sepp, *Görres*, 1896 (*Geisteshelden*, vol. 23)
W. Schellberg, *Josef v. Görres*, 1913; 2nd ed. 1926
F. Schultz, *Görres im Zusammenhang mit der jüngeren Romantik*, Pal.
    11, 1902
H. Kindt, *Görres Rheinischer Merkur und die Presse seiner Zeit*, diss.
    Berlin, 1936
R. Reisse, *Die weltanschauliche Entwicklung des jungen Josef Görres
    1776–1806*, 1926
R. Saitschik, *Josef Görres und die abendländische Kultur*, 1953
G. Bürke, *Vom Mythos zur Mystik. J. v. Görres' mystische Lehre und die
    romantische Naturphilosophie*, 1958
R. Habel, *J. v. Görres. Studien über . . . Natur, Geschichte und Mythos
    in seinen Schriften*, 1960
Cf. also *Görres-Festschrift*, ed. K. Hoeber, 1926. *Lit. wissenschaft-
    liches Jb. der Görres-Gesellschaft*, ed. G. Müller, 1926 ff.; new
    series, ed. H. Kunisch, 1960 ff.

JOHANN WOLFGANG (VON) GOETHE

Goethe was born on 28 Aug. 1749 in Frankfurt on Main of affluent parents. As a child he was mainly educated at home. The strongest impressions made on him in his early youth were the Lisbon earthquake and the coronation of Joseph II as Holy Roman Emperor in Frankfurt in 1764. In 1765 he began to study law at Leipzig university. During his stay he met Käthchen Schönkopf (who inspired his first collection of poems *Annette*) and took drawing lessons from Oeser who was also Winckelmann's teacher. An illness took Goethe to Frankfurt in 1768: he now came under the influence of the Pietist lady, Susanne von Klettenberg, in whose image he drew the 'schöne Seele' of *Wilhelm Meisters Lehrjahre*; he also began his studies of magic and mysticism.

From April 1770 until Aug. 1771 he continued his legal studies in Strasbourg. Here he associated with Herder and members of the 'Sturm und Drang', and met Friderike Brion at Sesenheim. In 1772 he spent the months from May to September at the 'Reichskammergericht' in Wetzlar and here met Charlotte Buff and her fiancé Kestner. He continued his training as advocate in Frankfurt from 1773 until 1775, met Maximiliane von La Roche and became engaged to Lilli Schönemann; the engagement was broken off in the autumn of 1775. From Frankfurt Goethe made journeys on the Rhine in the company of Lavater and Basedow in 1774 (see the poem 'Diner zu Koblenz') and to Switzerland with the brothers von Stolberg in 1775.

In December 1774 Prince Karl August visited him in Frankfurt and invited him to Weimar where he arrived on 7 Nov. 1775. His friendship with Charlotte von Stein began in 1776. At this time, too, he started his scientific investigations, different aspects of which were to occupy him for virtually the rest of his life. During the first ten years in Weimar he devoted a considerable amount of time and energy to his administrative duties as 'Geheimer Legationsrat'. In 1780 he became 'Geheimer Rat' and in 1782 'Kammerpräsident' in charge of finances. In this year he was also raised to the rank of nobleman.

He made important journeys to the Harz Mountains in 1777 (cf. the poem 'Harzreise im Winter'), 1783 and 1784, and to Switzerland in 1779 and 1797. His first Italian journey took place between September 1786 and June 1788 with visits to Verona, Vicenza, Padua, Venice, Bologna, Rome, Naples, Paestum, Sicily and Florence (see his account in *Italienische Reise*); the second, far less significant one, in 1790. From 1791 until 1817 he directed the Weimar theatre. He took part in the war against France in 1792 and 1793 (see *Die Campagne in Frankreich* and *Die Belagerung von Mainz*). His friendship with Schiller began in 1794.

The following are the most important events in Goethe's life after 1800: Visit of Mme de Staël, 1803–4; marriage to Christiane Vulpius, 1806; friendship with Minna Herzlieb, 1807; meeting with Napoleon, 1808, and with Beethoven, 1812; death of his mother, 1808, and of Christiane, 1816; journey to the Rhine and friendship with Marianne von Willemer, 1814–15; journey to Marienbad and friendship with Ulrike von Levetzow, 1823; visits from Emerson, Carlyle, Heine, Grillparzer, Turgenev, Thackeray and other literary figures, 1820–30; death of Duke Karl August, 1828; death of his son August in Rome, 1830. Goethe died in Weimar on 22 Mar. 1832.

Collected works
*Vollst. Ausg. letzter Hand*, 1827–42
*Weimarer Ausg.*, 1887–1920
*Jubiläumsausg.*, ed. E. v. Hellen, 1902–12
*Festausg.*, ed. R. Petsch, 1926–8
*Hamburger Ausg.*, ed. E. Trunz, 1948–60
*Gedenkausg.*, ed. E. Beutler, 1948–60
*Werke*, ed. *Dt. Akad. der Wiss.*, 1952 ff.

Dramas
*Die Laune des Verliebten*, 1767
*Die Mitschuldigen*, 1768
*Götz von Berlichingen*, 1773
*Clavigo*, 1774
*Erwin und Elmire*, 1775
*Claudine von Villa Bella*, 1776
*Stella*, 1776
*Die Geschwister*, 1776
*Lila*, 1776
*Der Triumph der Empfindsamkeit*, 1777
*Jery und Bätely*, 1779
*Iphigenie auf Tauris*, 1779–86
*Egmont*, 1775–88
*Faust. Ein Fragment*, 1790

*Torquato Tasso*, 1780–90; ed. E. L. Stahl, 1962; ed. C. P. Magill, 1969
*Der Gross-Cophta*, 1787–91
*Der Bürgergeneral*, 1793
*Die Aufgeregten*, 1793
*Die natürliche Tochter*, 1801–3
*Faust. Der Tragödie erster Teil*, 1808
*Pandora*, 1809
*Des Epimenides Erwachen*, 1815
*Faust. Der Tragödie zweiter Teil*, 1833

Poetry
*Das Buch Annette*, 1767
*Neue Lieder*, 1768
*Reineke Fuchs*, 1794
*Römische Elegien*, 1795
*Alexis und Dora*, 1796
*Venezianische Epigramme*, 1796
*Hermann und Dorothea*, 1796–7
*Xenien* (with Schiller), 1797
*Ballads*, 1797
*West-östlicher Divan*, 1814–19

Novels and Tales
*Die Leiden des jungen Werthers*, 1774, revised 1787; ed. E. L. Stahl, 1942
*Wilhelm Meisters theatralische Sendung*, 1776 pass. (publ. 1911)
*Unterhaltungen deutscher Ausgewanderten*, 1795
*Wilhelm Meisters Lehrjahre*, 1795–6
*Die Wahlverwandtschaften*, 1809
*Wilhelm Meisters Wanderjahre*, 1821
*Novelle*, 1828

Literature: General works
F. Gundolf, *Goethe*, 1925
E. Kühnemann, *Goethe*, 1930
K. Viëtor, *Goethe*, 1949
B. Fairley, *A study of Goethe*, 1947
E. Staiger, *Goethe*, 1957–9
P. Stöcklein, *Wege zum späten Goethe*, 1960

W. Mommsen, *Die Entstehung von Goethes Werken in Dokumenten*, 1958 ff.

E. Beutler, *Essays um Goethe*, 1957

*Goethe Handbuch*, ed. A. Zastrau, 1955 ff.

*Aesthetics*

Goethe's contribution to aesthetics is mainly in two fields: first, in the conception of artistic form and secondly in that of symbolism. In the first instance a development may be traced from his 'Sturm und Drang' days when he valued expressiveness and what he called 'characteristic' form, to his Classical period when he demanded adherence to formal principles such as symmetry and parallelism. The notion of 'Innere Form' remained an abiding conviction, although he emphasized different sides at different times. His scientific studies allowed him to gain insights into the similarity as well as, more particularly, the difference between forms produced in nature and in art. Here his discovery of the symbol is of especial interest. The formative arts, above all architecture, played an important part in the development of his aesthetic views. Their main import lies in Goethe's recognition of aesthetic autonomy. This becomes evident, for example, in his dramatic theories, most notably in his interpretation of catharsis as meaning 'Ausgleichung' and 'aussöhnende Abrundung'. Some of his other literary principles are best studied in his autobiography, *Dichtung und Wahrheit*.

Works

'Zum Shakespeare Tag', 1771

'Von deutscher Baukunst'. 1773

*Zur Theorie der bildenden Kunst*, 1788

'Einfache Nachahmung, Manier, Stil', 1788

'Über Wahrheit und Wahrscheinlichkeit der Kunstwerke', 1797

'Über epische und dramatische Dichtkunst' (with Schiller), 1797

'Der Sammler und die Seinigen', 1798–9

*Winckelmann und sein Jahrhundert*, 1804–5

'Shakespeare und kein Ende', 1813–16

*Aus meinem Leben, Dichtung und Wahrheit*, 1808–31

'Shakespeare als Theaterdichter', 1815

'Nachlese zu Aristoteles Poetik', 1827

Ed. *Propyläen*, 1798–1800

*Jenaische Literaturzeitung*, 1804–7
*Über Kunst und Altertum*, 1816–28

Literature
W. Bode, *Goethes Ästhetik*, 1901
F. Weinhandl, *Die Metaphysik Goethes*, 1932
H. Sudheimer, *Der Geniebegriff des jungen Goethe*, 1935
C. Müller, *Die geschichtlichen Voraussetzungen des Symbolbegriffs in Goethes Kunstanschauung*, 1937
H. v. Einem, 'Goethes Kunstphilosophie', *Goethe und Dürer*, 1947
O. Stelzer, *Goethe und die bildende Kunst*, 1949
E. R. Curtius, 'Goethe als Kritiker' in *Kritische Essays zur europäischen Literatur*, 1950
E. M. Wilkinson, 'Goethe's Conception of Form', *Proceedings of the British Academy*, 1953
M. Jolles, *Goethes Kunstanschauung*, 1957
P. Menzer, 'Goethes Ästhetik', *Kantstudien, Ergänzungsheft* 72 (1957)

*Science*
For the student of Goethe's literary work his scientific writings are often invaluable aids to understanding and appreciating much of his imagery and his symbolism. Some of his key concepts in both realms belong closely together and may be explained in mutual terms, for example 'Bildung' and 'Metamorphose'.

Works
'Über den Zwischenkieferknochen', 1784
*Versuch, die Metamorphose der Pflanzen zu erklären*, 1790
*Entwurf einer Einleitung in die vergleichende Anatomie*, 1795–6
*Zur Farbenlehre*, 1810
*Zur Naturwissenschaft überhaupt, besonders zur Morphologie*, 1817–24
'Versuch einer Witterungslehre', 1825

Literature
H. Helmholtz, 'Über Goethes naturwissenschaftliche Arbeiten' in *Vorträge un Reden*, 1896
R. Magnus, *Goethe als Naturforscher*, 1906
G. Müller, *Die Gestaltfrage in der Literaturwissenschaft und Goethes Morphologie*, 1944
K. Hildebrandt, *Goethes Naturerkenntnis*, 1948

FRIEDRICH WILHELM GOTTER

Born 3 Sep. 1746 in Gotha, studied law in Göttingen, edited *Göttinger Musenalmanach* with C. H. Boie, associated with Goethe and Jerusalem in Wetzlar, travelled in France and Switzerland. Gotter encouraged the court theatre in Gotha, which was directed by Ekhof and then by Iffland. He translated plays from French, and his own dramas and 'Singspiele' were in the French taste. He died 18 March 1797.

Works
*Tom Jones*, 1772 (operetta)
*Die Dorfgala*, 1772 (comedy)
*Die falschen Entdeckungen*, 1774 (comedy)
*Medea*, 1775 (drama)
*Mariane*, 1776 (tragedy)
*Romeo und Julia*, 1799 (drama)
*Gedichte*, 3 vols., 1787–1802
*Die Erbschleicher*, 1789 (comedy)
*Schauspiele*, 1795
*Die Geisterinsel*, 1797 (operetta based on Shakespeare's *Tempest*)

Literature
R. Schlösser, *F. W. Gotter, sein Leben u. seine Werke*, 1894

JEREMIAS GOTTHELF (ALBERT BITZIUS)

Bitzius, who took his pseudonym from his own first novel, was born 4 Oct. 1797 in Murten, Switzerland, and followed in the footsteps of his father, who was Protestant minister in Utzenstorf; he studied theology in Berne, went to the University of Göttingen in 1821 and after travelling in Germany was appointed assistant minister in Herzogenbuchsee. He was transferred to Lützelflüh in the Emmental in 1831 and succeeded to the living there in the following year. From 1840–5 he was editor of the *Neuer Berner Kalender* and virtually its sole contributor. He died in Lützelflüh, 22 Oct. 1854. Gotthelf regarded his stories primarily as a means of moral instruction and a weapon in the conservative cause for which he stood, but they far transcend the mere propagandistic purpose. Gottfried Keller, a political adversary, considered him 'ein originales, grosses, episches Genie'.

## Works

*Der Bauernspiegel oder Lebensgeschichte des Jeremias Gotthelf*, 1837
*Wie fünf Mädchen im Branntwein jämmerlich umkamen*, 1838
*Leiden und Freuden eines Schulmeisters*, 1838
*Dursli der Branntweinsäufer*, 1838
*Wie Uli der Knecht glücklich wird*, 1841
*Bilder u. Sagen aus der Schweiz* (inc. *Geld und Geist*; *Die schwarze Spinne*), 1842–6
*Wie Anne Bäbi Jowäger haushaltet*, 1843 f.
*Der Geltstag*, 1846
*Jakobs des Handwerksgesellen Wanderungen in der Schweiz*, 1846
*Käthi die Grossmutter*, 1847
*Hans Joggeli*, 1848
*Uli der Pächter*, 1849
*Die Käserei in der Vehfreude*, 1850
*Zeitgeist und Berner Geist*, 1852
*Gesammelte Erzählungen u. Bilder aus dem Volksleben der Schweiz* (inc. *Elsi die seltsame Magd*), 5 vols., 1850–5
*Historisch-kritische Gesamtausgabe*, ed. R. Hunziker, H. Bloesch, 36 vols., 1911–51

## Literature

W. Muschg (ed.), *Jeremias Gotthelfs Persönlichkeit. Erinnerungen von Zeitgenossen*, 1944
G. Muret, *Jérémie Gotthelf, sa vie et ses oeuvres*, 1913
R. Hunziker, *Jeremias Gotthelf*, 1927
W. Muschg, *Gotthelf. Die Geheimnisse des Erzählers*, 1931
H. M. Waidson, *Jeremias Gotthelf. An introduction to the Swiss novelist*, 1953
W. Muschg, *Jeremias Gotthelf. Eine Einführung in seine Werke*, 1954; 2nd ed. 1960
W. Günther, *Jeremias Gotthelf. Wesen u. Werk*, 1954
K. Fehr, *Jeremias Gotthelf*, 1954
W. E. Peuckert, 'Jeremias Gotthelf', *ZfdPh* 74 (1955)
K. Fehr, *Das Bild des Menschen bei Jeremias Gotthelf*, 1954
W. Günther, *Neue Gotthelf-Studien*, 1959
F. Sengle, 'Zum Wandel des Gotthelfbildes', *GRM* 38 (1957) or *Arbeiten zur dt. Lit.*, 1965
K. Fehr, *Jeremias Gotthelf (Albert Bitzius)*, 1967
A. Reber, *Stil u. Bedeutung des Gesprächs im Werke Jeremias Gotthelfs*, 1967

JOHANN CHRISTOPH GOTTSCHED

Born on 2 Feb. 1700 at Judittenkirchen near Königsberg, where he studied theology and philosophy. In 1724 he fled to Leipzig when he was in danger of being drafted into Frederick II's chosen regiment because of his size. He became Professor of Poetry in 1730, Professor of Logic and Metaphysics in 1734. His influential work on literary theory and criticism should be viewed against the background of his philosophical studies which do not lack historical interest. He died in Leipzig on 12 Dec. 1766.

Works

*Redekunst*, 1728
*Versuch einer critischen Dichtkunst vor die Deutschen*, 1730; repr. 1962
*Erste Gründe der gesammten Weltweisheit*, 1734
*Grundlegung einer deutschen Sprachkunst*, 1748
*Gesammelte Schriften*, ed. E. Reichel, 1902–6
*Ausgewählte Werke*, ed. J. Birke, 1968 ff.

Literature

E. Reichel, *Gottsched*, 1908–12
A. Peiz, *Die vier Auflagen von Gottscheds Critischer Dichtkunst in vergleichender Betrachtung*, 1929
W. Kuhlmann, *Die theologischen Voraussetzungen von Gottscheds Critischer Dichtkunst*, diss. Münster, 1935
U. Lehmann, *Der Gottschedkreis u. Russland*, 1966

CHRISTIAN DIETRICH GRABBE

Born at Detmold of very poor parents, 11 Dec. 1801. He studied law at Leipzig in 1820 and at Berlin university in 1822, where he met Heine. In 1823 he returned to Leipzig and later went to Dresden, Hanover and Bremen, with the intention of becoming an actor. When his plans failed he went back to Detmold in 1824 and completed his studies. He began practising and was appointed to a post as 'Militärauditor' in 1827. His life became more and more dissolute after the failure of his marriage with Luise Closter-meier, the daughter of his patron. He was dismissed from his post in 1834. Immermann vainly tried to help him by obtaining em-ployment at the Düsseldorf theatre for him. He returned to

Detmold after quarrelling with Immermann and died of alcoholic excess on 12 Sept. 1836.

Works

*Herzog Theodor von Gothland*, 1827
*Scherz, Satire, Ironie und tiefere Bedeutung*, 1827
*Marius und Sulla*, 1827
*Don Juan und Faust*, 1829
*Die Hohenstaufen*, 1829–30
*Napoleon oder die hundert Tage*, 1831
*Hannibal*, 1835
*Sämtliche Werke*, ed. S. Wukidanowié, 1912
*Werke und Briefe*, ed. A. Bergmann, 1960 ff.

Literature

A. Kutscher, *Hebbel und Grabbe*, 1913
F. J. Schneider, *C. D. Grabbe. Persönlichkeit und Werk*, 1934
E. Dieckmann, *C. D. Grabbe. Der Wesensgehalt seiner Dichtung*, 1936
E. Busch, 'Geschichte und Tragik in Grabbes Dramen', *Dichtung und Volkstum*, 1941
W. Hollerer, 'C. D. Grabbe', *Zwischen Klassik und Moderne*, 1958
D. Schmidt, *Die Problematik des Tragischen in den historischen Dramen Grabbes*, 1965
A. W. Hornsey, *Idea and Reality in the dramas of C. D. Grabbe*, 1966
R. A. Nicholls, *The dramas of C. D. Grabbe*, 1969

FRANZ GRILLPARZER

Born in Vienna, 15 Jan. 1791. He studied law from 1808 until 1811. After a year's tutorship he entered the civil service in 1813 first in the State Library and then, from 1832 until 1856, in the archives of the Ministry of Finance. In 1818 he was also appointed official poet at the Burgtheater. The suicide of his mother in 1819 had a lasting effect upon his life and work. In 1819 he went on a journey to Italy and visited Trieste, Venice, Ferrara, Rome, Naples and Florence. He also travelled in Germany in 1826 and visited Goethe in Weimar, Tieck in Dresden, Fouqué and Chamisso in Berlin. In 1836 he travelled to Paris, where he met Heine and Börne, and to London. On the way back he visited Uhland in Stuttgart. In 1843 he made a journey to Turkey and Greece, in 1847 a second journey to Germany. After writing the poem 'Die Ruinen des Campo vaccino' he was in constant difficulties with the censorship authorities and when the first performance of *Weh dem, der lügt* proved a failure, he withdrew more and more from public acclaim. Nonetheless he was highly esteemed for his dramatic work and was elevated to the rank of 'Hofrat' in 1856 and to that of 'Reichsrat' in 1861, and was given the freedom of the city of Vienna in 1864. None of his travel experiences or the honours bestowed on him, however, mitigated his hypochondria, a side of his personality which comes out in his relations with women, particularly with Katharina Fröhlich whom he met in 1821. It is also a feature of his poetry, especially his epigrams and satirical verse. His diaries are a valuable source of information. Grillparzer died in Vienna on 21 Jan. 1872.

Works

*Die Ahnfrau,* 1817
*Sappho,* 1819
*Das goldene Vliess,* 1822
*König Ottokars Glück und Ende,* 1825
*Ein treuer Diener seines Herrn,* 1828
*Das Kloster bei Sendomir,* 1828 (Novelle)
*Der Traum ein Leben,* 1834; ed. W. E. Yuill, 1955; repr. 1964
*Weh' dem, der lügt,* 1838; ed. G. Waterhouse, 1923; repr. 1962
*Des Meeres und der Liebe Wellen,* 1820–9
*Der arme Spielmann,* 1847 (Novelle)
*Libussa,* 1872
*Ein Bruderzwist in Habsburg,* 1872
*Die Jüdin von Toledo,* 1872
*Sämtl. Werke,* ed. A. Sauer and R. Backmann, 1909–48; ed. P. Frank and K. Pörnbacher, 1960
*Gespräche und Charakteristiken seiner Persönlichkeit,* ed. A. Sauer, 1904; repr. 1941
*Briefe und Tagebücher,* ed. C. Glossy and A. Sauer, 1903

Literature

E. Reich, *Grillparzers Dramen,* 1894
O. Katann, ed., *Grillparzer-Studien,* 1924
I. Münch, *Die Tragik in Drama und Persönlichkeit Grillparzers,* 1931
O. Zausner, *Grillparzers Lyrik als Ausdruck seines Wesens,* 1933
A. Sauer, *Franz Grillparzer,* 1941

K. Vancsa, *Franz Grillparzer. Bild und Forschung*, 1941

R. Peacock, in *The Poet in the Theatre*, 1946

D. Yates, *Franz Grillparzer. A critical biography*, 1946

J. Nadler, *Franz Grillparzer*, 1948

E. E. Papst, 'Franz Grillparzer', *German Men of Letters, I*, 1961

G. Baumann, *Franz Grillparzer*, 1966

B. Breitenbach, *Ethik und Ethos bei Grillparzer*, 1966

U. Helmensdorfer, *Grillparzers Bühnenkunst*, 1960

J. Kaiser, *Grillparzers dramatischer Stil*, 1962

U. Fülleborn, *Das dramatische Geschehen im Werk F. Grillparzers*, 1966

G. A. Wells, *The plays of Grillparzer*, 1969

Bibliographies by K. Vancsa, 1937 and E. Hock, *GRM* 35 (1954)

## JAKOB GRIMM

Born 4 Jan. 1785 in Hanau. Grimm studied law in Marburg and Heidelberg, where he associated with the group of Romantic writers that included Brentano and Arnim. In 1808 Grimm became librarian to the King of Westphalia, moving to a similar post in Kassel when this Napoleonic régime collapsed. In 1829 he became professor of Germanic antiquities in Göttingen but was dismissed along with six other professors ('Göttinger Sieben') because of his liberal views. From 1841 he was a member of the Prussian Academy of Sciences and held a chair at the University of Berlin. He was a delegate to the abortive Frankfurt Parliament of 1848. With his brother Wilhelm, Jakob Grimm edited the great *Deutsches Wörterbuch* that goes by their name and the two men may be considered the major founders of modern Germanistic studies.

Works (many in collaboration with Wilhelm Grimm)

*Kinder- und Hausmärchen*, 3 vols., 1812, 1815, 1823; repr., ed. F. Panzer, 1955

*Lieder der alten Edda*, 1815

*Deutsche Sagen*, 2 vols., 1816–18

*Deutsche Grammatik*, 4 vols., 1819–37; latest reprint 1967

*Deutsche Mythologie*, 1833

*Geschichte der deutschen Sprache*, 2 vols., 1848

*Kleine Schriften*, 8 vols., 1864–90; repr. 1965–6

*Briefe der Brüder Grimm*, ed. A. Leitzmann, 1923

*Briefwechsel der Brüder Grimm mit K. Lachmann,* ed. A. Leitzmann,
2 vols., 1927

Literature

W. Scherer, *Jakob Grimm,* 1885; repr. 1921
A. Duncker, *Die Brüder Grimm,* 1884
A. E. Schönbach, *Die Brüder Grimm,* 1948
G. F. Hering, *Jakob Grimm,* 1948
H. Gerstner (ed.), *Die Brüder Grimm. Ihr Leben und Werk in Selbst-
zeugnissen, Briefen und Aufzeichnungen,* 1952
W. Schoof, *Jakob Grimm. Aus seinem Leben,* 1961
W. Schoof, *Die Brüder Grimm in Berlin,* 1964
W. Schoof, *Zur Entstehungsgeschichte der Grimmschen Märchen,* 1959
J. Bolte, G. Polivka, *Anmerkungen zu den Kinder- und Hausmärchen
der Brüder Grimm,* 3 vols., 1914–18
F. v. d. Leyen, *Das deutsche Märchen und die Brüder Grimm,* 1964
Cf. also W. Fraenger, W. Steinitz (eds.), *Jakob Grimm Festschrift,*
1963

WILHELM GRIMM

Wilhelm was born on 24 Feb. 1786 at Hanau, a younger brother
of Jakob and his life-long partner in philological research. After
studying law in Marburg Wilhelm became secretary of the library
in Kassel in 1814 and followed his brother to Göttingen in 1830,
where he worked as sub-librarian before being appointed
professor in 1830. He was expelled in 1837 along with his brother
and five other professors whose liberal opinions he shared.
Wilhelm died in Berlin on 16 Dec. 1859. He edited many Middle
High German texts and wrote mainly on the heroic sagas.

Works
*Altdänische Heldenlieder, Balladen und Märchen,* 1811
*Die deutsche Heldensage,* 1829
*Kleinere Schriften,* ed. G. Hinrichs, 4 vols., 1881–7

Literature
C. Zuckmayer, *Die Brüder Grimm,* 1948
W. E. Peuckert, 'Wilhelm und Jakob Grimm', *Die grossen Deut-
schen,* ed. H. Heimpel, T. Heuss, B. Reifenberg, vol. 3, 1956
W. Schoof, *Wilhelm Grimm. Aus seinem Leben,* 1960
Cf. also under Jakob Grimm

KARL GROSSE (pseud. GRAF VON VARGAS)

Born 1761 in Magdeburg, studied medicine, led an irregular life
and eventually vanished in Spain. Author of sensational tales;
his *Genius* impressed the youthful Tieck deeply.

Works
*Der Genius*, 4 vols., 1791–4
*Novellen*, 2 vols., 1792
*Kleine Romane*, 4 vols., 1793 f.
*Spanische Novellen*, 4 vols., 1794 f.
*Liebe u. Treue*, 2 vols., 1796 f.
*Des Grafen von Vargas Versuche*, 2 vols., 1811

Literature
J. W. Apell, *Die Ritter- u. Räuberromantik*, 1859

ANASTASIUS GRÜN (ANTON ALEXANDER GRAF AUERSPERG)

Born in Laibach in Austria, 11 April 1806; studied engineering,
philosophy and law at Vienna and Graz universities. He travelled
in Germany, Italy, France and England from 1830 to 1838 and
then became a member of the Frankfurt Parliament and of the
Austrian 'Herrenhaus'. Died 12 Sep. 1876.

Works
*Spaziergänge eines Wiener Poeten*, 1831
*Sämtliche Werke*, ed. E. Castle, 1909

Literature
F. Riedl, *Anastasius Grün*, 1909
R. Wächter, *Anastasius Grüns politische Dichtung*, 1933

KAROLINE VON GÜNDERODE

Born in Karlsruhe, 11 Feb. 1780, grew up in Hanau and entered
a Protestant religious foundation in Frankfurt am Main at the
age of eighteen. It was here that she made the acquaintance of the
Brentanos and formed a close sentimental friendship with Bettina.
Her lyric poetry and dramas, published under the pseudonym of
Tian, are Romantic in idiom, sentimental or quasi-mystical in

tone; at their best they lend some colour to the reputation she enjoyed as 'the German Sappho'. In consequence of an unhappy love affair with the Heidelberg mythologist, Professor G. F. Creuzer, she stabbed herself to death in Winkel am Rhein on 26 July 1806.

## Works

*Gedichte und Phantasien*, 1804
*Poetische Fragmente*, 1805
*Gesammelte Dichtungen*, ed. F. Götz, 1857
*Werke*, ed. L. Hirschberg, 1920–2

## Literature

B. v. Brentano, *Die Günderode—ein Briefwechsel*, 1840; repr. 1890
L. Geiger, *Karoline von Günderode und ihre Freunde*, 1895
G. Bianquis, *Caroline de Gunderode*, 1910
M. Mattheis, *Die Günderode*, 1934
A. Neumann, *Caroline von Günderode*, diss. Berlin, 1957
M. Preitz, 'Karoline von Günderode in ihrer Umwelt', *Jb. des des freien dt. Hochstifts*, 1962; 1964

## JOHANN CHRISTIAN GÜNTHER

Born 8 April 1695 at Striegau, studied medicine in Wittenberg and Leipzig but fell into dissipated ways. He forfeited an appointment as court poet in Dresden through the untimely publication of a satire and moved to Breslau, where the efforts of friends to help him failed. Disowned by his father, Günther died in Jena on 15 March 1723. He was undoubtedly one of the most gifted lyric poets in the age before Goethe.

## Works

*Die Eifersucht*, 1715 (tragedy)
*Deutsche und lateinische Gedichte*, 4 vols., 1724–35
*Curieuse und merkwürdige Lebens- und Reisebeschreibung*, 1732
*Gedichte*, 1735; ed. J. Tittmann, 1874, L. Fulda (DNL 38), 1883
*Sämtliche Werke*, ed. W. Krämer, *Bibliothek des lit. Vereins in Stuttgart*, 6 vols., 1930–7; repr. 1964

## Literature

A. Heyer, A. Hoffmann, *Günthers Leben auf Grund seines handschriftlichen Nachlasses*, 1909

C. Wittig, *Johann Christian Günther*, 1909

A. J. P. Crick, *Die Persönlichkeit J. C. Günthers*, diss. Heidelberg, 1938

W. Krämer, *Das Leben des schlesischen Dichters J. C. Günther*, 1950

H. Dahlke, *J. C. Günther. Seine dichterische Entwicklung*, 1960

F. Delbono, *Umanità e poesia di Christian Günther*, 1959

W. Krämer, 'Probleme u. Ergebnisse der Günther-Forschung', *GRM* 18 (1930)

J. Klewitz, *Die Natur in Günthers Lyrik*, 1911

I. S. Stamm, 'Günther and Leibniz-Wolff', *GR* 23 (1948)

G. Gillespie, 'Suffering in Günther's poetry', *GQ* 41 (1968)

A. Hoffmann, *J. C. Günther. Bibliographie*, 1929; repr. 1965

S. Lupi, 'Güntheriana', *Studi Germanici* 4 (1940)

E. Dürrenfeld, *Paul Fleming und J. C. Günther*, diss. Tübingen, 1964

P. Kirchner, 'Lomonosov und J. C. Günther', *Zs. f. Slavistik* 6 (1961)

## KARL GUTZKOW

Son of a groom in the royal stables, born 17 March 1811 in Berlin, studied in Berlin, became prominent as a publicist for the liberal Young German movement. His works were banned by the Bundestag in 1835 and *Wally, die Zweiflerin* cost him three months in a Mannheim prison. Gutzkow, who led a restless life, was for some years Dramaturg at the Hoftheater in Dresden. Following an attempted suicide in 1865 he spent a year in a mental hospital and, after his discharge, continued a nomadic existence, living in Switzerland, Berlin, Italy, Heidelberg and Frankfurt a. M. He died, apparently accidentally, of carbon monoxide poisoning in Sachsenhausen on 16 Dec. 1878. Much of Gutzkow's vast literary production was inevitably ephemeral, his novels are mostly too prolix and too superficially tendentious for the modern reader; only *Wally*, in spite of its makeshift form, retains its interest as a psychological study. A number of Gutzkow's historical dramas have, however, retained their popularity.

### Works
*Briefe eines Narren an eine Närrin*, 1832

*Maha Guru, Geschichte eines Gottes*, 1833

*Wally, die Zweiflerin*, 1835; repr. ed. J. Schillemeit, 1965

*Hamlet in Wittenberg*, 1835 (drama)
*Blasedow und seine Söhne*, 1838–9
*Richard Savage oder der Sohn der Mutter*, 1839 (tragedy)
*Werner oder Herz und Welt*, 1840 (drama)
*Die Schule der Reichen*, 1841 (comedy)
*Zopf und Schwert*, 1844 (comedy)
*Das Urbild des Tartüffe*, 1844 (comedy)
*Uriel Acosta*, 1846 (tragedy)
*Der Königsleutnant*, 1849 (comedy)
*Die Ritter vom Geiste*, 1850–1
*Aus der Knabenzeit*, 1852 (autobiography)
*Der Zauberer von Rom*, 1858–61
*Hohenschwangau*, 1867–8
*Die Söhne Pestalozzis*, 1870
*Rückblicke auf mein Leben*, 1875
*Gesammelte Werke*, 12 vols., 1872–6
*Dramatische Werke*, 20 vols., 1873–5
*Werke*, 4 vols., ed. H. H. Houben, 1910

Literature

W. Höllerer, 'Gutzkow', *Zwischen Klassik u. Moderne*, 1958
H. H. Houben, *Gutzkow-Funde*, 1901
A. Caselmann, *Gutzkows Stellung zu den religiös-ethischen Problemen
    seiner Zeit*, 1900
P. Westra, *Karl Gutzkows religiöse Ansichten*, 1947 (inaugural lec-
    ture, Groningen)
J. Dresch, *Gutzkow et la jeune Allemagne*, 1904
O. P. Schinnerer, *Women in the life and work of Gutzkow*, 1924
M. Schönfeld, 'Gutzkows Frauengestalten', *Germ. Stud.* 133 (1933)
H. Gerig, *Karl Gutzkow. Der Roman des Nebeneinander*, diss. Berne,
    1954
P. Hasubek, *Karl Gutzkows Romane Die Ritter vom Geiste und der
    Zauberer von Rom*, diss. Hamburg, 1964
K. Freiburg-Rüter, *Der literarische Kritiker Karl Gutzkow*, 1930
E. Melis, *Karl Gutzkow als Dramatiker*, 1915


FRIEDRICH WILHELM HACKLÄNDER

Born 1 Nov. 1816 at Burtscheid near Aachen. After experience in
the army and commerce became secretary to the crown prince of

Württemberg, later clerk of works to the King of Württemberg. War correspondent at Radetzky's headquarters in Italy in 1849, then founder and editor of various family magazines in 1849. Hackländer's journalistic training stood him in good stead in his stories of urban life and in his successful plays, he was hailed as the German Dickens but soon forgotten. Died 6 July 1877 at Leoni on the Starnbergersee.

Works

*Bilder aus dem Soldatenleben im Frieden*, 1840
*Bilder aus dem Soldatenleben im Kriege*, 2 vols., 1849 f.
*Handel und Wandel*, 1850
*Der geheime Agent*, 1851 (comedy)
*Europäisches Sklavenleben*, 1854
*Monsieur de Blé*, 1857 (comedy)
*Der Wechsel des Lebens*, 1861
*Das Geheimnis der Stadt*, 1868
*Der letzte Bombardier*, 4 vols., 1870
*Der Sturmvogel*, 1871
*Werke*, 1860–73
*Kainszeichen*, 1874
*Der Roman meines Lebens*, 1878

Literature

C. Pech, *Hackländer u. der Realismus*, diss. Kiel, 1932
T. Heuss, 'Der Hack', *Schattenbeschwörung*, 1948

ERNST HAECKEL

Born Potsdam, 16 Feb. 1834, doctor, then professor of zoology in Jena; populariser of the philosophy of monism, influenced Naturalist writers like G. Hauptmann. Died Jena, 9 Aug. 1919.

Works

*Der Monismus. Glaubensbekenntnis eines Naturforschers*, 1892
*Die Lebenswunder*, 1900

Literature

W. Bölsche, *Ernst Haeckel, ein Lebensbild*, 1900
W. May, *Ernst Haeckel. Versuch einer Chronik seines Lebens u. Wirkens*, 1909

WILHELM HÄRING: see WILLIBALD ALEXIS

## FRIEDRICH VON HAGEDORN

Born 23 April 1708 in Hamburg where he lived most of his life; he died there on 28 Oct. 1754. He studied law at Jena for one year and became secretary to the Danish ambassador in London in 1729. Thereupon he took a position as secretary to an English firm in Hamburg. These connections made him an influential intermediary between English and German literature.

### Works

*Sämtliche poetische Werke*, ed. J. J. Eschenburg, 1800
*Versuch einiger Gedichte*, 1738–50; ed. A. Sauer, 1883
*Versuch in poetischen Fabeln und Erzählungen*, 1738–50
*Sammlung neuer Oden und Lieder*, 1742–52
*Moralische Gedichte*, 1750

### Literature

K. Epting, *Der Stil der lyrischen und didaktischen Gedichte Hagedorns*, 1929

## IDA GRÄFIN HAHN-HAHN

Born 22 June 1805 at Tressow, Mecklenburg, married a wealthy cousin in 1826, divorced 1829, converted to Roman Catholicism 1850; indefatigable traveller and campaigner, first for the emancipation of women, then for the Church. Her flamboyant personality caused a sensation in her time; her novels, which clearly reflect her abrupt change of outlook, retain interest as social documentation. Died in Mainz, 12 Jan. 1880.

### Works

*Gedichte*, 1835
*Lieder und Gedichte*, 1837
*Ilda Schönholm*, 1838
*Gräfin Faustine*, 1841
*Ulrich*, 1841
*Gräfin Cecil*, 1844
*Aus der Gesellschaft*, 1845
*Sybille*, 1846

*Von Babylon nach Jerusalem,* 1851
*Die Liebhaber des Kreuzes,* 1852
*Maria Regina,* 1860
*Peregrin,* 1864
*Die Glöcknerstochter,* 1871
*Vergib uns unsere Schuld,* 1874
*Wahl und Führung,* 1878
*Gesamtausgabe* (Protestant works), 21 vols., 1851
*Gesammelte Werke* (Catholic), ed. O. von Schaching, 45 vols., 1930 ff.

Literature

M. Helene, *Gräfin Ida Hahn-Hahn: ein Lebensbild,* 1869
P. Haffner, *Gräfin Hahn-Hahn, eine psychologische Studie,* 1880
O. Denke, *Ida Gräfin Hahn-Hahn, eine biogr.-lit. Skizze,* 1903
M. Koher-Merzbach, 'Ida Hahn-Hahn', *Monatshefte* 47 (1955)

JOHANN CHRISTIAN LUDWIG HAKEN

Born 28 March 1767 at Jamund, near Köslin, rose to eminence in the Protestant Church, friend of Schleiermacher; historian and scholar, founded *Pommerische Provinzblätter.* Haken's novels and moral tales show powers of social observation and talent for characteristic dialogue. He died 5 June 1835 as 'Superintendent' at Treptow in Pomerania.

Works

*Die graue Mappe aus Ewald Rinks Verlassenschaft,* 4 vols., 1790–4
    (novels and tales)
*John Byrons Schiffbruch und Drangsale,* 1793
*Romantische Ausstellungen,* 1797–8
*Phantasus,* 1802
*Bibliothek der Robinsone,* 5 vols., 1805–8

ALBRECHT VON HALLER

Born 16 Oct. 1708 in Berne and studied medicine at Tübingen and Leipzig, anatomy, physiology and botany at Leiden, where he obtained his doctorate in 1727. In 1728 he went to London and to Paris and in the following year began practising medicine in Berne. He became librarian there in 1735 and in 1736 was appointed professor of medicine at Göttingen. He returned to Berne in 1753 and died there on 12 Dec. 1777.

## Works

*Versuch schweizerischer Gedichte,* 1732
*Die Alpen,* 1729; repr. ed. H. Betteridge, 1959
*Die Alpen und andere Gedichte,* ed. A. Elschenbroich, 1965

## Literature

C. Siegrist, *Albrecht v. Haller,* 1967
O. v. Greyerz, *Albrecht von Haller als Dichter,* 1902
K. S. Guthke, *Albrecht von Haller und die Literatur,* 1962
W. Kohlschmidt, 'Hallers Gedichte und die Tradition' in *Dichter, Tradition und Zeitgeist,* 1965

## JOHANN GEORG HAMANN

Born in Königsberg, 27 Aug. 1730, studied theology, law and Oriental languages and, after teaching in Riga, took up a commercial career. This brought him to London where he experienced a 'Pauline' conversion in 1758. Returning to Königsberg in 1759 he continued his studies in Oriental languages while occupying minor administrative posts in customs and excise departments. He was retired in 1787 and died on a visit to Jacobi in Münster, 21 June 1788.

## Works

The most important writings on aesthetic subjects in which
   Hamann expresses his 'irrationalist' attitude are contained
   in *Sokratische Denkwürdigkeiten* (1759) and in *Aesthetica in nuce*
   (part of *Kreuzzüge des Philologen,* 1762)
*Hauptschriften,* ed. O. Mann, 1938
*Sämtliche Werke,* ed. J. Nadler, 1949–57
*Briefwechsel,* ed. W. Ziesemer and A. Henkel, 1955 ff.

## Literature

R. Unger, *Hamann und die Aufklärung,* 1925
T. Hank, *Hamann als Ästhetiker,* 1947
J. Nadler, *Johann Georg Hamann,* 1949

F. Blanke, *Hamann-Studien*, 1956
H. A. Salmony, *Hamanns metakritische Philosophie*, 1958
W. Hilpert, *J. G. Hamann als Kritiker der dt. Literatur*, 1933
R. G. Smith, J. G. Hamann: a study in Christian existence, 1960

FRIEDRICH LEOPOLD VON HARDENBERG ('NOVALIS')

Born on 2 May 1772, son of a pietistic landowner in Oberwieder-stedt, Thüringen, Hardenberg studied in Jena, Leipzig and Wittenberg, making the acquaintance of Schiller and F. Schlegel. After training in the mining academy at Freiberg he entered the Saxon administration of mines at Weissenfels and was promoted Amtshauptmann shortly before his death there on 25 March 1801. Along with Tieck and the Schlegels, to whose periodical *Das Athenäum* he contributed, Novalis was a founder of the first Romantic School, its most distinguished lyric poet and a thinker with an encyclopaedic range of interests. The mysticism of Jakob Böhme and the idealist philosophy of Fichte were influential in the development of his philosophy of 'magischer Idealismus'. Hardenberg seems to have been deeply affected by the death of his fiancée, Sophie v. Kühn, at the age of fifteen, and the memory of this experience is fused with quasi-mystical religious sentiment in his poems and fragmentary novels. His political essay, *Die Christenheit oder Europa*, foreshadowed the Roman Catholic trend of later Romantic thinking.

Works

*Blütenstaub* (Fragmente), 1798
*Die Christenheit oder Europa*, 1799 (publ. 1826)
*Hymnen an die Nacht*, 1800
*Heinrich von Ofterdingen*, 1802
*Schriften*, ed. F. Schlegel, L. Tieck, 1802
*Schriften u. Briefe*, ed. P. Kluckhohn, R. Samuel, 4 vols., 1929; rev.
    ed. R. Samuel, 1960 ff.

Literature

W. Dilthey, 'Novalis', *Das Erlebnis u. die Dichtung*, 1906
H. Lichtenberger, *Novalis*, 1912
E. Hederer, *Novalis*, 1949
F. Hiebel, *Novalis. Der Dichter der blauen Blume*, 1951
H. Ritter, *Der unbekannte Novalis*, 1967

R. Peacock, 'The poetry of Novalis', *Germ. Studies in honour of H. G. Fiedler*, 1938

M. Dick, *Die Entwicklung des Gedankens der Poesie in den Fragmenten des Novalis*, 1967

H. Ritter, *Novalis' Hymnen an die Nacht*, 1930

T. Haering, *Novalis als Philosoph*, 1954

L. Albrecht, *Der magische Idealismus in Novalis' Märchentheorie u. Märchendichtung*, 1948

A. Reble, 'Märchen u. Wirklichkeit bei Novalis', *DVLG* 19 (1941)

M. Besset, *Novalis et la mystique*, 1947

W. Feilchenfeld, 'Der Einfluss Jakob Böhmes auf Novalis', *Germ. Stud.* 22 (1922)

W. Malsch, *Europa. Poetische Rede des Novalis*, 1965

F. Hiebel, 'Novalis and the problem of Romanticism', *Monatshefte* 8 (1947)

W. Vordriede, *Novalis u. die französischen Symbolisten*, 1963

W. Müller-Seidel, 'Probleme neuerer Novalis-Forschung', *GRM* 34 (1953)

## WILHELM HAUFF

Born 29 Nov. 1802 in Stuttgart, studied in Tübingen and travelled in France and Northern Germany before returning to Stuttgart to become editor of Cotta's *Morgenblatt für gebildete Stände*. He died 18 Nov. 1827. Hauff's *Lichtenstein* has remained one of the most popular German historical novels, and his Märchen are still favourites with children. Some of Hauff's lyrics, e.g. 'Steh ich in finstrer Mitternacht' and 'Morgenrot, Morgenrot, leuchtest mir zum frühen Tod', have acquired the status of folk-songs.

## Works

*Mitteilungen aus den Memoiren des Satans*, 1826 f.
*Märchenalmanach auf das Jahr 1826*
*Der Mann im Monde*, 1826
*Lichtenstein*, 1826
*Phantasien im Bremer Ratskeller*, 1827
*Jud Süss*, 1827
*Die Bettlerin vom Pont des Arts*, 1827
*Die Sängerin*, 1827
*Das Bild des Kaisers*, 1827

*Phantasien und Skizzen*, 1828
*Sämtliche Werke*, 36 vols., ed. G. Schwab, 1830
*Werke*, 2 vols., ed. B. Zeller, 1969

Literature

H. Hofmann, *Wilhelm Hauff*, 1902

F. Zinkernagel, *Wilhelm Hauff*, 1921

H. Binder, *Wilhelm Hauff*, 1940

E. Sommermeyer, 'Hauffs Memoiren des Satans', *Germ. Stud.* 129 (1932)

H. Schulhof, 'Hauffs Märchen', *Euph* 29 (1928)

O. Plath, 'Washington Irvings Einfluss auf Wilhelm Hauff', *Euph.* 20 (1913)

J. H. Haussmann, 'E. T. A. Hoffmanns Einfluss auf Wilhelm Hauff', *JEGP* 16 (1917)

P. Roggenhausen, 'Hauff-Bibliographie', Archiv 157 (1930)

CHRISTIAN FRIEDRICH HEBBEL

Born on 25 March 1813 at Wesselburen in Holstein, the son of a bricklayer. After earning his living as a scribe he was assisted by Amalie Schoppe, editor of a fashion journal in Hamburg, and by Elise Lensing, a seamstress who bore him two illegitimate children. He went to Hamburg university in 1835 and to Heidelberg and Munich in 1836 to study law, history and philosophy. He returned to Hamburg in 1842 where Elise Lensing supported him while he began writing. In 1843 he went to Copenhagen and in the same year received a grant from King Christian VIII. He first travelled to Paris where he met Heine, then to Rome, Naples and Vienna. He married Christine Enghaus, an actress at the Burgtheater, in 1846. Apart from several journeys, for example to Paris and London in 1862, he lived in Vienna and in his cottage near Traunsee. He died in Vienna, 13 Dec. 1863.

Works

*Judith*, 1840
*Gedichte*, 1842
*Genoveva*, 1843
*Maria Magdalene*, 1844
*Der Diamant*, 1847

*Neue Gedichte*, 1848
*Herodes und Mariamne*, 1849
*Der Rubin*, 1851
*Ein Trauerspiel in Sizilien*, 1851
*Agnes Bernauer*, 1852
*Erzählungen und Novellen*, 1855
*Gyges und sein Ring*, 1856
*Mutter und Kind*, 1859
*Die Nibelungen*, 1862
*Demetrius*, 1864
*Sämtliche Werke*, ed. R. M. Werner, 1911–20 (including diaries)
*Werke*, ed. B. v. Wiese, 1941; ed. G. Fricke and K. Pörnbacher, 1965

Literature

E. Kuh, *Friedrich Hebbel*, 1912
R. M. Werner, *Friedrich Hebbel*, 1913
O. Walzel, *F. Hebbel und seine Dramen*, 1913
E. Dosenheimer, *Das zentrale Problem in der Tragödie F. Hebbels*, 1925
H. Henel, 'Realismus und Tragik in Hebbels Draman', *PMLA* 53 (1938)
K. Ziegler, *Mensch und Welt in der Tragödie Hebbels*, 1938
P. Bornstein, *Hebbels Persönlichkeit*, 1944
I. Braak, 'Hebbel als Lyriker', *Hebbel-Jahrbuch*, 1954
J. Müller, *Das Weltbild Hebbels*, 1955
G. Fricke, *F. Hebbel und sein Zeitalter*, 1956
H. Kreuzer, *Die Tragödien F. Hebbels*, 1957
H. Stolte, *F. Hebbel Welt und Werk*, 1965
E. Purdie, *F. Hebbel*, 1932
   id., 'Hebbel. Some aspects of research and criticism, 1953–1963–4', *Euph* 60 (1966)

JOHANN PETER HEBEL

Hebel was born on 10 May 1760 in Basel of Protestant peasant stock. He studied theology in Erlangen (1778–80), became vicar in Herlingen and then a teacher in the seminary at Lörrach. In 1791 he moved to the Gymnasium in Karlsruhe, eventually achieving the title of Professor and becoming its head-master in

1808. In 1819 he was elevated to the dignity of 'Prälat' in the Protestant church and received an honorary doctorate of the University of Heidelberg in 1821. He died in Schwetzingen on 22 Sep. 1826. Hebel is the most talented of Alemannic dialect poets and a master of the anecdote and moral tale, but his literary significance extends well beyond the bounds of his native locality. Allowing for his very different moral views, Hebel's standing may perhaps be compared with that of Robert Burns in English literature.

## Works

*Alemannische Gedichte,* 1803
*Schatzkästlein des rheinischen Hausfreundes,* 1811
*Rheinländischer Hausfreund,* 1808–11
*Rheinischer Hausfreund,* 1814 f.
*Sämtliche Werke,* 8 vols., 1832–4
*Briefe, Gesamtausgabe,* ed. W. Zentner, 1939; 2nd ed., 2 vols., 1957–8

## Literature

W. Altwegg, *Johann Peter Hebel,* 1935
W. Zentner, *Johann Peter Hebel,* 1965
R. M. Kully, *Johann Peter Hebel,* 1969
T. Heuss, C. J. Burckhardt, et. al., *Über Johann Peter Hebel,* 1964
H. Uhl, *Hebeldank,* 1964
R. Minder, 'Heidegger und Hebel oder die Sprache von Messkirch', *Dichter in der Gesellschaft,* 1966
W. Zentner (ed.), *Johann Peter Hebel und seine Zeit. Fs. zur 200. Wiederkehr seines Geburtstages,* 1960
H. Pross, 'Johann Peter Hebel 1960. Ein bibl. Bericht', *Studien zur neueren dt. Lit.,* ed. H. W. Seiffert, 1964

## HEINRICH HEINE

Born 13 Dec. 1797 in Düsseldorf where he went to school until 1816. After an apprenticeship in the bank of his uncle Salomon Heine in Hamburg and an abortive attempt to run a business of his own, he began in 1819 to study law and literature at Bonn, where he attended A. W. Schlegel's lectures. In 1820 he went to Göttingen and was sent down for a duelling offence. He continued his studies in Berlin during the years 1821 to 1823 and attended Hegel's lectures. In Berlin he also was a member of Rahel Varnhagen's salon. In 1824 he returned to Göttingen and made a walking tour in the Harz mountains which gave rise to the first of his 'Reisebilder'. He qualified as a lawyer in 1825 and in this year joined the Protestant faith in order to facilitate his career. He made journeys to England, Heligoland and Italy in 1827 and 1828. In 1831 he went to Paris as the correspondent of the Augsburg 'Allgemeine Zeitung' and, except for brief visits to Germany in 1843 and 1844, lived there for the rest of his life, mainly on a pension from the French government. He married Eugénie Mirat ('Mathilde') in 1841. During the illness which kept him in his 'mattress grave' for eight years, he was tended by Elise Krinitz, the 'Mouche' of his late poetry. His very large circle of acquaintances in Paris included Karl Marx, Victor Hugo, Meyerbeer, Dumas, George Sand and Balzac. Heine died on 17 Feb. 1856.

## Works

*Junge Leiden*, 1821
*Lyrisches Intermezzo*, 1823
*Reisebilder*, 1826–31
*Das Buch der Lieder*, 1827
*Französische Zustände*, 1833
*Der Salon*, 1834–40
*Die Romantische Schule*, 1836
*Der Rabbi von Bacharach*, 1840
*Atta Troll: Ein Sommernachtstraum*, 1843
*Neue Gedichte*, 1844
*Deutschland. Ein Wintermärchen*, 1844
*Romanzero*, 1851
*Die Harzreise*, 1853
*Letzte Gedichte*, 1869
*Conversations*, ed. H. Houben, 1948
*Selected Poems*, ed. B. Fairley, 1965
*Atta Troll: Ein Sommernachtstraum. Deutschland*, ed. B. Fairley, 1966
*Sämtliche Werke*, ed. E. Elster, 1887–90; ed. O. Walzel, 1910–15; ed. F. Strich, 1925–30; ed. H. Kaufmann, 1961 ff.

Literature

A. Strodtmann, *Heinrich Heine, Leben und Werke*, 1867–8

M. J. Wolff, *Heinrich Heine*, 1922

U. Belart, *Gehalt u. Aufbau von Heines Gedichtsammlungen*, 1925

M. Brod, *Heinrich Heine*, 1934; repr. 1956

C. Andler, *La poésie de H. Heine*, 1948

L. Marcuse, *Heinrich Heine*, 1951

B. Fairley, *Heinrich Heine. An interpretation*, 1954

E. M. Butler, *Heinrich Heine*, 1956

W. Rose, *Heinrich Heine: two studies of his thought and feeling*, 1956
  id., *The early love poetry of Heinrich Heine*, 1962

L. Hofrichter, *Heinrich Heine*, transl. B. Fairley, 1963

S. S. Prawer, *Heine, the tragic satirist: a study of the later poetry 1827–1856*, 1961

## JOHANN JAKOB WILHELM HEINSE

Born on 16 Feb. 1749 in Langenwiesen, Thüringen, Heinse studied in Jena and Erfurt; he was encouraged to embark on a literary career by the poet Gleim and by Wieland, who had taught him at Erfurt, and was later employed by J. G. Jacobi on his periodical *Iris*. In 1780 Heinse travelled to Italy and spent some three years in Venice, Florence and Rome before returning to Düsseldorf, where he wrote his highly successful novel, *Ardinghello*. In 1786 he became reader and librarian to the Elector of Mainz, Friedrich von Erthal. It was in Mainz that Heinse made the acquaintance of the widely travelled revolutionary enthusiast Georg Forster. After the Peace of Basel in 1795 the Elector moved his court to Aschaffenburg, where Heinse continued to serve him and his successor, Fürst Dalberg, until his death there on 22 June 1803. During his later years Heinse was converted to Roman Catholicism. Heinse was a man of problematic character who was in many ways in advance of his time: much of his writing challenged accepted moral standards in its praise of uncompromising vitality. The erotic hedonism of *Laidion* is manifestly copied from Wieland, but in *Ardinghello* cultivated sensuality is made the main principle of an artistic Utopia; this was the first work in Germany to glorify the Italian Renaissance as an age of virtuosi modelling their lives on the example of the ancient Greeks. Many of Heinse's contemporaries were scandalized by what they considered to be Heinse's immorality but *Ardinghello* came into its own during the Young German period, when it was hailed as an adumbration of the 'emancipation of the flesh'. In an age still dominated by Winckelmann's idea of Classical 'edle Einfalt und stille Grösse' Heinse attributed to Greek life and art a dionysiac spirit and thus anticipated the ideas of Nietzsche nearly a century later. His intuitive insight into the thought and art of the ancient world, although less mystically sublime than that of Hölderlin, is nevertheless remarkable. The elaborate discussions of art in *Ardinghello* and, even more, the figure of the musician-hero and the view of music in *Hildegard von Hohenthal* anticipate later Romantic novels by Tieck and E. T. A. Hoffmann.

## Works

*Sinngedichte*, 1771
*Laidion oder die eleusinischen Geheimnisse*, 1774
*Erzählungen, für junge Damen und Dichter gesammelt*, 1775; repr. 1967
*Torquato Tassos Befreites Jerusalem*, 1781 (transl.)
*Roland der Wütende, ein Heldengedicht von Ludwig Ariosto*, 1782 f.
*Ardinghello und die glückseligen Inseln*, 1787
*Hildegard von Hohenthal*, 1795–6
*Anastasia und das Schachspiel. Briefe aus Italien*, 1803

## Literature

J. Schober, *J. J. W. Heinse, sein Leben und seine Werke*, 1882
E. Sulger-Gebing, *Heinse, eine Charakteristik*, 1903
K. D. Jessen, *Heinses Stellung zur bildenden Kunst und ihrer Ästhetik*, 1901
E. Utitz, *J. J. W. Heinse und die Asthetik zur Zeit der dt. Aufklärung*, 1906
W. Brecht, *Heinse und der ästhetische Immoralismus*, 1911
E. Nikefeld, *Heinse als Musikschriftsteller und Musikästhetiker*, diss. Vienna, 1937
M. L. Baeumer, *Das Dionysische in den Werken W. Heinses*, 1964
H. R. Sprengel, *Naturanschauung und malerisches Empfinden bei W. Heinse*, 1930
A. Zippel, *W. Heinse und Italien*, 1930
H. W. Kruft, 'Wilhelm Heinses italienische Reise', *DVLG* 41–2 (1967/8)

H. Horn, *Heinses Stellung zur dt. Klassik*, 1936–7

H. Rosenfeld, *Heinses Leben und Kunstanschauung und die Romantik*, 1939

F. Petitpierres, *Heinse in den Jugendschriften der Jungdeutschen*, 1915

E. Riess, *W. Heinses Romantechnik*, 1908

B. v. Wiese, 'Heinses Lebensanschauung in *Ardinghello*', *Zs. f. Deutschkunde* (1930)

E. E. Reed, 'The transitional significance of Heinses *Ardinghello*', *MLQ* 16 (1955)

P. Grappin, '*Ardinghello* und *Hyperion*', *WB* 2 (1956) (transl. from *EG* 10 (1955))

H. v. Hofe, 'Heinse, America, and Utopianism', *PMLA* 72 (1957)

M. L. Baeumer, *Heinse-Studien* (inc. bibl.), 1966

## JOHANN GOTTFRIED HERDER

Born in Mohrungen, East Prussia, 25 Aug. 1744. He was at the University of Königsberg from 1762 to 1764, studied medicine, theology and philosophy and attended Kant's lectures, but never became a disciple. Instead he came under the influence of Hamann who remained his life-long friend and mentor, although he disagreed with him on important theological issues. From 1764 until 1769 he held educational and ecclesiastical posts at the 'Domschule' in Riga which he resigned after a feud with C. A. Klotz whose work he later publicly criticized in *Kritische Wälder*, just as Lessing had done before him. Herder undertook a voyage to Nantes in 1769 during which he wrote his seminal *Journal meiner Reise*. After visiting Hamburg, where he met Lessing, he was commissioned in 1770 to accompany the young Prince of Holstein-Eutin on a journey to Italy, but was stopped in Strasbourg where he had to undergo an eye operation. Here he became the intellectual leader of the 'Sturm und Drang' group. From 1771 until 1776 he held ecclesiastical posts at Bückeburg, where he wrote some of his most important works. On Goethe's recommendation he was called to Weimar in 1776 to fill the posts of church superintendent and preacher. He remained there for the rest of his life with the exception of a journey to Italy in 1788. He died on 18 Dec. 1803. His aesthetic thought, as distinct from his literary criticism, began with his elaborating Lessing's distinctions in *Laokoon*. The first of Herder's *Kritische Wälder* argues in favour of differentiating between painting and sculpture by postulating for the latter the category of 'das In- und Hinterein-ander' to include the third dimension, a point that is further developed in *Plastik*. In treating the Laokoon subject Herder also made a distinction between poetry and music by assigning the principle of 'Energie' to the former. His later aesthetic writings frequently dealt with music as an individual art form, thus preparing the way for the Romantics, although he held controversial views on the nature of musical form.

Works

*Über die neuere deutsche Literatur*, 1767–8
*Kritische Wälder*, 1769
*Journal meiner Reise*, 1769; ed. A. Gillies, 1947
*Abhandlung über den Ursprung der Sprache*, 1772
*Von deutscher Art und Kunst*, 1773; ed. E. Purdie, 1924
*Älteste Urkunde des Menschengeschlechts*, 1774–6
*Auch eine Philosophie der Geschichte zur Bildung der Menschheit*, 1774
*Ursachen des gesunkenen Geschmacks*, 1775
*Plastik*, 1777
*Vom Erkennen und Empfinden der menschlichen Seele*, 1778
*Vom Geist der Ebräischen Poesie*, 1782–3
*Ideen zur Philosophie der Geschichte der Menschheit*, 1784–91
*Gott*, 1787
*Briefe zur Beförderung der Humanität*, 1793–7
*Metakritik*, 1799
*Kalligone*, 1800
*Adrastea*, 1801–3
*Sämtliche Werke*, ed. B. Suphan, 1887–1913
*Werke*, ed. W. Dobbek, 1957

Literature

W. Kohlschmidt, *Herder-Studien*, 1929
R. Haym, *Herder nach seinem Leben und seinen Werken*, 1877–85; repr. 1954
E. Kuhnemann, *Herder*, 1895; repr. 1927
G. Weber, *Herder u. das Drama*, 1922
F. McEachran, *The life and philosophy of Herder*, 1939
H. Franz, *Von Herder bis Hegel*, 1938
A. Kathar, *Herders Literaturkritik*, 1969

A. Gillies, *Herder*, 1945; repr. 1953
R. Pascal, *The German Sturm und Drang*, 1953
R. T. Clark, *Herder. His Life and Thought*, 1955
E. Baur, *J. G. Herder. Leben und Werk*, 1960
K. May, *Lessings und Herders kunsttheoretische Gedanken*, 1923
A. Closs, 'Joh. Gottfr. Herder,' *German Men of Letters*, ed. A. Natan, 1961

## JOHANN TIMOTHEUS HERMES

Hermes was born on 31 May 1738 at Petznick near Stargard. He followed in his father's footsteps and studied theology in Königsberg. After employment as a teacher and military chaplain he was eventually appointed preacher in Breslau, where he finally became church superintendent and Oberkonsistorialrat and where he died on 24 July 1821. Hermes was a persistent imitator of Richardson and Fielding and very popular during his lifetime. Apart from the picaresque *Sophiens Reise*, which retains its interest as a reflection of social conditions during the Seven Years War, his novels must now be considered unreadable—not only because of their excessive length and prosaic style but also because of their obtrusive rationalism and didacticism. Hermes sometimes wrote under the anagrams Heinrich Meister and T. S. Jemehr and also used the pseudonyms F. Bothe and Cyllenius.

Works
*Geschichte der Miss Fanny Wilkes*, 1766
*Sophiens Reise von Memel nach Sachsen*, 1769–73; repr. in abridged version, DL, 1941
*Für Töchter edler Herkunft*, 1787
*Manch Hermäon*, 1788
*Zween literarische Märtyrer und deren Frauen*, 1789
*Für Eltern und Ehelustige*, 1789
*Lieder der besten bekannten Kirchenmelodien*, 1800
*Anne Winterfeld*, 1801
*Verheimlichung und Eil*, 1802
*Mutter, Amme und Kind in der Geschichte Herrn Leopold Kerkers*, 1811

Literature
G. Hoffmann, *J. T. Hermes*, 1911
K. Muskalla, *Die Romane von J. T. Hermes*, 1912

R. Prutz, *Sophiens Reise*, 1848

K. L. Cholevius, *Die Verkehrssprache in Sophiens Reise*, 1873

E. T. Voss, *Erzählprobleme des Briefromans*, diss. Bonn, 1958

G. Schulz, 'Hermes und die Liebe,' *Jb. der schlesischen Frdr.-Wilh.-Univ. zu Breslau* 6 (1961)

## GEORG HERWEGH

Born in Stuttgart, 31 May 1817, studied theology at the 'Tübinger Stift'. After being sent down from there he earned his living by his writings. From Stuttgart he went to Switzerland in 1840 and then to Paris in 1842. King Frederick William IV granted him an audience in 1842 but he was exiled from Prussia after writing an offensive letter to the king. From 1843 he lived mainly in Paris and Zürich. He led an armed band of French and German workers into Baden in 1848 and was defeated at Schopfheim. He then lived in Berne, Geneva and Nice and, after the 1866 amnesty, settled near Baden-Baden, where he died on 7 April 1875.

### Works

*Gedichte eines Lebendigen*, 1841-3

*Neue Gedichte*, 1877

*Werke*, ed. H. Tardel, 1909

### Literature

V. Fleury, *Le poète Herwegh*, 1911

H. E. Hirschfeld, *Politische Zeitdichtung in Herweghs Gedichten eines Lebendigen*, 1921

G. Wilson, *Herwegh: a critical introduction to the later lyric poetry*, 1948

F. Notter, in *Eduard Mörike und andere Essays*, 1966

## CHRISTIAN LEBERECHT HEYNE ('ANTON WALL')

Born 1751 at Leuben, near Meissen, studied in Leipzig, author of comic novels and moral tales, often in Oriental costume. Died at Hirschberg, Vogtland, 13 Jan. 1821.

### Works

*Miss Sara Salisbury, eine engländische Begebenheit*, 1782

*Ämilie*, 1781

*Der Herr im Hause*, 1783 (comedy)
*Amathonte*, 1799
*Körane*, 2 vols., 1801
etc. etc.

Literature
R. Fürst, *Die Vorläufer der modernen Novelle im 18. Jh.*, 1897

## PAUL HEYSE

Born 15 March 1830 in Berlin, took his doctorate in philology at University of Berlin, travelled in Italy, for which he conceived a lasting love, went to Munich in 1854 at the invitation of King Maximilian II and became a leader of literary life in the city. He died 2 April 1914. Heyse was much admired as a stylist, especially for his Novellen; it was he who stated the so-called 'Falkentheorie', which stressed the importance in this genre of a central symbol. His novels are characterized by a specious 'modernity', and his ambitious dramas have long since vanished from the repertoire. Heyse was awarded the Nobel prize for literature in 1910, but his inflated reputation barely survived his death. His elegant translations from Italian have lasting merit, however.

Works
*Francesca von Rimini*, 1850 (tragedy)
*Novellen*, 20 vols., 1855–95
*Die Sabinerinnen*, 1858 (tragedy)
*Novellen in Versen*, 1864; 2nd series 1870
*Colberg*, 1865 (tragedy)
*Hans Lange*, 1866 (drama)
*Gedichte*, 1872
*Kinder der Welt*, 1873
*Im Paradies*, 1875
*Der Roman einer Stiftsdame*, 1887
*Merlin*, 1892
*Über allen Gipfeln*, 1895
*Jugenderinnerungen u. Bekenntnisse*, 1900
*Gesammelte Werke*, 38 vols., 1899–1914
*Paul Heyse. Die Reise nach dem Glück. Auswahl aus dem Werk*, ed. G.
    Manz, 1959

Literature

V. Klemperer, *Paul Heyse*, 1907

H. Raff, *Paul Heyse*, 1910

H. Spiero, *Paul Heyse. Der Dichter u. seine Werke*, 1910

L. Ferrari, *Paul Heyse u. die lit. Strömungen seiner Zeit*, diss. Bonn, 1938

A. v. Ian, *Die zeitgenössische Kritik an Paul Heyse*, diss. Munich, 1966

M. Schunicht, 'Der "Falke" am "Wendepunkt". Zu den Novellen-theorien Tiecks u. Heyses', *GRM* 41 (1960)

K. Negus, 'Paul Heyse's Novellentheorie. A revaluation', *GR* 40 (1965)

E. Petzet, *Paul Heyse als Dramatiker*, 1904

## THEODOR GOTTLIEB VON HIPPEL

Born 31 Jan. 1741 at Gerdauen in East Prussia, studied theology and law in Königsberg; Frederick the Great appointed him Kriegsrat and Stadtpräsident in Königsberg, where he died on 23 April 1796. Wrote lyric poetry, dramas and novels.

Works

*Der Mann nach der Uhr oder Der ordentliche Mann*, 1765 (comedy)

*Geistliche Lieder*, 1772

*Über die Ehe*, 1774

*Lebensläufe nach aufsteigender Linie*, 4 vols., 1778–81

*Kreuz- u. Querzüge des Ritters A bis Z*, 2 vols., 1793 f.

*Sämtliche Werke*, 14 vols., 1827–38

Literature

T. Hönes, *T. G. von Hippel*, diss. Bonn, 1910

F. J. Schneider, *Theodor Gottlieb von Hippel*, 1911

M. Greiner, *T. G. von Hippel*, 1958

H. Deiter, 'T. G. von Hippel im Urteil seiner Zeitgenossen', *Euph* 16 (1910)

J. Cerny, *Hippel u. Jean Paul*, 1904

F. J. Schneider, 'Studien zu Hippels Lebensläufen', *Euph* 23 (1921)

T. G. van Stockum, *T. G. von Hippel u. sein Roman, Lebensläufe nach aufsteigender Linie*, 1959

H. Vormus, 'T. G. von Hippels Lebensläufe. Eine Interpretation', *EG* 21 (1966)

## Johann Christian Friedrich Hölderlin

Born 20 March 1770 at Lauffen on the Neckar. He went to school in Nürtingen, Denkendorf and Maulbronn. In 1788 he entered the 'Tübinger Stift' where Hegel and Schelling were his contemporaries and where he also met L. Neuffer and R. Magenau. In 1793 he was given the post of tutor to Charlotte von Kalb's son in her home at Waltershausen near Jena. He also attended Fichte's and Schiller's lectures at the university. After leaving Waltershausen he took a similar post in 1796 in the home of Suzette Gontard, the wife of a Frankfurt banker. During a stay at Kassel with the family he met Wilhelm Heinse. A quarrel with the husband led to Hölderlin's leaving the post in 1798. Until 1800 he stayed mainly in Homburg with his friend Isaac Sinclair. In 1801 he took up a tutorship in Hauptwil near St. Gallen, in 1802 a similar post in Bordeaux. He returned to Nürtigen late in 1802 in a state of tension and distress. He recovered temporarily and through Sinclair obtained a post as librarian in Homburg in 1804. His health broke down completely in 1806. From 1807 he lived in the home of the carpenter Zimmer in Tübingen. Hölderlin died on 7 June 1843. His essays on philosophical and aesthetic subjects are abstruse and hermetic exercises which he did not get ready for publication but which are considered by many to be of great importance.

### Works

*Hyperion,* 1797–9
*Empedokles,* 1797–1800; *Der Tod des Empedokles,* ed. M. B. Benn, 1968
*Hymnen des Pindar* (translation)
*Ödipus der Tyrann,* 1804 (translation)
*Antigone,* 1804 (translation)
Philosophy and aesthetics:
   *Über den Begriff der Strafe*
   *Über das Gesetz der Freiheit*
   *Über religiöse Vorstellungen*
   *Über das Werden im Vergehen*
   *Über die verschiedenen Arten zu dichten*
   *Über den Unterschied zwischen lyrischer, epischer und dramatischer*
      *Dichtung*
   *Grund zum Empedokles*
   *Über die Verfahrungsweise des poetischen Geistes*

*Gedichte*, ed. L. Uhland and G. Schwab, 1826

*Sämtliche Werke*, ed. C. T. Schwab, 1846; ed. N. v. Hellingrath and others, 1913–23; ed. F. Beissner, 1943 ff.

*Werke* (1 vol.), ed. F. Beissner, 1961; ed. M. Hamburger (with translations), 1966

Literature

K. Viëtor, *Die Lyrik Hölderlins*, 1922

W. Böhm, *Friedrich Hölderlin*, 1928–30

P. Bertaux, *Hölderlin*, 1936

P. Böckmann, *Hölderlin und seine Götter*, 1935

R. Peacock, *Hölderlin*, 1938

R. Guardini, *Hölderlin. Weltbild und Frömmigkeit*, 1939; repr. 1955

E. L. Stahl, *Hölderlins Symbolism*, 1944

A. Pellegrini, *Hölderlin. Storia della critica*, 1960

M. Kohler, A. Kelletat (ed.), *Hölderlin-Bibliographie*, 1953

P. Kluckhohn (ed.), *Hölderlin-Gedenkschrift*, 1943

E. Müller, *Hölderlin*, 1944

A. Closs, *F. Hölderlin: Gedichte*, 1944

A. Stansfield, *Hölderlin*, 1944

B. Allemann, *Hölderlin und Heidegger*, 1954

V. Erdmann, *Hölderlins ästhetische Theorie im Zusammenhang mit seiner Weltanschauung*, 1923

K. Hildebrand, *Hölderlin: Philosophie und Dichtung*, 1939

L. Ryan, *Hölderlins Lehre vom Wechsel der Töne*, 1960

U. Gaier, *Das gesetzliche Kalkül: Hölderlins Dichtungslehre*, 1962

L. Salzberger, *Hölderlin*, 1952

J. C. Hammer, *F. Hölderlin in England*, 1966

## LUDWIG CHRISTOPH HÖLTY

Born at Mariensee near Hanover 21 Dec. 1748. He studied theology at Göttingen from 1769 until 1775. Here he became a founder member of the Hainbund and a co-editor of the Musen-almanach. In 1774–5 he made a journey to Leipzig, Hamburg and Wandsbeck and finally went to Hanover where he vainly sought a cure from tuberculosis; he died there on 1 Sept. 1776.

Works
*Gedichte*, ed. F. L. Stolberg and J. H. Voss, 1783
*Sämtliche Werke*, ed. W. Michael, 1914–18

Literature
E. Albert, *Das Naturgefühl L. C. Höltys*, 1910
T. Simon, *Stil und Sprache der Poesie Höltys*, 1923

## AUGUST HEINRICH HOFFMANN VON FALLERSLEBEN

Born 2 April 1798 in Fallersleben (Lüneburg), author of the national anthem 'Deutschland über alles' (1841). In spite of his manifest patriotism Fallersleben was suspected of dangerous democratic tendencies; his *Unpolitische Lieder* were banned and he was dismissed from the chair of German at the University of Breslau; reinstated and awarded a pension in 1848. Fallersleben contributed to the study of folk-lore by the collection of popular poetry, particularly that of the Low Countries. Died at Corvey, Westphalia, 19 Jan. 1874.

Works
*Geschichte des dt. Kirchenliedes bis auf Luthers Zeit*, 1832; repr. 1965
*Holländische Volkslieder*, 12 vols., 1833–62
*Unpolitische Lieder*, 1840–1
*Die dt. Gesellschaftslieder des 16. u. 17. Jhs*, 2 vols., 1844; repr. 1966
*Mein Leben*, 6 vols., 1868
*Gesammelte Werke*, 8 vols., ed. H. Gerstenberg, 1890–3

Literature
A. Hüllbrock, *Hoffmann von Fallersleben*, 1896
H. Gerstenberg, *Deutschland, Deutschland über alles! Ein Lebensbild des Dichters Hoffmann von Fallersleben*, 1916
F. A. Löffler, *Der Einfluss des Volksliedes auf H. v. Fallersleben*, diss. Heidelberg, 1919
W. Schoof, 'H. v. Fallersleben u. die holländische Volkslied-forschung', *Zs. f. Volkskunde* 52 (1955)
P. Brachin, 'Les Pays-Bas vus par H. v. Fallersleben', *EG* 20 (1965)
P. H. Nelde, *Flandern in der Sicht Hoffmanns v. Fallersleben*, 1967
U. Gunther, . . . *über alles in der Welt? Studien zur Gesch. u. Didaktik der dt. Nationalhymne*, 1966

ERNST THEODOR AMADEUS HOFFMANN

Born on 24 Jan. 1776 in Königsberg, Hoffmann appears to have inherited a neurotic disposition from his father and no doubt suffered also from the separation of his parents. After studying law in Königsberg he began a career in the Prussian civil service at Glogau, moving in 1800 to Berlin, then to Posen. From there he was relegated to the obscure provincial town of Plozk for the untimely and insubordinate exercise of his talent as a caricaturist. At this time he broke his engagement to Minna Doerffer and married a handsome but ill-educated Polish girl. The Prussian defeat of 1806 wrecked Hoffmann's career and he was obliged to seek a living as composer, artist and journalist. In 1807 he returned to Berlin, where he formed a close friendship with Julius Eduard Hitzig. He moved in 1808 to Bamberg where he had been offered employment as music teacher and Kapellmeister, and where he subsequently experienced an unhappy passion for a certain Julia Marc. It was now that Hoffmann began to write his first poetic works. From 1813 he was associated with the Seconda troupe of actors in Leipzig and Dresden. After the collapse of the Napoleonic régime Hoffmann returned to Berlin, where he was re-instated in his post of Regierungsrat and obliged against his will to conduct investigations into the allegedly subversive liberal movements of the succeeding years. Hoffmann's life was henceforth divided between the court-room and Lutter und Wegner's Weinstube, where in the company of Hitzig and other 'Serapionsbrüder' like the actor Ludwig Devrient he inflamed the imagination which inspired such stories as *Die Elixiere des Teufels*, *Der Sandmann* and *Die Abenteuer der Sylvester-Nacht*. He died on 25 June 1822. Hoffmann's stories reflect in their mingling of realism and macabre fantasy the ambivalence of his personality and eccentric way of life. The psychological authenticity of his stories and Märchen as accounts of mental or artistic crises explain his appeal to writers and artists of many nations. Byron, Scott, Gautier, Balzac, Baudelaire, Poe and Wilde were among those influenced by him.

Works
*Fantasiestücke in Callots Manier*, 1814
*Der Dey von Elba in Paris*, 1815
*Nachtstücke*, 1817

*Seltsame Leiden eines Theaterdirektors,* 1818
*Klein Zaches genannt Zinnober,* 1819
*Die Serapionsbrüder,* 1819–21
*Lebensansichten des Katers Murr nebst fragmentarischer Biographie des
    Kapellmeisters Kreisler,* 1820
*Prinzessin Brambilla,* 1821
*Meister Floh,* 1822
*Aus Hoffmanns Leben und Nachlass,* ed. J. E. Hitzig, 2 vols., 1823
*Die letzten Erzählungen,* ed. J. E. Hitzig, 2 vols., 1825
*Sämtliche Werke,* ed. W. Harich, 15 vols., 1924

Literature

G. Ellinger, *E. T. A. Hoffmann. Sein Leben und seine Werke,* 1894
W. Harich, *E. T. A. Hoffmann. Das Leben eines Künstlers,* 2 vols.,
    1920
E. Heilborn, *E. T. A. Hoffmann. Der Künstler und die Kunst,* 1926
E. v. Schenck, *E. T. A. Hoffmann. Ein Kampf um das Bild des
    Menschen,* 1939
H. W. Hewett-Thayer, *Hoffmann, author of the tales,* 1948
J. F. A. Ricci, *E. T. A. Hoffmann, l'homme et l'oeuvre,* 1947
H. Ehinger, *E. T. A. Hoffmann als Musiker und Musikschriftsteller,*
    1927
J. Reddick, 'E. T. A. Hoffmann', *German Men of Letters,* vol. 5,
    ed. A. Natan, 1969
O. Klinke, *E. T. A. Hoffmanns Leben und Werke vom Standpunkte
    eines Irrenarztes,* 1903
H. Müller, *Untersuchungen zum Problem der Formelhaftigkeit bei
    E. T. A. Hoffmann,* 1964
K. G. Negus, *E. T. A. Hoffmann's other world,* 1965
A. Sakheim, *E. T. A. Hoffmann. Studien zu seiner Persönlichkeit und
    seinen Werken,* 1908
J. Voerster, *160 Jahre E. T. A. Hoffmann-Forschung. Eine Biblio-
    graphie,* 1967
G. Wittkopp-Ménardeau, *E. T. A. Hoffmann in Selbstzeugnissen und
    Bilddokumenten,* 1966
T. Cramer, *Das Groteske bei E. T. A. Hoffmann,* 1966
L. Köhn, *Vieldeutige Welt. Studien zur Struktur der Erzählungen
    E. T. A. Hoffmanns,* 1966

HEINRICH HOFFMANN (also: HOFFMANN-DONNER)

Born 13 June 1809, Frankfurt a. M., died there 20 Sep. 1894.
Director of mental hospital in Frankfurt, author of *Struwelpeter*
and interesting memoirs.

Works
*Struwelpeter*, 1847
*Struwelpeter-Hoffmann erzählt aus seinem Leben*, ed. E. Hessenberg,
   1926

Literature
G. A. E. Bogeng, *Der Struwelpeter u. sein Vater*, 1939

KARL VON HOLTEI

Born 24 Jan. 1798 in Breslau, Holtei had a varied career as
student, soldier, actor, journalist and novelist, in which capacities
he roamed through Germany and Austria. As secretary and
producer of the Königsstädtisches Theater in Berlin he had considerable popular success with his sensational dramas (*Lenore*;
*Lorbeerbaum und Bettelstock*), frequently acting in them himself.
After managing theatres in Riga and Breslau he moved to Graz
then back to Breslau, where he turned to the writing of novels
and where he died, 4 Feb. 1880. His memoirs shed an interesting
light on literary and theatrical life. Along with G. Freytag
Holtei did much to stimulate interest in Silesian dialect poetry
and folk-lore.

Works
*Gedichte*, 1827
*Theater*, 1845
*Erzählende Schriften*, 37 vols., 1861–6
*Haus Treustein*, 1868
*Erlebnisse eines Livreedieners*, 1868
*Eine alte Jungfer*, 1869

Literature
M. Kurnik, *Karl von Holtei*, 1880
P. Landau, *Holteis Romane*, 1904

A. Moschner, *Holtei als Dramatiker*, 1911

M. Back, *Holteis Stellung zu den politischen Strömungen seiner Zeit*, diss. Münster, 1914

K. B. Beaton, *Der Tendenzroman zwischen 1848 u. 1866, unter besonderer Berücksichtigung der konservativen Romane K. v. Holteis*, diss. Birmingham, 1964-5

## WILHELM VON HUMBOLDT

Born in Potsdam 22 June 1767, studied law at Frankfurt and Göttingen. After travelling in France and Switzerland and brief sojourns in Erfurt and Weimar he settled in Jena in 1794 where he became an intimate friend of Schiller. He also knew Goethe and the Schlegels. From 1797 until 1799 he lived in Paris and in Spain; between 1801 and 1808 he occupied diplomatic posts and represented Prussia in Rome. In 1809 he was appointed Prussian minister of education and during his term of office completely reformed the system of higher education. In 1810 he founded the University of Berlin. Later he held ambassadorial posts in Vienna and London. He retired to his estate at Tegel in 1819 in order to pursue his literary researches and died there on 8 April 1835. He made notable contributions to knowledge with his investigations into language, and influenced political thought with an essay defining the limits of state interference in cultural affairs. He wrote an important essay on Schiller's development as a thinker and a penetrating analysis of *Hermann und Dorothea* (1799). Another of his accomplishments is as a sonetteer.

Works

*Über die Verschiedenheit des menschlichen Sprachbaues und ihren Einfluss auf die geistige Entwicklung des Menschengeschlechts* 1836; repr. 1960

*Ideen zu einem Versuch die Grenzen der Wirksamkeit des Staats zu bestimmen*, 1851; repr. 1946

*Über Schiller und den Gang seiner Geistesentwicklung*, 1830; repr. 1952

*Correspondence:* with Schiller, ed. A. Leitzmann, 1900; with A. W. Schlegel, ed. A. Leitzmann, 1908; with Goethe, ed. L. Geiger, 1909

Literature

R. Haym, *Wilhelm v. Humboldt*, 1856

A. Leitzmann, *Wilhelm v. Humboldt*, 1919
  id., *Wilhelm v. Humboldts Sonettendichtung*, 1912
E. Spranger, *Wilhelm v. Humboldt und die Humanitätsidee*, 1928
  id., *Wilhelm v. Humboldt und die Reform des Bildungswesens*, 1960
E. Howald, *W. v. Humboldt*, 1944
P. B. Stadler, *W. v. Humboldts Bild der Antike*, 1959
C. Menze, *W. v. Humboldts Lehre und Bild vom Menschen*, 1965

## CHRISTIAN HUNOLD ('MENANTES')

Born 1680 at Wanderleben, died 16 Aug. 1721 in Halle. Studied law in Jena, settled in Hamburg but was forced to leave because of his scurrilous *Satirischer Roman*; lectured at university in Halle. Author of 'galant' verse and novels.

### Works
*Die verliebte u. galante Welt*, 1700
*Edle Bemühungen in galanten . . . Gedichten*, 1702
*Der törichte Pritschmeister*, 1704
*Salomon*, 1704 (Singspiel)
*Satirischer Roman*, 1705
*Theatralische, galante u. geistliche Gedichte*, 1706
*Die allerneueste Art zur reinen u. galanten Poesie zu gelangen*, 1707
*Akademische Nebenstunden*, 1713

### Literature
H. Vogel, *Christian Hunold, sein Leben u. seine Werke*, diss. Leipzig, 1897
H. Singer, *Der galante Roman*, 1961

## AUGUST WILHELM IFFLAND

Born 19 April 1759 in Hanover. He fled from his home in 1777 to become an actor, first at Gotha under Ekhof and later at Mannheim under Dalberg. He took the part of Franz Moor in the first performance of *Die Räuber*. From 1796 onwards he directed the National Theatre in Berlin and promoted, in opposition to Goethe's classical Weimar style, a realistic manner of presentation. He was a prolific writer of plays (65 in number) and gained enormous success, mainly in the genres of sentimental comedy and domestic tragedy. He died in Berlin on 22 Sep. 1814.

Works
Some of the best known plays were:
*Albert von Thurneisen. Ein bürgerliches Trauerspiel in 4 Aufzügen*, 1781
*Verbrechen aus Ehrsucht. Ein ernsthaftes Familiengemälde*, 1784
*Die Jäger. Ein ländliches Sittengemälde*, 1785

Literature
A. Stiehler, *Das Ifflandsche Rührstück*, 1898
B. Kipfmuller, *Das Ifflandsche Lustspiel*, 1899
K. H. Klingenberg, *Iffland und Kotzebue als Dramatiker*, 1959; repr. 1962

## KARL LEBERECHT IMMERMANN

Born 24 April 1796 in Magdeburg, studied law in Halle, fought in the war against Napoleon but opposed the radical ideas of the Burschenschaft, entered Prussian civil service and became Landgerichtsrat in Düsseldorf, where he also took a leading part in organizing and reforming the theatre. Immermann died in Düsseldorf, 25 Aug. 1840, leaving unfinished his verse romance, *Tristan und Isolde*. Immermann's *Epigonen* and the *Oberhof* episodes of *Münchhausen* initiated a trend to increasing realism, but he was by no means lacking in vision and poetic imagination. His satirical humour is aimed at outmoded feudalism as well as reckless industrialization and commercialism.

Works
*Die Prinzen von Syrakus*, 1821 (comedy)
*Trauerspiele*, 1822 (*Das Tal von Ronceval*; *Edwin*; *Petrarca*)
*Die Papierfenster eines Eremiten*, 1822
*Gedichte*, 1822
*Ein Trauerspiel von Pater Brey*, 1823
*König Periander und sein Haus*, 1823 (tragedy)
*Cardenio und Celinde*, 1826 (tragedy)
*Das Trauerspiel in Tirol*, 1828; as *Andreas Hofer*, 1834
*Kaiser Friedrich II*, 1828 (tragedy)
*Gedichte. Neue Folge*, 1830
*Tulifäntchen*, 1830 (comic epic)
*Merlin*, 1832 (drama)
*Alexis*, 1832 (dramatic trilogy)

*Die Epigonen*, 1836
*Münchhausen*, 1838–9
*Die Opfer des Schweigens*, 1839
*Memorabilien*, 1840–4; repr. ed. E. Laaths, 1966
*Tristan und Isolde*, 1841
*Sämtliche Werke*, 20 vols., ed. R. Boxberger, 1886
*Werke*, DNL 159–60, ed. M. Koch

Literature
G. v. Putlitz, *Karl Immermann. Sein Leben u. seine Werke*, 1870
S. v. Lempicki, *Immermanns Weltanschauung*, 1910
A. W. Porterfield, *K. L. Immermann: a study in German Romanticism*, 1911; repr. 1966
H. Maync, *Immermann, der Mann u. sein Werk*, 1921
W. Höllerer, 'Immermann', *Zwischen Klassik u. Moderne*, 1958
M. Windfuhr, *Immermanns erzählerisches Werk*, 1957
L. Lauschus, *Über Technik u. Stil der Romane u. Novellen Immermans*, 1913
K. Jahn, *Immermanns Merlin*, Pal 3 (1899)
H. Moenkemeyer, 'Immermanns Merlin. Das Problem des selbsternannten Erlösers bei Immermann', *JDSG* 5 (1961)
H. Mayer, 'Karl Immermanns Epigonen', *Von Lessing bis T. Mann*, 1959
F. Rumler, *Realistische Elemente in Immermanns Epigonen*, diss. Munich, 1965
B. v. Wiese, 'Immermanns Münchhausen', *Der dt. Roman*, I (1963)
M. Scherer, 'Immermanns Münchhausen-Roman', *GQ* 36 (1963)
E. Guzinski, *Karl Immermann als Zeitkritiker*, 1937
J. Kuczynski, 'Immermann u. die industrielle Revolution', *WB* 5 (1959)

## Friedrich Heinrich Jacobi

Born on 25 Jan. 1743 in Düsseldorf, Jacobi was destined for a commercial career and after an apprenticeship in Geneva took over the family business in 1764. In 1772 he abandoned commerce for the customs service of Jülich-Berg and—briefly—for a similar post in Bavaria. His abiding interest was, however, literature and he was acquainted with almost all the leading writers of his time, many of whom visited the estate at Pempelfort that formed a significant intellectual centre until Jacobi moved to Munich in 1805 where he held the post of professor of philosophy and president of the Academy of Sciences until retirement in 1812. He died in Munich on 10 March 1819. Jacobi's warm and impulsive nature expressed itself in a cult of sentimental friendship that plays a large part in lyrical novels which have many autobiographical features. *Eduard Allwills Papiere* reflects the impression made on Jacobi by Goethe as the epitome of the Sturm und Drang genius. *Woldemar* attempts to qualify this admiration of genius and reconcile it with the idea of social responsibility. It was Goethe's ridicule of *Woldemar* that put an end to the friendship of the two men; Jacobi's devout Christian faith would no doubt have estranged him from Goethe sooner or later in any case. As a philosopher Jacobi was never much more than a dilettante; he opposed a philosophy of faith and feeling to the systematic pantheism of Spinoza and conducted an acrimonious dispute with Moses Mendelssohn on this issue, he also fought against the critical idealism of Kant, Fichte and Schelling.

Works

*Aus Eduard Allwills Papieren*, 1775 (rev. 1776, 1781, 1792); repr. 1962

*Freundschaft und Liebe*, 1777

*Woldemar*, 1779; 1794–6; repr. 1969

*Über die Lehre des Spinoza in Briefen an Herrn Moses Mendelssohn*, 1785, 1789

*Auserlesener Briefwechsel*, 2 vols., ed. F. Roth, 1825–7

Literature

E. Zirngiebl, *F. H. Jacobis Leben, Dichten und Denken*, 1867

F. A. Schmid, *F. H. Jacobi*, 1908

G. Fricke, 'F. H. Jacobi', *Studien und Interpretationen*, 1956

O. F. Bollnow, *Die Lebensphilosophie F. H. Jacobis*, 1933; repr. 1966

R. Hassencamp, *Der Düsseldorfer Philosoph F. H. Jacobi und sein Heim in Pempelfort*, 1898

H. Schwarz, *F. H. Jacobis Allwill*, 1911

F. David, *F. H. Jacobis Woldemar*, 1913

O. Heraceus, *F. H. Jacobi und der Sturm und Drang*, 1928

T. Bossert, *Jacobi und die Frühromantik*, diss. Giessen, 1926

H. Nicolai, *Goethe und Jacobi*, 1965

H. v. Hofe, 'Jacobi, Wieland and the New World', *Monatshefte* 49 (1957)

A. Hebeisen, *F. H. Jacobi. Seine Auseinandersetzung mit Spinoza*, 1960

G. Fittbogen, 'Die Hauptschriften zum Pantheismusstreit zwischen Jacobi und Mendelssohn', *Euph* 22 (1921)

## JOHANN GEORG JACOBI

Johann Georg, the elder brother of F. H. Jacobi, was born in Düsseldorf on 2 September 1740, studied theology, law and philosophy and became professor of philosophy at Halle in 1766. In 1768 he settled in Halberstadt, where he was intimately associated with Gleim. In 1774 Jacobi founded the journal *Iris* in Düsseldorf and counted Goethe, Gleim and Heinse among his contributors. After *Iris* ceased publication Jacobi collaborated with Wieland on *Der teutsche Merkur*. In 1784 he became professor of aesthetics in the University of Freiburg im Breisgau, where he published a series of *Taschenbücher*—from 1803 under the old name of *Iris*. Jacobi died in Freiburg on 4 Jan. 1814. His early lyric is anacreontic in the manner of Gleim—he is satirized by Nicolai in *Sebaldus Nothanker* as the foppish poet, Säugling—but later, particularly after his acquaintance with Goethe, it became more original. Some of his poems (e.g. 'Sagt, wo sind die Veilchen hin'; 'Willst du frei und lustig gehn') enjoyed great popularity in musical settings.

Works
*Poetische Versuche*, 1763
*Abschied von Amor*, 1769
*Winterreise*, 1769
*Sommerreise*, 1770
*Auserlesene Lieder*, 1784
*Phädra und Naide*, 1788
*Theatralische Schriften*, 1792

Literature
U. Schober, *Jacobis dichterische Entwicklung*, diss. Breslau, 1938
J. Longo, *L. Sterne und J. G. Jacobi*, 1898
O. Manthey-Zorn, *Jacobis Iris*, diss. Leipzig, 1905
H. Bräuning-Oktavio, 'J. G. Jacobis *Schreiben eines Freidenkers an seine Brüder*', *WB* 7 (1961)

JOHANN HEINRICH JUNG-STILLING

Jung-Stilling, who was born on 12 Sept. 1740 in the humble circumstances of a charcoal burner's family, contrived to educate himself and gained a living by teaching, tailoring and farming until he was able to set up a practice as an ophthalmic surgeon in Elberfeld in 1772. In 1778, when he already had a great reputation for his operations on cataracts, he began a new career with an appointment as professor of economics at the Kameralakademie in Kaiserslautern, moved in 1787 to Marburg, then in 1803 to Heidelberg, where he was the trusted advisor of Karl Friedrich, Grand Duke of Baden. Jung-Stilling died in Karlsruhe on 2 April 1817. Goethe, who knew him in Strasbourg' and arranged for the publication of his first novel, was impressed by Jung-Stilling's self-confidence and by his conviction that his whole life was guided by divine Providence. Jung-Stilling's novels, the best of which combine autobiography and fiction, testify to the powerful influence of pietism: they described and appealed to sections of the population normally remote from literary experience. The freshness and verve of *Heinrich Stillings Jugend* and *Heinrich Stillings Jünglingsjahre* give way in the later works, however, to a harshly dogmatic tone. In his later years Jung-Stilling applied his writings and his prestige to a crusade against rationalism and waning faith; like many others of his persuasion at this time he was fascinated by somnambulism and other alleged evidences of the supernatural.

Works
*Heinrich Stillings Jugend,* 1777
*Heinrich Stillings Jünglingsjahre,* 1778
*Heinrich Stillings Wanderschaft,* 1778
*Geschichte des Herrn von Morgenthau,* 1779
*Die Geschichte Florentins von Fechtendorn,* 1781–3
*Lebensgeschichte der Theodore von der Linden,* 1783
*Heinrich Stillings häusliches Leben,* 1789
*Das Heimweh,* 1794
*Der graue Mann,* 1795–1816 (periodical)
*Schlüssel zum Heimweh,* 1797
*Szenen aus dem Geisterreich,* 1797–1801
*Heinrich Stillings Lehrjahre,* 1804

*Theorie der Geisterkunde,* 1808
*Erzählungen,* 1814
*Heinrich Stillings Alter,* 1817
*Chrysäon oder das goldene Zeitalter,* 1818
*Gedichte,* 1821

Literature

W. Jörn, *Jung-Stilling, ein Pilger zur ewigen Heimat,* 1923
H. Müller, *Jung-Stilling,* 1941
E. Schick, *Jung-Stillings Heimweh und Heimat,* 1943
H. R. Günther, *Jung-Stilling: ein Beitrag zur Psychologie des Pietismus,* 2nd ed., 1948
M. Geiger, *Aufklärung und Erweckung,* 1963
E. Benz, *Jung-Stilling in Marburg,* 1949
H. Grollmann, *Die Technik der empfindsamen Erziehungsromane Jung-Stillings,* diss. Greifswald, 1924
L. M. Price, 'The pilgrim journeys of Bunyan and H. Jung-Stilling', *CL* 12 (1960)

## GOTTFRIED KELLER

Born 19 July 1819 in Zürich, died there 15 July 1890. He was orphaned when he was five years old and was brought up in reduced circumstances and with an indifferent education at several elementary schools and institutions. He was expelled from the Cantonal 'Industrieschule' in 1834 and became apprenticed to the painters Peter Steiger and Rudolf Meyer. In 1840 he went to Munich to continue his studies but began to take up writing instead when he lost confidence in his talent for painting on his return to Zürich in 1842. After a period of political activity in association with Freiligrath and Herwegh he went to Germany on a scholarship from his native city to study history, philosophy and literature. In Heidelberg he came under the influence of the philosopher Ludwig Feuerbach and the literary historian Hermann Hettner. The most formative years of his life as author began now and when he lived in Berlin from 1850 until 1855. He returned to Switzerland to earn his living by writing but in 1861 was appointed to a secretarial post by the city of Zürich which he held until 1876. He was on terms of friendship with Jacob Burckhardt, A. Böcklin and C. F. Meyer and corresponded on literary topics with Storm and Heyse.

Works

*Gedichte*, 1846
*Neuere Gedichte*, 1851
*Der grüne Heinrich*, 1854 f.
*Die Leute von Seldwyla*, 1856 and 1874
*Sieben Legenden*, 1872
*Zürcher Novellen*, 1878
*Das Sinngedicht*, 1881
*Gesammelte Gedichte*, 1883
*Martin Salander*, 1886
*Sämtl. Werke* ed. J. Fränkel and C. Helbling, 1926–49; ed. C. Heselhaus, 1958
*Correspondence*, ed. C. Helbling, 1950–54; ed. C. Heselhaus, 1956–8

Literature

A. Frey, *Erinnerungen an G. Keller*, 1919
H. Maync, *G. Keller, Sein Leben und seine Werke*, 1922
E. Korrodi, *G. Kellers Weltanschauung*, 1932
R. Faesi, *G. Keller*, 1942
G. Lukács, *G. Keller*, 1946
H. Boeschenstein, *G. Keller, Grundzüge seines Lebens und Werkes*, 1947
H. W. Reichert, *Basic Concepts in the Philosophy of G. Keller*, 1949
L. Wiesmann, *Gottfried Keller*, 1967
M. Lindsay, *Gottfried Keller: Life and Works*, 1968
H. Brockhaus, *Kellers Sinngedicht*, 1969

JUSTINUS KERNER

Born 18 Sept. 1786 in Ludwigsburg, studied medicine in Tübingen and ultimately settled as doctor in Weinsberg, where he developed an interest in spiritualism and mesmerism, spending years in recording the visions of the mystic 'Seherin von Prevorst', Friederike Hauffe. Kerner was a central figure of Swabian Romanticism, a close friend of Uhland, Gustav Schwab and Karl Mayer. His prose writings are a strange blend of fantasy, science and superstition, but some of his poems have achieved the immortality of folk-songs: they include 'Wohlauf, noch getrunken', 'Dort unten in der Mühle' and 'Preisend mit viel schönen Reden'. Kerner died in Weinsberg on 21 Feb. 1862.

## Works

*Reiseschatten*, 1811; repr. 1964
*Geschichte zweier Somnabülen*, 1824
*Gedichte*, 1826
*Die Seherin von Prevorst*, 1829
*Dichtungen*, 1834
*Lyrische Gedichte*, 1847; 1854
*Bilderbuch aus meiner Knabenzeit*, 1849
*Der letzte Blütenstrauss*, 1852
*F. A. Mesmer, der Entdecker des tierischen Magnetismus*, 1856
*Winterblüten*, 1859
*Sämtliche Werke*, ed. W. Heichen, 8 vols., 1903

## Literature

F. Heinzmann, *Justinus Kerner als Romantiker*, 1918
F. Kretschmar, *Die Seherin von Prevorst u. die Botschaft J. Kerners*, 1930
O. Ackermann, *Schwabentum u. Romantik*, 1939
H. Büttiker, *J. Kerner: ein Beitrag zur Gesch. der Spätromantik*, diss. Zürich, 1952
E. Staiger, ' "Der Wanderer in der Sägemühle" ', *Kunst der Interpretation*, 1955
A. P. Cottrell, 'J. Kerner, *Der Grundton der Natur*', GQ 39 (1966)
K. Pörnbacher (ed.), *Das Leben des J. Kerner. Erzählt von seiner Tochter Marie*, 1967

## EWALD VON KLEIST

Born on the family estate Zeblin in Pomerania on 7 March 1715. He studied law, philosophy and mathematics at Königsberg and in 1740 became an officer in Frederick II's army. He began writing poetry when he met Gleim and Ramler in Potsdam. He was sent to Zürich in 1752 and there met Bodmer and Breitinger. In 1758 he met Lessing in Leipzig and became his intimate friend. Mendelssohn and Lessing addressed the 'Literaturbriefe' to him and he is said to have been the model for Tellheim in *Minna von Barnhelm*. He died on 24 Aug. 1759 from wounds received in the battle of Kunersdorf in the Seven Years War.

## Works

*Der Frühling*, 1749

*Gedichte*, 1756
*Neue Gedichte*, 1758
*Cissides und Paches*, 1759
*Sämtliche Werke*, ed. K. W. Ramler, 1760; ed. A. Sauer, 1883

Literature
H. Guggenbühl, *E. v. Kleists Weltanschauung als Schicksal*, 1948
H. Stümbke, *E. v. Kleist. Krieger, Dichter, Denker*, 1949

## HEINRICH VON KLEIST

Born in Frankfurt on Oder, 18 Oct. 1777. From 1792 until 1799 he served in the Prussian army, taking part in the 1793/4 campaign. He resigned his commission in 1799 and began to study philosophy, physics and mathematics at Frankfurt university. During this time he studied Kant's writings which affected him profoundly. At the same time his engagement with Wilhelmine von Zenge took place but was broken off in 1802. He discontinued his studies in 1800 and in the autumn made a journey to Würzburg with his friend L. Brockes. He travelled with his sister Ulrike to Paris and Switzerland in 1801 and 1802, and again in 1803. On this occasion he suffered a spiritual collapse in Paris. He formed a plan to join Napoleon's projected invasion of England. He entered the Prussian civil service in 1805 and left it again in 1807. In this year he was arrested by the French near Berlin for alleged espionage and imprisoned in Fort de Joux. From August 1807 until April 1809 he lived in Dresden where he was in the company of Tieck, Adam Müller, G. H. Schubert and Varnhagen von Ense. Here he edited the journal *Phöbus*. After a journey to Austria in 1909 he returned to Berlin and, with Adam Müller, edited the *Berliner Abendblätter*. The failure of this venture, rejection of his application to re-enter the Prussian army and friendship with Henriette Vogel combined to induce his committing suicide with her at Wannsee, 21 Nov. 1811.

Works
*Aufsatz, den sichern Weg des Glücks zu finden*, 1799
*Robert Guiskard*, 1801–08 (drama)
*Die Familie Schroffenstein*, 1803

*Erzählungen*, 1804–11:
  *Michael Kohlhaas* (1804–8)
  *Die Marquise von O.* (1806–7)
  *Das Erdbeben in Chili* (1807)
  *Die Verlobung in San Domingo*
  *Das Bettelweib von Locarno*
  *Die heilige Caecilie*
  *Der Findling*
  *Der Zweikampf*
*Amphitryon*, 1807
*Penthesilea*, 1808
*Der zerbrochene Krug*, 1808
*Das Käthchen von Heilbronn*, 1808
*Prinz Friedrich von Homburg*, 1810
*Gesammelte Schriften*, ed. E. Schmidt, G. Minde-Pouet, R. Steig,
  1904–5; repr. 1936
*Sämtliche Werke und Briefe*, ed. H. Sembdner, 1961; repr. 1965
*Lebensspuren, Dokumente, Berichte von Zeitgenossen*, ed. H. Sembdner,
  1957
*Berliner Abendblätter*, repr. ed. H. Sembdner, 1960
*Phöbus*, repr. ed. H. Sembdner, 1961

Literature
H. Meyer-Benfey, *Kleists Leben und Werke*, 1911
  ibid., *Das Drama Heinrich von Kleists*, 1911–13
F. Gundolf, *Kleist*, 1922
G. Fricke, *Gefühl und Schicksal bei Heinrich von Kleist*, 1921
I. Kohrs, *Das Wesen des Tragischen im Drama H. v. Kleists*, 1951
E. L. Stahl, *The dramas of Heinrich von Kleist*, 1948; repr. 1961
H. Mayer, *Heinrich von Kleist, Der geschichtliche Augenblick*, 1962
W. Müller-Seidal, *Heinrich von Kleist. Aufsätze und Essays*, 1967
W. Silz, *Heinrich von Kleist, Studies in his works and literary characters*,
  1961
J. Geary, *Heinrich von Kleist: a study in tragedy and anxiety*, 1968
M. Garland, *Kleist's Prinz Friedrich von Homburg*, 1968

While not dealing directly with aesthetics, Kleist's essay *Über das Marionettentheater* has considerable relevance for a discussion of topics in the subject as treated during the 18th century and in the Romantic movement. Other important essays are *Über die allmähliche Verfertigung der Gedanken beim Reden* and *Brief eines Dichters*.

Literature

*Kleists Aufsatz über das Marionettentheater. Studien u. Interpretationen*, ed. H. Sembdner, 1967

R. E. Helbling (ed.), *Heinrich von Kleist. Novellen u. ästhetische Schriften*, 1967

H. M. Brown, Kleist's *Über das Marionettentheater:* 'Schlüssel zum Werk', or 'Feuilleton', *OGS* 3, 1968

## FRIEDRICH MAXIMILIAN KLINGER

Klinger was born on 17 Feb. 1752 in Frankfurt-am-Main; his father, a town constable, died when he was eight, but his mother contrived to have him educated and he studied law in Giessen. Klinger spent a tumultuous youth in the company of his fellow-countryman Goethe and other young bloods of the 'Sturm und Drang'—a movement which took its name from one of Klinger's dramas. Klinger failed to establish himself as a protégé of Goethe in Weimar, but Goethe's brother-in-law, Schlosser, procured him a commission in the Imperial army and Klinger subsequently pursued a brilliant military career in Russian service, being ennobled in 1780, appointed curator of the University of Dorpat in 1803 and promoted to lieutenant-general in 1811. He died in Dorpat on 3 March 1831. Apart from Goethe, Klinger was practically the only 'Sturm und Drang' 'genius' who fulfilled his early promise and proved capable of maturing and adapting himself to the changing demands of life. He was a man of robust health, tremendous energy and unbounded ambition, admired as a demi-god even by his youthful peers; the exultant vitality of his early work matches that of Goethe's. His dramas, many of them composed while he was associated with the Seyler troupe of actors in Leipzig and Mainz, were typically inflammatory products of the age, but with the novel *Plimplamplasko*, a satire on the turgid heroics of the 'Sturm und Drang', and hence on himself, there are signs of increasing maturity and detachment. Even in his later works Klinger never entirely belied his passionate temperament, dimmed his vivid imagination or denied his youthful faith in the teachings of

Rousseau, but the novels of the Faust cycle show at least a less explosive and more discursive concern with social and philosophical problems.

Works

*Otto. Ein Trauerspiel*, 1775; repr. DLD, 1881
*Das leidende Weib. Ein Trauerspiel*, 1775
*Die Zwillinge. Ein Trauerspiel in fünf Aufzügen*, 1776
*Die neue Arria. Ein Schauspiel*, 1776
*Simsone Grisaldo. Ein Schauspiel in fünf Akten*, 1776
*Sturm und Drang. Ein Schauspiel*, 1776
*Stilpo und seine Kinder. Ein Trauerspiel in fünf Akten*, 1780
*Orpheus, eine tragisch-komische Geschichte*, 1778
*Der Derwisch. Eine Komödie in fünf Aufzügen*, 1780
*Prinz Formosos Fiedelbogen und der Prinzessin Sanaclara Geige*, 1780
*Plimplamplasko, der hohe Geist*, 1780; repr. DN, 1966
*Die falschen Spieler*, 1780 (drama)
*Elfride*, 1782 (drama)
*Der Schwur gegen die Ehe. Ein Lustspiel in fünf Aufzügen*, 1783
*Konradin*, 1784 (drama)
*Der Günstling*, 1785 (drama)
*Die Geschichte vom goldnen Hahn*, 1785
*Der verbannte Göttersohn*, 1787
*Neues Theater*, 1790 (*Aristodemus, Trauerspiel; Roderiko, Trauerspiel; Damokles, Trauerspiel; Die zwei Freundinnen, Lustspiel*)
*Oriantes, Trauerspiel*, 1790
*Medea in Korinth und Medea auf dem Kaukasus. Zwei Trauerspiele*, 1791
*Fausts Leben, Taten und Höllenfahrt*, 1791
*Geschichte Giafars des Barmeciden. Ein Seitenstück zu Fausts Leben usw.*, 1792
*Geschichte Raphaels de Aquillas ... Ein Seitenstück zu Fausts Leben usw.*, 1793
*Reisen vor der Sündflut*, 1795
*Der Faust der Morgenländer*, 1797
*Der Kettenträger*, 1797
*Sahir, Evas Erstgeborner im Paradies*, 1798
*Geschichte eines Teutschen der neuesten Zeit*, 1798
*Der Weltmann und der Dichter*, 1798
*Betrachtungen und Gedanken über verschiedene Gegenstände der Welt und der Literatur*, 1803–5

Literature

M. Rieger, *Klinger in der Sturm- und Drangperiode*, 2 vols., 1880 f.

O. Smoljan, *F. M. Klinger. Leben und Werk*, 1962

C. Hering, *F. M. Klinger. Der Weltmann als Dichter*, 1966

H. M. Waidson, *Klingers Stellung zur Geistesgeschichte seiner Zeit*, diss. Leipzig, 1939

O. Smoljan, 'Klinger in Russland', *WB* 4 (1958)

R. Philipp. *Beiträge zur Kenntnis von Klingers Sprache und Stil*, diss. Freiburg i. Br., 1909

J. Müller, *F. M. Klingers kulturphilosophische und politische Anschauungen*, diss. Munich, 1921

J. Bollag, *F. M. Klingers Kulturprogramm in seiner Abhängigkeit von Rousseau*, diss. Basel, 1922

H. Steinberg, *Studien zu Schicksal und Ethos bei Klinger*, Germ. Stud. 234, 1941

H. M. Waidson, 'Goethe and Klinger', *PEGS* 23 (1953–4)

E. Sturm, *F. M. Klingers philosophische Dramen*, diss. Freiburg i. Br., 1916

H. Ziegler, *Zeittendenzen und Charaktere in Klingers Dramen*, diss. Breslau, 1921

H. Wahn, *Die Medea-Dramen von F. M. Klinger*, diss. Greifswald, 1924

O. A. Palitzsch, *Erlebnisgehalt und Formprobleme in Klingers Jugenddramen*, 1925

H. Zempel, *Erlebnisgehalt und ideelle Zeitverbundenheit in F. M. Klingers Medeendramen*, 1929

A. Keller, *Die literarischen Beziehungen zwischen den Erstlingsdramen Klingers und Schillers*, diss. Berne, 1914

F. Prosch, *Klingers Romane*, 1882

M. M. Heise, *Der Kultus der Persönlichkeit in den Romanen Klingers*, diss. Munich, 1929

E. Volhard, *F. M. Klingers philosophische Romane*, 1930

H. J. Geerdts, 'F. M. Klingers Faust-Roman', *Zs. f. dt. Lit. Gesch.* 6 (1960).

G. Zilk, *Faust und Antifaust*, diss. Munich, 1965

## FRIEDRICH GOTTLIEB KLOPSTOCK

Born at Quedlinburg, 2 July 1724. He was educated at Schulpforta between 1739 and 1745 and studied theology at Jena and

Leipzig; here he associated with the 'Bremer Beiträger' in whose journal the first three cantos of *Der Messias* appeared in 1748. In 1750 he stayed in Zürich as Bodmer's guest and in the following year went to Copenhagen on a salary from King Frederick V. After the king's death he went to Hamburg where he lived for the rest of his life except for brief sojourns in Göttingen (where he was warmly received by the members of the 'Göttinger Hain') and to Frankfurt (where he met Goethe). Klopstock died on 14 March 1803.

His writings on poetics, including subjects like artistic presentation, poetic vocabulary, word order and syntax, and suggestions for German prosody and orthography, are of considerable historical importance. The central concept of his poetics is contained in the term 'Darstellung' with which he opposed the current notion of imitation.

Works
*Der Messias*, 1748–1800
*Der Tod Adams*, 1757 (drama)
*Salomo*, 1764 (drama)
*Hermanns Schlacht*, 1769 (drama)
*Oden und Elegien*, 1771
*David*, 1772 (drama)
*Hermann und die Fürsten*, 1784 (drama)
*Hermanns Tod*, 1787 (drama)

Theoretical writings
    *Von der Sprache der Poesie*, 1758
    *Gedanken über die Natur der Poesie*, 1759
    *Die deutsche Gelehrtenrepublik*, 1774
    *Über deutsche Rechtschreibung*, 1778
    *Von der Darstellung*, 1779
    *Vom edlen Ausdruck*, 1779
    *Über Sprache und Dichtkunst*, 1779
    *Grammatische Gespräche*, 1794
*Sämtliche Werke*, ed. F. Muncker, 1887
*Ausgewählte Werke*, ed. K. A. Schleiden, 1962

Literature
F. Muncker, *Klopstock*, 1900
W. Lich, *Klopstocks Dichterbegriff*, 1934

K. Kindt, *Klopstock*, 1941
K. A. Schleiden, *Klopstocks Dichtungstheorie*, 1954
J. Murat, *Klopstock. Les thèmes principaux de son oeuvre*, 1959
K. L. Schneider, *Klopstock u. die Erneuerung der dt. Dichtersprache
     im 18. Jh.*, 1960
G. Kaiser, *Klopstock. Religion und Dichtung*, 1963
A Klopstock-Gesellschaft with its seat in Berlin was founded in
     1929.

ADOLF FREIHERR VON KNIGGE (pseud. JOSEPH ALOISIUS MAIER)

Born 16 Oct. 1752 at Schloss Bredenbeck near Hannover, studied
in Göttingen, held administrative posts in Kassel, Weimar and
Bremen, where he died, 6 May 1796. Knigge was a prominent
member of the 'Illuminati' and suspected of revolutionary
activities because of his satires on the reactionary nobility. His
name has become synonymous with correct manners but in fact
his *Umgang mit Menschen* is more than a manual of etiquette; it
was intended to encourage spiritual and intellectual self-improvement and designed to raise the self-esteem of the middle-class
in a society still much dominated by feudal conventions.

Works

*Der Roman meines Lebens*, 4 vols., 1781-3
*Die Verirrungen des Philosophen oder Gesch. Ludwigs v. Seelberg*, 1787
*Über den Umgang mit Menschen*, 1788; innumerable later eds.
*Geschichte des armen Herrn v. Mildenberg*, 3 vols., 1789 f.
*Des seligen Etatsrats v. Schaafkopfs hinterlassene Papiere*, 1792; repr.
     ed. I. Fetscher, 1965
*Die Reise nach Braunschweig*, 1792; repr. 1956
*Geschichte des Amtsrats Gutmann*, 1794
*Reise nach Fritzlar*, 1794
*Schriften*, 12 vols., 1804-6

Literature

K. Goedeke, *Adolf Freiherr von Knigge*, 1844
J. Popp, *Die Weltanschauung Knigges*, diss. Munich, 1931
K. Spengler, *Die publizistische Tätigkeit des Freiherrn A. v. Knigge
     während der französischen Revolution*, diss. Bonn, 1931
B. Zaehle, *Knigges Umgang mit Menschen u. seine Vorläufer*, 1933

Heinrich Josef König

Born 19 March 1790 in Fulda, radical publicist, dismissed from his post as Obergerichtssekretär in 1847; author of novels, plays and historical works of a tendentious kind. Died in Wiesbaden, 25 Sept. 1869.

Works
*Die hohe Braut*, 1833
*Die Waldenser*, 1836
*Die Clubisten in Mainz*, 1847
*Gesammelte Schriften*, 20 vols., 1854–68
*Ausgewählte Romane*, 15 vols., 1875

Literature
H. Halbeisen, *H. J. König. Ein Beitrag zur Gesch. des dt. Romans im 19. Jh.*, diss. Münster, 1915
G. Hohmann, *Heinrich König. Leben u. Werk des Fuldaer Schriftstellers*, 1965

Karl Theodor Körner

The son of Schiller's friend Christian Gottlieb Körner, born in Dresden on 23 Sep. 1791. He studied science, law, philosophy and history at Leipzig and Berlin. In 1811 he went to Vienna where he met W. v. Humboldt, F. Schlegel and Eichendorff. After the successful performance of his tragedy *Zriny* in 1813 he became 'Theaterdichter' at the Burgtheater, a post Kotzebue had held. In 1813 he joined Lützow's 'Freischar' and was killed in action 26 Aug. 1813. In addition to *Zriny* he wrote a tragedy *Toni*, based on Kleist's 'Die Verlobung in St. Domingo'.

Works
*Werke*, ed. H. Tardel, 1909; ed. E. Wildenow, 1913

Literature
E. Zeiner, *Körner als Dramatiker*, 1900
K. Berger, *T. Körner*, 1912
J. Töpfle, *T. Körner*, 1943

## August von Kotzebue

Born in Weimar, 3 May 1761, studied law at Jena. After being in practice in Weimar he entered Russian services in 1781 and occupied several influential posts. He retired in 1790 to Reval until 1797 when he was appointed to a post at the Burgtheater. He returned to Weimar in 1799 and in 1800 went back to Russia. For offending the Czar in his play *Der alte Leibkutscher Peters des Dritten* he was sent to Siberia but was soon recalled by Czar Paul and put in charge of the German theatre in St. Petersburg. From 1802 until 1806 he lived in Berlin. In 1813 he was made Russian Consul in Königsberg and in 1817 was appointed to report to Czar Alexander I on German affairs. He incurred the hatred of German Liberals by his attack on the Burschenschaften and was suspected of espionage. He was assassinated by a student of theology, K. L. Sand, on 23 March 1819. He was a prolific writer of plays and novels. His most successful dramas are *Menschenhass und Reue* (1789) and *Die deutschen Kleinstädter* (1803).

Works
*Sämtliche dramatischen Werke*, 44 vols., 1827–9

Literature
J. Minor, *Kotzebue als Lustspieldichter*, 1911
R. L. Kahn, *Kotzebue. His social and political attitudes*, 1950
K. H. Klingenberg, *Iffland und Kotzebue als Dramatiker*, 1959; repr. 1962

## Gustav Kühne

Journalist and author of novels and tales, early works in the manner of Tieck, latterly tendentious in the Young German fashion. Born 27 Dec. 1806 in Magdeburg, died 22 April 1888 in Dresden.

Works
*Eine Quarantäne im Irrenhaus*, 1835
*Weibliche und männliche Charaktere*, 1838
*Die Rebellen von Irland*, 1840
*Die Freimaurer*, 1855
*Gesammelte Schriften*, 12 vols., 1862–7

Literature
E. Pierson, *Gustav Kühne*, 1890
W. P. Hanson, 'F. G. Kühne, a forgotten Young German', *GLL*
17 (1963-4)

## AUGUST LAFONTAINE

Born 20 Oct. 1758 in Braunschweig, rose to eminence in the
Protestant church under patronage of King Frederick William
III of Prussia. Author of over 160 stories which met popular
demand for sentimental and sensational fiction. Died 20 April
1831.

Works
*Der Naturmensch*, 1791
*Die Tochter der Natur*, 1806
*Familienpapiere*, 1806
*Eugunie oder der Sieg der Liebe*, 1814
*Agathe oder das Grabgewölbe*, 1817
*Das heimliche Gericht des Schicksals*, 1817
etc., etc.

Literature
J. G. Gruber, *A. Lafontaines Leben u. Wirken*, 1833
H. Ishorst, 'August Lafontaine', *Germ. Stud.* 162 (1935)

## SAMUEL GOTTHOLD LANGE

Born at Laublingen in 1711, studied theology at Halle. He
entered the church and later became an inspector of schools. A
member of the Halle group of poets, he collaborated with Pyra
in founding the 'Gesellschaft zur Förderung der deutschen
Sprache, Poesie und Beredsamkeit'. His translations of Horace
provoked Lessing's adverse criticism. Lange died at Laublingen
on 25 June 1781.

Works
*Thyrsis und Damons freundschaftliche Lieder* (with Pyra), 1745; ed.
    A. Sauer, 1885
*Horazische Oden*, 1747

Literature
H. Gepfert, *Samuel Gotthold Lange*, 1923
W. P. Hanson, 'Lange, Pyra and "Anacreontische Tändeleien" ',
     *GLL* 18, 1964/5

## SOPHIE VON LA ROCHE

Sophie von La Roche, born in Kaufbeuren on 6 Dec. 1731, was
the daughter of the Augsburg doctor Georg Friedrich Gutermann.
In her youth she formed a sentimental friendship with Wieland
that lasted until the end of her life and survived her marriage in
1754 to Georg von La Roche, the factor of Wieland's patron,
Graf Friedrich von Stadion. Sophie's home in Ehrenbreitstein
was for a number of years a centre of literary life and when her
husband fell on evil days she supported the family by her writing.
Her daughter Maximiliane, a noted beauty admired by Goethe
in his youth, married the Frankfurt banker Brentano and was
the mother of Clemens and Bettina Brentano. Sophie died in
Offenbach on 18 Feb. 1807. Sophie von La Roche was much
concerned with the education of women; her stories place
unremitting stress on maidenly virtue and maternal duties.
Along with the journal *Pomona* which she edited (1783–4) they
constitute a vademecum of womanly conduct as well as of
domestic management.

## Works

*Geschichte des Fräuleins von Sternheim*, 1771; repr. DLD 138 (1907),
     DL 14 (1938)
*Der Eigensinn der Liebe und Freundschaft*, 1772
*Rosaliens Briefe*, 1779–81
*Moralische Erzählungen*, 1782–4
*Briefe an Lina als Mädchen, als Mutter*, 1785–97
*Neuere moralische Erzählungen*, 1786
*Geschichte von Miss Lony*, 1789
*Rosalie von Cleberg auf dem Lande*, 1791
*Schönes Bild der Resignation*, 1795–6
*Erscheinungen am See Oneida*, 1797–8
*Mein Schreibtisch*, 1799
*Fanny und Julia*, 1803

*Liebe-Hütten*, 1803
*Herbsttage*, 1805
*Melusinens Sommerabende*, 1806

Literature

L. Assing, *Sophie von La Roche*, 1859
W. Milch, *Sophie von La Roche*, 1935
K. Ridderhoff, *Sophie von La Roche, die Schülerin Richardsons und Rousseaus*, diss. Göttingen, 1895
W. Spickernagel, '*Die Geschichte des Fräuleins von Sternheim*' von *Sophie von La Roche und Goethes 'Werther*', diss. Greifswald, 1911
C. Riemann, 'Die Sprache in Sophie von La Roches Roman "Geschichte des Fräuleins von Sternheim" ', *Wiss. Zs. der Univ. Jena, Gesellsch. und Sprachw. Reihe 8* (1958–9)

## HEINRICH LAUBE

Born 8 Sept. 1806 in Sprottau, Silesia, turbulent youth as Young German journalist and novelist, banned, arrested and imprisoned, exiled in Paris and Algiers, member of Frankfurt Parliament. From 1850–67 Laube was director of the Viennese Burgtheater. Laube's youthful novels and short stories are the expression of his liberal views, diffuse and often jejune in situation and characterization; he later turned to the historical novel. His dramas, realistic in characterization, are Schillerian in inspiration and style (*Die Karlsschüler* is a dramatization of Schiller's youth in Karl Eugen's academy). His history of the Burgtheater is important as a study of theatrical methods and practice. Laube died in Vienna, 1 Aug. 1884.

Works

*Das junge Europa*, 1833–7
*Reisenovellen*, 6 vols., 1834–7; 10 vols., 1847 f.; sel.: *Reise durch das Biedermeier*, ed. F. H. Körber, 1965
*Moderne Charakteristiken*, 1835
*Die Bandomire*, 1842
*Die Bernsteinhexe*, 1846 (tragedy)
*Struensee*, 1847 (tragedy)
*Die Karlsschüler*, 1847

*Graf Essex*, 1856 (tragedy)
*Der deutsche Krieg*, 9 vols., 1863–6 (historical novel)
*Das Burgtheater*, 1868
*Die Böhminger*, 3 vols., 1880 (historical novel)
*Theaterkritiken u. dramaturgische Aufsätze*, ed. A. v. Weilen, 1906
*Gesammelte Werke*, ed. H. Houben, 50 vols., 1908 ff.

Literature

H. Andree, *H. Laube als jungdt. Journalist*, diss. Tübingen, 1923
L. M. v. Gersdorff, *Laubes Reisenovellen u. das Junge Deutschland*, diss. Breslau, 1923
B. v. Wiese, 'Zeitkrisis u. Biedermeier in Laubes Das junge Europa u. Immermanns Epigonen', *Dichtung u. Volkstum* 36 (1935)
W. J. Becker, *Zeitgeist u. Krisenbewusstsein in H. Laubes Novellen*, diss. Frankfurt a. M., 1960
K. Häberle, *Individualität u. Zeit in Laubes Jungem Europa u. K. Gutzkows Ritter vom Geist*, diss. Erlangen, 1938
F. Brosswitz, *Laube als Dramatiker*, diss. Breslau, 1906
P. Weiglin, *Gutzkows u. Laubes Literaturdramen*, Pal 103 (1910)
R. Junack, *H. Laubes Entwicklung zum Reformator des dt. Theaters*, diss. Erlangen, 1922
S. D. Stirk, *Kritiken von Heinrich Laube*, 1934
E. Ziemann, *Heinrich Laube als Theaterkritiker*, 1934
Cf. also *Maske u. Kothurn* 2 (1956) *passim*

## JOHANN KASPAR LAVATER

Lavater was born on 15 November 1741 in Zürich; he was taught by Bodmer and Breitinger and entered the Protestant church, being appointed 'Diakonus' of the Waisenhauskirche in Zürich in 1769. He became the incumbent there in 1775 and was elected preacher in the city's Peterskirche in 1786. Originally a supporter of the French Revolution, Lavater developed a keen patriotism during the Napoleonic wars, was imprisoned by the French for 3 months in 1799 and died on 2 Jan. 1801 in consequence of a wound received during the French entry into Zürich. Lavater was a man of generous feeling and liberal sympathies; he travelled widely in Germany and was for a time a close friend of Goethe. The divergence of their views on religion led, however, to later hostility. Lavater was most influential as a writer on education and a prolific author of religious works. His theories on the relation of physiognomy and character became a subject of controversy throughout Europe. His literary works are derivative: the fervent tone of his lyric reminiscent of Klopstock, his Biblical epics and dramas seemingly modelled on Bodmer.

Works
*Schweizer Lieder*, 1767
*Aussichten in die Ewigkeit*, 1768–78
*Physiognomische Fragmente zur Beförderung der Menschenkenntnis und Menschenliebe*, 1775–8
*Christliche Lieder*, 1776–80
*Abraham und Isaak*, 1776 (drama)
*Jesus Messias oder die Zukunft des Herrn*, 1780 (poems)
*Poesien*, 1781
*Neue Sammlung geistlicher Lieder und Reime*, 1782
*Pontius Pilatus oder die Bibel im Kleinen*, 1782–5
*Jesus Messias oder Die Evangelien- und Apostelgeschichte in Gesängen*, 1783–6
*Lieder für Leidende*, 1787
*Joseph von Arimithia*, 1794 (poems)

Literature
F. Muncker, *J. K. Lavater*, 1883
H. Funck, *J. K. Lavater*, 1902
E. Castle, *Lavater und die Seinen*, 1922
A. Bömel, *Lavaters Leben*, 1923; 2nd ed. 1927
O. Guinaudeau, *Etudes sur J. C. Lavater*, 1924
C. Janentzky, *J. C. Lavater*, 1928
M. Lavater-Sloman, *Genie des Herzens. Die Lebensgeschichte J. K. Lavaters*, 1939; 5th ed. 1955 (fictionalized biography)
T. Hasler, *J. Lavater*, 1942
J. Forstmann, *Lavater und die religiösen Strömungen des 18. Jhs*, 1935
E. v. Bracken, *Die Selbstbeobachtung bei Lavater*, 1932
C. Janentzky, *Lavaters Sturm und Drang im Zusammenhang seines religiösen Bewusstseins*, 1916
H. Funck, *Goethe und Lavater*, 1901
S. Atkins, 'Lavater und Goethe: Die Leiden des jungen Werther', *PMLA* (1948)

O. Guinaudeau, 'Les rapports de Goethe et de Lavater', *EG* 4 (1949)

O. Huppert, *Humanismus und Christentum. Goethe und Lavater*, 1950

F. Götting, 'Die Christusfrage in der Freundschaft zwischen Goethe und Lavater', *Goethe* 19 (1957)

E. v. der Hellen, *Goethes Anteil an Lavaters Physiognomischen Fragmenten*, 1888

J. Graham, 'Lavater's Physiognomy in England', *JHI* 22 (1961)


JOHANN ANTON LEISEWITZ

Born 9 May 1752 in Hannover, studied law in Göttingen, where he was a member of the 'Hainbund', settled in Braunschweig in 1775, visited Berlin and Weimar, where he met Goethe. In 1786 Leisewitz became tutor to the crown prince of Braunschweig-Lüneburg, in 1790 he became a member of the ducal administration, advanced to Geheimer Justizrat in 1801 and, in 1805 to president of the Obersanitätskollegium. He died in Braunschweig on 10 Sept. 1806. His early promise as a dramatist was not sustained.


Works
*Julius von Tarent*, 1776; repr. ed. R. M. Werner, DLD 32 (1889)
*Sämtliche Schriften*, ed. Schweiger, 1838; ed. A. Sauer, 1883

Literature
G. Kraft, *Johann Anton Leisewitz*, 1894
W. Kühlhorn, *Leisewitzens Julius von Tarent*, 1912
E. H. Zeydel, 'Neues zu Leisewitzens Julius von Tarent', *ZfdA* 56 (1931)
P. Spycher, *Die Entstehungs- u. Textgesch, von Leisewitz' Julius von Tarent*, diss. Zürich, 1951


NIKOLAUS LENAU (N. NIEMBSCH EDLER VON STREHLENAU)

Born at Csatad near Temesvar in Hungary 13 Aug. 1802, the son of an officer belonging to the Prussian nobility. He studied philosophy, law and medicine at Vienna, Pressburg and Heidelberg universities without taking a degree. He was an accomplished violinist and when he was in Vienna met Strauss as well as

Grillparzer and Anastasius Grün. He became financially independent on the death of his mother in 1830. In 1832 he went to America hoping to begin farming on a property he bought in Pennsylvania. When this venture failed he returned to Europe and lived at different times in Austria and Germany. He had unhappy love affairs with Sophie, wife of his friend Max Löwenthal, and with Karoline Unger, a singer. His health broke down before his marriage to Marie Behrends in 1844. He died in an asylum at Ober-Döbling near Vienna on 22 Aug. 1850.

Works
*Gedichte*, 1832
*Faust: Ein Gedicht*, 1835
*Savonarola*, 1837
*Neuere Gedichte*, 1838
*Die Albigenser*, 1842
*Gedichte*, 1844
*Sämtliche Werke*, ed. E. Castle, 1910–23

Literature
A. X. Schurz, *Lenaus Leben*, 1855; ed. E. Castle, 1913
M. Butler, 'Nikolaus Lenau', *German Men of Letters*, vol. 5, ed. A. Natan, 1969
E. Greven, *Lenaus Naturdichtung*, 1910
H. Bischoff, *Lenaus Gedichte*, 1920–1
L. Wege, *Hegel und Lenau*, 1929
H. Vogelsang, *N. Lenaus Lebenstragödie*, 1952
W. Martens, *Bild und Motiv im Weltschmerz: Studien zur Dichtung Lenaus*, 1957

JAKOB MICHAEL REINHOLD LENZ

Born at Sesswegen on the Baltic, 12 Jan. 1751. He studied theology at Dorpat and Königsberg. In 1771 he joined the circle of writers in Strasbourg and in 1776 followed Goethe to Weimar. He was expelled for dissolute behaviour. The first signs of madness appeared in 1778. After a brief period of recuperation he went to St. Petersburg and to Moscow in 1781 where he died in utter poverty, 24 May 1792.

Works

*Der Hofmeister*, 1774
*Das leidende Weib*, 1775
*Die Freunde machen den Philosophen*, 1776
*Der neue Menoza*, 1776; repr. ed. W. Hinck, 1965
*Die Soldaten*, 1776
*Der Engländer*, 1777
*Pandaemonium Germanicum*, 1819; repr. ed. E. Schmidt, 1896
*Gesammelte Werke*, ed. L. Tieck, 1828
*Werke und Schriften*, ed. B. Titel, H. Haug, 1966
*Gesammelte Werke*, ed. F. Blei, 1909


Literature
H. Kindermann, *Lenz und die dt. Romantik*, 1925
W. Wien, *Lenzens Sturm u. Drang Dramen innerhalb seiner religiösen Entwicklung*, 1934
G. Unger, *Lenzens Hofmeister*, 1949

Lenz's *Anmerkungen übers Theater*, 1774, shows the important influence of Mercier's writings on the generation of the 'Sturm und Drang'. See *Aus Goethes Brieftasche*, 1775.

M. N. Rosanow, *J. M. R. Lenz*, 1909
J. San Giorgiu, *Sebastien Merciers dramaturgische Ideen im Sturm und Drang*, 1921

## GOTTHOLD EPHRAIM LESSING

Lessing was born on 22 Jan. 1729 in Kamenz, Saxony. From 1741 to 1746 he attended the Meissen 'Fürstenschule' and from 1746 to 1748 studied theology and medicine at Leipzig where he also took an active interest in the theatre. From 1748 he was a freelance writer and journalist in Berlin. Here he met Nicolai, Mendelssohn, Ramler and other writers of the day. After renewing his studies at Wittenberg in 1751 he took a secretarial post with General Tauentzien in Breslau (1760–4). In 1767 he was called to Hamburg as literary adviser at the newly established 'Nationaltheater'. He became librarian in Wolffenbüttel in 1770. In 1775 and 1776 he made journeys to Vienna and Rome. In the latter year he married Eva König, who died two years later. Lessing himself died in Braunschweig on 15 Feb. 1781.

Lessing's main work on aesthetics is *Laokoon*. Its principal contribution to the subject lies in the distinction he made between painting and sculpture, art forms whose presentation is effected through coexistence in space ('Nebeneinander im Raum') and poetry and music, whose effects are produced through succession in time ('Nacheinander in der Zeit'). This fruitful distinction, the first of its kind, allowed him to deny the validity of the Horatian 'ut pictura poesis' principle and to curtail the prevalent vogue of descriptive poetry. It also permitted the presentation of painful impressions in poetry (while excluding them from the formative arts), so that Lessing's theory of tragedy can be seen to form part of his general aesthetic theory.

In his theological writings Lessing followed the same line of independent enquiry as in his literary criticism. He was not an orthodox believer, but it is wrong to say that Lessing's main purpose in writing his tracts was to undermine the Christian religion. Rather, he attempted to turn it into a 'Religion der Vernunft' without sacrificing at least some of its essential dogmas. His controversy with Goeze concerned the fundamental ideas of Christianity outside its institutionalized forms. This is the point of his distinction between 'die Religion Christi' and 'die christliche Religion', and his rejection of historical evidence as the basis of faith. The most important aspects of his thought in *Die Erziehung des Menschengeschlechts* are the relation between Revelation and Reason, the postulation of 'das dritte Evangelium' and the doctrine of immortality linked with that of metempsychosis.

Works

*Der junge Gelehrte*, 1748
*Der Freygeist*, 1749
*Die Juden*, 1749
*Die alte Jungfer*, 1749
*Beiträge zur Historie und Aufnahme des Theaters*, 1749–54
*Miss Sara Sampson*, 1755
Correspondence with Nicolai and Mendelssohn on tragedy, 1756–7; ed. R. Petsch, 1910
*Philotas*, 1759
*Fabeln*, 1759
*Briefe die neueste Literatur betreffend*, 1759–65

*Laokoon*, 1766; repr. ed. H. Blumer, 1880; ed. D. Reich, 1965
*Minna von Barnhelm*, 1767
*Hamburgische Dramaturgie*, 1767–9; repr. ed. J. Petersen, 1925;
   ed. O. Mann, 1958
*Emilia Galotti*, 1772
*Fragmente eines Ungenannten*, 1774
*Eine Duplik*, 1778
*Eine Parabel*, 1778
*Anti-Goeze*, 1778
*Die Christenheit der Vernunft; Ernst und Falk*, 1778
*Nathan der Weise*, 1779
*Die Erziehung des Menschengeschlechts*, 1780
*Werke*, ed. J. Petersen, W. Ohlshausen, 1925–35; ed. P. Rilla,
   1954–8

Literature
E. Schmidt, *Lessing*, 1884–92; repr. ed. F. Schultz, 1923
G. Kettner, *Lessings Dramen im Lichte ihrer und unserer Zeit*, 1904
W. Oehlke, *Lessing und seine Zeit*, 1919
J. Clivio, *Lessing und das Problem der Tragödie*, 1928
B. v. Wiese, *Lessing. Dichtung, Aesthetik, Philosophie*, 1931
H. Rempel, *Tragödie und Komödie im dramatischen Schaffen Lessings*,
   1935
H. B. Garland, *Lessing*, 1937
O. Mann, *Lessing. Sein und Leistung*, 1949; repr. 1961
O. Walzel, 'Lessings Begriff des Tragischen', *Vom Geistesleben
   alter und neuer Zeit*, 1922
K. May, *Lessings und Herders kunsttheoretische Gedanken*, 1923
J. G. Robertson, *Lessing's dramatic theory*, 1939
F. O. Nolte, *Lessings Laokoon*, 1940
M. Bieber, *Laokoon. The influence of the group since its rediscovery*,
   1942
F. Leander, *Lessing als ästhetischer Denker*, 1942
M. Kommerell, *Lessing und Aristoteles*, 1940; repr. 1957
A. Baumann, *Studien zu Lessings Literaturkritik*, 1951
E. M. Szarota, *Lessings Laokoon*, 1959
C. Schrempf, *Lessing als Philosoph*, 1921
G. Fittbogen, *Die Religion Lessings*, 1923
K. Aner, *Die Theologie der Lessingzeit*, 1929; repr. 1964
H. Leisegang, *Lessings Weltanschauung*, 1931

S. Pons, *G. E. Lessing et le Christianisme*, 1964
H. Thielicke, *Offenbarung, Vernunft und Existenz. Studien zur Religionsphilosophie Lessings*, 1957

## DANIEL LESSMANN

Born of Jewish parents, 18 Jan. 1794 at Soldin (Neumark), died by his own hand near Wittenberg, 2 Sep. 1831. Lessmann spent his life as tutor and travelling companion in Italy, France, Spain and England. His work is influenced by the example of Heine.

Works
*Amathusia*, 1824
*Zwölf Wanderlieder eines Schwermütigen*, 1826
*Luise von Halling*, 1827 (novel)
*Biographische Gemälde*, 2 vols., 1829 f.
*Gedichte*, 1830
*Aus dem Wanderbuch eines Schwermütigen*, 2 vols., 1831 f.
*Nachlass*, 3 vols., 1837 f.
*Die Heidemühle*, 1838 (novel)

Literature
H. Schumann, *Daniel Lessmann*, diss. Leipzig, 1920

## HEINRICH LEUTHOLD

Born Witzikon near Zürich, 9 Aug. 1827, author of lyric and grandiose verse epics in Classical style; pessimistic, occasionally satirical tone; translator of French lyric in collaboration with E. Geibel. Something of a Bohemian, Leuthold became insane and died in a Zürich mental hospital, 1 July 1879.

Works
*Fünf Bücher französischer Lyrik*, 1862 (translations)
*Penthesilea*, 1868 (epic)
*Die Schlacht bei Sempach*, 1870 (epic)
*Hannibal*, 1871 (epic)
*Gedichte*, 1879 (preface by G. Keller); 2nd ed. by J. Baechtold, 1884

*Gesammelte Dichtungen,* ed. G. Bohnenblust, 3 vols., 1914
*Der schwermütige Musikant,* ed. H. Hesse, 1934
*Ausgewählte Gedichte,* ed. A. Guggenbühl, 1946

Literature
A. W. Ernst, *Heinrich Leuthold,* 1891; 2nd ed. 1893
K. E. Hoffmann, *Das Leben des Dichters H. Leuthold,* 1935
M. Plüss, *Leutholds Lyrik u. ihre Vorbilder,* diss. Berne, 1908
K. A. v. Müller, 'Leutholds Penthesilea', *Neue Schweizer Rundschau*
    18 (1950–1)
H. Schneider, *Die freundschaftliche Begegung H. Leutholds u. E.*
    *Geibels in München,* 1961

AUGUST LEWALD

Born 14 Oct. 1792 in Königsberg, where he studied; fought in
the War of Liberation, subsequently went on the stage and
became director of the theatre in Nürnberg in 1824. Later settled
in Stuttgart, where he founded the magazine *Europa, Chronik der*
*gebildeten Welt.* In 1849 was appointed editor of the conservative
*Deutsche Chronik* and later became director of the Stuttgart
court theatre. Converted to Roman Catholicism in 1852, died
10 March 1871. Author of topical novels, Novellen and 'Zeitbilder'.

Works
*Schattierungen,* 1836
*Aquarelle aus dem Leben,* 4 vols., 1836 f.
*Der Diwan,* 1839 (Novellen)
*Mörder u. Gespenster,* 1840
*Theaterroman,* 1841
*Die Geheimnisse des Theaters,* 1845
*Klarinette,* 1863
*Der Insurgent,* 1865
*Moderne Familiengeschichten,* 1866
etc., etc.

Literature
A. Rosenthal, *Convertitenbilder aus dem 19. Jh.,* 1872

FANNY LEWALD (FANNY STAHR)

Born 24 March 1811 in Königsberg, daughter of a Jewish business-man called Markus, cousin of August Lewald, whose name she assumed. Converted to Protestant faith in 1828, travelled in France and Italy, where she met the scholar Adolf Stahr, who divorced his wife and married her in 1854. Prolific novelist and supporter of women's emancipation. Died in Dresden, 5 Aug. 1889.

Works
*Clementine*, 1842
*Jenny*, 1843; repr. ed. T. Erler, 1967
*Diogena*, 1847
*Italienisches Bilderbuch*, 1847; repr. ed. T. Erler, 1967
*Erinnerungen*, 1850
*Deutsche Lebensbilder*, 1856
*Von Geschlecht zu Geschlecht*, 1864
*Die Familie Darner*, 1887; repr. ed. H. Spiero, 1925
*Gesammelte Werke*, 12 vols., 1871–75

Literature
M. Weber, *Fanny Lewald*, diss. Zürich, 1921
M. Steinhauer, *Fanny Lewald*, 1937
H. Hettner, 'Fanny Lewald', *Schriften zur Lit. u. Philosophie*, 1844–1853; repr. 1967

GEORG CHRISTOPH LICHTENBERG

Lichtenberg was born on 1 July 1742 at Oberramstadt, near Darmstadt; he grew up to be a hunch-back, a condition to which some of his contemporaries were inclined to attribute his satirical vein. After studying mathematics and science in Göttingen Lichtenberg became professor there, first of mathematics, then of physics. The political connection between Hannover and England favoured Lichtenberg's interest in a country that, with its tradition of empirical thought, was to some extent his spiritual home. He was for a time public teacher of English at the University of Göttingen, spent a year in England (1774–5), acted as tutor to three English princes during their stay in Göttingen and was elected a Fellow of the Royal Society in 1793. His knowledge of English life is reflected in his commentaries on Hogarth's engravings and his characterization of the actor, David Garrick. At the end of 1775 Lichtenberg returned to Göttingen, where he remained until his death on 24 Feb. 1799. As one of the most brilliant representatives of the 'Aufklärung' Lichtenberg directed his sardonic wit against religious zeal, the cult of sentimentality— practised, for example, by the poets of the 'Göttinger Hainbund' —and the quasi-mystical ideas of Lavater. His literary work consists mainly of short satirical pieces and an enormous number of aphorisms compiled throughout his life. From 1778 he was editor of the Göttingen *Taschenkalender* and in 1780 he founded, with Georg Forster, the *Göttingisches Magazin*.

## Works

*Timorus, das ist Verteidigung zweier Israeliten, die durch die Kräftigkeit der Lavaterischen Beweisgründe, und der Göttingischen Mettwürste bewogen, den wahren Glauben angenommen haben, von Conrad Photorin*, 1773

*Patriotischer Beitrag zur Methyologie der Deutschen*, 1773

*Briefe aus England*, 1776–8

*Über Physiognomik; wider die Physiognomen*, 1778

*Fragment von Schwänzen*, 1783

*Ausführliche Erklärung der Hogarthischen Kupferstiche*, 1794–9

*Georg Christoph Lichtenbergs auserlesene Schriften*, 1800

*Georg Christoph Lichtenbergs Aphorismen*, ed. A. Leitzmann, DLD 123, 131, 136, 140, 141 (1902–8)

## Literature

V. Bouiller, *G. C. Lichtenberg. Essai sur sa vie et ses œuvres littéraires*, 1914

W. Grenzmann, *G. C. Lichtenberg*, 1939

A. Schneider, *Lichtenberg. Précurseur du romantisme*, 1954

A. Schneider, *Lichtenberg penseur*, 1954

C. Brinitzer, *Lichtenberg. Die Geschichte eines gescheiten Mannes*, 1956 (transl. B. Smith: *A reasonable rebel: G. C. Lichtenberg*, 1960)

J. P. Stern, *Lichtenberg. A doctrine of scattered occasions*, 1959

W. Promies, *Lichtenberg*, 1964

F. H. Mautner, *Lichtenberg. Gesch. seines Geistes*, 1968

P. Rippmann, *Werk und Fragment. G. C. Lichtenberg als Schrift-steller*, diss. Berne, 1953

J. D. Workman, 'Lichtenberg's irrationalism', *Monatshefte* 39 (1947)

H. Schöffler, *Lichtenberg. Studien zu seinem Wesen und Geist*, 1956

W. Rödel, *Forster und Lichtenberg*, 1960

W. A. Berendsohn, 'Lichtenberg und der junge Goethe', *Euph* 23 (1921)

M. L. Mare, W. H. Quarrel, *Lichtenberg's visits to England*, 1938

A. Marshall, 'Lichtenberg on Chodowiecki and Hogarth', *PEGS* 36 (1966)

F. H. Mautner, 'Lichtenberg as an interpreter of Hogarth', *MLQ* 13 (1952)

G. Betz, 'Lichtenberg as a critic of the English stage', *JEGP* 23 (1924)

W. Preisendanz, 'Lichtenberg. Ein Forschungsbericht', *GRM* 37 (1956)

## HERMANN VON LINGG

Born 22 Jan. 1820 in Lindau, died 18 June 1905 in Munich; army medical officer, member of the Munich literary circle 'Das Krokodil'; lyric, ballads and epics, mostly on vast and sombre themes; also abortive dramas.

### Works

*Gedichte*, 1854; 1868

*Die Völkerwanderung*, 1866–8 (epic)

*Vaterländische Balladen*, 1869

*Schlußsteine*, 1878 (poems)

*Byzantinische Novellen*, 1881

*Meine Lebensreise*, 1899

*Dramatische Dichtungen*, 2 vols., 1897 ff.

*Ausgewählte Gedichte*, ed. P. Heyse, 1905

### Literature

F. Port, *Hermann Lingg*, 1912

E. Pfaff, *H. Lingg als epischer Dichter*, diss. Giessen, 1925

H. Rothärmel, *Die Völkerwanderung von H. Lingg*, diss. Munich, 1925

A. Sonntag, *H. Lingg als Lyriker*, 1908
W. Knote, *H. Lingg u. seine lyrische Dichtung*, diss. Würzburg, 1936

## JOHANN MICHAEL VON LOEN

Great-uncle of Goethe, born 11 Dec. 1694 in Frankfurt am Main, publicist of enlightened views, attracted the attention of Frederick the Great, who appointed him Regierungspräsident of Tecklenburg. Mentioned in *Dichtung und Wahrheit* and possibly the model for the 'Oheim' in *Wilhelm Meisters Wanderjahre*. Died in Frankfurt, 24 July 1776.

### Works
*Der Graf von Ribera oder Der redliche Mann am Hofe*, 1740; repr., ed. K. Reichert, DN (1966)
*Gesammelte kleine Schriften*, 1750
*Moralische Gedichte*, ed. Naumann, 1851

### Literature
H. Haeckel, 'J. M. v. Loen u. die dt. Aufklärung', *Zs. f. Relig.-u. Geistesgesch.* 6 (1954)
E. Beutler, 'Goethes Ahne in Mörfelden', *Essays um Goethe*, 5th ed., 1957
K. Reichert, 'Utopie u. Satire in J. M. v. Loens Roman, Der redliche Mann am Hofe', *GRM* 15 (1965)

## OTTO LUDWIG

Born 12 Feb. 1813 at Eisfeld (Thuringia), died 25 Feb. 1865 in Dresden. Ludwig was orphaned when he was twelve years old and suffered since childhood from a nervous complaint. He was meant to take up a commercial career but in 1839 received a grant from the Duke of Meiningen and studied music in Leipzig under Mendelssohn-Bartholdy. He then took up writing and settled in Dresden in 1849. King Maximilian of Bavaria granted him a pension in 1856.

### Works
*Die wahrhaftige Geschichte von den drei Wünschen*, 1842
*Maria*, 1843

*Die Torgauer Heide*, 1843 (drama)
*Die Rechte des Herzens*, 1845 (drama)
*Der Engel von Augsburg*, 1846 (drama)
*Die Pfarrose*, 1847 (drama)
*Das Fräulein von Scudéri*, 1848 (drama)
*Der Erbförster*, 1853 (drama)
*Die Makkabäer*, 1854 (drama)
*Die Heiterethei*, 1854
*Aus dem Regen in die Traufe*, 1855
*Zwischen Himmel und Erde*, 1856
*Shakespeare-Studien*, 1871; ed. A. Stern, 1891
*Gesammelte Werke*, ed. A. Stern, E. Schmidt, 1891; ed. P. Merker,
    1912–22, repr. 1961 ff.
*Tagebücher*, ed. K. Vogtherr, 1936

Literature
L. Mis, *Les Études sur Shakespeare d'Otto Ludwig*, 1921
    id., *Les œuvres dramatiques d'Otto Ludwig*, 1922
R. Adam, *Der Realismus Otto Ludwigs*, 1938
H. Reuter, *Otto Ludwig als Erzähler*, 1957
E. Witte, *Otto Ludwigs Erzählkunst*, 1959
A. Meyer, *Die ästhetischen Anschauungen Otto Ludwigs*, 1957
For further lit. on Ludwig see: *Otto Ludwig-Kalender* 1–4 (1929–32)


HERMANN MARGGRAFF

Born Züllichau, 14 Sept. 1809, died 11 Feb. 1864 in Leipzig.
Journalist, author of humorous tales as well as historical tragedies.

Works
*Bücher und Menschen*, 1847
*Johannes Mackel*, 1841
*Politische Gedichte aus Deutschlands Neuzeit*, 1847
*Fritz Beutel*, 1856
*Hausschatz der deutschen Humoristik*, 2 vols., 1858–60

Literature
P. Berland, *Hermann Marggraff*, 1942

## August Gottlieb Meissner

Born 3 Nov. 1753 in Bautzen, professor of aesthetics and classical philology in Prague, then director of Lyzeum in Fulda; translator and author of comedies and librettos as well as numerous novels and tales of an enlightened and rationalistic kind. Died in Fulda, 18 Feb. 1807.

Works
*Sämtliche Werke*, ed. F. Kuffner, 56 vols., 1811 f.

Literature
R. Fürst, *August Gottlieb Meissner*, 1894
S. Hock, 'Zur Biographie A. G. Meissners', *Euph* 6 (1899)

## Moses Mendelssohn

Born 6 Sept. 1729 in Dessau. He had no formal education and earned his living first as a tutor, then in commerce. He died in Berlin on 4 Jan. 1786. He was a close friend of Lessing, with whom he conducted a fruitful debate on topics of art and philosophy. His views on some aspects of aesthetics have more than historical interest.

Works
*Philosophische Gespräche*, 1755
*Briefe über die Empfindungen*, 1755
*Über die Hauptgrundsätze der schönen Künste und Wissenschaften*, 1757
*Betrachtungen über das Erhabene und Naive in den schönen Wissenschaften*, 1757
*Gesammelte Schriften*, ed. I. Elbogen, J. Guttmann, E. Mittwoch, 1929 ff.
*Schriften zur Philosophie, Ästhetik and Apologetik*, ed. M. Brach, 1880

Literature
L. Goldstein, *Moses Mendelssohn u. die dt. Ästhetik*, 1904
E. H. Zeydel, 'Moses Mendelssohn', *GQ* 3 (1929)
F. Bamberger, *Die geistige Gestalt Moses Mendelssohns*, 1929
H. Behrens, *Moses Mendelssohn u. die Aufklärung*, 1940
L. Richter, *Philosophie der Dichtkunst. Moses Mendelssohns Ästhetik zwischen Aufklärung und Sturm und Drang*, 1948

JOHANN HEINRICH MERCK

Merck was born in Darmstadt on 11 April 1741. He studied at the Universities of Giessen and Erlangen and the Academy of Art in Dresden; after a spell as private tutor he became a civil servant in his native town and was granted the title of 'Kriegsrat' in 1767. Merck's intellectual position was ambivalent: he was a central figure in the complex of sentimental friendships that included Goethe and Herder, but his sardonic temperament caused Goethe to give him the nickname Mephistopheles. Merck probably influenced Goethe in his youth more than any other single person, and it was he who published Goethe's *Götz von Berlichingen*. He was certainly one of the most knowledgeable men of his time and enjoyed the esteem and patronage of many eminent people. His most important work is in the form of reviews on topics ranging from fine art to palaeontology and geology in leading periodicals like the *Frankfurter gelehrte Anzeigen*, Nicolai's *Allgemeine deutsche Bibliothek* and Wieland's *Teutscher Merkur*. Merck's later life was plagued by domestic and financial cares that finally drove him to suicide on 27 June 1791.

Works
*Fabeln*, 1770
*Rhapsodie*, 1773
*Pätus und Arria, eine Künstler-Romanze*, 1775 (satire on the *Werther* furore)
*Geschichte des Herrn Oheims*, 1778
*Lindor. Eine bürgerlich-deutsche Geschichte*, 1781
*Herr Oheim der Jüngere*, 1781–2
*Akademischer Briefwechsel*, 1782 (short novel)
*Ausgewählte Schriften zur schönen Lit. u. Kunst*, ed. A. Stahr, 1840; repr. 1965
*Fabeln und Erzählungen*, ed. H. Bräuning-Oktavio, 1962

Literature
H. Prang, *J. H. Merck. Ein Leben für andere*, 1949
M. Ludewig, *Merck als Kritiker*, diss. Münster, 1930
K. Beckmann, 'J. H. Merck als Dichter', *Jb. des Kölnischen Geschichtsvereins* 14 (1932)
V. Tornius, *Die Empfindsamen in Darmstadt*, 1911

H. Bräuning-Oktavio, 'Der Einfluss von J. H. Mercks Schicksal auf Goethes *Faust* und *Tasso*', *Jb. des freien dt. Hochstifts*, 1962

H. R. Vaget, 'J. H. Mercks Kunstanschauung', *Monatshefte* 60 (1968)

## CONRAD FERDINAND MEYER

Born 11 Oct. 1825 in Zürich, member of an old patrician family, studied in Lausanne and Zürich but was prevented by his neurotic disposition from taking up a career. The friendship of the historian, Louis Vulliemin, rescued him from the depression which forced him to spend a year in a mental hospital at Préfargier. The suicide of his mother, although it haunted him for years, had some kind of liberating effect on Meyer, and travels in France and Italy opened up new horizons, stimulating his interest in art and providing material for the colourful descriptions in his subsequent works. By 1860 Meyer had compiled his first collection of poems, but it was the Franco-Prussian War of 1870 which stirred his enthusiasm for the German heritage and inspired the long poem, *Huttens Letzte Tage*. Meyer had a close relationship with his sister Betsy and it was not until he was fifty that he took the decisive step of marriage to Luise Ziegler. He settled in Kilchberg, near Zürich, and his later years saw the renewed onset of melancholia. In 1892 he returned to Préfargier and although he was discharged within the year his literary career was virtually at an end. He died 28 Nov. 1898. Meyer's historical tales are remarkable for formal perfection. They are crowded with virile characters and violent action, furnished with sumptuous descriptions; in their obsessive symbols they reflect the writer's psychological conflicts and his wrestling with the concepts of fate and free-will, suffering and guilt. His lyric is fashioned with careful craftsmanship, tensely statuesque rather than musical in its effect, haunted by melancholy.

Works
*Zwanzig Balladen von einem Schweizer*, 1864
*Romanzen und Bilder*, 1871
*Huttens letzte Tage*, 1871
*Engelburg*, 1872
*Das Amulett*, 1873

*Jürg Jenatsch*, 1876
*Der Schuss von der Kanzel*, 1878
*Der Heilige*, 1880; repr. ed. W. A. Coupe, 1965
*Gedichte*, 1882
*Plautus im Nonnenkloster*, 1882
*Gustav Adolfs Page*, 1882
*Die Leiden eines Knaben*, 1883
*Die Hochzeit des Mönchs*, 1884
*Die Richterin*, 1885
*Die Versuchung des Pescara*, 1887; repr. ed. W. D. Williams, 1958
*Angela Borgia*, 1891
*Sämtliche Werke*, 4 vols., ed. R. Faesi, 1926
*Historisch-kritische Ausgabe*, ed. H. Zeller, A. Zäch, 1959 ff.


Literature

B. Meyer, *C. F. Meyer in der Erinnerung seiner Schwester*, 1903

R. d'Harcourt, *C. F. Meyer. Sa vie, son œuvre*, 1913

F. F. Baumgarten, *Das Werk C. F. Meyers*, 1917; ed. H.
    Schumacher, 1948

M. Nussberger, *C. F. Meyer. Leben u. Werke*, 1919

W. Linden, *C. F. Meyer. Entwicklung u. Gestalt*, 1922

H. Maync, *C. F. Meyer u. sein Werk*, 1925

A. Burkhard, *C. F. Meyer. The style and the man*, 1932

R. Faesi, *Conrad Ferdinand Meyer*, 1948

H. v. Lerber, *C. F. Meyer. Der Mensch in der Spannung*, 1949

H. Henel, *The poetry of C. F. Meyer*, 1954

L. Hohenstein, *Conrad Ferdinand Meyer*, 1957

L. Wiesmann, *C. F. Meyer, der Dichter des Todes u. der Maske*, 1958

W. E. Yuill, 'C. F. Meyer', *German Men of Letters*, ed. A. Natan,
    1961

W. D. Williams, *The stories of C. F. Meyer*, 1962

J. Fährmann, *Bildwelt u. symbolische Gestaltung in der Dichtung
    C. F. Meyers*, diss. Freiburg, 1964

M. Shaw, 'C. F. Meyer's resolute heroes', *DVLG* 40 (1966)

E. Staiger, 'Das Spätboot. Zu C. F. Meyers Lyrik', *Kunst der
    Interpretation*, 1955

H. Henel, *Gedichte C. F. Meyers. Wege ihrer Vollendung*, 1962

W. P. Bridgwater, 'C. F. Meyer and Nietzsche', *MLR* 60 (1956)

W. Oberle, 'C. F. Meyer: ein Forschungsbericht', *GRM* 37
    (1956)

EDUARD MÖRIKE

Born in Ludwigsburg, 8 Sept. 1804. From 1822 to 1825 he was educated at the Tübinger Stift where D. F. Strauss and F. T. Vischer were his contemporaries. At that time he met Maria Meyer, the 'Peregrina' of his poetry. From 1826 he occupied clerical positions in different places, including Nürtingen. He became engaged to Luise Rau in 1829 but the engagement was broken off in 1833. From 1834 until 1843 he was vicar at Cleversulzbach where he lived with his mother and sister. He gave up the vicarage in 1843 and went to live in Schwäbisch Hall. In 1851 he took up a teaching post in a girls' school in Stuttgart. His marriage to Margarethe von Speeth took place in 1851 and was dissolved in 1873. After giving up his teaching post in Stuttgart he lived in retirement there and later at Nürtingen. He died in Stuttgart, 4 June 1875.

Works

*Maler Nolten*, 1832

*Gedichte*, 1838

*Die Idylle vom Bodensee*, 1846

*Das Stuttgarter Hutzelmännlein*, 1852

*Mozart auf der Reise nach Prag*, 1856

*Werke*, ed. H. Maync, 1924

*Werke und Briefe*, ed. G. Baumann, 1960

*Sämtliche Werke*, ed. H. G. Göpfert, 1965

Literature

H. Maync, *Eduard Mörike. Sein Leben und Dichten*, 1902; repr. 1944

J. M. Lindsay, 'Eduard Mörike', *German Men of Letters*, vol. 5, ed. A. Natan, 1969

E. F. Heilmann, *Mörikes Lyrik und das Volkslied*, 1913

V. Sandomirski, *Mörike u. sein Verhältnis zum Biedermeier*, 1935

G. Schutze, *Mörikes Lyrik u. die Überwindung der Romantik*, 1940

H. Vetter, *Mörike und die Romantik*, 1940

H. Oppel, *Peregrina*, 1947

B. V. Wiese, *Eduard Mörike*, 1950

H. Meyer, *Eduard Mörike*, 1950; repr. 1965

H. Emmel, *Mörikes Peregrinadichtung u. ihre Beziehung zum Noltenroman*, 1952

A. Beck, 'Peregrina', *Euph* 47 (1953)

L. Dieckmann, 'Mörike's presentation of the creative process' *JEGP* 53 (1954)

S. S. Prawer, *Mörike und seine Leser*, 1960

H. Meyer, *Eduard Mörike*, 1961; repr. 1965

F. Noller, *Eduard Mörike und andere Essays*, 1966

H. Uhde-Bernays, 'Schriften über Mörike', *Deutsche Beiträge* 4 (1950)

F. Sengle, 'Mörike-Probleme', *GRM* 33 (1951)

H. H. Krummacher, 'Zu Mörikes Gedichten. Ausgaben u. Überlieferung', *JDSG* 5 (1961)

  id., 'Mitteilungen zur Chronologie u. Textgesch. von Mörikes Gedichten', *JDSG* 6 (1962)

H. Henel, 'Mörike's "Denk' es o Seele"; Ein Volkslied?' Festschrift f. R. Alewyn, 1967

## JUSTUS MÖSER

Möser is closely identified with Osnabrück, where he was born on 14 Dec. 1720 and where he spent his life in various administrative posts. His historical studies praising the sturdy traditions of his native province constitute an aspect of the general enthusiasm for the German heritage exemplified in Herder's *Von deutscher Art und Kunst*. Möser's *Osnabrückische Geschichte* emphasizes the part played by folk traditions in the evolution of culture in his own age. His periodical, *Osnabrückische Intelligenzblätter*, is modelled on the 'moral weeklies' of the Enlightenment and it shares with them the purpose of popular instruction, but its appeal to national sentiment rather than universal reason foreshadows Romantic notions of 'Volkstum'. In his essay *Über deutsche Sprache und Literatur* Möser was bold enough to reply to Frederick the Great's disparaging account of German literature. Möser died in Osnabrück on 8 Jan. 1794.

Works
*Osnabrückische Geschichte*, 1768; 2nd ed. 1780
*Patriotische Phantasien*, 1774–86
*Über deutsche Sprache und Literatur*, 1781

Literature
P. Klassen, *Justus Möser*, 1936
L. Bäte, *Justus Möser. Advocatus patriae*, 1961

H. Zimmermann, *Staat, Recht und Wirtschaft bei Justus Möser*, 1933
W. Hollmann, *Justus Mösers Zeitungsidee*, 1937

## KARL PHILIPP MORITZ

Moritz was born in Hameln on 15 Sept. 1757. *Anton Reiser* gives an account of his upbringing in a family dominated by a neurotically pietistic father, his privations as apprentice to a hatmaker and as a charity scholar and the re-direction of his histrionic ambitions from the pulpit to the stage. After an attempt to join Ekhof's company in Gotha Moritz studied in Erfurt and became a teacher, first at Badedow's progressive Philanthropinum in Dessau, then at the military orphanage in Potsdam and the 'Graues Kloster' in Berlin. He travelled to England in 1782 and on his return became a master at the Köln grammar school in Berlin as well as editor of the *Vossische Zeitung*. In 1786 he was driven by restlessness and ill-starred love to Italy, where he was befriended by Goethe. After his return from Italy Moritz was Goethe's guest in Weimar for two months, and it was in part Goethe's influence which secured for him in 1789 a post at the Akademie der Künste in Berlin, where he died on 26 June 1793. Moritz turned to literary ends the pietistic practice of self-observation that he had known in his youth; both as an imaginative writer and as editor of the *Magazin für Erfahrungsseelenkunde* (1783–93) he anticipated techniques and findings of modern psychiatry. His interest in practical psychology and educational reform is characteristic of the Enlightenment, but on the other hand the awareness of the sombre recesses of the soul bred into him in his youth foreshadows Romantic irrationalism. His glorification of Greek art as embodying a psychic balance between reason and potentially destructive energy is no doubt relevant to this inner conflict. For Goethe, Moritz's treatise *Über die bildende Nachahmung des Schönen* was a manifesto of Classicism, 'das Fundament unserer nachher entwickelten Denkart'.

## Works

*Beiträge zur Philosophie des Lebens*, 1781
*Blunt oder der Gast*, 1781 (drama)
*Reisen eines Deutschen in England*, 1783; repr. DLD 126 (1903)
*Anton Reiser*, 1785–90; repr. DLD 23 (1886)
*Andreas Hartknopf*, 1786; repr., ed. H. J. Schrimpf, 1968

*Denkwürdigkeiten*, 1786–8

*Versuch einer deutschen Prosodie*, 1786

*Über die bildende Nachahmung des Schönen*, 1786; repr. DLD 31 (1888)

*Fragmente aus dem Tagebuch eines Geistersehers*, 1787

*Götterlehre oder mythologische Dichtungen der Alten*, 1791

*Vorlesungen über den Stil*, 1791

*Reisen eines Deutschen in Italien in den Jahren 1786–88*, 1792–3

*Die neue Cäcilie*, 1794

*Launen und Phantasien*, 1796 (ed. K. F. Klischnig)

A generous selection of Moritz's critical writing is available in *Schriften zur Ästhetik und Poetik*, ed. H. Schrimpf, NDL 7 (1962)


Literature

H. Henning, *Karl Philipp Moritz*, 1908

F. Ernst, 'Karl Philipp Moritz', *Essays II*, 1946

E. Naef, *K. P. Moritz. Seine Ästhetik*, diss. Zürich, 1930

R. Minder, *Die religiöse Entwicklung von Karl Philipp Moritz*, 1936

E. Catholy, *Karl Philipp Moritz und die deutsche Theaterleidenschaft*, 1962

W. Altenberger, *K. P. Moritz' pädagogische Ansichten*, diss. Leipzig, 1905

G. Hinsche, *K. P. Moritz als Psychologe*, diss. Halle, 1912

E. Moritz, *K. P. Moritz und der Sturm und Drang*, diss. Marburg, 1958

H. J. Schrimpf, 'Anton Reiser', *Der dt. Roman*, I, ed. B. v. Wiese, 1963; 2nd ed. 1965

H. Glogau, *Anton Reiser*, 1903

H. Eybisch, *Untersuchungen zur Lebensgeschichte Moritzens und zur Kritik seiner Autobiographie*, 1909

E. H. Zeydel, 'The relation of Moritz's *Anton Reiser* to Romanticism', *GR* 3 (1928)

H. J. Schrimpf, *K. P. Moritz. Studien zum Wirklichkeits- und Kunstbegriff der deutschen Frühklassik*, 1963–4

JULIUS MOSEN

Born 8 July 1803 at Marieney (Vogtland), Mosen studied in Jena and travelled in Italy, where he came across the material for his verse epic *Lied vom Ritter Wahn*, before returning to study in Leipzig. He occupied administrative posts in Kohren and Dresden before becoming artistic director of the court theatre in Oldenburg. He died in Oldenburg on 10 Oct. 1867.

## Works

*Das Lied vom Ritter Wahn*, 1831
*Georg Venlot*, 1831 (Novelle)
*Heinrich der Finkler*, 1836 (historical drama)
*Gedichte*, 1836
*Novellen*, 1837
*Ahasver*, 1838 (epic)
*Der Kongress zu Verona*, 1842
*Theater*, 1842
*Bilder im Moose*, 1846 (Novellen)
*Herzog Bernhard von Weimar*, 1855 (tragedy)
*Der Sohn des Fürsten*, 1855 (tragedy)
*Sämtliche Werke*, 8 vols., 1863; repr. ed. R. Mosen, 6 vols., 1880 ff.
*Ausgewählte Dichtungen*, ed. M. Rudolf, 1905
*Julius-Mosen-Buch*, ed. K. A. Findeisen, 1924

## Literature

F. A. Zimmer, *Julius Mosen*, 1938
F. Welsch, *Julius Mosen*, 1953
A. Fehn, *Die Geschichtsphilosophie in den historischen Dramen Mosens*, 1915
K. Basse, *Mosens Theorie der Tragödie*, diss. Münster, 1915
W. Schwelje, *Naturgefühl in Mosens Novellensammlung Bilder im Moose*, 1916
H. Schuller, 'Zu Mosens Georg Venlot', *Euph* 23 (1921)
   id., 'Mosen u. E. T. A. Hoffmann', *Euph* 24 (1922)
F. Wittmer, *Studien zu Mosens Lyrik*, diss. Munich, 1924

## ADAM HEINRICH MÜLLER

Born 30 June 1779 in Berlin, prominent political and economic theorist of the Romantic era. Influenced by Burke in his conservative idea of an organic state, embracing, in opposition to the rational theories of Montesquieu and Adam Smith, 'die Totalität des gesamten Lebens'. Müller helped Kleist publish *Phöbus* and the *Berliner Abendblätter*; in 1811 he entered the Austrian civil service, was employed as a diplomat and ultimately worked in the Staatskanzlei under Metternich. He died in Vienna on 17 Jan. 1829.

## Works

*Die Lehre vom Gegensatz*, 1804
*Elemente der Staatskunst*, 1809; repr. ed. J. Baxa, 1922
*Theorie der Staatshaushaltung*, 1812
*Versuche einer neuen Theorie des Geldes*, 1816; repr. ed. H. Lieser, 1922
*Von der Notwendigkeit einer theologischen Grundlage der gesamten Staatswissenschaften*, 1819
*Ausgewählte Abhandlungen*, ed. J. Baxa; 2nd ed. 1931

## Literature

J. Baxa, *Adam Müller*, 1929
H. Schröder, *Adam Müller*, 1930
L. Sauzin, *Adam-Heinrich Müller, sa vie et son œuvre*, 1937
K. Wolff, 'Staat u. Individuum bei Adam Müller', *Hist. Vierteljahrsschrift* 30 (1935)

## FRIEDRICH MÜLLER ('MALER MÜLLER')

Born 13 Jan. 1749 at Kreuznach. He was trained as a painter and engraver and enjoyed the patronage of Goethe and Dalberg. He went to Rome in 1778 and was converted to Catholicism. In 1798 he was expelled because of his anti-republican activities. King Ludwig I of Bavaria granted him a pension and appointed him court painter. His literary works fall almost entirely within the 'Sturm und Drang' era. He died in Rome on 23 April 1825.

## Works

*Der Satyr Mopsus, Idylle*, 1775
*Bacchidon und Milon, Idylle*, 1775
*Das Nusskernen*, 1776
*Balladen*, ed. M. Oeser, 1916–18
*Idyllen*, ed. O. Heuer, 1914

Literature

W. Oeser, *Maler Müller*, 1928

  id., 'Maler Müllers Stellung in der Entwicklung des musikalischen Dramas', *GRM* 40 (1940)

W. Renwanz, *Maler Müllers Lyrik und Balladendichtung*, 1922

F. A. Schmidt, *Maler Müllers dramatisches Schaffen*, diss. Göttingen, 1936

F. Meyer, *Maler-Müller-Bibliographie*, 1912

## JOHANN GOTTWERT MÜLLER

Born Hamburg 17 May 1743, often called Müller von Itzehoe after the town where he settled as a bookseller and where he died, 23 June 1828. Friend of F. Nicolai, whose 'enlightened' views he shared, collaborated on *Allgemeine dt. Bibliothek* and took over Nicolai's *Straussfedern* from Musäus. Lichtenberg admired his novels and compared him to Sterne. The best-known of them, *Siegfried von Lindenberg*, satirizes the manners of an eccentric backwoods squire and attacks literary foibles like the cult of Klopstock and the 'Geniebewegung'.

Works

*Gedichte*, 2 vols., 1770 f.

*Der Ring*, 1777

*Siegfried von Lindenberg*, 1779–81; abridged repr. ed. E. Weber, 1966

*Komische Romane*, 8 vols., 1784–91

*Die Herren von Waldheim*, 1786

*Emmerich*, 1786–9

*Sarah Reinert*, 1791; 1806

*Ferdinand*, 1809

Literature

A. Brand, *Müller von Itzehoe. Sein Leben u. seine Werke*, 1901

## WILHELM MÜLLER ('GRIECHENMÜLLER')

Born 7 Oct. 1794 in Dessau, studied philology at Berlin University. After teaching in Italy he became a teacher and later a librarian in Dessau. He is best known as the author of the

*Schöne Müllerin* and *Winterreise* cycles set to music by Schubert. Müller died in Dessau, 30 Sept. 1827.

Works
*Lieder der Griechen*, 1821–4
*Vermischte Schriften*, ed. G. Schwab, 1830
*Gedichte und Briefe*, ed. P. Wahl, 1931

Literature
F. M. Müller, *Wilhelm Müller*, 1885
H. Lohre, *Wilhelm Müller als Kritiker und Erzähler*, 1927

ADOLF MÜLLNER

Born 18 Oct. 1774 in Langendorf, near Weissenfels, where he practised as a lawyer, founded an amateur theatre and was active as a journalist. Leading practitioner of the 'fate tragedy' some of whose works were produced by Goethe in Weimar. Died 11 June 1829.

Works
*Der 29. Februar*, 1812
*Die Schuld*, 1816
*König Yngurd*, 1817
*Der Wahn*, 1818
*Die Albaneserin*, 1820
*Dramatische Werke*, 8 vols., 1828; supplementary vols. 1–4, 1830

Literature
J. Minor, *Die Schicksalstragödie in ihren Hauptvertretern*, 1883
O. Weller, *Müllner als Dramatiker*, diss. Würzburg, 1922
G. Koch, *A. Müllner als Theaterkritiker, Journalist u. lit. Organisator*, diss. Cologne, 1939 (*Die Schaubühne*, vol. 38)

THEODOR MUNDT

Leading Young German writer, born 19 Sept. 1808 in Potsdam, edited liberal journals, all of which had difficulties with the censor, held academic posts in Breslau and Berlin, but was forced to retire because of his radical views. Married the popular historical novelist Luise Mühlbach, died in Berlin, 30 Nov. 1861.

Works

*Moderne Lebenswirren*, 1834
*Madonna*, 1835
*Charlotte, ein Denkmal*, 1836
*Charaktere und Situationen*, 1837
*Die Kunst der deutschen Prosa*, 1837
*Thomas Münzer*, 1841 (novel)
*Geschichte der Gesellschaft*, 1844
*Ästhetik*, 1845; repr. ed. H. Düvel, 1966
*Allgemeine Literaturgeschichte*, 1846
*Dramaturgie*, 1848
*Die Matadore*, 1850
*Graf Mirabeau*, 1858

Literature

O. Draeger, *Mundt u. seine Beziehung zum Jungen Deutschland*, 1909
H. Knudsen, 'Mundt u. Gutzkow', *Euph* 24 (1922)
W. Grupe, *Mundts u. Kühnes Verhältnis zu Hegel u. seinen Gegnern*, diss. Halle, 1928
W. Dietze, 'Theodor Mundt u. Gustav Kühne', *Junges Dt. land u. Klassik*, 1958

JOHANN KARL AUGUST MUSÄUS

Born 29 March 1735 in Jena, where he studied; became teacher at the Gymnasium in Weimar. Musäus is a typical representative of the Enlightenment, his style is that of the Rococo. Contributed to Nicolai's *Allgemeine Deutsche Bibliothek* and *Straussfedern*; parodied Richardsonian sentimentalism as well as the physiognomic theories of Lavater. His versions of German folk-tales have a moralizing and sometimes ironical tone. He died in Weimar, 28 Oct. 1787.

Works

*Grandison der Zweite*, 3 vols., 1760–2; as *Der dt. Grandison*, 1781 f.
*Physiognomische Reisen*, 4 vols., 1778 f.
*Volksmärchen der Deutschen*, 8 vols., 1782–6; repr. ed. P. Zaunert, 1912
*Straussfedern*, 1787
*Nachgelassene Schriften*, ed. A. Kotzebue, 1791

Literature

M. Müller, *J. K. A. Musäus*, 1867

A. Ohlmer, *Musäus als satirischer Romanschriftsteller*, diss. Munich, 1912

E. Geschke, *Untersuchung über die zwei Fassungen von Musäus Grandisonroman*, diss. Königsberg, 1910

G. Stern, 'A German imitation of Fielding. Musäus' Grandison der Zweite', *CL* 10 (1958)

A. Richli, *J. K. A. Musäus. Die Volksmärchen der Deutschen*, 1957

D. Berger, 'Die Volksmärchen der Deutschen von Musäus, ein Meisterwerk der dt. Rokokodichtung', *PMLA* 69 (1954)

## BENEDIKTE NAUBERT

Born 13 Sep. 1756 in Leipzig, daughter of an eminent physician, Johann Ernst Hebenstreit, married first to Lorenz Holderieder then to Johann Georg Naubert. She died in Leipzig on 12 Jan. 1819. Naubert was an indefatigable translator and the author of numerous medieval romances.

Works

*Geschichte Emmas, Tochter Karls des Grossen*, 1785

*Amalgunde, Königin von Italien*, 1786

*Walther von Montbarry*, 1786

*Neue Volksmärchen der Deutschen*, 5 vols., 1789–93

etc., etc.

Literature

K. Schreinert, *Benedikte Naubert*, 1941

## JOHANN NEPOMUK NESTROY

Born in Vienna, 7 Dec. 1801, studied law but did not go into practice. Instead he became an opera singer and then took up an acting career. In 1831 he went to the Theater an der Wien, in 1845 to the Leopoldstädter Theater, of which he was appointed director in 1854. He retired in 1860 and lived at Ischl and in Graz. He died 25 May 1862 in Graz. His works are in the best tradition of the Vienna theatre.

Works

*Der böse Geist Lumpazivagabundus*, 1835
*Zu ebener Erde und im ersten Stock*, 1838
*Einen Jux will er sich machen*, 1844; repr. ed. W. Zentner, 1965
*Der Zerrissene*, 1845
*Judith und Holofernes*, 1849
*Freiheit in Krähwinkel*, 1949
*Sämtliche Werke*, ed. O. Rommel, F. Brukner, 1924–30
*Gesammelte Werke*, ed. O. Rommel, 1948; repr. 1962
*Werke*, ed. O. M. Fontana, 1962

Literature

W. Höllerer, 'J. N. Nestroy', *Zwischen Klassik u. Moderne*, 1958
O. Forst de Battaglia, *Johann Nestroy*, 1962
G. Seidmann, 'Johann Nestroy', *German Men of Letters*, vol. 5, ed. A. Natan, 1969
L. Langer, *Nestroy als Satiriker*, 1908
F. H. Mautner, *J. N. Nestroy und seine Kunst*, 1937
A. Hämmerle, *Komik, Satire und Humor bei Nestroy*, 1947

FRIEDRICH NICOLAI

Nicolai was born in Berlin on 18 March 1733 and trained in the booktrade for eventual employment in the family business. He showed great capacity for self-education and after becoming head of the firm in 1758 used its publishing facilities to disseminate his rationalistic views. The *Bibliothek der schönen Wissenschaften und Künste* and the *Allgemeine Deutsche Bibliothek*, which he edited, included Lessing, Moses Mendelssohn and many other distinguished writers among their contributors. Nicolai, who played a leading part in the social and intellectual life of Berlin, died on 8 Jan. 1811. The rational liberalism of this 'Prince of the Enlightenment' made him the butt of more agile spirits: Goethe ridiculed his naive materialism and anti-clericalism in the Walpurgisnacht scene of *Faust* and in the *Xenien*, while Tieck, who began his literary career as Nicolai's hack, caricatured his philistinism in *Prinz Zerbino*. Nicolai did much to discredit himself in his later years by a vehement polemic against the Kantian philosophy. However, he did not himself lack a satirical gift, his *Sebaldus Nothanker* does not lack literary merit, and the *Beschreibung einer Reise* is a monument to uncommon intellectual curiosity and powers of observation.

### Works

*Briefe über den itzigen Zustand der schönen Wissenschaften in Deutschland,* 1754

*Briefe, die neueste Literatur betreffend,* 1759–65 (with Lessing)

*Allgemeine Deutsche Bibliothek,* 107 vols., 1765–1806

*Leben und Meinungen des Herrn Magister Sebaldus Nothanker,* 1773–6

*Freuden des jungen Werthers: Leiden und Freuden Werthers des Mannes,* 1775

*Ein feiner kleiner Almanach,* 1777–8

*Beschreibung einer Reise durch Deutschland und die Schweiz im Jahre 1781,* 1783–96

*Geschichte eines dicken Mannes,* 1794

*Leben und Meinungen Sempronius Gundiberts, eines deutschen Philosophen,* 1798

*Vertraute Briefe von Adelheid S. an ihre Freundin Julie B.,* 1799

*Philosophische Abhandlungen,* 1808

### Literature

F. Meyer, *Friedrich Nicolai,* 1938

K. Aner, *Der Aufklärer Nicolai,* 1912

F. C. A. Philips, *Nicolais literarische Bestrebungen,* diss. Amsterdam, 1925

M. Sommerfeld, *Friedrich Nicolai und der Sturm und Drang,* 1912

E. Altenkrüger, *Nicolais Jugendschriften,* 1894

M. Kupfer, *Die literarische Kritik in Nicolais Allgemeiner Deutscher Bibliothek,* diss. Leipzig, 1922

R. Schwinger, *Nicolais Roman Sebaldus Nothanker,* 1897

Ernst Elias Niebergall (pseud. E. Streff)

Born 18 Jan. 1815 in Darmstadt, talented writer of dialect comedies. Died Darmstadt, 19 April 1843.

### Works

*Des Burschen Heimkehr oder Der tolle Hund,* 1837

*Datterich,* 1841; repr. 1965

*Dramatische Werke,* ed. G. Fuchs, 1894 (with biography)

*Erzählende Werke,* ed. K. Esselborn, 3 vols., 1925

Literature

K. Esselborn, *Ernst Elias Niebergall*, 1922
M. Z. v. Zobeltitz, 'Zu Niebergalls Lustspielen', *ZfdPh* 62 (1937)
W. Höllerer, 'Gutzkow, Raimund, Nestroy, Niebergall', *Zw. Klassik u. Moderne*, 1958
G. Hensel, *Rede auf Niebergall*, 1965

JEAN PAUL

'Jean Paul' was the pseudonym of Johann Paul Richter, born at Wunsiedel in the Fichtelgebirge on 21 March 1763. He spent his youth in his father's remote parsonage at Schwarzenbach, studied theology at Leipzig and after a spell as private tutor established an elementary school in Schwarzenbach, where he taught from 1790 to 1794. He subsequently led a restless life, living first with his mother in Hof and moving after her death in turn to Leipzig, Weimar, Berlin, Meiningen, Koburg and Bayreuth. In 1808 Jean Paul was granted a pension by the Prince Bishop of Mainz, Karl Theodor von Dalberg, and this was renewed by the Bavarian government until his death in Bayreuth on 14 Nov. 1825. His works are a bizarre mixture of fantasy, sentiment, humour, satirical comedy and brooding anxieties. They abound in eccentric characters, and the style and narrative technique, which owe much to Laurence Sterne, are wilfully tangled, whimsical and filled to overflowing with reference, jocular or learned, that testifies to the author's capacity for acquiring 'curious' information and impressions. He combines the idealism and enlightened didacticism of Weimar Classicism with the fantasy characteristic of the Romantics. His practical interest in education is reflected in novels that show the influence of Rousseau and Goethe's *Wilhelm Meister*. Goethe detested Jean Paul's unruly style, but Herder ranked him as a poet superior even to Goethe; he was much read during his life-time, but his popularity faded immediately after his death until it was revived by the Young Germans, who saw him as a champion of the poor and a radical educational reformer. His influence affected many later novelists, including G. Freytag, F. T. Vischer, G. Keller, W. Raabe, F. Reuter and H. Seidel.

Works

*Grönländische Prozesse*, 1783–4
*Auswahl aus des Teufels Papieren*, 1789
*Die unsichtbare Loge*, 1793
*Hesperus oder 45 Hundsposttage*, 1795
*Leben des Quintus Fixlein*, 1796
*Blumen-, Frucht- und Dornenstücke oder Ehestand, Tod und Hochzeit des Armenadvokaten Fr. St. Siebenkäs im Reichsmarktflecken Kuhschnappel*, 1796–7
*Der Jubel-Senior*, 1797
*Das Kampaner-Tal oder Über die Unsterblichkeit der Seele*, 1797
*Palingenesien*, 1798
*Titan*, 1800–3
*Vorschule der Ästhetik*, 1804
*Flegeljahre*, 1804–5
*Levana oder Erziehungslehre*, 1807
*Des Feldpredigers Schmelzle Reise nach Flätz*, 1809; repr. ed. J. Smeed, 1966
*Doktor Katzenbergers Badereise*, 1809
*Poetische Fastenpredigten während Deutschlands Marterwoche*, 1817
*Der Komet oder Nikolaus Marggraf*, 1820–2
*Selina oder Über die Unsterblichkeit der Seele*, 1827
*Der Papierdrache*, 1845 (ed. E. Förster)


Literature

J. Alt, *Jean Paul*, 1925
W. Harich, *Jean Paul*, 1925
M. Kommerell, *Jean Paul*, 1933; 3rd ed. 1957
J. Smeed, *Jean Paul's Dreams*, 1966
H. Keith, *Spiel und Spiegelung bei Jean Paul*, diss. Munich, 1965
R. Grötzebach, *Humor und Satire bei Jean Paul*, diss. Berlin, 1966
W. Harich, 'Satire und Politik beim jungen Jean Paul', *SuF* 19 (1967)
M. Kommerell, *Jean Pauls Verhältnis zu Rousseau*, 1925
J. Cerny, *Sterne, Hippel und Jean Paul*, 1904
B. Brandi-Dohrn, *Der Einfluss Laurence Sternes auf Jean Paul*, diss. Munich, 1964
E. Engel, *Jean Pauls Schulmeisterlein Wuz*, 1962
H. Bach, *Jean Pauls Hesperus*, 1929
R. Rohde, *Jean Pauls Titan*, 1920

E. Berend, *Jean Pauls Ästhetik*, 1909

P. H. Neumann, *Jean Pauls Flegeljahre*, *Pal* 245 (1966)

W. Rehm, *Jean Paul und Dostojewski*, 1962

J. Smeed, 'Jean Paul und die Tradition des theophrastischen Charakters', *Jean Paul Jahrbuch* 1 (1966)

E. Berend, *Jean Paul-Bibliographie*, 1963

E. Fuhrmann, 'Jean Paul-Bibliographie 1963–5', *Jean Paul-Jb.* 1 (1966)

G. Wilkending, *J. Pauls Sprachauffassung in ihrem Verhältnis zu seiner Ästhetik*, 1968

Cf. the following publications passim.:

*Hesperus. Blätter der Jean Paul-Gesellschaft*, 1951 ff.

*Fs. Eduard Berend*, 1959

*Jean Paul-Sonderheft*, *EG* 18 (1963)

*Jahrbuch der Jean-Paul-Gesellschaft*, 1966 ff.

## Johann Heinrich Pestalozzi

Born 12 Jan. 1746 in Zürich, educational reformer influenced by Rousseau's ideas and the Classical notion of 'Humanität'. Most of Pestalozzi's practical projects failed but his theories, deployed in didactic stories, remained influential. He died in Brugg, 17 Feb. 1827.

### Works

*Lienhard u. Gertrud*, 3 vols., 1781–5

*Wie Gertrud ihre Kinder lehrt*, 1801

*Buch der Mutter*, 1803

*Meine Lebensschicksale*, 1826

*Gesamtausgabe*, 15 vols., 1819–26

*Gesammelte Werke*, 10 vols., ed. E. Bosshardt et al., 1944 ff.

### Literature

F. Medicus, *Pestalozzis Leben*, 1927

W. Leibersberger, *Pestalozzis socialpolitische Anschauungen*, 1927

A. Buchenau, *Pestalozzi-Studien*, 1927 ff.

K. Silber, *Pestalozzi: the man and his work*, 1960

J. Benrubi, 'Pestalozzi u. Rousseau', *DVLG* 11 (1933)

A. Stein, *Pestalozzi u. die Kantische Philosophie*, 1927

E. Spranger, *Pestalozzis Denkformen*, 1959

H. Hoffmann, *Die Religion im Leben u. Denken Pestalozzis*, 1944
I. Rappard, *Die Bedeutung der Mutter bei J. H. Pestalozzi*, 1961
A. Israel, *Pestalozzi-Bibl.*, 3 vols., 1903–4
W. Klinke, *Pestalozzi-Bibl.*, 1923

## LUISE PETERS (LUISE OTTO-PETERS; OTTO STERN)

Born Luise Otto 26 March 1819 at Meissen; agitated for women's rights in her *Frauenzeitung*, married the radical writer August Peters in 1865, became president of the 'Allgemeiner Deutscher Frauenverein' which she had founded. Novels of social criticism, but also two opera librettos, *Die Nibelungen* and *Theodor Körner*. Died 19 March 1895 in Leipzig.

Works
*Schloss und Fabrik*, 1840
*Ludwig der Kellner*, 1843
*Privatgeschichten der Weltgeschichte*, 6 vols., 1868–82
*Frauenleben im Deutschen Reich*, 1876
*Das erste Vierteljahrhundert des Allgemeinen Frauenvereins*, 1890
*Mein Lebensgang*, 1893 (poems)

Literature
A. Schmidt, H. Rösch, *Luise Otto-Peters*, 1898
H. Lange, *Luise Otto-Peters u. die erste dt. Frauenzeitung*, 1927
G. Bäumer, *Luise Otto-Peters*, 1939
L. Mallachow, 'Biographische Erläuterungen zu dem lit. Werk von L. Otto-Peters', *WB* 9 (1963)

## AUGUST GRAF VON PLATEN-HALLERMÜNDE

Born in Ansbach, 24 Oct. 1796. He entered the Bavarian Kadettenkorps in Munich in 1806 and took part in the campaign against France. He was granted extended leave and from 1819 to 1826 studied law, philosophy and science at Würzburg and Erlangen, attending lectures by Schelling and G. H. Schubert. He became librarian in Erlangen in 1826 and subsequently went to Italy which became his home except for brief visits to Munich between 1832 and 1834. At different times he lived in Florence,

Rome, Venice and Sicily. He died in Syracuse on 5 Dec. 1835 while seeking refuge from an outbreak of cholera in Florence.

Works
*Ghaselen*, 1821
*Lyrische Balladen*, 1821
*Neue Ghaselen*, 1823
*Sonette aus Venedig*, 1825
*Die verhängnisvolle Gabel*, 1826 (drama)
*Gedichte*, 1828
*Der romantische Ödipus*, 1829 (drama)
*Die Abassiden*, 1835 (epic)
*Sämtliche Werke*, ed. M. Koch, E. Petzet, 1910
*Dichtungen*, ed. G. Voigt, 1957
*Gedichte*, ed. C. Fischer, 1958

Literature
M. Koch, *Platens Leben und Schaffen*, 1909
R. Schlösser, *August Graf von Platen*, 2 vols., 1910
W. D. Williams, 'August von Platen', *German Men of Letters*, vol. 5, ed. A. Natan, 1969
K. Steigelmann, *Platens Ästhetik*, 1925
H. L. Stoltenberg, *Platens Oden und Festgesänge*, 1929
V. Jirát, *Platens Stil*, 1932
W. Heuss, *Platens dramatisches Werk*, 1935
F. Redenbacher, *Platen-Bibliographie*, 1936
A Platen-Gesellschaft, founded in 1925, has its seat in Erlangen and has published a number of papers on Platen.

KARL ANTON POSTL: see CHARLES SEALSFIELD

ROBERT PRUTZ

Scholar and writer of liberal persuasion, born 30 May 1816 in Stettin, charged with lèse-majesté because of a dramatic satire, *Die politische Wochenstube*, pardoned by Frederick William IV on intercession of A. v. Humboldt. Founded the periodical *Deutsches Museum* in 1851. Was Professor of German Literature in Halle from 1849. Translated the Danish dramatist Holberg. Died 21 June 1872 in Stettin.

Works
*Die politische Wochenstube*, 1843
*Das Engelchen*, 1851 (novel)
*Felix*, 1851 (novel)
*Der Musikantenturm*, 1855 (novel)
*Helene, ein Frauenleben*, 1856 (novel)
Also political lyric

Literature
E. Hohenstatter, *Über die politischen Romane von R. Prutz*, diss.
   Munich, 1918
K. H. Wiese, *Prutz' Ästhetik u. Literaturkritik*, diss. Halle, 1934

HERMANN LUDWIG FÜRST VON PÜCKLER-MUSKAU

Born in Schloss Muskau in Saxony on 30 Oct. 1785 and
died in Schloss Branitz near Kottbus, 4 Feb. 1871. He was
educated at Pietist institutions and studied law in Leipzig. He
entered the Saxon army and resigned his commission in 1804.
After travelling in France and Italy he resumed his military
career first in the Russian army and later in the service of the
Duke of Sachsen-Weimar. After the end of the Napoleonic wars
he travelled in England, France, Algiers, Egypt, Asia Minor and
Greece. He is best known for his accounts of these travels, his
writings on landscape gardening (a subject he took up after his
visits to England) and his diaries which he published under the
title *Briefe eines Verstorbenen*.

Works
*Briefe eines Verstorbenen*, 1830
*Andeutungen über Landschaftsgärtnerei*, 1834; repr. 1939
*Jugendwanderungen*, 1835
*Vorletzter Weltgang von Semilasso*, 1835
*Semilasso in Afrika*, 1836
*Aus Mehemed Alis Reich*, 1844
*Die Rückkehr*, 1846

Literature
F. Zahn and R. Kalwa, *Fürst H. v. Pückler-Muskau als Garten-
   künstler*, 1928

A. Ehrhard, *Le Prince de Pückler-Muskau,* 1929
E. M. Butler, *The tempestuous Prince,* 1929

## IMMANUEL JAKOB PYRA

Born in Kottbus, 25 July 1715, and studied theology at
Halle. He earned his living as a private tutor and collaborated
with S. G. Lange in writing volumes of poetry. He also wrote
*Der Tempel der wahren Dichtkunst* (1737) in imitation of Pope's
*The Temple of Fame,* and in 1744 published an attack on Gottsched
under the title 'Erweis, dass die Gottschedianische Sekte den
Geschmack verderbe'. Pyra died in Berlin, 14 July 1744.

Works
See under S. G. LANGE

Literature
G. Wanniek, *J. Pyra und sein Einfluss auf die dt. Literatur des
18. Jhs.,* 1882
W. P. Hanson, 'Lange, Pyra and "Anacreontische Tändeleien",'
*GLL* 18 (1964/5)

## WILHELM RAABE

Born 8 Sep. 1831 at Eschershausen near Holzminden, educated
at the Gymnasium in Wolfenbüttel, apprenticed to the book-
trade in Magdeburg. Two apparently aimless years in Berlin
culminated in his first novel, *Die Chronik der Sperlingsgasse,* which
pictures his own frugal existence. In 1856 he returned to Wolfenbüttel, where he became a free-lance journalist, employed mainly
by *Westermanns Monatshefte.* After extensive travels through
Germany and Austria he married and settled in Stuttgart, where
he lived from 1862 until 1870. Disappointed by his relative lack of
success he moved to Braunschweig and spent the remaining forty
years of his life there until his death on 15 Nov. 1910. Raabe's
mature novels represent the victory of equanimity and sound
good-nature over the malevolence of man and fate alike. He
appeals to inner values threatened by the onrush of commercialism and the vanity of modern society, but his austere and often
sombre outlook is illuminated by shafts of humour. Raabe's deep

historical sense and his attachment to his native Lower Saxony are manifest in nearly all of his stories. His fondness for eccentric character and on occasion the Jean Paulesque involved whimsicality of his style give his works the superficial appearance of Biedermeier idylls, but his use of symbolic incident, the profound ambiguities of his language and his intricate narrative technique increasingly attract contemporary critics.

## Works

*Die Chronik der Sperlingsgasse*, 1856
*Ein Frühling*, 1858
*Die Kinder von Finkenrode*, 1859
*Nach dem grossen Kriege*, 1861
*Verworrenes Leben*, 1862 (short stories)
*Unseres Herrgotts Kanzlei*, 1862
*Die Leute aus dem Walde*, 1863
*Der Hungerpastor*, 1864
*Abu Telfan oder die Heimkehr vom Mondgebirge*, 1868
*Der Regenbogen*, 1869 (short stories)
*Der Schüdderump*, 1870
*Meister Autor*, 1874
*Horacker*, 1876
*Wunnigel*, 1878
*Krähenfelder Geschichten*, 1878
*Deutscher Adel*, 1880
*Alte Nester*, 1880
*Das Horn von Wanza*, 1881
*Prinzessin Fisch*, 1882
*Pfisters Mühle*, 1884
*Unruhige Gäste*, 1886
*Im alten Eisen*, 1887
*Das Odfeld*, 1889
*Stopfkuchen*, 1891
*Die Akten des Vogelsangs*, 1896
*Gesammelte Erzählungen*, 4 vols., 1896–1900
*Hastenbeck*, 1899
*Altershausen*, 1911
*Gedichte*, 1912
*Sämtliche Werke*, 18 vols., 1913–16; 15 vols., 1938
*Braunschweiger Ausgabe*, ed. K. Hoppe, 1951 ff.

## Literature

W. Fehse, *Wilhelm Raabe. Sein Leben u. seine Werke*, 1937

H. Pongs, *Wilhelm Raabe. Leben u. Werk*, 1958

S. Hajek, *Der Mensch u. die Welt im Werk Wilhelm Raabes*, 1950

G. Mayer, *Die geistige Entwicklung Wilhelm Raabes*, 1960

A. Helmers, *Wilhelm Raabe*, 1968

J. H. Reid, 'Wilhelm Raabe', *German Men of Letters*, vol. 5, ed. A. Natan, 1969

E. Klopfenstein, *Erzähler u. Leser bei W. Raabe*, 1969

B. Fairley, *Wilhelm Raabe. An introduction to his novels*, 1961

H. Meyer, *Der Sonderling in der dt. Dichtung*, 1943; 2nd ed., 1963

R. Pascal, *The German novel: Studies*, 1956

H. Helmers, *Die bildenden Mächte in den Romanen Wilhelm Raabes*, 1960

G. Lukács, *Dt. Realisten des 19. Jhs.*, 1951

F. Martini, 'Wilhelm Raabe u. das 20. Jh.', *ZfdPh* 58 (1933)

F. Martini, 'Das Problem des Realismus im 19. Jh. u. die Dichtung Wilhelm Raabes', *Euph* 30 (1935)

H. Meyer, 'Raum u. Zeit in Wilhelm Raabes Erzählkunst', *DVLG* 27 (1953)

H. Oppermann, 'Zum Problem der Zeit bei Wilhelm Raabe', *Jb. der Raabe-Gesellschaft*, 1964

R. Pascal, 'The reminiscence technique in Raabe', *MLR* 49 (1954)

F. Meyen, *Wilhelm Raabe-Bibliographie*, 1955

K. Hoppe (ed.), *Jb. der Raabe-Gesellschaft*, 1960 ff.

## GOTTLIEB WILHELM RABENER

Born at Wachau near Leipzig, 17 Sep. 1714. He studied law and philosophy and entered the civil service as a tax inspector. He is one of the foremost satirists of the period. He died in Dresden, 22 March 1771.

## Works

*Sammlung satirischer Schriften*, 1751–5

## Literature

P. Richter, *Rabener und Liscow*, 1884

A. Biergann, *G. W. Rabeners Satiren*, 1961

FERDINAND RAIMUND

Born in Vienna, 1 June 1790. He was apprenticed to a baker from 1804 until 1808 and then took up acting on different stages in the provinces. In 1813 he joined the 'Josephsstädter Theater', in 1817 the 'Leopoldstädter Theater' of which he became the director in 1828. He gave guest performances in Berlin, Munich and Hamburg. His literary career began in 1823. He retired to the country in 1834 and committed suicide on 5 Sep. 1836 fearing that he would contract hydrophobia after having been bitten by a dog. Raimund considerably enlarged the scope of Austrian dramatic literature while remaining true to the tradition of the Vienna stage.

Works

*Das Mädchen aus der Feenwelt oder der Bauer als Millionär*, 1826
*Der Alpenkönig und der Menschenfeind*, 1828
*Der Verschwender*, 1834
*Sämtliche Werke*, ed. F. Brukner and E. Castle, 1924-34
*Werke*, ed. F. Schreyvogel, 1960

Literature

K. Fuhrmann, *Raimunds Kunst und Charakter*, 1913
R. Smekal, *Grillparzer und Raimund*, 1920
A. Moller, *F. Raimund*, 1923
K. Vancsa, *F. Raimund*, 1936
H. Kindermann, *Raimund*, 1940
W. Erdmann, *F. Raimunds dichterische Entwicklung, Persönlichkeit und Lebensschicksal*, 1944
W. Höllerer, 'F. Raimund', *Zwischen Klassik und Moderne*, 1958

ERNST RAUPACH (pseud. E. LEUTNER)

Popular romantic dramatist, born 21 May 1784 at Straupitz, near Liegnitz, died 18 March 1852 in Berlin. His 117 published plays include almost every form of dramatic entertainment from pseudo-Shakespearean and Schillerian historical tragedy to low comedy. Raupach wrote no fewer than 16 Hohenstaufen dramas. His *Der Müller und sein Kind* (1835) has attained the status of a 'Volksstück'.

GL—P

Literature
D. Raupach, *Ernst Raupach*, 1853
E. Wolff, *Raupachs Hohenstaufendichtungen*, diss. Leipzig, 1912
K. Kohlweyer, *Raupach u. die Romantik*, diss. Göttingen, 1923
J. M. Leaver, 'Hebbel's "Genoveva" and "Nibelungen" and Ernst Raupach', *MLR* 55 (1960)

## PHILIPP JOSEPH (VON) REHFUES

Born 2 Oct. 1779, son of the Bürgermeister of Tübingen, spent much time in Italy during his youth, became court librarian in Stuttgart in 1806. Rehfues played an important part in founding the University of Bonn and became its 'Curator'. His determined opposition to Roman Catholic influences led eventually to his retirement in 1842. He died in Bonn on 21 Oct. 1843. Rehfues was an influential mediator between Germany and Italy. His historical novels are modelled on those of Sir Walter Scott.

Works
*Briefe aus Italien*, 1809
*Die Brautfahrt in Spanien*, 1811 (comic novel)
*Scipio Cicala*, 1832; repr. ed. L. Passarge, 1888 (historical novel)
*Die Belagerung des Kastells von Gozzo*, 1834
*Die neue Medea*, 1836
*Denkwürdigkeiten des spanischen Hauptmanns Bernal Diaz del Castilla*, 1838

Literature
I. E. Heilig, *Philipp Joseph von Rehfues*, diss. Breslau, 1941

## FRITZ REUTER

Born 7 Nov. 1810 in Stavenhagen, Mecklenburg-Schwerin, studied in Rostock and Jena but was arrested in Berlin in 1833 and charged with complicity in the alleged conspiracy of the Burschenschaften. The death sentence passed on him was commuted to thirty years' imprisonment, but Reuter was pardoned in 1840 by the Grand Duke of Mecklenburg. He led an unstable life as farmer, portrait-painter and private tutor until he ventured to publish his first verses and tales in the local Low

German dialect. His marriage to Luise Kunze in 1851 seems to have saved him from incipient dipsomania and provided the incentive for a literary success that was recognized eventually in the conferment of an honorary doctorate on him by the University of Rostock in 1863. In the same year Reuter moved to Eisenach, and, apart from a journey to Greece and the Holy Land, lived there until his death on 12 July 1874.

Works

*Läuschen un Rimels*, 1853; 2nd series 1858
*De Reis' na Belligen*, 1855 (comic verse tale)
*Keen Hüsing*, 1857 (verse epic)
*Olle Kamellen*, vol. 1, 1859
*Hanne Nüte un de lütte Pudel*, 1860 (verse fable)
*Schurr-Murr*, 1861 (short stories)
*Ut mine Festungstid* (*Olle Kamellen*, vol. 2), 1862
*Ut mine Stromtid* (*Olle Kamellen*, vols. 3–5), 1865
*Dörchläuchting* (*Olle Kamellen*, vol. 6)
*De mecklenbörgschen Montecchi un Capuletti oder De Reis' na Kon-
    stantinopel*, 1868
*Urgeschicht von Mecklenborg*, 1874
*Sämtliche Werke*, 13 vols., 1863–8
*Nachgelassene Schriften*, 2 vols., ed. A. Wilbrandt, 1874–5

Literature

K. T. Gaedertz, *Reuter-Studien*, 1890
K. T. Gaedertz, *Aus F. Reuters jungen und alten Tagen*, 3 vols.,
    1897–1901
K. T. Gaedertz, *Im Reiche Reuters*, 1905
J. Hunger, *Fritz Reuter. Lebensbild*, 1952
F. Griese, *Fritz Reuter. Leben u. Werk*, 1938; 3rd ed., 1960
J. S. Andrews, 'The reception of Fritz Reuter in Victorian
    England', *MLR* 56 (1961)
I. Barnikol, 'Fritz Reuter-Bibliographie', *Fritz Reuter, Fs. zum
    150. Geburtstag*, ed. Reuter-Komitee der DDR, 1960

WILHELM HEINRICH RIEHL

Author of an ethnic theory of sociology based on historical study of the German people and illustrated in realistic 'kulturgeschicht-

liche Novellen'. Born in Biberich (Rhein) 6 May 1823, studied
theology and history and, after experience as a journalist, became
director of Wiesbaden theatre, ultimately, in 1859, professor of
cultural history in Munich. He was a delegate to the Frankfurt
Parliament of 1848–9, but his mild Young German sentiments
soon gave way to a chauvinistic conservatism that endeared his
work to the National Socialists. He died 16 Nov. 1897.

Works

*Die Naturgeschichte des deutschen Volks als Grundlage einer deutschen
    Sozialpolitik*, 1851–69; repr. 1925–30; ed. G. Ipsen, 1935,
    repr. 1939, 1944
*Kulturgeschichtliche Novellen*, 1856
*Musikalische Charakterköpfe*, 1853 ff.
*Die Pfälzer*, 1857
*Die deutsche Arbeit*, 1861
*Geschichten aus alter Zeit*, 1862 ff.
*Neues Novellenbuch*, 1867
*Am Feierabend*, 1880
*Lebensrätsel*, 1888
*Religiöse Studien eines Weltkindes*, 1894
*Geschichten und Novellen*, 7 vols., 1898 ff.; repr. 1923

Literature

V. v. Geramb, *W. H. Riehl: Leben und Wirken*, 1954
M. Janke, *W. H. Riehls Kunst der Novelle*, diss. Breslau, 1918
K. Ruprecht, *Riehls kulturgeschichtliche Novellen mit Berücksichtigung
    ihres Verhältnisses zur Quelle*, diss. Königsberg, 1936

JOHANN FRIEDRICH ROCHLITZ

Born 12 Feb. 1770 in Leipzig, where he studied at the University.
Founded *Leipziger Allgemeine Musikalische Zeitung*. Wrote short
stories and plays of an improving sort. Died 16 Dec. 1842 in
Leipzig.

Works

*Lustspiele für Privattheater*, 1794
*Amaliens Freuden und Leiden*, 1795
*Erinnerungen zur Beförderung einer rechtmässigen Lebensklugheit in
    Erzählungen*, 4 vols., 1798–1800

*Charaktere interessanter Menschen*, 4 vols., 1799–1803 (short stories)
*Familienleben*, 2 vols., 1801–3
*Lustspiele*, 1803
*Glycine*, 1805
*Kleine Romane u. Erzählungen*, 1807
*Neue Erzählungen*, 1816
*Ausgewählte Schriften*, 6 vols., 1821 f.

Literature
A. Stern, *Friedrich Rochlitz*, 1893


PETER ROSEGGER

Born 31 July 1843 at Krieglach in Styria, died there 26 June 1918. The son of poor peasants, he received a rudimentary education and mainly taught himself. In 1864 he became a bookseller in Laibach and from 1865 to 1869 attended an academy in Graz. In 1870 he won a scholarship and for two years travelled in Germany, Holland, Switzerland and Italy. Later he settled in Graz where he did most of his writing and edited the journal *Heimgarten*. He was a highly popular writer of humorous, sentimental and didactic tales dealing realistically with life in his native Styria.

Works
*Zither und Hackbrett*, 1869
*Schriften des Waldschulmeisters*, 1875
*Der Gottsucher*, 1883
*Jakob der Letzte*, 1888
*Peter Mayr*, 1893
*Das ewige Licht*, 1897
*Gesammelte Werke*, 1914–16

Literature
J. Nadler, *Peter Rosegger*, 1923
F. Pock, *Rosegger. Ein Lebensbild*, 1943
O. Janda, *Peter Rosegger. Das Leben in seinen Briefen*, 1948
R. Latzke, *Der ältere u. der jüngere Rosegger*, 1953

430     SELECT BIBLIOGRAPHY

JOHANN LEONHARD ROST ('MELETAON')

Born 14 Feb. 1688 in Nürnberg, studied in Leipzig and Jena,
returned to his native city in 1712; died 22 March 1727. Besides
scientific works on astronomy he published at least nine 'galant'
novels, taking Bohse and Hunold as his models.

Works
*Die getreue Bellandra*, 1707
*Die unglückliche Atalanta*, 1708
*Die türkische Helena*, 1710
*Der verliebte Eremit*, 1711
*Die durchlauchtige Prinzessin Tamestris aus Egypten*, 1712
*Die Helden- u. Liebes-Geschichte dieser Zeiten*, 1715

Literature
H. Singer, *Der galante Roman*, 1961

FRIEDRICH RÜCKERT (pseud. FREIMUND RAIMAR)

Born at Schweinfurt in Bavaria, 16 May 1788. He studied law
and philology at Würzburg and Heidelberg from 1805 to 1808.
In 1811 he began lecturing on Greek and Oriental mythology at
Jena, taught at a school in Hanau and then travelled in Italy.
In 1818 he went to Vienna to study Oriental languages under
J. v. Hammer-Purgstall. He became Professor of Oriental
philology at Erlangen in 1826, and was elected to a similar post
in Berlin in 1841. He retired to his estate near Koburg in 1848
and died there on 31 Jan. 1866.

Works
*Deutsche Gedichte*, 1814
*Die Makamen des Hariri in freier Nachbildung*, 1826–37
*Die Weisheit des Brahmanen*, 1836–9
*Saul und David*, 1843 (drama)
*Kaiser Heinrich der Vierte*, 1844 (drama)
*Christofero Colombo*, 1845 (drama)
*Kindertotenlieder*, 1872
*Gesammelte poetische Werke*, ed. H. Rückert, 1881–2; ed. G. Ellinger,
    1897
Selections, ed. J. Kühn, 1959

Literature
F. Muncker, *Friedrich Rückert*, 1890
G. Voigt, *Rückerts Gedankenlyrik*, 1891
H. Behr, *Zeit-Lyrik Rückerts, 1848–66*, diss. Greifswald, 1937
R. Ambros, *Rückert als Dramatiker*, 1922
M. Duttle, *Rückerts Verskunst*, 1937
H. Prang, *Friedrich Rückert. Geist und Form der Sprache*, 1963

## FERDINAND VON SAAR

Born in Vienna, 30 Sep. 1833. He was a cadet in the Imperial army but resigned his commission in 1859, since when he lived as a free-lance writer alternately in Vienna and on estates in Moravia. He contracted an incurable disease and committed suicide on 24 July 1906.

Works
*Kaiser Heinrich IV*, 1867 (tragedy)
*Gedichte*, 1881
*Wiener Elegien*, 1893
*Sämtliche Werke*, ed. J. Minor, 1909
*Auswahl aus dem lyrischen Werk*, 1962
Correspondence with Marie Fürstin zu Hohenlohe, ed. A. Bettelheim, 1910
Correspondence with Marie von Ebner-Eschenbach, ed. H. Kindermann, 1957

Literature
K. Pfitzer, *Ferdinand von Saars Lyrik*, 1930
M. Lukas, *Ferdinand von Saar*, 1947
H. Kretzschmer, *Ferdinand v. Saar. Eine Zusammenstellung der seit seinem Tode erschienenen Ausgaben seiner Schriften u. der Literatur über ihn*, 1965

## MORITZ GOTTLIEB SAPHIR

Born Lovas-Berény, near Budapest, 8 Feb. 1795, originally called Moses, converted to Christianity in 1832. Journalist and critic, famed and feared for his mordant wit, active in Berlin, Vienna and Munich; one of the founders of 'Der Tunnel über der Spree'. Died 5 Sep. 1858 in Baden, near Vienna.

Works
*Poetische Erstlinge,* 1821
*Poesien,* 1824
*Humoristische Abende,* 1830
*Humoristische Damenbibliothek,* 6 vols., 1838–41
*Konversationslexikon für Geist, Witz und Humor,* 5 vols., 1851 f.
*Schriften,* 10 vols., 1826 f.; 26 vols., 1886–8

Literature
K. Glossy, 'Saphir', *Österreichische Rundschau* 16 (1908)
S. Kösterich, *Saphirs Prosastil,* diss. Frankfurt, 1934
I. Müller, *Saphir in München,* diss. Munich, 1940
W. Zitzenbacher (ed.), *Moritz Gottlieb Saphir: Halbedelstein des Anstosses,* 1965

## ADOLF FRIEDRICH, GRAF VON SCHACK (pseud. FELIX ADOLPHI)

Born 2 Aug. 1815 in Schwerin, widely travelled and cultured diplomat, patron of the arts who founded the Schack-Galerie in Munich; translator of Spanish and Persian poetry, author of lyric, drama and tales in the Classical taste. Died 14 April 1894 in Rome.

Works
*Gedichte,* 1867
*Lothar,* 1872 (epic)
*Nächte des Orients,* 1874 (epic)
*Die Pisaner,* 1876 (drama)
*Die Plejaden,* 1881 (epic)
*Lotosblätter,* 1882
*Ein halbes Jahrhundert,* 1887 (memoirs)
*Geschichte der Normannen in Sizilien,* 1889
*Gesammelte Werke,* 6 vols., 1882–3; 3rd ed., 10 vols., 1897–9

Literature
F. W. Rogge, *Graf A. F. v. Schack,* 1885
W. J. Mannsen, *Schack,* 1888
M. Armi, 'Graf Schack u. der Orient', *Germ. Stud.* 154 (1934)
E. Walter, *Schack als Übersetzer,* diss. Breslau, 1907
O. Schoen, *Gehalt u. Gestalt im dramatischen Schaffen des Grafen Schack,* diss. Breslau, 1938

JOSEPH VIKTOR (VON) SCHEFFEL

Born 16 Feb. 1826 in Karlsruhe and died there, 9 April 1886. He studied law in Munich, Heidelberg and Berlin between 1843 and 1847. After travelling in Italy he gave up a legal post he had held in Säckingen and in 1856 went to Munich where he associated with members of the 'Münchener Dichterkreis'. From 1857 to 1859 he was librarian in Donaueschingen and from 1864 lived in Karlsruhe.

Works
*Der Trompeter von Säckingen,* 1854
*Ekkehard,* 1855
*Frau Aventiure,* 1863
*Gaudeamus,* 1868 (poems)
*Gesammelte Werke,* ed. J. Proelss, 1907; ed. F. Panzer, 1925
Correspondence with Paul Heyse, ed. C. Höfer, 1932

Literature
J. Proelss, *Scheffels Leben und Dichten,* 1887
W. Klinke, *Scheffels Lebensbild in Briefen,* 1947
A. Breitner, *J. V. v. Scheffel u. seine Literatur. Prodromos einer Scheffel-Bibl.,* 1912
M. Lechner, *J. V. v. Scheffel. Eine Analyse seines Werkes u. Publikums,* diss. Munich, 1962

FRIEDRICH WILHELM SCHELLING

Born 27 Jan. 1775 in Leonberg, Württemberg, fellow-student of Hegel and Hölderlin at the Tübingen Stift, appointed professor in Jena in 1798, subsequently professor in Würzburg (1803), Munich (1827) and Berlin (1841). Died in Ragaz, Switzerland, 20 Aug. 1854. It was in Jena that Schelling first met the leading Romantics, including A. W. Schlegel, whose wife, Karoline, he married in 1803 after her divorce. Schelling was one of the most dynamic thinkers of the Romantic era. The interest in natural science which brought him close to Goethe inspired the 'Natur-philosophie' of his youth, which was succeeded by an 'Identitäts-philosophie' that postulated the common ground of subject and object in the Absolute. In his later years Schelling developed a philosophy which stressed the organic unity of religion, art and social life. He placed throughout great emphasis on art as 'das einzig wahre und ewige Organon der Philosophie' and himself possessed literary and critical talent, so that his influence on literary development was considerable.

Works

*Über die Möglichkeit u. Form der Philosophie überhaupt*, 1794
*Vom Ich als Prinzip der Philosophie*, 1795
*Ideen zu einer Philosophie der Natur*, 1797
*Von der Weltseele*, 1798
*Erster Entwurf eines Systems der Naturphilosophie*, 1799
*System des transzendentalen Idealismus*, 1800
*Darstellung des Systems meiner Philosophie*, 1801
*Bruno oder über das göttliche u. natürliche Prinzip der Dinge*, 1802
*Philosophie der Kunst* (lectures 1802 f.), 1809
*Philosophie u. Religion*, 1804
*Philosophische Untersuchungen über das Wesen der menschlichen Freiheit*, 1809
*Philosophie der Mythologie*, 1842
*Philosophie der Offenbarung*, 1854
*Gesamtausgabe*, ed. M. Schröter, 12 vols., 1927 ff.

Literature

H. Zeltner, *Schelling*, 1954
L. Noack, *Schelling u. die Philosophie der Romantik*, 1859
A. Allwohn, *Schelling u. die Romantik*, 1925
K. Klein, *Die Universalität des Geistes im Lebenswerk Goethes u. Schellings*, 1934
E. Staiger, *Der Geist der Liebe u. das Schicksal: Schelling, Hegel u. Hölderlin*, 1935
E. Staiger, *Das Apollinische u. das Dionysische bei Nietzsche u. Schelling*, 1935
G. Schneeberger, *F. W. Schelling. Eine Bibl.*, 1954

## MAX VON SCHENKENDORF

Born Tilsit 11 Dec. 1783, died Koblenz 11 Dec. 1817. Romantic poet whose patriotic lyric (e.g. 'Freiheit, die ich meine', 'Wenn

alle untreu werden') roused German youth during the War of
Liberation against Napoleon.

Works
*Christliche Gedichte*, 1814
*Gedichte*, 1815
*Poetischer Nachlass*, 1832
*Sämtliche Gedichte*, 1837
*Werke*, ed. E. Gross, 1910

Literature
E. v. Klein, *Schenkendorf*, diss. Vienna, 1908
P. Czygan, 'Neue Beiträge zu Schenkendorfs Leben, Denken u.
 Dichten', *Euph* 13, 14 (1906–7)
G. Köhler, *Die Lyrik Schenkendorfs*, diss. Marburg, 1915


JOHANN CHRISTOPH FRIEDRICH (VON) SCHILLER

Born at Marbach in Württemberg 10 Nov. 1759, went to school
in Ludwigsburg. From 1773 until 1780 he studied law and
medicine at the 'Karlsschule' there by order of Duke Karl Eugen.
In 1780 he became an army doctor with very poor pay and it was
at this time that he wrote *Die Räuber*. He attended the first
performance in Mannheim without leave and was accordingly
forbidden by the Duke to do any more writing. In 1782 he fled to
Mannheim and from December of that year stayed on the estate
of Henriette von Wolzogen near Bauerbach. He returned to
Mannheim in July 1783 and was appointed 'Theaterdichter',
a post from which he retired in 1785. An invitation from
Christian Gottfried Körner took him to Gohlis near Leipzig and
later to Dresden. He went to Weimar in 1787 and met Herder
and Wieland while Goethe was in Italy. In January 1789 he was
appointed Professor of History at Jena university. He married
Charlotte von Lengefeld in February, 1790. After a serious illness
in 1791 (from which he never completely recovered) he visited
Körner in Dresden and his homeland in 1793. His friendship with
Goethe began in 1794. He worked in Jena until 1799 when he
transferred to Weimar. The remainder of his life was spent quietly
there except for a journey to Berlin in 1804. He died on 9 May
1805.

Works

*Die Räuber*, 1777–80
*Fiesko*, 1782
*Kabale und Liebe*, 1782–3
*Don Karlos*, 1783–7
*Der Verbrecher aus verlorener Ehre*, 1785 (story)
*Der Geisterseher*, 1788 (novel)
*Wallenstein*, 1796–9
*Maria Stuart*, 1800
*Die Jungfrau von Orleans*, 1801
*Macbeth*, 1801 (translation)
*Die Braut von Messina*, 1802
*Turandot*, 1802 (translation from Gozzi)
*Wilhelm Tell*, 1804
*Demetrius*, 1804 (unfinished)
*Phèdre*, 1805 (translation from Racine)
*Säkularausgabe*, ed. E. v. Hellen, 1904–5
*Nationalausgabe*, ed. J. Petersen, H. Schneider and others, 1943 ff.
*Werke*, ed. G. Fricke, H. G. Göpfert, 1965–6
Correspondence, ed. F. Jonas, 1892–6
Correspondence with Goethe, ed. G. Gräf and A. Leitzmann, 1912, repr. 1955
Correspondence with Körner, ed. K. Goedeke and L. Geiger, 1893
Correspondence with W. v. Humboldt, ed. S. Seidel, 1962


Literature

K. Berger, *Schiller. Sein Leben und seine Werke*, 1905–9
L. Bellermann, *Schillers Dramen*, 1911
G. Fricke, *Der religiöse Sinn der Tragödie Schillers*, 1927
G. Storz, *Das Drama Schillers*, 1938
   id., *Der Dichter F. Schiller*, 1959
H. B. Garland, *Schiller*, 1949
W. Witte, *Schiller*, 1949
E. L. Stahl, *Friedrich Schillers Drama. Theory and Practice*, 1954, repr. 1961
M. Gerhard, *Schiller*, 1959
W. Mainland, *Schiller and the Changing Past*, 1957
B. v. Wiese, *Schiller*, 1959
Bibliographies by H. Marcuse, 1925, and W. Vulpius, 1959

R. Pick, *Schiller in England, 1787–1960. A bibliography,* 1961
Cf. also *Jahrbuch der dt. Schillergesellschaft,* 1957 ff. passim
H. B. Garland, *Schiller. The Dramatic Writer,* 1969

*History*
The significance of Schiller's historical writings for his development consists in the fact that they mark his transition from 'Sturm und Drang' subjectivity to Kantian idealism. Apart from being outstanding examples of prose composition, they conditioned his future dramatic work by supplementing his theoretical concepts with carefully accumulated documentary material.

Works
*Geschichte des Abfalls der vereinigten Niederlande,* 1788
*Was heisst und zu welchem Ende studiert man Universalgeschichte?,* 1879
    (Schiller's Inaugural lecture at Jena).
*Geschichte des dreissigjährigen Krieges,* 1791–3

Literature
J. Janssen, *Schiller als Historiker,* 1879
F. Ueberweg, *Schiller als Historiker und Philosoph,* 1904

*Drama*
Schiller's principal essays on dramatic theory deal largely with the tragic emotions and with the use of 'das Pathetische and 'das Erhabene': they show a clear line of development in the views he expressed during the years from 1791 to 1801 when he assimilated first Lessing's and then Kant's doctrines and proceeded to evolve a theory characteristically his own. His achievement of an independent line of thought is even more striking in his writings on aesthetics beginning with *Über Anmut und Würde* (1793). The salient features of his aesthetic thought are his dialectic approach and his attempts to reconcile the fundamental differences constituting the essence of human nature and of the cultural history of man. These aspects of his endeavour are most tellingly in evidence in *Briefe über die ästhetische Erziehung des Menschen* and in *Über naive and sentimentalische Dichtung.*

Works
*Über das gegenwärtige deutsche Theater,* 1782
*Die Schaubühne als moralische Anstalt betrachtet,* 1784

*Philosophische Briefe,* 1786
*Briefe über Don Carlos,* 1788
*Über Bürgers Gedichte,* 1790
*Über den Grund des Vergnügens an tragischen Gegenständen,* 1791
*Über die tragische Kunst,* 1792
*Über das Pathetische,* 1793
*Vom Erhabenen,* 1793
*Über Anmut und Würde,* 1793
*Über Matthissons Gedichte,* 1794
*Briefe über die ästhetische Erziehung des Menschen,* 1795; ed. L. A.
    Willoughby and E. M. Wilkinson, 1968
*Über naive und sentimentalische Dichtung,* 1796; ed. W. Mainland,
    1951
*Über epische und dramatische Dichtung* (with Goethe), 1797
*Über das Erhabene,* 1801
*Über den Gebrauch des Chors in der Tragödie,* 1803
(The so-called 'Kallias Briefe' contained in Schiller's correspon-
    dence with C. G. Körner are also of considerable importance.)


Literature
O. Pietsch, *Schiller als Kritiker,* 1898
K. Berger, *Die Entwicklung von Schillers Ästhetik,* 1894
V. Busch, *La Poétique de Schiller,* 1902
B. Mugdan, 'Die theoretischen Grundlagen der Schillerschen
    Philosophie', *Kantstudien, Ergänzungsheft* 19 (1910)
W. Böhm, *Schillers Briefe über die Erziehung des Menschen,* 1927
M. Weber, 'Schiller als Kritiker', *Dichtung und Forschung, Fest-*
    *schrift für E. Ermatinger,* 1933
H. Meng, *Schiller. Abhandlung über naive und sentimentalische Dich-*
    *tung,* 1936
S. S. Kerry, *Schiller's writings on aesthetics,* 1961
J. M. Ellis, *Schiller's Kalliasbriefe and the study of his aesthetic theory,*
    1969

AUGUST WILHELM SCHLEGEL

Born 5 Sept. 1767 in Hannover, studied theology and philology in
Göttingen, collaborated with Schiller on his *Horen* and *Musen-*
*almanach* but later fell out with him and, along with his brother
Friedrich and Novalis, founded *Das Athenäum* (1798–1800),

principal organ of early Romanticism. After a brief spell as Privatdozent in Berlin he became companion to Mme de Staël in her journeys round Europe and at her home in Coppet. In 1819 Schlegel became professor in Bonn and helped to establish the study of Sanskrit and ancient Indian literature. He died in Bonn on 12 May 1845. His reputation rests on his brilliant critical essays, his lectures on literary history, which display enormous erudition, and on his translations of Shakespeare and the Spanish dramatists.

Works

*Shakespeares dramatische Werke*, 9 vols., 1797–1810

*Gedichte*, 1800

*Charakteristiken u. Kritiken*, 2 vols., 1801 (with Fr. Schlegel)

*Ion*, 1803 (drama)

*Spanisches Theater*, 2 vols., 1803–9

*Lacrimas*, 1803 (drama)

*Blumensträusse italienischer, spanischer u. portugiesischer Poesie*, 1804

*Vorlesungen über schöne Lit. u. Kunst*, lectures, Berlin 1801–4, ed. J. Minor, DLD 17–19, 1884

*Rom*, 1805 (elegy)

*Über dramatische Kunst u. Lit.*, 3 vols., 1809–11; ed. G. V. Amoretti, 1923

*Poetische Werke*, 2 vols., 1811

*Kritische Schriften*, 2 vols., 1828

*Sämtliche Werke*, ed. E. Böcking, 12 vols., 1846 ff.

Literature

B. v. Brentano, *A. W. Schlegel*, 1943

J. Körner, *Romantiker u. Klassiker*, 1924

J. Körner, *Die Botschaft der dt. Romantik an Europa*, 1929

A. Besenbeck, 'Kunstanschauung u. Kunstlehre A. W. Schlegels', *Germ. Stud.* 87 (1930)

O. Brandt, *A. W. Schlegel, die Romantiker u. die Politik*, 1919

O. F. Walzel, *Frau v. Staëls De l'Allemagne u. A. W. Schlegel*, 1898

W. F. Schirmer, 'A. W. Schlegel u. England', *Shakespeare-Jb.* 75 (1939)

R. Genee, *A. W. Schlegel u. Shakespeare*, 1903

M. C. Lazenby, *The influence of Wieland and Eschenburg on Schlegel's Shakespeare translation*, 1942

## Friedrich Schlegel

Born 10 March 1772 in Hannover, younger brother of August Wilhelm, studied in Göttingen and Leipzig, joined his brother in Jena where he formed friendships with Tieck and Novalis and contributed critical essays and aphorisms to *Das Athenäum*. After the affair with Dorothea Veit which forms the basis of *Lucinde* and which led to her divorce, Schlegel married her in 1804. Both were converted to the Roman church in 1808 and Schlegel gave up his insecure career as lecturer and journalist for a post in the Austrian civil service. As a conservative publicist associated with F. Gentz and Adam Müller he edited the *Armee-Zeitung* and the *Österreichischer Beobachter* and founded the journal *Concordia*. Schlegel died on 12 Jan. 1829 in Dresden where he had been lecturing. He was the most brilliant critic amongst the members of the early Romantic school and did much in his later years to stimulate studies in Oriental literature and comparative philology.

Works

*Über das Studium der griechischen Poesie*, 1797
*Geschichte der Poesie der Griechen*, 1798
*Lucinde*, 1799; repr. ed. K. K. Polheim, 1963
*Alarcos*, 1802 (tragedy)
*Von der Sprache u. Weisheit der Inder*, 1808
*Gedichte*, 1809
*Vorlesungen über die neuere Geschichte*, 1811
*Geschichte der alten u. neueren Literatur*, 1815
*Philosophie der Geschichte*, 1829
*Sämtliche Werke*, 10 vols., 1822–5; 2nd ed., 15 vols., 1846
*Kritische Ausgabe*, ed. E. Behler, H. Eichner, J.-J. Anstett, 22 vols., 1959 ff.
*Literary Notebooks, 1797–1801*, ed. H. Eichner, 1957

Literature

K. Enders, *F. Schlegel. Die Quellen seines Wesens u. Werdens*, 1913
O. Mann, *Der junge Friedrich Schlegel*, 1932
E. Behler, *F. Schlegel in Selbstzeugnissen u. Bilddokumenten*, 1966
W. Mettler, *Der junge F. Schlegel u. die griechische Lit.*, diss. Zürich, 1955
J.-J. Anstett, *La pensée réligieuse de F. Schlegel*, diss. Paris, 1941
K. Briegleb, *Ästhetische Sittlichkeit*, 1962

P. Klaus, *F. Schlegels ästhetischer Intellektualismus*, 1965

H. E. Hugo, 'An examination of Schlegel's Gespräch über Poesie', *Monatshefte* 40 (1948)

E. Behler, 'F. Schlegels Theorie der Universalpoesie', *JDSG* 1 (1957)

K. K. Polheim, *Die Arabeske. Ansichten u. Ideen aus F. Schlegels Poetik*, 1966

H. Nüsse, *Die Sprachtheorie F. Schlegels*, 1962

H. Henel, 'F. Schlegel u. die Grundlagen der modernen lit. Kritik', *GR* 20 (1945)

R. Immerwahr, 'The subjectivity or objectivity of F. Schlegel's poetic irony', *GR* 26 (1951)

G. P. Hendrix, *Das politische Weltbild F. Schlegels*, 1962

F. Schleiermacher, *Vertraute Briefe über Schlegels Lucinde*, 1800; repr. 1964

W. Paulsen, 'Schlegels Lucinde als Roman', *GR* 21 (1946)

J.-J. Anstett, ' "Lucinde: eine Reflexion": essai d'interpretation', *EG* 3 (1948)

E. Behler, 'Der Stand der Schlegel-Forschung', *JDSG* 1 (1957)

E. Behler, 'Neue Ergebnisse der F. Schlegel-Forschung', *GRM* 39 (1958)

## JOHANN ADOLF SCHLEGEL (pseud. HANS GÖRG)

Born in Meissen, 18 Sept. 1721, brother of J. E. Schlegel and father of Friedrich and August Wilhelm Schlegel, studied theology in Leipzig. He was one of the founders of the *Bremer Beiträge*. Apart from volumes of poetry he wrote on theoretical topics. He died in Hannover, 16 Sept. 1793.

### Works
*Vermischte Gedichte*, 2 vols., 1787–9

### Literature
H. Bieber, *J. A. Schlegels poetische Theorie*, 1912

## JOHANN ELIAS SCHLEGEL

Born in Meissen, 17 Jan. 1719, educated at Schulpforta at the same time as Klopstock. He studied law in Leipzig from 1739 to

1742. In 1743 he was appointed secretary to the Saxon ambassador in Copenhagen and became professor at an academy in Soröe. Apart from his dramas, his principal contribution is in aesthetics where he showed remarkable originality, particularly in the theory of imitation. Schlegel died in Soröe on 13 Aug. 1749.

Works

*Orest und Pylades*, 1739 (tragedy)
*Vergleichung Shakespeares and Andreas Gryphs*, 1741
*Abhandlung von der Nachahmung*, 1742
*Hermann*, 1743
*Der geschäftige Müssiggänger*, 1743
*Gedanken zur Aufnahme des dänischen Theaters*, 1747
*Die stumme Schönheit*, 1748; ed. W. Hecht, 1962
*Werke*, ed. J. H. Schlegel, 1761–70
*Ästhetische und dramaturgische Schriften*, ed. J. v. Antoniewicz, 1887

Literature

J. W. Eaton, *J. E. Schlegel and German literature*, 1929
H. Schonder, *J. E. Schlegel als Ubergangsgestalt*, 1940
E. M. Wilkinson, *J. E. Schlegel. A German pioneer in aesthetics*, 1945

## JOHANN GOTTFRIED SCHNABEL ('GISANDER')

Born 7 Nov. 1692 at Sandersdorf, near Bitterfeld, surgeon in the army of Prinz Eugen during War of the Spanish Succession, practised in Hamburg and Stolberg, where he edited the *Stolbergische Sammlung neuer u. merkwürdiger Weltgeschichte*. Schnabel's *Insel Felsenburg* was the most original and successful of 'Robinsonaden'; in the version published by Tieck in 1828 it is still read. He died some time after 1750.

Works

*Die wunderliche Fata einiger Seefahrer ... auf der Insel Felsenburg*, 4 vols., 1731–43; repr. ed. H. Ulrich, DLD 108–20, 1902; ed. P. Gugisch, 1966
*Lebensgeschichte Prinz Eugens*, 1736
*Der im Garten der Liebe herumtaumelnde Kavalier*, 1738

Literature

F. K. Becher, *Die Romane J. G. Schnabels*, diss. Bonn, 1911

K. Schröder, *Die Romane J. G. Schnabels*, diss. Marburg, 1912

H. Mayer, 'Schnabels Romane', *Studien zur dt. Lit. gesch.*, 1954; 2nd ed., 1955

I. Weinhold, *Johann Gottfried Schnabels Insel Felsenburg*, diss. Bonn, 1964

R. Haas, 'Die Landschaft auf der Insel Felsenburg', *ZfdA* 91 (1961–2)

F. J. Lamport, 'Utopia and "Robinsonade". Schnabel's Insel Felsenburg and Bachstrom's Land der Inquiraner', *OGS* 1 (1965)

M. Stern, 'Die wunderlichen Fata der Insel Felsenburg. Tiecks Anteil an der Neuausgabe von J. G. Schnabels Roman', *DVLG* 40 (1966)

## CHRISTIAN FRIEDRICH DANIEL SCHUBART

Born at Obersontheim in Württemberg, 24 March 1739. He studied theology at Erlangen and became organist and conductor at the court in Ludwigsburg in 1769. He was dismissed and exiled because of immorality and disrespect. He stayed in Heilbronn, Mannheim and Munich during the next few years. In 1774 he founded an outspokenly anti-clerical journal *Deutsche Chronik*. He was enticed to Württemberg in 1777 by an agent of Duke Karl Eugen, arrested and imprisoned in the fort Hohenasperg for ten years. Here he wrote some of his most trenchant poems denouncing tyranny and social abuses (esp. 'Die Fürstengruft', 'Kaplied', 'Der Gefangene'). He was released in 1787 and appointed musical director at the Stuttgart court. Until his death he renewed the editorship of his journal under the title *Vaterlandschronik* in a mood of submission. As a personality and a poet he has a prominent place among the rebellious spirits of the 'Sturm und Drang' era and had a particularly strong influence on the young Schiller and on Hölderlin. He was also an eminent musician. His *Ideen zur Ästhetik der Tonkunst* (ed. R. Walter, 1924) contains much original thought, especially on the work of J. S. Bach. Schubart died in Stuttgart on 10 Oct. 1791.

Works
*Gesammelte Schriften*, 1839–40
*Gedichte*, ed. G. Hauff, 1884
Selections ed. U. Wertheim and H. Böhm, 1959

Literature
D. F. Strauss, *Schubarts Leben*, 1849
S. Nestriepke, *Schubart als Dichter*, 1910
E. Thorn, *Genius in Fesseln*, 1935

JOHANN GOTTLIEB SCHUMMEL

Born 8 May 1748 at Seidendorf, near Hirschberg, studied in Halle, became teacher in Magdeburg and Liegnitz, finally professor at Elisabeth-Gymnasium in Breslau. Editor of Magdeburg *Wöchentliche Unterhaltungen*, 1777–9. Educational reformer and satirical opponent of Enlightenment. Mainly novels and dramas. Died in Breslau, 23 Dec. 1813.

Works
*Empfindsame Reisen durch Deutschland*, 3 vols., 1770–2
*Begebenheiten des Herrn Redlichs*, 1771
*Das Duell*, 1773 (comedy)
*Die unschuldige Frau oder Viel Lärm um Nichts*, 1773 (comedy)
*Fritzgens Reise nach Dessau*, 1776; repr. ed. A. Richter, 1891
*Die Eroberung von Magdeburg*, 1776 (drama)
*Spitzbart, eine komi-tragische Geschichte für unser pädagogisches Jahrhundert*, 1779
*Wilhelm von Blumenthal oder Das Kind der Natur*, 2 vols., 1780 f.
*Reise durch Schlesien*, 1791

Literature
G. Weigand, 'J. G. Schummel. Leben u. Schaffen eines Schriftstellers u. Reformpädagogen', *Dt. Forschungen* 13 (1925)

CHARLES SEALSFIELD

Sealsfield's real name was Karl Anton Postl. He was born on 3 March 1793 at Poppitz in Moravia and entered the Catholic order of the Kreuzherren in 1813. He deserted the order in 1823 and after trying to find employment in Germany and Switzerland emigrated to America where he spent altogether some fifteen years of his life. He returned to Europe in 1832 and settled in Switzerland. He shows an astounding insight into the rapidly developing political, social and economic life of the United States and great ingenuity in embodying his observations and theories in exciting novels, some of them in English. He died at Solothurn in Switzerland on 26 May 1864.

Works
*Tokeah*, 1829
*Der Legitime und der Republikaner*, 1833
*Der Virey und die Aristokraten*, 1834
*George Howards Brautfahrt*, 1834
*Ralph Doughbys Brautfahrt*, 1835
*Lebensbilder aus beiden Sphären: Morton*, 1835
*Nathan, der Squatter-Regulator*, 1837
*Das Kajütenbuch*, 1841
*Gesammelte Werke*, 18 parts, 1844–6

Literature
L. Smolle, *Sealsfield*, 1875
V. Hamburger, *Charles Sealsfield*, 1879
E. Castle, *Der grosse Unbekannte. Das Leben von Charles Sealsfield*, 1952
  id., 'Charles Sealsfield in Amerika', *ZfdPh* 67 (1942)
F. P. Knöller, *Charles Sealsfields Werke*, diss. Munich, 1924
E. Aufderheide, *Das Amerika-Erlebnis in den Romanen Charles Sealsfields*, diss. Göttingen, 1947
M. Gjorgjevic, *Charles Sealsfields Auffassung des Amerikanertums u. seine literarhistorische Stellung*, 1931
H. Zimpel, *K. Postls Romane im Rahmen ihrer Zeit*, diss. Frankfurt, 1941
G. W. Thompson, *An enquiry into the sources of Charles Sealsfield's novel Morton oder Die grosse Tour*, 1910
O. Heller, T. H. Leon, *Charles Sealsfield. Bibliography*, 1939
F. Bornemann, H. Freising, *Sealsfield-Bibliographie 1945–65*, 1966
A Charles Sealsfield-Gesellschaft was founded in Stuttgart in 1964

FRIEDRICH SPIELHAGEN

Successful novelist whose liberal opinions on political and social issues of the day were reflected in stories of a somewhat sensational kind. Born 24 Feb. 1829 in Magdeburg, brought up in Stralsund, studied in Berlin, Bonn and Greifswald. *Problematische Naturen* seems to be based on his experiences as a private tutor. He later became a teacher and journalist before devoting himself entirely to writing. His works include plays, lyric poetry and translations as well as treatises on the novel and drama. Spielhagen died in Berlin, 25 Feb. 1911.

Works

*Problematische Naturen*, 1861
*In Reih und Glied*, 1867
*Hammer und Amboss*, 1869
*Sturmflut*, 1877
*Beiträge zur Theorie und Technik des Romans*, 1883; repr. ed. H. Himmel, 1967
*Was will das werden?*, 1887
*Finder und Erfinder, Erinnerungen aus meinem Leben*, 1890
*Neue Beiträge zur Theorie und Technik der Epik und Dramatik*, 1898
*Sämtliche Romane*, 16 vols., 1871; 28 vols., 1900 ff.
*Meisterromane*, 3 vols., 1929

Literature

H. Henning, *Friedrich Spielhagen*, 1910
V. Klemperer, *Die Zeitromane F. Spielhagens u. ihre Wurzeln*, 1913
H. Schierding, *Untersuchungen über die Romantechnik F. Spielhagens*, diss. Münster, 1914
M. Geller, *F. Spielhagens Theorie u. Praxis des Romans*, 1917
W. Hellmann, 'Objektivität, Subjektivität u. Erzählkunst. Zur Romantheorie F. Spielhagens', *Wesen u. Wirklichkeit des Menschen* (Fs. H. Plessner), ed. K. Ziegler, 1957
H. W. Seiffert, 'Fontanes Effi Briest u. Spielhagens "Zum Zeitvertreib" ', *Studien zur neueren dt. Lit.*, ed. H. W. Seiffert, 1964

CHRISTIAN HEINRICH SPIESS

Born 4 April 1755 in Freiberg, Saxony, actor in touring companies before he made his reputation as author of historical thrillers and ghost stories which helped to establish the fashion for tales of medieval chivalry. Of his dramas, *Klara von Hoheneichen*, which impressed the youthful Grillparzer, was the most successful. Spiess died at Klattau, Bohemia, 17 Aug. 1799.

## Works

*Maria Stuart*, 1784 (tragedy)
*Biographien der Selbstmörder*, 4 vols., 1785
*Klara von Hoheneichen*, 1790
*Die Löwenritter*, 4 vols., 1794 f.
*Biographien der Wahnsinnigen*, 4 vols., 1795 f.
*Der Ritter mit dem goldenen Horn*, 1799
etc., etc.

## Literature

K. Müller-Fraureuth, *Die Ritter- u. Räuberromane*, 1894
C. Quelle, *C. H. Spiess als Erzähler*, diss. Leipzig, 1925
O. Rommel, 'Rationalistische Dämonie', *DVLG* 17 (1939)

## KARL SPINDLER (pseuds. C. SPINALBA, M. HUFNAGL)

Born 16 Oct. 1796 in Breslau, took up his parents' calling of strolling player, then turned to the writing of highly successful historical novels in the manner of Scott. After a restless life he died on 12 July 1855 in Bad Freiersbach, Baden.

## Works

*Sämtliche Werke*, 102 vols., 1831–54
*Ausgewählte Romane*, 34 vols., 1875 f.

## Literature

J. König, *Karl Spindler, ein Beitrag zur Gesch. des histor. Romans u. der Unterhaltungslektüre in Deutschland*, 1908

## ADALBERT STIFTER

Born at Oberplan in Bohemia, 23 Oct. 1805, and died in Linz, 28 Jan. 1868. He was educated at the Benedictine school in Krebsmünster and from 1826 until 1830 studied law, mathematics and science at Vienna university. His aim was to become a painter. At first he earned his living as tutor in aristocratic Viennese families including that of Fürst Metternich. In 1850 he became a school inspector, an occupation which gave him little satisfaction. He retired from it in 1865. He suffered from an incurable illness and is believed to have committed suicide.

## Works

*Studien,* 1844–50 (including *Der Condor,* 1840, *Das Heidedorf,* 1840, *Feldblumen,* 1841, *Die Mappe meines Urgrossvaters,* 1841–2, *Der Hochwald,* 1842, *Abdias,* 1843, *Brigitta,* 1844, *Der Waldsteig,* 1845, *Zwei Schwestern,* 1846, *Der beschriebene Tännling,* 1846)

*Bunte Steine,* 1853 (including *Granit,* 1849, *Kalkstein,* 1848, *Bergkristall,* 1845, *Turmalin,* 1852, *Katzensilber,* 1852, *Bergmilch,* 1843)

*Nachsommer,* 1857

*Witiko,* 1865–7

*Erzählungen,* ed. J. Aprent, 1869 (including *Prokopus,* 1848, *Die drei Schmiede ihres Schicksals,* 1844, *Der Waldbrunnen,* 1866, *Der Waldgänger,* 1848, *Der fromme Spruch,* 1866, *Zuversicht,* 1846, *Die Barmherzigkeit,* 1843, *Der späte Pfennig,* 1843, *Der Tod einer Jungfrau,* 1847)

*Sämtliche Werke,* ed. A. Sauer, F. Huller and G. Wilhelm, 1901–60

*Leben und Werk in Briefen und Dokumenten,* ed. K. S. Fischer, 1962

*Gesammelte Werke,* ed. K. Steffeny, 1965–6

Correspondence, ed. J. Aprent, 1869

## Literature

E. A. Blackall, *Adalbert Stifter: a critical study,* 1948

J. Michels, *Adalbert Stifter. Leben, Werk und Wirken,* 1949

H. Kunisch, *Adalbert Stifter. Mensch und Wirklichkeit,* 1950

W. Rehm, *Nachsommer,* 1951

W. Kosch, *A. Stifter als Mensch, Künstler, Dichter u. Erzieher,* 1952

U. Roedl, *Adalbert Stifter in Selbstzeugnissen u. Bilddokumenten,* 1965

L. Stiehm (ed.), *A. Stifter. Studien und Interpretationen,* 1968

K. Spalding, 'Adalbert Stifter', *German Men of Letters,* vol. 5, ed. A. Natan, 1969

J. Kuhn, *Die Kunst Stifters,* 1943

E. Staiger, *Stifter als Dichter der Ehrfurcht,* 1943

A. v. Grolman, *Stifters Romane,* 1926

E. Eisenmeier, *Adalbert Stifter-Bibliographie,* 1964

E. Lunding, 'Probleme und Ergebnisse der Stifterforschung 1945-54', *Euph* 49 (1955)

There are 'Adalbert Stifter-Gesellschaften' in Vienna (founded 1918) and Munich (founded 1946)

## FRIEDRICH LEOPOLD GRAF ZU STOLBERG

Born in Schloss Bramstedt (Holstein), 7 Nov. 1750. Together with his brother Christian (1748–1821) he studied law at Halle and Göttingen. Here they became members of the 'Hainbund'. They travelled with Goethe to Switzerland in 1775. Friedrich Leopold entered the diplomatic service in 1777. He lived in Copenhagen until 1781 and in Berlin from 1789 until 1791. In 1800 he retired to Münster where he joined the circle of Gräfin Gallitzin. His conversion to Catholicism in 1800 became a cause celèbre, largely owing to J. H. Voss's reactions to it. Apart from his lyric poetry his most important literary work is his translation of the Iliad (1778) and of Aeschylus (1802). He also wrote two influential theoretical essays: *Vom Dichten und Darstellen* (1780), *Über die Begeisterung* (1782). He died at Schloss Sondermühlen near Osnabrück, 5 Dec. 1819.

Works
*Der Brüder Christian und F. L. Grafen zu Stolbergs gesammelte Werke*, 1820–5
Selections, ed. O. Hellinghaus, 1921
*Oden und Lieder*, ed. T. Haecker, 1923

Literature
W. Keiper, *Stolbergs Jugendpoesie*, 1893
J. Janssen, *F. L. Graf zu Stolberg*, 1910
E. Holtz, *Stolbergs Odenlyrik*, 1924
P. Brachin, *Le cercle de Munster*, 1951

## THEODOR STORM

Born 14 Sept. 1817, at Husum in Schleswig which at that time was Danish territory. He studied law at Kiel university from 1837 until 1842 and then practised as an advocate in Husum. In 1852 he was expelled for his pro-German activities. From 1853 until 1856 he was an assessor at the Potsdam law courts and in Berlin joined the literary society 'Tunnel über der Spree'. After transferring to a post in Saxony he returned to Husum in 1864 and in 1880 settled in Hademarschen in Holstein, where he died, 4 July 1888.

Works

*Liederbuch dreier Freunde* (with Tycho and Theodor Mommsen), 1843

*Immensee*, 1850

*Sommergeschichten und Lieder*, 1851

*Gedichte*, 1852, 1856, 1864, 1885

*Späte Rosen*, 1859

*Viola tricolor*, 1873

*Aquis submersus*, 1875–6

*Renate*, 1877–8

*Die Chronik von Grieshuus*, 1883–4

*Ein Fest auf Haderslevhuus*, 1885

*Vor Zeiten*, 1886

*Ein Doppelgänger*, 1887

*Ein Bekenntnis*, 1888

*Der Schimmelreiter*, 1888

*Sämtliche Schriften*, 1867–89

*Sämtliche Werke*, ed. A. Köster, 1919 f.; ed. C. Jenssen, 1958

Correspondence with Mörike, ed. J. Baechtold, 1891

Correspondence with Heyse, ed. G. J. Plotke, 1917

Correspondence with G. Keller, ed. A. Köster, 1924; ed. P. Goldhammer, 1960

Correspondence with Fontane, ed. E. Gulzow, 1948

Literature

A. Biese, *Th. Storms Leben und Werke*, 1921

W. F. Mainland, 'Theodor Storm', *German Men of Letters*, vol. 1, ed. A. Natan, 1961

J. A. Alfero, *La lirica di Storm*, 1924
    id., *Storm novelliere*, 1928

E. D. Wooley, *Studies in T. Storm*, 1942

F. Stuckert, *Th. Storm. Sein Leben und seine Welt*, 1955

C. Bernd, *T. Storm's craft of fiction*, 1966

E. A. McCormick, *T. Storms Novellen*, 1964

DAVID FRIEDRICH STRAUSS

Born 27 Jan. 1808 in Ludwigsburg, educated at the Tübingen Stift, studied under Schleiermacher in Berlin and returned as a teacher to the Stift. Public outrage over his rationalistic and critical *Leben Jesu* forced him to abandon his post and a later appointment as professor of dogmatics and church history in Zürich was similarly terminated. In his later years Strauss leaned towards a shallow materialistic humanism which was attacked by Nietzsche in his *Unzeitgemässe Betrachtungen*. He wrote some excellent historical biographies. Died in Ludwigsburg, 8 Feb. 1874.

Works
*Das Leben Jesu, kritisch bearbeitet*, 2 vols., 1835 f.
*Die christliche Glaubenslehre u. ihre gesch. Entwicklung*, 2 vols., 1840 f.
*Leben u. Schriften des Dichters u. Philologen Nicodemus Frischlin*, 1855
*Ulrich von Hutten*, 2 vols., 1858 ff.
*H. S. Reimarus*, 1861
*Kleinere Schriften*, 2 vols., 1862 ff.
*Voltaire*, 1870
*Der alte und der neue Glaube*, 1872
*Poetisches Gedenkbuch*, 1876
*Gesammelte Schriften*, ed. E. Zeller, 12 vols., 1876–8
*Werke*, 5 vols.; *Ausgewählte Briefe*, ed. E. Zeller, 1895
*Briefwechsel mit F. T. Vischer*, ed. A. Rapp, 2 vols., 1952

Literature
F. Hettinger, *D. F. Strauss u. die Theologie seiner Zeit*, 2 vols., 1876 ff.
T. Klaiber, *David Friedrich Strauss*, 1920
O. Walzel, 'Der Begriff des Mythus bei D. F. Strauss', *N*26 (1941)

HELFERICH PETER STURZ

Born 16 Feb. 1736 in Darmstadt, studied law in Jena, Göttingen and Giessen, entered Danish diplomatic service and accompanied King Christian VII to England and France. Dismissed after the fall of Struensee, Sturz settled in Oldenburg, where he sadly missed the stimulus of the European society he knew as a diplomat. He died 12 Nov. 1779 in Bremen. Urbane and cultivated author of essays, tales, travel journals and occasional satires in the manner of Lichtenberg.

Works
*Julie*, 1767 (tragedy)
*Erinnerungen aus dem Leben des Grafen v. Bernstorff*, 1777
*Schriften*, 2 vols., 1779–82
*Gedichte*, DNL, vol. 135

Literature
M. Koch, *H. P. Sturz*, 1879
A. Schmidt, *H. P. Sturz*, 1939
L. Langenfeld, *Die Prosa H. P. Sturz'*, diss. Köln, 1935
R. Riemeck (ed.), *H. P. Sturz. Auf dem Wege zur klassischen Form*, 1948

## JOHANN GEORG SULZER

Born 16 Oct. 1720 at Winterthur in Switzerland. He was educated in Zürich and became a teacher, first in Magdeburg and later in Berlin. His encyclopaedia on aesthetics and poetics was a unique and influential work, although some of his articles provoked Goethe's criticism. Sulzer died in Berlin, 27 Feb. 1779.

Works
*Allgemeine Theorie der schönen Künste*, 1771–4; later eds. 1786–7, 1792–4

Literature
K. J. Gross, *Sulzers Allgemeine Theorie der schönen Künste*, diss. Berlin, 1905
H. Fausten, *J. G. Sulzer*, diss. Berlin, 1921
A. Tumarkin, *Der Ästhetiker J. G. Sulzer*, 1933
O. Walzel, 'J. G. Sulzer über Poesie', *ZfdPh* 62 (1937)

## MORITZ AUGUST VON THÜMMEL

Thümmel was born on 27 May 1738 at the manor of Schönefeld, near Leipzig. He studied law at the University of Leipzig, was taught by Gellert amongst others and formed friendships with such literary men as Weisse, Garve, Rabener and Ewald von Kleist. In 1768 Thümmel became privy councillor and minister in Sachsen-Coburg. The years 1772–7 he spent travelling in France and Italy. From 1783 he lived a retired life in Gotha, Altenburg, Sonneborn and Berlin. He died in Koburg on 26 Oct. 1817. His principal models were Wieland and Laurence Sterne: to the urbanity and stylistic elegance of the former and the piquant mixture of satire and whimsy characteristic of the latter he added a modicum of reason and patriotic pride. His greatest success was achieved with the miniature comic epic in prose *Wilhelmine*, which is perhaps the best example of a much-favoured contemporary genre, but his quasi-sentimental journal was also widely appreciated.

## Works

*Wilhelmine oder Der vermählte Pedant*, 1764; repr. DLD 48 (1894)
*Die Inoculation der Liebe*, 1771 (verse tale)
*Zemire und Azor*, 1776 (German version of Marmontel's opera)
*Kleine poetische Schriften*, 1782
*Reise in die mittäglichen Provinzen von Frankreich im Jahre 1785–6*, 1791–1805
*Der heilige Kilian und das Liebespaar*, ed. F. F. Hempel, 1818

## Literature

J. E. v. Gruner, *M. A. Thümmels Leben*, 1820
H. Heldmann, *M. A. v. Thümmel: Sein Leben, sein Werk, seine Zeit, Teil I*, 1964
H. Rochocz, *Thümmels Wilhelmine und das komische Heldengedicht des 18. Jhs*, diss. Leipzig, 1911
R. Kyrieleis, *Thümmels Roman: Reise in die mittäglichen Provinzen*, 1908
G. Bianquis, 'Un allemand dans le midi de France au 18ième siècle', *RLC* 25 (1951)

## JOHANN LUDWIG TIECK

Born in Berlin on 31 May 1773, Tieck began to write while still at school, studied in Halle, Erlangen and Göttingen, where he developed an interest in medieval literature and Renaissance art. He became a professional writer, dramatist and critic, travelling widely in Germany, Italy and England before settling in Dresden in 1819, where he became Dramaturg to the court theatre. In 1842 Frederick William IV summoned him to Berlin as his personal reader and theatrical adviser. Tieck died in Berlin on 28 April 1853. He was an impressionable character who reflected in his works the changing literary modes of his long life. His earliest dramas and tales either echo the rationalism of his employer, Friedrich Nicolai, or reproduce the horrific atmosphere of the popular 'Gothic' novel. A visit to South Germany in 1793 and the influence of his friend Wackenroder, however, opened his eyes to the glories of Renaissance and Baroque art and to the aesthetic values soon to be embodied in Romanticism. After the death of Wackenroder in 1798 Tieck joined forces with the Schlegels and Novalis and, as a facile lyrical talent, probably did more than anyone else to popularize Romanticism. The transition from Romanticism to the more realistic idiom of Biedermeier is reflected in the short stories and historical novels of Tieck's later years. His translation of *Don Quixote*, his work on the translation of Shakespeare by A. W. Schlegel and his daughter Dorothea Tieck, his critical writing on Elizabethan drama and the superb dramatic recitations he gave in the drawing-rooms of Dresden and Berlin made Tieck an international celebrity in his lifetime, but of his vast output only some of the earliest Romantic Novellen and satirical comedies and the later historical novels may be regarded as of the highest quality. Tieck rendered important services to posterity by editing and publishing the works of Novalis, Kleist and Lenz.

Works

*Peter Leberecht. Geschichte ohne Abenteuerlichkeiten,* 1795–6
*Geschichte des Herrn William Lovell,* 1795–6
*Volksmärchen von Peter Leberecht,* 1797
*Der gestiefelte Kater,* 1797 (comedy)
*Franz Sternbalds Wanderungen,* 1798
*Die verkehrte Welt,* 1798 (comedy)
*Phantasien über die Kunst,* 1799
*Prinz Zerbino,* 1799 (comedy)
*Der getreue Eckart und der Tannhäuser,* 1799
*Leben und Tod der heiligen Genoveva,* 1799 (drama)
*Historie von der Melusina,* 1800

*Kaiser Oktavianus*, 1804 (drama)
*Phantasus* (collected plays and stories), 3 vols., 1812–16; repr. 1912
*Gedichte*, 3 vols., 1821–3
*Novellen*, 7 vols., 1823–8
*Shakespeares dramatische Werke* (transl. with A. W. Schlegel, Dorothea Tieck and Graf Baudissin), 9 vols., 1825–33
*Der Aufruhr in den Cevennen*, 1826
*Gesammelte Novellen*, 14 vols., 1835–42
*Vittoria Accorombona*, 1840
*Schriften*, 20 vols., 1828–46
*Gesammelte Novellen*, 12 vols., 1852–4
*Nachgelassene Schriften*, ed. R. Köpke, 2 vols., 1855
*Werke*, ed. M. Thalmann, 1963–6

Literature

R. Köpke, *Ludwig Tieck, Erinnerungen aus dem Leben des Dichters*, 2 vols., 1855
F. Gundolf, 'Ludwig Tieck', *Jb. des freien dt. Hochstifts*, 1929
E. H. Zeydel, *Tieck, the German Romanticist*, 1935
R. Minder, *Un poète romantique allemand: Ludwig Tieck*, 1936
M. Thalmann, *Ludwig Tieck, der romantische Weltmann aus Berlin*, 1955
M. Thalmann, *Ludwig Tieck, der Heilige von Dresden*, 1960
H. Hammer, *Die Anfänge Tiecks u. seiner dämonisch-schauerlichen Dichtung*, 1910
J. Trainer, *Ludwig Tieck. From Gothic to Romantic*, 1964
M. Thalmann, *Probleme der Dämonie in Tiecks Schriften*, 1919
A. E. Lussky, *Tieck's approach to Romanticism*, diss. Michigan, 1926
J. Budde, *Zur romantischen Ironie bei Tieck*, 1907
R. Lieske, 'Tiecks Abwendung von der Romantik', *Germ. Stud.* 134 (1933)
M. Hasinsky, *Tiecks Verhältnis zum Jungen Deutschland*, diss. Breslau, 1920
E. H. Zeydel, 'Ludwig Tieck u. das Biedermeier', *GRM* 9–10 (1938)
R. M. Immerwahr, *The aesthetic intent of Tieck's fantastic comedy*, Washington Univ. Studies, Lang. and Lit., 22 (1953)
P. J. Arnold, 'Tiecks Novellenbegriff', *Euph* 23 (1921)
E. H. Zeydell, *Tieck and England*, 1931

H. W. Hewett-Thayer, 'Tieck and the Elizabethan drama', *JEGP* 34 (1935)

P. Matenko, *Ludwig Tieck and America*, 1954

E. C. Stopp, 'Wandlungen des Tieck-Bildes', *DVLG* 17 (1939)

M. Thalmann, 'Hundert Jahre Tieckforschung', *Monatshefte* 45 (1953)

## FRIEDRICH VON UECHTRITZ

Born 12 Sept. 1800 at Görlitz, legal career in Berlin, where he frequented literary circles that included Hitzig, Rahel von Varnhagen, Heine, Grabbe, and in Düsseldorf, where he was a friend of Immermann. Although admired by Hebbel, Uechtritz's Schillerian tragedies enjoyed little popular success and he later turned to the novel. The popularity of Young Germany and the radicalism of 1848 confirmed him in his conservatism. Died in Görlitz, 15 Feb. 1875.

### Works
*Alexander und Darius*, 1827 (tragedy)
*Das Ehrenschwert*, 1827 (tragedy)
*Rosamunde*, 1833 (tragedy)
*Albrecht Holm*, 1852 f. (historical novel)
*Der Bruder der Braut*, 1860 (novel)

### Literature
W. Steitz, *Uechtritz als dramatischer Dichter*, 1909

K. Meyer, *Die Romane von F. von Uechtritz*, 1911

H. W. Keim, *Beiträge zur Düsseldorfer Literaturgeschichte*, 1927

## LUDWIG UHLAND

Born 26 April 1787 in Tübingen, studied law and philology there. In 1810 he went to Paris to study medieval French and German manuscripts. From 1812 to 1814 he worked in the Ministry of Justice in Stuttgart; from 1819–39 he was an active Liberal member of the Württemberg Parliament. He also took part in the proceedings of the Frankfurt Parliament of 1848. He was Professor of German Literature in Tübingen University from 1829 to 1833, but resigned from the post when he was forbidden to hold it jointly with his parliamentary seat. He made an important collection of 'Volkslieder'. Uhland died in Tübingen on 13 Nov. 1862.

Works
*Gedichte*, 1815
*Vaterländische Gedichte*, 1817
*Ernst, Herzog von Schwaben*, 1819 (drama)
*Ludwig der Baier*, 1819 (drama)
*Alte hoch- und niederdeutsche Volkslieder*, 1844
*Gedichte und Dramen*, 1863
*Schriften zur Geschichte der Dichtung und Sage*, 1865–73
*Werke*, ed. H. Fischer, 1892
*Dichtungen, Briefe, Reden. Eine Auswahl*, ed. W. P. H. Scheffler, 1963

Literature
W. Bernhardt, *Uhlands politische Betätigung*, 1910
H. Haag, *Uhland. Die Entwicklung des Lyrikers*, 1907
A. Thoma, *Uhlands Volksliedsammlung*, 1929
H. Schneider, *Uhland. Leben, Dichtung, Forschung*, 1920
L. Fränkel, 'Bibliographie der Uhland-Literatur', *Germania* 34 (1889)

ALEXANDER VON UNGERN-STERNBERG

Born 22 April 1806 in Estonia, conservative publicist with wide acquaintance in literary circles of Dresden and Berlin. The satirical wit and brilliance of his many novels and Novellen made him the favourite of elegant society. Died at Dannenwalde, Mecklenburg, 24 Aug. 1868.

Works
*Die Zerrissenen*, 1832
*Palmyra oder Das Tagebuch eines Papageis*, 1838
*Alfred*, 1841
*Diana*, 1842
*Jena und Leipzig*, 1844 (novel)
*Wilhelm*, 1849
*Der deutsche Gil Blas*, 1851
*Macargan oder Die Philosophie des 18. Jhs*, 1853
*Erinnerungsblätter*, 5 vols., 1855–60; repr. ed. J. Kühn, 1919

Literature

E. Weil, 'Alexander von Ungern-Sternberg', *Germ. Stud.* 130 (1932)

A. Molsberger, *Adel und Adelsgesinnung in den Zeitromanen A. v. Ungern-Sternbergs*, diss. Halle, 1929

T. Geisendörfer, *Dickens Einfluss auf Ungern-Sternberg u. andere*, 1915

## JOHANN PETER UZ

Born in Ansbach 3 Oct. 1720, studied law, philosophy and history at Halle. He began his career as a lawyer in 1748 and rose to the rank of 'Wirklicher Geheimer Justizrat'. He died in Ansbach, 12 May 1796.

Works
*Lyrische Gedichte*, 1749
*Lyrische und andere Gedichte*, 1755
*Sämtliche Poetische Werke*, 1768; ed. A. Sauer, 1890

Literature
E. Petzet, *Johann Peter Uz*, 1896; repr. 1930
A. Ewald, 'Uz und Goethe', *Euph* 20 (1913)

## CARL FRANZ VAN DER VELDE

Born 27 Sept. 1779 in Breslau, died there on 6 April 1824. He was the author of popular historical stories which earned him the title of 'the German Scott'. Many of them were successfully dramatized.

Works
*Sämtliche Schriften*, 27 vols., 1830–2

Literature
W. Matthey, *Die historischen Erzählungen des C. F. van der Velde*, 1928

## KARL AUGUST VARNHAGEN VON ENSE

Was born in Düsseldorf 21 Feb. 1785, and died in Berlin 10 Oct. 1858. He studied medicine at the universities of Berlin, Halle and

Tübingen. From 1809 until 1812 he had a military career and then entered the Prussian diplomatic service. He attended the Congress of Vienna and from 1816 acted as Minister in Karlsruhe. He was dismissed from the service in 1819 because of his Liberal leanings. He settled in Berlin, where his wife Rahel (née Levin) was a prominent literary hostess. Varnhagen von Ense wrote short stories, poetry and plays, but is best remembered for his diaries and memoirs.

Works
*Erzählungen und Spiele*, 1807
*Gedichte*, 1814
*Deutsche Erzählungen*, 1815
*Vermischte Gedichte*, 1816
*Biographische Denkmale*, 1824–30
*Rahel, ein Buch des Andenkens*, 1834
*Denkwürdigkeiten und vermischte Schriften*, 1837–46; 1859; ed. J. Kühn, 1922–3; Leutner, 1950
Correspondence with A. v. Humboldt, 1860; with Rahel, 1874 f.

Literature
C. Misch, *Varnhagen in Beruf und Politik*, 1925
F. Römer, *Varnhagen als Romantiker*, diss. Berlin, 1934

FRIEDRICH THEODOR VISCHER (pseuds. PHILIPP ULRICH SCHWARTENMAYER; DEUTOBOLD SYMBOLIZETTI ALLEGOROWITSCH MYSTIFIZINSKY)

Born 30 June 1807 in Ludwigsburg, studied at Tübingen Stift but had no vocation for the ministry and developed in fact marked anti-clerical views. Appointed professor of aesthetics in Tübingen in 1837 but suspended from his office following his inaugural lecture. Delegate to the Frankfurt Parliament in 1848. In 1855 Vischer became professor at the Zürich Polytechnic but returned to Tübingen in 1866 and ended his career at the Technische Hochschule in Stuttgart. He died in Cannstatt, 14 Sept. 1887. Vischer was an influential aesthetic theorist and a witty controversialist; his satirical novel, *Auch Einer*, attacks the modish adulation of the national past and Germanic legends but appeals chiefly because of its ill-starred hero for whose constant battle against a malign fate and the intractable physical universe Vischer coined the expression 'Tücke des Objekts'.

Works

*Kritische Gänge*, 1844; repr. ed. R. Vischer, 6 vols., 1922 ff.
*Ästhetik oder die Wissenschaft des Schönen*, 1846–57; repr. ed. R. Vischer, 6 vols., 1922 ff.
*Faust, der Tragödie dritter Teil*, 1862 (parody)
*Auch Einer, eine Reisebekanntschaft*, 1879
*Lyrische Gänge*, 1882
*Allotria*, 1892
*Dichterische Werke*, 5 vols., 1917
*Ausgewählte Werke*, ed. T. Kappstein, 1920
*Briefwechsel mit E. Mörike*, ed. R. Vischer, 1926
*Briefwechsel mit D. F. Strauss*, 2 vols., ed. A. Rapp, 1952–3

Literature

F. Schlawe, *F. T. Vischer*, 1959
E. Heyfelder, *Klassizismus u. Naturalismus bei F. T. Vischer*, 1901
F. Reich, *Die Kulturphilosophie F. T. Vischers*, diss. Leipzig, 1907
W. Oelmüller, *F. T. Vischer u. das Problem der nachhegelschen Ästhetik*, 1959
F. Feilbogen, *Vischers Auch Einer*, 1916
H. W. Hewett-Thayer, 'The road to "Auch Einer" ', *PMLA* 75 (1960)


JOHANN HEINRICH VOSS

Born at Sommersdorf in Mecklenburg of humble parentage, 20 Feb. 1751. After going to school at Neubrandenburg and working as a teacher he went to Göttingen university where he studied theology and philology from 1772 to 1775 and, with Boie, founded the 'Hainbund'. He occupied clerical posts at Otterndorf and Eutin (where he renewed his friendship with Stolberg) which he resigned in 1802 in order to devote his time to writing. He retired first to Jena and later to Heidelberg. Apart from his poetry and his polemical writings against Stolberg and against the Romantics, his fame rested on his translations of Homer, Vergil and Horace which for many years formed the basis of the knowledge of these authors among wider circles of the German reading public. He died in Heidelberg, 29 March 1826.

Works

*Gedichte*, 1785–95
*Homers Werke*, 1793
*Idyllen*, 1801
*Sämtliche Gedichte*, 1802
*Wie ward Fritz Stolberg ein Unfreier?*, 1819
*Sämtliche poetische Werke*, ed. A. Voss, 1835

Literature

W. Herbst, *J. H. Voss*, 1872–6
K. Kahnis, *Stolberg und Voss*, 1876
F. de Broissia, 'Le lyrisme de J. H. Voss', *Revue Germanique* 16 (1925)
K. Aner, *J. H. Voss*, 1928
E. Metelmann, 'Voss und Goethe', *ZfdPh* 62 (1937)

## CHRISTIAN AUGUST VULPIUS

Born 22 Jan. 1762 in Weimar, brother of Christiane Vulpius who was first the mistress then the wife of Goethe. Vulpius studied in Jena and Erlangen and taught in Bayreuth, Würzburg, Erlangen and Leipzig before returning to Weimar in 1790. He became secretary to the Weimar ducal library in 1797 and eventually rose to the dignity of Grossherzoglicher Rat. He died in Weimar on 26 June 1827. Vulpius was one of the most successful writers of popular thrillers.

Works

*Skizzen aus dem Leben galanter Damen*, 4 vols., 1789–93
*Romantische Geschichten der Vorzeit*, 10 vols., 1792–8
*Rinaldo Rinaldini, der Räuberhauptmann*, 1797
*Orlando Orlandini*, 1802
*Kuriositäten der physisch-literarisch-artistisch-historischen Vor- und Mit-welt*, 10 vols., 1811–23

Literature

J. W. Appell, *Die Ritter-, Räuber- u. Schauerromane*, 1859
K. Müller-Fraureuth, *Die Ritter- u. Räuberromane*, 1894

W. Vulpius, 'Bibl. der selbständig erschienen Werke von C. A. Vulpius', *Jb. der Sammlung Kippenberg* 6 (1927)

## WILHELM HEINRICH WACKENRODER

Born 3 July 1773 in Berlin, school-fellow of Tieck, with whom he studied in Erlangen and Göttingen. He had scarcely embarked on his career as a civil servant when he died in Berlin on 13 Feb. 1798. Wackenroder's sensitive response to medieval and Renaissance art and literature not only influenced Tieck but set the tone for the Romantic school as a whole: it has been said that with the *Herzensergiessungen* he founded Romanticism without knowing it. The conflict between the rapture of the musical artist and the harsh realities of life, which Wackenroder experienced himself, initiated a fruitful theme of Romanticism.

Works
*Herzensergiessungen eines kunstliebenden Klosterbruders*, 1797; repr. ed. A. Gillies, 1948
*Phantasien über die Kunst*, ed. L. Tieck, 1799; repr. DNL 145 (1886)
*Werke u. Briefe*, ed. F. v. d. Leyen, 2 vols., 1910; ed. L. Schneider, 1938
*Reiseberichte*, ed. H. Höhn, 1939

Literature
B. Tecchi, *Wilhelm Heinrich Wackenroder*, 1926; transl. C. Riessner, 1962
R. Wenzel, *Wackenroders Weltanschauung*, diss. Münster, 1925
H. Lippuner, *Wackenroder, Tieck u. die bildende Kunst*, 1965
W. D. Robson-Scott, 'Wackenroder and the middle ages', *MLR* 50 (1955)
G. Fricke, 'Bemerkungen zu Wackenroders Religion der Kunst', Fs. Kluckhohn/Schneider, 1948
D. Hammer, *Die Bedeutung der vergangenen Zeit im Werk Wackenroders*, diss. Frankfurt a. M., 1960
K. Thornton, 'Wackenroder's objective Romanticism', *GR* 37 (1962)
E. Hertrich, *Joseph Berlinger. Eine Studie zu Wackenroders Musikerdichtung*, 1969

LEONHARD WÄCHTER (pseud. VEIT WEBER)

Born 25 Nov. 1762 at Uelzen, studied in Göttingen, served in the
French revolutionary army, returning to his parents' home in 1793
after being wounded. Wächter travelled in England, Austria and
Switzerland before settling again in Hamburg, where he died on
11 Feb. 1837. His historical tales are influenced by ideas of the
Enlightenment and by the English sentimental novel.

Works
*Sagen der Vorzeit*, 7 vols., 1787–98
*Wilhelm Tell*, 1804
*Ulrich von Hutten*, 1818
*Historischer Nachlass*, ed. C. F. Wurm, 2 vols., 1837 f.; repr. 1904

Literature
W. Pantenius, *Das Mittelalter in L. Wächters Romanen*, 1904


HEINRICH LEOPOLD WAGNER

Born 17 Feb. 1747 in Strasbourg where he studied and practised
law. Wagner was a lesser known 'Stürmer und Dränger' associated
with Lenz und Klinger. Goethe accused him of plagiarizing
scenes from *Faust* for his *Kindermörderin*. He died in Frankfurt am
Main, 4 March 1779.

Works
*Konfiscable Erzählungen*, 1774
*Vermischte Gedichte*, 1774
*Prometheus Deukalion und seine Rezensenten*, 1775 (on Goethe's
    *Werther*)
*Die Reue nach der Tat*, 1775 (drama)
*Die wohltätige Unbekannte*, 1775 (drama)
*Die Kindermörderin*, 1776 (tragedy); repr. ed. E. Schmidt, DLD 13
    (1883)
*Leben und Tod Sebastian Silligs*, 1776 (novel)
*Gesammelte Werke*, ed. L. Hirschberg, 1923

Literature
E. Schmidt, *Heinrich Leopold Wagner*, 1875
J. Froitzheim, *Goethe und Wagner*, 1889

## GEORG WEERTH

Born 17 Feb. 1821 in Detmold, worked in the textile trade in Germany and England. Between 1843 and 1848 Weerth published a number of sketches of industrial conditions and social life in Great Britain and in 1848–9 was literary editor of Karl Marx's *Neue Rheinische Zeitung*. His principal model seems to have been Heine. The satirical novel *Leben und Taten des berühmten Ritters Schnapphahnski* earned him three months' imprisonment in Cologne. After a further spell in England he travelled to South America on business and died in Havana on 24 July 1856.

### Works

*Leben und Taten des berühmten Ritters Schnapphahnski*, 1849
*Die ersten Gedichte der Arbeiterbewegung*, sel. and ed. H. Pross, 1956
*Fragment eines Romans*, ed. S. Unseld, 1965
*Sämtliche Werke*, 5 vols., ed. B. Kaiser, 1956–7
*Ausgewählte Werke*, ed. B. Kaiser, 1966

### Literature

K. Weerth, *Georg Weerth*, 1930
H. Bunke, *Georg Weerth. Ein Überblick über sein Leben u. Wirken*, 1956

## FRIEDRICH LUDWIG WEIDIG

Born 17 Feb. 1791 at Oberkleen, near Wetzlar, teacher and then parson; forerunner of socialism, edited the revolutionary *Hessische Landbote* with Georg Büchner, arrested, committed suicide in prison at Darmstadt, 23 Feb. 1837.

### Works

*Gedichte*, 1847
*Der hessische Landbote*, ed. with comm. by H. M. Enzensberger, 1965

### Literature

O. Ruhle, 'Friedrich Ludwig Weidig', *Religion in Gesch. u. Gegenwart*, vol. 5, 1931

## CHRISTIAN FELIX WEISSE

Born at Annaberg, 18 Jan. 1726. He studied theology at Leipzig where Lessing was his contemporary. He went to Paris in 1759 and in 1761 became an inspector of taxes in Leipzig. From 1759 he edited Nicolai's *Bibliothek der schönen Wissenschaften und der freien Künste*. His position was unusual in that he equally opposed Bodmer and Gottsched and wrote dramas interchangeably in alexandrines and blank verse. He also made a contribution with his 'Singspiele'. Lessing took the opportunity of a performance of his *Richard III* in Hamburg to develop his theory of tragedy. Weisse died at Stöttwitz near Leipzig, 16 Dec. 1804.

Works
*Die verwandelten Weiber*, 1752
*Der Dorfbarbier*, 1759
*Scherzhafte Lieder*, 1758
*Komische Opern*, 1768–71
*Trauerspiele*, 1776–80
*Lustspiele*, 1783

Literature
J. Minor, *C. F. Weisse*, 1880
W. Martinsen, *Gottscheds Singspiele im Verhältnis zu den Weisseschen Operetten*, 1887
C. G. Zander, *C. F. Weisse und die Bühne*, 1949

## ZACHARIAS WERNER

Born in Königsberg, 18 Nov. 1768, studied law and philosophy there from 1784 to 1789 without completing the courses. He occupied minor posts in Warsaw and Berlin between 1796 and 1807. After the failure of his third marriage he travelled to Switzerland and visited Mme de Staël at Coppet. He joined the Catholic Church in 1810 and became a fashionable preacher in Vienna where he died on 17 Jan. 1823.

Works
*Die Söhne des Tals*, 1803; ed. W. J. Stein, 1927
*Das Kreuz an der Ostsee*, 1806

466     SELECT BIBLIOGRAPHY

*Martin Luther oder die Weihe der Kraft*, 1807
*Attila, König der Hunnen*, 1808
*Der 24. Februar*, 1815; ed. E. Kilian, 1924
*Die Mutter der Makkabäer*, 1820
*Ausgewählte Schriften*, ed. F. J. K. Schutz, 1840–1
*Dramen*, ed. P. Kluckhohn (*Dt. Lit. in Entwicklungsreihen*), 1937

Literature
P. Hankamer, *Zacharias Werner*, 1920
I. Maione, *Zacharias Werner*, 1954
G. Gabetti, *Il dramma di Zacharias Werner*, 1916
F. Stuckert, *Das Drama Zacharias Werners*, 1926
L. Guinet, *Zacharias Werner et l'ésotérisme maçonnique*, 1962
G. Kozielek, *Friedrich Ludwig Zacharias Werner. Sein Weg zur Romantik*, 1963


JOHANN KARL WEZEL

Born 31 Oct. 1747 in Sondershausen, studied in Leipzig, visited London, Paris and Vienna, returned to Leipzig. Went mad and from 1786 until his death in 1819 lived as an eccentric recluse in Sondershausen. Wrote mainly satirical novels in the manner of Sterne and Fielding.

Works
*Lebensgeschichte Tobias Knauts des Weisen, sonst der Stammler genannt*, 4 vols., 1773–6
*Belphegor oder die wahrscheinlichste Geschichte unter der Sonne*, 1776; repr. ed. H. Gersch, 1965; W. Dietze, 1966
*Ehestandsgeschichte des Herrn Philipp Peter Marks*, 1776
*Satirische Erzählungen*, 2 vols., 1777 f.
*Lustspiele*, 4 vols., 1778–87
*Hermann und Ulrike*, 1780
*Der Weltbürger oder Briefe eines chinesischen Philosophen aus London*, 1781
*Wilhelmine Arend oder Die Gefahren der Empfindsamkeit*, 1782
*Kakerlak*, 1784
*Versuch über die Kenntnis des Menschen*, 1784 f.

Literature

S. Kampe, *J. K. Wezels Leben u. Schriften*, diss. Königsberg, 1911
G. Kreymberg, *J. K. Wezel, sein Leben u. seine Schriften*, diss. Münster, 1913
A. Völker, *Empfindsamkeit u. Aufklärung in Wezels Wilhelmine Arend*, diss. Münster, 1934
K. Adel, 'Eine vergessene Faustdichtung des 18. Jhs. J. K. Wezels Kakerlak', *Jb. des Wiener Goethe-Vereins* 66 (1962)
W. Dietze, 'Elend u. Glanz eines "Deutschen Candide". Vorläufige Bemerkungen zu Wezels Belphegor', *Wiss. Zs. der Univ. Leipzig* 14 (1965)

## CHRISTOPH MARTIN WIELAND

Like many German writers of the eighteenth century Wieland was a son of the manse, born on 5 Sept. 1732 in Oberholzheim, Swabia, and brought up in the small imperial city of Biberach nearby, where his father had become 'Oberpfarrer'. His home background and his schooling in Kloster Berge near Magdeburg exposed him to pietistic influences and it is not surprising that, when he began to compose poetry during his years as a student in Tübingen (1750–2), he modelled himself on the more devotionally coloured works of Klopstock and Bodmer rather than on the rational Leipzig school. His works attracted the attention of Bodmer who invited the 'zweiten jungen Klopstock' to Zürich in 1752. Wieland adopted the enthusiastic or sanctimonious tone current in Zürich patrician circles and laboured to realize Bodmer's literary ambitions—'acting the nun to please old Widow Bodmer', as Nicolai put it—but this overwrought piety ran counter to his true nature and he felt himself enervated by Platonic friendships with soulful matrons; during the years 1757–8 a 'great revolution' marked the end of his 'seraphic phrase', and it was with some relief that he moved to Berne in 1759. In 1760 he returned to his native town as 'Kanzleidirektor', where the mondaine atmosphere of Graf Stadion's neighbouring estate at Warthausen completed his conversion to worldly pleasures. In 1765 he terminated a series of more or less ill-starred love-affairs by a marriage which turned out to be a long and happy one. Despite official duties he found time in Biberach not only to publish some of his most significant original works but also to translate 22 of Shakespeare's plays. After a brief interlude as professor of philosophy in Erfurt (1769–72), Wieland was invited by the Duchess Anna Amalia of Weimar to act as tutor to the princes Karl August and Konstantin. He retired from this post in 1775 but remained in Weimar devoting himself to literary and journalistic work—particularly the writing and editing of *Der Teutsche Merkur*, which for nearly forty years played a large part in spreading enlightenment and raising standards of middle-class taste. For some years Wieland owned a small estate at Ossmanstädt, near Weimar, but he returned in 1803 to the town, where he died on 20 Jan. 1813. In embracing the Enlightenment's faith in human progress through reason and refining it by his urbanity, wit and elegance of expression Wieland became the first founder of Weimar Classicism. His *Agathon* is the first of the great German 'Bildungsromane' that set out to establish the ideal of balanced and integrated human personality, and as such it achieves both unprecedented psychological insights and a universal validity hitherto unknown in the novel. His *Oberon* is the last great allegorical verse epic in German, but it also fore-shadows many features of Romanticism; *Musarion* epitomizes perfectly Wieland's doctrine of compromise between the demands of nature and the claims of reason; *Die Geschichte der Abderiten* is a masterly satire on the undying philistinism of German provincial life. Wieland belonged historically and temperamentally to a rococo tradition in which didactic purpose and polished regularity were rated higher than self-expression and spontaneity. He was not a highly original poet: he drew his themes from a vast knowledge of literature ancient and modern, his philosophy owes much to Shaftesbury, his narrative style a great deal to Laurence Sterne. Nevertheless, in spite of his apparent frivolity and an occasional lubricity too mild to raise an eyebrow in any enlightened society, Wieland's ideal of the moderate cosmopolitan has a rare wisdom and there is evidence enough of his personal integrity and practical humanity. In his own time he raised German literature to new stylistic heights, leavened its ponderous mass, warded off the puritanical blight that threatened it and brought it international acclaim. In return he was assaulted successively by the 'Göttinger Hain', the 'Sturm und Drang' and the Romantics, while his reputation suffered even more in the century that followed his death from the nationalistic spleen of strait-laced

German critics, for whom he was 'undeutsch' and 'französierend' —or at best 'unproblematisch'. It may be that German history would have taken a happier course had Wieland's countrymen adopted the tradition of Horace and Lucian, which he sought to popularize and on which he hoped to base a 'Philosophy of the Graces', rather than the faith in 'Volkstum', that deformed offspring of Romanticism.

## Works

*Lobgesang auf die Liebe*, 1751
*Die Natur der Dinge*, 1752
*Zwölf moralische Briefe in Versen*, 1752
*Anti-Ovid oder Die Kunst zu lieben*, 1752
*Briefe von Verstorbenen an hinterlassene Freunde*, 1753
*Der geprüfte Abraham*, 1753 (epic in 4 cantos)
*Sympathien*, 1756
*Empfindungen eines Christen*, 1757
*Lady Johanna Gray. Ein Trauerspiel*, 1758
*Cyrus*, 1759 (fragment in 5 cantos)
*Clementina von Porretta*, 1760 (drama)
*Araspes und Panthea*, 1760
*Shakespeares theatralische Werke*, 1762–6 (translations)
*Die Abenteuer des Don Sylvio von Rosalva*, 1764
*Geschichte des Agathon*, 1766 (revised and augmented 1777, 1798)
*Idris und Zenide*, 1768 (comic epic)
*Musarion oder Die Philosophie der Grazien*, 1768
*Combabus*, 1770
*Die Dialogen des Diogenes von Sinope*, 1770
*Die Grazien*, 1770
*Der neue Amadis*, 1771 (comic epic in 18 cantos)
*Der goldne Spiegel oder die Könige von Scheschian*, 1772
*Der Teutsche Merkur*, 1773–89; *Der neue Teutsche Merkur*, 1789–1810
*Alceste*, 1773 (Singspiel)
*Die Geschichte der Abderiten*, 1774–81
*Rosamunde*, 1778 (Singspiel)
*Oberon*, 1780
*Horazens Briefe, aus dem Lateinischen*, 1782
*Horazens Satiren*, 1786 (translation)
*Dschinnistan oder Auserlesene Feen- und Geistermärchen*, 1786–9
*Lucians von Samosata Sämtliche Werke*, 1788–9 (translation)

*Geheime Geschichte des Philosophen Peregrinus Proteus*, 1791 (novel)
*Agathodämon*, 1799 (novel)
*Aristipp und einige seiner Zeitgenossen*, 1800–1 (novel)
*Ciceros sämtliche Briefe*, 1808–21 (translation)


Literature

J. G. Gruber, *Wielands Leben*, 1827–8

F. Sengle, *Christoph Martin Wieland*, 1949

D. van Abbé, *Christoph Martin Wieland*, 1961 (in English)

J. Hecker, *Wieland*, 1966

V. Michel, *C. M. Wieland. La formation et l'évolution de son esprit jusqu'en 1772*, 1938

E. Ermatinger, *Die Weltanschauung des jungen Wieland*, 1907

K. Hoppe, *Der junge Wieland. Wesensbestimmung seines Geistes*, 1930

H. Wolffheim, *Wielands Begriff der Humanität*, 1949

L. F. Ofterdinger, *C. M. Wielands Leben und Wirken in Schwaben und der Schweiz*, 1877

F. Budde, *Wieland und Bodmer*, 1910

E. Springer, 'C. M. Wieland als Kanzleiverwalter in Biberach', *Württ. Vierteljahrshefte f. Landesgesch.*, new series, 22 (1913)

F. Sengle, 'Wieland und Goethe', *Arbeiten zur dt. Lit.*, 1965

H. Grudzinski, *Shaftesburys Einfluss auf C. M. Wieland*, 1913

A. Behmer, *Laurence Sterne und C. M. Wieland*, 1899

P. Michelsen, 'Welt und Sonderling. C. M. Wieland', *L. Sterne u. der dt. Roman des 18. Jhs.*, 1962

A. Fuchs, *Les apports français dans l'œuvre de Wieland 1777–89*, 1934

K. Otto, *Wielands Romantechnik*, diss. Kiel, 1922

C. J. Jacobs, *Der Roman der schönen Gesellschaft*, diss. Köln, 1965

F. Martini, 'C. M. Wieland und das 18. Jh.', *Fs. Kluckhohn u. Schneider*, 1948

C. Sommer, *Wielands Epen und Verserzählungen*, diss. Tübingen, 1966

F. Beissner, 'Poesie des Stils', *Wieland. Vier Biberacher Vorträge*, 1954

H. W. Seiffert, 'Wielandbild und Wielandforschung', ib.

M. C. Lazenby, *The influence of Wieland and Eschenburg on Schlegel's Shakespeare translation*, 1942

J. Scheidl, *Verhältnisse und Beziehungen zu den antiken Quellen in Wielands Agathon*, diss. Munich, 1904

E. Gross, *Wielands Geschichte des Agathon. Entstehungsgeschichte*, Germ. Stud. 86 (1930)

L. Stettner, *Das philosophische System Shaftesburys und Wielands Agathon*, 1930

H. W. Reichert, 'The philosophy of Archytas in Wielands Agathon', *GR* 1 (1949)

R. Schindler-Hürlimann, *Wielands Menschenbild. Eine Interpretation des Agathon*, 1963

W. Buddecke, C. M. *Wielands Entwicklungsbegriff und die Geschichte des Agathon*, 1966

E. Staiger, 'Wielands Musarion', *Kunst der Interpretation*, 1955

D. Vogt, *Der goldne Spiegel und Wielands politische Anschauungen*, 1904

A. Fuchs, *Geistiger Gehalt und Quellenfrage in Wielands Abderiten*, 1934

B. Seuffert, *Wielands Abderiten*, 1878

F. Martini, 'Die Geschichte der Abderiten', *Der dt. Roman*, ed. B. v. Wiese, 1963

W. E. Yuill, 'Abderitis and Abderitism', *Essays in Germ. Lit.*, ed. F. Norman, 1965

J. Müller, 'Wielands Versepen', *Jb. des Wiener Goethe-Vereins* 69 (1965)

M. Koch, *Das Quellenverhältnis von Wielands Oberon*, 1879

G. Raederscheidt, *Entstehungsgeschichte, Analyse und Nachwirkung von Wielands Oberon*, diss. Frankfurt, 1930

H. P. H. Teesing, 'Die Motivverschlingung in Wielands Oberon', *N* 31 (1947)

H. P. H. Teesing, 'Wielands Verhältnis zur Aufklärung im Agathodämon', *N* 21 (1936)

H. Berger, *Wielands philosophische Romane mit besonderer Berücksichtigung des Aristipp*, diss. Munich, 1944

O. Bautel, *Wieland und die griechische Antike*, diss. Tübingen, 1953

J. Steinberger, *Lucianus' Einfluss auf Wieland*, 1902

W. Monecke, *Wieland und Horaz*, 1964

A. Pellegrini, *Wieland e la Classicita Tedesca*, 1968

LUDOLF WIENBARG (pseuds. L. VINETA, FREIMUND)

Born in Altona, 25 Dec. 1802, died in Schleswig, 2 Jan. 1872. He studied theology and philosophy at Kiel, Bonn and Marburg. He became a lecturer on aesthetics at Frankfurt University: his lectures formed the basis for his influential book *Ästhetische Feldzüge*. He was a leading member of 'Das junge Deutschland'. The movement in fact took its name from the dedication of his

*Feldzüge*: 'Dem jungen Deutschland widme ich diese Reden und nicht dem alten.'

Works
*Ästhetische Feldzüge*, 1834; repr. ed. W. Dietze, 1964
*Zur neuesten Literatur*, 1835
*Die Dramatiker der Jetztzeit*, 1839
*Vermischte Schriften*, 1840

Literature
V. Schweizer, *Ludolf Wienbarg*, 1897
L. Burkhardt, *Ludolf Wienbarg*, 1956
A. Graf, *Freiheit und Schönheit bei L. Wienbarg*, diss. Bonn, 1952

ERNST VON WILDENBRUCH

Born 3 Feb. 1845 in Beirut, grandson of Prince Louis Ferdinand of Prussia, son of the Prussian Consul General (later Ambassador) in Constantinople. Wildenbruch had a military education and became a Lieutenant in the Prussian Guards in 1863; he resigned his commission two years later, however, in order to study law, and after service in the Franco–Prussian War became a judge in Eberswalde and Berlin. In 1877 he entered the Foreign Office and achieved the rank of Geheimer Legationsrat in 1897. He retired in 1900 and died on 15 Jan. 1909. Wildenbruch is most notable as a dramatist and his plays express well the patriotic self-confidence and energy of the Wilhelminian era.

Works
*Spartakus*, 1873 (drama)
*Lieder und Gesänge*, 1877
*Die Karolinger*, 1882 (tragedy)
*Harold*, 1882 (tragedy)
*Der Mennonit*, 1882 (tragedy)
*Novellen*, 1882
*Väter und Söhne*, 1882 (drama)
*Opfer um Opfer*, 1883 (drama)
*Dichtungen und Balladen*, 1884
*Christoph Marlowe*, 1885 (tragedy)
*Neue Novellen*, 1885
*Die Herrin ihrer Hand*, 1885 (drama)

*Das neue Gebot*, 1886
*Humoresken*, 1886
*Der Fürst von Verona*, 1887 (tragedy)
*Die Quitzows*, 1888 (drama)
*Der Generaloberst*, 1889 (tragedy)
*Die Haubenlerche*, 1891 (drama)
*Der neue Herr*, 1891 (drama)
*Meister Balzer*, 1893 (drama)
*Eifernde Liebe*, 1893 (novel)
*Schwester-Seele*, 1893 (novel)
*Heinrich und Heinrichs Geschlecht*, 1896 (drama)
*Tiefe Wasser*, 1897 (short stories)
*Gewitternacht*, 1898 (tragedy)
*Die Tochter des Erasmus*, 1900 (drama)
*König Laurin*, 1902 (tragedy)
*Der unsterbliche Felix*, 1904 (comedy)
*Das schwarze Holz*, 1905 (novel)
*Die Rabensteinerin*, 1907 (drama)
*Lucrezia*, 1907 (novel)
*Letzte Gedichte*, 1909
*Der deutsche König*, 1909 (drama)
*Gesammelte Werke*, ed. B. Litzmann, 17 vols., 1912–19
*Ausgewählte Werke*, ed. H. M. Elster, 4 vols., 1919

Literature

B. Litzmann, *Ernst von Wildenbruch*, 2 vols., 1913–16
H. Maync, 'Ernst von Wildenbruch', *Dt. Dichter*, 1927
E. A. Morgan, *Wildenbruch as a naturalist*, diss. Madison, 1930
J. Röhr, *Wildenbruch als Dramatiker*, 1908
U. Mannes, *Wildenbruchs dramatische Technik*, diss. Jena, 1934
A. M. Morisse, *Die epische Kunst und Technik Wildenbruchs*, diss. Bonn, 1912
F. Schlosser, *Wildenbruch als Kinderpsycholog*, 1919
A. Fries, *Beobachtungen zu Wildenbruchs Stil und Versbau*, 1920; repr. 1967

## ERNST ADOLF WILLKOMM

Journalist and author of novels, short stories and plays in the spirit of Young Germany and socialism. Born 10 Feb. 1810 near Zittau, died Zittau, 24 May 1886.

Works
*Julius Kühn*, 1833
*Bernhard Herzog von Weimar*, 1833 (tragedy)
*Die Europamüden*, 1838
*Eisen, Gold und Geist*, 1843
*Weisse Sklaven*, 1845
*Moderne Sünden*, 1861
*Wunde Herzen*, 1875

Literature
F. Heimnach, *Ernst Adolf Willkomm*, 1915

## JOHANN JOACHIM WINCKELMANN

Born on 9 Dec. 1717, the son of a cobbler in Stendal. He studied without conspicuous success in Halle and Jena and eventually became 'Konrektor' in Seehausen. He did not discover his true vocation, however, until he was appointed librarian to Graf von Bünau in Nöthnitz near Dresden in 1748; here he was able to gratify his interest in art and conceived his ardent admiration for the sculpture of Classical Greece. In order to pursue his study of the ancient world Winckelmann embraced Roman Catholicism and became curator of Cardinal Albani's gallery in Rome, where he wrote his *Geschichte der Kunst des Altertums*. He came to a tragic end on 8 June 1768, being murdered in Trieste on his way back from Austria. The systematic study of archaeology and art history owes much to Winckelmann, who developed important techniques of chronological and aesthetic classification. Hardly less important was the influence of his style on the development of German as the language of Classical scholarship. His conception of the Classical aesthetic ideal as the epitome of 'edle Einfalt und stille Grösse' formed one of the main pillars in the edifice of German literary classicism erected by Goethe and Schiller. His view of Greek art as the product of an ideally harmonious ethnic community held sway in Germany until it was radically called in question by Nietzsche. It was with Winckelmann's interpretation of Greek statuary in these terms that Lessing took issue in his *Laokoon*.

Works
*Gedanken über die Nachahmung der griechischen Werke in der Malerei und Bildhauerkunst*, 1755; repr. DL (1935)

*Anmerkungen über die Baukunst der Alten*, 1762
*Abhandlung von der Fähigkeit der Empfindung des Schönen in der Kunst
    und dem Unterricht in derselben*, 1763
*Geschichte der Kunst des Altertums*, 1764
*Anmerkungen über die Geschichte der Kunst des Altertums*, 1767

Literature
J. W. v. Goethe, *Winckelmann und sein Jahrhundert*, 1805
K. Justi, *Winckelmann, seine Werke und Zeitgenossen*, 1866–72; 5th ed.
    W. Rehm, 1956
W. Zbinden, *J. J. Winckelmann*, 1935
L. Curtius, *Winckelmann und seine Nachfolge*, 1941
A. Schulz, *Winckelmann und seine Welt*, 1962
H. Koch, *J. J. Winckelmann, Sprache und Kunstwerk*, 1957
W. Rosshard, *Winckelmann. Ästhetik der Mitte*, 1960
W. Rehm, *Winckelmann und Lessing*, 1941
H. C. Hatfield, *Winckelmann and his German critics*, 1943
H. S. Schultz, 'Winckelmanns Griechenbild und die neuere
    deutsche Literatur', *Dt. Beiträge zur geistigen Überlieferung*,
    1953
M. Dietz, 'Anschauungen von italienischer Kunst von Winckel-
    mann bis zur Romantik', *Germ. Stud.* 94 (1930)
H. Ruppert, 'Winckelmann-Bibliographie', *Jahresbericht der
    Winckelmann-Gesellschaft*, 1924
C. Vinz, 'Eine Winckelmann-Bibliographie' (seit 1945) *Börsen-
    blatt f. den dt. Buchhandel* 23 (1967)
L. Curtius et al., *Johann Joachim Winckelmann*, 1968

AUGUST VON WITZLEBEN (pseud. AUGUST VON TROMLITZ)

Born 27 March 1773 at Tromlitz between Weimar and Jena,
educated as a page at the Weimar court where Herder and
Musäus were his teachers. Witzleben became an officer in the
Prussian army and, after being captured by the French in 1806
was commissioned in the army of Murat, finally changing sides
again to serve in the Russian army. He died in Dresden on
5 June 1839. His historical novels and dramas are imitations of
Sir Walter Scott.

Works
*Das stille Tal,* 1798
*Frauenwert,* 1823
*Die Douglas,* 1825 (drama)
*Historisch-romantische Erzählungen,* 7 vols., 1826–8
*Sämtliche Schriften,* 1829–41; 3rd ed., 20 vols., 1860–4

Literature
H. Morawetz, *August von Witzleben,* diss. Breslau, 1934

HEINRICH ZSCHOKKE (pseuds. JOH. V. MAGDEBURG, L. WEBER)

Born 22 March 1771 in Magdeburg, left school to become an
actor but reverted to academic life when the troupe was dissolved
and gained his doctorate at Frankfurt on Oder. In 1792 he
became a parson in Magdeburg and also acquired the right to
lecture in Frankfurt. In 1795 he travelled via Switzerland to
France and Italy, then settled in Switzerland as a publicist in the
service of the Helvetian government and was subsequently
appointed to high administrative posts. After the collapse of the
regime he was dismissed but soon re-established himself as
journalist, author and editor and was eventually made a member
of the Grand Council of Canton Aarau. Zschokke writes in the
socially didactic tradition of Pestalozzi, Hebel and Gotthelf but
he was also the author of sensational thrillers and comic tales.
He died on 27 June 1848 in Aarau, where he had lived since
1807. He was a friend of H. v. Kleist, and like him wrote a work
called *Der zerbrochene Krug.*

Works
*Aballino, der grosse Bandit,* 1794
*Stunden der Andacht,* 1809–16
*Erzählungen,* 1811–27 (mostly in the magazine *Erheiterungen*)
*Das blaue Wunder,* 1813
*Der zerbrochene Krug,* 1813
*Das Goldmacherdorf,* 1817
*Das Abenteuer in der Neujahrsnacht,* 1818
*Der tote Gast,* 1821
*Der Freihof von Aarau,* 1823 f.
*Addrich im Moos,* 1825–6

*Spruch und Schwank des Schweizerboten,* 1825
*Die Branntweinpest,* 1837
*Eine Selbstschau,* 1842 (autobiography)
*Gesammelte Schriften,* 35 vols., 185–4; 36 vols., 1856–9
*Ausgewählte Schriften,* 12 vols., ed. H. Bodmer, 1910

Literature

J. J. Bäbler, *Heinrich Zschokke,* 1884
M. Scheidereit, *Zschokkes Weltanschauung,* 1904
C. Günther, *H. Zschokkes Jugend- u. Bildungsjahre,* diss. Zürich, 1917–18
E. Reichmann, *Zschokkes Weltanschauung in seinen Jugendjahren,* diss. Berlin, 1936
M. Schulz, *Zschokke als Dramatiker,* diss. Breslau, 1914
M. Prieger, *H. Zschokkes Erzählungskunst,* diss. Munich, 1924
P. Schaffroth, *H. Zschokke als Politiker u. Publizist,* diss. Berne, 1949
E. Dietsch, *H. Zschokkes Rechts- u. Staatsdenken,* 1957

# APPENDIX I

## GERMAN PAINTING*
### by
### Hannah Priebsch Closs

Moral conscience and inhibitions, added to the menace of the French Revolution, too soon assert themselves against the frivolities of the French rococo, whose influence permeated German art, while Neo-classicism, as it were an artistic parallel to the *Aufklärung*, preached the gospel of uplift. These new ideals are reflected particularly in the art of Anton Raphael Mengs (1728–79), whilst a simpler matter-of-fact conception characterizes the portraits of Anton Graff (1736–1813) and the engravings of Daniel Chodowiecki (1726–1801), a typical representative of the '*Zopfstil*', in which reminiscences of Watteau and the classic intermingle with great naivety. Once more classicism manifests itself in its northern capacity as an influence of restraint. But now, united to no sensuous affirmation of the present but to a pessimistic longing for a world of beauty that has died, it results in the affectations of Angelica Kaufmann (1741–1807) or the lifeless archaeology of a Jakob Carstens (1754–98) and a J. H. Wilhelm Tischbein (1751–1829), whom the patronage of Goethe raised to an unmerited fame . . .

The religious-nationalistic dream of the '*Nazarener*' Overbeck, Schnorr v. Carolsfeld, Cornelius, and those other members of the little company which gathered together in Rome with the aim of regenerating art by a pious discipline of life (a parallel to the original idea of the English Pre-Raphaelites) soon lost its specific-

* *General Editor's Note:* This is a continuation of the section that appeared in Vol. II and is a reprint with some slight alterations and omissions from *Germany: a Companion to German Studies* 1955, revised edition, J. Bithell. It is reprinted by kind permission of Messrs Methuen.

An early death prevented the author from dealing with the most recent painters, such as Ernst W. Nay (1902–1968), Fritz Winter (b. 1905) and Hans Hartung (b. 1904).

ally romantic character through a gradual subservience to Italian form. Alfred Rethel (1816–59), alone amongst historical painters, rising above the mediocrity of the Düsseldorf school, was able in the *Rathaus of Aachen* to transfuse Raphaelian form with a sternness characteristically German, whilst finding a yet freer scope for dramatic emotion in the woodcut series of the *Totentanz*, symbol of the revolution of 1848. Indeed where the painters Adrian Ludwig Richter (1803–84) and Moritz von Schwind (1804–71) allow their fancy free play in their intimate illustrations of folk-life, fairy-tale and legend, nineteenth-century Romanticism produced an art of true German sincerity, a perfect expression of the trim comfort and homely piety of the *Biedermeier* style of Schubert's time . . .

Karl Spitzweg's (1808–85) humorous paintings of philistine fads and foibles are rendered more artistic by an interest in the effect of light. Already before him Karl Blechen (1798–1840) seems in some of his landscapes to foreshadow the naturalism of the later nineteenth century, whilst in Philipp Otto Runge (1778–1819) we find not only the various tendencies which later Romantic painters developed but a sensibility to atmospheric light and colour which make him appear almost a forerunner of the impressionists. He maintained for instance that an admixture of white dulls the radiancy of the pigment. Yet Runge's attitude to painting remains fundamentally romantic or even mystic. His *Four Seasons* were intended as a fantastic musical poem. With the poet Tieck and the philosopher Jakob Böhme he dreamed of the unification of all the arts, the *synæsthesia*, in subordination to a higher Being, God-Nature.

His theory of colours and his 'colour-globe' brought him into contact with Schelling. Regarding colour as a mystery which we can only apprehend through flowers, he interpreted it as a symbolic manifestation of the Trinity, 'for Light itself lies beyond our realization'. In many ways Runge recalls the visionary painter Samuel Palmer, with whom he may indeed have had some direct or indirect contact, though the English artist's 'supernatural moonscapes' may suggest also an affinity with those of Kaspar David Friedrich (1774–1840). Whilst Palmer's creative anguish, however, found release in mystically exalted Virgilian idylls, Friedrich's spirit is weighed down by the realization of man's solitariness, his nothingness in face of infinity. Thus his figures, seen nearly always in back-view, rise as dark silhouettes against a waste of sky, watching a sail far out at sea at sunset, or stand lost in contemplation, gazing at the rising moon. Once more, as with Grünewald and the school of the Danube, these landscapes with their rocks and moss-clad conifers, half-shrouded by wraiths of mist, remind one of Asiatic art, though the European Romantic cannot attain the Oriental's detachment nor his self-annihilation before the mystery of the infinite. But there is, too, a strange rectangular simplicity and stillness about some of K. D. Friedrich's landscapes and interiors which seem to make them precursors of certain modern movements in German art.

The revolt against the poetic sentimental conception of painting which gave birth to the great movement of nineteenth-century naturalism was carried on in Germany by individuals rather than centres as in France, though Düsseldorf, under French and Belgian influences, specialized in *genre*. Something of the spirit of the Barbizon school is reflected consciously or unconsciously in most German landscape painting of the time, as for instance in that of the Austrian Ferdinand Waldmüller (1793–1856), with his pictures of children playing in the sun-lit Vienna woods. Champion of dawning realism, Adolf Menzel (1815–1905), whose woodcuts illustrate Kugler's *History of Frederick the Great*, found inspiration not only in the glories of the past, but in actual impressions such as the *Potsdam Railway*. His early landscapes are reminiscent of Constable, whose paintings he studied at the Berlin exhibition of 1839, but, characteristically German, his linear accents are sharper in contrast to the atmosphere. Sometimes dramatic sense and colour, as in the *Théâtre Gymnase*, suggest Delacroix. In the *Balkonzimmer* no trace is left of the sentimental conception of the romanticists (Schwind's young girl at the window greeting the morn); instead, we see a muslin curtain blown in the wind—the silhouette of a dark chair—light, air, and movement. *The Flute Concert of Frederick the Great* shows all interest in anecdote subordinated to the visual impression of transient motion and scintillating tremulous light. The realism of Wilhelm Leibl (1844–1900) provides a parallel to that of Courbet, but without the Frenchman's pathos. He moulds the figures of his peasants (*Drei Frauen in der Kirche, Das ungleiche Paar*) in a strict counterpoint of line and mass, light and colour, exaggerating the smooth strength of Holbein's objective form. But in his earliest portraits, perhaps the finest of nineteenth-century Germany, surface and a feeling for the atmospheric predominate. Under his influence Wilhelm Trübner (1851–1917), applying himself to the problem of *plein-air*, gave his landscapes fine construction and space through the bold use of strips of brilliant colour.

But the naturalistic cause was not allowed to attain victory unimpeded, and the middle of the nineteenth century rallied to the call of German idealism. Once again a number of artists, hoping to escape the pest of materialism, found their way to Rome. But their artistic conception was still bound to a realism that could not digest dogmatic poetic sentiment. Thus Anselm Feuerbach (1829–80), all too conscious of his lofty mission, struggled in vain to reconcile the momentary impression with a slowly evolved intellectual ideal, his would-be epic style degenerating into an ever bleaker pathos. The sensual vision of Arnold Böcklin (1827–1901), intoxicated by nature, sought to personify elementary forces. In the play of the waves he sees Triton and mermaid at their watery sport. Meadow and wood are filled with the music of Pan's pipes. His idylls are the dreams of one who beholds the south with the eyes of the northerner, recognizing therein not static perfection but the mystery of the infinite. But Böcklin, like so many before or since, was unable to assimilate Italian form, and an ever-growing yearning for monumentality led to the domination of the figures over the landscape and a use of unbroken colour that destroy the very rhythm of nature he had sought to create. Thus also Hans Thoma (1839–1924)—with his strange admixture of realism and fairytale, his landscapes that are the purest embodiment of German *Volkstümlichkeit*—was wrecked on the same rock in his striving to translate into visible form the gigantic musical visions of Richard Wagner. One painter alone during this idealistic intermezzo came near a realization of his dreams, Hans von Marées (1837–87), whose poetic art seems born, not of external literary influences, but of true creative vision, of imagination rather than fancy.

In the meantime the realists, absorbed in problems of *plein-air*, had embarked upon impressionism proper. Beholding the world almost scientifically in terms of atmosphere and light, its true devotees cared little for subject-matter or the relation of volume to space. Hence object and picture lose their tectonic structure, a fragment of nature disintegrated is reconstructed as a process of colour atoms, and the individuality of the artist manifests itself almost entirely in his technique. Supremely analytical, impressionism was developed to perfection by the logical genius of the French, whilst the Germans, in need of a more direct and subjective form of expression, were unable to fulfil the finest possibility of this passive art—its exquisite sensibility.

Max Liebermann's (1847–1935) early realism, which, in pictures such as the *Goose-pluckers* (1872, Berlin National Gallery) or *Brother and Sister* retains a certain monumentality in the design and pose of figures, gradually shows an increasing delight in the accidental and the transient impression. In the *Munich Beer Garden* (1883, Berlin), which suggests Manet and Renoir, a crowd of people are viewed collectively as a succession of tones and colour patches beneath the changing effect of light. But the comparative distinctness of single objects appears as a relic of that love for characterization which in his early works had sometimes almost amounted to caricature. Now, it is less an interest in the individual than a sociological tendency which insists on the theme *Großstadtleben*, and so causes this and other paintings of the period to betray more than purely aesthetic feeling. Even later, linear tension and sharp delineation divide such works as the *Polo Players* (Hamburg) from the purest conception of impressionism with its complete disintegration of form. Still less compatible with the French ideal is the sentimentality of Fritz von Uhde (1848–1911), which vacillates between Tolstoyan ethics in sympathy with the workers and the oppressed, and the salon idealism of Hans Makart (1840–84).

The art of Lovis Corinth (1858–1925) is not based on rationalism but on a baroque idealism akin to that of Rubens which, like the latter's final style, makes use of impressionistic technique. Dynamic form and an almost brutal sensuality of vision are far removed from the subtle nervosity of the French. Not always in this religious and mythological pictures are realism and imagination blended to a perfect unity, but the demonic power of such late portraits as *Bernt Grönvold*, the impassioned abandonment to nature in his last landscapes and flower-paintings with their broad surfaces of pure colour, prove Corinth's power to reawaken a fundamentally German conception of art.

A growing sensibility to the epidermis of things tended with many to a sensual suggestivity, an eroticism that ends in the decadent and the perverse. A would-be Satanism inspires Franz von Stuck (1863–1928), whilst a predilection for the Salome theme discernible in literature and music of the period is found also in the paintings of various artists, including Max Slevogt (1868–1932). However, impressionistic technique proved a means of salvation to the latter, enabling him to imbue fantastic etchings and drawings with a vitality that Max Klinger's (1859–1920), burdened by their intellectual content, had lacked.

Literary and illustrative tendencies, united to a reviving desire for a more linear or flat decorative treatment of the surface, were in the meantime giving birth to a German version of the style often designated as 'L'Art Nouveau', its greatest exponent being perhaps the Austrian painter Gustav Klimt (1862–1918), who through his prodigious sense of colour raised his somewhat Beardsleyan vision to monumental proportions.

In the field of book-illustration, which proved perhaps the happiest medium for exponents of a decorative symbolist outlook, mention may be made of Heinrich Vogeler (1894–1924), whose dreamy, Maeterlinckean visions have been recorded by Rainer Maria Rilke in his monograph on the group of artists who, from the year 1895 onward, gathered in a colony in the moorland village of Worpswede near Bremen. On the whole this group tend towards a freer naturalism, though the landscapes of Otto Modersohn (1865–1943) reflect a poetic spirit, haunted by the elfish world of German fairy-tale, whilst his wife Paula Modersohn-Becker (1876–1907), whose passionate devotion to art found a moving record in her autobiography, possessed perhaps the most sensitive eye in the Worpswede school.

But a revolt against the relative passivity of pure impressionism had already manifested itself throughout Europe in attempts at firmer construction, bolder colour, and increased spiritual activity. In Switzerland the new ideals find a champion in Ferdinand Hodler (1853–1918), who dreams of a formal and moral regeneration of art. Here, plastic figures, whose anatomy is tortured like Signorelli's, whose hard modelling is reminiscent of Witz and Pacher, are subordinated to a decorative scheme, a symmetrical, chequer-board treatment of the surface. An expressive treatment of line in which old German traditions reassert themselves replaces the flaky illusionistic technique of impressionism. With his paradoxical theory of *parallelism*, which demands individual characterization within universal abstraction, freedom within rule, Hodler hoped to restore to fresco its lost monumentality. Thus: *Swiss on the Retreat after the Battle of Marignano* (Zurich Museum), and the *Revolt of the Students of Jena* (Jena University). A tendency towards symbolism, here apparent, is accentuated in the ensuing artistic development of Central Europe. It is significant that whilst in France and Italy post-impressionism recognized a goal in cubism and futurism, it adopts in the German-speaking countries more especially the extreme form of expressionism.

This new movement was heralded by the Norwegian Edvard Munch, who had been living in Berlin for some years. His work (at first repudiated) found recognition in the *Sezession* of 1902, a society of anti-academic independents which had branches in Berlin, Munich and Vienna. Soon afterwards, three German architectural students at Dresden, Ernst Ludwig Kirchner (1880–1938), Erich Heckel (1883–), Karl Schmidt-Rotluff (1884–), inspired by a passion for painting, founded a group *Die Brücke* which, holding its first exhibition in Dresden in 1905, was joined by Emil Nolde (1867–1956) and Max Pechstein (1881–1955).

A similar movement, *Die neue Künstlervereinigung*, made its appearance in Munich in 1909, a Russian emigrant, Wassily Kandinsky (1866–1955) being one of the leaders.

Other members included Alexander Kanoldt (1881–1939), and Alfred Kubin (1877–), the latter a book-illustrator of demonic power, who together with Kandinsky later separated from the NKV and formed a third group named *Der blaue Reiter*, which was augmented first by Franz Marc (1882–1916) and August Macke (1887–1914) and subsequently by Paul Klee (1879–1940).

All three groups, as was the case with the 'Expressionists' in general, were concerned in the creation of an antinaturalist art in which the painter, beholding nature only as a medium of subjective expression, seeks to bind arbitrarily selected objects to an abstract unity, thus reducing the representational element in design to a minimum. Whilst for the impressionist objects were passive to the natural influences of light and atmosphere, they become for the expressionist the active symbol of an idea, e.g. the expressionist, striving to penetrate the essence of things, sees the town concentrated to a knot of cubic and crystalline blocks (Alexander Kanoldt: *Subiaco* and *San Gimigniano*), or again, as a chaos of reeling edifices consuming space. His imaginative vision seeks, not the superficial appearance, but the underlying idea which is in truth a phantom of the brain, excited by the tumult and fever, the hysteria of the city (Conrad Felixmüller: *Stadtmensch*). So, too, in landscape the expressionist explores the primeval forces of nature, the dynamic energy of growth. Trees writhe in horrid spasm, ejected from a soil rent as in travail, the ears of the corn hang heavy with ripeness, we feel the generation of things (Christian Rohlfs, 1849–1938). Or in mystic studies of animals he tries to submerge his will in that of the beast, seeking not the actual physical appearance but the mystery of instinct (Franz Marc: *The Bull*).

Marc too, even if he employs a rather more distinct 'pattern', seems to have set out in quest not so much of a formal as of a spiritual 'absolute'. The primal force which threw up the gigantic folds of the mountains curves no less the necks of the horses, spans the rainbow arch between heaven and earth. One is reminded of the poem 'Mensch' by the expressionist poet Kurt Heynicke. Wassily Kandinsky, indeed, upheld that 'the artist must have something to say, as his duty is not to control form but to match the form to the subject concerned'. The 'subject', however, is as far removed from representational standards as possible, 'inner' or emotional states being translated direct into line, form and colour rhythms according to a system of musical harmony and counterpoint, which he described in a treatise, whilst his paintings bear such titles as 'Symphony in colour', etc.

Strange to relate, it was not only absolute painting but the 'distortions' of such artists as Nolde that National Socialist propaganda banned as 'decadent and Bolshevik', evidently unaware that non-representational art is far more akin to Germanic and Nordic tradition than the amalgam of realism and neo-classicism it sought to set up as model. Ironically, the Soviet Union itself has been following in the same footsteps . . .

It is perhaps significant that two of the greatest artists of irrational fantasy should have sprung from the roots of German expressionism. Thus with Max Ernst (1891–) zoomorphic and anthropomorphic images move through a world in sequences as illogical as those of dream, though subordinate to an exquisite law of colour and texture, whilst the Swiss painter Paul Klee spins the thread of his cobweb fantasies across page or canvas, and through contrast of surface, lineal crescendo and diminuendo renders each encounter with the improbable inevitable as in the realm of fairy-tale. Paul Klee amongst all modern artists was indeed perhaps the happiest in reawakening the old Gothic-Nordic dynamism of line.

But what, we may ask, is the trend of German art today? The spiritual upheavals of two wars and the years between have caused such havoc that it is difficult to tell. Many are trying to recover the line of development arbitrarily cut short . . . Amongst the refugees, the Viennese painter Oskar Kokoschka (1886–) has continued to show signs of maturing from the uncanny psychological penetration of his early portraits, in which he lays bare the pathological secrets of the soul hidden behind the mask of convention, through the darker passion of his second period (an analogy is afforded by the expressionist pathos of his plays) and thence to a new reverence for Nature. None the less, his nervous energy, wedded to remains of expressionist and impressionist technique, render his landscapes very different from the calm, objective and rectangular simplicity of a Georg Schrimpf (1889–1938), or Franz Lenk (1898–), whose art reminds us almost of the landscapes of Kaspar David Friedrich . . .

Max Beckmann (1884–1950), on the other hand, the exponent of new realism (represented also by Otto Dix (1891–) and Karl Hofer (1878–)), was perhaps the most forceful of all German artists in rendering the horror and 'anxiety' of our mechanized, dehumanized age, though his power of vision prevented him from becoming an infuriated satirist as was the case with Georg Grosz (1893–) or from falling into the naturalistic though sincere reform propaganda of Käthe Kollwitz (1867–1945).

Recent publications on the drawings of the sculptor Ernst Barlach (1870–1938) with their intense yet formally powerful humanity show from what recent sources German art may still draw and yet remain essentially true to itself.

# APPENDIX II

# THE ARCHITECTURE AND
# SCULPTURE OF GERMANY
by
## M. Q. Smith M.A., Ph.D.

'He had been to places that people had written books about,
and they were not a bit like the descriptions. To see for
yourself—that was the great thing. He always tried to see
for himself.'—HENRY JAMES: *Washington Square*

The best Roman remains in Germany are at Trier. First to impress
the traveller is the massive yet beautifully articulated Porta Nigra,
the fourth-century north gate of Augusta Treverorum. Even
though its prime function was defensive, the relationship of
projecting towers before an inner courtyard with the inner gates
provides a most memorable architectural experience. The
unfinished detailing of the huge capital blocks sets, by an historic
accident, the tone of a millennium of German architecture. The
Roman Imperial traditions of a monumental style prevailed
well into the age of the mature Gothic.

Trier was to the Romans an important bridge-point, and part
of the Roman bridge still survives. Nearby are parts of ware-
houses. More impressive are the two sets of baths and an earth-
banked amphitheatre. But it is in the fine museum and in
excavation reports that one has to study such important sites
as the Temple Area.

The same is true of the recent discoveries made beneath the
cathedral and Liebfrauenkirche: a most important group of
Constantinian wall-paintings has been re-assembled and displayed in the Bishop's Museum. The palace from which they
come was flattened to provide a site for the two churches, begun
in about 325; part of the northern church as altered in about 380
survives, incorporated in the present Romanesque cathedral. The
famous Basilica was the audience room of another palace;

although partly rebuilt, it remains a dominant feature of the city, nearly a hundred feet high.

An immediate derivative of the Roman Imperial architecture of Trier was the Carolingian palace at Aachen. Though now transformed into the Town Hall, it is still possible to recognize the basic form of the great half-drum swelling from the end wall, and additional ones at the middle of each side wall. The exterior had the tall blank wall-arcades and cantilevered wooden galleries found also at Trier.

The antecedents of the palace chapel are to be found in the other Imperial capitals, notably Ravenna. But the basic architectural forms remain more Roman than Byzantine, with a weightiness which foreshadows the manner of the mature German Romanesque. The distinctive design of ambulatory and gallery arranged around an octagon is found again at Ottmarsheim, Nymwegen and in the westwork at Essen. The two-storey palace chapel long remained popular in Germany; typical ones will be found in Nuremberg castle and at Speyer and Mainz but the finest of the Romanesque examples is Schwarzrheindorf which retains its wall-paintings of subjects from Ezechiel and the Apocalypse.

Since so much of the architecture of the middle ages has necessarily been so often altered, restored and repaired, it is important that visitors should not neglect the considerable riches displayed in cathedral treasuries and various national museums and libraries. The gold, ivory and manuscripts of early medieval Germany represent one of the greatest periods of European art, and to neglect them would lead to a complete misinterpretation of the civilization of the period. For example, the Cross of Lothair at Aachen gives a clear impression of the glittering and essentially tactile qualities of the art of the German goldsmith. Any feeling that the great Romanesque churches may have been grim and bare is finally dispelled once one has seen the stupendous embroidered copes and cloaks of Henry II and Kunigunde. In the mind's eye one can see these being worn, scarlet and gold on deep blue, and at the altar a great gold antependium like that from Basle, now in the Hotel de Cluny, Paris.

Many ninth-, tenth- and eleventh-century examples of these so-called minor and applied arts have survived as complete, undamaged works; but few buildings of the period remain in anything like their original forms. Some evidence has been recovered in excavations at Cologne and Fulda; at Corvey on the Weser is a characteristic westwork, and Steinbach is a reasonably well-preserved example of the basilican form of church. The precisely decorated monumental gateway at Lorsch indicates the high quality of design and workmanship. But by far the most attractive group are the three basilicas on the enchanting island of Reichenau, Lake Constance. St Peter and Paul retains a monumental Vision of the Almighty in the apse, Ss Mary and Mark in the middle of the island is larger and grand in its proportions, but most impressive of all is St George with its walls completely covered by a series of scenes to a monumental scale, in many ways so similar to what can be seen on the page of a manuscript but so much more powerful in impact.

St Cyriakus at Gernrode, founded in 961, is basilican in form, like the Reichenau churches, but with galleries over the aisles in the Roman fashion. Influence from Italy is seen too in the decoration of the walls with pilaster strips and arcading, a fashion appearing at about the same date on St Pantaleon in Cologne. Alas, most of the finest and most important churches of Cologne were destroyed or severely damaged by bombing. The traveller will find many of the famous city churches of Germany rebuilt, restored or even now in a web of scaffolding.

Mainz, Speyer, Worms and other churches of the period, such as those at Hildesheim have all been very much altered during the thousand years of their history. One of the most important, Limburg-an-der-Hardt has been a ruin for hundreds of years. But as a group these fine churches have few equals. Mainz (of 978–1009, and 1060–1137) is particularly memorable for its extraordinary silhouette, a combination of nineteenth-century restoration and eighteenth-century bravura on a medieval theme. Its interior is outstanding for the way in which its history is reflected in a splendid sequence of monuments. Speyer gives most clearly the impression of majesty. Cushion capitals, spurred bases, groin-vaults and semi-circular arches are all so large that they dwarf every English example. The Imperial form of giant blank arcading found on the Basilica at Trier and in Milan reappears on the inner walls of the aisles and is adapted to provide a staggeringly tall enclosing order for the nave elevation.

The effect of five great bays of domical groin-vaulting over a hundred feet tall is unparalleled in Romanesque. Worms is of particular interest for the building is its own historian: in the nave elevation can be seen a whole set of variations on a simple theme, culminating in a west choir with orgies of zig-zag. The cumulative effect of a square-ended sanctuary set between circular turrets with conical tops, an octagonal pyramid over the east crossing and the almost baroque group of the west choir, apsidal beyond its octagonal crossing pyramid and another pair of cylindrical towers is quite unlike anything encountered in England.

The severely damaged Holy Apostles, Great St Martin's, St Pantaleon and St Gereon, all at Cologne, showed a similar sensibility for the grouping of volumes. At the abbey of St Maria Laach there is a rich grouping of vertical elements to balance the horizontals of nave and aisle roofs. At the east, the crossing tower is octagonal and the minor towers are square; at the west, the central tower is square but its flanking turrets are cylindrical. The design is a derivative of that used earlier for St Michael at Hildesheim; fortunately the Romanesque painted ceiling here—the finest in Europe—was removed for safety's sake, and after a very successful restoration has been put back in the rebuilt church. Hildesheim boasts three other great treasures, the bronze column and bronze doors made for Archbishop Bernward in about 1020, and the bronze font. The other important doors in Germany are the wooden ones in St Maria in Capitol, Cologne, and the bronze ones at Aachen and Augsburg. (Those of St Zeno, Verona, were in fact made in Germany, and there are connections with those made by Bonannus for Pisa and Monreale.) It is in metal that the German sculptor achieved his most memorable works during the Romanesque period; the stone sculpture carved around the windows of such cathedrals as Speyer plays little part in the achievement of architectural effects. Much of the detailing is reminiscent of Italian work, and there are probably connections with England. But the character of German Romanesque remains unique, distinguished by its sense of mass.

Signs of the transition from Romanesque to Gothic appeared in Germany by about 1125, and many major Romanesque churches, such as Mainz, acquired during the course of their construction or reconstruction features typically Gothic, such as rib-vaulting. But such individual features could not at the latest stages of the construction of a church alter its general character. For several decades German architects managed to assimilate a whole range of Gothic features within the context of a mature Romanesque.

Magdeburg cathedral is sometimes described as the first Gothic church of Germany, but this is too simple a view: the majority of the Gothic features date from the later stages of its construction. Nonetheless it is a fascinating example of the way in which a locally accepted mature style is transformed as knowledge of the latest developments in the Isle de France reaches the Elbe. A much better integrated building is Limburg an der Lahn, an outstandingly satisfying work of art. There is no need to make comparisons with the very latest in glazed triforia and banked flying buttresses; the true context of Limburg is German Late Romanesque. Both exterior and interior are integrated in terms of volume; the towers and turrets, nave, aisles, transepts and apse are closely grouped in an unforgettable way on a steep hill above the roofs of the city and above the river. The detail is equally satisfying in its homogeneity.

Bamberg cathedral is also well sited above its beautiful old city. Its lively towers were, of course, almost the latest part of the building, and the cathedral like Worms presents a fine sequence of parts illustrative of the change from Romanesque to Gothic, but in sculpture as well as architecture. The Bamberg sculptures, although not far apart in date, show considerable stylistic changes. The latest of them are as individual pieces fully Gothic; it is unfortunate that so few of them should be in their original positions, for this makes it difficult to assess the relationship of one figure to another.

The sculptures may be divided into two main groups. Alternate columns at the sides of the Fürstenportal are enlivened with figure sculpture, apostles standing precariously but elegantly on the shoulders of prophets. They are elegant examples of the transition from the formalism and decorative art of the Romanesque into the new naturalism of Gothic. The faces of the figures are individually characterized; the poses are, considering the proportions of the scheme as a whole, wonderfully free and varied. But the freedom with which the draperies are cut into deep folds is for decorative rather than naturalistic ends. Similarly the pairs of apostles and pairs of prophets on the choir-screen, though less elongated and no longer confined to columnar shapes, are still seen as types rather than as living persons; their draperies (which need to be studied individually, for they are not all of exactly the same style) are less formal than those of the Fürstenportal, and the ways in which each pair is shown disputing are very varied. Some of the figures, particularly the Jonah, are quite classical in spirit.

A further change can be seen in the work of the Bamberg Master. It is generally assumed that this artist had worked at Reims, for the drapery-styles he employs, both smooth and broken, had been used on works at Reims dated before 1231. His work at Bamberg has been dated to the years just before the dedication of 1237. The clearest indebtedness to Reims is to be seen in the Visitation group; with them are the pair of Ecclesia and Synagogue. But the best-known and most popular figure is the Bamberg Rider, a figure which defies identification; with another of the same sort at Magdeburg it conveys a similar ideal as Durer's Knight, Death and the Devil or Bernt Notke's St George at Stockholm. Finally at Bamberg, we come to the almost life-size nude Adam and Eve, Ss Stephen and Peter, Henry II and Kunigunde on the Adamspforte: with these works Germany achieves the position in the forefront of Gothic sculpture which it never loses.

If it were possible, one would wish to be able to travel directly from Bamberg to Naumburg. Its west towers were obviously modelled on those of Bamberg, but the major interest is again in the sculpture concentrated, as at Bamberg, round the choir. The Naumburg sculptor worked in the cathedral from about 1249 to 1270; his earlier career can be traced back to Noyon in the 1230s and Mainz (see the beautiful fragments in the Dommuseum) in about 1240. The sculptures at Naumburg show the influence of a training in the workshops of High Gothic France, but the statues are placed in a way that is characteristically German. Each figure, marvellously individualized, stands round the altar. Such figures as Ekkehard and his wife Uta mark a high point in European sculpture. Yet the Passion reliefs of the screen, and the poignant figures of the Virgin and St John, seem to foreshadow all the art of German Late Gothic sculpture, that peculiarly intense and dramatic art from which the restrained portraits in the choir seem so far removed.

Up-to-date Parisian architectural forms appeared in the new churches needed by the friars—the Dominicans at Regensberg, Koblenz and Esslingen, the Franciscans at Cologne, Freiburg and Ulm, for instance, all of about 1245. This introduction of a new style by a religious order can be compared with the introduction of the Burgundian half-Gothic by the Cistercians in the previous century, as at Maulbronn. The cathedral of Magdeburg (begun 1209) and the Elisabethkirche at Marburg (1235) demonstrate how, even in thirteenth-century churches, the German Romanesque traditions still remained strong. Magdeburg uses the old-fashioned groin vault, and the whole massing of walls and openings is in the Speyer tradition. Marburg has an east end in the trefoil form of Holy Apostles or St Maria in Capitol at Cologne. Its best parallel is not with any French church, but with the Liebfrauenkirche at Trier. In each case the structure is undeniably Gothic, but the rejection of the structural system of flying buttresses means that neither church attains the airiness of Reims or Amiens. For this sort of effect, one must turn to the choir of Cologne cathedral. Its interior is even more coolly precise than that of Amiens, all on tip-toe. Not far from Cologne is the Cistercian church of Altenberg, the design of which has sometimes been attributed to Gerhard, the designer of the cathedral. If Cologne repels a little by the regularity of its repetitious design (not completed till recently), Altenberg satisfies for the same reason: there is an attraction in the precision of a smaller work of art which becomes uninspiring as the scale is enlarged. Altenberg appeals too for the greenness of its setting: architecture cannot be judged, as can a painting in its frame, independent of its environment. Alas, at Cologne the old skyline has been greatly altered, but even now the ranks of flying buttresses around the apse of the cathedral and the two tall west spires provide an exciting Gothic vision across the Rhine.

Whether we are conscious of it or not, our attitudes to Gothic owe something to Goethe's essay on Strasbourg cathedral, 'Von deutscher Baukunst', written in 1770. The youthful joy in Gothic still communicates itself to the reader: 'My soul was filled by a whole and great impression, which, because it consisted of a thousand harmonizing details, I could indeed taste and enjoy, but by no means comprehend or explain. They say it is thus with the joys of heaven . . .' After being temporarily forgotten during a romantic Classical phase, Goethe's youthful enthusiasm for Gothic reappeared in the *Elective Affinities* of 1809, where his preference continues to be for Strasbourg rather than Cologne.

Strasbourg is a much more complex building than Cologne, the proportions of the Gothic have been related to the earlier east end. Particularly memorable is the quantity and quality of the glass of the nave. But the feature which most attracted Goethe (and which should appeal to eyes trained on Perpendicular) is the west façade. Freiburg, with a single west tower, and Ulm can be mentioned in this context: the manner of combining portals, towers, soaring octagon and perforated spire is typically German. The sculptures of the Ecclesia Master at Strasbourg, whether in the individual figures of Ecclesia and Synagogue from which he takes his name or in the tympanum of the Death of the Virgin, have some connections with Chartres; but more important parallels are with Bamberg and Naumburg. The transformation of Gothic sculpture between 1230 and 1290 can be seen by comparing these pieces with the Prophets and Virtues of the west front. Ulm portal is justly famed, and with that at Freiburg (which is coloured—dark and pale blues, red and gold are less garish in fact than they would seem in a mental reconstruction) and the entrances of Holy Cross at Schwäbisch Gmünd and of St Lorenz at Nuremberg come as a surprise, almost an embarrassment to an English visitor unused to a fully sculptural architecture.

The revolution in sculpture which was taking place at this time was part of an architectural revolution which is connected with the name of the Parler family. Prime among their works is the Holy Cross at Schwäbisch Gmünd. This, like the Wiesenkirche at Soest, a church of particularly felicitous proportions, is a häll church, having aisles and central nave rising to the same height. The volumes of these churches are integrated beneath vaults of great ingenuity, going far beyond the innovations made by the designer of the choir of Bristol cathedral. The two häll churches at Nuremberg illustrate the way the form was developed. The choir of St Lorenz, begun in 1439, is larger, more complex, more muscular than that of St Sebald of 1361–79, and beautiful in an entirely different way. The whole structure is tense, and the expertise of the masoncraft no small part of the pleasure. As with rococo, the visitor is carried away, and ready to accept the life-size portrait figure of Adam Kraft supporting the Sacrament House, raising it so high that the topmost pinnacle, though of stone, has to be bent over to avoid the tall arch of the main arcade.

The list of other fine late Gothic buildings in Germany is daunting. Works such as the choir of Aachen, St Lambert at Münster, Ulm cathedral, St Martin and the Spitalkirche at Landshut, St Martin at Amberg and St George at Nordlingen—all these and many more ought to be kept in mind. Although not strictly German, Prague and Vienna cathedrals cannot be omitted from consideration, for it is in these churches that a number of important innovations are first to be recognized.

One of the places at which one can gain a proper idea of the richness of German Late Gothic art is Freiburg: Ulm and Nuremburg, alas, suffered heavily in the bombing. The Minster is the completest example in Germany of a mature Gothic church; it has its sculpture including the great west portal; it has a wide variety of good glass, and on its altars a whole series of painted and sculptured altarpieces. Moreover, in the Augustinermuseum are beautifully displayed gold and silverwork, embroidery, panels of glass, and panels by such artists as the Housebook Master, Hans Baldung Grien and Grünewald, and wood-sculptures—all magnificent examples illustrative of the variety and liveliness of German Late Gothic culture.

The sculpture on buildings is of the same stone as the buildings, often red sandstone; but the altarpieces, often with painted wings, are of wood. The same artists can be found carving both stone and wood, and both materials were frequently coloured. Probably Master Bertram and certainly Michael Pacher (on his St Wolfgang altar) were both sculptor and also panel-painter. There are from about 1400 a number of single figures of the Madonna (Schonen Madonnen), reliquary busts of almost portrait likeness, and Pietà groups: but the major works are the great altars. An initial distinction can be made between the problems facing the designer of groups of standing figures and the rather different problems involved in designing narrative scenes, whether on a large scale or more intricately. In Germany itself, Michel and Gregor Erhart's altar at Blaubeuren (1493–4) is greatly admired: in the centre is a formal group of standing figures, and the wings have narrative panels in relief. The carved figures by Nicholas von Hagenau were provided by Grünewald with shutter-wings famous throughout the world (Colmar). The work of Veit Stoss in Nuremberg—such as the Passion reliefs in St Sebald, the Annunciation and Crucifix in St Lorenz—and the triptych at Bamberg demonstrate the extraordinary power of his vision. His supreme masterpiece is the huge altarpiece of the Passion, and of the Life and Coronation of the Virgin at St Mary, Cracow (1477–89). Quite different in personality—almost a German Botticelli—is Tilman Riemenschneider (d.1531). Especially notable is the way he uses his materials—limewood and sandstone are given surfaces which are both as distinct from each other and alike as wood-cuts and engravings. Many pieces are in museums (including complete altars at Heidelberg and Munich) but much remains in small and rather remote churches. Among other particular pleasures are the choir stalls—as at Basel, Überlingen and Constance (and in this context, see the fine Madonna at Downside Abbey, Somerset). Finest of all are the stalls at Ulm, the work of Jörg Syrlin: the series of busts on these are among the supreme works of Late Gothic. With the opening of the sixteenth century, Renaissance influences begin to be seen. Connections with Italy had been close: Michael Pacher's paintings of the previous thirty or forty years show the strong influence of Mantegna, but there is in his sculpture, some of it south of the Brenner, no sign of the influence of Donatello. The mixture of Renaissance detail within a fully Gothic context is beautifully illustrated by the shrine of St Sebald at Nuremberg, cast by Peter Visscher in 1508–9.

There could be no true revival of Classical architecture in Germany as there could in Italy; every classical detail had, so to speak, to be imported, usually along the important commercial routes from North Italy, particularly Venice, to such centres as Nuremberg and Augsburg. The first work to concern us is the chapel of St Anna at Augsburg, built in 1509–18 for the Fuggers. On a larger scale, the detailing and decorative effects used at the castle at Heidelberg are justly famous. Augsburg remained in the forefront of the renaissance movement, and the finest evidence of this can be seen in London in the Victoria and Albert Museum—the Christopher Fugger altar from St Magdalena (1581–4), the work of Hubert Gerard, who with Adrian de Vries and Hans Reichle was responsible for bringing Italian

High Renaissance sculptural styles into Germany. The prolixity of the earlier Renaissance style finally disappears with the work of Elias Holl. His Town Hall at Augsburg is Italian and classical in proportion as well as detail; the sculptural detail is restricted to the architectural members—windows, cornices, main entry and pediment. The break from the Late Gothic of Ss Ulrich and Afra is complete. Even more Italian in its effects, and more monumental, is the Town Hall at Nuremberg (1616–22) by Jacob Wolff the Younger. Here the balance of blank wall and modelled detail achieves a completely harmonious unity. Nuremberg was very seriously damaged, but Augsburg, with the Fugger alms-houses of 1519, the long street of palatial houses, the fountains, the Romanesque cathedral, the late Gothic Ss Ulrich and Afra and the movingly efficient Lutheran preaching hall, Heilig Kreuz (1693), gives the traveller a good impression of the development of a rich merchant city with international connections.

The history of the Baroque in Germany is immediately connected with the allegiance to Roman Catholicism, especially through the influence of the various Orders whose centres were in Rome. St Michael's, the Jesuit church in Munich, for example, is a derivative of Il Gesu, though the proposed dome between the broad tunnel-vaulted nave and the conched apse was never built. Rome again provided the model for the Theatinerkirche, of 1663–71, eighty years later than St Michael. The effect of a centralizing dome reminds one immediately of Rome; the volumes of the interior are Roman, but the stucco is fruity and vegetable-like where Rome would have had marbles and gilding. The present contrast between the richness of the modelling and the pristine, almost puritan whiteness creates a curiously ambiguous effect.

The development of South German Baroque as an independent style can be divided into three major phases. After its beginnings in the seventeenth century, the major period can be considered under the sub-title Rococo; this in turn gives way towards the end of the century in the face of a renewed Classicism. Rome is, of course, the fons et origo; the art of Bernini as architect-sculptor and the spatial ingenuity of Borromini indicate the trends which were further to be explored not only in North Italy but throughout Germany, Austria and Switzerland as well as farther east. Not only are the main architectural forms Italianate, but the decoration is regularly based on the innovations and expertise of such artists as Mantegna and Correggio, Pozzo or Tiepolo.

The greatest of the true Baroque architects is Fischer von Erlach (1656–1723), whose education included (as should every European's) a long stay in Rome. After the Dreifaltigkeitskirche at Salzburg (1694, and a variation on Borromini's St Agnese of forty years earlier), the Kollegienkirche in the same city shows how a Roman feeling for masses was adapted in a personal way. The Karlskirche at Vienna (begun 1716) is an outstanding example of the Baroque use of a dome, here seen rising above the taut façade stretched between turrets and set back behind a pair of triumphal columns, Roman in derivation but creating the sort of effect found also in the relation of dome to minaret in the mosques of Sinan, the great Turkish architect. The secular work of the period is illustrated by the Imperial Library, the finest part of the great palace complex in the centre of Vienna. As with the Belvedere outside the walls, a work by Lucas van Hildebrandt, many visitors to a modern museum collection will find that the building itself is no less impressive than the contents. The third great architect of the Austrian Baroque was Jacob Prandtauer, responsible for the reconstruction of two great abbeys: Melk, superbly designed to make the most of its cliff-edge site above the Danube, and St Florian.

In Franconia, the façade of St Martin at Bamberg, built by Georg Dientzenhofer, is typical of a developed Baroque, robust and vital, quite distinctive from the quiet precision of Elias Holl. Bamberg is one of the most attractive of German cities, retaining an interesting variety of seventeenth- and eighteenth-century work to complete a sequence beginning with the cathedral. Georg Dientzenhofer was one of a family of architects; his younger brother Johann rebuilt the cathedral at Fulda. This is rather a solemn church, not so much in the ordering of the parts as in the lighting. More exciting is the abbey of Banz, where the plan is more complex, and the volumes are expressed in the rhythmic forms of the vaults. Thirty or so miles south of Banz is Johann Dientzenhofer's secular masterpiece, the Schloss Pommersfelden of 1711–18.

Greatest of the architects of this first group was Johann

Balthasar Neumann (1687–1753). In 1719 he began the Residenz at Würzburg, his major commission, a work whose design was altered during execution: it was damaged in the war. The exterior is grand without being pretentious, the central section being linked to the end wings beneath a richly moulded roof. The first surprise is the chapel, so complex in form and so colourful within the rectangular greyish walls of the exterior. From the main entry in the central block one reaches the grand stairway; in form, the room and stairs are not quite coherent; but this is quickly forgotten for the whole ceiling is covered by painting, Tiepolo's masterpiece. With *joie de vivre* the artist has created a decoration combining history, geography and allegory with a certain amount of flattery. The full impact of this entry is most marvellously maintained by the contrast made as one enters at the top of the stairs the ante-room, the White Hall. This has no colour; all the decoration is in stucco, left white, the frenzied seven months' work by Antonio Bossi. Appropriately the major emphasis is on military trophies, but the effect is less martial than decorative. Next one enters the oval Kaisersaal, where sunlight streams in from the gardens, glistening in chandeliers and shining back from the mirrors. For the first time in this sequence of rooms, the order is coloured; the fluted columns are warm against the cooler walls, their bases and capitals golden like the mirror frames and other decorative mouldings. Above the entablature which encircles the room, architectural space is dissolved by pictorial space created, again with absolute fluency, by the unequalled Tiepolo.

Neumann's church of Vierzehnheiligen, on the opposite side of the valley to Banz, dates from the 1740s; it is a standard example of the genius of the architect as he combines and reconciles the volumes of a standard transepted church with the requirements of a shrine set in the nave. The ways in which the five continuous areas of the ground-plan are transformed so that at vault level there are only three reminds one of the less complex attempts at Banz. Perhaps the best way to sort out this complex and beautiful building is to begin by studying the design-model still preserved in the museum at Bamberg, concentrating on purely architectural features without the lively distractions of the stucco saints. Like Fischer von Erlach, Neumann remains always and primarily an architect, where some of his contemporaries, like the Asams or the Zimmermanns, were decorators more than modellers of space.

The usefulness and dangers of making such a distinction can easily be realized by making a comparison between two small churches at Munich, both of about 1735–50. First, in Sendlinger-strasse in the busy centre of the city is the church of St John Nepomuk, built and decorated by the Asam brothers at their own expense; as a personal offering, it may be taken as indicative of the ideals of the architects. The whole aim seems to have been to persuade the congregation to suspend for a little any belief in the mundane view that the tangible is real and the real tangible. The ambiguities are concentrated at the altar end, where beyond spiralling columns the eye is led and misled by a variety of visual stimuli so that the brain hardly knows which is architectural space and which pictorial, which light is daylight and which artificial. By contrast, the very fine frescoes by J. B. Zimmerman and the equally splendid statuary by J. B. Straub found adorning the interior of Johann Michael Fischer's St Michael at Berg am Laim are used more purely as adornment within the context of distinct architectural volumes, altar, octagonal choir and larger octagonal nave. The interest of the design is in the reconciliation of the east–west axis and the centrifugal tendencies of the nave and choir; wherever one sits, one is firmly placed in a defined space. But the Asam brothers' effect is achieved by placing the congregation in the space possible on a tiny, cramped site, hoping that they will allow themselves to accept the further space created by pictorial and architecturally ambiguous means.

The Zimmerman brothers, of whom Johann Baptist has already been encountered as a decorator at Berg am Laim, were also architects, and in their work there is a complete fusion between architecture and decoration. The Wieskirche of 1745–54, near Oberammergau, is locally praised as the greatest of their works. Like Steinhausen, it is a pilgrimage church built on an oval plan with the long axis from entry to altar. An ambulatory encircles the churches, the central space being supported by an inner oval of pillars, single at Steinhausen but paired at the Wies. Above all floats the dome; at the Wies especially the architectural forms seem to defy gravity—an effect but partly achieved by the use of wood. Effects of lightness are further enhanced by the mobile forms of the stucco and the merriness of the coloration—pale pinks and greens, bluish white and gold. The shapes of the windows filled with clear glass are lively too, their curious shapes emphasized by the stucco woodpecker or magpie placed at the edge where the light half illumines and half dazzles, casting shadowy blue silhouettes across the white walls.

Of all the Baroque churches, and there are many fine ones including St Gall and Zwiefalten, none can rival J. M. Fischer's Ottobeuren, built to celebrate the millennium of the abbey and restored on its twelve-hundredth anniversary in 1964. The bold exterior gives little indication of the interior riches. Great coloured columns around the walls of nave and transepts and choir support an uninterrupted entablature, and the highly decorative altars, confessionals, pulpit, font, wooden stalls and organs are all kept subordinate to the architectural members. Shadows of leafy capitals, gesticulating putti, shadows of the geometrical patterns of window-leads and shadows of tormented St Sebastian tied to a gilded tree enliven the whitewashed flat planes of wall between the giant order. Only where the form of vault is dissolved by pictorial means is the spectator taken unawares, so that he hesitates where coloured stucco putti clutch a garland of flowers whose other end is held by irreverent painted putti in a painted sky.

Ottobeuren is however more than just a church: like any large abbey it has its domestic parts, and among them the great ceremonial Kaisersaal and a cool, elegant library. Perhaps the finest of the monastic libraries is that of St Gall, both for the splendour of the woodwork but also for the treasures displayed— metalwork, ivories, manuscripts and the famous Carolingian plan of an ideal monastery. The libraries of Wiblingen and Schussenreid—the latter a charming interior, mostly pink in tone, with a complex programme in honour of Wisdom by Dominikus Zimmerman—are both to the same basic design, a rectangular hall with a gallery all round, and stairs hidden by bulging bookcases in the end walls. The word rococo becomes too loose a term to use in describing such rooms; the eye is soon able to distinguish varieties of rococo-ness, with here the capitals more restrained and there the bookcases more exuberant. Indeed at Schussenreid the books themselves were considered too untidy as they rested on their shelves, so the bookshelves have become cupboards and the doors are painted with false books whose whitish backs and reddish labels complete the harmony of pinks and whites, pale blue and gold of the painted architecture and ceiling.

There is little to distinguish the art of such rooms from that found in secular palaces. At Vienna and Munich and elsewhere one encounters the familiar fashions for chinoiserie, the gilded furniture and the porcelain elegance. The Residenz Theatre at Munich is one place where the adjectives rococo and theatrical may be linked appropriately. Mock curtains of bluish silver and metallic scarlet are fringed and tasselled with gold; white and gilded stucco is modelled into trophies of trumpets and drums, horns and violins; lively caryatids, trumpeting putti and cherubs proffering crowns cavort above the satins and chandeliers. The atmosphere is quite magical. A similar magic enchants one at the Amalienburg, the finest of the pavilions at Nymphenburg. This is the work of the same artist, François de Cuvilliés. Such places as Nymphenburg were designed for a leisurely life, and they deserve an unhurried visit, wandering from the Amalienburg to the true rococo grotto of the Magdalen chapel and then on to the mock Chinese of the Pagodenburg. Nothing can be more pleasant on a hot day than to leave the bustle and noise of a busy city centre and to wander at will round the semi-rustic paths of Nymphenburg or the more formal walks of the great park at Hannover.

The Revival styles of Germany are not in themselves perhaps of sufficient interest to the average visitor for them to be sought after, but they will be frequently encountered. Neo-classicism seems nowhere more appropriate than at the Glyptothek at Munich. Revivals of the medieval styles will be encountered at other museums, and though many a Gothic Revival church will be passed over without note, many a time the visitor will be startled to find Carolingian or Romanesque designs used for railway stations or for the piers of a bridge. In Germany the Rundbogenstil was assiduously cultivated, and whether the results seem commendable, boring or hilarious will depend on the visitor's sensibilities. Nothing can better illustrate the great confidence of the nineteenth century than the construction of the Ring at Vienna on the site of the old enclosing walls and ditches—a practice taken up at many other cities. Classic Parliament,

Gothic Rathaus and Votivkirche stand proudly beyond the roaring traffic. Beyond each Ring stretch the great expanses of the modern cities.

One of the major centres of the international movement known as Art Nouveau or the Jugendstil was Vienna, with such works as Olbrich's building for the Vienna Secession of 1898-9 and the Hochzietsturm of two years later. In Munich, Endell's Elvira studio (although now destroyed) is by now a text-book example of the decorative features of the style. The further course of the development of the modern movement, the formation of the International Modern style, has attracted much attention from historians. The tendency to reject any richness or extravagance in linear or other decorative effects such as can be found in the works of Otto Wagner, or of Olbrich and Hoffman can be traced through to the absolute clarity of cubical forms preferred by such designers as Adolf Loos, particularly in the design of private houses. Although the main line of development is clear, there were diversions, especially in an Expressionist phase, exemplified in some of the buildings of Mendelsohnn and in the moving figure-sculpture of Ernst Barlach. In sculpture and architecture, as in the paintings and graphic work of the period, German traditions of linear design and forceful expression were not easily forgotten. But the major developments—for ever connected with the names of such theorists, teachers and designers as Gropius, Mies van de Rohe and Mendelsohnn—remain relevant today. The examples of works in Berlin and Stuttgart, of factory designs by Behrens, or by Gropius and Meyer are basic to the modern situation. Indeed, no better introduction to modern architecture, to the aims and ideals of the modern architect or designer, can be found than in the lucid statements of Walter Gropius and the Bauhaus.

Not the least stimulating of problems facing the traveller in Germany is that of sorting out the original parts of a building from all its alterations and additions. Many medieval churches have been brought up to date, the Romanesque made Gothic, and churches of both styles altered in the sixteenth, seventeenth and eighteenth centuries before being restored and rebuilt in the nineteenth and twentieth. Romanesque Freising has a charm all of its own in the finery of the Asam brothers' stucco; the Michaelsberg at Bamberg is dressed up in an almost Strawberry

Hill rococo. Authors of text-books tend to concentrate on the identification and analysis of the pure style, but the traveller will probably find that it is not only the 'pure' building (like Ottobeuren, with its organs making eighteenth-century music) which please and remain in the mind: it may be the lively silhouette of Mainz, the solid nave and airy choir of St Sebald at Nuremberg, the sequence of buildings along the streets of Augsburg or Bamberg, the contrasting heights of the octagon and choir at Aachen, the tiny but fine Carolingian church next the baroque cathedral at Fulda, the Bishop's Palace at Trier overshadowed by the Constantinian basilica, or the once-deserted church in Freiburg revived and re-enlivened as an elegant modern museum.

There cannot, of course, be any substitute for walking in and around a building; and sculpture in Germany, particularly in the Gothic and rococo periods, is usually misinterpreted unless seen in its intended architectural setting. But there is no shortage of useful books to guide one: the only danger is that one could so easily spend all one's time and money on them and never be able to go all over Germany to see for oneself.

# INDEX

This index embraces the Appendices on German Painting, Architecture and Sculpture but not the General Editor's Preface. References are confined mainly to personal names of writers and artists; some terms relative to literary movements and genres have been included, but for the most part movements and genres may be traced from the Table of Contents. The Select Bibliography is not indexed as author entries are in alphabetical order